The Law of Blood

The Law of Blood

Thinking and Acting as a Nazi

Johann Chapoutot

Translated by Miranda Richmond Mouillot

The Belknap Press of Harvard University Press
CAMBRIDGE, MASSACHUSETTS • LONDON, ENGLAND
2018

First Printing
This book was originally published as *La loi du sang: Penser et agir en nazi* © Éditions Gallimard, Paris, 2014

Library of Congress Cataloging-in-Publication Data

Names: Chapoutot, Johann, author. | Richmond Mouillot, Miranda, translator.
Title: The law of blood : thinking and acting as a Nazi / Johann Chapoutot ; translated by Miranda Richmond Mouillot.
Other titles: Loi du sang. English
Description: Cambridge, Massachusetts : The Belknap Press of Harvard University Press, 2018. | "This book was originally published as La loi du sang: Penser et agir en nazi © Éditions Gallimard, Paris, 2014." | Includes bibliographical references and index.
Identifiers: LCCN 2017039800 | ISBN 9780674660434 (alk. paper)
Subjects: LCSH: National socialism—Historiography. | National socialism—Moral and ethical aspects. | Antisemitism—Germany—History—20th century. | Germany—Politics and government—1933–1945.
Classification: LCC DD256.5 .C547513 2018 | DDC 940.53 / 43—dc23
LC record available at https://lccn.loc.gov/2017039800

To Marie Anna —J.C.

To Armand Jacoubovitch —M.R.M.

Contents

Introduction   1

PART I: PROCREATING

1. Origins: Nature, Essence, Genesis   23

2. Alienation: Acculturation and Denaturing   64

3. Restoration: Renaissances   112

PART II: FIGHTING

4. "All Life Is Struggle"   155

5. The War Within: Fighting the *Volksfremde*   194

6. The War Outside: "Harshness Makes the Future Kind"   242

PART III: REIGNING

7. The International Order of Westphalia and Versailles:
   Finis Germaniae   277

8. The Reich and Colonization of the European East   321

9. The Millennium as Frontier   353

Conclusion   405

Notes   *417*
Bibliography   *457*
Glossary   *483*
Index   *489*

Introduction

In 1945, eighteen physicians from Hamburg, all of them on the staff of the Rothenburgsort Pediatric Hospital, were brought before the German criminal justice system at the behest of the British Occupying Forces. All eighteen were charged with murdering, or acting as accessories to the murder of, fifty-six children who had been diagnosed as permanently unfit between 1939 and 1945, by means of lethal injection. In 1949, the *Landgericht* (regional court) of Hamburg dismissed the charges. Yes, "it has been objectively verified" that "at least fifty-six children were killed at the Rothenburgsort Pediatric Hospital." Yes, these acts were "against the law." The judges argued, however, that "all of the defendants . . . deny their guilt . . . and contest the charge that they committed any acts in objective violation of the law, explaining that they believed their actions to be permitted under the law."[1]

The physicians' arguments were in fact sound. In his exchanges with the British investigators, the hospital's director, Dr. Wilhelm Bayer, objected strenuously to the charge of a "crime against humanity." "Such a crime," he asserted, "can only be committed against people, whereas the living creatures that we were required to treat could not be qualified as 'human beings.'"[2] Dr. Bayer, with great sincerity, kept reiterating that doctors and legal experts had for decades been advising modern governments to shed the weight of useless mouths, burdens that hampered their military and economic performance. These beings were barely human, they asserted; they were corrupted biological elements, and their defects and pathologies risked being passed on if they reproduced. The doctor's words reflect the recent discovery of the laws of heredity, as well as lingering fear from the panics that swept European society at the close of the nineteenth century and in the aftermath of the First World War. On July 14, 1933, the Nazi government had responded to these concerns by passing a "law for the prevention of hereditary disease," which required the sterilization of individuals identified as diseased by a "hereditary health court." The law remained in effect until October 1939, when Hitler issued an executive order that these individuals be put to death instead.

In 1949, the Hamburg judges found nothing in the physicians' arguments worthy of objection. Four years after the war's end, they ruled that their colleagues in the medical profession were not guilty. The court accepted even the most peculiar of their arguments: "The elimination of lives not fit to be lived was the norm in Classical Antiquity. One would not venture to claim that the ethics of Plato or Seneca, both of whom defended these views, are any less elevated than those of Christianity."[3] The humanities, vague recollections from high school lessons trotted out regularly by these doctors to justify what might appear to be shocking acts, were also the intellectual heritage of the judges before whom they appeared. They shared both a culture and a point of view: "biology" was their only law. Endorsed by the Ancients, they stood against the norms adopted in subsequent eras, which they regarded as hostile to life itself.

Bayer was dismissed from his position as director of the Rothenburgsort Hospital, but he was allowed to keep his medical license. His license was renewed by the Hamburg Medical Board in 1961, which had undertaken to review his case following the publication of a series of articles on the doctor by the weekly newspaper *Der Spiegel* in 1960. A few years later, in 1964, Werner Catel, a professor of pediatrics, gave a long interview to this same newspaper. He had acted as a medical consultant to the Third Reich for its Aktion T4 program, the Nazis' involuntary euthanasia project. In this role, he had been responsible for the murder of sick children, a responsibility he acknowledged openly, dismissing all disapproval or rebuke. Indeed, he persisted in proposing that mixed panels of doctors, mothers, lawyers, and theologians be assembled to rule on the elimination of terminally ill children—a chilling echo of the health courts established by the 1933 law. When the journalist conducting the interview reminded him that the death penalty had been abolished in West Germany, Catel demurred:

> Don't you see that when a jury makes a decision it is always judging human beings, even if they are criminals? We are not talking about

humans here, but rather beings that were merely procreated by humans and that will never themselves become humans endowed with reason or a soul.[4]

The physician and the state must therefore intervene out of pure "humanity," in order to avoid needless suffering on the part of patients, families, and the community.[5] Neither Dr. Bayer nor Dr. Catel could understand how they could be guilty of anything: contemporary culture, their own humanity, and the state had all led them to act as they did. These arguments still carried enough weight after the war's end to be accepted by the court and reprinted in the columns of a respectable daily newspaper. These men were—and remained—obstinately committed to this line of reasoning.

With this story in mind, we should return and listen once more to the steady refrain of "not guilty" that echoed through the courtroom at the beginning of the Nuremberg Trials. *Nicht schuldig* sounded out each time the court asked the defendants for their plea. Every one of them was the same: *Nicht schuldig.* "Not guilty." By now we have heard this refrain all too many times. Even today, it never fails to provoke our outrage and anger at its apparent cynicism. Eichmann's assertions, all the way to the gallows, that he had done no wrong, are troubling to the reader of history. In his own personal writings and his conversations with friends and loved ones, Eichmann claimed to have only one regret, which was that he had contributed to the murder of just five million people, rather than ten or twelve, a number that, according to the estimates of the RSHA (Reichssicherheitshauptamt; Reich Main Security Office), would have accounted for the entirety of Europe's Jewish population.[6]

Similarly, one can only feel stunned by the words of Otto Ohlendorf's final statement to the court when he was tried at Nuremberg. Ohlendorf, an economist, had joined the NSDAP (Nationalsozialistische Deutsche Arbeiterpartei; National Socialist German Workers' Party, or the Nazi Party) in 1925. As the chief of the mobile killing unit Einsatzgruppe D, he had been responsible for the murder of ninety thousand people in Ukraine and the Caucasus. He denied nothing over the course of the trial, cooperated fully with the court, then concluded his oral arguments with a defense and an illustration of his commitment to Nazism—which was, to him, the only valid response to the distress of his generation.

These stories are in no way exceptional. *Nicht schuldig:* the pleas of these defendants were not cynical or provocative, nor were they made in denial or dishonesty—these men truly believed what they were saying. Most of them were convinced that they were *doing the right thing.* Ohlendorf asserted this in a statement to the court that he knew would earn him the death sentence. Eichmann repeated it right to the very end of his life. And in 1949, 1961, and 1964, the doctors and jurists involved in the case of the Rothenburgsort Pediatric Hospital remained committed to what they had heard, uttered, and written since well before 1933. In other words, the acts they committed made sense to them. Posterity either couldn't, or wouldn't, see their point of view. I grew up in France in an era in which universalism and liberal thought had been chosen as my country's founding principles. In France and in the rest of Western democratic society, universal human equality and political freedom are the cornerstones of our laws and institutions; they underpin our schools and university systems. From this perspective, the intensity and scope of the Nazis' crimes are totally incomprehensible: the NSDAP's violence and radicalism, its complete denial of humanity, are staggering, outrageous.

As soon as Nazism and its crimes are mentioned, "we"—this "we" includes the press, editorialists, commentators, and all those engaged in public expressions of informed opinion—mobilize batteries of explanations that, in the end, explain nothing at all. The perpetrators of Nazi crimes were madmen, we say—but a top-to-bottom review of the Nazi hierarchy leaves a psychiatrist nearly empty-handed. Some Nazis may indeed have been madmen, but there were no more madmen among their ranks than in any other group of human beings. This places most everything that was said and done during the Third Reich in the historian's jurisdiction.

Barbarity is a seductive explanation, because of its tremendous dialectic appeal. At the heart of Europe, in the middle of the twentieth century, at the very moment when—this discourse is rooted in the Enlightenment and stretches all the way to Norbert Elias—Western civilization was making great progressive strides, a terrible exception arrived to prove the rule. In Germany, no less: Europe's most literate nation, home to so many Nobel laureates, became the perpetrator of unspeakable crimes. This seems less paradoxical once the argument of German exceptionalism has been applied: off in their forests, sheltered from the influence of the Roman Empire, the Germans had always been a singular people. Historians convinced of Germany's *Sonderweg,* or "special path," have advanced this line of reasoning in a slightly more sophisticated form, while others, less scrupulous and more sensationalistic, have connected Luther to Hitler with a single stroke.

But the argument of German exceptionalism is fundamentally unsound. Culturally speaking, the Nazi ideology advanced by the NSDAP contained only an infinitesimal number of ideas that were genuinely German in origin. Racism, colonialism, anti-Semitism, social Darwinism, and eugenics did not originate between the Rhine and the Memel. Practically speaking, we know the Shoah would have been considerably less murderous if French and Hungarian police forces—not to mention Baltic nationalists, Ukrainian volunteer forces, Polish anti-Semites, and collaborationist politicians, to name only a few—had not supported it so fully and so swiftly: whether or not they knew where the convoys were headed, they were more than happy to rid themselves of their Jewish populations. In all these nations, men and women from all walks of life brutalized, arrested, and killed far more Jews than Martin Luther or Friedrich Nietzsche ever did.

For both the historian and the reader of history, once these pseudo-explanations have been examined and dismissed, perplexity—and even despair—are all that remain. It is a fifteen-minute bus ride from Weimar to Buchenwald; the distance has been noted a thousand times and has inspired myriad vertiginous reflections on humanity and its Others, on the dialectics of culture and barbarity, and, most often, on the radical impossibility of saying or concluding anything at all. The very idea that the horrors written down, proclaimed, or committed by the Nazis were the work of human beings is difficult to comprehend—and that is a good thing. As madmen, as barbarians, or, for followers of certain strains of theology and the occult, as incarnations of some kind of radical "evil," the authors of these crimes are inevitably placed outside the bounds of our shared humanity. In both France and Germany, the reception of films such as *Downfall* (2004), which portrayed Hitler's final days in his bunker, has contributed to this phenomenon of circumscription and rejection: it has been deemed indecent, and even intolerable, to show Hitler munching cookies, chatting affably to his secretary, and playing with his dog. Giving human—all too human—traits to the absolute monster in this way can seem quite dangerous, particularly from a pedagogical standpoint. But if history can and must take this perspective into consideration—and this is another debate entirely—its study most definitely is not served by the dehumanization of those who participated in the Nazis' crimes. Excluding these people from our shared humanity exonerates us from any serious reflection on humankind, Europe, modernity, the West—in sum, it makes it impossible to rigorously study any aspect of the world the Nazi criminals inhabited and participated in, a world that we might have in common. Certainly, skating around this point is both convenient and comfortable: the idea that we might share anything at all with the authors of statements and crimes as monstrous as theirs is repugnant to us. But it is unlikely that the cause of historical understanding—or understanding of any kind—can be served if questions that touch on our own time and place in this way are avoided or overlooked.

In addition to confronting the fact that they were twentieth-century Europeans, we must come to terms with the fact that the Nazis were, quite simply, people. They were people who came of age and lived in a specific set of circumstances, and one job for historians is to shed light on these circumstances. But beyond that, the Nazis have in common with all other humans, including ourselves, the fact that their lives took place within a universe of meaning and values. Put another way, it is unlikely that Franz Stangl, at Treblinka; Rudolf Höss, at Birkenau; or Karl Jäger, the head of the Einsatzkommando 3 of Einsatzgruppe A, woke up delighted each morning at the thought of the abominations they were about to commit. These men were not madmen. They did not see their actions as criminal. Rather, they were accomplishing a task, an *Aufgabe*—perhaps unpleasant, but necessary nonetheless.

Here, the sources all concur: private correspondence, personal diaries, and memoirs; public speeches such as the one Heinrich Himmler delivered to his superior officers and fellow generals in Posen (Poznań) in October 1943—they all bear witness to this point. Although there was nothing glorious or pleasant about this day-to-day work; although it could—Himmler himself conceded it—weigh on a man's conscience; although it could be grueling; it was carried out and held meaning in the context of a grander plan, one that was "historic" and "glorious." In this light, these actions take on meaning and value: they were committed by people, and as such they must be reclaimed from the domain of the psychiatrist or the zoologist and placed—at long last—where they belong, in the sphere of the historian. If they were committed by people, they must be examined within the context of the story being told about them, and the project they were intended to advance. If they were committed by people, it must be acknowledged that they were responses to hopes and fears. To say this of Nazi crimes may surprise or even shock the reader, and for this reason, historians have generally avoided doing so—both because of their own revulsion and because any comprehensive approach has, in the case of Nazism, always been ruled out. If the words of the old adage are true, and (attempting) to understand really is to forgive, then to do so would simply be going too far.

In his book *Ordinary Men*, on the officers of Reserve Police Battalion 101, Christopher Browning spends little time examining the meaning these men's acts might have had in their own eyes. His understanding of "ideology" is largely one of simple "inculcation," or even "brainwashing"—something ineffectual and imposed from the outside.[7] He does not portray these acts as signifying the actors' participation in a larger project, or even a partial adherence to elements borrowed by Nazi discourse from other imaginations, epochs, or rhetorics. As for German historians, since 1990 the majority of them have focused their attention on the archives discovered in East Germany after the end of the Soviet era. Their work on Nazism has defused and distanced it as a subject by focusing primarily on the logic of managerial and genocidal praxis: administrative procedures, relationships among institutions, and chains of command.

This approach certainly offers a form of protection from the subject and its reverberations—a way of absorbing the shock, the emotion, and the pain in order to carry out the work of history. With the threat of Holocaust denial and revisionism never far off, "documenting" (*dokumentieren*) the crime—assembling data, reconstituting contexts, tracking the executioners—remains a worthy task. At the same time, it has made it possible to largely sidestep the question of meaning, and the Nazi mental and intellectual universe still remains, for the most part, unknown. Certainly, the overarching principles of the Nazi "worldview" are familiar enough—although not always correctly explicated in history books. Certainly, too, influential historians have examined the genesis of these ideas, their formulation, their appropriation, and their dissemination. In passing, a few biographies of those who played central or supporting roles in the Third Reich have also referred to Nazi discourse and writing, citing them to support their arguments.

But, to my knowledge, no one has ever yet attempted to map out what might be called the mental universe in which Nazi crimes took place and held meaning. In addition to the reasons cited earlier, it must be acknowledged that historians have every reason to avoid this territory: why strain your eyes over the gothic characters and flimsy paper of this ersatz literature? The beetle-browed, crew-cut officers of the SA (Sturmabteilung; Brown Shirts) were rarely great philosophers. As for the intellectuals—for there were many—their work was at once cynical and superficial, an intolerable cosmetic smeared by monsters over what truly counts in the eyes of historians, which is praxis.

Reams of this literature exist, a whole vast continent neglected and dusty from disinterest. Its shores hold no interest for philosophers and intellectual historians; the Nazis were far too boorish for them to waste time investigating their writings. Historians have no time for it either; their concern is with social dynamics and practices. This continent is not entirely unexplored, however: specialists in a variety of disciplines have ventured through certain regions of it. Legal scholars, most notably, have worked for decades on the social and intellectual history of their field under the Nazi regime; the theoretical texts of the era, as well as their jurisprudential application, have been the subject of numerous studies.

For the most part, however, historians have remained cautious in their explorations. Among the many who have participated in writing the history of the Third Reich, only a small minority have taken a cultural approach to Nazism. No one taking this approach has claimed to be undertaking a comprehensive study. Research into the culture of Nazism all postdates 1995. The explanation for this is twofold. The first has to do with archival sources: the mass of documentation discovered following the end of the Soviet era has expanded our understanding of Nazi crimes, as well as of the Nazi project in the East, leading numerous historians to reexamine what might have motivated the Third Reich's gargantuan efforts to conquer, colonize, and eradicate, while at the same time attempting a biological reconstruction of their own society. The other reason may best be explained by German reactions to a traveling exhibit that toured the country between 1995 and 2000. Titled *Verbrechen der Wehrmacht* (The crimes of the Wehrmacht), its launch coincided with the publication of a critically acclaimed book which argued that Nazi crimes were the inevitable consequence of an essentialist version of German history whose sole grammar, since the sixteenth century at least, had been a radical and messianic anti-Semitism.[8] The book was a tidy response to the questions so violently raised by the traveling exhibit, which included a display of enlargements of photographs taken by troops, showing ordinary soldiers witnessing and participating in massacres and genocidal acts.

The effect of these photographs and the facts they revealed—which had been well known to historians for many years—were quite painful. How could ordinary Germans have ended up in these pictures? This question, asked by the exhibit's visitors and the media, was distressing to historians, who had for a long time been contesting discourses that contrasted the white knights of the Wehrmacht (the German armed forces) with the fanatical murderers of the SS (Schutzstaffel; Protection Squadron). No matter how carefully these historians analyzed the sources (where and when the photographs had been taken) and attempted to contextualize them (showing that these massacres had convincingly been presented to troops as operations required to maintain order and to secure the rear lines, which justified them in the eyes of the men carrying them out), their efforts were in vain: even as the extreme Right marched to defend the honor of the German private, the pendulum was swinging far in the other direction among the members of the public most strongly affected by these images. Their sincere and horrified response seemed to be that if nearly every German citizen had been a monster, it was because Germans had, since time immemorial, wished to kill the Jews and bring Europe to its knees.

The generalizations and the essentialist view of history that emerged from all this amounted to a call to historians to return to work. The goals, contexts, and fears of the Nazi era, including the mental universe of its actors, are better understood now than ever before. In the wake of Omer Bartov's superb study of the German Army on the Eastern Front, a great deal of research has been published, including Christian Gerlach's work on Belarus, Dieter Pohl's on Galicia, and Christoph Dieckmann's on Lithuania.[9]

In parallel to this work, a group of historians has developed a long-term study of the ideological motivations of the conquerors and colonizers of the East. Jürgen Förster, Jürgen Matthäus, and Richard Breitmann, historians based at the MGFA (Militärgeschichtliches Forschungsamt), a German research institute devoted to military history, have explored the formulation, dissemination, and reception of Nazi precepts and projects in the combat units of the Wehrmacht and the SS.[10] They have successfully shown that ideology was a significant motivator, all the more so because Nazi ideas were not unusual in Germany, Europe, and the West at that time. Recent audience reception studies, notably those using information gathered from prisoners of war who were being held by Britain and the United States, have established that these ideas were a component in actors' frames of reference (Referenzrahmen).[11]

Increasingly, the question of ideological conviction is also being used as a lens to examine the Nazi elite. Michael Wildt, for example, devoted an impressive doctoral thesis to the RSHA elite, the "generation of the absolute," who were haunted by distress over a Germany they saw as besieged, diminished, and threatened by a panoply of perils, a country these men had made it their mission to save once and for all.[12] In Believe and Destroy, Christian Ingrao offers a precise and rigorous social and intellectual history of high-ranking officials in the SD (Sicherheitsdienst; Security Service, the intelligence wing of the SS).[13] He, too, emphasizes that these men were intellectuals who inscribed their actions in a universe of meaning enriched by the fact that the nature of their work and human resource management policy within the SS required them to alternate time in the office and time in the field. Ulrich Herbert, in his biography of one of these men, Werner Best, paints a portrait of an "intellectual in action" deploying a set of principles and impeccable reasoning to justify his own actions and the projects of the Third Reich.[14]

Taken together, these studies, and the conclusions that could be drawn from them, were sufficient reason for certain historians to take up the question of the Nazi conception of values and meaning. American historian Claudia Koonz paved the way in 2003 with a book whose intentionally provocative title, *The Nazi Conscience*, distills the book's argument, which is that there was such a thing as an internally coherent Nazi morality.[15] A few years later, Raphael Gross, who had published a book on the political theorist Carl Schmitt's relationship to the Jews, edited a volume titled *Moralität des Bösen* (The morality of evil) and then put together a collection of articles on the ethics of National Socialism.[16]

This attention to the logic and the internal coherence of Nazi discourse as meaningful took place in the context of other, older work that, in the 1980s, had ventured to investigate what people at the time might have found attractive in Nazism. Exploring the "fascination of Nazism" and its "beautiful appearance" opened the way to exploring Nazi responses to contemporary concerns.[17] For, as curious as this may seem today, Nazism was not merely an aesthetic. It was also an ethic, offered up to a generation at sea.

The values and moral imperatives of the era in which Nazism emerged have been studied extensively. For Germans, the end of the First World War was a catastrophe that reopened old wounds: those of the Thirty Years' War, of the defeat of Prussia by Napoleon in 1806, of all of the apocalyptic moments that had been regular fare in Germany since the time of the Lutheran Reform. The fall of the empire; the near civil war that raged between 1918 and 1923; the Versailles treaty of 1919, which put an end to Germany as a world power; the hyperinflation of 1922–1923—all these events inspired apocalyptic prophecies, cultural pessimism, and a generation of artists who observed and depicted the ways in which chaos was supplanting the ordered cosmos of the prewar era. Painters such as Otto Dix transferred their experiences in the trenches to canvas, showing dismembered corpses and putrefying flesh; writers churned out disillusioned indictments of the era's decaying values; filmmakers described the triumph of crime, of dissembling, of gambling. The film *Dr. Mabuse the Gambler* (1922) was Fritz Lang's "portrait of his time": in it, the invisible and elusive Dr. Mabuse, with his cunning intellect and genius for disguise, reigns over a rapidly degenerating society, left without bearings by the dissolution of all fiduciary and moral value. Widespread devaluation, according to one contemporary, had transformed Germany into a theater of vast and unceasing "saturnalia":

> All peoples have known world war; most have known revolutions, social crises, strikes, reversals of fortune, and devaluations. But none other than Germany in 1923 has experienced the grotesque madness of all of these phenomena at once. None before has experienced this massive, carnivalesque *danse macabre*, the extravagant and unceasing saturnalia in which all values, not only monetary, have been debased.[18]

This was the situation at the end of the 1920s, when economic and social crisis struck Germany yet again. The popular *Emil and the Detectives*, adapted for the screen in 1931, was a children's story only in appearance: the author, Erich Kästner, wrote of how a community of children banded together to defend its members and fight crime. The underlying theme was the same as that of Fritz Lang's *M*, released the same year. *M* also depicts a counterculture, in this case the mob, which bests the impotent forces of the police and the state in nabbing a child killer. In the end, Commissioner Lohmann carries the day, but for how long? A year later, *The Testament of Dr. Mabuse*, Fritz Lang's sequel to *Dr. Mabuse the Gambler*, showed terror and crime continuing to mushroom.

The mob, the underworld, the mafia: like Berthold Brecht in *Arturo Ui*, Lang was referring to the rise of the NSDAP. If its enemies saw the Nazi Party as a criminal counterculture, its members saw it as the only community that was actually generating and proposing values that were relevant to contemporary problems. Jean Genet noted in his fictionalized memoir *The Thief's Journal* that of all the countries he had traveled through, Germany was the only one where he did not dare steal a thing: to him, crime seemed to be the only law of the land, spoiling any pleasure he might have taken in transgression. But if the values and norms of Nazism seemed criminal from outside the world the Nazis were building, from the inside they offered the reassuring coherence of a closed system, founded on a handful of particularistic principles and the inexorable conclusions that were to be drawn from them.

In 1919, as the NSDAP was coming together, Max Weber observed in *Science as a Vocation* that a "struggle of the gods" was under way: the more the Renaissance and modernity had undermined society's certainties, the more difficult it had become to know which saint, which church, or which school to believe in. The struggle of the gods was further amplified by what Kant referred to in his eponymous text as "The Conflict of the Faculties." Neither gods nor certain knowledge could offer safe refuge from these doubts, conflicts, and struggles, which could no longer be quelled—not by reason, not by religion, not by the Great War or its aftermath, not by the fallen empires of a bygone era. To many at the time, the NSDAP had the tremendous merit of clearing a straight path through a confusing world, with tangible and easily comprehensible guideposts.

What should we do? How should we act? Why are we here? The Nazis answered these questions with a large body of texts, speeches, and images, exhorting people to look to what was most concrete, closest to home, most tangible: from a welter of contradictory ideas, all of which seemed to carry the same weight, from the clang and clash of warring religious faiths, blood, flesh, and "race" were held out as a reference, as a beacon. Biological substance offered a further advantage: it was not strictly personal. It was shared by members of the same family, the same "community," the same "race"—members living and dead, and those yet to be born. To preserve and foster this substance was a clear and easy-to-understand goal. It created a community; it gave meaning to an individual's private existence.

Keeping the race alive was the founding principle and the end goal of this openly particularistic and holistic set of norms: we must act for the Germanic-Nordic race alone (or for the German people)—not for humanity, which is a dangerous and dissolving chimera—and we must act for the community, not for our own personal interest. These simple principles gave people answers to the questions raised by modernity. Wilhelm Frick, a lawyer by training and by profession, was appointed minister of the interior on January 30, 1933. In this capacity, he convened a group of biologists and legal experts to discuss the implementation of eugenics legislation and offered them this striking summary of the ways in which the damaging course of nineteenth-century history had "shaken the moral structure" of the German people:

> Observe German history and you will note that we have shifted from
> an agrarian state to an industrial people. [Karl] Hardenberg set the
> growth of the industrial state in motion in Prussia in 1807. The

moment he liberated the soil so that it could become private property, the liberal economic system was made possible. As this money economy grew, Germany urbanized and industrialized. This put an end to the natural growth of our people, to farm families and to the efficient natural selection that is so vital to our countryside! Our legal relations, the money economy, and social welfare legislation have upended our understanding of morality, the sexes, family, and children. It was the beginning of individualism, of class warfare, of Marxism, of Communism. After the war, the mechanization of labor, economic enslavement, and the Marxist economy completed this process of destruction, which has led our people to the edge of the abyss. What ensued was the moral decadence of our people. The liberal mind poisoned its soul and killed off all sense of family and child.[19]

This flow of change, it must be noted, had a source (the French Revolution), as well as an outlet (the First World War and its aftermath). The Nazis claimed to be taking a stand against these "one hundred and fifty years of error," as the Nazi theorist Alfred Rosenberg called them; more, indeed, than a hundred and fifty years, since many believed that the problem dated back to the reception of Roman (and Jewish-influenced) law during the Early Medieval period, or earlier than that, to the evangelization of Germania. Some traced it even further, to the torrent of Germanic blood spilled during the Peloponnesian Wars. The practical and moral errancy of the Germanic and the German people went back a long way: for centuries, lacking in roots, structure, and solidarity, they had been required to obey rules that were an open threat to their very lives—and this phenomenon had only intensified since 1789.

Christianity had imposed monogamy and the obligation to care for the weak and the sick; then the Enlightenment and the French Revolution injected these religious injunctions with liberalism and universalism; then international law and order had further sapped the people's strength—the clear aim of all this being the extinction of the German people as a political power, and even as a biological reality. The norms that structured German culture and governed its actions were thus harmful, hostile to its very existence (*lebensfeindlich*). The Nazi corpus proposed that these values be revisited on the grounds that blood was the only tangible reality. It called for the establishment of a new normativity, one that would be benevolent toward the German people, that would nurture and care for them rather than fettering and annihilating them, both legally and morally.

The historical work mentioned earlier decisively opened the way to approaching and understanding how and why the criminal violence of the Nazis came to be deployed. My goal here is to follow in its footsteps by pursuing and deepening the study of the norms, imperatives, and duties that underlie Nazi discourse. This study is all the more warranted by the fact that norms appear to have played a crucial role in mobilizing people to act in situations that pushed at the limits of what was morally acceptable—that is, to commit these crimes. To the extent that we are engaging in the study of history, that is, that we believe ourselves to be considering human beings, and not madmen or monsters, we cannot avoid the observation that killing is an unpleasant and difficult thing to do—all of the sources attest to this. Formulating a discourse that conveys meaning, and even transmits imperatives, maxims, or duties, facilitates the act of killing by establishing, at the very least, the conditions in which it becomes possible.

Initially, this book was intended to be a highly systematic and technical study of Nazi morality. Very rapidly, however, the sources led elsewhere: their intellectual and ethical content was indeed very thin. Nazi morality—for such a thing does exist—is holistic, particularistic, heroic, and sacrificial, which is interesting, but hardly original.

Little by little, I widened my focus and embarked on a comprehensive study of Nazi normativity. Such a project required taking into account not only sources whose contents and aim were explicitly ethical, but also all other types of normative discourse, which, whatever their form, described what was *normal*, stated was *desirable*, and formulated what was *imperative*—in short, all discourse that in any way gave indications or orders as to what to do, how to do it, and why. The field from which this project drew is vast, profuse, and diffuse.

I examined printed sources, texts, images, and films, both fictional ones and those that claimed to document or inform. The texts were taken from the reference works of Nazi ideology, but also from pedagogical literature (from both schools and the NSDAP), from daily newspapers, from academic literature in fields as diverse as law—fiscal,

administrative, real estate, and criminal—legal theory, biology, philosophy, history, race "science" (or "raciology" as it was called), and others.

The corpus from which these sources are drawn is colossal: 1,200
books and articles and some fifty films. The abundance of material
alone shows that the authors clearly had a lot to say, and that they felt
the need to do so. In my previous work, I noted that references to Greek
and Roman Antiquity also served as tools to justify, in the eyes of the
actors themselves, what was not self-evident in a cultural universe built
on Judeo-Christian and Kantian principles.[20] Seeing high-profile
scholars of eugenics call on the even higher profiles of Seneca and Plato
invited further study.

The authors or producers of these sources include, first, the inner
circle of the Nazi leadership. Hitler, in his private communications as
well as his published writings and his speeches, was not content to
merely give orders. He argued and held forth extensively on the harmful
ways in which German cultural norms had changed. We also find
Goebbels, in his speeches, his writings, and his *Journals*; Himmler, at
once the SS's chief, patriarch, and schoolmaster, who offered a profusion of ideological and moral lessons; and Rosenberg, who, in his
writing, deployed a *Kulturkritik* more expansive and carefully argued
than is generally recognized.

Second, in addition to the highest-ranking members of the Nazi
Party, the corpus studied here contains works by numerous academics
in a wide range of fields: legal experts, of course, but also anthropolo-
gists of race (*Rassenkunde*), historians, and even geographers and landscape architects. Some of them were eager to reach beyond their field
of expertise: the physician and eugenicist Fritz Lenz, for example, held
forth on "gentilist" morality, a term he had invented to describe what
he saw as a necessary antidote to the era's harmful '-isms' (collectivism,
individualism, and humanism), while historian Theodor Schieder ear-
nestly offered advice on how best to carry out a sustainable Polish
occupation.

The third group of contributors to this corpus, all university educated and for the most part ennobled by doctorates, were high-ranking
officials, members of a skilled intellectual elite who gave force to the
political projects of the Nazi Party, grounding and justifying them by
mobilizing law, biology, and history. Werner Best, a lawyer and a high-

ranking member of the SD, is an excellent example of such men—not content to merely act, he accompanied his actions by numerous articles in which he explained just why and how he acted.

A fourth cohort in this corpus is composed of the publicists and ideologues who devoted their time to popularizing and disseminating this normative system and its founding principles in newspaper articles, brochures, books, and classes in ideology. This cohort includes journalists, teachers, and essayists, who, from their positions in the party or thanks to their access to a publisher or the media, explained to the people the right way to act.

Many of these authors have been the subject of biographies or at least have an entry in the various reference works that identify key actors in the Third Reich. The others have been the subject of studies in social history: the groups to which they belonged (*Akademiker*, university educated people, high-ranking officials, university professors, journalists, and so on) have been investigated in numerous books, which have reconstructed their career paths and mapped out the networks in which they lived and worked. What remained was the task of reading their intellectual output—truly reading it.

Journal by journal, headline by headline, publisher by publisher— and with the help of the bibliographies these texts contained—I have attempted to identify everything that was written on the necessary reconstruction of norms in the new Germany as constructed by the National Socialists. Step by step, as I became familiar with the subject matter and reasoning in these texts, I widened my scope of interest, and the themes I examined proliferated: from animal protection in ancient India to nudism, from the conversion of Greenland to witch hunts, from the Nuremberg Laws to the (rudimentary) labor laws applied to Polish workers, or—still more elliptical—those applied to Soviet prisoners in the territories of the Reich. Nazism was nothing less than a rereading of all history, and my project was to follow it through each era and theme of this ambitious revisionist process.

There may be some objections to calling such a vast and varied collection of texts a corpus. But all of these textbooks, manuals, treatises, pamphlets, doctrinal articles, brochures, films, and more were, to some degree, offering an answer to the same question, raised tacitly or in so many words: what must be done to keep Germany from dying? What norms should be followed so that German life would be fruitful and multiply, so that the Germanic race would have a long and certain—and even an unending—future ahead of it? Furthermore, as I read and examined these writings, common themes emerged: Germany's political and biological distress; the necessity of responding to that distress with actions that would no longer be undermined by injunctions that further contributed to that distress; the primacy of the group over the individual and the indisputable superiority of the Germanic race, which had given birth to all culture. Despite the diversity of the authors and the heterogeneity of the media in which they worked, these common denominators provide the keys to understanding the core of the Nazi *Weltanschauung*, to understanding the components of this core that, despite internal contestations and debate, were agreed to by all and upheld in the face of the enemy, of history, and of the death thought to be in store for the *Volk* if nothing was done.

This welter of words, so widely seen as soporific and uninteresting, turned out to be more than worthy of further examination: the study of this discourse makes it possible to reconstitute a "worldview" and to place the actions of the Nazis where they belong, within a vast design drawn up using a specific critique of the past and with precise plans for the future. This is not to say that the images and texts examined here were the sole or direct motivation for all that went on between 1933 and 1945 in Germany or between 1939 and 1945 in Europe—far from it. The link between discourse and practice is not a direct one, and obviously the foot soldiers of the Reich on the Eastern Front were not packing texts by the theorists of *Rassenhygiene* in their kits. It is clear, however, that they were familiar with the ideas produced by Nazi legal experts, planners, biologists, and historians, which were disseminated in the press and on film; incorporated into agendas and taught in instructional courses on Nazi ideology; and printed up and distributed in brochures, booklets, pamphlets, and tracts for military use. Not everyone was intimately familiar with the complete works of the Nazi theorist and agriculture minister Richard Darré, but his ideas seeped through myriad channels of communication. Furthermore, ideas such as his were, generally speaking, neither unheard of nor particularly original; it was therefore all the easier to penetrate a social space in which they were, to a degree, already present.

This body of texts and images thus interested me as a symptom, a matrix, and a project. It was symptomatic of a time and a place—the West in the first half of the twentieth century, and, more specifically, Germany from the 1920s to the 1940s. It formed a matrix of ideas that were promoted, repeated, and developed, and, as reception studies have shown, offered meaning and structure to the experiences that individuals lived through, the crimes they committed, and even the traumas they suffered. Finally, this corpus formed the bedrock of a very long-term vision. The "thousand years" touted by the Reich was much more than a slogan: it was a project for a cultural revolution, for the overturning and replacement of one normative universe by another in the centuries to come. Nazi ideologues and cadres knew all too well that it would take the German people several generations to accomplish such a revolution, besotted as they were with Judeo-Christian values, Kantian ethics, and the liberal worldview. Everything that I read, saw, and watched was thought out, written, and filmed to help Germans of the time accomplish a difficult task—but, more than that, it was intended to acculturate the generations to come and cleanse them of the dross of harmful norms. A revolution in culture and norms is a long-term goal. The authors of the body of texts studied here worked toward this revolution valiantly, offering up a highly developed *Kulturkritik* that consisted of measuring inherited norms by a single yardstick—that of the life of the race. Once inherited values had been evaluated and discredited, once the traditions of (Judeo-) Christianity, the Enlightenment, and the dominant world order had been repudiated, it was possible, having opposed them, to establish and offer up a new discourse, one that offered not a bewildering profusion of words and ideas, but instead a carefully and coherently argued *logos*.

I have been able to identify three foundational categorical imperatives in the Nazi project—three types of action that were intended to ensure eternal life for Germany.

The first was that of procreation: the Aryan race had to be fertile and to produce as many children as possible, especially as a defense against the Slavic enemy; it also had to be attentive to the quality of the biological substance it produced, which was to be free of all foreign and degenerate elements. Everything that governed procreation was intimately linked not only to the origins of each child, but also to the origins of the race itself, and, by the same token, to the norms governing the life of the race: What had the race looked like in its infancy, and what had its original laws been? How and why had the Aryan race been denatured? How could its authenticity be restored? These questions were given abundant attention in this corpus, and Part I of this book attempts to offer an account of it.

After the moment of origin came the moment of history. The (natural) law governing History was the law of conflict, of unceasing racial war: all life was struggle. Part II of the book treats this theme of war. Norms hostile to life had sapped the strength of the Aryan race as it engaged in this struggle, threatening its very survival. Acknowledging nature's unyielding imperatives—natural selection and a struggle to the death among racial principles—meant fighting according to the laws dictated by blood, not those dictated by humans or by false gods.

Part III turns to the aftermath of this struggle. Winning this war, if it could be done, would put an end to the "six thousand years of racial war."[21] It would allow the Germanic race to escape History and enter the triumphal, eschatological moment of its reign. Emerging victorious into the vast reaches of the East and of time which its struggle had opened up, the race would finally be able to inhabit the infinite time of the millennium and of the eschatological promise. This space, too, was to be governed by new norms, so that this domination could be perpetuated for centuries of centuries.

PART I

Procreating

CHAPTER ONE

Origins: Nature, Essence, Genesis

ACCORDING TO NAZI WRITERS, even the most disinterested and un-prejudiced of minds agreed that a German man was a brave man, and a good one. Brave, valorous, a good warrior, but not excessively war-like: left to his own devices, he would devote himself to agriculture and to culture and would take up arms only rarely, to conquer a bit of living space for himself—after all, one does have to live.

In this respect, Nazi discourse followed a *völkisch* tradition whose roots stretched back into the nineteenth century.[1] As early as 1919, the Nazis were already going to great lengths to prove how good and mild Germans really were: far from the image of the blood-drinking, raping, pillaging barbarian that had been spread by depictions of the sack of Rome, they were actually peaceable, affable peasant-soldiers. In their natural state, these powerful, handsome children of nature (*Naturmenschen*) lived in a state of bliss so pure that even Rousseau would have struggled to imagine it. The infancy of the race was a happy time of healthy, pure humans reveling in their existence and their lives, "just as the innocent child rejoices in his existence, so much that he even shouts for joy."[2] The Germanic people, at the time of their birth, were close to nature and could freely express their essence, without any alteration or mediation.

Birth and Essence: Germans, Nature, and Animals

Then as now, if one chose a single flag to brandish in order to provoke anti-Semitic sentiment, it would most likely be that of ritual animal slaughter and the biblical-veterinary injunctions upon which the laws of Kashrut are founded. The NSDAP took on this issue very early and deployed an unnuanced campaign against "the torture of animals"

(*Tierquälerei*). In 1931, a physician who was a member of the Nazi Party published a pamphlet on the topic of "the NSDAP fight against animal cruelty, animal torture, and ritual slaughter."[3] It bore the Führer's stamp of approval, in the form of a letter from Hitler to the author in which he expressed his support and promised that "in the future National-Socialist state, all of these things will be rapidly brought to an end."[4] The author, Albert Eckhard, reminded his readers that it was "part of the very essence of what it means to be German to condemn and combat any torture inflicted on a human being or a defenseless animal." The NSDAP had "emblazoned on its standards the combat against evil and for good" and therefore had no choice but to make this just cause its own and to fight against torturers of all stripes, cruel beings lacking in all "empathy."[5]

Ritual slaughter is "a horror" that "goes against the requirements of humanity," said Eckhard. Fueled by indignation, the author went on to oblige his readers with the story of a poor cow's escape from some abhorrent rabbis who had slit its throat: the animal made a break for it, shedding blood over the last two hundred meters it managed to run, its carotid artery flapping in the breeze. This true fact, the author noted, careful to cite his sources, had been reported in the *Völkischer Beobachter*.[6] A decade later, in 1941, German cinemagoers could enjoy fainting at the sight of ritual slaughter as depicted by Fritz Hippler, who featured the slitting of animal throats in his film *Der Ewige Jude* (The eternal Jew). The film, shot for the sole purpose of demonstrating the fundamental otherness and the essential criminality of the Jews, devoted ten minutes out of seventy to a gory scene in which two cows were bled to death with a knife. The defenders of these practices provoked the audience's ire when they appeared on screen—ire quickly soothed by a voice-over reminding viewers that the procedure had been prohibited in one of the first laws passed by the Führer, on April 21, 1933—in the name of "the German people's well-known love of animals."[7] The denunciation of this so-called ritual cruelty is a constant in Judeophobic discourse: here, as is so often the case, the Nazis were hardly innovating; they employed ideas and vocabulary that one encounters elsewhere.

More interesting is the insistence on an alleged trait in Jewish, and then in Christian, culture, that this supposed cruelty revealed. Here, it is exposed and criticized in the SS journal *Das Schwarze Korps* (The black corps), in an article titled "Trouble in the Blood: This World and the Next":

> We all know that this horrifying mistreatment of animals so often observed in so-called Catholic countries is based on the idea that animals have no soul. This mechanistic view of the world, which sees animals as machines with no feelings, is particularly offensive to the faith unique to our race. To us, God is manifest everywhere in nature, because nature is sacred, and we worship in it the revelation of an eternal will. Seen in this light, the animal is, in our eyes, actually a "little brother," and our sensibility considers that assaulting a man able to defend himself is more morally acceptable than any cruelty towards a defenseless creature.[8]

By constructing a God that was one and absolute, Jews, and their Christian epigones and avatars, were taking sacredness from the world. Long ago, in the happier days of Germanic antiquity, in the ancient woods of Saxony, in Greece, or in Rome, the divine had been present everywhere. But that was all in the past—God had now withdrawn to the heavens, where He lived alone and jealously. Now all the firmament and perfection belonged to the hereafter, and all that remained in this world was substance and sin. Animals had been among the victims of this great schism between nature and the divine; now, they were nothing but animal-machines. And this was just what Albert Eckhard deplored, noting, "In our supposedly German laws, which in fact can hardly be described as German, and which await reform, animals are not considered to be living beings, but things."[9]

Clearly, this rhetoric goes much further than the habitual critiques of ritual slaughter: animals were mistreated by Jews (and Christians) because, like the natural world to which they belonged, they had been stripped of all enchantment, reigned over and ruled by a far-off God. This idea recurs throughout the texts devoted to this issue: the Jews were materialists (they considered the world to be pure matter) because they were metaphysical (they had imposed a separation between nature and the divine).

Germanic religious sentiment, by contrast, was profoundly animist, perceiving and revering the divine wherever life was manifest. Whereas for Germanic peoples nature was a manifestation of the divine, and was for this reason to be worshiped as sacred, Judeo-Christians had come up with a materialism that was brutal and coldhearted. The world, to them, was nothing but disenchanted matter, from which God had retreated to a distant place, making it the object of humankind's destructive and exploitative actions. An unrestrained passion for money was not the only manifestation of the materialism that characterized this race; it could also be seen in the metaphysical worldview of the Jews, according to which the physical world and spiritual principles were separate.

Held up in opposition to this separation was "Northern European man, who . . . perceives the world as all one," in the words of Dr. Lothar Stengel von Rutkowski, a eugenics specialist, sometime professor at the University of Jena, a poet and a thinker, a lyricist of the German race—and during the war a practitioner in the medical service of the Waffen-SS (literally "armed protection squadron"; that is, the military branch of the SS).[10] Contemporary science, he wrote, had confirmed this intuition by showing that humans and their environment are both ruled by "natural law," at the microcosmic and macrocosmic levels, in nature and in culture. Without citing him, Stengel von Rutkowski lifted Kant's famous words for his conclusion, which was that "natural law" reigned over the "starry heavens above us and the moral law within us."[11]

The biologist Heinz Graupner devoted many pages to his attempt to distinguish the animal kingdom from the plant kingdom, to discriminate among life's various manifestations, before concluding that the task was impossible: "When we attempt to draw borders between the different organic kingdoms, we perceive an image of a grand unity of all living things, because we can detect no fundamental difference among the organisms" themselves. Contrary to the affirmations of Christians—and all those who professed their belief in specific difference—"there is no human exception." To support his argument, the biologist cited the use of animal extracts such as hormones in the medical treatment of humans. Humans, as a part of the great unity of all living things, were therefore subject to the laws of nature: "Our shared experience shows that everywhere we come up against the oneness of all life, and the universality of its laws. This must be the precept of our thoughts and our actions": "the oneness of all living things requires us to act and behave in ways respectful to the laws of life."[12]

This idea was dear to Himmler, who, in the hours following the funeral of assassinated Nazi intelligence chief Reinhard Heydrich, gave his audience his own personal version of *vanitas vanitatum:*

> It is time to break with the folly of these megalomaniacs, in particular these Christians, who speak of dominating the earth; all of that must brought back into perspective. There is nothing particular about man. He is but a part of this world. In the face of a good storm, he can do nothing. He cannot even predict it. He does not even know how a fly is made—as disagreeable as it may be, it is a marvel—or how a flower is organized. Man must relearn how to see the world with worshipful respect. Only then will he be able to perceive things as they are; only then will he see to what extent we are caught up in a system [greater than us].[13]

Against the artificial and senseless individualism of the -isms of the past (Christianity, humanism, liberalism), it is a strictly holistic vision of the world that is defended in this passage. Up against nature, individualism became a chimera. Nature taught that the individual was nothing, that the world was to be thought of, seen, and treated as a whole. The *SS-Leitheft,* a journal for SS officers, affirmed this view:

> It goes against nature's will for man, imprisoned by the folly of his own importance, to decide to live the life he wants. For what is man, taken on his own? Observing nature teaches us that the leaf on the tree exists only through the branch on which it grows. That the trunk gives life to the branch, and in turn owes its growth to the root, which itself draws its forces from the earth. As for the tree, it is but a member of the forest.[14]

The analogy of the people and the race was then drawn explicitly:

> A people, too, is a living, organic whole. Just as the tree is not a sum of its branches, its offshoots, and leaves, but rather an organic product of all its parts, a people is not merely a mass of individuals brought together by chance, but an organic entity.[15]

Logically, one could induce from this natural reality "consciousness of racial duty," a "duty of race," which was to "advance the race into eternity." In other words, "We exist on this earth to give our people eternal life."[16] A striking summary of Nazi religiosity: the same thing that bound the living to the dead bound the living to the living. To be sure, those now living would die, but biological substance was eternal, as long as its health and purity were preserved.

Contrary to what all churches descended from Jewish stock claimed, man did not have any "special position" in "nature's reign," as a publication by the Hanover section of the NSDAP explained: "Man is integrated into nature, he is part of the great family of living things. He is subject to the law of the preservation of the race, to the struggle for life, to the law of heredity," which is valid for both plants and animals.[17] One had only to observe the vital phenomena of breathing and digestion to be convinced: they obeyed "the same laws" in all living things.[18] The religiosity of bondedness and a system of thinking based on connectedness and fusion were thus held up against dialectical Jewish thought and its focus on forming judgments through logic and process, perpetual disjunction, and constant separation. Indeed, what was being criticized in Judaism was the very existence of metaphysics (there could be no such thing in animism, for which nothing existed beyond physical reality—no *meta*, in other words), and of speculative intelligence itself.

Many texts leveled this kind of charge against metaphysics. At the core of all their critiques was a repudiation of the idea expressed in the very prefix meta- (above or beyond). Writing on the notion of *Volk*, Stengel von Rutkowski recalled, "man . . . obeys the same laws as animals and plants."[19] As part of an overarching whole, man could not break free from this natural law. Nor could he argue that there was a radical ontological difference between himself and an animal or a plant. The very idea of "metaphysics," that there could be a discipline devoted to exploring what was beyond or outside nature, was therefore completely absurd: "The *physis;* that is, nature, is everywhere for us! That is why our humanities and our philosophy must also be rooted in this *physis* and in this natural law." Anything "supernatural" was in fact "non-nature; against nature."[20] Here, Stengel von Rutkowski echoed his friend and collaborator Karl Astel, a professor of eugenics at the University of Jena, who, in his opening remarks for the 1937 school year, assigned human intelligence a clear mission: to serve life, not "any sort of 'meta' that destroys life and burdens it with sickness and stupidity." For Astel,

> *physis* means nature, and we are all a part of nature, we result from nature's law. Why should our intelligence deviate from under-standing nature's laws to explore any kind of "metaphysics," any-thing "supernatural," which, until now, has always degenerated into "non-nature" and anti-nature?[21]

This Jewish disenchanting of the world demeaned the animal kingdom, objectifying and shamelessly exploiting it. If animals were being treated so poorly, according to this discourse, it was because the Nordic race had been stripped of its natural sensibilities and its inborn instincts. Here is Heinrich Himmler's description of the pain and sorrow he felt when he saw a deer shot or a snail crushed, as recounted to his masseur, Felix Kersten, who treated him for various aches and pains, including stomach trouble:

> How could you feel any kind of pleasure in shooting these poor beasts from behind as they graze innocently and defenselessly, so unsus-pectingly, at the edges of the forests, my dear Kersten? Because it is in fact murder, pure and simple. . . . Nature is so beautiful, and every animal has the right to live. It's a way of seeing I admire very par-ticularly in our ancestors. . . . You find this respect for animals every-where among the Indo-Germanic peoples. I was quite interested to hear recently that even today, Buddhist monks, on their evening walks through the forest, carry a little bell with them to warn the woodland creatures so that they can run away and not be stepped on. Here, we tread thoughtlessly on every snail, we crush any old worm.[22]

Buddhist monks, according to Himmler, represented a branch of the Nordic race that had emigrated to Asia in prehistoric times, and were therefore living examples of the race's culture in its primitive state, preserving practices that had long disappeared in the West. Judeo-Christian acculturation was to blame for this: it led to a disre-gard for animals, not to mention the innocent loss of earthworms' lives during people's crepuscular perambulations.

Himmler, who had sent raciologists on a high-profile expedition to examine the skulls of contemporary Tibetan farmers, was not the only one looking to India or Tibet for evidence of the practices of the Nordic race.[23] In 1939, a student at the Leipzig School of Medicine presented a doctoral thesis on "The Protection of Animals in Ancient India."[24] His long detour through space and time had brought him up close to an essential quality of the Nordic race: "The German [sic] has for all time loved animals."[25] This, he explained, could be observed in India, because the ancient Indians had been "Indo-Germanic," a population of peasant-soldiers who had subjugated the "original population," which was of lesser biological quality, then inhabited the subcontinent. The Indo-Germans, who were as close to nature as all original Germanic peoples, were convinced that between "man and nature, there exists no significant difference."[26] This explained their belief—neither exotic nor outrageous—in "the transmigration of souls," a religious affirmation of "the unity of all living things," a faith that could only be fully realized "among Aryans, with an Aryan worldview, and this high consideration for life, for all forms of life, that is unique to them."[27]

Attitudes toward animals were thus presented as evidence of an ethical and intellectual divide between the Nordic and Jewish races, as well as of extremely different ways of relating to the world: the Jewish person refused nature and mistreated animals; the Nordic individual, by contrast, celebrated nature and believed that the difference between humans and animals was negligible (because humans *are* animals)—far too negligible to justify assaulting their physical integrity. In addition to the law of April 23, 1933, the Third Reich vaunted its Reichstierschutzgesetz (Reich Animal Protection Act, passed on November 24, 1933), whose first article prohibited inflicting pain on or otherwise mistreating animals. In this way, justice was done to an inborn sentiment that was unique to the Nordic race: exalting the closely linked nature of bipeds and quadrupeds.

Hunting, however, was a noble and revered pastime—so much so that Hermann Goering, never able to pass up a fancy title, had himself named the Reich's master huntsman. Not that hunting was contradictory to this "love of animals . . . which is German in its essence": it was merely necessary to respect "the foundational laws of the hunt," a custom "which we may proudly claim as a German virtue and which is based on respect for the animal, for this creature who is our sister."[28] The "Reich hunting law" proclaimed at the impetus of Field Marshal

Goering, was, moreover, a faithful transcription of these "customary laws of the hunt."[29]

These texts and legal measures sketched out a hierarchy of living things that was unique to Nazism. Contrary to what is often claimed, this hierarchy was not a scale with Aryans at the top and Jews at the bottom. Rather, it was a far more complex topology, with Aryans and all apex predators at the top, followed by mixed peoples, and then, at the bottom, Slavic, Black, and Asian individuals. Jews had no place in it at all—they belonged to bacteriology more than to any shared biological law. This distinction was a structural one in the Nazi imagination, as Hitler himself emphasized in his endeavor to convince Admiral Horthy to intensify the persecution of Hungarian Jews:

> They must be treated like tuberculosis bacilli, which can infect a healthy body. There is nothing cruel about that when one thinks that innocent animals such as rabbits or deer have to be culled to avoid any damage. Why should we, then, spare the horrible beasts who wanted to bring us Bolshevism?[30]

Were the Nazis really animal lovers? We often hear that this was the case: after all, Hitler and Himmler were vegetarians, and their animal protection laws were considered remarkable enough that they were left in place in West Germany until 1972. But, as with all nature protection regulations, the Nazis relied on texts that had already been written—and they rarely applied them.[31] The fate of animals in Germany was no more enviable after 1933 than it had been before, and it deteriorated considerably after the war began in 1939. It should not be forgotten that 80 percent of the transport of the Wehrmacht was powered by horses. The German armed forces were great consumers and destroyers of creatures of war, particularly horses and dogs.

Their affection for animals also did not prevent the Nazis from biological and "medical" experimentation. Before 1933, they denounced "Jewish medicine" and its sadistic practices, notably its use of vivisection. After 1933, however, animals were no less subject to this sort of practice. Even worse, when it came to research of strategic interest to the state (resistance to poison gas, biological weapons, and so on), animal experimentation was widespread and uncontested.[32]

Not all animals found favor in the eyes of the Nazis. Predators
(*Raubtiere*) were seen as fighters demonstrating superior strength in the
struggle for life, and were held in great esteem. At the same time, certain domestic animals were dismissed as having been alienated and
enslaved by a life of weakness and dependence on humans. *Alles Leben
ist Kampf* (All life is struggle), a 1937 documentary that promoted eugenics and the practice of sterilization for "useless lives," praised
stags—in particular, the alpha male victors in mating combats—then
flashed an image of a coddled, curly haired poodle onto the screen. It
was, the film explained, the perfect example of culture's role in coun-
tering natural selection: "Once, we believed that we could preserve all
useless life, even encourage it. Left to their own devices, none of these
pathetic creatures would emerge victorious" in the struggle for life.

Nazis' love of animals, just like their enchantment with the mystery of the natural world, had its limits: there is no absolute valorization
of animals in Nazi texts. Nazi esteem for animals was relative, and depended on an animal's life force and capacity for aggression. A poodle,
from this perspective, deserved only the cruelest Darwinian sarcasm.

Nudity, Nature, Authenticity

Nature, of course, had its physical trappings. Victorian as it was, the
Nazi leadership supported nudist movements, which were often closely
tied to the nationalist and racist right wing. The idea was to experience life as nature had made you—not, perish the thought, as the Judeo-
Christian God made you—in direct contact with the elements and
with Mother Nature. This was thought to encourage the body's healthy
development, which could then be exhibited as inspiration to others
to cultivate their own healthy bodies. In his magazine *Deutsche
Leibeszucht*, as well as numerous other, highly popular, publications,
Hans Suren, Nazi Germany's foremost and best-known promoter of
nudist sport, offered readers a plethora of nudes: photographed by forests, lakes, or at the seaside, these naked bodies were shown as at one
with the sand and the water whence they had come. In harmony with
the elements, tanned, fulfilled, and happy, the subjects of these images
offered dwellers of the strait-laced and blacktopped cities a sense of recovered communion with Mother Nature in all her cosmic grandeur.

The Party's censors had nothing to say against them: if—as one would wager was the case—these (beautiful) images evoked certain feelings and sensations in the *Sommerlager* (summer camps) of the Hitlerjugend, officially they were devoid of all eroticism. The innocent depiction of nudes was merely the faithful and authentic display of a race of beautiful-bodied people. Close to nature, men and woman could mix: because Mother Nature—contrary to what the unhealthy and repressive cultures of East claimed—sees nothing wrong with that. Indeed, nudity was to be a cornerstone of a renewed morality. According to the Nazi journal *Neues Volk*, promoting and appreciating Nordic nudity allowed the people "to think and to formulate moral judgments in concert with nature," rather than against it.[33]

Taking a stand against certain art critics who had expressed offense at the proliferation of nudes in official art since 1933, *Das Schwarze Korps* attacked these Christian and Jewish hypocrites. Nudity had been banished from art as from life by "foreign doctrines" that had "torn our country apart," to the point that "many Germans no longer know what is honest and what is not":

> The pure and the beautiful have never been a sin in the eyes of the German people. Just as the Greeks knew how to represent the harmoniousness of the Nordic body, the duty of our art is to represent the ideals of the German people in sculpture and painting. We vigorously reject the prudishness that helped to destroy in our people the instinct for the noble and the beautiful in our bodies. Here again, we should look to the Greeks, who knew how to cultivate biological selection among their people through athletic contests held in the nude during the Olympic Games, which encouraged racial selection.[34]

The SS publication firmly condemned "morality foreign to the race" (*artfremde Moral*), deploring an acculturation that had, over the centuries, alienated the Nordic race from its roots and its nature. The contamination was everywhere:

> Even the healthiest among us is haunted by this centuries-long permeation, by an education that has spanned multiple generations. A shame of being truly sincere towards our bodies inhabits us. . . . This is why the Greek concept of the beautiful and the good as a force that

preserves and governs the world is also our ideal of life . . . as opposed
to medieval obscurantism.[35]

The aesthetic and ethical legitimacy of the Greek forebear dispelled
any shame: followers of Johann Joachim Winckelmann should be taken
at their word![36] If the *Bildungsbürgertum*, Germany's cultivated bourgeoisie, were swooning before marble nudes carved by the Greeks, the
Greek nude should also be taken as a practical imperative, not merely
a scholarly one. A biological one, as well, for Judeo-Christian culture
was deadly: this "mortification of the flesh is a total destruction of . . .
all vital forces."[37]

The Nordic race was a race that hid nothing, dissembled nothing;
its spirit was pure and guileless, like a child's. *Deutsche Leibeszucht*,
the Nazi nudist movement's magazine, argued staunchly that "nudity
in nature is not in any way immoral. . . . Liberated from the shackles
imposed on them by civilization and culture," humans could experience "freedom" and "health" in all the places nature had to offer, such
as, continued the author, apparently suffering from a surfeit of clichés:
"a meadow filled with flowers, beneath the foliage of the forests, at the
edge of the waters of a lake sparkling with blue, on the burning sand,
or on the rugged mountaintops that rub shoulders with the sky."[38]

Nudism, in addition to being a physical, aesthetic, and moral choice,
was an ontological attempt to return to one's core being, "an urge to
heal ourselves, a liberation that sweeps away the debris deposited by
the centuries." Only in this condition could one recover one's humanity:
"Only he who builds his life on life's foundations and who acknowledges and respects the laws of nature is a [true] man. He is a healthy and
fully viable man when he has (again) become a natural man."[39] Nudism
was not simply a matter of skipping around without a bathing suit—it
was a form of asceticism. It made it possible for the race to return to
its own essence, its own authentic state:

> To consciously live such a life, a powerful reform of beliefs must no
> doubt take place. . . . One must disrobe on the inside first, be naked
> spiritually—that's it! All the layers imposed by education and up-
> bringing, by religion, by all of the -isms that man, over time, has
> seen imposed upon him like the rings accumulated by trees as they
> age—all of these must fall away. Man must return to his nudity, in-
> tact [that is, healthy . . .], holy, and pure, as nature created us.[40]

Nudism represented a path away from the hypocrites and the sermonizers who, having constrained and repressed it, distrusted the nature within them. By striving to be saintly and fleeing their animal nature, they had lost their way: nudism is "the beginning of the path home. As we walk along it, all other signs of our wanderings will also fall away of their own accord." Along with clothing, "concupiscence" and "lust in all its forms" would be cast off. The old man leering at Bathsheba in the baths was, of course, a Jew. At the end of this path is "the essence of our self, in all its purity," the being "we have lost, but will find anew."[41]

The nudism promoted by *Deutsche Leibeszucht* was thus fully aligned with the principles and goals of National Socialism. The journal's subtitle—translated as a "life close to nature and in keeping with the race"—shows its adherence to the Party agenda, and to its laws.

The Archetype and the Archaic: Toward a Normative Archaeology

How to access the moment of origin? Nothing to it, really: one simply had to dig, to practice a legal and moral archaeology that sought to unearth the archaic. From this primal, original, natural version an archetype could be constituted, the first and most natural specimen of the Nordic race. "Renewal" was less a matter of creating or instituting something new and more about restoring something ancient.

"Layer after layer," it was necessary to clear away "the sediment" in order to "bring to light the precious treasures of German legal thought."[42] The metaphorical language of burial is present everywhere. Everything relating to this original Germanic culture had undergone "burial" (*Verschüttung*), was buried treasure (*verschütter Schatz*). This was to be regretted, of course, but offered some hope, since this culture could then be unearthed or exhumed (*ausgraben*) and brought to light (*ans Licht tragen*). Indeed, wrote the legal scholar Roland Freisler, the problem was simple: "The continuity of German legal life and its growth has been buried" beneath the silt and sediment of history.[43] In the foreword to an essay series titled "Political Biology" put out by the publisher Lehman, a patron of racist and eugenicist thinkers since the 1920s, the collection's stated mission to restore this

Aryan wisdom, which has been buried and misunderstood by our
people for so long . . . , which National Socialism was able to discern,
and whose vigor it has reestablished. . . . National Socialist policy can
only be . . . biological; that is, it must obey the laws of life. This must
be the overarching principle commanding every other aspect of
German life, [for it is only] by observing the foundations of all (biological) life that we will be able to preserve the foundations of the
(political) life of our people.[44]

In the absence of excessive mixing and contamination, races remain stable. Their spirits do, too: "German legal sentiment has remained true to itself" throughout the centuries, in spite of history's
vicissitudes, as a "race-based history of the law" could prove: "According
to the Indo-Germanic understanding of the law; or, to speak in terms of
race, to the way the Nordic race understands the law, it must obey the
laws of life, or to employ foreign terms, fulfill an exclusively 'biological'
function." By returning to this definition of law, "National Socialism
constitutes a return to our race's authenticity, a rediscovered meditation on what our German race is, of what our German being is."[45] Minister of the Interior Wilhelm Frick, also a lawyer, contributed to the
same line of thinking in "Nordic Thought in the Legislation of the
Third Reich":

> To our people, we have given laws that correspond to our Germanic
> culture. We wish to liberate our people from the folly of crossing and
> mixing races internationally—we wish to bring [our people] back to
> the purest sources of its being.[46]

Finding inspiration in the primal instinct of race both promised an
authentic practice of customs and politics and made possible a return
to knowledge and behaviors that science had come to confirm millennia later, in the nineteenth century. If, over time, instinct had
dulled to the point that people were no longer able to locate the path
that nature showed them, then knowledge could help. Ernst Lehmann,
a biologist specializing in heredity, was delighted to observe that humankind finally had access to an understanding of nature and race that
made it possible to find a way back to the laws of nature that harmful
traditions and cultural sedimentation had obscured from view: "The
mission of biology is to use research to track down . . . the eternal laws

of nature and to spread knowledge of these laws in an era when, for all too many people, instinct has been lost." Biology was a kind of buttress to nature and life; it could "illustrate how to live according to the laws of nature."[47] Happily, "National Socialism has taken very seriously the teachings of biology. It truly wishes to reestablish harmony between our people's vision of the world and the laws of life."[48]

The Germanic people were right about everything, as the study of heredity had shown in the decades preceding the Nazis' rise to power: "We must once again serve our race and return to the admirable view of the world held by our ancestors, who, millennia ago, had already observed that men were unequal" in race and in health. The standards of behavior that could be deduced from this primitive and instinctive knowledge had now been confirmed by science, whose findings validated Germanic morality. In the words of Arthur Gütt, a doctor and eugenicist who was an SS member and one of the guiding forces behind the Sterilization Law of July 14, 1933:

> Since the science of heredity allows us to understand the laws of natural heredity . . . , we must have the courage to do what, by simple racial intuition, appeared obvious to our Germanic ancestors in the millennia preceding the Christian era.[49]

Since intuition was now knowledge, since science had vindicated conscience, there were no remaining impediments to this knowledge becoming the groundwork for a political system; that is, norms and practice, law and custom. The rational justification and the scientific foundation were irrefutable: "Only a legal order that does not contradict scientific findings on heredity and race can be qualified as just, and therefore true and in keeping with the race, by the German people."[50]

To look back to the ancient in order to reconnect with instinct, to restore the archaic in order to recover the archetype—this was a mission that Himmler assigned to the SS. In one of his notoriously lengthy speeches, Himmler explained that each stage in life should be marked by an archaic rite, which it was the organization's mission to revive: "Everything in life must be ordered by customs," but customs, "you may be certain, that are in keeping with ancient norms and with the ancient laws of our age-old past": "each moment of our lives must, little by little, come to correspond once again, and to correspond deeply, with our race."[51] To this end, Himmler was reviving the summer solstice as a holiday, and working to ensure that every holiday in the Christian calendar be returned to its origins, and to its original meaning (the winter solstice, for example, had been Christianized into Christmas). Additionally, he ordered that SS members and their wives were to receive a silver goblet for their wedding and that SS members should be buried with their heads to the north. Their funeral wreaths, moreover, were not to be made from flowers, which were both showy and in poor taste: in winter they were to be crafted from braided "conifer needles" culled from native trees such as "spruce, fir, and pine"; in summer, from twined "oak and beech leaves."[52] In the press and in the SS literature, a welter of articles and texts explained the meanings of the *Julleuchter* (ritual candelabrum), the various shapes of Christmas cake, and the many runic symbols that adorned rings, daggers, and collars; an official guide provided an educational exegesis of the holiday calendar.[53] Even today, these publications, talks, and practices continue to fuel an inexhaustible chronicling of the supposed occultism of the SS. It should be borne in mind that they do not represent the intense Germanophilia of a small minority, nor a kitschy esotericism, but rather a coherent desire to return to the moment of origin, and, through ritual, to fall into step with true rhythms of the race and of the world. As a phrase from a solstice fire ritual proclaimed, "We feel the pulse of millennia within us."

Himmler was careful to state that he wanted to avoid offending anyone's conscience or sensibilities. With a fair dose of condescension, he argued that the old world could be left to its mistakes and its chimeras: if the wife of a deceased member of the SS wanted a priest to be present at the funeral, no one "had the right" to try and talk her out of it. By the same token, "the elderly must be left . . . to their ideas."[54]

> I have always understood when someone came to me and said: "Out of respect for my parents, I must baptize my child." Please, by all means, do! We cannot change a seventy-year-old person. It makes no sense to trouble the inner peace of people in their sixties or seventies. Neither destiny nor our most distant ancestors would want that. They only want us to do better in the future.[55]

The Ahnenerbe, the SS center for scientific research, and its journal, *Germanien*, as well as countless other publications distributed or financed by the SS—including publications by groups such as the "believers in God" (*Gottgläubige*), racist anti-Christians who prayed to a Germanic divinity—all tirelessly explored the existence and meaning of such rites. According to Himmler, their goal was to "rediscover . . . and re-awaken our pre-Christian ancestors' worldview and to create from it a guide to our own existence." In a continuous dialectic of present and past, these studies explored "pre-Christian German-ness as the original image of our vision of the world," as the underpinning of "the universe of National-Socialist values," to allow "a fundamental reevaluation of nearly all past centuries."[56]

Germanic Immediacy

"The soul of the Germanic race is the source of all moral life and of all of our values," wrote the philosopher Georg Mehlis, a professor at the University of Freiburg who specialized in neo-Kantianism and the editor of the prestigious journal *Logos*.[57] He sought to explain the foundations of National Socialism in *Führer und Volksgemeinschaft* (The Führer and the community of the people), published in 1941. "The concept of race," wrote the ethics specialist, "is, at its root, a conception of sciences and of nature, and, as such, is axiologically neutral." The Nordic race, he added, possessed a soul that "knows honor, liberty and duty" by its very nature—from birth, in other words.[58] The soul of the Nordic race was born with these values and was by nature pure. The Germanic race was ontologically and biologically moral. It was logical, therefore, that "the natural sciences become a foundational value of the community of the people," and that "the highest and most sacred of duties is to serve the people."[59]

The highest morality was—quite literally—consubstantial with the Germanic race. This had to do with its biological excellence, which placed it in harmony with the laws of nature, but also, as we shall see, with the difficult climate that had fashioned its ethos, making it naturally and spontaneously moral. This discursive context makes it easier to understand the surprising affirmations that one observes so consistently in legal publications, moral treatises, and courses of ideological instruction, which all proclaimed that "the Germans are known and appreciated throughout the world for their clear sense of justice."[60]

Germanic people, in other words, possessed an unwavering moral instinct. Walther Merk, a lawyer, professor at Marburg, and influential
member of extreme-right-wing circles before 1933, was certain of this:
"Historically, the root of law is not cold and calculating understanding,
but a feeling for what is right." This feeling was never wrong in Germanic people of good racial composition, homogeneous biological
makeup, and unmixed blood: "A sure feeling of justice and an innate
sense of what is right is rooted in the original foundation of the race."[61]

Traditional and authentic German justice was not a cold, dry
succession of articles of the law to be learned by heart, but a "lyrical"
literature whose "spontaneous flow of poetry and humor" had for centuries brought joy to lovers of German literature and legal experts
alike.[62] Merk, fashioning himself into a historian of usage, observed
that "in the language of our medieval legal sources, the law is spoken
of as found, drawn, shown," not instituted or proclaimed. This was
proof that "its wellspring is not the will of whoever is prince at that
moment, but rather the sense of justice and the legal consciousness of
the community."[63]

A Germanic person in the moment of origin was not far from the
birth of the race, and therefore was close to nature. He or she was an authentic expression of the Nordic essence, and acted in keeping with it.
This was legal scholar Helmut Nicolai's argument in the first text ever
devoted to a description of Nazi legal theory. Nicolai, a lawyer and a
veteran of the *Freikorps* (right-wing paramilitary units) had been excluded from any government-related work because of his membership
in the NSDAP. By 1932, Nicolai was an *alter Kämpfer*, a longtime Party
member, and in this capacity had been invited to explain "the foundations of a National Socialist philosophy of law" in the prestigious
"National Socialist Library" put out by the Party's publisher, Franz
Eher. Titled *Die rassengesetzliche Rechtslehre* (A biological doctrine
of the law), the text explained that "before the introduction of Christianity, the legal life of our Germanic ancestors was steeped in biology."
Indeed, "biological" thinking was so consubstantial with Germanic
culture that the author chose to follow the excellent example of Hermann Gustav Prost Holle, who in 1925 had Germanized "the foreign
word 'biological'" as *lebensgesetzlich*, meaning "belonging to the laws
of life/vital-legal."[64]

Certainly these Germanic ancestors did not have written and formally formulated laws, but "no laws did not mean that no legal system existed. The law at that time was one of custom." Things had, moreover, remained that way for a long time: "The *Sachsenspiegel* was not a legal code in the current sense of that term, but simply a restitution of the people's law as it existed then, which had been in place for centuries, and which had not been invented or dreamed up by any legislator."[65] This argument was contradicted by other authors, who pointed out that the *Sachsenspiegel*, far from being a monument to the Nordic legal mind, was a written text—not only written, but written in paragraphs!—and thus Romanized, contaminated, and unusable. Even so, most literature on the *Sachsenspiegel* produced between 1933 and 1945—no fewer than eighteen essays, theses, and books—marveled at the genius of the race as expressed in this Saxon text. If the law came from the people, then an extremely different kind of relationship was implied between the state and its citizens, normativity and the law, and legality and morality. The Germanic people were free because they were the true legislators:

> On one side, the law is what the State, arbitrary and imperious, orders; on the other, the law is an eternal moral value, superior to the power of the State, which cannot alter it . . . . On one side, the law is what is posited by laws—*positum*, hence "positivism"—on the other, the law is what hews to the eternal idea of what is right . . . —hence legal idealism. On one side, morality is entirely separate from the law; on the other, the law is the expression of the moral order and the world order.[66]

Thus, "what was just and good was not that which was not forbidden—that is the Roman understanding of the law, and became our own—but what moral law ordered us to do."[67] The original Germanic understanding was active and *bejahend* (affirmative), as opposed to the passive and repressive understanding of the law as a standard designed to set external limitations and to alienate, imposed by an institution with a monopoly on constraint.

True, it was challenging to access the race's original law of custom, because of the lack of written sources: after all, custom implies orality. The "law of life" was as fleeting (and as eternal!) as life itself, a case-by-case legal process that was forgotten as quickly as the situation it addressed was resolved. Luckily, this law "still lives among the healthiest of our people," that portion of the people who, unmixed and unblended, had remained faithful to the spirit of the Nordic race.[68] Furthermore, it was possible to practice legal and cultural archaeology:

> Since we have learned that the Germanic people are just one branch of the original Nordic people, and that this people originally included the ancient Indians and Persians, the ancestors of the Greeks and the Romans, the Celts, and the Slavs, we are . . . better able to comprehend ancient German law.[69]

The relatively numerous extant sources regarding legal life could be relied on, because

> these peoples, originally, . . . before they lost their hereditary nature, were the flesh of our flesh, the bone of our bone; they spoke our language, they possessed the same soul and the same mind as our Germanic ancestors, and, consequently, the same fundamental understanding of the law.[70]

Plunging into the race's past, one swiftly concluded that "the law . . . , according to the German understanding, was considered to be innate. One was subject to the law by blood, and one transmitted it by heredity."[71] The law was the very lifeblood of the race. In 1931, Helmut Nicolai enthusiastically proclaimed,

> On one side, rigid legal paragraphs; on the other, the law of life. On one side, the State; on the other, the people. On one side, the letter; on the other, the consequence. On one side, a static legal system; on the other, a dynamic one . . . . The day the NSDAP takes power will not only mark the arrival of a new government. That day will see the overturning of the Judeo-Roman understanding of the law. The idea of German law, in keeping with the laws of life, will be returned to its rightful place.[72]

Nature as a higher authority? There was nothing outlandish about this idea when one recalled that, like a newborn child, the Germanic race at the moment of origin knew no other law. An article titled "Natur," published by *Neue Brockhaus* in 1938, reminded readers that

for the ancient Greeks, nature was the living, dynamic, and spiritu-
alized foundation of all things. In the Germanic religion, nature was
reality suffused with the divine, and thus an object of worship. In the
eyes of Christianity, nature became a foreign force, one that was
hostile to the divine, the realm of the devil. . . . Our era has re-
appropriated the ancient Greek understanding of nature. . . . More
and more, nature has come to designate all of life's phenomena, such
that the opposition between nature and mind may now be considered
to have been surmounted,[73]

thanks to a political movement that was restoring Nordic-ness to
its rightful place—and restoring its laws. Alfred Rosenberg wrote,
"Nordic man believes deeply in the eternal laws of nature."[74] Hans
Frank solemnly proclaimed that: "We, the Germanics, believe in a
legal order, a truly divine institution, which came before us and which
transcends us."[75]

To bring the race back to its true state, it was necessary to research
and think deeply about the origins of the Nordic race, its birth and its
nature. Slogans that merely brushed the surface of beings and behaviors were not enough; they could not restore the race's authenticity. The
Reichsärzteführer (Reich chief physician) Gerhard Wagner called for "a
complete revolution in feeling and in thinking," for the "revitalization
of the forces that lie dormant in our unconsciousness and in our sub-
consciousness, and which alone" would be able "to resuscitate in our
people this instinct for racial self-affirmation . . . which had been de-
liberately stifled by foreign forces hostile to our race."[76] In another
speech, Wagner stated that "we will have achieved our goal when we
no longer have any need for racial laws" and when the principles of nature "have been firmly anchored in each young German man and
woman, such that it will become instinct *again*" to respect nature and
the race.[77]

Happily, the time had come for a "revolution in the law." Thanks
to the challenges and the traumas endured by Germany, it was now
possible to observe "an awakening of a German feeling for the law, of
a German legal sensibility, of a German love of the law, of a German
understanding of the law," which was simply a right and healthy return to the German self.[78] After all,

the National-Socialist ethic was born of a revolution. These are norms that . . . generally should not be considered as a reevaluation of existing values. Hitler did not wish to write new Tablets of the Law. He only underlined and illuminated the old eternal values that Germanic man worshiped and loved. The National-Socialist ethic is an ethic of war, a soldier's ethic. It breathes with the spirit of Frederick the Great. Against the Christian ethics of the West, which seeks to place notions such as love, humility, and pity above all other ethical norms, its focus is on pride, honor, and heroism.[79]

Unity, Separation, Mediation

The first separation had most likely been between God and the world. The Jews, with their strict monotheism, their rejection of pantheism and animism, had chased the divine from the world. The caste of rabbis, which had given birth to the Catholic clergy, also had created a regrettable mediation between God and man, who, deprived of any direct relationship, was required to pass through the tollbooth of the minister, the intercessor, the mediator. Man had also been separated from himself— from his own sinful, shameful body, and from the other sex—and from the nature within and around him. These many separations were like so many plagues inflicted on man, a mutilation of his nature, a permanent distinction that dissected and dislocated him.

And yet, at the dawn of the race, all had been fusion and ferment. Law, for example, had not been distinct from morality. The inspiration, intuition, and instinct of the people proclaimed what was good, beautiful, right, and just. "The law's commandments," like the "maxims of morality," wrote Roland Freisler, were dictated by "the people's conscience and by the arm of the people. This conscience, which is the voice of morality, is also the matrix of the law."[80] In the plasma of Mother Nature, nothing was distinct, separated, or discrete. The people were both nomothetic and subject to the law; morality was the law, and vice versa; the norm *was* the fact. Any sane norm thus expressed the "vital order of the people." Nature, and by extension the norm, was "the living organism of the people itself."[81] Freisler railed against distinctions, which had been put in place to "dissect, then pulverize, and ultimately atomize" the body of the people.[82] This "dissection"—the autopsy-like treatment of the corpse of the *Volksgemeinschaft* by an intellect hostile to life—was denounced in much of his writing. Just as there was no distinction between law and morality in the state of nature, the "separation between state and society" was artificial and false. Reinhart Höhn, a professor of law at the University of Berlin and a member of the SS, was categorical on this point:

> Law, culture, mores, and language are expressions of the community of the people. . . . They are not juxtaposed but intertwined, entangled in such a way that all of the distinctions and differentiations of traditional systemic thinking have lost all their meaning.[83]

Criticism of "separation" was a commonplace. In 1939, Otto Brunner, a legal historian who specialized in the medieval period, wrote a book called *Land und Herrschaft* (Land and lordship), which was awarded the "Verdun Prize," presented by Walter Frank, the director of the Reich Institute for the History of the New Germany. After 1945 Brunner would go on to become one of the founding fathers of German *Begriffsgeschichte* (conceptual history), and *Land und Herrschaft* was ideologically well received as well as historiographically significant. In it, he argued that historians were mistaken in attempting to comprehend the realities of the Middle Ages by using categories forged in and by the modern era. Understanding the medieval era, or phenomena peculiar to it, such as sovereignty in a feudal world, required abandoning modern, contemporary words and ideas. One had to examine and speak of the era in medieval terms. In his dizzying and erudite writing, Brunner showed that contemporary historians were obsessed with and distracted by categories and distinctions inherited from liberal times—from the nineteenth century. He retraced the epistemological and sociopolitical process that, since the birth of the state in the modern era, had made it impossible to think in terms other than those of the separation of state and society:

> This process came to an end only in the mid-nineteenth century, when the state and society were conceived of as distinct realities and as the objects of completely distinct knowledge. It was at this time that science began to be disaggregated into a large number of scattered disciplines and that a "disjunctive mode of thought" (*Trennungs-denken*) became prevalent. Among these seemingly autonomous

disciplines there began a chaotic struggle for supremacy; one that, moreover, reflected the struggle among political powers in the nineteenth century. By dint of this fundamental separation between State and society, the State became a simple legal structure and a normative order, while society became the domain of spiritual and material values.[84]

For Brunner, "the weakness of our historical concepts, . . . which are cut from the cloth of the modern era," was clear. The Middle Ages had been a time of fusion and ferment, when "the distinction between the profane and the sacred was unknown," as was the classic modern distinction between "law and justice." The medieval era had been ruled by "popular sentiment, which could not, and did not wish to, distinguish between positive and ideal law, for the law was the law of the people."[85] Brunner indicted the modern era for its harmful preoccupation with division and distinction. Ernst Forsthoff, a student of Carl Schmitt and a professor at the University of Koenigsberg, shared this view. In a lecture on modern rationality given as part of a tribute to Kant organized in 1941, he paid a series of double-edged compliments to the author of the three *Critiques*. Kant, he asserted, had participated fully in a modern age that had brought about the "separation between legality and morality, the inner and the outer self," as well as between "law and morality," an unhappy era that had given birth to the "technical age of the nineteenth century," a mechanized and rationalized world characterized by the automation (of individuals), by mathematical discreteness, and by uprootedness.[86] Very luckily, "the struggle to transcend the dualism of law and ethics, the legal order and material justice" had begun.[87]

Historians had to work hard to reorient themselves and had to exercise some semantic imagination to think about the Middle Ages in its own terms. Medieval sovereignty and politics could not be imagined using terminology inherited from the modern "sovereignty of princes" and the "liberal age" that had followed.[88] Brunner's claim that the disjunctive categories created in a bourgeois, liberal age were useless for understanding medieval organicism, and ought therefore to be rejected, was not a surprising one for the times. By contrast, his critical attitude toward the era of princes and of pre- and post-Westphalian absolutism differed from much Nazi discourse, where it was often employed as a handy foil to contest the claim that the Führer's regime was a dictatorship. Widespread "mediation" had caused a welter of separations, a real *vivisection*. All had been separated—all that had been organically linked, all that had lived and grown together in life's pure and innocent movement, all that had been one in life's dynamic substance—man from woman, body from spirit, norm from action.

In his arguments for "an education faithful to the laws of life," Lothar Stengel von Rutkowski called for an epistemological revolution. To close the chasm of this separation and return to an organic and unified understanding of reality, millennia of alienation had to be overcome. The minds of Germany's youth had been poisoned by education as it had emerged at the close of the Middle Ages, in an era when "there was no biology, but a theology," an "Eastern and monastic culture" that had destroyed "the ancient union of body and soul that characterized all robust Aryanness, and was unique to the Greeks and the Romans." In addition to the religious, cultural, and social damage caused by this great separation, Stengel von Rutowski pointed out the intellectual damage wrought by this "Church dogma, incompatible with a biological understanding of the laws of nature." In this "clear opposition between the Germanic consciousness of unity and of the wholeness of all that is living and the clerical-Eastern separation of sinful flesh and pure spirit," Stengel von Rutkowski perceived a "confrontation among racial souls." It was one in which the Eastern soul had come out ahead, moreover, since "still today" the school and the university systems, the very organization of knowledge, was dominated by this "separation between the natural sciences and the spiritual sciences."[89]

The time had come to end this "unhealthy division" "between mind and nature, between culture and the laws of life"; society had to learn to think in terms of "the biological unity of all things," to realize that "men, animals, and plants are all subject to the same laws of nature."[90] Here was "the only certain path our instinct and our biological heritage can follow, despite Rome and despite Jerusalem."[91] For this to occur, it was necessary to pare back the teaching of abstract and scholastic subjects, of literature and the humanities. In high school, Stengel von Rutkowski had not studied "Latin and Greek with displeasure," for these eminently useful subjects had allowed him to "access our own

most ancient sources."[92] That being said, the same could be done with
the ancient languages of India and Iran. And in all seriousness: "It is far
less important to study their languages than their history, which is so
rich in biological and racial teachings, and to consider this history as an
integral part of the general history of Indo-Germanic humanity."[93]

Higher education was to be renewed according to the same principles: knowledge, which had been fragmented and separated, needed to
reunify and to serve life. In his inaugural lecture as a professor of
medicine at the University of Jena, Karl Astel revealed to his listeners
the foundations of scientific values in the National Socialist Reich:
"The preservation of the race, and of healthy life, is the sure criterion of
value that allows for the evaluation of science, research, and the University."[94] The fundamental and cardinal value was the life of the Nordic
race, its preservation, and its improvement. This was the sole criterion
needed to reevaluate science, to restore its value, and to renew German
universities.[95] Taking a stand against the *Universitas literarum* of the
past, with its rabbis parading as clergymen and clergymen parading as
professors, Karl Astel called for a *Universitas vitae.*[96]

Nordic Piety: Serenity, Friendship, Harmony

Each race had its own representation of man, community, and the
world. The same was true of religious sentiment, the most primitive
means of interrogating possible links between the living and the dead,
and life and death, which was not entirely the same thing. Hans Günther, the pope of Nordic raciology, the major inspiration behind the
Nordic-racist right wing of the SS, devoted a portion of his abundant
bibliography to this Nordic religious sentiment, both in chapters of his
treatises on raciology as well as in a brief essay titled "Frömmigkeit
nordischer Artung" (The piety of the Nordic race), which came out in
1934, in a context of "debate and dispute over the German people's religious values."[97] This was an allusion to the serious skirmishes
taking place between the Deutsche Christen (German Christians), who
were Protestant Nazis seeking to purge the Gospel of its Jewishness,
and various other churches that were more circumspect in their views,
all of which took place beneath the mocking gaze of hardline defenders
of Nordic religion. For Günther, the authentic piety unique to the

Nordic race was the exact opposite of what was preached by the Jews, and in their wake, by Christians.

Germanic religiosity was characterized first and foremost by the close link between man and the divine. In the Eastern religions (Judaism, Christianity, and so on), God was a "powerful lord" and his follower was his "slave": "In Semitic languages, the verb 'to pray' is derived from the root *abad*, which means 'to be a slave.' "[98] Showing humility to God, as these religions instructed, was utterly "foreign to the Indo-Germanic mind . . . an effect of Eastern piety": "Because he is not the vassal to his lord, the Indo-Germanic Man prays most often not on his knees and gazing at the ground, but standing, and gazing upwards, his palms raised to the sky," a pose best exemplified by the statue of the Apollo Belvedere so often depicted in Nazi publications.[99]

The relationship between the divine and man was a friendly one, bathed in a sort of confident companionship, the polar opposite of the emotions inspired by the vengeful, terrible, and terrifying god of the Jews, "Yahweh," "the monstrous demon of the desert."[100] For men of the Germanic-Nordic race, "God is always a friend and comrade," as shown in "Plato's *Symposium*" as well as in "the *Bhagavad-Gita*."[101] In the absence of written Germanic sources, "ancient India, ancient Persia, and ancient Greece help us to reconstruct our own self."[102] Because they did not serve one God, jealous of His uniqueness, the Germans did not proselytize. Their fatherly, benevolent tolerance extended freedom of religion to all, a freedom that did not bother them in the least: to each race its gods! Christian vices such as "evangelical ardor and intolerance have always been foreign to Nordic piety."[103] By the same token, temporal structures such as the Church and the "clericalization of faith," which buttressed and supported intolerance, were, according to Günther, "once again, an expression of the spirit of the Eastern (desert) race, or of the interaction between the spirits of the Eastern races and of Asia Minor."[104]

The closeness of man and the divine, of the world and the human spirit, tolerance and peaceful coexistence among men and gods: Nordic religiosity was all peace and harmony. It inhabited a pacified world and certainly did not seek to upset or deny the order of the world, to unsettle nature in the name of something that transcended or opposed it. Nordic piety was "a religion of the here and now," a theme that Günther tirelessly developed in his many books and in a highly illuminating article written for *Germanien*.[105] In it, he accused Christianity of having based its success on ideas of "redemption" and "deliverance" (*Erlösungsgedanke*), ideas that the racial theorist Ludwig Ferdinand Clauss had shown were products of the Semitic-Asiatic race.[106] Broadly speaking, it seemed evident to these authors that "religious concepts" had "a biological root" and were determined by race. In *Der Biologe*, a journal published by the National Socialist Association of Professors of Biology, Wilhelm Hauer, a high-profile proponent of the Germanic religion, even spoke of "racio-religious concepts." Race determined worldview, religion, and morality. Contrary to the factual judgment of science, value judgments "have no foundation in things, but in the individual who judges; that is, in his essence, in his race." Therefore, "depending on whether he assigns more value to humility or to honor, to courage or to kindness, depending on whether he deems it more worthy to serve the Reich and the people or to lead a monastic life in order to reach a supernatural world," an individual was not expressing "an objective criterion" but "an elementary yes or no in keeping with the necessity unique to his race."[107]

Citing the Book of Revelation, Günther showed that the eschatological Christian hope was for deliverance from this world to the next, having shrugged off the bonds "of his race, of his language, and of his people." Jews and Christians had been weakened by deep despair, the despair of being of this world, from which they hoped to depart because they hated it and themselves—their only salvation was to flee as far as possible from the self. And

> now Germans ought to believe that their race, their language, and their people are things from which they must be delivered? . . . But delivered from what? From what evil, and to pass on to what world and what life? *Midgard*, the world of just order, the mother country built by man, was not an evil in their eyes. . . . For them there was no better life.[108]

The German, a pure and harmonious being, both loved others and loved himself. He did not suffer from a troubled and divided self, did not suffer from any internal imbalance so intolerable that his only hope was in its end. As Lothar Stengel von Rutkowski effused in the pages and verses of a collection of poetry perpetrated in 1937, titled *Das Reich dieser Welt: Lieder und Verse eines Heiden* (The reign of this world: Songs and verses of a pagan):

> More ancient than the churches and the cloisters is our motherland
> Our blood unites us more firmly than the baptism of priests.
> Our kingdom, my brothers, is of this world!
> God enjoined us to build it![109]

Nordic Morality, or the Instinct for Good

Each race possessed its "value system" (*Wertordnung*): race produced culture; values were dictated by blood.[110] There was no need for lengthy reflection: natural norms were instinctive—immediate, animal, spontaneous—they "do not think, they do not split hairs, they don't hesitate." A sound mind born of unmixed biology and still faithful to its racial identity would produce pure thoughts and know how to act: "A thought is instinctive if the soul producing it still obeys the values unique to its race."[111] This made things quite simple: "Rights are, plain and simple, a matter of what's right."[112] No need to be a lawyer to understand that.

Formulating norms, writing legal codes, establishing collections of maxims—all of these were purely inductive, empirical exercises. Ludwig Ferdinand Clauss devoted his academic work to showing that each race possessed its own spirit, its own psyche, its own style. His benefactor, Friedrich Wilhelm Prinz zur Lippe, enthusiastically praised both Clauss and the "science of the racial soul" (*Rassenseelenkunde*) that Clauss had founded. It had proven, in the words of Nicolai, that "it is from living and lived life, and from their lifestyles, that the normativity of the different races emanates." *A contrario*, any "doctrine not taken from lived life is nonsense, a harmfully stupid thing . . . , a feeble theory," and therefore necessarily enfeebling.[113]

Pureblooded Germans, by dint of their biological substance, were confident, healthy beings, able to act without feeling any turmoil or doubt. The purity of one's blood guaranteed a total absence of doubt or misgiving. A Germanic person was capable of developing an immediate relationship from self to self, which allowed his or her decisions to be sure and pure. Albrecht Hartl, a specialist in religious questions for the SS, explained that by following "the most natural and most basic norms in the world . . . , he is capable of making clear, calm decisions . . . , without falling into the moral doubt so often experienced by beings who adhere to artificial, anti-natural doctrines" or who were themselves "racial bastards" whose heterogeneous biological substance had plagued their minds with schizophrenia.[114] A natural and homogeneous being followed the law of nature and knew no misgivings, no moral dilemmas, no remorse: "A man of pure race decides on an action without artifice, unhesitatingly, in a manner in keeping with his instinct."[115] This was one of the problems afflicting "racial bastards," whose motley biological substance deprived them of any sure instinct for what was true and right. They were frail crafts, without rudder or compass, and had to steer by external rules that were learned and applied without any thought:

> This is why the Jew clings to his external laws, to the law, to dogma, to the letter. He does not feel what is right and good: he must arrive at it through reason, and it must be told to him by others. This is also why the Jew builds a legislative machine for himself that tells him what is forbidden and what is permitted on every occasion.[116]

The Jew, a heteronomous being (one who is subject to a law or standard external to oneself), could only follow the Decalogical and Talmudic handbooks, which he or she took as literal teachings, a kind of conscience by default. Indeed, Nazi raciology saw Jews as the ultimate example of mixed blood, because the Jews were not a race at all. Instead, they were a "non-race," an "anti-race," a mishmash of varied flesh and blood deposited in the Jewish vessel over millennia of Diaspora and wandering. It was for this reason, the author added, "that we encounter in all racially mixed people this idea that the law must be set from on high, from outside, by the State, by a power" of some kind, imposed by "paragraph fiddlers" upon "a mass lacking in instinct."[117] In the absence of a natural coherence and homogeneity that no longer existed in miscegenated peoples, only "the external power of the State and its coercive force can hold men together."[118] People of mixed blood were lacking in pure consciences and clear wills, so they relied on a Law to guide them, and on interpreters—rabbis or princes—to state this Law to them.

All of this made it easier to understand what gave rise to constraint and dictatorship, to the servile alienation so characteristic of the Roman state and Roman law: "racial mixing" had dissolved the Roman people, transformed it into a "plebian mass . . . that no natural ties, no ties of blood" held together any longer. Roman law, as the *Corpus juris* of Justinian showed, was not dictated by an "innate feeling for the law" but by a "logical, punctilious, chattering, hair-splitting under-standing."[119] The Germanic people, by contrast, were autonomous be-ings. The law was not external to them, but inborn in each person and internal to the community: "This instinct, which shows us what is right, is called conscience," and this instant agreement between a person and him- or herself was true freedom. A Germanic person at the moment of origin was not a deliberating subject, a being that was uncertain and devoured by misgiving. Quite the contrary, that person acted without hesitating, in a state of immediacy that was the mani-festation of his or her authenticity. This was because that person had been cut from a single block of stone, pure and unadulterated, because his or her spirit had no cultural or psychic rifts. A German could thus act with great vigor, in full accord with the self, when procreating, fighting, and hunting. The immaculate German, with a pure race mixed only with itself, was utterly immediate. Any gap, any screen separating that person from himself or herself could be blamed on harmful imports from foreign places: "Mediation came late to the North, through evangelical missions sent out to the Nordic populations by Rome."[120]

The Germanic Race, the Only Moral Race

"The law is what the Aryan man feels is right," wrote Reinhard Höhn, for whom tautology appeared to be synonymous with ontology. He was not alone in this view. Roland Freisler believed that "respect for jus-tice is an essential feature of our people," while Hans Frank spoke rap-turously of "the eternal moral law unique to our German people."[121]

Free of all mixing, the original Nordic race was free from all psychic
and moral troubles. In its very essence, it was the natural race. Its moral
excellence was due to its blood, but also to the climatic and natural
conditions to which the Germanic peoples had been subjected. The
hostile environment of cold and ice had led them to develop and maintain physical and ethical virtues that pitiless natural selection had
transmitted from one generation to the next. The white plagues of the
ice and the wind had drawn the people together and populated their
ranks with the toughest, strongest, and most unified of men. According
to Karl Astel,

> among the men of yesteryear, the one who did not enjoy robust health
> died off, and could not pass on his hereditary dispositions to his de-
> scendants. . . . A man who abandoned his comrades, who lied to them
> and tricked them, that man was abandoned, and rightly so, when he
> in turn needed his comrades, and he died off. And so he, too, could
> not pass on to his descendants his hereditary penchant for dishon-
> esty, lying, and treason.[122]

Germanic people had an innate sense and an immediate appercep-
tion of honor, which the SS made synonymous with "fidelity" in its
motto. As an instructional text for German police and SD officers explained, "all honor comes from fidelity." Fidelity to what? The manual
continued, "Service to the community is always the decisive sign that
identifies an honorable member of the community of the people."[123]
Honor, which Nazi discourse celebrated worshipfully, was thus the exercise of fidelity (*Treue*), embodied in the practice of service (*Dienst*),
in all its forms, for under the Third Reich everything fell more or less
into the category of *Dienst:* the soldier's *Dienst*, for example, could be
broken down into strictly military service (*Wehrdienst*), work service
(*Reichsarbeitsdienst*), and intellectual service. Invitations to participate in intellectual service were a common theme in the commence-
ment remarks and lectures of university professors.[124]

The "community" in question was the race, which transcended the
individual because it gave each individual meaning and existence, and,
unlike each individual, was neither finite or limited in time: "An action
may be considered honorable when its consequences may be justified
before what is eternal"—the race, in other words. By contrast, "a man

without honor is one who violates the duties imposed by the preservation of eternal values."[125] Race, community, eternity: Germanic honor commanded obedience to nature and its laws. It was, by the principles of equivalence and transitivity, "fidelity to the order of divine creation, fidelity to the laws of life, to the voice of blood, to oneself," "fidelity to nature, to oneself, to one's people."[126]

Honor as fidelity was so fundamental, claimed Anton Holzner, that "the ancient Germanic people punished deception more harshly than theft," unlike the laws of the Jews and the "Jewified law," which were so materialistic and so divorced from questions of honor that they did not punish insult.[127] Johann von Leers claimed to have observed that in the Bible and the Talmud, insult or verbal offense was not punished, because the Jews had no sense of honor.[128] For Germanic people, however, "the emphasis placed on honor and fidelity . . . the North Stars of the Germanic feeling for what is right," revealed the race's "fundamentally moral character," its superior ethical quality.[129] With these prolegomena exposed and understood, the reader is less surprised to see that "the law can only be known, laid out, proclaimed, and spoken by Aryan, Nordic man. Nordic man is the only man called to create law, that is, to draw the law from the original wellspring of his wisdom."[130] Long ago, there had been no distinction between wisdom and norm, morality and law. Everything was melded together in the great wholeness of life and in its safeguarding: "To be a guardian of the law meant to preserve life," for "all law was vital law."[131]

Everything was interconnected—honor, fidelity, morality, law, and life. It was because the foundational values of the Nordic race were fidelity and honor that morality, and therefore law, served life, the only authority that could dictate the norm: "All of law was suffused with morality. At the center, fidelity and honor, these pillars of the German race, values dictated by blood itself, and which, a constant flow, link the living to eternity."[132] Moral values and the knowledge of these values were inherent to the Nordic race. They were one of its defining qualities. Racial and cultural authenticity was therefore the only sure path to the right way to act. With the prophetic affectation of a bard, the Nordicist poet Gustav Frenssen, already well known during the reign of Kaiser Wilhelm as a champion of the *völkisch* cause, wrote, "When a Germanic man follows . . . the pull and the exigency of the real, the good, and the beautiful, . . . he is healthy and strong, he knows his path and does not err."[133]

Spontaneity and natural movement were far more important than reflection, scruples, and conscience. Body and soul, full of blood and meaning, pulsing to the heartbeat of the world, were called to take a stand against the tormented and mortified conscience of the follower of the Talmud or the religious believer, against the nullifying self-criticism and the eternal struggle of the supposed angel with the imagined beast. Hans Johst, a poet and an SS general, sounded the call: "Follow your own heart unreservedly! It is the command post of divine nature within you. By obeying it, you place yourself at the heart of the living law! If you are disciplined and moral in the way you live, you will bring justice to your people, and to your race."[134] Morality, law, and norms were well and truly a matter of instinct, of affect, and of the body, which was the seat of all affect.

The laws of life were the most basic form of reality, the most immediate experience of one's own existence. They could be felt in the immediate experience of the internal rhythms of the body, in its very pulse: these laws were "laws as simple as breathing, as the circulation of blood, etc., which govern an individual's body," as well as "higher laws, such as the struggle for life and the principle of evolution." They left great margin for interpretation and great exegetic freedom: "The laws of life are proteiform and elastic. They never rigidify into dead dogma. They are as diverse as life itself."[135] An SS textbook taught that it was indeed this heart, whose pulse beat in time to the rhythm of the world, that was to be followed:

> Fidelity is an affair of the heart, never of belief. Belief can be mistaken. . . . As for the heart, it must always beat at the same rate. If it stops, man dies, just as a people does, when it betrays and . . . breaks with its fidelity to its blood, to its ancestors, to its children and grandchildren.[136]

To betray, to lie, to violate the bond of fidelity that bound each man to his ancestors, to his descendants, and to his people, was to create an infarction, a dangerous blockage in the flow of blood, in the body of the people, or *Volkskörper*. Morality was a vital biological function that regulated and fed the body, so to violate this fidelity to the body was to threaten the homeostasis of the blood and of the race, that is, to cause a biological shock to the body. Betrayal meant mixing one's blood with an allogenic fluid, or breaking rank in any way with the greater body of the race.

The Order of the World

Heart, body, and cosmos: if the Nordic race was the only moral race, it was because its norms were derived inductively from the law of the universe. Nordic religion, morality, and law were one and the same, because nature was one. For the Nordic race, God's commandments were "the actual order of the world," not the phantasmagorical vaticinations of a self-proclaimed and generally drug-addled prophet of the kind so appealing to the Eastern peoples, with their taste for oracles and saviors. A historian of the law knew why the Germanic people had heeded the order of the world and made it their law: a people of farmers, they had been obliged to listen to nature, to feel its pulse, to understand its rhythms and its laws, and to act in consequence, in order to live and survive.[137]

According to the Germanic worldview, the law was derived from the order of the whole. In a poetic vein, Johann von Leers affirmed that "the law lies curled in the palm of the world," for it had been "inferred from the world's order, which is good."[138] Carl Schmitt translated this idea into more technical terms. Seeking to order and establish a typology of legal thinking, he argued that it was necessary to distinguish between legal cultures in which "the law is understood as a rule, as a decision, or as an order"—in the sense of an objective order—and those in which the law was a "concrete order."[139] Dominant legal scholarship pertained to these two categories: "Nineteenth-century legal positivism is the combination of decision and law, of decisionism and normativism," as if it were possible to create law *ex abstracto* and *ex nihilo*, by making decisions and by constructing abstract hierarchical structures of super- and subordinate norms that had no foundation in concrete, real orders.[140] To Schmitt, the "victory of the French Revolution, which had imposed a society of citizens and individuals," and "the liberal 'Ideas of 1789,'" had led to "a disintegration of order thinking"; that is, of concrete legal thinking about the nature of order.[141]

The French Revolution had designated the individual as the beginning and ending of the law. It made the law—something voted on and therefore decided by Parliament—into the only valid norm. In this, the French Revolutionaries were the heirs of a long tradition, one that Carl Schmitt traced back to the Stoics, and specifically to the scholar and Stoic philosopher Chrysippus, according to whom the law was "king, overseer, ruler, and master over morality and immorality, right and wrong."[142] This had been followed by the natural law of the Classical and Enlightenment ages, "the rational law of the seventeenth and eighteenth centuries, . . . which is part abstract normativism, part decisionism." A good Catholic, Schmitt did not condemn "the Aristotelian-Thomistic natural law of the Middle Ages." This law, which was a law of nature above all, and a theoretical consecration of the order willed by God, was, "from the point of view of legal science, the concrete order."[143] Just as, politically, Nazism had reestablished the hierarchy of the part and the whole, in the legal world, "concrete-order thinking" had returned the standard or the norm to its place: "For concrete-order thinking, order is not . . . above all a rule or a summation of rules; to the contrary, the rule is merely a component or a means to order."[144] The objective order—of nature, of the world, of the hierarchy of the sexes—had preceded the rule ontologically, logically, and chronologically. It had not been created or invented by legal scholars; they had derived it inductively from the concrete order of the world.

Norms, People, and Life

Fundamentally, and foundationally, life was what dictated the norm. Past generations, alienated by the Judeo-Christian enterprise of cultural domination, had lost their instinct for what was beautiful and good. Rudolf Viergutz, a propagandist of Nordic religiosity, was unequivocal in his affirmation:

> The values set by life are different from those imposed by the mind, whose norms came late and, for the most part, are hostile to life. A man who truly wants to be himself—and all natural peoples are com-

prised of such men—must be as good and as bad as nature herself. Life arrives, quite simply, without any concern for absolute values. . . . Rarely do we act in order to respect acquired and learned values, either. We act because an impulse pushes us to do so, because a slope leads us there: "It is an impulse; it is therefore a duty" (Goethe).[145] What is natural is at the same time what is healthy, good, and useful.[146]

To act in the right way, it was therefore necessary to reject the "mind," the ratiocinating of moralizers and any authority that required the mortification of the body to grow and govern. If primitive peoples, "people of nature" (Naturvölker), were the only ones who acted in the right way, this was because they followed the nature within them. Their impulse was correct; it was life's unadulterated gesture, the most pertinent and immediate expression of life. This meant that for them, action "comes, as with all that is living, from beyond good and evil." Far from being a reference to Nietzsche, "beyond good and evil" was a common expression in German. In the context of this argument, it was a way to express that the pure actions of the living could not be assigned to a spectrum of values marked by the artificial poles of moral "good" and "evil." Life was located beyond this axiology, which could not be used to enframe it. Therefore, any ethics dictated by reason and any value system that claimed to proceed from anything other than the animal life contained in mankind was rejected, on the grounds that ethics, which formulated prohibitions and taboos, prevented life from unfolding freely and wholesomely:

> If life truly unfolds beyond good and evil, this is proof that all "ethics" are morbid and lacking in life force. Ethics is a product of the mind: the fact that animals do not possess it and that they are not any worse for it is sufficient proof. Furthermore, the incompatibility of ethics and life may be identified in the fact that the former consists only of prohibitions.[147]

Animals were to be envied their happy ignorance of the Ten Commandments and the penal code: their beauty and wholesomeness were direct results of the natural freedom that they enjoyed, much like primitive peoples. If ever there was any original sin, Walther Buch, the president of the NSDAP's internal tribunal, believed it was the separation of man from nature, of human nature from animal nature.

We, the National Socialists, have appropriated the laws that animals follow unconsciously for ourselves. Transgressing the boundaries drawn by nature and coupling blindly was a possibility reserved for men "endowed with reason." This is how these famous mixed races came to be.[148]

Reason betrayed instinct; it was good to return to immediacy and animality. Were combat, war, or the elimination of the weak problematic or shocking? No, Buch replied: "such is life, and life is right. To live according to its laws is good."[149] Failing that, life eliminated you; its laws had no pity. Morality did exist, but "racial consciousness is to be clearly distinguished from the bad conscience of educated morality. It reflects the axiological instincts of race in our conscience."[150] Conscience, the examination of the conscience, bad conscience—these had been banished: the only "sacred commandment," according to Gustav Frenssen, "was to respect the laws of life," laws that were not laid out in any code or catechism, but which, invisible and structuring, were the cause of everything that is.[151]

Law as Folklore

The original law of the Nordic race, Heinrich Himmler recalled, was unwritten, and respect for this unwritten law above all things had to be relearned: "we must return to our ancestors' ideas; we can no longer live content to merely follow the written laws; we must always act so that we never contravene the unwritten laws of our people."[152] "German law," explained one legal historian, was instinctive and spontaneous, a true, free, and immediate expression of the race, "not a written law, but an oral law," customary in its principles and oral in its procedures. The reason for this was that "a word of honor was worth more than a letter or a seal."[153] "Nowhere can it be read, but everyone knows it": it is "drawn from the very source of the people."[154] To recover the right law, the authentic law, it was necessary to return to the people and to their proverbial wisdom, to give less credence to lawyers than to laymen, for therein lay the race's past and its authenticity: "Less legal science and more law, this is the future."[155]

When the professor of law Justus Wilhelm Hedemann presented the groundwork for a "People's Code of Law" (*Volksgesetzbuch*), whose very title suggests his agenda, he proudly evoked the idea of a prestigious assembly that "held court in life's midst," and whose "academic members were not merely learned men who sit in their offices and see life only through foggy windowpanes." Much to the contrary, they were to be "fully present in the life of the German man" and would thus understand the needs of Germans.[156] For Hedemann and for Freisler, "The law is quite simply the reality of life."[157] Its subject was "the German people, a real, living . . . and eternal being, whose vital oneness relies on a community of blood."[158]

Here again, we see the same transitivity: the law was the people's life. To formulate norms, it was best to return to the people, and to listen to them. Accordingly, "the convictions of the people are the true source of criminal law," as well as for all other branches of the law, and for morality.[159] As Freisler wrote, "we understand an offence to be any violation of the commandments of the moral order of the people and the race," as well as anything in "contradiction with the will of the community of the people."[160] The law was "an integral part of the life of our people. The legislator does not create it. He draws it from the wellspring of our people; he harvests it from the mouth of the people's conscience. This is where it grows, constantly and organically."[161]

The people were the soil from which the norm grew. The image of the people as "source" or "wellspring" recurred often. While legal scholars today still use the term "sources of the law," its meaning is now purely metaphorical. But in the discourse of Nazi legal scholars, the image was—as many such images were—to be taken literally: legal norms poured and flowed like the blood from which they originated. German legal scholars were to be faithful to the work of Jacob Grimm, who had been both a lawyer and a folklorist. In addition to collecting the tales and legends of Germanic culture from the people, he also, as a legal romanticist, believed that legal norms were dictated by the soul of the people, by their proverbs, customs, and usages. In a book called *Rechtliche Volkskunde* (Legal ethnology), the celebrated legal historian Eberhard von Künssberg, a professor at the University of Heidelberg, argued that "legal science and folklore share the same substance."[162] In "more ancient times, morality and law, popular usage and legal usage, were not separate." The task of the legal scholar, therefore, was

to gather "the law that is rooted in the people's morality," to study the
"living legal customs," and to "bring them together . . . in order to
codify a law in accord with the race."[163] This "study of the living law"
made it possible to understand "our people's most venerable legal concepts, where they have been buried or deformed."[164] For "the source of
customary law is the people's legal conscience, the people's spirit."[165]

Falk Ruttke, like Heinrich Himmler, called for the rehabilitation
of "legal proverbs" that had survived in popular language and culture,
"in spite of all the influences of Judeo-Roman law." They praised the
poetic creativity, the sense of humor, and the rhymes in these invalu-
able proverbs, which instructed, for instance: "If on the dung heap you
should wed, then you will know what lies ahead."[166] Abiding sources
of wisdom indeed, and indispensable in daily life.

Just as Leni Riefenstahl's camera was sweeping over the medieval
buildings of Nuremberg with its elegiac caress, a legal system that was
the last word in modernity was being grown from the most ancient of
traditions. The links in the chain of time had been restored. Walter
Gross, a doctor and the head of the NSDAP's Office of Racial Policy,
was pleased to note, "[Since 1933,] we have been formulating moral
judgments in a modern, or an immemorial way, as you will." He explained this way of thinking by affirming that the morality ensuing
from the Nazi worldview was "modern; that is, culled from the very
depths of our history."[167] If this seemed paradoxical, it was only at first
glance: since contemporary science had confirmed that the original
views of the Germanic race were correct, the ultramodern dovetailed
with the race's prehistory.

This renewal of the law was therefore a revolution in the sense that
it was a return to the beginning. Taking a stand against "the lawyer
bureaucrat who despised the law unique to the race," the Nazi renewal
of the law promised a return to birth and to nature. "A people that does
not constantly recall what the law of its own race demands is without
direction and headed for extinction." Against these positivist confab-
ulations and successive alienations, "it is from the furthest depths of
the race's conscience and soul that the legal scholar draws the law,"
according to the declaration of faith of the new journal *Recht der Rasse*
(Law of the race), founded in 1935.[168] According to Freisler, "the law

must draw from the wellspring of the German people's good sense," and "create a racially authentic law that corresponds to the German people's feeling for the just, create a law that is linked to our people. This is the task of German jurists."[169] A struggle against artifice, anti-nature, alienation.

CHAPTER TWO

Alienation:
Acculturation and Denaturing

UNDER THE INFLUENCE OF Jewish monotheism, then of its variant, Christianity, the divine had withdrawn from the world, or, rather, had been driven out of it. Judeo-Christianity "quite simply turns living nature into something inferior." This "contempt for nature," which went alongside a "contempt for the body peculiar to Christianity," had made the natural world—the only world there was—a universe of disenchanted despair, which gave rise to a typically "Eastern" need for a "savior" who would come to "deliver" (*erlösen*) us from this vale of tears. These were the terms an article in the *Schwarze Korps* employed to take to task "Judeo-Asiatic savior theories" that had been disseminated during the "Hellenistic era":

> [The] savior figure . . . was born on Asiatic-Babylonian soil before being thoroughly reshaped by the Aryan Cult of Mithras. . . . What became of it in the hands of Judeo-Hellenic Alexandrine Philosophy is clearly shown in the last book of the New Testament and its twisted phantasmagoria.[1]

This "Asiatic fable," based on "concepts alien to our race," did not deserve to be called religion.[2] The ethics derived from the Asiatic-Judeo-Christian understanding of the world and of man also went against nature, for it prescribed the negation of being, the disappearance of the self in a body-killing asceticism. It asked that man renounce the world and bade him, not to defend himself, but to turn the other cheek in humble resignation:

> All this was clear to the Greeks. Aristotle said, a hundred years after Confucius: we must behave toward others as we would have others behave toward us.[3] These principles proceed from a high degree of self-respect, which holds up one's own conscience and individual re-

sponsibility as the supreme judge. By contrast, Christian ethics holds the value of loving one's neighbor above all others as its governing principle, to the detriment of self-respect.[4]

This was "an inadmissible and shameful injunction to be cowardly and humble." It commanded you to "give the entire coat to the man who takes a bit of fabric from you," which, when carefully considered, was nothing short of an "invitation to steal."[5] By renouncing nature, by being torn from nature by people whose interest it was to denature others, an upside-down world had been created—an anti-nature.

Denaturing Little Germans

What evil spells had caused young Germans of good race, who ought to love the life in and around them and to love the world and their bodies, to become denatured and see the world as a vale of tears and their bodies as the source of sin? Their Christian upbringing, of course, that Jewish ruse. Unable to vanquish Germanic-Nordic power honorably, the Jews had decided to sap its strength through cultural contamination. A text published for the ideological instruction of police officers affirmed:

> Germans have suffered atrociously from the importation of a foreign world view, the Jewish view, which was inculcated in their souls by the boundless violence of the Churches: the repression of the race's authentic culture, the falsification of the German language, the destruction of all evidence of our pre-history. For centuries, German man has been subjected from earliest childhood to ideas that are alien to his race, in such a way that he has never since been capable of thinking for himself—and if he attempted to, he was condemned, even eradicated, as a "pagan" or a "heretic." . . . Nevertheless, the voice of his blood has never been stilled. It is now stronger than ever and cannot be stifled again.[6]

This process was described over and over. But even more effective in beginning the process of winning back hearts and minds may have been a novel by a certain Anton Holzner, published in 1939. The book, titled *The Law of God*, recounted the adventures of a young German seminary student who becomes a priest and then, over time, discovers

God's true law, that of nature, and condemns the false one, that of the Church. "Holzner" was speaking from experience: the man writing under this pen name was Albrecht Hartl, a member of the NSDAP since 1933 and an SS officer since 1934. Ordained to the priesthood in 1929 by Monseigneur Faulhaber, Hartl found himself questioning the precepts of the Church and ultimately decided to leave one faith for another one that, in his eyes, hewed more closely to the immortal decrees of the only true divine will, that of nature. As a member of the SD, he was assigned to the *Gegnerbekämpfung* (a unit dedicated to preemptively combating political enemies) and worked under Franz Six, gathering information on "political Catholicism" as one of the major experts on the topic for the SS.[7] At the same time, the former priest published numerous works intended to popularize ancient Germanic nature worship. In 1936, he even went so far as to hold his wedding at a supposed Paleo-Germanic religious site in the Harz Mountains.

The Hartl-Holzner story opened with a foreword that presented it as a fictionalized memoir based on personal experience and the experiences of "a dozen or so friends." The text, designed as a weapon in the fight against Catholic education, took aim at all the expected targets: the wretchedness of a cloistered life, the stupidity and violence of teachers who were not always well-meaning, the abuses of trust and conscience committed against youth left in the hands of teachers who demanded faith, obedience, and complaisance of all sorts. Against this depressing and stereotypical backdrop, a young man awakens to himself (and comes of age), then discovers the outside world and politics at the end of the Weimar Republic.

In the grips of a growing crisis of faith, Peter Schädl, the young priest depicted by Hartl, attempts to "reconcile the natural laws decreed by God and the teachings of the Church," an effort that is destined to fail given the deep chasm between the two. As he grows increasingly skeptical of church dogma, the priest is no longer able to speak to his catechumens of anything but "the works and the power of God in this splendid natural world, of the beauty of the flowers and the plants . . . , of the laws obeyed by all of nature, and of the All-Powerful, who reigns over all this."[8]

These "fundamental truths of a natural faith in God" were held in contempt, even denied, by the faith of prophets, the Messiah, and the saints. Such faith led to the repression of emotions, contempt for the body, and confinement of the individual.[9] All of this stifles our young priest, who needs air and can no longer stand to chant Jewish texts. Awareness dawns when, as he performs his sister's wedding ceremony, he must recite the ritual phrase *ut Rachel, ut Rebecca, ut Sara*.[10] "These three Jewesses from Old Testament, Rachel, Rebecca, and Sarah, should therefore be models for his sister? . . . These Jewesses should be models for all Catholic women?"[11] It was too much: the young priest refuses to continue reciting "Jewish psalms written in Latin, stories and poems taken from Jewish history," all "these prayers with foreign content in a foreign tongue."[12] Not only that, Jewish piety is expressed in a Jewish way, "with the lips alone," for "inner participation is not required" in all this play-acting: "the paragraphs of the law" were recited during an hour of apparent piety that was purely mechanical, the very height of artifice and hypocrisy, when, all the while, outdoors, nature glowed on in its abandoned splendor.[13]

The young priest's internal turmoil mirrored the political turmoil raging outside the seminary. The novel tells of how he is drawn to the Nazi movement, sparking the ire of his superiors. Schädl ultimately decides to follow his heart, Mother Nature, and the nation, and leaves the cloth, to the great consternation of his family and the Church, which is by turns menacing and cajoling as it attempts to bring its lost sheep back to the fold. Threatened with hellfire and brimstone, Schädl ignores its lies and revels in his rediscovery of the truth hidden deep inside himself, observing that "German blood and natural sentiment are alive within him." When his mother asks him whether he still believes in God, he presents her with his new declaration of faith: "My heart belongs to faith in God alone, an ancient and indestructible faith that every German man carries inside him. This God decreed his laws in the laws of nature. They are sacred in my eyes, and I will respect them for as long as I live." Now that he is "finally a member of his people" once again, he understands that "the highest moral law is our duty toward the German people, to whom we are linked by the chain of our ancestry, and from which all moral responsibility results."[14]

The youth of Germany had been subjected to the brainwashing of Judeo-Christian alienation, trussed and tied and handed over to priests who were nothing but rabbis in disguise. And all of them, along with all of the books and texts to which these poor youth had been exposed, sought to make good Aryans into obedient little Jews. A 1942 article in the *SS-Leitheft* insistently denounced this process, calling for the "de-Judaization of German mental imagery."[15] Very cleverly, the author took aim at everyday commonsense expressions that everyone, without meaning any harm, employed in daily life, out of "fecklessness, out of indolence, out of sloppiness"—rich as Cresus, old as Methuselah, since Adam and Eve, and so on.[16] What did these expressions show, if not an intolerable alienation? While it was true that Aryan and Jewish bodies and blood had been forbidden to mix since 1935, minds were a different story. The Nuremberg laws, alas, could not fight acculturation to all things Jewish: "since our childhoods, we have unconsciously swallowed notions and names" to such an extent that, even if Jewish bodies had been contained, and, since 1942, were being definitively removed, "extracting the Jewish mind and the Jewish essence from our thinking and our beliefs, from Germanic mental representations" was a project that was far from complete.[17]

As for Adam and Eve, progress in "prehistoric research" had now clearly shown that Germanic peoples had played no part in the Adamic genesis narrative with which the Church had attempted to indoctrinate them: "Can we still tolerate our children being obliged to learn that Jews and Negroes, just like Germans or Romans, are descended from Adam and Eve, all because a Jewish myth says so?" What a pity it was that German children knew so much of Genesis and nothing at all of the Eddas (Old Norse literary works), that they were steeped in the lives of the saints without learning even the rudiments of the great sagas! This acculturation explained why "our representations are still largely dominated by Jewish names and concepts." This "Judaization" had to be "fought," for "it is as impossible . . . to trace the variety of birds in this world back to a single, original ornithological paradise as it is foolish to believe that Noah was the ancestor of Siegfried and Hector, Goethe and Beethoven."[18]

This alienation was so ancient, so deep, and so massive that everything, or nearly everything, had been adulterated, even the things that seemed most authentic. Vigilantly, rigorously, and with tremendous precision, the purity of the notions, ideas, and idols that made up Germanic cultural heritage had to be examined before they were taught to innocent souls. Luther, for example, that ostensible hero of Germanic liberty and Nordic honor, had in truth been thoroughly Judaized. The Lutheran Reform, wrote Stengel von Rutkowski, had been an aborted emancipation:

> Time passed, but the priest remained
> To steal the soul of the people
> Roman or Lutheran,
> He preached the Jewish faith.[19]

Luther had not gone far enough, for he had remained prisoner of the Judeo-Christian world. Today "the Nordic soul is rising up to complete the Reform, not by fighting to impose a primitive oriental culture, but against it, to restore Nordic morality and ways of life to their rightful position."[20] After Luther, Wotan himself was held up to the vigilant scrutiny of raciologists such as Hans Günther: "So many of the depictions of the Indo-Germanic god Odin (Wodan, Wuotan) seem no longer to be Indo-Germanic or Germanic! . . . Already, Wotan is no longer an Indo-Germanic or Germanic god."[21] Karl Kynast, who had already separated the Apollonian wheat from the Dionysian chaff in a celebrated book, thoroughly agreed.[22] His claim was that just as the Greek pantheon had been altered by the immigration of the Asian Dionysus, the Germanic pantheon had been contaminated by Jewish influences.

Everything was suspected of miscegenation: according to Lippe, the Prussian mind was contaminated, even if it had been extensively praised as a sublime conquest of man over his own human weakness. Lippe did not hesitate to write that "there is something alien to the Nordic race in this Prussian notion of duty," and that it had really been to "overcome the biblical condemnation of labor that the Nordic mind had invented the Prussian concept of duty."[23] This concept, therefore, only made sense in the Jewish and Eastern framework in which it originated: its invention had been necessary because work and effort were condemned. The supreme effort of self-mastery, the moral asceticism of abnegation, and the sacrifice that constituted the Prussian spirit "revealed the struggle of the Nordic mind with Eastern morals, to reconcile its value system with the value system peculiar to the Nordic race."[24]

The Catholic Church, like other Christian institutions, was an instrument of the Jews used to poison the German people. In the merciless battle that the SS claimed to be waging against "political Catholicism," in other words, against the political institution and project that the Catholic Church represented and pursued, Catholicism was portrayed as a black-hearted International wielding the universalism proclaimed by the children of God / Yahweh against German particularism.[25] The fight against the dissolution of the German nation that this universalism threatened was in fact a struggle against a Jewish idea, a Jewish weapon:

> The Jewry uses the Church as a political institution . . . to infect other peoples with the Jewish mindset. The Old Testament, which is one of the religious cornerstones of Christian churches, glorifies the Jewish people and bears the heavy imprint of the Jewish mind.[26]

This meant that churches looked favorably on mixed marriages, so long as the Jews in question had been baptized—as if their otherness were cultural (a matter of faith) and not biological (a matter of race). Further proof of the collusion of Jews and Christians—poor fools so useful to their masters—could be seen in the strong Jewish presence in the Catholic political apparatus, similar to their presence in the institutions of Moscow:

> The Jew has also made his nest in the political organization of the Church. Many popes, such as Alexander VI and Callixtus III, were Jews—as was Loyola's successor, Laynez, the General of the Jesuits, and the infamous Grand Inquisitor Torquemada.[27]

The *SS-Leitheft* illustrated this argument with a coin showing the profile of Alexander VI. The peculiar prominence of the Borgia proboscis was considered ample proof of his Semitic nature.[28] The outcome of this Semitic-Christian acculturation was summed up for police and SD officers in a table that gave a synoptic overview of the key differences between Christian and National Socialist values, set out line by line in an irreconcilable face-off (see Table 2-1): "The doctrine of Christianity . . . may be summed up as follows in its opposition to the Nordic-German view of the world."[29]

Table 2-1   The Nazi juxtaposition of National-Socialist values (left-hand
column) and false Christian values (right-hand column)

The people as a racial cell (*sic*)	Christianity equals racial chaos
Determination by blood	Alien to the soil
German mind	Jewish demon
Germanic values	Jewish history and tradition

Their opposing consequences

Dynamic	Static
Organic	Mechanical
Faithful to the reality of life	Unnatural (anti-natural)

Their opposing values

The nation as value	International doctrine
Pride of character	Servility of the faithful
Freedom of thought	Dogmatism
Honor	Love
Duty	Pity
Dignity	Humility
Affirmation of the self	Renunciation
Performance	Aspiration to salvation
Life	Preaching melancholy

Their opposing significance for the state and the people

Racial	A-racial
Awakening of the race	Global apostolicism
Creation of the state	Dissolution of states
Affirms life	Denies life

Their opposing enumeration of religious values

Authentic religion	Rigid faith
Will	Abulic alienation
Heroic conception of life	Sinful sentiment
Religion in keeping with blood and race	Negative religion
Service to the nation	Worship of the written word
Church of the German people	Miscegenated humanity
Community of German souls	A-racial system
National honor	Universal love of one's neighbor
Profession of the Nordic faith	Judeo-Eastern ideology

The Jews, People of the Law

In the beginning was *the law*, the direct expression of a natural morality that obeyed the laws of life. The German people were now slave to a multitude of abstract *laws*, and had forgotten the concrete law governing its life. Much ink has been spilled over Nazi anti-intellectualism: after all, Hitler did admit his preference to boxing over grammar lessons in *Mein Kampf*. Eternal fascism?[30] Of course. At the same time, however, one must look deeper than the—very real—hatred of intellectuals, and push past the—just as real—inferiority complexes of parvenus and the way they affected their attitudes toward the academic elite. What was described earlier, a return to nature with the goal of directly and instinctively apprehending it, goes much further than that, and the program that lay behind it is far more than just a simple, banal form of "fascist" anti-intellectualism.

Very classically, at a conference of jurists, Hans Frank declared, "Jewish domination sought to imprison the clergy in their libraries and cut them off from the people. It was even affirmed that being foreign to the race and to the people was a criterion of intellectual excellence. Professors, National Socialism is asking you for a science that comes from the people and serves the people." The people, here, were understood as a racial reality and a biological imperative. The enemies of this people were designated over the course of this conference, which was devoted to "The Jewry in the German Legal Sciences": "The time for daydreaming, meditation, and reverie, the time for formalist debates over abstraction and for excessive systemization, for verbose ratiocination, is well and truly over."[31]

Jews were beings of abstraction, for they hated what was real. This hatred had led them to invent artifice, to take refuge in what did not exist, in phantasmagoria confabulated in their poor sick heads. It was the Jews who had written the laws: they were the "people of the Law" because they were incapable of living and thinking the law—the natural law, that is, which was the pure expression of the natural world they were defying. The Jews knew they were inferior and incomplete. They hated nature and the world, as well as nature's greatest achievements, chief among these the Nordic race.

Unable to live happily with nature and its laws, they had created and formulated artificial laws that were a negation of the natural world.[32] Moreover, these mixed and unstable beings had bound themselves with the constraining and inanimate written word, for they— anarchic, nervous, and sickly—mistrusted life, which offered them neither essence nor constancy. Incapable of governing themselves, the Jews had taken refuge in a set of words that was their only touchstone and source of stability. Their geographical wanderings, combined with their psychological instability, truly left them with no respite and no bearings. As Carl Schmitt put it, "There are peoples that, without a territory, without a state, and without a church, exist only through 'law.' To them, normativist thought is the only reasonable legal approach."[33]

As a miscegenated people, the Jews were, furthermore, intellectually and psychologically schizophrenic, because they were substantively mixed. According to raciologists, the Jews were, as we have seen, a non-race (*Unrasse*) or a counter-race (*Gegenrasse*). Jews were always described as a coagulated jumble of different racial elements, never whole, never complete: "The Jew is a bastard," taught the SS department of racial expertise, an aggregate "of the Oriental, the Asian of Asia Minor, the Hamitic, the Negro."[34] This meant that diverse and contradictory beings coexisted and warred within them. They could not trust their own instincts, because they did not have any. Instinct, after all, was the direct expression of a racial identity not afflicted by contradictions or problems. A racially mixed being, then, was by nature contradictory and even schizophrenic: "Natural harmony is upset by the crossing of races, which produces imbalance." This imbalance was hematic, endocrinal, and therefore psychological. Within human groups and countries, this gave rise to revolutionary entities, and countries whose "development is hampered by riots, revolutions, and power struggles."[35] At the individual level, miscegenation produced beings whose blood and psyches bore the same taint. "Racial bastards" suffered from psychologies that were "divided and torn apart," because "two beings are at war within them"—at the very least. "Another sad story of the betrayal of the white race" was that of the "Rhineland bastards," the result of France's criminal policy of stationing African troops in

Germany and the irresponsibility of certain German women, who had conceived children with these "Negroes." The "sad life" of these unhappy creatures could be blamed on the shameful incompetence of certain women and the malevolence of a hostile power that had sought to pollute the Nordic race in order to corrupt it.[36] These poor beings, unhappy and schizophrenic, required merciful treatment, which state medical services would soon administer, mostly by sterilizing them.

The Jew was the ultimate mixed being, and had to follow a law, a code, a written norm. No instinct would ever dictate this law to him; he had to refer to a text, which explained the cultural and psychological importance to the Jewish people of rabbis and exegetes, of education and reading, and of the written word. The Jews were a people of the yeshiva and of the Torah—all because they were an unsettled, troubled, and troubling people. Beyond the law, the Jews had generated the hypertrophy of the law and of legalism that was formalism. The two *bêtes noires* of the "renewers" of "German law," positivism and formalism, were thus Jewish creations.

The ontology of the Jew and juridical epistemology were linked, according to Carl Schmitt: "Jewish law is . . . a polarity [*sic*] between Jewish chaos and Jewish legality, between anarchist nihilism and positivist normativism, between a crudely sensual materialism and the most abstract moralism."[37] Chaos indeed! A potpourri of antagonisms: from Marx to Rothschild, the Jew was everything and its opposite, a formidable screen onto which every phantasm—and its opposing one, depending on the era, the place, and the social group—could be projected; a chimera. In legal terms, the Jew was both anarchist and hypernormativist, or, as Hans Frank put it, "liberal-Marxist"—an odd association, but, from the Nazi perspective, not at all contradictory.[38] The Jew, by this definition, had no form. Jews were chaotic, because of the mixing that characterized their substance.

This formlessness had led the Jews to seek refuge in formalism: since their ontology was labile and uncertain, they found reassurance and structure in and through the rigidity of unquestioned and imperative norms. The Jews were the people of the law because they needed its normative backbone to live. This law did not lead them to construct a cosmos, however; instead it commanded them to act in keeping with its nature, which was to sow chaos and devastation. Formless, deformed, the Jew deformed and destroyed, unlike the Aryan, who informed and conformed. Seen in this light, the need to rid German legal life of all Jewish elements was understandable. The Jewish mind had to be hunted down, and practitioners of Judaism mercilessly expelled.

Jewish men of law were rabbis pure and simple: they alienated German intelligence with a redoubtable and perverse intelligence. They were to be excluded through provisions in the law passed as public health measures: a law issued on April 7, 1933, barred Jews from entering the magistracy and the law, and from holding positions as university professors.[39] These legal provisions had been preceded by harassment and physical violence that sought to drive Jews out of the places where justice was practiced in Germany. In 1933, Sebastian Haffner, a young *Referendar* (legal intern), described the SA's assault of the Berlin *Kammergericht* (Court of Appeals), where he worked.[40] Such incidents of intimidation and violence increased in the spring of 1933. In Cologne, for example, a legion of brown-shirted strongmen took the courthouse by force with the stated intent of "Aryanizing" it on March 31, 1933.[41]

The law—that is, nature's original law—was Germanic and a living thing, whereas laws—as in corpuses of individual laws—were rabbinic ooze, a dead and deadly matter. This conception of the relationship between justice and the law allowed Himmler to appropriate the notion of law with complete sincerity while heaping scorn on individual laws. He was by no means being cynical when he wrote of the German police and their activities:

> We, the National Socialists—it seems strange to be saying this here, before the Akademie für Deutsches Recht (German Academy of Law), but all will soon be clear to you—we have gone to work, not without respect for the law, for we carry it within us, but without respect for laws. I decided immediately that if a paragraph in a law caused us to deviate from our path, I would ignore it entirely, and that, in order to accomplish my work in the service of the Führer and the people, I would do what my conscience and good common sense commanded me to do. There were people who, in the months and years during which the life and death of the German people were at stake, bemoaned this "violation of the laws"; this mattered not one whit to me. Abroad . . . , naturally, there was talk of a lawless police state.

There was talk of lawlessness because what we were doing did not correspond to what they understood by the word *law*. But in truth, with our work, we were laying the foundations of a new law, the German people's right to life [in other words, the most basic and ancient of laws, forgotten for centuries].[42] . . . We have limited ourselves, quite simply, to restoring the most ancient law of our people: this is what the police are doing.[43]

Himmler asked the jurists he was addressing in this speech to do the work necessary to simplify German law so that it would be congruent with the laws of nature and the laws of the race, as had once been the case, long ago:

The basic concepts of the law must correspond with the blood and the spirit produced by the body of our race. If you can formulate that law, and sum it up in a corpus of maxims—not in paragraphs, but in aphorisms brimming with wisdom and intelligence, understandable to the simplest of men with no legal training—you will have accomplished a tremendous task.[44]

French Revolution, Jewish Revolution

Slowly, over time, legalism, formalism, and positivism had penetrated the Germanic-Nordic body. The history of this contamination, which began with the evangelization of Germania, and with the adoption of Judaicized Roman law, continued during the Renaissance and the Enlightenment, and then on through the French Revolution and its fallout. "The French Revolution," Hitler proclaimed, "formulated verbose theories and grandiloquent proclamations that the Jewish intellectualism of centuries past, with its fussy systematism, transformed into the sacred dogma of the Revolutionary International."[45] According to Roland Freisler, the "French Revolution . . . was an attack on life itself by what was alien to the race." The result had been, "in the end, the amorphous, the indefinite, the unformed."[46] The French Revolution, with its chimerical principles, had sown chaos, undermining the natural order. Before 1789, blood, land, and membership in a group had been one and the same thing; afterward, the Revolution had left things in an unprecedented shambles, jumbling identities and muddling bloods. As a textbook for SS officers-in-training lamented:

Following the French Revolution, civil law progressively insinuated itself into every State, which had the effect of detaching the legal concept of citizenship from racial belonging. Birth and race no longer carried any weight in the attribution of citizenship: "Anyone wearing a human face"—it was now said—"is equal."[47]

But, warned Walther Buch, "the affirmation that anyone with a human face is equal is not compatible with real life. . . . The essence, not only of men, but also of all things, is difference."[48] The French Revolution, therefore, had imposed illusions that even a child would know to condemn, and that a peasant, armed with nothing but his own good sense, would find stupid. Liberty? "It is not permissible to any individual to leave his family and his people." After all, a branch will wither if cut from the tree. Equality? "But look around you! . . . There is no identity, no equality. Nature does not will it." As for fraternity, the third part of the credo,

And fraternity, then! . . . A buzzard will never share its nest with a bat. By the same token, an Eskimo from the frozen North will feel no fraternity with a Negro from Somalia, who is at home in the hot sun of the tropics. They are all obliged to live according to the laws of their life, of their race.[49]

To lend validity to these revolutionary follies, which had no rhyme or reason, apologists of the Enlightenment and the Revolution had twisted themselves into imaginative intellectual knots. To explain the objective differences that could be observed among beings, the same people who had brought about the French Revolution, although they postulated universal equality, had also "invented as a panacea the doctrine of the environment, still known as the theory of the inheritance of acquired traits, elaborated by the French zoologist Lamarck," in order to avoid any contradiction between the beautiful and lofty principles of 1789 and the stubbornly persistent fact that people did not resemble one another and were not equal.[50] SD police were taught that while they had no need for the social sciences, they could not afford to ignore biology:

A good number of our enemies teach that all men are equal. But as [men] are White, Black, Yellow, and Brown, they have sought to explain racial differences through the alleged theory of environment or surroundings. They have affirmed that Negroes are black because the hot sun of Africa has burnt their skin, and that criminals are not guilty because of their own malignancy but because their "delirious imaginations," bad novels, or detective films provoked their crime.[51]

On November 28, 1940, from a highly symbolic position on the dais of the Palais-Bourbon, Alfred Rosenberg delivered a speech to the former Chamber of Deputies of the defunct French Republic, in German-occupied Paris. Standing before walls hung with Nazi flags, he drove the last nails into the coffin of the French Revolution, and affirmed that the war still raging around them, now against England alone, was a "global struggle between gold and blood": against the gold of Judaized British plutocrats, but also against gold as a financial instrument—as a quantitative, democratic, universal equalizer that dissolved all hierarchies, especially those of race and blood.[52] The French Revolution, Rosenberg declared, had meant "triumph [for] the supposedly liberal idea of the most important commandments of national life":

> The emancipation of the Jews was followed, a hundred years later, by the emancipation of the Negroes. The French minister's declaration claiming that there was no difference between Whites and Blacks and that France was no longer a nation of forty, but of one hundred million inhabitants, was the logical consequence of the ideas of 1789 and a racial capitulation of the worst kind, [in keeping with] the infamous slogan of Liberty, Equality, Fraternity.[53]

Luckily, the Führer had arrived. And even more than 1933 had been, 1940 was a victory over 1789, as well as over the harmful events and changes that had led up to that infamous year. The victory of German forces had been

> a decision in history comparable to the one, more than a thousand years ago, that led Christianity to triumph in Europe. . . . For the first time, a movement was born within the very bosom of life . . . , driven by the most implacable will that ever reigned in Germany and constituted by the awakening of the biology and the character of eighty million men and a race that will use this vital force against all forces of destruction.[54]

Mass and power, race and will: there was no doubt that "this war between the eighteenth and the twentieth centuries will end in the triumph of blood" over gold, of the Nordic race over its enemies, of 1933 and 1940 over 1789.[55] "With the National Socialist revolution, the philosophy and legal thought of the French Revolution are coming to an end, as are other, earlier eras."[56] That is, "the French Revolution has been liquidated, defeated by fighting spirits on the front and in the trenches, which have brought renewal to all things." Against alienation, "National Socialism re-discovers: it brings German sources to light, digs up the elements that compose the eternal German being, and then builds an edifice with these immemorial elements."[57]

This past reached very far back. In a vast survey published in 1937 that reviewed the history of philosophy of law "from the Greeks to today," Professor Kurt Schilling rejoiced that, thanks to Adolf Hitler, the German people "had been saved from extremely threatening dangers"—those of legal abstraction and inveterate egalitarianism.[58] In erudite, compelling terms, Schilling traced this mania for abstraction back to the Stoics, those anemic philosophers "in whose arteries not a single drop of blood still ran"—that is, not a single drop of pure, authentic blood.[59] The noxious Jean-Jacques Rousseau had been the *Stoa*'s rightful heir, and his *Social Contract* horrified our author all the more in that it had been put into practice by proponents of the French Revolution, which had led to "an excessive politicization of the people in the form of the State," as well as in "this idiotic principle of the majority" that was the foundation of democracy.[60]

Democracy, majority, the parliamentary model—these were all key components of a new era of humanity, of an unprecedented and terrifying anthropology that had been enframed by mathematics. The liberal, industrial, and commercial nineteenth century, as our perspicacious professor noted, was both the age of democracy and that of science: "Life became science, and science, statistics."[61] With this transitive leap, he argued, the mystery of life in its organic and biological reality had become a simple matter of numbers, data, averages, and standard deviations. This mathematical age was characterized by abstraction, which was hostile to life. The dictatorship of reason had disenchanted the world, it had oppressed men: the principle of majority rule, so dear to the mathematical democracy of contemporaries, had led to "a violent and blind constraint that effectively excludes a portion of citizens from the life of the state"—which was, yet again, entirely contrary to "Germanic liberty."[62]

Luckily, "this world crumbled during the World War. During the conflict, the German people proved to . . . be an authentic community, both at the front lines and the rear," a community under attack by a handful of traitors and enemies. This stab in the back had been possible because of the tremendous weakness of "the State and political power," which, contrary to the unvanquished people, had failed.[63] The *Volk* were thus, and rightly so, the touchstone once again: the norm's principle and its end was not a regime, not the state, but the people.[64]

Gustav Adolf Walz, a professor of public law and chancellor of the University of Breslau, a brilliant and sought-after legal scholar, incriminated the mathematical reason of the Enlightenment and liberal democracy in an abstruse and jargon-filled work titled *Racial Equality against Equality in Principle*, in which he sought to rehabilitate the biology of difference as an argument against the mathematics of equality, and to use it as a new foundation for the law. Walz observed that all legal systems could be divided into two simple categories: first were those legal systems which "regulated on a leveling principle of equality," such as the old Judeo-liberal law; and second, those founded on "the principle of differentiation determined by race," such as the emerging National Socialist legal system.[65]

For Walz, there could be no doubt that "the regulating idea of equality is a product of the rationalist mentality of European man as it was formed in the seventeenth and eighteenth centuries."[66] For understandable, logical reasons, the thinkers of the Enlightenment had wished to awaken humanity from its dogmatic slumber. To do so, they had made use of the admirable faculty known as reason, which they had "enthroned" over dogma. Thereafter, "mathematics became the alpha and the omega of thought" in all areas of human creation, including the law: "The law, the rational rule, appeared as the juridical expression of this way of thinking," marked by abstraction and by individualism—reason was, after all, the human faculty that fostered individual autonomy and helped people to throw off their cultural and political chains. This "legal understanding based on the individual is a system of subjective private rights," although entirely contestable, had been in keeping with the ambitions and the spirit of the age.[67] Such law was both the matrix and the expression of a society (as opposed to a community) that was liberal (and not organic), free (and not determined), mercantile and account-keeping (and not founded on solidarity). Under such conditions, "the law is a utilitarian rationalism intended to regulate relationships among individuals," because individuals were the only acknowledged reality, and their egotistical and private interests the only ones to be defended—both against those of others and against the potentially tyrannical state.[68]

Like the French revolutionaries fired with the zeal of Rousseau's philosophy, the Stoics had also been fervent defenders of this "legal mathematics."[69] Their secret goal had been to promote this legal equality, which was couched in mathematical terms—in other words, in terms of universal equivalence. In general, fanatical believers in equality were failures, beings of low biological, intellectual, and racial value who, eager to overturn the existing biological order, mobilized equality to destroy the hierarchical structure that maintained them in this state of legal inferiority and political subordination. For Walz, any legal scholar "who attempts, through the principle of equality, to lift himself up to [the level of] legal equality," was "typically morally defective, a physical failure, and racially mediocre." It was obvious, therefore, that "anywhere logic reigns supreme, one finds a biological failure or a secret political Messianism"—since the latter is the deplorable, but logical, outcome of the former.[70]

Racial Insurrection, Universalism, and Liberalism

The French Revolution had put an end to the Middle Ages, much to the chagrin of Roland Freisler, a legal scholar fond of old-fashioned turns of phrase as well as sayings in *Althochdeutsch* (Old High German). According to Freisler, the Middle Ages had, despite growing alienation, managed to preserve something of the old ethical and legal spirit of the ancient Germanic race—until the French Revolution had come and swept it all away. The corporatist, and therefore organicist, legal order of the medieval era had been characterized by "a very sound natural character," one that had placed skills at the service of the community in the context of guilds and brotherhoods, with its "indentures," its entrepreneurial liberty, its freedom to employ (and to employ oneself) bearing witness to the "anarchist and destructive" tendencies that were a defining feature of the abstract, individualist, liberal law of the nineteenth century, with its political and "legal atomization."[71] There was every reason to deplore the long "dissolution of the Middle Ages" that the French Revolution had set in motion.[72]

Fredrich Jess, a doctor and teacher of racial theory at the NSDAP *Hohe Schule* (Advanced School) in Bochum, also heaped criticism on the French Revolution. To his mind it had been a political and cultural cataclysm that had created an anti-natural order at the heart of Europe. Luckily, Jess continued, the "National Socialist revolution" was there to vanquish the Revolution of 1789, which had "applied Rousseau" as rigorously as the Reich was accused of implementing "the theories of Mendel."[73] Rousseau had been the hero of the French Revolution because he had proclaimed universal human equality and exalted mediocre and failed humans, who had been endowed with inalienable dignity according to natural law. The French Revolution, like all revolutions, had been the insurrection of the weak and the miscegenated against a Germanic racial aristocracy; consequently, an "Aryan elite" had been "massacred" by the Parisian "plebs."

Jess described the hysterical and evil joy of the racial rabble "when a blond head fell at the chopping block" of the executioner. He wrote of how, to put an end to a veritable racial genocide whose aim was, quite simply, the extinction of the Frankish—and therefore Germanic—aristocracy, "the white Charlotte Cordey [sic], beautiful as an angel with her blue eyes," had "planted her dagger in the heart of the Sardinian Jew Marat, thus becoming a martyr of her blood."[74]

A terrifying era indeed, during which, *Neues Volk* reminded its readers, "blond hair and blue eyes were enough to send you to the guillotine, because they made you an aristocrat, a member of the Frankish elite, whose extermination the fanaticized masses demanded." The Revolution and the Terror had provoked the final "de-Nordification" of France, which, from then on, was at the mercy of Negroes and Jews.[75] The SS even had images to support these texts: Slide Series Number 10 in the "Jewish" file, created by the RuSHA (*Rasse- und Siedlungshauptamt* der SS, the SS Central Office on Race and Colonization), presented terrifying pictures of the three major massacres perpetrated by the Jews against Nordic humanity: the Purim "pogrom" against the original Persians, who had come from the North; the Russian Revolution of 1917; and 1793, when the Jews had unleashed "a war of extermination against the bearers of Germanic blood."[76] The French Revolution, that "infection from the West," was the stench rising from the "swamp of blood" of the racial plebs, frustrated and humiliated by their own mediocrity and awakened by the "principle of equality" that had "excited the unsatisfied popular classes," who were "scorned and socially oppressed."[77]

This "revolution" had in fact been a counter-revolution. The true revolution of modern times was the pacific and liberal insurrection of the Germanic mind in favor of freedom of thought. It had been led by "heroes of our people and of our blood," notably by the "blond Galileo," with his "eyes as blue" as those of the lovely Charlotte Corday. From Kepler to Kant, these heroes had fought against obscurantism of all varieties to "reveal the truth of the laws of nature and the cosmos."[78] Against this intelligent revolution, though, a new obscurantism had prevailed, and the "bio-racial consequences" of the dogma of universal equality, warned Neues Volk, were nothing short of dramatic.

The French Revolution and its principles had created a synergy of forces hostile to the Nordic race, which had come together to annihilate it: "the modern era saw Roman law, natural law, economic liberalism and individualism, and capitalism come together to destroy" for good the Germanic order so unique to the Germanic culture and race.[79]

The civil law expert Heinrich Lange, a jurist and a member of the Nazi Party who served as a judge in Saxony before becoming a professor at the Universities of Breslau and then Munich, devoted a good deal of attention to the question of legal liberalism and its normative transposition of the principles of the French Revolution. Writing in 1933, the year his university career began, the Saxon civil servant called for a strict application of the law of April 7, 1933, the so-called Law for the Restoration of the Professional Civil Service—which, incidentally, had opened a number of previously filled university professorships to civil servants such as himself—and decried the "liberalism" of "civil law." "Liberalism is the degenerate product of the idea of liberty [and has] become hyperbolic individualism, contaminated with materialism."[80]

Faithful to the precepts of his party, the author added that as a true Nazi, he had nothing against "the idea of liberty," which indeed he hailed for having "separated the modern era from the Middle Ages." "Freedom of conscience was the fruit of the Reform, freedom of thought was willed to us by the Enlightenment." The problem was that freedom had "become an end in itself." The "overvaluing of rights and the undervaluing of responsibilities" had unleashed an "individualism and materialism" that had sapped away national solidarity. Against the dissipating forces of this culture, "the Prussian doctrine of duty and community" had been erected, a doctrine embodied, notably, in the person of Otto von Bismarck.[81]

Among these platitudes, Lange produced an original thesis: "Liberalism and the law are, by their very essence, antithetical to each other." What was important to the individual and the individualist actor, after all, was "legal security," "the predictability of the results of his action. The ideal of liberalism is therefore the codification, regulation, and setting" of laws. For the liberal citizen of the nineteenth century, who sought to conduct his affairs without interference from brigands and princes, and for whom "time is money," legal security was crucial to the function of these affairs, and widespread codification of the law had been undertaken to meet his needs—but it had "drowned the law in positivism."[82] By contrast, "the [Germanic, foundational] law is a subspecies of the vital and moral order. For this reason, the principle of good faith and respect for the word of others is the fundamental law of the life of our community—specific norms do nothing but translate and disseminate it." Things were actually very simple: good faith, giving one's word—and the *clausula rebus sic stantibus* left for dead by liberalism," which should "by all rights" be rehabilitated and reactivated.[83] This was true because "the law is the order of life and of our community. Like it, the law is not a set thing, but constantly fluid."[84]

Returning to the law of the community, to this good and life-giving original law, not only meant "readjusting a few hundred or a few thousand articles of law." To understand it in these terms would be to "fall back into positivism." Lange, like so many others, called instead for a "re-forging of our law," a normative revolution—that is, a cultural revolution that would necessarily upend and annul existing positive law:

The application of the principle of duty toward the community destroys the law in its current form. The rigid, clear, distinct, and logical structure of our legal system, which speaks only to understanding, must give way to a living, fluid organism, which rambles and drifts without logic, but which is underpinned by the feeling of justice. Understanding must blend with and into feeling: *pectus jurisconsultum facit* (the heart makes the jurist).[85]

To break with this essentially artificial order of things, with its poisoned origins and harmful consequences, Walz proposed to replace equality (*Gleichartigkeit*) with racial identity (*Artgleichheit*), which was to be used as the foundation of the law. To him, this was simply a return to the original, correct order of things. Racial identity was an incontestable and irrepressible biological reality, and one that had, for millennia, provided a solid base for healthy, happy Germanic communities: "This vital sentiment dominated the dawn of Germanic time," a happy time when "a sureness of original instinct had no need to be formalized in conscious principles."[86] Without falling back on such mediating forms as language, intelligence, or formal rules, the Germanic people, down to a person, knew in and through their bodies what was right both for themselves and for the Germanic race.

"Race . . . gave form to the whole legal order according to its law alone. Family, clan, race determined the law." For millennia, the Germanic race had known what to do and how to do it, until the day "that legal sensibility . . . disappeared during the Roman-Byzantine racial chaos and the heightened mixing unique to this era" occurred.[87]

This terrifying history had a reassuring flipside: what had been demolished could be restored. The race was still there. It was under threat, to be certain, but it had endured. Its spirit, too, was still alive. History was not destiny, nor was it fate. Its path could be reversed. The Third Reich could make possible the renaissance of true, original, Germanic normativity, which grew from racial identity, rather than being founded on interracial equality: "Wherever racial identity reappears, one finds the original vital type, the vital community of race . . . which determines the legal order according to this vital original feeling that is unique to it."[88]

Universalism and Its Contradictions

Alone in the world, unmixed, gathering from nature the laws it was to follow, the Nordic race had once known nothing of the perversion of human intelligence that would one day become universalism. As was so often the case, it was the Jews who had promoted this idea in the guise of Christianity. As the *SS-Leitheft* affirmed:

> the doctrine of the equality of all men that was preached among the nations by the Churches and by the apostles of Bolshevism sought to supplant original racist thought and to lift the natural barriers that existed among peoples, barriers that followed the natural laws of life.[89]

Universalist Christian egalitarianism had played a decisive role in the emergence of the idea of equality. According to one NSDAP publication,

> it is the Jew Paul who must be considered as the father of all this, as he, in a very significant way, established the principles of the destruction of a worldview based on blood. Instead of an evaluation of peoples and bloods, his political Church decided to consider only individuals.[90]

The Church had spurned all of the natural evidence and assembled men of different races in "a community of faith, and, if one were to believe the priests' pastorals, a Negro baptized as a Catholic was closer to a young German Catholic girl than a non-Catholic German man, even if they shared the same blood." Christianity had thus opened the way to the racial abomination of "mixed marriages" among people of different blood. Worse still, the church defined mixed marriage as "the union between two Germans when one of them sang Lutheran hymns in his childhood, and the other Marian hymns."[91]

In the footsteps of Christianity, communism, its present-day avatar, had completed the task of promoting equality and universality against hierarchy and difference: "Bolshevism, which, like all clericalism, comes from Jewish culture, finished toppling the natural barriers among races and peoples," since its "supreme objective was racial chaos."[92] Universalism had always been a weapon in the hand of Germany's enemies, from Christian universalism, the weapon of the cosmopolitan and miscegenated masses to dissolve Nordic racial excellence, all the way to Bolshevism, a conspiracy against the Nordic race—not to mention the Enlightenment, the French Revolution, the "great nation," and the Wilsonian United States. In 1933, the doctor and celebrated eugenicist Fritz Lenz published a slim volume titled *Die Rasse als Wertprinzip: Zur Erneuerung der Ethik* (Race as a moral principle: For a restructuring of ethics). It included an essay he had written as a young military doctor in the trenches in 1917, and his comments on it. As a young doctor, he had wondered about the meaning of such a murderous war, and had concluded that the Germans were fighting in the name of the people, of their people, whereas their enemies were fighting in the name of "humanity."

> Here and there, you could see doubts being expressed: the people, the race, were they so worthy that it was necessary to sacrifice everything for them? What was this race, after all? What was it made of? Was it an essence? Before the war, many had doubted that race could be [considered] a value [in itself]. It was said that humanity ought to be the end of all moral action. But now it seemed that the majority of this "humanity" was fighting us or had taken sides against us. . . . Our enemies never tired of preaching that they were fighting for humanity, freedom, and culture. Of what value was our race, if hundreds of thousands of men died or were mutilated to defend it? Devotees of humanity, those who deny the value of race, those who assert that differences among men are morally invalid, could only see this war as nameless idiocy. We, however, see this understanding as a profanation of our dead. It is not humanity that refutes this war: in our eyes, this war refutes humanity. The goal of this war does not lie in humanity, but in the good of our own people. And this supreme goal represents the supreme morality.[93]

"Humanity," held up as a standard by enemies of Germany and of the race, was a dangerous trap: the only reason to live and die was for the German people. In addition to humanity, that monstrous fraud, Fritz Lenz refuted other "values" promoted by modernity. Individualism, so highly prized since the end of the nineteenth century, was banished without trial because "it does not fit our [German] moral conscience." The "collectivism" that emerged in 1917 was refuted as well, for it was a kind of "collective individualism"; that is, the individualism of the group: "The value of the race as a supra-individual organic entity stands in even greater opposition to collectivism than to individualism." Fritz Lenz contrasted these with his own "ism," which he called *gentilism:* "The gentilist system describes a vital order that places the biological community at the heart of law and of morality." Gentilism, from the Latin *gens* (people), was the classical moral system of the "Chinese," who originally were a Nordic people, "and of the ancient Germanic tribes as well as of other Indo-Germanic peoples."[94]

Between the two extremes—of the insignificant individual, and of nonexistent humanity—the only truth was race. Gentilism gave meaning to the life and death of the men who had fought in the Great War, but it also offered meaning to contemporaries—a meaning that individualism, collectivism, and universalism could neither conceive of nor offer. "The individual person cannot be an ethical end," Lenz argued. This end "could only be what is organic in race, whose vital flow traverses centuries and in which individuals are merely passing waves. It is the people as an organism that is our ethical end."[95] The defeat at the end of the First World War had been caused by "the influence of a non-German ideology and moral values" that were alien to the race: "the Christian understanding of man, which leads us astray in affirming that all races, all peoples, and all men must be considered as equals" and "the vision of the Enlightenment, which comes to us from the West."[96]

Friedrich Berger agreed with Lenz: race was the only reality that it was valid to live and die for. It was "a biological and empirical reality," not a Christ-like chimera or some Marian apparition—and one that had been elevated to the ranks of religion by the terrible carnage of the Great War: "The myth of blood replaced the myth of the cross. This is the major legacy of the heroes who died in the Great War." Men had died, had passed on, had disappeared. But "the people is what persists, what is, what endures."[97]

> Filled with sacred respect, we see this flow of blood that is our own, this blood that comes from the depths of time and goes toward the end of time, and which, for a time, has honored us as its trustees. We are only the servants, way stations for a formidable will that mani-

fests itself in and through our blood. [To be] worthy [of it is a] sacred obligation.[98]

The race's "path toward eternity" now "passed through the concrete and practical commitment to serve our people." Adolf Hitler's declaration that "it is not necessary that one of us live, but it is necessary that Germany live" should be understood in this light.[99] There had been no fight "for human rights"—Germans had been fighting for Germany's right to live. A 1934 film ironically titled *Um das Menschenrecht* (For the rights of men) offered a striking, caricatured image of this way of thinking: in it, demobilized soldiers returning to Bavaria become the despairing witnesses to a communist revolution in what was threatening to become the Bavarian Soviet Republic.[100] "The *Internationale*/is fighting for the rights of men"—strains of the chorus of the German version of the revolutionary anthem echo through the film as bare-bosomed Red women shout "Liberty, Equality, Fraternity" as part of the wild celebrations held in the soviets as the revolution progresses. The Red Terror, with its thick Eastern accent, is all set to execute its unarmed civilian hostages when the returning German soldiers step in. Falling back into the ranks of their *Freikorps* units, they take up arms once more to defend the nation against international peril.

Against this universalism, defined as both the symptom and the matrix of a mixed and muddied biology, Nazi discourse unhesitatingly held up its noisy particularism. An ideological instructional text on Bolshevism put out by the RuSHA informed its readers that, unlike communism, "National Socialism is not export merchandise. It is exclusively intended for the German people and its goal is the good of the German nation alone."[101] This repudiation of universalism even led some to declare that philosophy was dead. As Ernst Krieck, a popular philosopher and a professor at the University of Berlin, put it:

> Philosophy as it is generally understood is characterized by a universalist principle. The fact that the National Socialist worldview . . . puts an end to all universalism and replaces it with the principle of race logically should lead to the declaration of philosophy's end . . . so that it can be replaced with a racist cosmology and anthropology.[102]

"Philosophy" in the Stoic, Renaissance, or *aufklärerisch* sense of that term was a thing of the past. Wisdom demanded a revolt against mixed-blood ideologies, that Plato be deployed against Chrysippus, Darwin against Voltaire.

A single member of the Nazi leadership attempted to save philosophical universalism, using an intriguing redefinition of the concept. His name was Otto Dietrich, and he served as the head of the NSDAP press service. A journalist and former soldier, Dietrich held a doctorate in political science, and was interested enough in philosophy to have published in 1935 *Die philosophischen Grundlagen des Nationalsozialismus: Ein Ruf zu den Waffen deutschen Geistes* (The philosophical foundations of National Socialism: A call to arms for the German mind). In it, Dietrich argued that it was necessary to find the right words to explain Nazism outside of Germany. Dietrich the communications specialist was concerned with publicizing Nazism, while Otto the philosopher wanted to universalize the ideology that was galvanizing Germany's rebirth. The author deplored "the lack we have noted until now of an internationally comprehensible language" that would make it possible to speak about Nazism. Such a language would provide an answer to a universal question, one that every people was facing due to the widespread crisis of "individualism, which is also a crisis of individualist philosophy."[103]

The profound idiocy of this individualism could be observed at the ground level of individual and political experience, since "man does not appear to us in the world as an individual, but as a member of a community." Dietrich argued against this individualism and for the promotion of what he called "universalist thinking," which redefined universalism as "the conscious thinking of the community."[104] So defined, universalism became a synonym for "communitarian" and "organicist."[105] In this way, "universalism" was redefined by the limits of the "community"—gentilism, to return to Lenz's term—and from this perspective, one sees how it could restrict moral duty to the *Volk* alone. With the help of Otto Dietrich, Kant's "categorical imperative" and "universal law" became the Nazi Golden Rule: "Kant's moral law [*Sittengesetz*]—'Act only according to that maxim by which you can at the same time will that it should become a universal law'—is the appropriate and classical formulation of National Socialist ethics."[106]

From an epistemological, rather than an ethical, view, one also understands that Dietrich would restrict the freedom to think and to teach to supporters of the Nazi Party, since anyone who thought or taught differently was mistaken.[107] This shift in the definition of the term *universalism* was so massive that the author felt obliged to clarify it in a paragraph that declared and delineated the new meaning:

> I would like above all to underline that the concept of "universalism" that I will use from now on has nothing to do with the vague and foolish concept of "human society" or "humanity": here, "universalism" is the opposite of individualism; it is a concept whose entire reality is to be located not in "society" but in "community."[108]

Dietrich was seeking nothing less than to put an end to the two centuries of misunderstanding that had followed the French Revolution: "The fact that individualist thought diverted the concept of universalism for its own benefit will not prevent me from restoring its true meaning."[109] Dietrich's philosophical and semantic battle was a lonely one, and in vain, for no one else was seeking to reconcile Nazism and universalism: in general, the radical particularism of the Nazi doctrine and project were openly asserted and accepted. Others were not so quick to bury philosophy. Georg Mehlis, for example, believed that National Socialism was itself a philosophy, a way of "thinking of life" that openly stated its vital particularism and joyfully cast off the deadly abstractions of universalism. There were moral and legal implications to this epistemology:

> [National Socialism] does not demand that other peoples and other races see the world with the same eyes. Yes, it is convinced that other nations see the world differently, and, consequently, that other values and other principles are valid for them. National Socialism therefore does not profess to be a universal ideology, a doctrine to which all peoples of the world should submit.[110]

Magnanimous, and in perfect coherence with racist thinking, Mehlis conceded that "all peoples are different and they profess values that correspond to their races. Each people—and this is true of all of them—creates a universe of values all its own."[111] Alfred Rosenberg repeatedly argued much the same thing in a series of newspaper articles devoted to the law and how it should be defined: "The individualist and universalist ideas dominant until now are ceding to a way of thinking based in biology":

> We do not believe that a legal norm should be thought of based on the individual abstracted from his blood. Nor do we believe that there are any so-called "eternal laws" or "eternal ideas" handed down from heaven and intended for all the peoples of the earth. Quite to the contrary, it is becoming clearer and clearer that legal cultures are born with a specific racial soul with which they perish or prevail.[112]

Mehlis warned, however, that the particularism he was proclaiming should not be mistaken for a synonym of relativism:

> This observation certainly does not lead us to insipid relativism: the "relative" is the enemy of all strong life. The National Socialist worldview is absolutely valid for each member of the German people. It is not only the best relative to others, but the only one that is right and the only one that is possible for anyone who identifies with authentic Germanity.[113]

The fact of race imposed the Nazi worldview in an absolute way, as the most fitting expression of the race, on each member of the *Volksgemeinschaft*. Such a thesis made it possible to be as implacable at home as one was magnanimous abroad. Asking Ethiopians or Turks to be Nazis was sheer madness. In 1938, as the Third Reich was dismantling the Treaty of Versailles, Hans Frank proclaimed a kind of minimalist fraternity of particularisms, with an unambiguous refusal of any outside interference:

> Other peoples and races have laws that correspond with their individuality, just as the German people has its own lifestyle. It is precisely because we consider races and peoples as biological entities that we uphold each people's right to live in keeping with the form its life takes.[114]

The Alienation of Law through the "Reception" of the Roman Law

There existed in Germany an ancient tradition of contestation, even rejection, of Roman law as it had been received in the fifteenth and sixteenth centuries.[115] The Nazis, who took care to criticize Roman law in Article 19 of their 1920 political platform, were following a well-worn path—and racializing it. In an article that is a tidy summation of the many treatises written on this topic, Hans Frank linked the arrival of the idea of sovereignty in Roman law to the development of the state—or rather, of states, which, in the Germanic sphere, grew from the ashes of the Holy Roman Empire starting in the fourteenth century, with a dramatic acceleration in the seventeenth century. The development of the state was, naturally, accompanied by the development of the legal theory of sovereignty as well as of a caste of legal scholars who worked in the service of the prince—both lawyers charged with conceptualizing the state and lawmakers whose task it was to ensure that it lived and maintained power. In the Germanic era, the concept of the state and Roman law had been imported via the Roman Catholic Church, which had followed the model of the late and decadent Roman Empire by preserving its legal traditions and its political concepts. This meant that Germany had undergone a kind of second evangelization: following in the footsteps of missionary bishops such as Ulfilas, *juris doctors* trained in "Italian universities" had surged to the north to "bring it typically Roman legal ideas." This new plague from Italy sought "to dominate and to shape real life through eternal values according to a concept of life, an abstraction of life, that expressed the rigid ritual mechanism of the Vaticanist regime."[116]

The clergy and scholars of canon law were ritual-obsessed zombies who mechanically followed liturgy, who recited masses now entirely devoid of meaning, and who shrouded the divine and all thinking related to the divine in deathly scholastic reasoning. Thus, "faith in God and in eternity had been calcified in the school of canon law into formal dogma"; and "life" had been shut away "in a logical system" that had transformed the "organic order" of life into a "mechanical order" manifested politically as "the state, in the modern sense of that term."[117] Today, "law was no longer a vital order," by nature *sui generis* and immediate, but "an artificial and formal world."[118]

Rome was to blame for this state of affairs: not only the Rome of popes and doctors of canon law, not only the Rome of the Italian universities that trained the *doctores utrique juris* who went on to counsel bishops and princes, but ancient Rome as well. Hans Frank, like all of his jurist colleagues, had nothing but harsh criticism for Roman law and its reception in Germany. It was as though German jurists, aware that the Führer had little love for them—Nazis preferred the word *Rechtswahrer* (guardian of the law) to the word *Jurist,* with its hated Latin roots—wished to shake off their academic robes and garb themselves anew in the vestments of National Socialism by repudiating what constituted the building blocks of their training: Roman law, Latin phrases—both abhorred signs of intellectual and social distinction accessible only to those who had obtained a baccalaureate from a *humanistisches Gymnasium.*

Roman law, therefore, was to be avoided like the plague—although Frank, good Nazi that he was, was careful to point out which Rome he was talking about. The "Roman law" that had contaminated Germanic law came from a Roman Empire that was decadent and on the wane, and so was an expression of degenerate biology. But heaven forfend it be confused with original Roman law, which was proud, noble, and sound. The racially pure roots of that Roman law were Germanic and Nordic, relics of the time when this great culture had colonized Italy and given birth to a glorious empire which had, alas, been slowly corrupted by the invasion of foreign bloods:

> The Roman law of the *doctores juris* was unnatural: it was no longer the authentic and proud law of the nobility, of Nordic Romans who had created the greatest empire in Antiquity. This law, organic, vital, was the law characteristic of a small racial entity based on the pure racial concept of the *civis romanus.* This term did not mean "inhabitant of Rome" or "Roman citizen," but rather expressed a belonging, through blood, to the Roman racial essence. So long as the law was an expression of the coarse and tough life of this racial cell, Rome was truly Rome, before the Romans' ill-considered extension of their Reich signed the death sentence of this original law. The vital law of a race certain of its own destiny deteriorated into an artificial principle of state domination. The racial citizen became a mere member of a Caracalla-style state.[119]

Caracalla, according to Rosenberg, was the "racial bastard" who had granted Roman citizenship to all free men in the Empire; under him, the Roman Empire had ceased to be a racial entity and become a simple political apparatus aggregating all of the races of the *oikoumenē* (the ancient Greek word for the known world, which in Roman times came to signify all parts of the world that fell under Roman imperial administration), which was one of the causes of the decline and fall, through biological degeneration, of Rome. Another Nazi publication, put out by the Association of National Socialist Jurists (NSRB), proceeded to mete out praise and blame using the same distinction:

> The Romans of Antiquity were very gifted, legally. But, by the fifteenth century, there were no more ancient Romans. . . . There was a deeply decadent science of law with late Antique origins. And it was this scientific system, foreign to our race, which became law in Germany. . . . The spirit of a decadent late Roman science dominated here unopposed for centuries.[120]

Original Roman law, the noble and proud expression of Germanic racial dominance, had become an egalitarian and universalist hodgepodge that offered safety and benefits to all of the Empire's inferior peoples: "When Roman racial foundations were diluted and Mediterranean-ized, the law of the Roman race was transformed into mere state regulation" of relationships among individuals. The "Jews, the Levantines, and the Greeks had their say in the formulation of 'Roman' law, and a maelstrom of noisy yawping was thus 'formulated' and 'systematized'" to favor the lowborn and the failures, who were thus able to insinuate themselves as citizens into the corridors of civil and military power.[121] Essentially, these Nazi legal scholars were arguing that the jurists of this decadent and harmful Roman law were, for the most part, Africans, Asians, and Jews.[122] These legal swindlers had replaced "family" and "community" with individual primacy, which became the core of legal and political life. Stripped of rights by dint of their own racial mediocrity, because they belonged to inferior biological communities, these (Levantine, Jewish, Asian, Arab, and so on) legal scholars of decadent Roman law had, by introducing "the concept of the legal personality as the holder of subjective and objective rights, as well as the concept of 'thing'"—all deplorable abstractions—managed to make themselves into individuals with rights that were natural, imprescriptible, universal, and other such nonsense.[123] It was very decidedly worth noting that the notion of the legal personality as defined by this legal system did not correspond to anything concrete or real: "The idea of the legal personality is completely detached from its physical being," Freisler objected. This "fiction of legal personality has been separated from the grounds from which it grew"; that is, from the concrete, physical beings who populated cities and towns:

> We find no trace of the race, of the people, of the difference between the sexes, in this fiction. These significant natural facts, which alone make a being into a person, were considered by the old law to be nonexistent. Taking them into account would have been a sin against the spirit of democracy [which considers that] all [beings] bearing a human face are equal.[124]

Ultimately, "the Roman law of Justinian," the law whose codes were studied, taught, and received in Germany, "contained as much Roman law as all the world's oceans conceal nuggets of gold."[125] The history of the "great reception" of Roman law was an unhappy one characterized by successive alienations: first that of the "late Roman" from the "Roman," then that of the "Germanic" from the late Roman.[126] Professor Walther Merk was another who deplored "this alienation of the law through the reception of late Roman and Byzantine law": "It was not the authentic and vigorous ancient Roman law . . . , but the highly Orientalized law of a population of degenerate European-Asiatic bastards" that had been received in Germany. Fundamentally foreign, this law "upset everything in the order created by the wisdom of our ancestors."[127]

The reception had created a formal system, stupefyingly abstract, universalistic, and egalitarian, "without the least breath of authentic, strong, and healthy Rome. It is in this form that it arrived in Germany. And it is for this—because of a Byzantine alienation—that our law was massacred" by separating "the law of the people" from the "law of the state, truly a law of jurists, formal and judicial." The importation of an artificial and complex law had created a double tyranny. Lawyers had created an increasingly absolute princely power, because no one understood the plan these jurists were hatching: the people, fit and pure, armed with good sense, had become the *Hanswurst*, the Punchinellos, of the courts, whose language and hairsplitting they could not understand.

At a deeper level, and far more seriously, life itself, in all its liberty and plasticity, in its labile and constantly moving indeterminacy, had been mortally stifled by the straitjacket of "paragraphs"—of writing, of death, of all that was fixed and unmoving. Frank noted with outrage that through the actions of these *doctores juris*, the subsuming "of particular cases (of life!) to articles of law had become the main mission of the justice" system. But, he added, life would take its revenge, because "one does not subject life to formal constraints" for long. Life's revolt against the formal tyranny of these eggheads, these rabbis of the law, these priests and princes, had begun in earnest in 1933: National Socialism required a "transition from formal law to the law of life, from Roman law to the communitarian law of the Germans," just as Article 19 of the NSDAP had declared in 1920.[128]

To reconnect with the spirit of the race required that not only Germanic legal theories and practices be studied and resuscitated, but those of the Romans as well, from the time before racial mixing had diluted their blood. Frank, with rudimentary Latin and hazy citations, affirmed that the origins of the maxim that expressed the foundations of Roman law were authentically Germanic: *Primum vivere, secundum philosophari*.[129] According to Frank, the "war that we have declared on Roman law has nothing to do with the law of ancient Rome. It targets the falsification of the Roman law that we appropriated a few centuries ago, in the form of a Romano-Byzantine bastardization."[130]

The willingness and energy with which these professional jurists went about discrediting and reviling their own profession is impressive. What curious brand of masochism could possibly lead those with doctorates in law, who had studied Latin and legal codes, to qualify themselves and their colleagues as a pile of positivist, nit-picking quibblers, as a bunch of degenerates to whom life itself was a foreign concept? Was it overwhelming self-hatred? Bad memories of their university years? Legal-digest-induced indigestion? Or rather were they scrambling to voice their agreement with what the Führer himself had so often repeated, that "jurists are the unending plague of humanity"?[131] Despite having defended their SA "comrades" before every court in Germany when they were charged with violence, conspiracy, and murder over the fourteen years of the *Kampfzeit*, Nazi lawyers remained unpopular within the movement.[132] Hitler despised them for their education and their degrees, just as he hated the academy-trained generals and diplomats for their pre-sumptuousness. In Germany, a country where a doctorate in law was the ultimate sign of intellectual standing as well as the swiftest road to higher social status, Hitler boasted that he was not a lawyer just as, in other lands, one might boast of not having attended an Ivy League school. In this spirit, he declared to a group of workers at the Borsig arms factory in Berlin:

> I am a humble man. . . . For the first time in our German history, we have a state that sweeps the slate clean of all of the social prejudices that until now dictated the attribution of places. . . . I am the greatest proof of this. I am not even a lawyer, think of what that means! And in spite of all that I am your Führer![133]

As legal matters became more and more complex, a caste of experts had arisen, people who spent all of their time reading the law, anno-tating and commenting on articles of the law, and producing paper ab-stractions. Ordinary people had been excluded from the law. The law had become "a specific technical profession reserved above all for classes who were educated and trained for it." The people had begun as the subject of the law, since they were the subject of their own lives; now, however, they had become the law's object, a mere thing dispos-sessed of itself, its liberty, and its life, dominated by specialists who led it astray with their trickery and scheming. As Frank wrote, "The vast majority of the people has become the object, pure and simple, of these abstractions" since the jurists had brought about the great "sep-aration of the soul of the law from that of the people." The "monsters of legal construction" had "pushed the law off into intellectual abstrac-tions that excluded the people's simple and basic truths about life from the sphere of the law."[134]

Frank was not seeking to throw the baby of ideal or idealist law out with the bathwater, however contaminated it might have been by dan-gerous and deadly abstractions. He was critiquing the militant and de-structive abstraction of life, not the idea of the law itself, for in the face of Jewish materialism—both capitalist and Bolshevik—the National Socialists, as he recalled, were modernity's idealists, faithful to the spirit of the race that had given birth to human culture—to Plato, to Bach, to Hegel. If lawyers were "called to leave behind the world of abstractions," it was so that they could return to the "positive and idealist politics of our National Socialism," based in the "soil, the race, honor, and work" that were at once concrete realities and high moral values.[135] To this end, there would always be a need for jurists—but only for those with actual life experience.

The letter of the law, the writing of legal codes, was a set legal standard that froze into the concrete present, and imposed on it, an abstraction from the past. As Frank put it, "the stasis of the past understanding of the law" implied the necessity of "always looking backward, toward the past," whereas life itself was above all a matter of the present and what was to come.[136] No lawyer could possibly predict and envision the myriad special cases that life, in all its indeterminacy and richness, would produce. It was necessary to "cast off the formalist prejudices of an outdated legal system." It was well and truly "the life of the people, the general interest of the community of the people," that was "more important, more essential, and more vital than the preservation of a formal legal order."[137]

In a file on "the Jewry," the SS Central Office of Race and Colonization included a slide that illustrated the difference between the " 'dead letter' of Jewish and Judaized law," represented by a closed law book, and a courtroom scene: "The introduction of Judeo-Roman law, foreign to our race and hostile to our peasant farmers, was a dangerous attack on the life of our people." Before this great alienation, the law had been "derived from popular good sense, from the just sense of the law of our pure blood."[138]

> [But] when Judeo-Roman law, this foreign law, replaced the one we inherited from our fathers, we began to trust only what was written in the law. The dead paragraph, the letter of the law, dominated legal life. The Jew, who knew so well how to interpret texts in the most unworthy way, to turn them to his advantage by detecting every possible chink and flaw, was the master and the beneficiary of this anti-German law. The clever and cunning Jewish lawyer was the typical representative of this law. As soon as a law alien to our race became dominant in Germany, the Jew prospered. From the moment a people's law becomes diseased, the Jew always becomes rich.[139]

The Acculturation and Denaturing of the German People

The corruption of the German people by foreign doctrines was denounced in numerous texts. The best-known and the most vitriolic
among them condemned the evangelization of Germania, decrying its
martyrization by violent, murderous proselytizers. *Der ewige Wald*
(The eternal wood), a film shot by Rosenberg's services in 1935, advanced the claim that the very same Christian axes that had deforested
Saxony from the south and from Asia had committed the Massacre of
Verden, thus transforming rich and verdant Germania into an Eastern
desert.

It had been the "Golgotha of the North," representing the agony of
the Germanic race, the slaughter of innocents delivered defenseless
into the malignant and hateful hands of the Jews. In an essay bearing
this very title, Werner Graul, one of the key propagandists of "Nordic
faith," recalled the birth of Christianity, a Jewish ruse invented to destroy the Roman Empire and subjugate Germanic populations the
world over. After evoking the conquest of the world by "Nordic Rome,"
the author pointed out that

> as invented by Jews and disseminated by Jews, Christianity stealthily
> insinuated itself into the heart of the eternal city. In the Roman Cata-
> combs, Jehovah's hatred ate away at the foundations of the temple of
> Jupiter, until it was converted into a church.[140]

Evangelization had "spiritually circumcised" the Germanic race,
which had had to "crawl before the cross," to convert, overcome by
Christian violence, confused by "the manipulative refinement of the
rabbis, which they could not resist," for, as was well known, the Germanic people were a nice people, a naïve people—and too trusting.[141]
And "the substance of the Christian message is Jewish. The Jewry is
the seed, Christianity is the fruit. . . . It is a not a religion in keeping
with the race of the German man."[142]

(Judeo-)Christian cruelty had targeted women in particular. "Witch
hunts" were a well-known phenomenon that had killed tens of thousands in a Germanic land torn by the Wars of Religion, by eschatological
anguish, and by the rifts of the Reformation and the Counter-Reformation
from the sixteenth through the seventeenth centuries. In 1935, Himmler

decided to devote considerable funding to a peculiar research project: for nine years, until the summer of 1944, the Sonderauftrag Hexen (Special Witch Mission) employed fourteen researchers to explore two hundred and sixty libraries and archives and establish a list of the female victims of Christian fanaticism. The project produced 34,000 precisely recorded individual profiles, each with thirty-seven subheadings (place, grounds for incarceration, method of torture, names of informers, executioners, and so on), spanning 3,621 German localities.

Directed by SS-Sturmbannführer Rudolf Levin, who had received his doctorate after defending—as one would expect—a thesis on the positivist method in history, the mission was an entirely secret one. Participating researchers worked under false identities and gave false grounds for their work. All of them were members of the SD and the SS, affiliated with the Gegnerforschung, the department of intelligence devoted to "ideological enemies," including Jews, Freemasons, Catholics, and members of the political opposition. This was, indeed, the core of their work: the mission's goal was to gather horrifying evidence of Christian barbarousness as it was unleashed—and not by chance—on women, the matrix and the future of the Nordic race. For the SS, the massacre of (no fewer than) 34,000 women had deadly significance: it was proof of the aggressive hatred of the Christians (the Jews, in other words), who were not content merely to soil Nordic women with *Rassenschande* (racial shame), thus rendering them unfit to procreate pure Aryans, but had actually sought to massacre them by delivering them to the vindictive, celibate priests. The parallel between the witch hunts and Jews' sexual commerce with Christians—or rather, the assimilation of one to the other—was drawn by another member of the SS, none other than Richard Walther Darré: "The profanation of the German woman by the Jews is similar to the witch hunts carried out by the Church. The two have the same spiritual father: Yahweh," the vengeful, Eastern, non-native god of the deserts, come to devastate the forests and lakes of verdant Europe.[143]

Ultimately, the project had to be made public. It had to be proven, as Himmler himself put it, that "all Christianity tends toward the absolute extermination of woman," and specifically of Aryan woman.[144] Himmler's idea was to produce a film and a book, and Rudolf Levin submitted a *Habilitation* on the subject at the University of Munich.

The results of this massive project fell short of the hopes and funds that had been invested in it: Himmler had hoped that the executioners would turn out to be priests and Jews, but the careful and honest work of the SS historian-recorders revealed no such thing. Mostly, the poor witches had been massacred by nice, long-skulled peasants. With a little imagination, Himmler might have been able to incriminate Christian culture all the same, since he had already gone so far to vilify it, but, like any good policeman, what he wanted was the names of priests and monks. Deeming the *Sonderauftrag* (special mission) a fiasco, the Reichsführer SS decided to put an end to it in the summer of 1944, and Rudolf Levin's *Habilitation* was not granted. The 34,000 files were shelved in a Polish archive near Poznań, where they remained hidden until they were stumbled upon by historians studying the medieval era, for whom they represented a veritable treasure trove.[145]

Other texts denounced the subsequent damage wrought by Christianity. Manfred Werner, for example, wrote about the evangelization of Greenland in the eighteenth century, claiming that the island, almost completely unsullied by contact with the outside world before then, was a magnificent test case for examining how Christian culture had altered and alienated a people still living in a natural state. Indirectly, of course, this was a way of describing the much earlier ravages of Christianity during the Germanic era. His study, titled *Natur und Sünde* (Nature and sin), purported to demonstrate how the notion of sin was totally unnatural; it was an evil invention of malevolent priests.[146] The subtitle, *Eine Studie zu der angeblichen* anima naturaliter christiana . . . (A study of the alleged *Anima Naturaliter Christiana . . .*), was a response to theologians who, in the spirit of Tertullian, affirmed that the human soul, in its virgin state, is "naturally Christian" (*naturaliter christiana*). The author insisted that the contrary was true, and that Christianization was denaturation: it made man a stranger to himself, alienating him from his own nature by distancing him from his natural state. The *anima christiana* was more than an invention, however: it was a poison, and because it inoculated crime into the conscience, it rendered a person criminal. This virgin population of native Greenlanders lived without boundaries, either among themselves or between themselves and the world.

The only thing that could explain that these men had no knowledge of sin was their total immersion in nature, of which they themselves were a part.[147] . . . [Pure] children of nature, who did not know the difference between life and faith, for whom life, in its wealth of manifestations, was a religion.[148] [The Greenlanders had been easy fodder for these missionaries, who came to teach them] the doctrine of original sin, of the fall of man, and of salvation in the suffering of Jesus Christ.[149]

No sooner had the priests taught the Greenlanders about the sinful nature of the world and about man's damnation than the simple, pure, and direct relationship they had once had with the nature around them was altered. Weakened by this message, they "resided no longer in the great, living whole."[150] Summing up his thinking in an apparent tautology, the author declared, "It is the knowledge of sin that makes man sinful."[151] He did not mean that people had become conscious of an evil of which they had hitherto been unaware. Rather, made vulnerable by the message of damnation, cut off from nature, urged to suppress their instincts and impulses, they had been denatured, and thus either spoiled by the suffering provoked by an unhappy conscience, or transformed into a perverse being who fell into evil ways:

> Before, man's intermingling with nature prevented the spread of anti-nature. And then foreigners arrived, with their gospel of sin: they sullied this pure nature, which had not before known sin. They preached this new notion, which was addressed to the subhuman in us.[152]

Werner, an ethnologist, focused on Greenland, while in 1931 the writer Wilhelm Vesper examined Iceland in *Das harte Geschlecht* (The tough race).[153] This novel about the Christianization of the island was hailed by the *Völkischer Beobachter* as a typical and remarkable "novel of the North" that was "soaked in the blood" of this unfortunate Germanic people, who had been forced against their wills to embrace a religion of the Jews.[154]

Inoculated with the fear of sin and schooled in foreign doctrines, these Germanic peoples had been successfully convinced that they were immoral brutes, and that they had become civilized only by learning the Jewish law of the Decalogue as it had been taught to them during their conversion. It could readily be observed that the very contrary of that had occurred, and continued to occur in every conscience and every heart under the influence of Christian education and upbringing. It was high time, wrote Friedrich Berger, one of the propagandists of the Germanic religious renewal, "to break free of Asiatic culture" and to stop believing that "if we gave up the Old Testament and the Ten Commandments, our moral life would be stripped of norms, of standards. . . . There is not enough trust in the German man and in Nordic blood." People claimed that "without the Jewish Tablets of the Law, we would never have been able to attain a moral existence," whereas in fact the ancient Germanic peoples were far more moral than the Jews—with some even going so far as to claim that the Ten Commandments of Moses had been inspired by an even older Nonalogue. This tablet of nine Germanic-Nordic commandments "proved that everything that seems valid to us in the Ten Commandments the Jews had borrowed from the primitive Aryan Nine Commandments."[155] These commandments, wrote Alfred Rosenberg, preexisted Moses's commandments, just as Nordic writing and civilization predated those of the Orient: "The table of the Ten Commandments is an adaptation of the system of the Nine Commandments, as testified by our Aryan humanity."[156] The fable of the Nine Commandments is found only, among high-ranking Nazi officials, in the writings of Rosenberg, who borrowed it from Wilhelm Erbt, one of the more prolix representatives of the Deutsche Christen movement.[157]

As Werner and Vesper wrote of Greenland and Iceland, Bernhard Kummer, a future professor of Nordic language and civilization at the University of Jena, was writing at length on the subject of the Germanic peoples in his doctoral thesis, titled "Midgards Untergang" (The decline of Midgard), which discussed "Germanic religion and faith in the last centuries of Paganism."[158] In it, the young Nordicist painted a picture of a paradise lost, and included a merciless indictment of Christian alienation, notably in chapter 19. In sum, Kummer was arguing that sin created sin. By producing taboos, setting up limitations, and problematizing the clear-cut, sin proscribed any direct interaction with the self, with one's own body, with nature, and with others, perverting these relations by declaring they were wrong. The direct and innocent relationship that had once existed with the body was illustrated in a practice observed by "Caesar . . . that Germanic people of both sexes bathed together."[159] This practice troubled no one. Only Christian interdictions regarding the body had made these social acts problematic by transforming bodies into sinful objects—forbidden, and thus desirable. With its unnatural prudishness, Christianity had, in aiming for the angelic, fallen toward the bestial. "Eyes famished by lucre were imported by the South. They cannot be found in the Pagan north. . . . Missionary Christianity definitively pushed converts into prostitution and a swamp of sexual degeneracy."[160]

Kummer in this way disputed the idea that Christianity had brought virtue to the people by eradicating supposedly pagan vices. In fact, the contrary had occurred:

> The absence of morality in sexual life is not an inherited legacy that Christianity should have painfully eradicated. It is rather a gift of conversion. . . . It is only where nature is called sin that, by dint of repression and taboo, eroticism emerges.[161]

This harmful separation between the here and now and the world to come, between body and soul, between substance and spirit, had been unknown to the Germanic people. Ascetic minds from the East had imported this illness into Europe, so that, alienated and deprived of the nature within himself, Germanic man had fallen into misfortune: "Christianity brought with it sinful flesh. . . . The separation between body and soul is foreign to the Germanic pagan, however, just as it was foreign to Greeks in the Classical era, or to Goethe."[162] As Greek art and civilization, or Goethe, proved, the eternal Germanic race was hostile to these Eastern importations: "The ideal of the mortification of the flesh to aid the soul, the notion of a body that would be the prison of the soul, finds in the Germanic Siegfried an enemy even more implacable than in the Greek Apollo."[163]

Most likely the Jews and the priests, men of the South, had distrusted the senses and affects because "in the hothouse atmosphere they knew," in the Eastern heat, these passions led to damages "from which only the punishment of the flesh could liberate them, whereas in the North, they fulfilled their natural roles in producing life" calmly and temperately.[164] But more than this climatic difference, it was the desire to harm that had led the Jew-Christians to condemn the body and the senses. Sin had been a redoubtable weapon for priests, who had taken advantage of it to subjugate Germanic peoples: "It was necessary to introduce sin and to make its influence felt before the desire for salvation could produce Christians." Christianity had imposed values and virtues, such as virginity and abstinence, which were of no value at all: "In the Pagan North, no one would have understood the meaning or the merits of virginity, not to mention the peculiar purity of an immaculate conception"—absurd dogma, but the logical consequence of the reasoning described earlier.[165] Christianity had perverted everything:

> It was necessary for it to demonize love and make it into a sin, through taboo and eroticism. The Nordic sagas contain no trace of eroticism. ... [Indeed,] the eroticism and Roman Christianity of the monks came and conquered together. They were fellow travelers and fellow fighters, and this is still the case today.[166]

Christianity, by constraining the direct expression of desire, by degrading nature into hateful sin, had created perversion.

Catholicism, Monasticism, and Anti-Nature

The ultimate outcome of this anti-nature was monastic life, the cenobitic existence that Christianity, the enemy of life, had elevated as the high road to holiness: "The ultimate goal of a well-ordered life," inveighed an SS textbook, "was to flee the world (celibacy, and in contemplative orders, the rejection of work)."[167] Renounced were sexuality, nature, life. And contaminated by these Eastern doctrines, Germanic man was lost:

> Man learned to disdain the laws of life, for he had lost all ties with nature and with life. The Churches convinced millions of members of our people that our faith in an eternity here on earth was false, so that countless men and women gave up becoming the parents of healthy children for belief in a heaven that did not exist. The Churches called our holy earth a vale of tears and made conception and birth a sin and an offence.[168]

SS publications repeated and circulated these critiques, explaining that Christianity had made the Nordic race foreign to itself and had alienated it from life by convincing its members that the pure, immediate life moving within them was wrong, offensive to a God that was the enemy of nature and the body. The different branches of Christianity, Protestant and Catholic alike, were equally responsible for this denaturing of the race. In an article titled "Artfremde Moral" (Morality alien to the race), the SS journal *Das Schwarze Korps* targeted the beliefs of the Evangelical Protestant Church and its definition of original sin as "not a sin one commits, but a sin inherent to nature, to the substance and the being of man."[169] This the journal qualified as crude and intimidating stupidity, given the extent to which nature, in a man whose blood was pure of all adulteration, was good and safe:

> Here is the very opposite of what we believe, on German soil, to be the foundation of worthy and moral behavior. We work from the principle that each of us bears in his heart the moral touchstone for good behavior and that each man must decide for himself what to do and what not to do. Nature, and this also implies human nature, is in our eyes holy and intangible, and we do not believe that a natural feeling could ever be bad or sinful. The very concept of sin . . . seems false to us and foreign to our being.[170]

In other words: "Our enemies speak of original sin, we speak of original and hereditary nobility."[171] Seen in this light, it was not surprising that monasticism represented the very height of vice. Starting in 1935, Catholic orders and clergymen were targeted in *Sittlichkeitsprozesse* (morality trials), which denounced *Doppelmoral* (moral doublespeak) in which the body was condemned and chastity was encouraged, while homosexuality and—above all—pederasty were tolerated. These trials sought to find—if not generally to fabricate—well-known practices, and were widely covered in the press.[172]

With their black garb and their Jesuit-tinged talk of "corpse-like obedience," was the SS the organization best qualified to criticize the Christian religious order? Yes, for while it did define itself as an *Orden,* both sexes were admitted to it: "The Church, in keeping with its negating views of life, founded orders that were built" on the strict separation of the sexes and "on the absence of marriage" and procreation. They had "ripped out humans' finest racial substance, and condemned them to sterility."[173] Unlike monastic orders, the SS mixed the two genders and brought the sexes together, so that they were positioned to fight for a single goal, "to accomplish the will of nature" by securing the eternal life of the race.[174] The SS was thus a "community of families" whose ambition was to recreate "the Germanic familial order."[175]

Himmler repeated this tirelessly; during a speech he gave while serving as a witness at the marriage of one of his officers, for example, he proclaimed: "The SS is an order of National Socialist soldiers, composed of Nordic men and a community of their families." The two necessarily went together, and the SS could not allow itself to be a mere order of soldier-monks: "We would not be fulfilling the duties of our will and of our activity if we did not include women. If we went about our historical and human mission as a mere order of soldiers, we would not meet our goal." The SS had to be a "familial order," and "it has become custom to welcome the young wife into the SS," which required that she be "faithful and obedient to the SS, to the movement, and to the Führer."[176] The SS was a natural order that respected and promoted the order of the world.

Thwarting Nature, Annihilating the Race

Anti-nature had triumphed in the cloisters and monasteries, where healthy human beings, encouraged to pursue the worst forms of depravity, were condemned to sterility; it had also emerged triumphant in every society in which the churches had succeeded in spreading their values. Well-meaning German "Michels" spouted their Christian virtues, forgetting that these very virtues had been proclaimed and passed on in order to kill the Nordic race.[177]

Volk in Gefahr (A people in danger), a collection of writings on population decline and the disappearance of the German people, featured an afterword by the influential author Arthur Gütt in which he explored the underlying causes of the phenomena that had just been described in fifty terrifying pages by the book's principal author, Otto Helmut. For Gütt, there could be no doubt: if "the German people [were] in the process of dying," it was in large part because "natural selection had been thwarted" by doctrines both deadly and foolish.[178] An attempt had been made to annihilate the German people "by imposing upon it, through the ideology of the past thousand years, the moral imperative to keep everything weak and sick alive."[179]

These "suicidal dogmas" induced from an "erroneous and faulty understanding of life" had nearly wiped Germany off the face of the map. Luckily, the Führer had not built his policy on this dogma. Instead, it was based in science, and had discarded "internationalism of every stripe, whether Jewish or [of the] international clergy," not to mention Bolshevism: the Nordic race had recovered its instinct and its authenticity, and had once again begun practicing ethics and politics that served life, instead of conspiring to bring about its own death, as had been the case before under the iron fist of the rabbis and priests.[180] The life of the race: "all other things must be subordinate to this, the sole end of racial politics . . . our custom and lifestyle, including the familial and sexual order."[181] This meant breaking with Judeo-Christianity, which had created an anti-nature, a counter-world, by substituting one legal frame of reference (false, artificial) for another (real, natural). One SS publication drove the point home in these terms:

> Our Germanic ancestors, who were pure men, accepted the laws of selection, for they had not yet been corrupted by these doctrines of pity, which are false, and hostile to life. The false image of God promoted by the churches succeeded in repudiating the divine laws of nature. Church doctrine was consciously opposed to the will of nature. Once it had been preached to the peoples that God had died on the cross out of pity for the weak, the ill, the sinners, and those who were seeking redemption, it was possible for a doctrine of unnatural pity and a misguided humanness to demand the protection of the congenitally diseased. It was even considered to be a moral duty to care for and nourish everything sick, retarded, afflicted, and simpleminded.[182]

The contamination of states and public policies by these doctrines was a catastrophe that "violates the order of life" and led to a "counter-selection" harmful to the "vital substance of the race."[183] Before this absurd encouragement of "life unfit to be lived," the race had been undermined by attempts to drain it of life through unnatural sexual practices. That Christian teachings were hostile to nature could be proven with a single fact: in addition to its attraction to death and the afterlife, to its disdain for flesh, Christian culture had divided Germanic nature against itself, not only by separating body from soul and the divine from the world, but also by dividing German from German. The division of faiths had sundered the "homogeneous substance" of the Nordic race into two religious groups.[184] The division was now so great that—the ultimate absurdity—"mixed" marriages between Catholics and Protestants were forbidden by their respective clergies.[185]

Celibate priests refused to marry Catholic men to Protestant wives, while thousands of young men and women cloistered themselves away, refusing to offer their bodies and their genetic material to the propagation of the species. It was only understandable that in the face of this terrible violence, nature had avenged itself in the burgeoning of homosexuality—a weapon of the Jews and the clergy to mortify the flesh and sap away Germanic life force. This homophobic psychosis and hatred of Christianity came together in the writing of Reichsführer-SS Himmler:

> I deeply believe that all of these priestly types and all of Christianity are nothing but an erotic *Männerbund* (virile community) [intended] to establish and maintain this bi-millenary Bolshevism. I tell you this because I am very familiar with the history of Christianity in Rome. I am convinced that the Roman emperors who eradicated the first Christians were doing exactly the same thing that we are doing with the communists. These Christians were, back then, the worst dregs of Rome, the most repugnant Jewish element, the most disgusting bunch of Reds.[186]

To recapitulate: the Christians, converted Jews or souls led astray by the messianic message spread by the Jew Saul-Paul, were the communists of antiquity. In order to destroy Germanic Rome, they had spread an egalitarian and universalistic message, while promoting celibacy—and therefore encouraging homosexuality—in order to hinder the reproduction of the Nordic biological force. The "Bolshevism of yesteryear had then had the force to grow on the corpse of Rome in its death throes."[187] To avoid perversion and homosexuality, it was necessary to allow nature to speak, to actively ignore the absurd and unnatural precepts of the Church. Here again, Himmler proposed a simple and commonsense solution to the problem of homosexuality: "In the country, these problems are unknown," for young men protected themselves from homosexuality through early sexual practice, albeit extramarital.

> In spite of the priest, in spite of Christian morality, in spite of religious teaching that has gone on for a thousand years, the boy goes to visit the girl, tapping at the window. This is how order is reestablished. So yes, there are a few children born out of wedlock, and two or three old ladies in the village get their noses bent out of shape about it. As for the priest, he is well pleased to have an edifying topic for his Sunday sermon. This doesn't keep the fellows from happily going about their business as they always have, since the beginning.[188]

This is how men naturally met women and German blood mixed only with German blood, without any need to look elsewhere or engage in homosexual relations: "All of this was natural. The order, back then, was proper and dignified. It respected the laws of nature. Not like today, when everything is done against the laws of nature."[189]

What to do with these children conceived out of wedlock? Their fate was not to be envied in a culture still steeped in petit-bourgeois taboos and Christian anathemas against free sexuality. No matter—these children ought to be cared for by the state, or, barring that, by the NSDAP. If racially pure, they would be housed, fed, and educated in order to preserve their good blood and to avoid any desperate recourse to abortion, a crime against the race: "We abhor the vice of abortion," the SS proclaimed.[190] Concerned for the fate of children born out of wedlock, it invested considerable resources in them, offering room, board, and health care to its happy parturients.[191] Far from being the stud farms that certain sensationalist publications painted them as, the *Lebensborn*, created in 1935, were maternity clinics and homes for all women in need, particularly women who had been the mistresses of SS members.[192]

[CHAPTER THREE]

Restoration: Renaissances

THE YEAR 1933 DID not, in the eyes of its actors, mark a simple change in head of state, but a veritable revolution, one whose aim was to restore nature to its rightful place. In a speech on January 30, 1937, in honor of the fourth anniversary of his accession to power, Hitler spoke proudly of the triumph of blood over ink: "Throughout a seemingly endless era, our legal life was troubled by the reception of foreign ideas and by the lack of a clear understanding of what the law was. The clearest example of this was our inability to understand the law's true end." Its end was not "to protect the individual in his person and in his property," but to "help to preserve and to protect the people against all of the elements" that threatened it: "Through this, we see that above person and property, there is now, in our legal life, the people."[1]

The people and its life: this was the law's end, served by the renaissance of the original norm, which commanded that the law be aligned with the law of nature, with biology. The *nomos* was the expression and the realization of the *bios:* "bionomy" was now anything but a nonsense word, and *Lebensrecht* (right to life) became a common term in political, legal, and geopolitical discourse. This, then, was the true Nazi revolution, in which members of its hierarchy, its intellectuals, and its legal scholars took such pride:

> To create a law that follows the laws of life, a law of the race, it is not enough to add the word "race" into past legal systems. Legal relations must be reorganized around a new nexus: the life of the German people. The vital, racial law of the German people must permeate and structure the law. A complete reevaluation must be undertaken.[2]

It was a Copernican revolution, according to Hitler, because the legal, political, and mental universe had changed its center: "Discovering that the Earth turned around the Sun led to a revolution in our understanding of the world. By the same token, the doctrine of blood and race that we uphold will lead to a revolution in knowledge."[3] The revolution was not only an epistemological one; it was practical, ethical, and legal, too: "Its only bedrock is the natural life of the people, structured by the Nordic race. The only valid criterion is utility to our people and its natural life."[4] Hans Frank returned to this frequently: "Law is what serves the people," he wrote, with "people" here understood to mean an organic and biological community.

Science (biological and medical) and law were in fact pursuing the same end: "The goal of German science must be to do everything to create the conditions for the eternal life of the German people" by "ensuring that we have, at all times, a sufficient number of pure, racially valid, and large families." Of course, it went without saying, "the way to achieve this is through the correct law (*das richtige Recht*)." It was by "ensuring the eternal life of the German people" that German law would fulfill "the original mission of the law: to serve living life [*sic*]."[5]

State and Nature: Restoring Original Norms

According to Helmut Nicolai, the state, a "system of legal constraints, was entirely unknown to the original Nordic peoples."[6] They had governed and regulated themselves very well indeed, and with complete autonomy and immediacy, because they obeyed the nature both outside and within themselves. The state had only appeared later on, through default, and as a result of the first racial mixing, which had clouded the mind of the Nordic race. The mixing of blood had deformed all intelligence, leaving it without bearings: "Racial degradation having dissolved all moral ties, individuals were connected only through an external power, by the coercive figure of the state." For those who worshiped at the altar of state, who were legion in Europe in the interwar period, "law is what state power commands arbitrarily."[7] For the Nazis,

> the law is an eternal and moral glory, superior to the state, which cannot alter it. For others, power is the law. For us, the law is power. . . . There, the law is what is posited in the laws—*positum*, from which comes positivism. Here, law is what is in keeping with

the eternal idea of the law . . . , which gives rise to our legal idealism. For others, morality is completely disconnected from the law. For us, the law is the expression of the moral order of the world.[8]

The state could hold just one function: "It does not create the law, it limits itself to formulating it."[9] The Nazi leadership's repeated attacks on the very idea of the state make more sense when examined through this intellectual lens. Hitler's famous speech at Nuremberg in 1934, immortalized on film by Leni Riefenstahl, was a denunciation of the idea of state. And in *Mein Kampf* he wrote,

The state is only a means to an end. Its end and its purpose is to preserve and promote a community of human beings who are physically as well as spiritually kindred. Above all, it must preserve the existence of the race.[10]

Institutions were subordinate to life; structure was subordinate to biology:

We must make a clear-cut distinction between the vessel and its contents. The state is only the vessel and the race is what it contains. The vessel can have a meaning only if it preserves and safeguards the contents. Otherwise it is worthless. . . . [Hitler] can consider the state only as the living organism of a people, an organism which does not merely maintain the existence of a people, but functions in such a way as to lead its people to a position of supreme liberty by the progressive development of the intellectual and cultural faculties.[11]

Wilhelm Frick, the minister of the interior, did specify that

the National Socialist idea requires that the state hold supreme authority. But at the same time, it asserts that the state is a mere means to serving the people, a tool that the party, the national Socialist Movement, uses to provide for the wellbeing and the life of the German people.[12]

Just as the NSDAP was less a "party" than a "movement," the state "must not become fossilized, but remain always and everywhere open to the movements of life."[13] Hans Frank pushed this idea even further: "The state is a means in view to an end," he repeated after Hitler and Frick. But he added: "It is an agency (*Anstalt*) that serves the people."[14]

In the 1930s, Reinhard Höhn, who after the war would become one of the fathers of a new discipline known as "management," was one of the theoretical architects of this decentralized, mobile, and ad hoc notion of state. According to this view, the state was divisible into a series of labile, flexible agencies that were as dynamic and responsive as the old state was inert and burdened by its immutable density. This deconstruction of the state horrified Carl Schmitt, who with his firm grounding in Roman law, Catholicism, and pontifical *summa potestas,* remained very Latin in this regard.

If political action sought to hew to life in order to protect and reinforce it, it required instruments as fluid as life itself. Critiques of statism and necrosis were a constant in texts and films. "Saint Bureaucracy is in charge here," laments Robert Koch, the scientist played by Emil Jannings in *Robert Koch, Bekämpfer des Todes* (literally, "Robert Koch, death-fighter"), when he realizes that the laboratories he has been appointed to lead close at five in the afternoon.[15] In his fight against tuberculosis, Koch comes up against the combined forces of the priests who denounce his experiments as satanic; of *Herr Rechnungsrat,* an accountant who keeps reminding him to stick to the rules; and of the big boss, Von Virchow, the "Pope of Medicine," who opposes the theory of bacillus infection and clings to the theory of internal degeneration. Two other celebrated films of the Third Reich, *Carl Peters* and *Kolberg,* also told the stories of civil servants straitjacketed by written rules and by death.

Cleaving to life, so that death did not strike at the quick of it: Achim Gercke, a chemist and genealogist who served as an expert in questions of racial heredity for the NSDAP, explained that "the law can only do justice to life and can only make the laws of nature into law if it follows biological thinking." To "think biologically means that we must consider the structure of our race organically, rather than organizationally."[16] Again, traditional legal thinking, in its static formalism and its focus on the state, had to be renewed and surpassed with an organic, biological, and dynamic understanding of racial reality. The state, in this context, did not appear to be the most efficient tool for governance, because "it is an organization, and not an organism."[17]

Erich Volkmar, a magistrate and a high-ranking government official, wrote extensively about the static/dynamic opposition in law.

According to him, the "dynamic" was gaining ascendancy over the "legal statism of the Romans": "The Roman understanding is static . . . , the Germanic is dynamic." The Roman was rigid and restrictive: it relied on the disembodied mechanism of an obligation to act that was guaranteed by the state; the Germanic was natural and ethical: it relied on mutual trust, "the bond of loyalty" (*Treueverhältnis*) that existed among the parts.[18]

Statism and rigidity were the consequences of the crazed abstraction that had governed late Roman law, which had been racially decadent. As the (execrable) symbol and example of this legal rigidity, Volkmar cited the "gold clause" or the "value conservation clause"— which stipulated that sums owed or outstanding were to be paid or reimbursed at face value, rather than at their actual value. Use of the clause had been widespread and rife during the hyperinflation that raged in 1922–1923, and was (in)famous for its power to magically efface debt, to the terrible detriment of lenders. The very concept of currency face value, when associated with the trauma of hyperinflation, constituted a powerful argument against the dangers of fiction and legal abstraction. In the summer of 1932, Alfred Rosenberg wrote an article condemning equations of monetary nominalism and legal egalitarianism, in which he argued that "a mark is a mark, and a man is a man," as Falk Ruttke would later write.[19] According to Volkmar, "this rigid clause . . . is the expression of a static way of thinking."[20] To say "a mark is a mark, even if the currency's value has changed completely," was an absurd and dangerous fiction. It was also, however, a sign that the law had remained fixed by and in writing—in this case by the face value of the coin, the note, or the debt. Rosenberg, in denouncing the verdict of the Potempa Murder, wrote that "during hyperinflation, this same 'justice' explained to us that a mark was a mark. The foolishness of this 'objective thinking' has been paid for with the lives of thousands of Germans and deprived the nation of all its savings."[21]

According to Volkmar, a living law, a breathing law, had to be composed of rules that were not "rigid, but flexible, so that they can be adapted to the time and the place of the case at hand."[22]

De-Judaizing Christianity?

If it was possible to align law with life, what about religious norms? In the words of many a tormented racist since at least the end of the nineteenth century, it was "impossible that Jesus was a full-blooded Jew."[23] How indeed could one be Christian and also German? Did a German of good stock and good race have any right to follow a Jewish prophet, the son of the God of the Jews, born in Judea and a resident of Jordan? This was a major question for racist and anti-Semitic groups.[24] As they recruited people into their ranks from nationalist and conservative circles, these racist groups showed themselves to be all the more eager to save Christianity because of the real services it had rendered to the wealthy and the powerful since antiquity. So how could the social order be maintained if its transcendent guarantor was called into question? This question became all the more and more pertinent and pressing after 1933.

One answer was that it was possible to be Christian and German if one were "Christian-German." The Deutsche Christen (German-Christian) movement drew from sources that dated back to the nineteenth century to lend credibility and legitimacy to the idea of a Christian and racist faith and a Christian-German church. The movement, which developed from the right wing of the Protestant Church, was embodied institutionally by the Reichskirche (Church of the Reich), led by Bishop Müller. It also had an intense intellectual life, with leaders going so far as to found the "Institute for the Exploration and the Elimination of the Jewish Influence in German Religious Life." At the head of this institute was the young and brilliant theologian Walther Grundmann. During his solemn investiture in Eisenach, the city where Luther had translated the Bible into German, Grundmann described "the de-Judaizing of religious life as the mission of German theology and the German church."

Grundmann believed that the "German revolution" could not take place without a "theology of the race."[25] Coopting Luther for the cause, he claimed that the "Reform" had been "a return to itself for the German soul" that presaged the revolution of 1933, which in turn had come about as a corrective for the mistakes of 1789.[26] The theologian recalled that "the beneficiaries of the French Revolution and the principal vector of its ideas were the Jews, for whom the ideas of 1789 threw the ghetto doors open wide," and then emancipated them legally. Only then had the Jews converted, the better to blend into post-Revolutionary society, which they both inhabited and subverted. The Jews had had themselves baptized and begun singing the praises of Jesus, despite having hated him so much before 1789 that they had killed him! In other words, Jesus was not Jewish. The hatred with which the Jews had pursued him proved this: the Judaizing of Jesus dated back to the nineteenth century, and indeed it had been "since this era [of the French Revolution and the emancipation] that the Jewish element had increasingly taken over Jesus to its own advantage."[27]

During antiquity, Jesus had been closer to the Greeks than to the Jews. Here, Grundmann based his claims in the work of the theologian Johannes Leipoldt, who in 1941 published *Jesu Verhältnis zu Griechen und Juden* (Jesus's relations with the Greeks and the Jews).[28] As an advertisement included in another work of Grundmann's proclaimed, Leipoldt's book showed how "Jesus's actions were directed against the Jews," that "Jesus's race was perfectly non-Jewish," and that "his thinking is in full agreement with that of the Greeks; that is, with the intellectually dominant Aryan people of his era."[29] Jesus was Aryan, and had thought and acted as an Aryan: this could be proved by observing that superficially Christianized Jews had fallen back into Judaism, whereas the Greeks, of Nordic blood, had converted to this authentic Aryan religion. The thesis of the Aryan Jesus was not merely the pious wish of Protestant theologians seeking to salvage what they could of their church and their faith. Hitler himself was convinced that Jesus was, at the very least, an Aryan bastard, that he had not been entirely Jewish, and perhaps not even Jewish at all. In private, the Führer confided to his table companions, "Jesus most likely was not Jewish. The Jews called him the son of a whore, the son of a prostitute and a Roman soldier."[30] Three years later, Hitler reiterated this hypothesis, this time in more detail:

> Jesus certainly was not Jewish, because the Jews would never have handed one of their own over to the Romans. They would have sentenced him themselves. It is likely that numerous descendants of legionnaires [from Gaul] lived in Galilee, and that Jesus was one of them. It is, however, possible that his mother was Jewish.[31]

As was often the case, the Führer's words echoed what was being said elsewhere—words that hypermnesic Hitler, who kept a finger in every pie, had read, heard, and retained. The idea that Jesus was Aryan was an old saw that allowed Christians to reconcile their love of Christ with their reverence for the Nordic race. It was in this spirit that the NSDAP platform of 1920 professed the party's commitment to "positive Christianity," with which Hitler was slow to break, for reasons both personal and politically opportunistic. It took until the mid-1930s, when the Vatican expressed reservations about his laws on eugenics, for the Führer to break privately with the Christianity of his childhood and to explicitly envision a future without Christianity. The "positive Christianity" of the Nazi Party was defined clearly by one of the best representatives of this Christian-Aryan sensibility, the lawyer Herbert Meyer, who, in 1925, published a dense work titled *Der deutsche Mensch* (The German man), an erudite volume devoted to "racist ideology" and "the community of the German people."

In it, Meyer wrote that "we, the racists, are the only ones who revere Christ as he deserves," by ceasing to consider him as a Jew and by taking his message seriously.[32] The author advocated a "circumcision of the Old Testament to recast our faith." The Old Testament, the Jewish Torah, "certainly belongs to religious history, but it no longer belongs to the living Christian faith. The God of the Jews is not actually the God of Christ."[33] The author did not deem it necessary to expand on this point. Christianity had been mutilated by Christ's epigones—first and foremost the Jew Saul-Paul—who had made the positive and vital religion of Jesus into a religion of death. No, man was not guilty; he had not fallen. Quite to the contrary, he was continually raising himself up in a process of "de-animalization." No, Christ "was not an ascetic. He lived with both feet firmly grounded in life and his people."[34] While the SS saw itself as firmly anti-Christian, it softened its message when it came to discussing Jesus Christ: in a circular, Reichsführer SS Himmler himself stated explicitly that in courses of ideological instruction, it was important not to cast aspersions on Jesus by suggesting that he had belonged to the Jewish people:

I forbid that, in the context of ideological instruction, you allow yourselves to attack Christ as a person, for such attacks, or the affirma-

tion that Jesus might have been Jewish, are below us, and probably
historically inaccurate.[35]

The fact remained, however, that Jesus had spent more time on the
shores of Lake Tiberias than among the sand dunes of Rügen. In his
remarks at the opening of his institute, Grundmann addressed this
issue head-on: "[One] cannot deny that the Holy Scriptures . . . are a
portrait of the Jewish spirit [and that] Christianity well and truly has
roots that stretch back to Palestine." This was why "historic-critical"
work was necessary. Through subtle racial exegesis, the divine and
Nordic wheat could be separated from the Eastern and Jewish chaff. As
a theologian and a historian, Grundmann raised the painful question:
to be certain, Christianity had been born in the land of the Jews, but did
"this undeniable moment truly belong to the essence and the truth of
the Christian faith?"[36] Buoyant, ardent Grundmann was convinced that
serious work would make it possible "to call these outdated facts into
question"—so convinced, in fact, that he repeated this claim six times
in two pages.[37] Grundmann invited his audience to "continue the Reform," an intellectual exercise whose "goal is to distinguish the eternal
truth from its different historical occurrences"—such as the unfortunate occurrence that had been Christ's inopportune birth in Judea,
a detail, a mere accident, in the eyes of the truth and the essence of
Christianity.[38]

The "Institute for the Exploration and the Elimination of the Jewish
Influence in German Religious Life" had a clear mandate: "As the Old
Testament does not have a monopoly on salvation," it was necessary
to engage in a "scientific edition of the four Gospels that questions the
most accepted ancient traditions."[39] This work of "de-Judaizing" (Entjudung) the Christian religion was one of the battlefields on which Germany's fight for survival against Jewish alienation and invasion would
take place:

> In the fight that Great Germany has undertaken for its destiny, in
> this fight against world Jewry and against all the forces of nihilism
> and destruction, the work of our institute provides all the weapons
> against religious alienation. . . . It thus represents a contribution to
> the war effort by the German religious sciences.[40]

The jurist Carl Schmitt was highly sympathetic to the German-Christian movement (Deutsche Christen), and shared a similar ambition to de-Judaize the law. A Catholic himself, Carl Schmitt invited representatives of Deutsche Christen to a major conference he organized in 1936 on the topic of "Jewishness in the Legal Sciences."[41] In his opening remarks, Schmitt cited *Mein Kampf* twice. In it, Hitler had written, "When I defend myself against the Jew, I struggle for the Lord."[42] Just as the Deutsche Christen were seeking to expel the Jewish spirit from Christian history, tradition, and substance, Carl Schmitt was seeking to liberate the law from Jewish alienation. In 1941, the Deutsche Christen published the *Volkstestament*, or the "(New) Testament of the People," which had been purged of all references to the Old Testament, followed by a catechism with no Jews in it and a completely *judenrein* psalter and hymnal.[43]

Despite all these ideological contortions and polemical acrobatics, the Deutsche Christen never fully succeeded in de-Judaizing Christ and Christianity. Grundmann and his friends would always stumble over that "undeniable moment" of the Jewish birth of Jesus, and over the organic link between the Hebrew Bible and the New Testament—which could not really be thought of without the Old. The SS greeted these dialectical contortions with skepticism, mincing no words in its assessment of the entire Deutsche Christen undertaking, which it deemed a "failure."[44]

Finding the Way within Race

The Reform, the "conflict of the faculties," and then the "war of the gods" had sown trouble and provoked chaos in German values. Luckily, Germany had found the center of gravity for all normativity: race. Not only did direct biological instinct indicate the path to follow, but race was, in itself, both the keystone and the touchstone of all ethical and legal norms: "National Socialism has placed the idea of race at the center of its view of the world and of life. . . . Race is, in the end, the effective foundation of every law enacted [since 1933]."[45]

In 1941, Justus Wilhelm Hedemann, a professor of civil law at the University of Berlin, published a report on "seven years of communitarian work," carried out by a special commission of the "Academy of German Law," which he directed, and which had been mandated to produce a "People's Law Code."[46] Its goal was to replace the BGB (Bürgerliches Gesetzbuch, the German civil code), not to "un-imaginatively copy the codes of the nineteenth century: henceforth, it is nature, and nature alone, which speaks."[47] In fact, this new code was to follow two principles: "the supreme law is the good of the German people," and "German blood, German honor, and genealogical health must be kept pure and protected. They are the foundation of German racial law."[48] For such resolute enemies of codification and abstraction, such an undertaking might seem strange. Let there be no doubt about it, though: "the dynamic of legal life will be recognized" by the code, which would neither constrain nor tether, but rather would serve as the "bed" over which "life's torrent" might flow. This was the metaphor developed by Freisler, citing Hedemann: "Today's legislation must be the guidepost and the riverbed of the vital needs and the growth of our race; it must make it a point of honor not to dam up the force of becoming, but rather to be a solid channel to reinforce and guide it."[49] Moreover, this form of codification expressed and reinforced "the unity of the German people" by fighting against the "the fragmentation of our legal life," which had for so long gone hand in hand with the scattering of the Germanic tribes and a lack of national unity.[50]

All normativity lived and lay in the race and in its innate values. The norms of the racial community were "honor, fidelity, truth." These "fundamental norms were ethically meaningful"; to violate them was "always a crime," for, as their name indicated, they were the bedrock of the community.[51] All other norms were both secondary and subsidiary. They were not fundamental, but rather only "ordering norms" that served the simple purpose of avoiding harm in human coexistence. Road rules were a case in point: "It simply matters that all drivers drive on the right or the left."[52] The choice of direction and handedness had to be made, but doing so was purely a matter of convention and had no biological significance.

The "substantive values" of the German people were "race, soil, work, community, honor," the five pillars of faith whose specific wording might vary, but which remained relatively consistent from one author and one discourse to another. It is worth noting that none of these terms was ever actually defined by these legal scholars: meaningful in and of themselves, they were repeated as a kind of incantation that was both rhetorically effective and intellectually convenient. Defined vaguely (if at all) they left extensive room for interpretation, just as, in judicial practice, *Generalklauseln*, or "general clauses"—so general that they were never specified—were promoted as the alpha and the omega of jurisprudence.[53]

In reality, the contents of these five pillars of faith were of little importance. Their value lay in their evocative power. Race, honor, work, soil, and the community of the people were concrete realities, not "anemic abstractions."[54] Unlike "formal values" promoted in the past, such as equality or universality, which did not correspond to anything tangible, these realities were "substantive values": "The concept of the people contains these values inherently. The mission of the law is not only to protect formal values, such as the legal order or the workings of the justice system, but also to extend its protection to these substantive values." It was by "resolutely turning its gaze to the substantive values of the German people" that "National Socialist legal policy" would succeed in aligning "the necessity of the laws of nature and human legal regulation."[55]

(Legal) culture had to be folded back into the (moral) nature of the German people. For justice to be reestablished and true law to triumph, it was necessary to return to that hallowed time before history began, before mixing and alienation. That original Germanity had had "a close bond to nature and the natural." Conversely, "the fact that our popular German law became foreign to us may be imputed to historical evolution, and that alone." Going back through time, diving into the depths of the German soul and the racial instinct of the *Volksgemeinschaft*, was enough to show that this "healthy people" possessed a "healthy intuition of the law." "True law" lay in the people alone; legislator and judge had to turn to them, to interrogate and seek out their good sense to produce "the organic alliance of the laws of nature and formal-legalism"; that is, to formalize natural laws in human regulations and judicial decisions.[56]

Finally, this law, which came from life, would serve life, and the virtuous cycle would be completed: "Only starting from the moment when the potentialities and the conditions imposed by the laws of nature on a community of people have found form in the legal order can this order be useful to the life of the people."[57] The ultimate example of the successful congruence of formal state laws and natural laws was the prohibition of all mixing between German blood and Jewish blood. Hans Frank, a devoted propagandist of the Nazi cause, frequently repeated that the Reich had passed the Nuremberg Laws not out of meanness, disgust, or even, God forbid, out of hatred for the Jews. They were a necessity of the biological and historical context: the Nordic race was wasting away, mixing, under ever-greater assault, creating a present and urgent need to act. In such a context, the Führer wished to ensure that "the laws of the race, the constituent elements of a people's existence, finally become state law."[58]

The Nuremberg Laws were held up as archetypes. They were touted as a text that merged and linked the natural necessity of biology with the formal obligations of law as written down by legislators who had finally understood their mission: to be nature's scribes. These laws were so natural that they actually contained nothing new. All of the wisest and the most sensible peoples, the ones closest to nature, possessed strict racial legislation, as the legal historian Johann von Leers sought to prove in *Blut und Rasse in der Gesetzgebung* (Blood and race in legislation), published in 1936. Indians, Iranians, Spartans, Athenians, Romans, the Medieval Germanic peoples—even the Jews themselves— were strictly opposed to procreation with people of other races. All of these examples, von Leers argued, proved that racial segregation was the oldest and most widespread phenomenon in the world.[59]

The task of legislators and judges was set by nature, which in turn had been revealed by the history of the original peoples. Frank concurred wholeheartedly: "Let us make sure that . . . the soul of our people, in its greatest depths, be the essential contents of our legal life. The soul of the people must be the soul of the law."[60] Only then would the norm serve life and be acknowledged and respected by the German people. The definition of the law, according to Frank, was to be found therein:

> We, the National Socialists, understand the law to be the vital order of our people, which develops from the foundations of our Germanic race and whose goal is to protect our community against the outside

as well as against internal threats, using rules acknowledged and respected by our people.[61]

Life to the People, Death to the Paragraph

Positive law as it was theorized and practiced in Germany before 1933
had been a catastrophe, an "immense burden of debt" left behind by a
past filled with mixing and alienation; it was a liability to be "liquidated" in every sense of that word.[62] The widespread reception of
Roman law from late antiquity, decadent and Judaized, followed by the
age of absolute monarchy, then by the French Revolution and its aftermath: all of this had made the Germans into "slaves of the paragraphs"
of the law. In the words of a publication by the National Socialist Association of German Legal Professionals: "The paragraph, that little
symbol, innocuous as it is on its own, which marks the ordinal succession of the articles of the law, has in the conscience of the people come
to symbolize a way of thinking about the law that is alien to life and
to reality."[63]

This symbol was so hateful that it became the object of iconoclastic
action: during a *Referendarlager*, a summer camp for lawyers and magistrates in training organized in Jüterbog, near Potsdam, a scaffold
was built to hang a poor cardboard "§" in effigy. This event even made
it into the newsreels: the *Deulig-Tonwoche* of August 2, 1933, featured
a report explaining the camp's purpose and the meaning of the symbolic execution. The narrator opened with an account of how "education for communal living" was one of the goals of the new state, after
which Staatssekretär Freisler explained how, for the first time, Hans
Kerrl, the minister of justice and Freisler's hierarchical superior, had
had the idea of "preventing candidates from studying for an exam" off
by themselves. Instead of spending the summer straining their eyes
over law codes, they could be found "out in nature," living "commu-
nally, among comrades," learning to be "soldiers of National Socialism
and the backbone of the new State" instead of selfishly working for
their own material and personal gain.[64] The news story closed with a
shot of the cardboard "§" swinging from the scaffold, while the "comrade" jurists sang of its death in the brilliant sunshine.[65] A photograph
in the federal archives of Lichterfelde shows Minister of Justice Hans

Kerrl smiling, his foot on the base of the scaffold, surrounded by the camp's leader, SA-Obersturmbannführer (attorney general) Dr. Christian Spieler, and his deputy, SA-Sturmführer Heesch, the camp's chief administrator.[66]

"Kill the paragraph so that the people may live: kill death (by abstraction) so that life may live." Once again, this ferociously tautological language was particularly effective. Frank, who so often rejected "the purely formal world of empty commentary, of sterile work on paper," joined in the call to bury the paragraph, with pomp and circumstance.[67] As the head of the Reich National Jurists' League, he urged government officials to take the greatest liberties with the texts that they were supposed to follow and that were supposed to direct their actions:

> It is not the paragraph in the material and liberal sense that should tyrannize life, no! We want the life of the nation to be the master of the paragraph. . . . This means, comrades of the people, that the future state will have to obey this principle: to preserve the bonds of the nation is more important than to respect an article of the law in the old sense of that term. This also means that nothing that hampers the people's growth can be considered as law; that the law is what serves the people, and that anything that harms the people is the contrary of the law. It must be made impossible, on German soil, for anti-German activity to benefit from the protection of German law, to the detriment of the German people itself.[68]

The death of the paragraph and the fall of the tyranny of the written word would set the law free as it was conceived and exercised. After centuries of domination, the written word was retreating, to the benefit of life: death would lose its grip on the living.

The Renaissance of German Law

How could true German law be brought into the concrete practice of jurists and courts of law? How could a renaissance of original Germanic law be brought about? As we have seen, one had to be a legal historian, a biologist of the race, as well as an ethnologist. And one should leap at the opportunity to study the living Germanic law as it was still being practiced—in England, for example.[69]

Armed with this knowledge, the next step was to entirely rethink legal categories, in order to subvert and redefine them. It would be unproductive to merely oppose current legal categories, Karl Larenz argued. Larenz, a widely respected jurist and a professor of civil law at the University of Kiel, was universally recognized as one of Germany's greatest academic talents. Starting in 1933, he devoted several books to the "renewal of the law" (*Rechtserneuerung*), in which he focused on redefining the concept of the "person" and the "thing," as well as the relationship between the two.

According to German positive law as it had existed before 1933, a "person" was said to be defined by his "freedom." Larenz denounced this "freedom" as utterly "abstract and negative," because it was often presented as protecting the subject from the state and from others. Larenz asserted that freedom was concrete and positive. He argued that rather than being linked to a status, a notion rooted in a static understanding of the law, freedom was a question of position, that of the "legal position of the individual, who is no longer a person, but a concrete being-member": "He is thus, for example, a farmer, a soldier, an intellectual worker, a spouse, a family member, a civil servant, and so on."[70] He did not enjoy absolute and inalienable rights as an abstract person, but concrete rights linked to his station—and his function— within the community of the people he served through his existence and his activity.

Larenz argued against the fantastical concept of an abstract universal subject who was, etymologically speaking, unbound from all ties to concrete reality (family, community, race). In its place, Larenz proposed what he believed was a more realistic and serious alternative: for jurists to return to reality as they could and ought to observe it, which was that man was born into a community, and that his meaning and existence were derived from his involvement in that community. In this way, "each member of the community of the people is obliged to serve the community in the role that the latter assigned to him" according to his physical and intellectual capabilities. It was easy to understand that the freedom enjoyed by a member of the community of the people was no more or less absolute and abstract than his "legal position" within that community: both were relative and concrete. This radical redefinition of the person as a legal entity had implications for the relationship between people and things. Once, this relationship had been known as "property." It had been an "abstract power, [concerning the] control and use of a defined object."[71] An abstract and absolute person, in other words, had absolute use of an abstract thing. Now, on the other hand, an interconnected and concrete person had use of a concrete thing relative to the needs of the community of the people.

Larenz cited the example of a farmer who was free to choose not to harvest his crop if he enjoyed no personal benefit from doing so. There was "no article of positive law that expressly enjoined a farmer to harvest."[72] If formal law as it had been inscribed in the laws and decrees still made no provision for this duty, then Larenz argued that it was necessary to appeal to "informal law." This was the law induced from the community's life and needs, according to which "such a duty on the part of the grower appears as an obvious imperative."[73] "Storing the harvest in a safe place is of vital importance to the community of the people, and this act is first and foremost the duty of a man to whom the community has entrusted some of its land."[74]

These ideas were also developed, albeit more assertively and less expressively, by Roland Freisler in *Nationalsozialistisches Recht und Rechtsdenken* (National Socialist law and legal thought). The "philosophy of law" that had predominated in the past was desperately "abstract, rational, intellectual," instead of being "founded in the concreteness of blood" and in the "life of the people."[75] Thought was abstract, couched in terms of law's subject and the citizen:

> It had been forgotten that behind this was the farmer and his farm, the tenant and his apartment, the craftsman and his workshop, the soldier and his mission, the factory and the community of men who worked there. One thought in terms of "plots of land" understood as "real estate"; in terms of "property" understood as the sovereignty of a "man" over a "thing"; in terms of very general types of contract, such as that of "hiring" and its variants, the "lease"—which might concern a student's furnished room, housing for the worker and his family, a library loan, or the use of labor.[76]

Against this absurd abstraction, which did not correspond to anything real, it made sense to return to the concreteness of things and beings: things had many natures and uses (a pen was not the same thing as a barn), and beings were assigned to a function within the community that best corresponded with their natural gifts—all of which were contained in their "legal position" (*Rechtstellung*) of farmer, soldier, professor, mother, and so on. Each "legal position" assigned a specific duty: "It is for this reason that the negligent farmer may see his land taken from him, that the incompetent factory director may be dismissed, that the government official who forgets his duties may be removed."[77]

These considerations did not remain purely formal: this new theory of law found legal and practical applications. When Freisler wrote that a farmer not up to the task of farming could be deprived of his land, he was referring to a disposition in the "law on inherited farms" (*Reichserbhofgesetz*) of September 29, 1933, that made the use of farmland contingent on the farmer's successfully discharging his duty to the community of the people, which was to feed it. The law stipulated that an incompetent farmer could be evicted from his land and stripped of the honorific title of "farmer."[78] Furthermore, on April 26, 1942, a "decision of the Greater German Reichstag" stated that "at the request of the Führer" the latter was "at any moment authorized, if necessary, . . . to dismiss from his office, strip of his rank and his position . . . any German—be he an ordinary soldier or an officer, a low- or high-ranking government official, judge, low- or high-ranking party functionary, worker, or employee"—if he did not adequately discharge his duties.[79]

For Freisler, the example of property law (land law, in other words) was an even better illustration of the redefinitions under way:

> Upon closer examination, the legal relationship that we call property is not a mere relationship between a person and a thing. . . . More than that, it is a relationship between a proprietor and the other comrade members of the legal community [*Rechtsgenossen*].[80]

It was not a direct relationship between a person and a thing—a relationship that would enshrine "the limitless absolutism of a domination by the thing"—but rather a mediated, triangular relationship that existed between the owner, the thing, and the community of the people.[81] The "owner" was now a "faithful administrator" (*Treuhänder*) more than he was an absolute owner free to do whatever he chose with, through, and to his thing: "Burning your own barn along with your harvest was permitted by our legal order, so long as the life and property of others were not threatened."[82] This was no longer possible: "you cannot do anything you want with your property"—and what was true for a harvest was true, for example, of "an investment property."[83] The true owner, in fact, appeared to be the *Volksgemeinschaft*, and it could ask for accounts from the trustee, because "the community of the people possesses an interest in all of this . . . , an ethical, cultural, and political interest that underpins the role of the cultural institution that we call 'property.' "[84] Since all institutions and cultural creations were expressions of the conscious or unconscious will of the community, property had an eminently communal purpose: it had been created for and was devoted to the service of the *Volk*. Furthermore, added Freisler, and contrary to the affirmations of the law and philosophy of law of the liberal age, "ownership is not the unlimited domination of a thing by a person." Moreover, he pursued, "I am of the opinion that the cultural institution of property exists for the community," or *Gemeinschaft*, the law's true subject.[85] This opinion echoes many theories of the social function of property, from Aristotle to Thomas Aquinas to Léon Duguit. But according to Freisler's thinking, its function was racial: what the farmer did with his harvest was a question of life and death for the race and for the *Volksgemeinschaft*, not merely a question of the just allocation of shared resources and goods. Here, ownership became a triangular relationship between the *Treuhänder* (trustee), the object, and the community, in which nature and the life of the race were at stake.

Jus soli, land law, land rights—roots, nutrition, birth—all of these now took on central importance, even more so because blood had been separated from soil by the French Revolution and by the geographic, demographic, and cultural changes it had brought about. Populations and their land had been made mobile, fluid. What had once been stable, immovable, and rooted was now labile: the immovable had become movable in the Saint Vitus's Dance of the Industrial Revolution. "Agricultural soil," although it needed "constant care," had become a "transferrable asset" from which "a rapid profit" was expected, as with a vulgar "packet of shares."[86] Because of the BGB, the legal expression of this capitalist and liberal age, "the constancy of the soil has become a source of constant liquidity."[87] This monstrous phenomenon violated nature, for as Darré lamented: "Liberal property law did not consider ownership of a farm or a field any different from a movable property, a share, and subjected it to the same legal regime and to the same estate provisions."[88] In the face of such aberrations, which threatened the life of the race, "National Socialist legislation seeks to reestablish stable property law," which would fix the land once again and bind the farmers to it. Not only the "nutritive policy" of the Reich, but also the "preservation of the peasantry as the source of the blood of our people" depended on this.[89]

Indeed, the entire focus of Darré's 1929 book on the subject was to establish historical proof of "the peasantry as the Nordic race's life source," confirm that "in a Germanic state of nature, blood is maintained and developed only in the country," and secure the idea that "the blood of a people, so to speak, flows from the soil of its farms like a bubbling, lively stream, while it drains away and runs dry in the cities."[90] The law of September 29, 1933, "consecrated the unity of the blood and the soil" by making "ancient custom and positive law" consonant once more, as it had been "since time immemorial German legal usage that the land and the soil were not to be counted as movable property."[91] Property law was important in that "it decides the manner in which the land and the soil are ordered with the biological forces of the people."[92] This view of property affected inheritance law: if "the owner is the administrator in the community's name" and if his property was to serve that community, then, Heinrich Lange concluded, the testation of land could not be left to the arbitrary will of the owner alone: "The absolute dominion" over property, this "individualist understanding," the "offspring of a feeble construction," was already obsolete during the owner's lifetime—and thus even more so after his death.[93] "The unlimited will of the testator" was no longer valid.[94] It was as invalid as a civil code that idiotically and mechanically privileged the most distant cousins, even if they were total strangers, over the devoted nurse who had cared for the invalid until his dying breath.[95] Distant cousins, once gratified by the arrival of good fortune in the form of a solicitor's letter, now had to step aside for the state; that is, for the community of the people:

Beside these relations, or behind them, is the community, the state. The rights that it may assert over inheritance are not based, as liberalism pretends, on fiscal greed, but upon the highly moral idea that the community of the people, which made it possible for the testator to act and to enrich himself, is closer to him than are indifferent and distant relations.[96]

This thesis was one of the arguments of Veit Harlan's famous film *Der Herrscher* (The master), released in 1937, which featured a keenly written screenplay by Thea von Harbou.[97] In it, Emil Jannings played Matthias Clausen, a worker who by hard work and merit has become the owner of an enormous foundry, with 20,000 employees working under him. The film's hero is surrounded by vultures: his board of directors whines that the factory is not earning enough dividends, while his family keeps a greedy lookout for the first signs of old age and the long-awaited moment when the great orgy of inheritance can finally begin. Clausen rails against the board of directors for their "abysmal egotism" and reminds them that they "work for the community of the people," not "to make percentages." And when his family try to have him placed under the care of a guardian so that they can become his trustees, he stands up to them by writing a will in which he leaves his fortune and his factories "to the state, and, in so doing, to the community of the people," as he proclaims in a long closing monologue that stuns the villains and the mercenaries. No one in his family is worthy to serve the interests of the *Volksgemeinschaft*. Clausen (played by Jannings), who "remained a worker," declares that he is certain another man like himself will rise from the ranks and show the "genius" necessary to run the Clausen factories. No other member of his family possesses this genius—in this bear garden of dullards and ectoplasms, each one is more lily-livered and pathetic than the rest. He reserves special scorn for his son-in-law, a particularly hideous and malingering "Herr Professor" who married his daughter to assure his own comfortable retirement:

> I leave my possessions to the state; therefore, to the community of the people. I am certain that, from the ranks of my workers and employees, from among those who helped me to build my business, a man will rise who is called to pursue my work. He will come from

the blast furnaces, he will stand up from the drawing tables, the laboratory, or the work benches. I will teach him very little: things that a man departing teaches a man arriving—a man who is born to be a leader (*Führer*) needs no professor to improve his own genius.

The Führer had been naturally selected.

Bringing the Law to Life: The Role of the Judge

Despite the intense legislative activity—regulatory activity, in fact—of the Nazi regime over its twelve years in power, despite the many successive editions of the *Reichsgesetzblatt* (the Reich's official statute book or law register) that were published, the accumulated volume of Nazi legal texts still was much less than the laws and decrees it had carried over from the Kaiserreich and the Weimar Republic. The regime's plan had been to create a legal system that was uniquely and entirely National Socialist, but this was a difficult undertaking. No matter how harshly the jurists working on the "renovation of the law" spoke about the written law, of "positivism," letters, and "codification," a new legal system meant new texts and new codes. In the interest of time—and, beyond that, because it was not actually legislatively pertinent to do otherwise—administrations and judges were invited to adapt existing positive law to the new principles.

In the central and eminently political case of criminal law, State Secretary of the Reich Ministry of Justice Roland Freisler dismissed out of hand the idea of a new criminal code. Judges were simply to renew existing law through judicial and praetorian practices that were in keeping with the spirit of the National Socialist revolution. Writing down laws would not only be long and tedious, it would also be silly: to be riveted to the fixed letters of a paragraph was an outdated attitude that imprisoned the reader in the past, in the moment when the letter had been written, and "The people does not live in the past, but in the present."[98] Life was in constant "evolution," perpetual "combat," a surging welter of events and situations that no legislator could predict. Judges were invited to practice "analogy," which represented an "emancipation from the law itself."[99]

Judges were also invited to "immerse [themselves] in the soul and the conscience of the people, which is the original wellspring (*Urquell*) of the law." Because the Führer, as the embodiment of the people and its representative, was the one who best understood and was best able to formulate the spirit that inhabited and defined the German soul, judges were also, naturally, to "plunge into the will of the Führer."[100] Judges were to base their practice on the law's four cornerstones: *generalklaussel*, or "general clauses"; the party's platform; the Führer's will; and "good common sense." These "general clauses are: good faith, good behavior, serious grounds, the payment or non-payment of a service, the greater interest of one of the two parties, public good, public order."[101] The basic notions of a pared-down, essential, original law, with general clauses such as "good faith, good behavior, etc.," as Carl Schmitt wrote carelessly, had a great advantage: they made it possible to "effectively change the entire law without needing to modify the least 'positive law.' "[102]

The party platform was also elevated to the rank of "general clause." Judges, wrote Freisler, should "rule according to an interpretation of the law induced from the National Socialist worldview."[103] This worldview was also expressed in the Führer's speeches, words, and instructions: because he was the faithful interpreter of nature's laws, Hitler's will was also a source for the law. Finally, "good common sense" bound the first three clauses together: the "general clauses," which were the founding principles of the most basic law; the NSDAP platform; and the Führer, who expressed the superior interests of the *Volk*—all of this derived from good common sense, the trustworthy intuition of the German people.

It could never be forgotten that "the source of all law is the moral conscience of the German people."[104] The administrative judge Robert Barth recalled this during his doctoral defense at the University of Hamburg in 1940, for a thesis on the subject of "good common sense in criminal law." The "pure feeling of the people" was the bedrock of the law, because the "community of blood" that bound Germans of good race together produced a community of values: "Racial identity . . . produces the same moral sentiments and the same ethical values" in everyone. The law's mission was to serve and protect this "community, unified by the same blood and . . . by the same ethics, which forms a vital organic unit."[105] The community, rather than the individual, was now at the center of legal and judicial life. The law's object and subject was the community and nothing else; it was the community that acted and judged. By relying on the "pure feeling of the people" and on good common sense, the judge made it possible for "the law to be created and uttered from the spirit of the people," and for the people, without mediation, to be the judge.[106] The judge and the court of law, by calling on "the moral idea that lives within the people," and on the "basic, innate moral and legal values that live in the people's conscience," were merely "making concrete," to use legal theorist Karl Larenz's language, what was already present but had not yet been formalized.[107]

Larenz's theoretical writing paralleled the practice of such jurists as Freisler or Barth. What he called "formalized law" (*geformtes Recht*) was necessarily always insufficient and incomplete. No mind was omniscient, even that of the wisest of legislators, and no one, therefore, could think of and predict life's every occurrence and its infinite configurations—it was life, after all, "this constant river that carries all phenomena." In judicial and jurisprudential practice, the judge's recourse to these four new sources of the law required that he engage in two simple praetorian practices: "Analogy, which draws from the coherence of existing laws," and "concretization, which draws from the non-formalized law of the community of the people."[108] Examining the case before him, the judge ought to ask "whether the conscience of the law that lives in the bosom of the people . . . would understand and accept" his decision.[109] To Larenz, "the law's function," particularly in its praetorian exercise, was "to extract from the community of the people the order that inhabits it and is unique to it."[110] Larenz nodded to Carl Schmitt in a footnote citing Schmitt's *Über die drei Arten des rechtswissenschaftlichen Denkens* (On the three types of juristic thought) and his "concrete order thinking," which informed Larenz's own approach.[111] In thinking in this way of the law and its practice, "certainly, we appear to lose some of the logical coherence of the system," but "we gain in proximity to life and therefore in true justice."[112]

A judge acting in this way would become the guardian and the practitioner of the people's law. The approach that Larenz and Freisler were proposing was simple and swift, and in this way close to life, because it would "fill in the lacunae of the laws" as they currently existed—lacunae that had been revealed by the National Socialist revolution. Before, no law had required a farmer to harvest his crop to nourish the people. The judge was now there to keep watch, "by recourse to the informal law of the community, and by making this law concrete" through a firm judicial ruling, where once it had existed only as an idea, an intuition, and an instinct.[113]

Otto Thierack, who became Reich minister of justice in August 1942, following Gürtner's death in January 1941, concurred with Larenz and Freisler in a column in the *Völkischer Beobachter*:

> The best judge is the one . . . whose decisions embody [sic] the legal sentiment of the people. Positive law must certainly help him in this, but it must not dominate the judge and make him lose all connection with his people's sensibility. The law is life, not the rigid shape of a juridical idea. To state the law is to put a vital justice into practice, not to perform exegesis of written texts. . . . Each judge is invited to come to me if he believes that the law requires him to hand down a ruling that is hostile to life. . . . I want, in every judge's decision, to recognize a German man who lives with his people.[114]

However surprising it may be to see a minister of justice inviting judges to emancipate themselves from the law, even to blithely transgress it, such a written injunction becomes far less disconcerting given what we know of the concept of law that the text employs, and from which it derives its meaning. Really, Thierack was only echoing all that we have read in the present chapter. He was in fact hewing quite faithfully to the ideas Hitler had laid out as a newly elected chancellor in 1933:

> Our legal system must first of all serve to preserve the community of the people. The life tenure of judges must be balanced by elastic jurisprudence, for the good of the community. It is not the individual who is the center of concern, but the German people.[115]

The Führer's decree nominating the new minister in fact specified that Thierack's mission was to "construct a National Socialist legal practice" and that he "could, in so doing, free himself of positive law."[116] This invitation did not go ignored. In the end, wrote the jurist Hans Fehr, "all common law is empirical law. Law on a case-by-case basis. Casuistry."[117] Did this mean that judges had been relieved of any obligation to obey norms that were external to their free will and their own pleasure? Did it mean that society was headed to legal confusion or the arbitrary will of the praetor? Not at all: judges, in their exercise of what Bernd Rüthers called "infinite interpretation," were obliged to do so on the basis of the four sources of the law described above.

While German society was happily evolving from "fixed law" toward "law on a case-by-case basis" (*Fallrecht*), there could be no question of falling into the capricious and discretionary excess of *Freirecht*, the "free law" theorized by Ernst Fuchs at the beginning of the twentieth century.[118] For Freisler, "the school of free law" was a touchstone of "anarchists determined by their blood, of Jews."[119] While *Freirecht* certainly liberated judges from written and fixed norms, it did so only, Freisler believed, in order to enshrine the sovereign individuality of a judge unbound from any norm at all, which led to "legal chaos, the death of the law."[120] It was out of the question to uphold "the law of the qadi [Islamic judge]."[121]

To see (and to remember) what Germanic *Fallrecht* had been, it is necessary not only to dive back into the race's past, but also to look to the English justice system. The Germanic Anglo-Saxons, protected from the ravages of legal and religious Romanization by their insular existence, had remained faithful to the ancient Germanic vision of the law. Thus, Hans-Otto de Boor, a professor of civil law at the University of Leipzig, advised his colleagues in the "Academy for German Law" to study British legal practice, with its "essentially German tradition," and which "emanates from the very same sources from which we wish to draw again today." While the "German people has distanced itself greatly from its law," the English had remained faithful to their racial culture. Whereas in Germany a "trial has become an act of paper," English rulings examined special cases "clearly and simply, without juridical quibbling." English jurisprudence was thus "worthy of a realist novel" and "reveals a very living [*sic*] juridical life." It constituted "a service rendered to the living life of our people," while the path Germany had chosen, that of codification, of carping, and of writing, "turns us away from the living life of our people."[122] To be close to the life of the people, the judge himself ought to be a full-fledged member of that people. Who indeed knew better the natural order expressed by the life of the people than the people itself? Who could be more faithful to the innate moral and legal instinct of the

German people than someone who had not been acculturated and alienated by legal studies? Some jurists jumped on this bandwagon, blithely undermining their own profession by demanding popular juries, and even popular judges. The legal historian Herbert Reier went so far as to note in a seminar given at the National Socialist Association of Legal Professionals that "the profession of judge" had emerged as a field during an unhappy period Reier dubbed the "Carolingian alienation," which he believed was an era of intellectual subversion caused by the importation of the Christian faith and late Roman law.[123] Before the advent of this professional specialization, which grew from the increasing complexity of legal matters—which had ceased to be instinctual and had become a matter of knowledge—every Germanic man had been a judge. Since then, sadly, "jurisprudence is no longer drawn from the sentiment of the people, but relies on the dictatorial will of the sovereign," to whom judges were bound and subject. Even so, the author remarked shrewdly, "our people does not tolerate any dictatorship," above all that of judges and their abstract codes.[124]

All dictatorship had been prohibited; the Führer himself had expressly forbidden it. One would be mistaken to believe that simply because the Third Reich had shaken up a few ingrained habits, it was a regime of satraps or *goldfasan* (party bigwigs, or literally, golden pheasants). Very much to the contrary, in fact; the arbitrary will of codes, jurists, and absolute monarchs was now a thing of the past: "Adolf Hitler has, since the first day he came to power, clearly stated that he did not want an arbitrary regime, but a National Socialist rule of law."[125]

To create a true justice system, of and for the people, professional judges ought to be brought together with "lay judges" or "nonprofessional judges," whom some wrongly called "popular judges" (as "if the professional judge was not just as much a popular judge" when he ruled in accordance with the people's good sense).[126] That legal laymen now sat in courts, no longer only as jurors but also at the magistrate's bench, was one of the great and noble advances of National Socialism, and it was a move inspired by a precedent in the history of Germanic judicial institutions. It was indeed the "municipal magistrate of ancient German law," a citizen assessor of the courts, who had inspired the idea of including laymen in the Tribunal of the People created by the law of April 24, 1934, a special jurisdiction that would, as time went by, include nearly all crimes and misdemeanors.[127] It went without saying that this assessor had to be "of Aryan blood" and a man, for—and this was the only explanation advanced—"good sense demands that a man, and only a man, sit as a magistrate."[128]

Himmler, speaking before the "Academy of German Law," recommended the reinstating of "justices of the peace, an old institution that has already existed for millennia within our people": "The justice of the peace could judge without written law, judge as an honest man, as a man who lived his life among the lives of every man, and who ruled in keeping with the law and good common sense."[129]

The special tribunals created by the *Erbhof* law of September 29, 1933—courts with the competence to strip a farmer of his land and his title of *Bauer* (farmer)—were composed of both professional magistrates and farmers. A simple man who was full of good sense was naturally just, as the ancients instinctively knew: "The protection of the Germanic life order was assured not by the paragraph, but by a guardian of the law (*Rechtswahrer*), who acted in accordance with the laws of the race."[130]

Who Has the Right to be Born? The Question of Sterilization

Meditating on one's essence, returning to one's birth, and entering anew into communion with nature and its laws—these were the secrets of Germanic life:

> National Socialism is always a meditation on the essence of the German people and the accomplishment of what the best representatives of our race have always wanted to do . . . : to protect and to make possible the life of the German people according to forms in keeping with our race, for the centuries of centuries.[131]

This noble intention was realized through the careful stewardship of births and a policy of selection that finally reestablished what private charity and public health policy had prevented: the elimination of all nonviable substance.

The sterilization of individuals whose reproduction was not desirable was mandated by law on July 14, 1933. The first article of the law stipulated that "anyone with a hereditary illness may be rendered sterile by means of surgical intervention if scientific medical experimentation has established a high probability that his descendants will suffer from hereditary physical or mental disorders."[132] State eugenic policy was rigorously scientific: medicine, through numerous studies, had established standards for diagnosis based on an extensive series of cases. This series made it possible to formulate "probabilities" that formed the basis of a prognosis, and the decision to intervene was based on this prognosis. The decision to sterilize or not was made by a special court also created by the law. "Hereditary health courts," or *EGG* (*Erbgesundheitsgerichte*), were composed of three members, a judge at the first level of jurisdiction assisted by two doctors.[133] These courts were set up in every local or district court (*Amtsgericht*). As the preamble to the law explained, "any resemblance to a criminal trial shall be avoided," since the unfortunate persons in question were diseased, and required support and treatment, not punishment.[134] The hearings were closed to the public, which allowed the witnesses, particularly doctors, to speak freely, without having to worry about patient confidentiality obligations or "professional secrecy."[135] A heredity health court of appeals was set up in each appellate court.[136] Its decision was final and could not be overturned. Appeals, which had to be filed within a month of the initial court decision, could only be for suspension. An amending law issued on June 26, 1935, hardened the provisions of the initial law, reducing the period of appeal to fifteen days and specifying in its tenth article that the decision to sterilize a pregnant woman "may" be accompanied "with the concerned party's consent, by a termination of the pregnancy, unless the embryo is already viable"; in other words, after the "sixth month." These provisions were, evidently, coercive in nature: "From the moment that the court has definitively ruled for sterilization, it shall be carried out against the patient's will when required," if necessary "by the employment of immediate constraint."[137]

This violent measure, to which 400,000 people fell victim in twelve years, was presented as the most humane possible solution to a serious public health problem, the claim being that the survival and reproduction of diseased beings was unnatural: unassisted by either charity or the state, they would have been eliminated by nature anyway. Indeed, the law's instigators never failed to show compassionate consideration for the "diseased." In this vein, Falk Ruttke, one of the fathers of the law of

July 14, 1933, who would go on to hold the chair of "Race and Law" at the University of Jena, declared to a conference of the International Federation of Eugenic Organizations, in Zurich on July 20, 1934:

> Everything should be done to avoid the conflation of the genetically diseased with the criminal. To be diseased is not a shameful thing, but it is incompatible with our moral understanding of the transmission of genetic disorders to generations to come.[138] . . . It is for this reason that in the law for the prevention of hereditarily diseased offspring, we have avoided saying anything at all regarding the castration of criminals [as the Law of November 24, 1933, would require a few months later].[139]

After all, Walter Gross remarked, these elements still belonged to Germanic biology. Their hereditary defects meant that they were deprived of their race and had become degenerated (entartet), meaning that they must be treated in a manner that ensured they "would be excluded from hereditary transmission."[140] This did not mean that they ought to be despised, because they could not be held responsible for their wrongs. And while they were certainly not useful elements, they ought to be granted compassion and respect for the sacrifice they were making by renouncing procreation. People who "within our own people must be eradicated," were "victims of the fate of being hereditarily diseased"; in other words, they were "bearers of a genetic makeup that made them unable to perform for the nation."[141]

> Such a hereditarily diseased person is not a bad man, nor is he the object of our recrimination or mockery, but a poor devil who is just as respectable as we are and to whom nothing but an incomprehensible fate has assigned such a burden. [Obligatory sterilization is] a real sacrifice . . . that state and legislator demand of him. He therefore has a right to our respect. He has the right to be treated with respect and decency . . . and perhaps doubly so, because of his sacrifice.[142]

Some, such as Ernst Rüdin, did not burden themselves with compassion, and refused any concession to "humaneness" or "humanity," arguing that that was not the issue at hand. The problem of the reproduction of diseased persons was not a moral one; there was no question of value judgments—it was a scientific, factual matter. Rather than awakening empathy or pity, it ought to mobilize reason: "In all questions regarding procreation among the hereditarily diseased, we must get over this supposed 'humanity.'"[143] A doctor carrying out his profession had to employ reason, and could not allow himself to be carried away by inappropriate feelings: "Just as the astronomer must employ the knowledge of his science when he is determining whether the Earth turns around the Sun or vice versa," biologists or doctors "not only have the right, but the obligation"—even the "sacred obligation," since it transcended individual destiny—to apply the conclusions of their science.[144]

Mostly, though, rhetoric tended toward compromise and avoided head-on confrontations with the moral sentiment of the German people. Negative eugenics was therefore generally presented as the highest form of moral action. It was the argument most often mobilized in the long campaign to promote the law of July 14, 1933, and the practices of the *EGG*. The SS journal *Das Schwarze Korps*, for example, featured an article titled "A Humane Law," elaborating on its title as follows:

> The German people must be firmly convinced that this is an authentically humane act. No longer will thousands of families have to suffer the unspeakable and to reproach themselves for the rest of their lives. As for the German people, it will in this way spare millions of people who will find better work elsewhere.[145] This law is a first step towards the healing and the strengthening of our people.[146]

These few lines were the core of the argument being mobilized. The law, which at first glance was harsh and severe, in that it mandated the violation of patient integrity, both physical and moral, was in fact the kindest of laws. It was kind to the families of these unfortunate humans, who would be saved from future generations of diseased individuals. It was kind to the German people, who would be liberated from the psychological and financial burden of these useless and suffering beings. And it was kind to the diseased themselves, who would have the satisfaction of knowing that their pathologies would not be transmitted to their innocent offspring; in other words, they would not be inflicting on others what the lack of foresight and irresponsibility of prior generations had inflicted on them.

The adjective "humane," systematically employed in these arguments—in both forms, *human* and *menschlich*—was an intriguing choice: if the only true and valid humanity was Nordic humanity, anything that contributed to its amelioration and protection necessarily had that quality. Indeed, the inhuman and the immoral were not what one might believe them to be: anything that opposed virile and resolute action was immoral—reproductive laxity, anti-eugenic negligence that misunderstood and violated the laws of nature, for example. This was Minister of the Interior Wilhelm Frick's explanation in a speech delivered to the first meeting of the "Expert Committee on Demographic and Racial Policy," which he convened in June of 1933: "This kind of modern humanism and social welfare for the diseased, the weak, and the inferior was a crime against the people, because it was leading to their doom."[147] Science was the trustworthy response to such dangerous foolishness; it was necessary to reconcile reason and pity by forging a superior moral system, one more honorable than the old moralistic saws of priests, pastors, and finicky churchgoers of every stripe:

> The science of heredity . . . gives us the right, but also imposes on us the moral obligation, to exclude the hereditarily diseased from procreation. We do not have the right to allow ourselves to be diverted from this duty by a poor understanding of brotherly love or by religious reservations, which are based on the dogmas of past centuries. To the contrary, it should be considered as going against Christian and social neighborly love to knowingly allow the diseased to reproduce, [as they] will pass on infinite sorrow to their loved ones and to future generations.[148]

Not surprisingly, the preamble to the law of July 14, 1933, presented its contents as "an act of brotherly love and of foresight for future generations . . . , a truly kind act for families touched by this disease."[149] Morality was not necessarily what it seemed to be at first glance. The focus was not the individual, but all that transcended the individual, all that gave meaning to individuals and allowed them to exist. This holistic view was key to understanding the Nazi message:

> It is foolish to allow the incurably diseased to irreversibly contaminate healthy men. Such humaneness destroys hundreds in order to

avoid harming a single individual. Forbidding defective individuals from giving birth to other dregs is the very definition of rationality and constitutes, if planned and carried out, humanity's most humane act.[150]

An SS publication commented, "That which is moral is that which benefits the racial preservation of the German people. That which is immoral is that which interferes with the preservation of the race."[151] Eugenics prevented the suffering of the diseased, of those around them, and of their racial community. It also ensured that their pathologies would not be transmitted to innocent future generations, thus avoiding future suffering. What could be more compassionate than that? Gross railed against people who professed to promote Christian charity: what good was a pity that produced more objects of pity? It was nothing less than a perversion, producing the very object it deplored, the very cause of its unhappiness: "True compassion seeks to prevent suffering and misery. This has far more value than coming and crying after the fact."[152]

In the context of twentieth-century Western society none of this was cynical, contradictory, or exceptional. Although France and England had no eugenics laws, reasoning of this sort had been common in those countries for decades; the United States, Switzerland, and the Scandinavian countries had all passed laws for "racial improvement." Germany was no exception, and in fact, it had not been the one to make the rule. Eugenicist discourse had intensified in Germany after 1918, however, following the demographic disaster—and what was often referred to as the counter-selection—of the First World War, which had destroyed the very best. The Nazis were not at all isolated in their views; consequently, for many eugenicists 1933 was an opportunity, much more than a revelation: in the 1920s there had been many indictments of "empty human envelopes" and "useless existences" and pleas for the "legal sterilization of the diseased."[153] These were often supported by the churches themselves, as was the case of theologian Joseph Mayer, whose 1927 essay on eugenics was blessed with the imprimatur of the Fulda Bishops' Conference of the German Catholic Church.[154]

For any eugenicist, the only relevant outlook was a holistic one. The subject of their ethics was the German people—the race, not the individual. All acts had to be carried out with reference to the group, rather than the individual; to the whole, rather than the part. Joseph Goebbels, for example, drew a clear distinction between the holistic ethic of the strong and the individualist morality of the weak:

> We do not start from the individual. We do not believe that the starving should be fed, that the thirsty should be given to drink, that the naked should be clothed. These are not valuable motives in our eyes. Our motives are of an entirely different nature. They may thus be summed up in a lapidary manner: "We must have a healthy people to dominate in the world."[155]

Gross continued in the same vein, taking those who preached pity at their word: "There are also duties of compassion and humanity toward healthy forces and healthy peoples."[156] Why think of the weak and the ill all the time? Why was there never a thought for the healthy forces that were being weakened and contaminated by the preservation of the degenerate and pathogenic elements among them?

And then again, what was the end goal? In July 1933, the weekly journal *Neues Volk*, published by Rassenpolitisches Amt, the NSDAP Office of Racial Policy, warned its readers of the limits of pity. The issue, published as the eugenicist law of July 14, 1933, was being passed, featured a charming cover image of the Pimpfe (the first sections of the Hitler Youth) assembled around a Christian roadside monument as its gigantic wooden cross went up in flames. The journal was not joking around: "The life of the nation is a question" that implies certain "rights" and "duties" on the part of the legislator.[157] While the law of July 14, 1933, may have shocked a few people with more delicate sensibilities, it was "nonetheless obeying prescripts of natural morality," since "the current situation is unnatural and shows the revolt of man against the eternal laws of nature." The National Socialist leadership, by enacting this kind of legislation, was merely "restoring the natural order of things."[158] In another article, *Neues Volk* hailed a recent sterilization order by an *EGG* in Munich with a headline that quoted *Mein Kampf*, describing it as "humanity's most humane act." The author set out to beat pastors, priests, and other pious folk at their own game:

> [The law of July 1933 is] a requirement of the clearest reason and signifies . . . humanity's most humane act. It will make it possible to

spare millions of unhappy lives. . . . Specifically moral and religious considerations ought to lead one to approve of the law on the prevention of inherited disease.[159]

How could God have done otherwise?

Procreation of the Pure and Strong

This eugenic and racial prophylaxis was advanced still further in 1935, to the level of marriage itself. Marriage legislation had been fundamentally altered by the laws of 1935, known as the Nuremberg Laws, passed in September of that year during a Party conference. The September laws prohibited all racial mixing by forbidding marriage between Aryans and Jews. These supposed health measures for racial hygiene were followed on October 18, 1935, by an expansion of the law of July 14, 1933. In order to avoid the procreation of diseased individuals and to relieve the *EGG*s of some of their work, the "law for the protection of the genetic health of the German people" forbade the marriage of individuals "suffering from hereditary diseases as defined by the law for the prevention of inherited disease" of July 14, 1933, and, more generally, of individuals "whose marriage appears undesirable for the community of the people."[160] That this was a question of protecting German biology was indicated in Article 5-1, which specified that "the provisions of this law do not apply when the engaged couple or the male fiancé are foreign nationals." Foreigners were welcome to degenerate as they pleased, and a non-German man was free to marry a diseased German person and breed corrupted offspring. That the contrary was true (that is, that a diseased foreigner could marry a healthy German woman) might seem surprising, but it should be recalled that the Nazis were above all concerned with the scarcity of males, because of the losses sustained during the First World War. Proportionally, women were an abundant resource, making legislators more tolerant toward their being led astray, and even lost. Further evidence of this may be found in the Third Reich's contradictory and relatively tolerant stance toward female homosexuality, which beyond obvious disapproval, did not raise any real hackles.

The subjects of the Nuremberg Laws no longer belonged to themselves in the most private and personal realm, that of their sexuality and choice of partner: "Any choice of spouse that goes against the race must be considered to be immoral and a violation of the vital order of our people."[161] By fighting these unnatural norms, nature would be restored to its inalienable rights, which were to be piously respected and cultivated if the people wished to live and not to die: "We have finally become aware that the laws of nature that we saw governing the lives of plants and animals were also valid for men," exulted Rüdin, Gütt, and Ruttke, delighted that science, good sense, and ancient wisdom were winning out over anti-nature, which for centuries had dominated Germany.[162]

The Jews knew what they were doing in forbidding the Germanic people to eliminate what ought to be eliminated and what, in nature, would not survive for an hour without help and care. It was they who, in evangelizing Germania, had imposed these suicidal laws on the Nordic people. Before that—among the Spartans, for example—they had exposed and left to die those who were meant to die. It was the Jews who had, through their travesty and conspiracy of Christianity, sought to kill off the Germanic-Nordic race. And it was "the repression of this Jewish influence that was qualified as inhumane," lamented Gerhard Wagner, the Reich's chief physician. Was it inhuman to want to live and to defend oneself against norms imposed by a race that willed your death? It was "not racial hatred" that motivated this rejection of the Jews, including their exclusion from the German medical profession, but "the survival instinct, pure and simple."[163] "We wanted, in our German homeland, very simply to be ourselves, and nothing else."[164]

If the various branches of Christianity were concerned about the principles and practices of the new state, they ought to be consistent with their own beliefs, not merely to render unto Caesar the things that were Caesar's, but also to realize that the laws of nature were laws desired and enacted by God—whatever entity was understood by that name—and that from now on, preaching the unnatural was a sin. Humanists and priests took umbrage at the Nuremberg Laws forbidding the mixing of the fluids, blood, and flesh of Aryans and Jews. But mixing with Jews "goes against the order of nature, which was the one to decree racial legislation." By solemnly reaffirming this legislation in Nuremberg in 1935, the Reich was only "acknowledging the inequality of men, a fact of nature desired by God."[165] Gerhard Wagner addressed priests and ministers in the bluntest of terms:

> When, dressed in the noble clerical robes of the two confessions, you preach that "your reign is not of this world," then go take care of your world, and leave us the right and the responsibility to regulate the governing of this world, our German state, according to our own laws and our own needs.[166]

In two articles, the SS journal *Das Schwarze Korps* concurred in a sarcastic and chilly tone:

> When someone says that man does not have the right to kill, let us reply to him that man has even less right to ruin the work of nature and to keep a being alive that was not born to live. This has nothing to do with Christian love of one's neighbor, for by one's "neighbor" we understand only the human being capable of feeling the love that is extended to him. . . . A law should be passed that returns nature to its rights. A being incapable of living would be left by nature to die of hunger. We can be more humane, and administer to him death without suffering. This is the only valid humanity; it is a hundred times nobler, more worthy, and more humane than the cowardice that hides behind a humanitarianism that imposes the burden of his own existence on this poor creature and the burden of his care on his family, as well as on the community of the people. Those who boast of their humanity are usually individuals who do nothing to preserve the force of the race and prefer a baptized idiot to a healthy pagan. From the line in Matthew 5:3, "Happy are the poor in spirit," no reasonable man could induce rights for idiots in the here and now. No one, on the other hand, contests their rights in the afterlife: the kingdom of heaven is wide open to them.[167]
>
> We stand tall, with both feet on the earth, and it is this earth we wish to govern. We do not profess the same faith as those who say, "Our Kingdom is not of this world." With pleasure we leave them the freedom to reign over their afterlife.[168]

Returning to the primal inspiration of nature meant breaking with millennia of wandering. For Hans Frank, "the law must be one of the lords," for, he wrote in virile tones, "the German Reich, placed under the command of Adolf Hitler, does not need helots or weaklings, but strong and healthy men of German race."[169]

The vocation of the law is not to educate. We do not want to protect the weak from the strong, we do not want to artificially preserve life that is unfit to live, to the detriment of healthy life. We simply wish, once and for all, to open the way to a healthy and fortifying selection for the racial structure of our people. Believe me: we are the ones who will be the face of the coming millennium.[170]

"National Socialist Revolution" and "Reevaluation of Values"

Edgar Tatarin-Tarnheyden, a professor of constitutional law and international law at the University of Rostock, took offense at the idea that the revolutionary quality of the political changes of 1933 might be questioned by some on the pretext that no blood had been shed. Tatarin, who equated revolution with the terror of 1793 or the bloody putsch of 1917, was pleased to note that for once, the order of things had been changed without anyone being killed! But this did not mean that 1933 had not been a revolution, for it had been an event brought about by a "movement of the people." The "national revolution" of 1933 had been an insurrection of the German people's body and soul against an order of things that was more than unsatisfying: against "the vacuity of the agnostic constitution of Weimar," 1933 had consecrated "the community of the people" as a "fundamental value."[171] Thanks to this "fundamental substantive norm," Germany had broken with the "formal values" of a decadent period and returned to the "people" as "sole end in itself."[172]

Tatarin, a conservative constitutionalist, still clung a little too firmly to the state to be fully Nazi, but he fully ordained—without entirely realizing it—the "community of the people," that is, "the idea of the national and social community of the people" as a "supreme value, which must serve as a beacon for all cultural creation, including, therefore, the law."[173] As a German conservative, he reviled the French Revolution; as a lawyer, he sought revenge against Hans Kelsen, whose constitutional thought had held sway from Vienna since 1919. Tatarin wrote off Kelsen's work as "formal-logical intellectual acrobatics" promoted by "non-German elements" and rejoiced to observe that law was now no longer a simple conceptual apparatus, a "reduction to the conceptual and to categories, which found its most monstrous hypertrophy in the formal, empty, abstract, and sterile doctrine of a certain Kelsen."[174]

Luckily, the law was once again "a juridical dynamic full of meaning," a "natural-organic whole."[175] "The legal order of the German people does not rest on . . . thousands of paragraphs, but on the solid whole of a worldview that conceives of the German people as a bionomic unit of Nordic blood and of ancient culture."[176] The term *bionomisch*, a neologism introduced by Tatarin, is striking: the German people was a vital reality (*bios*), and this life was prescriptive, a creator of norms (*nomos*). Better still: by the simple fact of its existence, governed by natural laws, the life of the German people was normative. If the German people lived this way (without mixing, without homosexuality, with the domination of men over women, and so forth) it was because the community had to live this way, to maintain itself, to reinforce itself, to perpetuate itself. Biology found the political fulfillment of its meaning in "bionomics": life was law; it was the law of a people that was itself a "vital bionomic whole."[177]

It was only logical, then, that there could be no distinction between law and morality: both were an expression of the bionomy, of the laws of life, laws induced from the very fact of life. True morality therefore was not, nor could it be, individualistic. It was necessarily holistic: "Morality is not a private affair. It is the affair of the whole of the people." Reciprocally, the law ought to locate the individual in his rightful place and in his rightful role within the community. There were no longer individuals, only members of the community of the people: "The perfect law, the truly national law . . . is the ethical law that leads the individual, as a member of a whole, a popular whole, to cease to orient himself morally in a solipsistic manner."[178]

Having broken with the Christian morality of sex and the body, having restored to the individual his consciousness of his holistic integration in a whole that transcended him and gave him meaning—having, in short, revived the original norm—it was now possible to increase the birthrate, to renew demographic abundance. Before 1933, Germans had produced few offspring and aborted frequently because "the German people was atomized." Germans had ceased to be the coordinated and organically united members of a racial body. The social and cultural mutations of modernity had caused them to lose their consciousness of their place in a whole that gave them both blood and meaning.

Contemporary man was an indivisible and absolute being; unbound, he had forgotten his unitary inclusion in a whole that transcended him and gave him life. He had forgotten that his sexuality and his procreation were governed by a racial imperative, that they were a duty. Himmler expressed great pleasure that this abnormality was finally coming to an end:

> One [man] will have a dog, the other a child. . . . These are self-centered motivations. This will always be the case with atomized men, with individuals. The liberal man is the mortal sin of liberalism and Christianity. They knew very well how to destroy everything that existed. What did the man of the past look like? He was horizontally integrated in a natural fabric of families, village communities, and regions. He was also vertically integrated in a long genealogical chain, with the conviction that he was called to rebirth each time his family produced offspring.[179]

It was possible, as we have seen, to build an ethics and a legal system on the ideas of blood and race. The progress of medicine and biology, "the discovery of hereditary traits, the idea of blood," had provoked a "total reevaluation of our values," so that, as Darré noted, "from the *danse macabre* of the ideas of a culture on its way to extinction appears a new worldview, that of the value and the eternity of blood, a sacred blood for our people."[180] In tones reminiscent of Ecclesiastes, Darré enjoined his readers to trust only their blood, for "nothing in this world is eternal that is made of the matter of this world . . . lest it be blood, alone eligible for eternity, if the people would only seek to obey the laws of life." In this world where everything was finite and passing, "blood is our people's unique and true treasure."[181] The new moral system had now naturally found its grammar, which specifically emerged from conception and childbirth:

> This idea that a child for whom we are answerable before his own ancestors gives us a criterion of value that allows us to locate, in the current maelstrom of opinions . . . , a sure foundation for judgment and for creating a German morality in keeping with and responsible to the race.[182]

The only "moral requirement of our times" was that "one must be able to answer to our ancestors for any child born within our racial community."[183]

> This acquiescence to the laws of life and of blood, this veneration of the ancestors . . . and this will to answer to our elders for our children and for their upbringing are the new tablets that open onto a German era.[184]

A grieving Himmler would return to this idea at Reinhard Heydrich's funeral, as he exhorted those present to believe in the future and in eternity:

> We must root ourselves once again in this eternal chain, in this eternal procession of our ancestors and our descendants. . . . Everything that we do, we must answer for it before our race, before our ancestors. If we do not find this moral anchor that is the deepest and the best, for it is the most natural, we will never be capable of . . . forming the Germanic Reich, which will be a benediction for this earth.[185]

PART II

Fighting

CHAPTER FOUR

"All Life Is Struggle"

Man Is Nature, Nature Is Struggle

THERE IS NO discontinuity between nature and culture: this was the central teaching of the social Darwinists, who since the late nineteenth century had transposed onto humankind the categories and concepts that Darwin had created to make sense of the plant and animal kingdoms. The same laws governed them all; they were, in fact, all one. Falk Ruttke, like Heinrich Himmler and nearly all of those involved in constructing Nazi normativity, wrote:

> National Socialism is a worldview that embraces all domains of life. In its eyes, life is a clash between the race and its environment. It asserts that our planet occupies no special place in the universe and that man is only one living thing among many.[1]

The documentary *Alles Leben ist Kampf* (All life is struggle), distributed starting in 1937 by the NSDAP Office of Racial Policy, offered a breakdown of these ideas in highly instructive images. The connection between the explicit images and the simple discourse was plain.

The film's opening sequence showed two stags in combat during mating season, angry monkeys, and vindictive birds, and then confirmed in its first title card, "All life is struggle." This law was valid for fauna as well as for flora; viewers should not be fooled by bucolic images of trees and meadows: "Forest and field struggle to secure their living space," the one spreading at the expense of the other, and vice versa. As for trees, they were engaged in a race for the light: those treetops that stretched their branches the farthest received more of the precious photons that made chlorophyll production possible. In this struggle for life, only the best—that is, those best adapted to struggle—would survive: "The weak and the nonviable must submit to the strong. Nature allows only the best vital force to survive," and "Anything that does not measure up to the conditions set by nature is eliminated with pitiless harshness." Should one complain or take offense? Find this cruel? No: "This struggle is a divine law. It makes possible the perfection of all living things." Impressive images of majestic elephants and tigers and robust rams poured onto the screen to prove this declaration.

Man did not escape this law of struggle, either: "Man must also assert himself against his environment"—this same environment, which, like nature in general, was entirely "animated by a will to extermination," for nature had made the "mortal combat of extermination" the "fate" of all things—here, the film showed gardeners, woodcutters, firefighters, laborers building a polder, and fishermen tossed by a wild storm.[2] These Frisian fishermen illustrated the next title card: "Each generation takes up arms yet again against the elements. Only the strong, resistant, and intelligent will prevail in this struggle for life." The doctors who appeared on the screen were warriors, too: "Our struggle against epidemics, illnesses, against everything that threatens life and the development of man is also of vital importance." After the white coats came the green uniforms of the police officers: "The struggle against criminality and inferior beings also contributes to building a healthy community of the people." Thus everything was marching toward strength and health, provided that the laws of nature were respected.

Certainly, Hitler conceded,

> one might find it horrifying to observe that in nature, one animal devours another. . . . But one thing is certain: nothing can be done to change that. . . . What I say to myself is that there is only one thing to do: to study the laws of nature to avoid ending up in contradiction with them. One cannot rise up against the firmament! If one must believe at all costs in a divine commandment, then it should be this one: to preserve the race.[3]

Since man was a natural being, the laws of nature applied to him—more so, even, than to animals. This was Hitler's private claim: "Apes massacre all fringe elements as alien to their community. What is valid for monkeys must be all the more valid for men."[4] It was irrefutable: man, as a superior ape, was subject to these same laws at a higher level. There was no point in getting upset over them. The ongoing war against the self, against others, and against the environment might be regrettable, but not in axiological terms, for it was mere fact: "Who is guilty? The cat or the mouse, when the cat eats the mouse? The mouse, even if it never hurt a cat?" demanded Hitler, to whom the Germans were the innocent mouse victims of the Jewish cats—it may be recalled in passing that cats, unlike dogs, were considered to be Eastern, even Jewish, animals.[5] On a deep level, no one was guilty. It was probably best to trust in nature:

> We do not know what it means when we see the Jews destroying peoples. Is it possible that nature created them so that, through the decomposition they provoke, they set [other] peoples in motion? In this case, Saint Paul and Trotsky were the most remarkable of the Jews, for they are the ones who contributed most to this.[6]

Could one blame nature for having provoked and created Jews and cats? Parasites and villains? Hitler preferred to wager that it had been nature's cunning trick, hiding a meaning by which the Jews served a purpose. If they were cruel and devious like cats, perhaps it was in order to provoke a healthy reaction among the people they gratuitously aggressed. War was actually the inescapable reality of all life, human or not, as an article in the *SS-Leitheft* titled "It's Him or Me" explained:

> Force against force, this is life's eternal character. . . . In nature, forces struggle against one another without end. The ocean throws itself unceasingly against a cliff that the earth erected to protect itself from it, the storm relentlessly attacks the forest to shatter the trees. . . . Eternal war is a law of life.[7]

Its logical conclusion:

> It is therefore not compassion, but courage and toughness that save life, because war is life's eternal disposition . . . and all of the harshness that war requires is just and justified.[8]

One had to fight in order to live—one even had to fight against oneself, against the dormant, whimpering weakling within. The Nordic race, confronted with a harsh climate, was the first to have fully understood this:

> We are duty-bound to be competitive, and this is why we are hard on ourselves and on others. This is one of the major traits of the Nordic ethos. A notion such as Kant's categorical imperative could only have grown in a Nordic soul.[9]

Here again, Kant, the liberal *Aufklärer* of the Enlightenment, had been coopted by the Nordic race. A shortcut through the Prussian Army was the quickest way to sidestep referencing the Konigsberg philosopher: "The Prussian sense of duty gave the German people the force to recover from the Peace of Westphalia and return to the path to establishing the Reich at Versailles, and then to creating the Greater German Reich" of the Führer.[10] Since the time of their Great Elector and Soldier-King, the Prussian Army had taught this duty to the Germans through the external constraints of sanction, discipline, and corporal punishment. In the wake of the destructive Thirty Years' War, which ended in 1648, these two great figureheads had whipped the Germanic people back into shape: "They paid no compliments and they did not say thank you. What the others did was self-evident, for it was their duty": "The driving force behind Prussian duty was without whimsy, bitter and tough."[11]

But this external constraint, "fear of punishment," was only an "expedient" required by the urgency of the moment: "Inner duty, from one's own impulse, soon replaced external coercion," implying that "the inner scoundrel had to be reduced to nothing."[12] It was necessary "to fight against oneself" in order to efface the *innerer Schweinehund* (literally, the "inner pig-dog") that SS sources sometimes evoke: inner weakness, mediocrity, and compassion were enemies to be vanquished in the war against the self.[13] The last shreds of Jewish, Judeo-Christian, and liberal alienation had to be destroyed, along with that particular brand of sentimentality that seemed to be the hallmark of the eternally dreamy German. This war, against everything old and vitiated in oneself, against that inner swine, made gangrenous by Christianity and crippled by humanism, was a form of asceticism, as well as a fight to the death. As Himmler declared:

We are living in the era of definitive confrontation with Christianity. Over the next fifty years, the vocation of the SS will be to provide non-Christian foundations for the German people that are in keeping with the race, and upon which it will be able to build its life.[14]

Humans, a mere part of nature's grand whole, had to avoid any hubris that might lead them to believe they were exempt from the laws that governed the existence of both the macrocosm and the microcosm. The documentary *Alles Leben ist Kampf* displayed the frightful consequences of this pseudo-emancipation: a world crawling with idiots, outcasts, and cripples, who are left to live and even helped to survive, even though they were supposed to die; apartments ornamented with ridiculous little poodles, though "none of these pitiful creatures would be capable of asserting its existence" on its own. These were the unsettling results of our hubris, the film explained, and yet we were "so proud of having outwitted the laws of nature and so puffed up with pride that we saw ourselves as little creators."[15] Nature pitilessly eliminated the weak and fortified the strong: "For as long as man lived in strictly natural conditions, the same was true for him. Natural man is dominated by the laws of fertility . . . and selection. . . . It is so-called culture that overturned these realities," wrote Richard Eichenauer in a textbook titled *Die Rasse als Lebensgesetz* (Race as natural law), originally published in 1934, and twice reprinted.[16] Culture had denatured man. In particular, "the ethical culture, the morality of pity," had led to "a counter-selective preference for the weak."[17] It was time for the "natural law" of the theologians, humanists, and philosophers of the classical era and the Enlightenment to give way to "the law of nature"—in other words, for society to look to nature as the sole foundation for the law.

The jurist Hans-Helmut Dietze wrote his doctoral thesis on contemporary issues surrounding the "law of nature," which he defended in Wurzburg in 1936 and published the same year.[18] That same year, in an article submitted to the journal of the Academy for German Law, Dietze recalled that, in its hubris, "liberal thought . . . denied that the natural world was the founding force of values." The "norm was purely a product of thought"; these "abstract laws" had been "produced by an international logic" in such a way that the law no longer was "the natural expression of concrete vital relationships."[19] Since 1933,

> a complete axial rotation has occurred. It is specifically in the field of law that a fertile bond with reality has replaced constructions that were far too artificial. The intellectual system of the law is now buttressed by our people's way of life. Scorn for the real, which was caused by a hypertrophy of the mind, has given way to a sacred respect for the laws of life.[20]

This "ground for the law in the laws of life" signified a

> resurrection of nature's law. Like all of those that preceded it, the new natural law seeks to translate the order that exists in nature into legal terms. Its immediacy distinguishes it from positive law, which, to be valid, must be decreed and written down. The law of nature, for its part, is valid immediately; that is, originally, without any human assistance.[21]

For Dietze, this resurrection brought only advantages: "By essence positive law is always rigid, lacking, and perishable, whereas nature's law is supple, valid in all cases, and as eternal as nature itself." At long last, nature was replacing artifice, thanks to racial legislation. The latter was "an allegiance to nature's laws," that is, "iron laws" that "teach us, notably, that only the pure and the strong can survive." Unafraid of self-contradiction, the author acknowledged that, "in this the new law of nature completely sets itself apart from other known versions of natural law," particularly those of the "Catholic Church" and its scholasticism, as well as from "Enlightenment" thinkers whose "anti-natural character" he denounced in cutting terms.[22] Priests and philosophers had gone wrong in trying to think up a "universalism that, like all universalism, is alien to the blood and therefore goes against nature." Unlike those who had placed their beliefs in peddlers of the Gospels and Diderot's *Encyclopédie*, "nature does not like simplification or abstraction, but that which comes from the blood, that which is concrete. It does not simplify, it specifies. It does not generalize, it distinguishes." This was why "the law of nature must be specific to race, but only to one race, and not to all of them."[23] He went on, citing Goering: "Our natural law is the law that was born with us." This law "speaks the language of our blood" and commands that the laws of nature, specifically those of hierarchy and the non-mixing of races, be scrupulously respected: "The preservation of this global racial order is a right and a duty of man. Anyone who contravenes this order is denying life itself."[24]

By the same token, in a preface written for a book on Nazi racial legislation, Hans Frank noted with pleasure that "the racial doctrine and National Socialist legislation would be the translation of nature's unwritten ancient and eternal laws."[25]

Man and Natural Law

We are nothing special in this universe, just one simple, small part of a great whole. This Hitler gravely explained in a speech on February 15, 1942:

> We are all beings produced by a nature that, as far as we can see, knows only one single and harsh law: the law that gives life to the strongest and takes it from the weakest. We men cannot free ourselves from this law. The planets turn around their suns and the moons around their planets according to the same eternal laws. In the infinitely large as in the infinitely small, one single principle reigns: the strong determines the course of the weak. And we, on this earth, are leading the eternal struggle of all living beings. An animal lives only by killing another animal. We may very well say that this world where the existence of one implies the destruction of another is cruel, horrible. We may even cut ourselves off from this world in thought, but in reality, we live right in its midst. To free yourself from it, if you wish to be consistent, would mean committing suicide. Because no one can ignore the fact that, since men have existed, [the law] that has emerged victorious is not some abstract and imaginary law they dreamed up themselves, but rather the survival of the fittest, that which succeeded in affirming and protecting its existence. . . . Nature, providence, does not ask for our advice, nor for our wishes. It knows only one law: "For heaven's sake, fight, affirm your existence, and you will live! Or then again, don't fight, don't defend your life, and you will die, and others will take your place." There is no vacuum on this earth. If ever man were to die of his pacifism, animals would take his place, because man did not become

dominant through pacifist reasoning; he ensured his sovereignty over the beasts by showing superiority in the way he struggled for life. Nothing about this will change. It has always been so, it is so, and it will remain so.[26]

By February 1942, Hitler was aware that the war in the East would be long, despite all the plans he had made a year earlier for a short end to the conflict. Moreover, the decision to murder all of Europe's Jews, not only those in the East, had most likely been made two months before this speech, in mid-December 1941. The winter of 1941, according to Hitler's thinking, was when the Reich had returned to the perilous circumstances that Germany had faced in 1917–1918, when it had been obliged to fight a war on two fronts. And the Jews, Hitler believed, had been the only ones to emerge victorious in 1918. Hitler pursued this exegesis on nature in a speech delivered a few months later, on May 30, 1942, to a class of young Wehrmacht officers assembled for the last time before their deployment to the Reich's fronts. Trotting out Heraclitus for their listening pleasure, the Führer opened by mixing up the pre-Socratics, who had hardly asked for such treatment, with Clausewitz, or perhaps Sun Tzu:

> According to a very deep saying by a great military philosopher, struggle, and therefore war, is the father of all things. A brief glance at the state of nature as it is confirms this saying, which is valid for all beings and for all the events . . . of this earth. . . . It produces a constant selection that in the end affords life and the right to live to the strongest and causes the weakest to die. Some say that nature is really cruel and pitiless, but others understand that nature itself is merely following an iron law of logic. True, the ones she strikes down will always suffer from it. But they will never be able to abolish this law through their suffering and/or by their protest, nor to rid the world of it as it has been given to us. The law remains. Anyone who believes that he can rebel against the law by his suffering, his sensibility, or his opinions will not eliminate the law, but will eliminate himself.[27]

It was useless to attempt to free oneself of the laws of life, to found any kind of humanity that was not solely animal, any culture that could not be dissolved into nature. Already, in *Mein Kampf*, his ideology-infused autobiography whose title clearly indicated that life was combat, Hitler had written,

> When man attempts to rise up against nature's iron logic, he enters into a war against the very principles to which he owes his existence as a man. His actions against nature necessarily lead him to his doom.[28]

The mere idea of attempting to rebel against the laws of nature was so absurd that the only response to it could be sarcasm. The jurist Günther Stier, for example, wrote:

> If our redressers of universal wrongs see any injustice there, they can always lodge a complaint against nature. But it's doubtful that this would be of any use.[29]

The Führer and his supporters leveled caustic and heavy-handed irony at any opposition to what they saw as necessary laws; such an attitude, to them, was unrealistic and irresponsible, and could only break a man's body and mind. There was no rebelling against the "firmament." In the speeches cited earlier, as in nearly all of his written and spoken discourse, Hitler used the word *Gesetz* (law) to mean natural law—that is, a law of necessity, rather than of obligation. The meaning that Hitler attributed to the word, stripped of all ambiguity, lurks behind his deep disdain for jurists: what good were these fussy hairsplitters who spent their days complicating principles and procedures in order to justify their own existences, when, deep down, things were so simple that observing how the world was and how it worked was enough to understand it? On February 10, 1933, in his first public address as chancellor—which was also the first campaign speech of that year's Reichstag elections, Hitler declared:

> The laws of life are always identical, they are always the same. We do not want to rebuild our people according to abstract theories elaborated by some foreign brain, but by following the eternal laws shown to us by experience and history, and which we know. . . . We do not live for ideas, for theories, or for phantasmagorical political platforms; no, we are living and we are fighting for the German people, to preserve its existence, to lead the battle it must fight for its life.[30]

Nature had to be seen and recognized for what it was—there was no point in dreaming of unworldly and anti-natural rights, moralities, and religions. A healthy, lucid, realistic vision of the world as it was—and of nature as it was governed by its own laws—had always been a signal quality of the Germanic race, before it had been alienated by foreign doctrines and false visions. In 1930, Alfred Rosenberg elaborated on this idea in *Der Mythus des 20. Jahrhunderts* (The myth of the twentieth century). There he claimed that the Semitic religions—both Judaism as well as the different forms of Christianity—imagined that an all-powerful God had created the world *ex nihilo* and sometimes professed that this God could intervene in the course of nature and the history of man. These religions were thus unable to see that nature governed itself: "It is the very idea of a legislation immanent in nature that is denied. That is the worldview of Semites, of Jews, and of Rome."[31] The opposition and the confrontation of God and the world, a world that could not be transcended, because there was nothing beyond or outside of it, led "these systems to ignore the idea of an organic law" belonging to the very organism of nature. Law, from this Semitic and Roman perspective, was no longer immanent in nature, but rather dictated by an exterior and transcendent God. Well apart from such nonsense, "Western Nordic man recognizes the existence of a legislation proper to and immanent in nature."[32]

Consequently, Germanic law was not a dreamlike fantasy or the creation of an over-imaginative mind, but well and truly the translation of the natural law that Germanics knew, recognized, and respected: "The idea of a law of the race is the consequence, morally speaking, of our scientific knowledge of objective natural legislation."[33] This was an opinion shared by Martin Staemmler, a professor of medicine at the University of Kiel and then of Breslau, and the editor of the journal *Volk und Rasse*. In 1933, Staemmler published a work titled *Rassenpflege im völkischen Staat* (Racial eugenics in the racist state), which also warned men against the consequences of their hubris: "disrespecting the laws of nature" had led to the disappearance of the greatest peoples of antiquity. Indeed, "great people of culture think, in their reckless fatuousness, that they can neglect the laws that otherwise rule nature." These laws, however, "are the most sacred of all laws, even more sacred than those of the religions, the people, and the societies of nations."[34]

What conclusions could be drawn from this science of nature and of human nature? The first was that the law could never be used to help stop war. The idea that the law could function as a third party empowered to impose mediation in order to pacify relations was false. Judge Walther Buch was categorical on this point: "to live is to fight!" This was life's only law, and "only the man who approves of these laws of eternal combat can be at peace with himself." These laws of nature were "the wellspring from which the law was drawn, for no single law is valid for all living beings. The law is determined by race. Law is and is only what is right for our species, our race, and which serves it."[35] To be certain, there could be relationships based in law, notably legal conventions of international law, or private law contracts among "different races," but these conventions and contracts could never have priority over the true law, the law of nature: "Above all this, there is the eternal law of nature that pushes each creature to fight in an endless war for the preservation of its race."[36] It was therefore possible to know how to act with regard to people outside the race, as a booklet published by the SS taught:

> Biological thinking creates reasonable criteria for evaluating things. It gives us the force to make clear decisions and shows us what we can and what we must do.[37]

For members within one's own group, the imperative was just as clear: "To serve the German people—this is the supreme moral law of all German men."[38] Care should be taken not to induce from the above statements that all-out war was a phenomenon dictated by nature. In fact, the contrary was true: races struggled with one another by birth and by nature, but solidarity necessarily reigned among members of a single race:

> The struggle for life should not be confused with lack of scruples, jockeying for position, exploiting others, etc. Here we see the behaviors of the ill adapted, of those incapable of living in community, of asocial and degenerate people. Life has wisely tempered the law of struggle for life with a sense of community, the communal instinct.[39]

The struggle for life therefore did not lead a person to slit the throat of someone within his own race. Only the Jews, those hateful beings, were capable of killing their own when they could find no enemies.[40] Germanic people would fight for their lives, but they were ethical beings who lived within a community and respected its rules. The struggle for life was about the group, not the individual within the group; the individual was called to find his place within the group in order to work for the common weal. Warfare was to be directed outward: "exploitation" and "lack of scruples" were permitted only toward non-members of the racial community.

Another consequence of this reasoning was the integration of law into warfare. Law was not meant to define norms for warfare so much as it was a recognition of and an adaptation to struggle as an unavoidable reality. The creation of the Wehrmacht and the reinstatement of the draft in 1935—in complete violation of the conditions of the Treaty of Versailles—gave rise to an abundant literature on *Wehrrecht*, which can be translated as "military law and the laws of war." This defense code was of enough interest to jurists for the "Academy for German Law" to create a special section for it, and to publish a specialized journal, *Zeitschrift für Wehrrecht*, from 1936 to 1944.

Otto Zschucke, a specialist in the field, attempted to offer a survey of *Wehrrecht* in 1944. In the context of the events of that year, he gave a wide scope to this area of the law, defining it as "the totality of legal norms . . . that serve the people's defense capacity and the defense of the country, in the broadest sense." Refusing "the typically liberal opposition of 'civil' and military,'" Zschucke claimed that *Wehrrecht* subsumed all legal norms. War was total, and the *Volksgemeinschaft*, de facto and de jure, was a community ready for combat: "Total war requires that the entire people form a unified community of defense and war."[41] No longer was *Wehrrecht* "exclusively military law," as it had been before 1933; it was now "the law that governs the nation as a whole, its security and its eternal future." The "entire legal order must be imbued with these norms, which govern our defense," so much so that this law was "the realization of the will for defense . . . of the entire community of the people." This was no doubt what Germany had lacked during the First World War: "The collapse of 1918" had occurred to a great extent because this law had been limited in its application to soldiers.[42] War had not been allowed to penetrate and permeate all areas of life. This reflected the adoption by legal thinkers of opinions of figures such as Erich Ludendorff and Ernst Jünger on the necessity of the military organization of society and the economy. Luckily, another specialist observed, German Wehrrecht resolved a problem that arose

> in all parliamentary states: that of the preeminence of civilian power or military power, that of the precedence of the demands of the state and the army during wartime. During the Great War, these contradictions between civilian and military authorities led to the harshest of confrontations.[43]

In Prussia, and then in the Reich, as Carl Schmitt noted in an article titled "Totaler Feind, totaler Krieg, totaler Staat" (Total enemy, total war, total state), "the Prussian Military state undertook a domestic policy struggle that lasted a hundred years against the constitutional ideals of the [Enlightenment] bourgeoisie." "Between 1848 and 1918, Prussian and then German domestic policy incarnated a continual conflict between the army and Parliament." Unfortunately, the Prussian military state, "in the spring of 1918, had succumbed" to political liberalism, which had led to its "collapse."[44] Subjecting the law and all legal and moral norms to the imperative of the defense of the race and the Reich should prevent all disasters of this type, Zschucke wrote in 1944.

This community of the people, under threat and under attack, was necessarily a *Leistungsgemeinschaft*, a "community of achievement," Zschucke explained. Consequently, he argued, *Wehrrecht* should also concern itself with the development and preservation of *Leistung* (effort, achievement, performance, service, merit), and so ought to rank people according to this criterion.[45]

Leistungsgemeinschaft: Who Has the Right to Thrive and Survive?

The principles of prophylaxis examined earlier had not offered a solution to every problem.[46] While the children of diseased persons did not have the right to be born, the diseased persons themselves still existed, and others continued to be born, despite the sterilization measures of the July 1933 law. The question of eugenic murder began to be raised with increasing intensity in the summer of 1939, as it became clear that the Reich would soon be going to war. More than ever, *Ballastexistenzen* (ballast existences) were seen as a burden to the community.

In October of 1939, Hitler made the decision to murder the genetically diseased, primarily the physically and mentally handicapped, and signed a written order that he backdated to September 1, 1939, the day the Reich had gone to war. Eugen Stähle, a physician, NSDAP member, and local leader of the operation, known as T4, in Wurttemberg, responded to the misgivings expressed by a Protestant leader over the murders carried out at Grafeneck and elsewhere with the following words:

> Where God's will truly reigns; that is, in pure nature, one finds no trace of pity for the weak and diseased. . . . You will not see a diseased rabbit survive more than a few days: it will fall prey to its enemies, and, in this way, will be relieved of its suffering. This is why rabbits are a society [sic] which is always 100% healthy. . . . The Fifth Commandment, "Thou shalt not kill," is not a commandment from God, but a Jewish invention through which the Jews, the biggest murderers history has ever known, always attempt to prevent their enemies from effectively defending themselves, all the better to exterminate them after that.[47]

To make the community of the people as healthy as the community of rabbits, doctors, jurists, and ordinary men had to shed these outmoded ideas. The film *Ich klage an* (I accuse), directed by Wolfgang Liebeneiner and released in 1941, dramatized this process on screen. In it, Hanna Heyt, a likable and lively young woman suffering from multiple sclerosis, asks her friend Dr. Bernard Lang to put her to death. He refuses, claiming that a doctor "serves life." So she turns to her husband, Thomas Heyt, a brilliant professor of medicine, who accedes to her request. After the young woman's death, the two men confront and confirm their deep difference of opinion:

> —Did you kill her?
> —I set her free, Bernard.
> —You call that setting someone free? You murdered her! You took from her the most precious thing she had, her life! You have dishon-

ored yourself as a doctor. She asked me to do the same thing. Because
I loved her, I did not do it.

—It is because I loved her far more that I did do it.

Then the affair passes into the hands of the law. During the trial,
neither the judges nor the lawyers hide their discomfort: they must
apply the law, despite their tremendous sympathy for the liberating act
of the physician-husband. In this way, the euthanasia trial becomes a
trial to determine whether the legislation is no longer adapted to the
ethical demands of modern biology. Professor Schlüter, a colleague of
Thomas Heyt's, indicts "an unnatural and inhuman legal order. Nature
allows those no longer fit to live to die quickly." Heyt's act had "been
beneficial, for it had liberated" his wife from "senseless suffering":

> Legislation that requires someone who is incurably ill to founder in
> unbearable suffering is a barbarous legal order. It is based on an un-
> healthy understanding of life: so the God of love would require man
> to die after infinite physical and moral suffering?

Before this indictment, even Hanna's pastor quietly acknowledges
that he is "the representative of an outdated understanding of life,
which lifted suffering above all else." Thomas Heyt delivers the closing
remarks for the defense. His action falls under Article 216 of the Criminal Code, concerning homicide committed at the victim's request, so
it is easy for Heyt to indict the article itself: a suffering person asks for
death, and the law would prohibit doctors from granting that request?
The defendant "accuses an article of the law that prohibits him from
placing himself at the service of the people."[48] It was up to the people,
therefore, as represented by the jury, to deliberate over the affair. A variety of opinions and personalities is represented, from an old major in
the Reichswehr who loved the hunt, to a high-school teacher arguing
in favor of euthanasia, to an elderly pious man horrified at this violation of the Ten Commandments, and so on. In a closed room that may
well have inspired the one in *Twelve Angry Men*, good common sense
slowly wins the day.[49] In a brief dialogue during which the old major
speaks of euthanizing his favorite hunting dog, *Rassenhygiene* emerges
victorious:

> —But all the same, men aren't animals!
> —That's just it: should we treat men worse than animals?

The argument for dignity is turned upside down with a dialectical force as devastating as the love story with which the film opens. The genetically and incurably diseased ought to benefit from the mercy of death (*Gnadentod*), which would deliver them from their suffering and free their families and community from the burden of their care. And what was to be done about the decline and degeneration of the elderly? To be granted a decent retirement, to be looked after in old age by the people and the state, one had to prove one's biological serviceability. In the context of racial war, in which the quantity and quality of biological substance, of fighting flesh, were of paramount importance, every man and woman capable of producing offspring had obligations, "duties to the German family, to the German people, and to the German future." In such a context, an individual "in his extreme old age only had the right to be assisted" if, and only if, "he had helped to provide children to the German people, and in so doing, had made possible his people's eternal youth."[50]

Being born on the right side of the racial fence did not give you any free passes in life. The very holistic "You are nothing, your people is everything" was not a mere slogan—it was a political program. People had a right to protection and sustenance from their community only if they served it, too: they were expected to give back what they had received in the form of nourishment and care in the time they themselves had spent as dependents. When their state of dependence returned in extreme old age, the services rendered by the whole to the part would be proportionate to the services the part had rendered to the whole. In a 1938 speech, the head of the Reich Medical Association, Gerhard Wagner, who was obsessed by health "performance" (*Leistungsfähigkeit*), went so far as to publicly express doubt over whether the elderly—who, like children, were useless mouths to feed, but who, unlike children, had no future, meaning that no cost amortization was possible—and the mentally ill—who, unlike the elderly, had not even served the Reich in the past—had any future in the *Volksgemeinschaft*, which, as a *Kampfgemeinschaft* (combat community), was a *Leistungsgemeinschaft* (community of achievement). In a speech delivered at the opening of an exhibit on work and health, Wagner was even bolder:

We firmly refuse to consider as ideal a situation in which we would have myriad diseased and invalid racial comrades in our German territories, merely because it is now scientifically possible to prolong their lives.[51]

The *Reichsärzteführer* said no more; his audience was free to induce his statement's theoretical—and, who knew, perhaps practical—implications for themselves. The philosopher Georg Mehlis was even more explicit: "Only our actions determine our value."[52] Falk Ruttke shared this opinion: "performance capacity" was a lucky biological attribute that made the Nordic race, qualitatively, the best in the world—the one that had created and developed all culture, and the one that, in the great struggle among the races, would triumph because of its innate value and its valorous nature. According to Ruttke, this capacity was "an obligation to perform" efficiently.[53] "Just as performance grants rights" to the capable individual, "by the same token, a right may be withdrawn based on an incapacity." Could this point be contested from a legal or a moral standpoint? Not at all, because "the moral anchoring of National Socialism" was expressed in "this deep awareness of responsibility, which National Socialism wants to and must awaken in everyone."[54]

Medical Ethics

Everything in the previous section was spoken, written, and carried out by doctors, which may seem surprising. What is a doctor? The Hippocratic Oath and its *primum non nocere* had not been forgotten, Gerhard Wagner insisted: they simply no longer had the same object. Before, "to be a doctor meant to care for a private individual." "Today, this is no longer the case. . . . To be a doctor is to serve the German people."[55] To a German doctor enlightened by racial science, this holistic understanding of his craft, the patient, and the body was obvious: "For us National Socialists, above the right to dispose of one's own body, there exists the right of the German people, this German people which National Socialism has placed at the center of its concerns."[56]

For this reason, a doctor's mission was to care for the whole and not the part; or, put another way, to care for the part for the good of the whole. Caring for an individual was not an end in itself: it was the body of the entire race that was being treated through the unique body of the individual patient. The doctor was called "to no longer consider only the diseased individual," but "behind him, the hereditary flow of the German people, governed by eternal laws."[57] The substance of the racial body as a whole was to be the sole object of his care and his craft. To this end, "We believe in the intimate organic solidarity of everything that life secretes."[58] Arthur Gütt also considered the medical arts as "a service to the race" and not to the individual: "A doctor's moral duty is to care for the individual and for humanity." He therefore was required to "no longer only . . . look after the health of an individual, but to think of the wellbeing and the prosperity of the people as a whole" by implementing the precepts of "racial hygiene; that is, in looking after the health of future generations."[59] This was an opinion shared by bacteriologist Hans Reiter, who served as president of the Reichsgesundheitsamt, the health bureau of the Ministry of the Interior. Reiter believed that doctors ought to rid themselves of the foolish ideas promoted by the French Revolution and to stop seeing their patients as atomized individuals. A doctor should see a patient as "the link in a generational chain. He must be evaluated based on the performances he is capable of developing in the present and for the future. He must be seen in connection to his parents and his grandparents, as well as to his children and his grandchildren."[60] In more metaphysical or exalted terms, Werner Kroll, one of the doctors in charge of the health institutions of the Nazi General Government, contended that a doctor "does not see the object of his art as the individual person, but has a duty . . . to serve eternal life," not in the sense of a "hypothetical hereafter," but in the sense of a "constant blood flow, the flow that supplies the body of our people."[61] As the *völkisch* bard Gustav Frenssen put it, "It is . . . true and just to eradicate" the diseased and the weak who threaten the health of the racial community. "What is good . . . is life itself," that is, the life of the great totality of the race, not a single one of its parts.[62]

This was why doctors were no longer only in charge of a posteriori "treatment"; they were now responsible for a priori "prevention" as well. Germans, to ensure their ongoing good health, were to visit the doctor on a regular basis, not only when they were ill. Any automobile or motorcycle owner, Wagner wrote, "has it checked regularly" to avoid breakdowns.[63] The same ought to be true of the human machine, which should be subject to regular checks, whose results would be stamped in a "health passport." To ensure an enduring "state of performance," "we wish to . . . practice examinations regularly, on an ongoing basis."[64] In this way, "we will have done all we can to improve the individual's health and performance, as well as to preserve them into the most advanced age."[65]

The goal of the doctor was well and truly "the eternity of Germany."[66] To this end, it was necessary to "bolster the strengths that will drive back all that is alien to our people, to our race, to our spirit."[67] Doctors were also to be demanding of their patients, who no longer existed in and of themselves, but only as members of a whole. Doctors were to remind patients that belonging to the German people required them to perform: "To be and to remain in good health is not your private affair; being healthy is your duty," because "each man must serve the life of his people and is to be protected by it according to his own performance."[68] From now on, doctors were to set aside their prejudices and their sentimentality in order to be the engineers of the health and the performance required by the German nation. Once doctors had shaken off the dust of the past, they could work together for the health of the race, alongside German men and women who had been restored to their instinctive nature:

> Our ideal is not, unlike other ideologies, of man as destined to live through this vale of tears with patience and humility, for the destiny that supposedly was imposed on him by his alleged god, but a healthy, performing, powerful man, ready to act, who masters his own destiny and proclaims his belonging to his blood, to his people, to his Führer, and to his god.[69]

Wagner could not speak and write more harshly about Christian religious culture, which he claimed "worshiped morbidity." "The thesis according to which sickness, pain, and suffering would be agreeable to God, because such trials would be the purification that would make one eligible for celestial beatitude"—this idea was the secretion of a diseased and wicked brain. Against this religion of death, Wagner affirmed a "fanatical will to make health triumph."[70] Not only were doctors engineers, they were also warriors: "Doctors fight as biological soldiers . . . for the health of their people."[71] In this war, there could be no trusting defectors, deserters, spies, and enemies. This was why Hans Reiter demanded the exclusion of all the Jews who still remained in the German medical profession: "We cannot ask men who are not German by biology or heredity to have a German mentality and morality."[72] Jews in white coats represented "alienation" within the German medical corps and culture, as well as the potential for the "moral rape of our youth."[73]

The Repudiation and Use of the Ten Commandments

It is hardly surprising that the Ten Commandments of the Hebrew Bible fell victim to Nazi iconoclasm: between 1933 and 1945, the tablets ornamenting the Bremen courthouse were covered, for example, because, as Eugen Stähle wrote, they were not divine commandments, but Jewish ones. The Tablets of the Law, dictated by God to Moses so long ago, were subject to the same symbolic rejection as the Hebrew characters that the Nazi press enjoyed pointing out on the facades of those churches whose seventeenth-century architects had foolishly adorned with the Hebrew Tetragrammaton wreathed in clouds. "God?" inquired a newspaper headline in 1938.[74]

The "Jewish" commandments were explicitly repudiated. As Rosenberg declared at a conference of pre-historians whom one imagines were delighted by the news, "the findings of prehistoric research are the Old Testament of the German people."[75] In a conversation recorded by Hermann Rauschning, Hitler even named the Decalogue as one of the main—if not the main—enemies of Nazism, declaring that the NSDAP was leading "a great battle to save humanity from the curse of Mount Sinai. . . . We are fighting against the Ten Commandments. Against them."[76]

> That damned "you must, you must!" and that stupid "you must not!" Out! Let us purge our blood of this curse from Mount Sinai! The Jews and the Christians have inoculated this poison into humanity to corrupt its magnificent, free instinct, to sully it, and to bring it down to the level of curs afraid of a good hiding.[77]

The Decalogue was a Jewish weapon for weakening the Nordic race, for replacing its instinct with conscience:

> Humanity has been misled for a long time. We are putting an end to this. The tablets of Mount Sinai are outdated. Conscience is a Jewish invention. It is like circumcision, a mutilation of human beings, [because] alleged morality, built as an idol to protect the weak from the strong, [denies] the eternal law of struggle, the great law of nature.[78]

While the Ten Commandments were removed from the facades of public buildings and "Thou shalt not kill" was rejected as a "Jewish commandment," other decalogues abounded in the Third Reich. They can be seen frequently in texts and archival resources as an expression of Nazi imperatives. Wheat production needed to go up? The Reichsnährstand issued "Ten Commandments for the production battle" in December 1934. German soldiers had to be protected from dysentery? Troops were issued "Ten Commandments for avoiding amoebiasis."[79] Also on the topic of health, an edifying compendium of hygienic commonplaces instructed the Hitler Youth to brush their teeth.[80] Once they grew up, these young men, with clean teeth and a diet of fresh fruit, needed wives. To help them in their search, the NSDAP Office for Racial Policy offered "Ten Commandments for finding a spouse," which enjoined its readers to "find a companion on life's journey, not a playmate," to "preserve the purity of mind and soul," and to choose a partner "of the same blood."[81]

So as not to be too tiresome, we will content ourselves by finishing with the "Ten Commandments of the SA," written in 1926 by Joseph Goebbels, then *Gauleiter* of Berlin, and, on the SS side, "The Fundamental Principles of Security Policy," and for jurists, "Ten Commandments of the arbitration judge."[82] Nazi rhetoric itself seemed marked by decimals, as in Hitler's repeated use of the anaphora "We want" in his first speech as chancellor to the newly elected Reichstag when it met in Potsdam on March 21, 1933.[83] Other decalogues appeared in the sources cited herein, and will be discussed later in the book.[84] Clearly, the decalogue model was important to the Nazis, who used it to formulate behavioral imperatives. That they coopted this style is intriguing: just as they voided Kant's categorical imperative of its original content and adopted it as an empty imperative form, so, too, did they adopt the Ten Commandments. The Decalogue, so present, and so familiar, had been widely taught and repeated by pastors and priests: its very form commanded obedience. Thus the redeployment of the Ten Commandment format was widespread, even to promote content that went directly against Jewish and Christian teachings.

The form appears significant in itself: the simple presentation of a text formulated in this way activated a reflex that signaled the need for unconditional obedience, recalling catechism classes in which a pastor or priest had students learn and recite a normative text by heart, allowing the text to be internalized without interference from critical thought. This use of a known and familiar form shows how the Reich went about acculturating the population to the new norms. The Nazis were all too aware that the norms they were promoting were unprecedented, surprising, and even shocking. After centuries, even millennia of Christian culture, they knew that it would take more than a few years to acculturate the German people. To ease the people's entry into this new normativity, the Nazis recognized that using known forms would be expedient—new norms would be easier to adopt when delivered wrapped in anything that evoked the nostalgia of schooldays and childhood. The foreignness of the contents would be offset by the familiarity of the container.

This same phenomenon is visible in the Nazis' purely instrumental use of Kantian formalism: known to the German people through their education and, for Protestants, even through their religion, it was deployed by the Nazis in a way that totally subverted its content. In their instrumental use of forms, the Nazis, who in fact rejected "formalism," were the André Chéniers of morality and law: on ancient forms, let us build new imperatives.[85]

Not: Distress, Urgency, Necessity

One of the most frequently employed words in the Nazi vocabulary is *Not*, a term that at once signifies distress in an objectively dangerous situation, the urgent need to act to remedy that distress, and the necessity of performing that required action. Since necessity was what underpinned all law, *Not* led to *Notzustand*, the state of emergency.

In their preface to their professional comments on the law of July 14, 1933, Gütt, Ruttke, and Rüdin justified eugenicist legislation by quoting the venerable formula used by the Roman Senate to proclaim a state of emergency: *Videant consules ne quid res publica detrimenti capiat* (Let the consuls see to it that the state suffer no harm). They explained that this, in sum, was what eugenics laws were proclaiming. In *Not-zustand*, a state of racial and biological emergency, the Führer was ensuring that nothing harmful befall the Reich.[86] The three jurist-physicians giving their blessing to the law of July 14, 1933, were merely repeating the words of Reich Minister of the Interior Wilhelm Frick, who had presented and signed the law: racial and eugenicist legislation was "not an act of hatred, but of legitimate defense (*Notwehr*)."[87] This was the very same *Notwehr* that Hitler, in chapter 15 of *Mein Kampf*, "Legitimate Defense as Law," had used as the foundation of all legislation and legality.[88]

The emergency was a demographic one: Germany was hemorrhaging blood and babies; its biology, exposed to the great migratory floods unleashed by the French and Industrial Revolutions, was mixing with that of others and becoming corrupt. What was more, the social and family policies of the welfare state, as well as institutional charities, which were generally religious and highly developed in Germany, had played a clear counterselective role: the diseased and the weak, living in palaces, were surviving and reproducing, when in any natural setting, they ought to die. Finally, the First World War had bled off the best German blood. When it was swift, war was both a sport and a testing ground; when it endured and killed en masse, then the best—those who rushed into the fray—were struck down.

In 1933, Lothar Tirala, an Austrian gynecologist and friend of Houston Chamberlain's, was appointed as a professor of eugenics at the University of Munich, on the recommendation of Julius Streicher. That same year, he published a worried and worrisome article in *Volk und Rasse* in which he wrote, "The political wellbeing of the German people is now assured within the Reich, but we have yet not done anything for its biological health. . . . From a biological standpoint, we are a dying people."[89]

In another issue, *Volk und Rasse* published a speech by Wilhelm Frick to members of the "Expert Committee on Demographic and

Racial Policy" on June 28, 1933. In it, the minister of the interior
painted a similarly catastrophic picture of the German people's biological state. According to Frick, "20 percent of the German population present genetic problems," and the current trend among healthy
individuals was not to reproduce. The country's weak population
growth was evidence of this—it lagged far behind "neighbors to the
east, who have double the procreative force and a birth rate—not
counting stillbirths—twice as high."[90] This qualitative and quantitative exhaustion of German vital substance could be blamed on the
ravages of modernity, on "individualism," on "mechanization," on the
"process of destruction" of traditional communities through the flight
of rural populations, on urbanization, and on massive and brutal industrialization. All of this had led to "the moral decadence of our
people," who were less focused on marriage and procreation and more
tempted by pleasure and even unnatural practices—all phenomena
"leading our people to death."[91]

Unfortunately, the countries that neighbored Germany, notably to
the East, were demographically robust: frightening statistics, bolstered
by artful graphics, showed cradles heaped with coffins, Germans
swamped by crowds of Slavic people, and healthy individuals draped
with sick ones. Diagrams and graphics using all the tricks of percep-
tual deception were employed to provide apocalyptic illustrations of
the country's demographic circumstances and future: "Our people is
dying," wrote the demographer Otto Helmut, who believed that "evolution is such that we can only look to the future with fear."[92] A series
called "Political Biology" published by Lehmann offered observations
and solutions. To Paul Danzer, demography was "absolutely, a war," a
"war for the life" of the German people, which implied a "vital duty,"
a "duty to the heritage of our ancestors and towards German life."[93]
Other titles in the series declared the "birth war" or the "war against
infant mortality."[94] It was, in other words, a war against the losses of
the Great War. According to Friedrich Burgdörfer, a demographic consultant to the Ministry of the Interior, a professor at the University of
Berlin and then of Munich, and a prolific author of pessimistic and vol-
untarist works, these losses came to "two million men on the field of
battle," plus "a million civilians, victims of the blockade," and "three

and a half million children not born during the war," a birth rate deficit that brought casualties to a total of "six and a half million lives."[95]

The astronomical costs of this war were ample proof that anti-Germanic hatred had reached its zenith in the contemporary era. For thousands of years, Germany had been under fire from enemies seeking its death. As the war's casualties proved, this death would mean not only its political destruction as a state, but also its biological disappearance as a people. If history could be summed up as "six thousand years of race war," the contemporary era represented the end stage of these wars, for the enemy was ever more numerous and powerful, and modern technologies had made this enemy capable of totally destroying the Nordic race, of biologically exterminating it.[96] The ultimate crime of physical eradication was now possible. Already in 1922, Hitler had warned:

> Long ago, when Rome was collapsing, an endless flow of Germanic hordes came from the North to save it. But if Germany disappears, who will come after? Little by little, Germanic blood is being drained from this earth, unless we pick ourselves up again and set ourselves free![97]

These prophecies became darker as the war continued. In a speech on January 30, 1944, Hitler ruminated on the apocalypse that would rain down if the Germans, who were unaware of what was at stake, did not stand firm against the Reich's enemies:

> If Germany does not win this war, the fate of the European nations to the East will be sealed, and the West will swiftly follow. Ten years from now, the most ancient continent of culture will be unrecognizable, the gains of the past two thousand five hundred years of material and intellectual evolution will be destroyed, and the peoples, like their leaders, artists, and scholars, will be dying like dogs in the forests or swamps of Siberia—if by chance they have not already taken a bullet to the head. The eternal Jew, that fomenter of destruction, will celebrate his second triumphal Purim among the ruins of a devastated Europe.[98]

The scope of the terrifying Judeo-Bolshevik menace to the East demanded a commensurable reaction. The distress of the German people required celerity: "Today, we face only two hundred million individuals. In 1960, they will no doubt number two hundred and fifty million," Himmler predicted in 1942.[99] "Believe me," he implored, "in a hundred years or in two hundred years, the mortal danger will have become even more pressing."[100] It was high time to take action in the East, given the Slavic and the Jewish threat. Distress and emergency meant that action was necessary (*Notwendigkeit*); in this case, to act without delay, for there was a very present danger of immobilization and death.

The moment of Adolf Hitler was the moment to act. The generation of the First World War and its children could not miss this call. Referring to the mass killings perpetrated by the *Einsatzgruppen* in Poland in September and October 1939, Himmler declared:

> Indeed, if we do not have the nerves solid enough for it, we shall will these mediocre nerves to our sons and to our grandchildren, and then we will start the same debacle that has been going on for the past thousand years all over again. We do not have the right to do this. We are lucky enough to be alive today, to have been educated by Adolf Hitler, and since we are lucky enough to be acting within the Reich of Adolf Hitler and under the Führer's orders, well then, please let us not be weak.[101]

This, to Himmler, was an obvious fact: "Germany will never again have the opportunity to solve this problem in the same manner as we are now able to, under the leadership of Adolf Hitler."[102] The Reich had to strike swiftly and hard, for time was short; the Nordic race risked ruin and the fortification of its enemies. The tremendous brutality and the extreme speed of German military operations were as much a response to a deep-seated anguish as they were a tactical decision: to shock the enemy, to paralyze and intimidate other belligerent states with the thunderous spectacle of German weaponry, and to act quickly, because time was pressing, for Germany and for the race.

Kampfgemeinschaft: The Community of Struggle

Biological urgency and the laws of nature, which willed that the strong live and the weak die, demanded that the community, the *Gemein-*

schaft, be organized. If it wished to survive, the *Volksgemeinschaft* had to pull itself together into a *Kampfgemeinschaft* or a *Frontgemeinschaft.* To the Nazis, the experience of the First World War had proven that the community of struggle (*Kampf*) was the most efficient and beautiful form of human organization: in the trenches, men lived in solidarity and discipline, and experienced the height of existence together. This large-scale experience of war had made it possible to overcome the sterile contradiction put in place in 1789, and then confirmed in 1917, which had set traditional monarchy and democracy in opposition to each other. The monarchy had disappeared in 1918, and history's decisions could not be repealed; if these regimes toppled, it was because they were meant to perish. In *Mein Kampf,* Hitler was unsparingly harsh in his critiques of the German and Austrian imperial dynasties. The Habsburgs and the Hohenzollerns, he declared, had been done in by their own mediocrity, which was an expression of their biological degeneracy. As for democracy, it was a waste of time and breath; it was an idea based in the illusions of equality and universality, and it placed power in the hands of masses whose weak biological and racial value fated them to submission and domination.

This did not mean, however, that it was possible to turn back time: since 1789 the masses had participated in politics, and the enormous sacrifices of men who had fought in the First World War required in return that they be honored and allowed to share authority. The only valid human organization, which had been tested in the extreme conditions of the trenches for four whole years, was the "community of struggle." It was the only one that combined the efficient authority of a leader and the participation of the masses, and that corresponded to nature—unlike monarchies, which were led by degenerates, and democracies, which functioned on the absurd postulate of equality.

The community of the people was therefore a "community of the front," which obeyed its Führer—a military title—just as in combat and mortal peril a unit blindly followed its leader: *Führerprinzip* and *Gefolgschaft,* principles of obedience to a leader, were not the megalomaniacal whims of a single individual, but principles of community organization designed to meet the demands of history and of nature. The same was true of Nazis' rhetoric and speaking style, which, along with their omnipresent uniforms, smacked of the barracks at every turn.

The cutting oratory and the harsh tone of NSDAP cadres and Nazi government officials were a constant reminder that orders could not be debated when the survival of the community was on the line. Constant peril required blind obedience to and trust in the leader.

Much like a pack of animals, this community based on struggle followed nature, both its principles and its ends. Scandalmongers who claimed that the Third Reich was a dictatorship were reminded that *germanische Demokratie* belonged to nature. It was nature that had elected and named the Führer, whose merits had raised him above all others: "The power of the Führer," Hans Frank wrote, "is not based in constitutional paragraphs, but in his manifestly superior acts and accomplishments."[103] Elected by nature—that is, by the exceptional gifts with which he had been born, the Führer understood nature and its necessity better than anyone. It was "not the arbitrary that dictates the law," but rather the will of the "Führer . . . who, better than anyone, knows what is necessary for the German people. And he is the Führer because he has been proven to have superior capabilities."[104] It was simply fact that "the men gifted by fate are the men fate designates as Führer of the people."[105]

The Third Reich was not a regime that fit into any known categories, such as dictatorship, oligarchy, or Caesarian monarchy. "It is an entirely new regime."[106] "Germanic democracy" did not rely on any constraint. The consent of the Reich's subjects to the power of the Führer was at once free, tacit, unconscious, and instinctive. Between the Führer and his subjects existed a preestablished harmony grounded in the community of race, which was the source of an "intimate connection" that excluded all possibility of mechanical, formalist, and police constraint. Loyalty to the leader was free in the sense that it was loyalty to oneself, and to the nature that lay within.

Since the Führer had laid bare the laws of history and nature, obedience to him was synonymous with obedience to the race, and thus with obedience to all that was purest and most authentic in oneself: "Servile and blind conformity is not demanded of those who accompany the Führer, but loyalty. And loyalty presupposes trust in the fact . . . that the Führer . . . knows, that he is wise."[107] The Third Reich could not imply submission, dictatorship, or the constraining power of the state—a Germanic person was a balanced being, master of him-

or herself, and had no need for constraint. There was nothing rebellious or anarchic about the Germanic man or woman. Easterners were beings of passion and affect, and miscegenated Easterners like Jews were all the more so; they had no mastery over themselves and had to be dominated by constraint. "Germanic loyalty is the exact antithesis of Eastern obedience."[108]

The immediate, spontaneous, and authentic participation that characterized "Germanic democracy" was a cornerstone of the *Führerstaat* and the opposite of the dictatorial constraint exercised by so-called liberal democracy, which was the true dictatorship: it was formalist, based in written law codes, and relied on police enforcement. With a hint of mischievousness, Carl Schmitt noted that the most punctilious democracies, the ones that were most zealous in their separation of powers, had not hesitated, "since the World War," in order to respond to the demands of contemporary life, to introduce "simplified procedures" that helped make possible "rapid adaptation to difficulties raised by shifting circumstances."[109] But the practice of issuing governmental decrees invalidated the theory—not to mention the dogma—of "constitutionalism that separates powers," in the way that legal formalism separated, distinguished, and dissected everything. The example of France proved that "no state on earth can escape the need for simplified legislation."[110] Schmitt particularly relished quoting treasured French colleagues who shared this opinion, from Carré de Malberg to René Capitant.[111]

Shedding Barriers, Eradicating Christianity

Erich Ludendorff, an expert in military affairs, and particularly in defeats, had identified the true cause of German defeat in World War I. He and his wife, Mathilde, argued in numerous works that Christianity had made the nation weak and pitiful, in every sense of that word. Hitler was convinced of this as well, telling Goebbels, "The most pious generals are the least successful ones. The pagans' army leaders are the ones with the greatest victories."[112] Hitler, Himmler, and Goebbels all had Catholic backgrounds, and, over the course of the 1920s, all of them progressively abandoned their faith and their Christian values. While Hitler, for reasons of political opportunism, remained prudent and continued promoting "positive Christianity," Himmler took a much more radical line, brooking no compromise with Christianity, which was forbidden in the SS, where yearly confession and communion—not to mention attending mass or baptizing one's children, were held in very low esteem:

> We are going to need to rid ourselves of Christianity even more force-fully than in the past. We must break with Christianity, which has made us weak in all struggles; this major plague, the worst that could strike us in the course of our history. If our generation does not do it, it will drag us down for a long time to come. It is on the inside, within ourselves, that we must be done with it.[113]

Christianity, with its emollient values of peace and pity, had disarmed the Nordic race. A religion created by Jews, it had been inoculated into these great blond animals to make them hesitant, scrupulous, and debilitated:

> Our Christianity is strongly tinged with Judaism. A religion that is based on the principle that you must love your enemies, that you must not kill, and that you must turn the left cheek when you are struck on the right, cannot serve as a virile doctrine of defense for the fatherland. . . . Its activity is treason.[114]

This was not a new idea, as reading Machiavelli or Nietzsche shows; both saw Christianity as the language of the weak and the weapon of the meek against the strong. Nazi discourse drew from these sources and radicalized them with racism and the extreme force of their rejection: "There have always been weak people, humble people, people who will stand anything. In the East, this fatalistic vision of life is common. But the Jew also comes from the East," along with his God, "Jehovah, the cruel, the wrathful."[115] It was

> in his quest to dominate the entire world that the Jew created a highly elaborate system of superstitions in the West, which relies on the spineless meek among every people he has infected with his Eastern-fatalistic ideas as he has insinuated himself everywhere. He convinced them that free will is an illusion, that they are predestined, and, with the slogan of "predestination," . . . he has paralyzed the deciding strength of men and of peoples.[116]

What to do? Very little, at first, other than removing younger generations from the harmful influence of their old teachers in the clergy. Direct conflict with the churches was not desirable: the Nazis had not been in power for very long and the Germans were not ready for a radical reform of their beliefs. Leave them their talismans, the incense and the magic of their childhoods, their Christian masses and midnights. What was more, the churches' open anti-communism and anti-Semitism made them first-rate allies. After the war, once victory had been won, the time would come to settle such accounts—not that there would be much to do, according to Hitler. He saw Christianity as an overripe, even a rotten, fruit that would fall from the tree on its own:

> We must ensure that in the future the churches do nothing other than what they are doing today: losing ground, step by step. What do you think? That the masses will become Christian again? Nonsense. Never again. That movie is over. No one is going to see it anymore.[117]

Hitler had come a long way from his electoral campaigns and their talk of "positive Christianity," and now paid little heed to reconciliation efforts by the *Deutsche Christen:*

> No future for religions . . . , not for the Germans, at any rate. Fascism, in Italy, may well make its peace with the Church in the name of the Almighty. I also will do it, why not? That won't prevent me from totally eradicating Christianity from Germany. . . . One is either Christian or German. One cannot be both. You may well try to throw that epileptic Saint Paul overboard, others have attempted it before us. . . . It's utterly useless. One cannot get rid of the Christian spirit, and that is really what this is about. We do not want people staring longingly at the hereafter. We want free men, who know and feel God in themselves.[118]

As time and the war went on, Hitler's attitude became more and more belligerent as he grew increasingly irritated by Germans' inability to take a stand against the Reich's enemies. By his calculation, the cause was religious and cultural—a Christian barrier. To definitively stamp out the Christian spirit, "the Führer is now inexorably determined to wipe out Christian churches after the victory."[119] Should the disappearance of Christianity lead to the revival of the old Germanic cults?

Certainly not! Hitler was unsparingly harsh and caustically sarcastic
in his ridicule of people who favored horned helmets and daydreamed
of slipping on "a bearskin to retrace the path of the Germanic migrations."[120] Rarely did he miss an occasion, in public or in private, to
slap these Germanic fantasies back into their past. A firm supporter of
life and its laws, he told his tablemates:

> It seems totally ridiculous to me to have the cult of Wotan celebrated
> again. Our old mythology is outdated; it wasn't even able to stay alive
> when Christianity arrived. What's ripe for death always disappears![121]

For Hitler, what was eternal—and should be eternal—was the life
of the Nordic race, not the forms that it might take over the ages. In
Nuremberg, he stormed against people who worshiped a static form
of Germanity:

> We are National Socialists and have nothing in common with that
> *völkisch* idea . . . , nor with that *völkisch*, petit-bourgeois kitsch or
> those bushy beards and long hair. We all had our hair cut nice and
> short.[122]

Rudolf Viergutz, herald of the *gottgläubig* (believers in God) movement, shared the opinion that reestablishing or reviving dead religions
was out of the question. Resurrecting Wotan or Edda "would be a reconstruction for a historical museum, a theater, but certainly not a
religion for our people."[123] Would that not show a lack of respect for the
Germanic gods? No, because Germanic religiosity required no figures
and no dogma: it respected and adored life itself, and was therefore as
plastic and labile as life itself. This handy plasticity made it possible
to see that the ancient German gods had been satisfactory expressions
of a life-feeling, but that they no longer were. "The gods are not rigid
and fixed. They are changing, like everything living." This was why it
"would be a mistake to become attached to old symbols" instead of
"inventing more new ones."[124] "The religion of the German people
must to the contrary . . . be authentic and living; it must spring from
the very motions of the German people's soul."[125]

This religion of the people and of life was, according to Hitler, a
faith in "God, God in nature, in the people, in our destiny, in our

blood."[126] A religion of immanence and not of transcendence, it was a faith in what was most intimate, most unique, and most authentic in man: his race, the nature within and around him. A religion of immanence might sound surprising, because those who understood religion according to the criteria of Christianity could not understand "that the religion of the German people now taking shape has no doctrine, no dogma, nor can it say exactly what is the object of its faith," other than nature and blood.[127] *Deus sive natura* (God or nature). Himmler delivered the credo of this faith:

> Just as I believe in God, I believe that our blood, Nordic blood, is the best blood on this earth. . . . We are superior to everything and everyone. When we are liberated from our inhibitions and the barriers holding us back, no one will be able to best us in quality and in strength.[128]

This cult of nature was a religion in the original Latin sense of that term: it was a link to nature, to origins, to birth.[129] The new faith, which was the most ancient and the most archaic of faiths, was a form of communication with the elements and with life. It offered a link to the race and to the dead, and gave meaning to man's life. As Himmler explained to his senior officers at Heydrich's funeral:

> In my speech, and quite intentionally, I expressed my deep faith in a god, in a destiny, in the Old One, as I call it—from the old Germanic word *Wralda*. Once again, we are going to have to find new touch-stones within our people for all that is, for the macrocosm and the microcosm, for the starry sky above us and the world within us, this world we see in the microscope.[130]

An individual was finite, but the eternity of his blood made him immortal through his *Sippe*, tribe, and his race. The great mystery had been revealed, and the question to end all questions, that of death, had found its answer in the perpetuation of *Erbgut*, genetic patrimony, which projected man into eternity. What was its teacher? Not four obscure Jews who demanded belief, because that was absurd, but rather the real world and its laws. Faith in nature was confirmed in all that was tangible and concrete (the flesh, the senses, water flowing, rock crumbling), not in a haze of incense. It was nature that ought to be believed in, nature that governed within us as it governed in the starry skies above our heads.

All of this required a fundamental reassessment of beliefs and values: "This kind of reassessment is the foundation of the German revolution, it is an assessment based on life itself, in the sense of a religion for the German people."[131] To relocate the path of authenticity, it was necessary, furthermore, to locate the healthiest elements of the German people, those most faithful to its roots:

> Our farmers have never forgotten their own faith. It still lives. It is merely buried. Christian mythology only covered it over like a layer of talc, but it preserved the original contents. I [Hermann Rauschning] said to Darré that the great reform should begin. . . . It will restore the ancient usages to their rights, by every means. . . . We shall remove the Christian patina and return to the faith unique to our race. . . . Our peasants still live with pagan representations, with pagan values . . . , an authentic faith, which is rooted in nature and in blood.[132]

It was not difficult to trace the course of alienation's path: one had only to observe what the Christians had degraded, and to restore authenticity to a people Christians had led astray. It was necessary to reproduce

> exactly what the church had done when it imposed its faith on the pagans: to preserve what could be preserved, and to reinterpret. We will follow the same path in reverse. Easter is no longer the resurrection, but the eternal regeneration of our people, and Christmas is the birth of our own messiah, our people's heroic spirit and freedom. . . . Instead of celebrating the blood of their redeemer, we will celebrate the blood of our people.[133]

The Correct Use of Pity

The eradication of Christianity would make it possible to do away with compassion (for the sick) and magnanimity (toward enemies). Questions of pity, of compassion, of empathy, and of the value of these concepts were raised by Nazi authors, leaders, and medical practitioners as soon as the first measures against people with hereditary illnesses were taken in 1933. The 1933 laws and the regulatory measures and practices that followed them sought to restore nature to its rightful place (by leaving to die all those who, in the state of nature, would have died anyway) and in this way to create a community of the people, a body of the people capable of the highest athletic, economic, and military performance, fit for the historic missions demanded of them.

Humanists and compassionate types might have been upset by all this, but "it is clear that the improvement of the species is only possible through pitiless selection. Any animal technician knows that."[134] Arthur Gütt, a doctor and a legal expert and one of the fathers of Nazi eugenicist legislation, made science and the real world as it existed the only acceptable axiological basis for all legislation and all policy:

> Genetic science of the past decades . . . gives us the moral sanction to evaluate any individual according to his physical and intellectual genetic disposition, whatever idiotic prejudices and totally outdated understandings may say about it.[135]

The feeble, compassionate, and individualistic morality of the past had been disqualified by the "supreme values" that were "the future of our people, the life or death of the German nation." These values— which were holistic because they took as their principle and end the whole, rather than the part, and realistic because they did not oppose any fantastical fiction to reality as it existed—were the ones with which the Reich's legislation and practices ought to be evaluated: "The elimination of damaged genetic stock . . . must be seen as an act dictated by neighborly love, by concern for the wellbeing of the generation to come."[136] Arthur Gütt was a firm proponent of this idea, which he developed in other publications, notably with his colleagues Ernst Rüdin and Falk Ruttke: "To purify the body of the people and to eradicate pathological genetic dispositions little by little" was an "act of solicitude towards the generations to come," as opposed to "the suicidal brotherly love that characterized past centuries": "these are superior ethical-racial goals which completely outclass the concepts of the liberal age as well as the Christian ethic of brotherly love that dominated the ancient era."[137] Whatever effort it took to overcome these outmoded

Christian and liberal ideas, "we must completely gauge our prior conceptions to the biology of heredity" and its conclusions for science, ethics, and politics.[138]

What good was any pity that prevented an appropriate response to the enemy as it smothered the race under cartloads of diseased people? These people would have been eliminated by nature had anti-natural pity not ordained that they be kept alive, cluttering up sick houses that cost the state a fortune, to the detriment of healthy individuals. As one SS publication recalled sententiously, "In nature, which has for all eternity been ordered by divine laws, the law of selection governs harshly and without pity. The constant struggle for existence kills off in the egg anything not fit to live."[139] Furthermore,

> our Germanic ancestors approved of the laws of natural selection, like all healthy men, like all who are not corrupted by false doctrines of pity that are hostile to life. This false idea of God preached by the churches has negated the divine laws of nature. . . . Harping on and on to the peoples that God died on the cross out of pity for the weak, the sick, and the sinners, they then demanded that the genetically diseased be kept alive in the name of a doctrine of pity that went against nature, and of a misconceived notion of humanity. Worse still, it was believed to be a moral duty to care for and help anyone who was sick, afflicted, or affected, either morally or physically.[140]

Photographs of people suffering from particularly deforming illnesses were printed in illustration of this argument. The good-natured German bumpkin sparked the ire of Nazi leaders and ideologues. This stereotype of bonhomie, which had spread during the Renaissance with the rediscovery of Tacitus's *Germania*, could be explained by the fact that Germanic people were superior beings, at peace with themselves and the world and thus magnanimous. This was a fine trait, but one that prevented them from perceiving the hatred confronting them and reacting appropriately. Nazi texts were constantly lamenting the supposedly German ailment of "sentimentalism," a soppy empathy that prevented them from striking the enemy with the force that was being used against them. The magnanimous German was also forgetful, and pardoned all too easily. Goebbels was infuriated by "this German illness of

ceding through sentimentalism," by this sappy and emollient pusilla-
nimity afflicting the "nice German chap."[141] The German bumpkin, a
friendly, foolish, sensitive boy, moved to tears by a Beethoven sonata
and vulnerable to the magnanimity of others, always acted in a "typically German way; that is, sentimental and sensitive."[142] Interestingly,
these indictments of German weakness were nearly all made after the
invasion of the Soviet Union and at the beginning of the genocide in
the East, or, at the very earliest, following the invasion of Poland in
September 1939.

This good-natured Germanic naïveté would be laughable if it did not
contain a mortal danger for the Nordic race. Even in his anger, though,
Himmler preferred to approach it with irony. In his famous speech on
the "Final Solution" at Posen, the Reichsführer SS relaxed the atmosphere and provoked laughter in the audience with a gentle but firm jab
at those good old Germans:

> It's one of those things it's easy to say: "The Jewish people must
> be eradicated. For sure! It's in our platform, come on, let's eliminate
> them, let's eradicate them, on with it, now! Just one thing!" And there
> they all are, those eighty million nice friendly Germans, all of them
> coming to see us because every one of them knows a very nice Jew. "I
> know, all the others are rubbish, but this one, he's a super Jew."[143]

This was an irresponsible attitude in a situation where, to use one of
Himmler's favorite adjectives, one had to be "consistent." The "Jewish
question" was not a problem of individuals, but of biology. It had to be
resolved as such, with no exceptions, even for a "super Jew"—whose existence was just as improbable as that of a "good Jew." One had to banish
pity about the "treatment" of the "Jewish question" for two reasons.
First, pity implied empathy: it was something to be directed at one's
neighbor. And Jews were not neighbors; they were not even human.
Second, pity implied reciprocity. And Jews had never pitied Aryans.

Who indeed had pitied Aryans? And when? In 1648, when the Holy
Roman Empire had been blown to pieces? In 1792, when France had at-
tacked Germany? At Versailles? Looking back through history, had the
Persians shown pity as they attacked Germanic Greece? And had the
Carthaginian Semites, when they had attacked Rome? Goebbels

deployed this argument as part of his thinking in 1938, when, as *Gauleiter* of Berlin, he began to envision the evacuation of all Jews living in the Reich's capital. It would have to be done, he noted, "with no sentimentalism! They aren't sentimental with us, either."[144]

When the decision was made to kill all of the Jews in Europe, most likely around December 11 or 12, 1941, Hitler told the *Gauleiters*, "We are not here to have pity on the Jews, but only to feel pity for the German people."[145] Jurist Hans Frank, by then the governor general of Poland, was present at the major informational meeting held on December 12. Four days later, during a meeting of the General Government's key police and administrative leaders in Kraców, he declared:

> I know there is criticism of the many measures that the Reich is taking against the Jews. There is talk of deliberate cruelty, of harshness, of I don't know what else. . . . But please agree with me on the following point: we want to have pity on the German people alone, and on no one else on this earth. No one has ever felt any pity for us.[146]

The argument Hitler advanced had been absorbed, and was being redeployed at every relevant occasion. Furthermore, pity was not even a valid category, since Jews did not belong to the human species. Images from the ghettos were ample proof of this. Ingrid Greiser, the daughter of Arthur Greiser, the *Gauleiter* of Wartheland, was revolted by the dirtiness and emaciation of the occupants of the ghetto of Łódź, and in April of 1940 wrote to one of her friends:

> there is nothing there but epidemics, and stench, because of the evacuation pipes. . . . No water, either: the Jews have to buy it, 10 pfennigs a bucket, so they wash even less than usual. . . . You see, one can't have any compassion for these people. I think they experience things differently from us and they don't feel the degradation and all that.[147]

If, unlike Miss Greiser, you could not take a personal tour of the ghetto, you could always go to the cinema and watch *Der Ewige Jude* (The eternal Jew), which was designed to provoke the same sentiment. In the first entry in his *Journals* that explicitly mentions the Wannsee Conference, Joseph Goebbels penned a medical argument to justify the solutions being adopted as suitable to himself: "One cannot leave any room for sentimentality in these questions. The Jews, if we did not defend ourselves against them, would destroy us. It is a life or death struggle between the Aryan race and the Jewish bacillus."[148] Did one pity the microbes one battled with an antiseptic? The very question was absurd.

Pity made no more sense when it came to the other enemies of the Nordic race, as Hitler pointed out to his general staff on August 22, 1939, in his Obersalzberg residence. Here, the source was written in a stenographic style, in notes taken by General Halder: "Close your heart to all pity. Act with brutality. Eighty million Germans must obtain what they have a right to. Their existence must be secured. The law is with the strongest. The greatest harshness is required."[149] There could be no pity. *Recht*, the German people's right to life, required that there be none.

From all of the premises laid out here, one conclusion was drawn, with apodictic force. It took the form of an openly asserted and highly particularistic ethics: because the other is a hostile force, and because anything outside the Nordic race wills its death, everything is legitimate defense. The clock was running out for Germany, and a preventive war could buy back time.

[CHAPTER FIVE]

The War Within:
Fighting the *Volksfremde*

The Concentration Camp: Protection and Rehabilitation

THE CONCENTRATION CAMP was a structure for the forcible detention of any person "hostile to the people and the state" who, "through his behavior, threatens its existence and its safety." These "elements dangerous to the people" were interned for "reasons of safety, of reform, or of prevention." Internment was not arbitrary, since the arrest and internment of these elements could only take place "on grounds of an order for security detention or a decision for internment issued by the Gestapo or by the Sicherheitspolizei."[1] Theodor Eicke's concentration camp regulations, in their updated and corrected 1941 edition, to which I shall refer here, set out three key concepts as foundational precepts: camps were institutions that protected the state and the *Volksgemeinschaft* from dangerous elements; their purpose was not to kill, but to rehabilitate whenever possible; and camp internment was not arbitrary, but followed a legal procedure, since a prisoner could only be interned there if the state secret police or the Sicherheitspolizei mandated it.

Although imprisonment followed a legal procedure, camps nevertheless were not prisons in the classic sense of that term: the camp guards, put in charge of these *volks- und staatsfeindlich* ("hostile to the people and the state") elements, were to "conscientiously discharge their duty like a soldier facing the enemy."[2] Prisoners were to be kept "in a subordinate position with no consideration for age, origin, or social status, and must obey the orders of their superiors swiftly and without question."[3] These prisoners were "obligated to salute" the guards while "marching with back straight or standing to attention and uncovering their heads."[4] Discipline was so strict that in many cases guards were instructed to "make immediate use of their weapon," most often "without warning."[5] "Sanctions" for breaches of camp discipline were numerous, progressively harsh, and standardized.[6] Reports of breaches and the punishments imposed for them had to be filled out in three colors: white for the prisoner's file, yellow for the camp commander's archives, and red for the IKL (Concentration Camp Inspectorate).[7] The major charges for breach of discipline were disobeying guards' orders (or failing to obey them immediately), disturbing the peace of camp dormitories, and laziness at work.[8] But just as judges under the Third Reich enjoyed infinite freedom of interpretation, camp guards could also employ a "general clause" of their own.[9] Punishment could be meted out to "anyone who infringes in any way on camp discipline, order, and safety."[10] Moreover, it was specified, "tolerance is a synonym for weakness."[11]

Theodor Eicke's regulations for the Esterwegen concentration camp, which went into effect on August 1, 1934, specified that prisoners were there to be cured of their desire "to die for the filthy Jewish International of some Marx or Lenin."[12] To understand the camp as an institution, it is necessary to seriously examine two phrases that would appear to encapsulate Nazi cynicism at its most cruel, brazen, and brutal. The first, *Arbeit macht frei*, was displayed above the entrances of many concentration camps. The second, *Jedem das Seine*, greeted prisoners entering Buchenwald. *Arbeit macht frei*, "Work sets you free," was the slogan of the concentration camp system as it was structured from 1933 and 1937. Although murderous in practice, in principle, the system's goal during this time was not actually to kill its *Häftlinge* ("detainees"). Certainly some of them, those considered irredeemable, would die there. Others would never be released. But until at least September 1939, most were. The "work" of rehabilitation to regain a place in the *Volksgemeinschaft* was in fact supposed to make you free.

The slogan over the entrance to Buchenwald was different: "To each his due" (*Jedem das Seine*). It was original in two senses of that word. The physical object was an original piece made by Franz Erlich, a well-known Bauhaus artist who spent two years in the Thuringian camp for his communist sympathies and his penchant for so-called degenerate art.[13] Its second layer of originality is more difficult to grasp. Again, the inscription seems to be dispensing an extra dose of Nazi humiliation and provocation. It appears to be saying that the camp's detainees deserved their internment, that the camp was governed by a principle of immanent justice that would give everyone precisely what he deserved, in both reward and punishment. This thought is unbearable to anyone visiting a place where 56,000 people died between 1937 and 1945. But the slogan meant exactly what it said. It was cast for the camp gates at the personal request of its commander, Karl-Otto Koch, who had been put in charge of this *Musterlager*, or "model camp" following a posting as director of Sachsenhausen, of which Himmler and Eicke were particularly proud. *Jedem das Seine* is as common an expression in German as it is in English or French, and translates the Latin expression *suum cuique*, which was the motto of the Order of the Black Eagle, the highest order of chivalry in the Kingdom of Prussia, established by King Frederick I in 1701.

Suum cuique tribuere is a Latin maxim frequently encountered in the writings of Roman philosophers and jurists, who themselves were quoting Plato (*Politeia*, 32). Later, in *De jure et justitia*, Leibniz would make it one of his three founding principles of justice. Karl Marx, with his abiding interest in redistributive justice, had it printed as his letterhead in the 1840s. In antiquity, "to each his due" was the basis of fairness. Christian theologians, theorists of the natural order, made it their credo, and Karl Marx, inspired by the materialist philosophy of antiquity, believed that each person should be remunerated according to his work, and that the vampires who merely fed off added value should be cut off from this source of nourishment. Although he was no great fan of Marx, had most likely never read Justinian's *Corpus juris civilis*, and probably knew little more of the hallowed expression than the words themselves, Karl-Otto Koch knew what he wanted to say: Nazism rejected and spurned equality, and stated a doctrine of fairness.[14]

"To each his due" was supposed to incarnate the basic principle of justice of the *Volksgemeinschaft*, which was, as we recall, a *Leistungsgemeinschaft*. Each member was to receive in proportion to his *Leistung*, his performance and production, and each member was to be evaluated according to the criterion of his race. The "due" of a Nordic man was not the same as that of a Jew. What was due to a deserving laborer and a tireless soldier was not the same as what was due to someone of good race who happened to be afflicted with a biological disease. Friedrich Jess summed up the idea in *Rassenkunde und Rassenpflege* (The science and care of the race): "A person can only become what his genetic patrimony destines him to become. Not everyone can become what he wants: it is not 'the same thing for everyone' but 'to each his due.'"[15] The principle governing the *Volksgemeinschaft* was valid both in and outside the community. The renowned jurist Edgar Tatarin-Tarnheyden, a specialist in international law, asserted that the basis of world order was "the organic idea of *suum cuique*."[16]

Criminal Law as War

The enframing (*gestell*) of German law by nature's laws extended to all areas of German law, from marriage to real estate, to cite some of the examples explored earlier. By all evidence, though, criminal law was a particularly central concern: it armed the state, the judiciary, and the police to win the war of the good against the bad. Critiques of the positive law and the philosophy of past law were more radical in this field than in any other.

Before 1933, under the reign of individualist liberalism, each person was considered a private individual, subject to the law and entitled to rights and protections. A criminal, even the most horrible of recidivists, thus benefited from the presumption of innocence, and was entitled to a competent defense and a fair trial. Roland Freisler could not say enough against such foolishness. The goal of the law, and particularly of criminal law, was "the protection of the people," not "of the criminal."[17] Therefore it was "the criminal" who should be "hindered," not "the judge."[18] Freisler argued in favor of a judicial practice he was given full powers to implement starting in 1942, when he left his role as secretary of state for the Ministry of Justice to preside over the "People's Court." Judges were to be relieved of all formalities and all formalism. "Form" had to be sacrificed in favor of "substance":

> In criminal law, National Socialism wishes to and must move beyond notions of formal law and formal injustice to replace them with the reign of material law and injustice.[19]

Matter, substance, substantive values: at its heart, substantive law was simply anything that served and protected the material, biological substance of the German people, that protected the race as a substantive organic community. The way to do this was to consecrate "the identity of the State's legal norms with the norms of popular morality, so that our people's conscience . . . effectively becomes the dominant factor" in law.[20] Out with paragraphs, form, and formalities: criminal judges should be free to be mobile, agile, and efficient. Freisler was particularly proud that the new state and its new justice system had tossed out the principles of legality and non-retroactivity: *"Nullum crimen, nulla poena sine lege!* This precept has been celebrated as the absolute safeguard of the freedom of citizens," whereas it had mostly guaranteed the freedom of rascals and scoundrels. Consequently, "to abandon the precept of *Nullum crimen sine lege* has liberated criminal jurisprudence of the notion of formal injustice."[21]

Judicial freedom, a lack of formalism in judicial decision-making, and the clauses set down as principles of the law (good common sense, the Führer's will, the party platform, "general clauses") made it possible to replace one precept with another. From now on, Hans Frank noted with pleasure, "The legal policy of the National Socialist Reich will no longer be dictated by the precept of 'No punishment without law,' but by another maxim: 'No crime without punishment.' "[22]

This precept was applied a month after the Reichstag fire, when a credible suspect, Marinus van der Lubbe, was arrested in the burning building on the night of February 27 to 28, 1933. The law of March 29, 1933, "regarding the infliction and execution of the death sentence" was a true case of legislation *ad personam*—and indeed rapidly became known as the 'Lex van der Lubbe.' Its first article determined that the sentences of the February 28, 1933, decree applied "to acts committed between January 31, and February 28" of that year.[23] The decree was thus made retroactive, and a law was created that openly violated the principles of non-retroactivity and legality.

Criminals were no longer protected by criminal law, but thoroughly endangered by it. The community, which had once been threatened, was now the one—the only one—to be protected. Solemnly, and once again backed by his Latin, Hans Frank wrote: "The criminal cannot and must not consider the Criminal Code as the *Magna Carta libertatum* to his profit," that is, as some grand charter of his personal liberties and safeguards.[24] The Criminal Code and the criminal judge were there to protect the community of the people, not the person endangering it. This was what Hitler had meant by a Copernican revolution, whereby the community, rather than the individual, was placed at the center of medicine, politics, and the law.[25] A judge's credo, wrote Walther Buch, was not "Everything for the individual," but "Nothing is more important to me than my people."[26]

The meaning of criminal law changed radically. Since Beccaria and the French Revolution, the goal of sentencing had been to improve and change the criminal, since man was flexible and able to evolve. Now, criminal law was based in the near-total determinism of "criminal biology" and could punish only to quarantine, or even to eradicate. Here, Falk Ruttke was categorical: "Criminal law means elimination." Moreover, "expiation and reform are not principles of criminal law; instead, quite simply, they are the eradication" of the bad and of villains, for the bad were fated to be bad by their biologically flawed nature.[27] From this perspective, the fantasy of improvement no longer made any sense. One could not change a biologically problematic element: it could only be treated medically, surgically, in order to remove it from the healthy body of the people.

Edmund Mezger, a professor of criminal law at the University of Marburg and then of Munich, also approved of the predominant role of "biology in the new criminal law." He viewed with particular favor the November 24, 1933, law on "dangerous recidivist criminals and on safety and reform measures."[28] Thanks to this law, "the biological understanding of the criminal has become a cardinal element in the National Socialist understanding of the law," not just in theory, but in (judicial) practice, since the law could protect the community from biologically degenerate elements that wronged and harmed it:

> The law's greatest failing, until recently, was that ideas of irresponsibility or partial irresponsibility could, during sentencing, lead to acquittal or to commutation. But it was impossible for the judge, in order to protect the community, to book a particularly dangerous criminal due to the very fact of his pathological penchants.[29]

That was the limit! A diseased person could be acquitted, because he was deemed irresponsible, while the community continued to suffer from a pathology that the individualist and liberal law, sublimely unaware of biology and its lessons, insisted on protecting. Now, however, the law offered a whole arsenal of weapons in the fight against someone's degenerate biology harming the community: a biologically determined criminal could be prevented from acting by safety measures such as preventive detention, castration, or safety detention at the end of his sentence.[30] As the jurist Günther Stier stated baldly, "guilt, according to our understanding, is synonymous with racial degeneracy," of which it was also the symptom.[31]

Friedrich Oetker, a leading expert in criminal law, professor at the University of Wurzburg, and, in 1933, president of the criminal law section of the "Academy for German Law," shared this opinion. Already advanced in years, Oetker represented an older generation of jurists, and believed that the goal of criminal law was to "fight the causes of the illness." From this perspective, an exclusively repressive and eradicative understanding of criminal law was therefore "neither backward nor barbarous," but, to the contrary, perfectly modern, since it was translating contemporary advances in the biological sciences into legal practice.[32]

Judges therefore acted as doctors who determined a diagnosis and acted in consequence by quarantining the unhealthy elements. Walther Buch, a career magistrate and "supreme NSDAP magistrate," staunchly defended this idea. "A judge, like a doctor, is a stakeholder in the bodily health of the German race" when he "eradicates pests with no conscience from the body of the people."[33] With no conscience and even with no free will. Nazi legal scholars took very little interest in the question of responsibility. The excessive attention once paid to this question had been based on two illusions: that of the individual, and that of freedom. Now, the law and judicial practice were holistic, not individualistic; they took the *Volk* as their principle and their end, and sought to protect it. Lothar Stengel von Rutkowski could now dismiss the question of responsibility as particularly pointless:

> It is not a question of holding a criminal responsible for behavior that harms the healthy order of the people. The question is: am I able to

remove from him the possibility of harming our genetic patrimony and our environment?[34]

The individual did not count. Imputing his act to one cause or another made no difference. What mattered was the fact of his misdemeanor or crime, which revealed a potential for causing harm that could always be renewed, since it had already acted in him. There was no need for the judge to waste time on useless questioning. The only interest to be defended here was that of the people in the present and in the future, in its descendants: biologically dangerous individuals ought to disappear not only from the "environment" of the people, but also from its "genetic patrimony" through measures, now provided for in the law, that intervened in his very body.

Rutkowski did temper his message: minor and unrepeated offenses such as stealing an apple or telling a lie did not indicate damaged biological substance. The police and the legal system therefore had to distinguish crime from crime, because criminality was not always a biologically determined inclination. For occasional delinquents, for those "whose malevolence is exclusively, or at least predominantly, conditioned by environment, order, justice, and sanction remain the most appropriate forms of intervention." The biologist thus acknowledged that not everything was biological or biologically determined. "Sentencing is an experiment," an "environmental stimulus" that could modify behavior. What mattered was accurately identifying the "environment" and the "genetic patrimony" as the only two "components of our will," so that "selective breeding," which was based on an a priori eugenics, and "education" could be the two pillars of an "ethics in keeping with the laws of life."[35] These were also two of the three pillars of a healthy legal order, alongside a criminal justice system designed, in theory and in practice, for the eradication of biologically unhealthy beings.

The "Armored Divisions" of the Law

To achieve this eradication, structures that were even more efficient than common law courts were created: the Sondergerichte (special courts) and the Volksgerichtshof (people's courts).

The offenses and crimes targeted in the rulings of February 28, 1933, and March 21, 1933, against *Heimtücke* (insidious treason) were handed over to the Sondergerichte, created by decree on March 21, 1933, and confirmed by the law of December 20, 1934. In parallel, the Volksgerichtshof were established on April 24, 1934, to handle a portion of crimes and offenses. The September 1939 decrees extended the competence of these special courts to nearly all offenses and crimes, including petty ones. This change in the criminal law system reflected the idea that it was unbearable for anyone to profit from the war, as evidenced by the extremely harsh sentencing of acts committed during *Verdunkelung* (air-raid-alert blackouts).

These special jurisdictions made it possible for criminal law to become as "harsh as war itself."[36] A World War I combat veteran and a dyed-in-the-wool Nazi, Roland Freisler described judges as "the soldiers of the home front," whether their benches happened to be in ordinary jurisdictions or special courts.[37] The special courts, in turn, were baldly described as "the court martials of the home front."[38] But the war metaphor, like all Nazi metaphors, was not actually a metaphor at all, as Freisler pointed out in no uncertain terms:

> The special courts . . . are in a way the armored divisions of the law. They must be as swift as assault tanks and have comparable firepower. . . . They must show the same ability to track the enemy, to flush them out, to overtake them, and possess the same capacity to destroy them, to annihilate them.[39]

These words were written in the euphoric midst of the successful *Blitzkrieg* against Poland, in which the tanks of the Wehrmacht played an illustrious role. They say a great deal about the concept of the "inner front" (*innere Front*) as developed by those responsible for Nazi law and jurisdictions. The idea was to ensure that "German men, in the rear as at the front, are at their combat posts," for "this is how the fighting bloc of a great people stands united and in solidarity behind its Führer."[40] But as early as 1935, in a context of international peace, Hans Frank had already stated aloud and on paper that judges were soldiers in a war against crime: "The guardians of the law are the soldiers of the law," a "combat unit" that sees to it that "German citizens of this Third Reich, this empire of honor, order, and decency, may once again feel safe."[41] This, then, was the true, literal, and faithful definition of "legal certainty" so dear to the jurists of yesteryear: "Legal certainty is only valid for the correct, honorable and sane majority of our people."[42] For Roland Freisler, the

> meaning of criminal law is . . . the protection and the reinforcement of the blood of our people and of its life force, . . . the reinforcement of this joyful disposition which the members of our race manifest in working for the reconstruction of our people [and the assurance] that the state, too, is fighting on the front lines.[43]

The war being waged by judges and police officers was a war against parasites, harmful elements, and brigands:

> We are waging a war of eradication, and we shall most energetically make sure that it is the criminal, not the state . . . , that is left to hang [sic]. We shall rid ourselves of these humanist and false ideas.[44]

Even more generally, it was part of the law's essence to be, quite literally, polemical. The law was not a judicative and neutral third party. It was a body of norms formulated and applied by men holding political power. It was an arm used by those in power to bolster and strengthen their domination. The law was never neutral; it was always partial and partisan, in its most ethereal formulation (philosophy of law) as well as in its most concrete and most brutal application (the criminal courtroom). The Nazis unequivocally favored this view, which seemed honest and just in their eyes: "The law is a means to assure the future of our people, or else to endanger and destroy it."[45] The law could be a weapon in the hands of Germany's opponents, as had been the case until 1933; before then it had been used to the detriment of the people and the race. Or it could be redefined and used by the best representatives of Germany's interests, in which case it would benefit and support the best in their struggle. During the affair of the Potempa Murder in the summer of 1932, the Nazis viewed the law's intervention as fully instrumental: to them, the death sentence handed down to the five SA members (who had trampled to death a Polish laborer and communist sympathizer) was proof that the law was in the hands of the Reds and the Blacks. Soon, however, it would be placed under the control of the Browns, who would reestablish legal harmony:

the state's laws would once again be congruent with the laws of nature, and the "enemies of the people" would once again be the "enemies of the state."[46]

The law was a weapon; the judge was a soldier, or rather a rogue non-commissioned officer lining the *Volksgemeinschaft* up for battle. This was the intriguing semantic argument proposed by Günther Stier in a book titled *Das Recht als Kampfordnung der Rasse* (The law as a battle order for the race), in which the author derived a plethora of words from the radical *Recht* to demonstrate the fertile semantic field it opened up:

> Just as an officer commanding a unit places his soldiers in a line, the task of a judge is to arrange the things that are presented to him. To judge (*richten*) therefore means putting things back in order (*zurecht-rücken*), putting them back in their place. When a soldier steps out of line, the corporal puts him back in his place; the judge puts the individual back in line when, on his own, he is not upright, he is lost, poorly positioned. This individual is then placed back on the straight and narrow.[47]

"Law" was "what makes [men] upright again" (*richtendes Recht*), and the "legal order" was a way to place them "in battle order."[48] Friedrich Oetker, a professor emeritus of criminal law at Würzburg and president of the criminal law section of the "Academy of German Law," said much the same thing: since life was a war of the races, and the individual's meaning and existence relied exclusively on his "position" as a "member of the community," the "categorical imperative" for each individual was "to return to his ranks in the community and to submit to its order." Now "anyone who forgets his position as a member of the community, anyone who lashes out at it, anyone who refuses to obey it, is an enemy of the people."[49] This was particularly true of judges. As another Nazi publication explained, "the fact that judges and prosecutors now march in the same ranks and in step with their comrades in the SA and the SS is evidence of a healthy change."[50]

Irritated and even exasperated by several legal cases he had heard of in which judges, to his mind, had taken too light a hand, Hitler came up with the idea of placing judges directly under his authority, with professional transfers, sanctions, and revocations possible in cases where judges were found to be lax or irresponsible. He had been particularly exasperated by the case of Ewald Schlitt, a man who had beaten his wife to death and whom a judge had sentenced to five years in prison for his crime. Hitler, who was particularly sensitive to these cases because of his own family history, learned of the affair through the press on March 21, 1942. It made him furious—so outraged that he threatened to do away with the courts entirely and hand the treatment of legal cases directly to the Reichsführer SS instead.[51] By order of the Führer, the Ministry of Justice transferred the case to the Leipzig Reichsgericht, which sentenced the defendant to death.[52] Hitler followed with this speech to the Reichstag, on April 26, 1942:

> No one, in the moments we are living, can brandish acquired rights. Everyone must know that from now on there are only duties. I therefore ask the Reichstag to expressly confirm that I hold the legal right to force each person to do his duty, or if the situation requires it, to demote or dismiss anyone who does not fulfill his duties, after a good conscience examination and with no consideration for his person nor any regard for any alleged legal rights.[53]

The German judiciary was included in this:

> I also expect the German justice system to understand that the nation is not there for it, but that it is there for the nation. This means that the world must not perish, nor must Germany, so that formal law can live, but that Germany must live at all costs, even when formalist understandings of justice must suffer for it.[54]

The last traces of procedural normality, of normalized administrative function, were now officially to disappear. They were to stand aside for the executive, legislative, and now the judicial supremacy of the Führer, who in his speech made explicit reference to the maxim *pereat mundus, fiat justitia* (let justice be done, though the world perish) in order to deny its validity. Paradoxically, the judiciary, most likely because as a professional body it had agreed so extensively with most Nazi ideas and proposals, had for many years been an island of excessive professional and decision-making autonomy. Judges ruled harshly, and if by chance their sentences displeased the Reich's secret police, then the Gestapo was there to nab any defendants who were discharged or let off too lightly, and to place them in *Schutzhaft* (protective detention) in a concentration camp.

In 1942, Hitler decided that he could and must do away with the last shred of respect that had once been granted to the judiciary. The fiction of a still-autonomous German judicial branch evaporated.

The Nature and Function of the German Police

During a 1936 conference in which he appeared in his new role as "chief of the German police," Heinrich Himmler offered some reflections on the genesis of the police over the long course of German history. These reflections were both etiological (why are we developing such a severe police force?) and ethological (because our behavior requires it): German history had been "incredibly painful," filled with war and misfortune, never peaceful enough to foster civil, polite officials. Germans had only ever fostered in their midst

> the German soldier and the German civil servant. We, the Germans, must be lucid on this point: we do not have steady-going knights or gentlemen, like other states of the Germanic race. . . . We weren't able to develop those types. For that, you need centuries of peace, without being disturbed. . . . And so we, the Germans, threw ourselves into regulations, and it is through regulations that, with an order and a discipline we stubbornly imposed on ourselves, we developed these two types, the civil servant and the soldier.[55]

German behavior and civilization had come about in this way, through lack of serenity and peace. The soldier and the civil servant had been its makeshift civilizers, and, doing the best they knew how, had nevertheless managed to help Germany survive and prosper in a hostile world.[56] Himmler, therefore, was not so much expressing regret over the backwardness of Germanic mores as he was admiring the German community's two types of executive. The German police, he believed, should specifically act as a junction to train a "civil servant militia."[57] This wartime civil service, come what may, was there to wage war:

> We are a people located at the center of Europe. The peoples surrounding us are not our friends. [They] would like to destroy this Germany . . . which is for us—and for the world: it is after all the heart and the brain of Europe!—a little more than a mere name on a map.[58]

This high-level mission gave the German police permission to take certain liberties. They were not there to protect society or the individual against the absolute state, but rather to look out for the health of the "community" as an "organic unit."[59] Their vocation was to ensure that the community would endure by requiring that each of its members fulfill the function that was assigned to him or her as a part of the whole, so that the whole might live:

> The individual's role as member of the community requires certain duties toward it. All of the duties an individual must discharge as a member of the community constitute the field that the police must survey, in the name of the state.[60]

The German police had to protect the life of Germany in a time of heightened, even paroxysmal danger. As Himmler inquired:

> What weight do the articles of the law carry? What weight do rulings carry? What weight do regulations and procedures carry? If, in one way or another, I succeed in helping my people, then I am acting in compliance with the law, in the most deeply divine and moral sense of that term.[61]

Himmler could thus proclaim boastingly, as we have seen earlier, that under his orders, the German police blithely violated "laws" in order to respect "the law"—"paragraphs" carried no weight in the face of "the German people's right to life":

> This is our way of thinking: we want only the laws of nature, the laws of life, which are simply there, which we did not create, but the Lord God, or nature, or destiny created, to be held back by stupid paragraphs of law.[62]

These "stupid laws" were the work of a bygone era, of which the majority of Reinhard Höhn's legal writing was a historical critique. The law the Nazis found themselves up against in 1933 had been "the expression of the ideology of the liberal bourgeoisie. The law that governed police activity had been the outcome obtained in the nineteenth century by the bourgeoisie in its struggle against the absolutist state." The bourgeoisie had been burned by absolutism and was therefore— legitimately—eager to prevent "any attacks on liberty and property":

"This was only possible once the state, and, with it, the police, was placed under a legal system that made it possible to evaluate, in each case, whether the police had acted arbitrarily or in compliance with the law."[63] The struggle against the arbitrary had thus given rise to legality—to submission to the law as a third party—the alpha and the omega of any judgment that could be passed on the actions of the police. To prevent the state from intruding into the private sphere—also an anti-absolutist legal construction—the bourgeoisie responsible for 1789 and the nineteenth century had also created a strict distinction between what was private and what was public. The police were limited to the public sphere alone, and were asked not to become involved in anything that was not their business. The private individual was thus free to go about this business, which he did, so long as he did not threaten public order in doing so, and the police had no say in the matter:

> Citizens expected the police to preserve public peace and safety so that they would be free to go about their economic and social occupations. Beyond that was the private sphere, which was not the business of the police.[64]

It was specifically this distinction between public and private that Höhn was calling into question. He proved its inanity not theoretically, but empirically, with a few memorable examples that ultimately allowed him to show that, contrary to the claims of the liberal bourgeoisie, nothing fell outside of the jurisdiction of the police. Before 1933, it had been believed that drunkenness was the private affair of an individual, who was free to drink as he pleased, even when "he was ruining his family" and causing desolation in his home. For indeed, "the idea that the family is a member of the community of the people, and that it must be protected, is foreign to a legal system that conceives of the family itself as a mere legal relationship."[65]

As a jurist, Höhn was more than likely aware that he was exaggerating, and that provisions in the former legal system made it possible to impose certain restraints on drunkenness. This is also true of Höhn's second example, that of suicide: before, he asseverated, the law prevented the police from intervening to prevent an unfortunate soul from carrying out his tragic project! To highlight the absurdity of this legal culture, Höhn insisted that the police had not had the authority to intervene unless the desperate act threatened to tie up automobile traffic. Here, once again, was the derisive caricaturing that Third Reich jurists enjoyed brandishing in their battle against the old legal order. Höhn concluded by lamenting: "that this man was a member of the community of the people, that he was perhaps a breadwinner, none of that could be taken into account in police officers' decisions."[66]

To Höhn, this handful of examples was ample illustration of the inanity and the stupidity of the public/private distinction and of the notion, however foundational it might be in the liberal understanding of the police, of "public order":

Public order comes from the concepts of the liberal bourgeoisie. This public order has no clear and firm grounding in the fundamental values, the racial values, of our people.[67]

The fact that "the liberal bourgeoisie had seized power over the rights of the police" as a kind of weapon for confronting the absolutist state might have been a good thing at the time, but their liberal understanding of the role of the police had led to abuses that became the rule:

The forces working to destroy the people and the state are hiding behind these laws governing the police to mask their plotting and to condemn the police to powerlessness in all issues pertaining to the very existence of the community of the people.[68]

The liberal understanding of the law and the police had made it possible for scoundrels to bring police officers before the courts, which could then investigate whether "the police had acted in compliance with the law; that is, in compliance with norms"—formalist legalism that had made it possible for swindlers with dishonest legal counsel to despoil the state and the community by reducing the police to inaction.[69]

Thankfully, the year 1933 had put an end to this aberration. Höhn recalled that President Hindenburg's decree of February 28, 1933, followed by Goering's ministerial order of March 3, 1933, had expanded the jurisdictions and intervention powers of the police force, notably for the Gestapo. This "exploded from all sides the legal framework once imposed on police activity," notably the infamous 1931 "Article 14 of the law regarding police administration."[70] This article had specified that "the police authorities must, according to the laws currently in effect, take all measures they deem necessary to protect the collective or an individual from dangers to public safety and order." Goering's decree thus lifted two conditions and checks by invalidating the distinction between public and private, and by removing the obligation to wait for an act to be committed to intervene. If, as Höhn had written, "the mission of the German police is to combat the enemy within," all barriers once imposed on their actions had to be removed.[71] A soldier's behavior under enemy fire was no longer determined by laws and regulations; by the same token, "for the first time, it has become clear that the highest mission of the police is the protection of the community, and that, from now on, their activity can only be dictated by that mission."[72] The police were no longer "reduced to the defensive," waiting for acts to be committed. Whereas previously they had been forced to wait for someone who had completed his sentence to commit another crime before they could arrest him again, the police force could now act on its own initiative:

> Professional criminals and perpetrators of dangerous moral crimes can be placed in preventive detention by the police without judicial intervention . . . , even if they have no prior criminal record, if they are suspected of planning serious crimes. In this, the idea that the police exists to protect the community fully prevails. This has made it possible to overcome the highly liberal Article 14.[73]

Did escaping liberalism mean returning to absolutism? Not at all! Absolutism made the state and its power absolute, whereas the real absolute was the people itself, conceived of as an organic, racial entity. The old "distinction" that had once prevailed between "individuals and the power of the state" had been useful for protecting individuals against the arbitrariness of that state, but it no longer had any reason to exist.[74] Free from these obsolete categories and rid of the confining norms that had been imposed on them, the police were now free to act and to serve the German people:

> National socialism has changed the police in its essence. From a mere administrative institution functioning by a set of rules, it was made into a reactive body serving the community of the people.[75]

If the mission of the German police was now to "fight the enemy within" (Höhn), then the Gestapo offered the troops best suited for the war on the home front. Its members were few and had been selected, for the most part, from agents of the secret police forces already in place under the Empire and the Weimar Republic. Now they were reorganized under young, new, highly trained Nazi chiefs.[76] Between 1933 and 1936, the different secret police forces were merged into the single entity of the Gestapo, considered to be the vanguard of the Nazi home front.

Werner Best, a lawyer, helped to design the organization and acted as its leader.[77] In his words, the Gestapo's mission was to fight against all "attacks on the state and the people." To be sure, it was not the first secret police force in the history of Germany—Best, who had a solid grasp of this historical background, cited the secret police of Metternich and the Deutscher Bund, the armed wing of the Restoration, notably after the Carlsbad Decrees of 1819. But, he added, the police forces of kings and princes "defended formal domination, and not a living idea," as was the case now.[78] Like an army, the Gestapo had to be empowered to act on its own initiative, rather than docilely waiting for an attack to strike: "More important than the repression of offenses already committed is their prevention." Indeed, "an act of high treason, once it has been committed, already signifies the death of the state."[79]

For this reason, all constraints had to be removed from the Gestapo's power to take action. "To uphold its mission, it must be able to apply means adapted to the ends it has set for itself, and this independent of all constraint." As he did in all his writing, Best recalled that the decree of February 28, 1933, suspended "until further notice" all basic rights accorded by Weimar's individualist-liberal constitution. At a deeper level, he pointed out the absurdity of any normative oversight for police action: "Using the law to impose norms on the means the secret police are empowered to employ is no more possible than it is to predict and describe each and every type of enemy attack on the state or every danger that may threaten the state in the future."[80]

Best, the lawyer, was demanding that the secret police be placed above the law, that they be granted exceptional status in relation to other state institutions. Fundamentally, he explained, there were two institutions that were free from the rules of common law—the two institutions at war with the enemies of the people and the state: the police and the army.

All state entities—with the exception of the army and the secret police—must absolutely work within the framework of firm and enduring legal structures, in order to avoid the weakening and the dismembering of the entire state apparatus. Only the Wehrmacht, which is fighting against the enemy abroad, and the Gestapo, which is fighting the enemy at home, must be free from these constraints so that they can carry out their mission.[81]

In the absence of a priori norms, how could one be sure that the secret police would do its job? Best believed that "the attentive selection of personnel" combined with "strict discipline and self-control within the corps" would guarantee competence, appropriate behavior, and quality. All this was crowned with "a bond of personal loyalty to the command" of the police and of the state, a long and quasi-feudal administrative chain that led straight to the Führer himself. And the Führer, as we have seen, could never be wrong, because he always acted in accordance with the laws of History—nature, in other words—with constant devotion to his people and their interests. These, then, were the foundational principles of "this new and unique type of protective body for the state."[82]

The Gestapo, in its essence and its mission, revealed the changes under way in the police force in general, according to Best. In a work titled *Die deutsche Polizei* (The German police), Best, as Höhn had, reminded his readers that "the bourgeoisie's 'liberal' understanding" had reduced the "prevention of dangers" described in the *Preussisches Allgemeines Landrecht* and by the Law of 1931 to the mere "role of night watchman."[83] They had been made into well-meaning guardians of the sleep and the interests of bourgeois liberals who cared only for their cozy privacy. Best, with striking pedagogical clarity, sought in this and in other texts to lay a new theoretical groundwork for the role of the police. At root, he wrote, two different and opposing anthropologies, two "ideas of life," had given rise to two opposing definitions of man, the group, and group regulation—and therefore also of the police.[84] The first was the "individualist-humanist" definition. It posited that the "unique individual is the highest life value," and that anything opposing "the preservation and the development" of this individual was "immoral."[85] Since all of "these individuals have the same value and are independent of one another," then "above them no vital human phenomenon [exists] that could be superior to them. Only the arithmetic sum of all of these individuals, which we call humanity, exists." This humanity had been held up as a "nebulous and controversial governing ideal." In this understanding of beings and things, the state was a mere creation of individual wills, freely assembled. Such a state's goal was thus "to protect, to encourage, and to preserve . . . the individuals participating in it."[86] They participated through the law, which expressed their will and their freedom. In such a context it was easy to see how "the legality of police activity would be subject, completely logically and with no exceptions, to the control of judicial authority."[87] The laws governing police action had been designed as a protective barrier, behind which individuals could move freely.

In opposition to this liberal understanding, Best described the contours and internal logic of a definition based on a "racial understanding." According to this understanding, the "people is the reality of human existence"—a people understood not in the terms of the French Revolution, but as "an entity that transcends individual people and has endured through time, an entity defined by a unity of blood and spirit." It was the "people"—as a whole—that was "the supreme life value." Not the individual—not the part, in other words. Anything that was a danger to the people's "preservation and development" was "immoral" and against the law. "All inferior life values, including individuals, must be subordinate to the preservation of this supreme life value. If necessary, they must be sacrificed to it."[88] In this context, "what is traditionally designated by the name of 'state' . . . is the group of institutions . . . through which the racial order is concretely implemented and serves the preservation and the development of our people's strength."[89] Among these institutions, at their forefront, the police ensured "the protection of the racial order against obstruction and destruction."[90]

Because "law" designated what was good for the people, Best rejected the liberal-humanist understanding of it, which confused "law" with "laws" and qualified as "a-legal, even illegal" anything that occurred outside the bounds of those laws. Now, at last, society could breathe again:

> The will of those commanding us, no matter what form its expression takes—be it a law, an order, a decree, a circumstantial order, a

general mission, a regulation regarding the organization and the attribution of competencies, etc.—this will creates law and abrogates
the preexisting law.[91]

Best, as a lawyer, tirelessly repeated this foundational idea of the
"racist-authoritarian state": "The precedence of laws as the source of
the law, which goes hand in hand with democratic-parliamentary control of legislation," coupled with judicial oversight to ensure that legislation was respected, very luckily no longer existed. Now "the will
of the supreme commander of the Reich is legislator"—and the police
had been set free.[92] The police could cast off the yoke of norms, rules,
and limits that had reined in its commitments and its action. Best
gratefully cited the decrees of March 18 and October 22, 1938, which
had defined the jurisdiction of the German police in territories annexed
by the Reich in 1938 (Austria and the Sudetenland). By these decrees,
"the *Reichsführer* SS and Chief of the German Police in the Reich Ministry of the Interior is empowered to take all necessary measures to
maintain safety and preserve order, even outside of the limits habitu-
ally set by the law."[93] In this way German police activity was completely unconstrained by borders (*Grenzen*), limits, or distinctions
(*Trennungen*), either geographical or legal.

The end of the distinction between public and private meant that a
person's (formerly inner) self belonged to him no more than his body did.
An article of the Heimtückegesetz, or Treachery Act, of December 20,
1934, specified: "all private declarations whose author knows or ought
to know that their utterance may be disseminated to the public are
considered public declarations."[94] Jokes about Goering's waistline or
Hitler's sexuality were potentially the business of the police, even
when made in the privacy of one's own home.

Best insisted on the legality of any action committed in compliance
with orders given by the Reich Oberste Führung (supreme command):
"The police are never acting outside the law or illegally when they
follow the rules set by their superiors—and this goes all the way to the
supreme command." The orders of the Oberste Führung "regulate and
link police action. So long as the police accomplish the will of their
command, they are acting in compliance with the law." If ever an

"agent of the police" overstepped that will, "he is no longer acting as a member of the police and . . . is guilty of professional misconduct."[95] Eichmann's argument that orders were orders may have dumbfounded the public at his trial in Jerusalem, but seen in this light, he was simply reciting regulatory catechism, making his words far less astonishing. From the theoretical and technical heights where they had been placed, jurists and intellectuals like Best set the tone and the rules by which the new police force was to function—a police force whose members, it should be recalled, had mostly been employed by at least one and in many cases two other regimes, one an authoritarian empire and one a democracy.

Unlike Eichmann, however, Best was arguing for and grounding his understanding of public service as it was carried out by the police, the chain of command in which they carried it out, and the legality of the actions they undertook, in a way of thinking about the constitution that, while certainly rudimentary, was clear-cut and firm. When Best wrote that "without regard to form," the will of the Führer and its expression had the force of law, he was stating the theoretical and practical consequences of the Enabling Act of March 23, 1933, which gave full power to the Reich's cabinet to enact laws by decree. In practice, by this time the cabinet met only episodically, so that in effect the law meant that all legislation was a direct result of the Führer's will. From then on, the form taken by his will mattered very little. Best could indeed conclude his inventories with a disdainful "etc.": all that mattered was that the will be expressed. The Enabling Act and the Reich's legislative practice sealed the theoretical and practical fate of the hierarchy of norms:

> There is therefore no longer any distinction between stronger and weaker norms, no longer any difference between constitutional law and common law, rulings and decrees, public law and private law.[96]

Thanks to the theory and practice of National Socialist law, all *Trennungen* had been left behind: norms had returned to the fluid fusion and intermingling of the beginning. The question remained of the fairness of the decisions made by the Oberste Führung, and Best, eager to ground the new discourse and its new practices, took care to address it:

That the command's will sets the "right" rules—that is, the rules necessary for the action of the police . . . —is not a question of the law, but of destiny. A Constitutional Court cannot sanction the abuse of legislative competence by the leaders of a people . . . , but well and truly destiny itself: the violation of the laws of life is inevitably punished, before history, by misfortune and catastrophe.[97]

Whereas a superior court was limited to ruling over whether an act did or did not comply with a system of norms whose postulates and reasoning might be false, because they were unnatural, the acts of the Third Reich and its Führer would be judged by history itself. Since the Führer had understood the laws of history and gave orders to his police and armed forces, as well as his state, in accord with the laws of nature, destiny would crown his actions with success. Before, when the Leipzig Reichsgericht had found the police guilty of violating the law, they were satisfying formal "laws" but scorning the German people's right to life; therefore, "misfortune and catastrophe were inevitable." Germany was no longer under threat from any such danger.

Kriminalbiologie: The Science of Crime Fighting

The work of the police, who defended the people in its struggle for life, was grounded in the laws of life as studied by *Kriminalbiologie*. Criminal biology became a popular discipline in Europe at the end of the nineteenth century. With medical advances and the first discoveries in the nascent field of genetics, the public, influenced by growing preoccupations with hygiene and biology and the rising popularity of social Darwinism, grew more and more interested in using science to answer social and criminal questions. The positivist age, in which taxonomies proliferated and living things were subject to conditioning and even to determinism, sought to diagnose and prognosticate on human and criminal matters.

Criminological positivists had high hopes that all this could be applied to their field. To this end, in Germany as in other Western countries, the field of *Kriminalbiologie* emerged in synergy with eugenics research as well as more general medical research. The Kriminalbiologische Gesellschaft (Criminal Biology Society) was founded in 1927;

its members came from the political Left and Right and included both Jews and non-Jews. Indeed, in 1933 its membership fell from one hundred and sixty-six to sixty-eight, meaning that nearly a hundred of them had departed or been removed or rejected for political reasons— or for racial ones.[98]

Criminal biology, already popular before 1933, was now in the limelight. The Reichsgesundheitsamt (Reich Department of Health), which was part of the Ministry of the Interior, included a "criminal biology research division," of which Robert Ritter was appointed director in 1940. The following year, on December 21, 1941, Heinrich Himmler also named Ritter chief of the all-new Kriminalbiologisches Institut der Sicherheitspolizei (Criminal Biology Institute of the Secret Police). Ritter and his team were assigned the mission of "providing expertise and counsel to the authorities and the services of the secret police."[99] In practical terms, this meant that Ritter and his collaborators would, between January 1942 and January 1945, produce an array of reports and memoranda for the Reichsführer SS and the Ministries of Justice and the Interior as part of the long process of preparing a law against "elements foreign to the community" (*Gemeinschaftsfremde*), as well as help to set up filters and criminological classification systems for the children and teenagers held in the Moringen and Uckermark juvenile concentration camps. After examining their history, their genealogical makeup, and their physiology, the experts would divide the young people into different categories ("unfit," "disruptive," "situational failure," "structural failure," "provisionally reformable," "reformable"), which determined their fate: either they would be sent to rehabilitative camp, or, once they reached adulthood, to another concentration camp.[100]

Here Reinhard Höhn was expressing a central idea in Nazi criminal biology: "in our people, the dispositions of race necessarily determine an identity of thought, feeling, and action."[101] There was no better way to express the idea that any political *divergence*—at the cultural level—was perceived and dealt with as a matter of biological *deviance*—at the level of nature—or, more specifically, as the symptom or manifestation of an organic pathology in the symbolic order of language, culture, and cultural choice. Werner Best expanded on this idea in an article on the Gestapo in the journal *Deutsches Recht:*

The National Socialist principle of wholeness, which corresponds to our organic and indivisible vision of the unity of the German people, cannot tolerate the formation of any political will outside of our own political will. Any attempt to impose—or even to preserve—another understanding of things will be eradicated as a pathological symptom threatening the unity and the health of the national organism. . . . It is based on these principles that National Socialism has, for the first time in Germany, developed a secret police that we see as modern; that is, as meeting the needs of our times. We have designed it as an institution that carefully surveys the political health of the German body, discerns in a timely fashion any symptoms of illness, and identifies and eliminates germs of destruction, whether they originated in internal degeneracy or from intentional contamination by outsiders. This is the idea and the ethics of the secret police in the racist state of our time, led by the Führer.[102]

As an SS instructional manual put it: "A member of the SS and of the police is proud of his race. . . . He is a friend to all that is healthy and the foe of all degeneracy."[103] The principle of Kriminalbiologie as revisited by the police officers and legal experts of the Third Reich was simple: biological defects provoked legal wrongdoing. The cause (the defect) had to be induced empirically from the effect (the wrongdoing), but this induction simply followed the basic rules of science. As the jurist Günther Stier explained, "criminal law is based on the laws of life," so that "one time does not count": only a series could determine the probability of a crime, and the legitimacy of "safety measures" taken to prevent it.[104] Probability was the law of criminal law: statistical recurrence made it possible to formulate a diagnostic of biological criminality that provided a legitimate prognosis of probable or even certain recidivism. Otto Thierack, who was appointed minister of justice in 1942, explained the idea to German judges in these terms:

It is not necessary for the reprehensible acts . . . to be serious in and of themselves. It is sufficient for the criminal, through his repeated violations of the law, to have proven that his character is dangerous to the community. If he has violated the law repeatedly and consistently . . . , a single new violation, even if it cannot be counted as criminality of the gravest kind, suffices as the last straw to isolate the criminal from the community forever.[105]

Notions of probability and inclination, and even of biological determination in the most serious cases, were used as the foundations
for criminal law. They also justified the eugenicist legislation of July
and November 1933. The preamble to the law of July 14, 1933, indeed
specified that

> hereditary disease courts must examine genetic probabilities on a
> case-by-case basis and rule in favor of surgical intervention when, ac-
> cording to the experience of medical science, it can be expected
> with the highest probability that descendants will be afflicted by se-
> rious physical or psychological pathologies.[106]

Reasoning according to type (criminal, biological, and so on) made
it possible to de-individualize cases, to establish series, and to target
an individual for belonging to a broader population. Police work, when
seen as a form of science, made it possible to define types of criminals
and probabilities through observation, statistics, and inductions, and
thus to engage in a priori police action—or prevention (*Vorbeugung*).

This was the stance of the new chief of the OrPo (Ordnungspolizei), the "order police," a gigantic organization that centralized the
command of all uniformed police forces at the level of the Reich, with
Himmler as its chief, via a decree issued on June 17, 1936. That same year,
Kurt Daluege published a book titled *Nationalsozialistischer Kampf
gegen das Verbrechertum* (The National Socialist struggle against criminality). If its title had not been clear enough, its highly expressionist
cover (a common feature of such works) filled in the gaps: a virile and
powerful forearm strangled a serpent against a red background.

According to Daluege, everything was quite simple: "criminality
caused by distress" had been reduced and even eradicated by the Führer's
policy of national economic recovery.[107] In other words, in the new Germany it was no longer necessary to steal to survive, or to eat. All remaining criminality and delinquency were therefore due to biological
flaws or defects. If, in the past, some delinquency had been provoked by
distressing social conditions, and therefore the context might have softened the police or stayed the judge's hand, the police were now fighting
hardened criminals who were incapable of falling back into line and
living worthy lives, unable to live at peace with a prosperous community that could easily ensure their livelihood if only they chose to work.

These recidivists were really "professional criminals," and the police and justice system of the liberal state were powerless against them. Daluege, seeking to promote an image of police practice as highly scientific, pretended to select a file at random from the police archives. Over two densely written pages, he sketched out the career of a certain "Ernst G.," who, since his birth in 1890, had required "mountains of paper and rivers of ink" and mobilized hundreds of police officers, judges, and lawyers.[108] All for nothing: his life path, marked with multiple offenses, was ample proof of the failure of "individualist-liberal society" in the face of a "born criminal" whose character was utterly impossible to reform.[109] Daluege deplored the "forbearance of the state" and the "waste of public funds," which were all the more "unjustifiable with regard to other citizens" because the response of these institutions had turned out to be so useless.[110] Worse, with a "corrupt Marxist state"—the Weimar Republic—in power, crimes and misdemeanors had doubled or tripled, because this liberal regime, founded by the "November criminals" (of 1918), had represented the zenith of laxity and tolerance, based on individualism and the theory of environment and upbringing.[111]

Since 1933, anyone living a criminal life was clearly one of the "voluntarily asocial enemies of the people," the "dregs of humanity," who had to be fought harshly.[112] Contrary to what a person might believe was indicated by a return to civil tranquility, public order, and economic growth, Daluege argued that police intervention ought to be tougher, because now the police were up against the dense and unforgiving core of the criminal element:

> We are living in a state at war. With gritted teeth, we are building a new house, solid as steel, on the ruins and the ashes of the old state, a rotten state, that crumbled away. Our era is a harsh era. There is no place for tenderhearted sensibilities and for teary laments—and certainly not for those people who, through their own wrongdoing, have excluded themselves from the community of citizens ready and willing to rebuild our state.[113]

This criminality was the symptom of a degenerate biology and the product of rotten organic elements. It was also due to the "infection" caused by the arrival of "foreign immigrants . . . whose activity often contains the seeds of crime"—in particular, Daluege recalled the "highly deleterious influence of Jewish immigrants from the East arriving under the Weimar Republic."[114] In 1936, Daluege was echoing what Reinhard Heydrich, his counterpart at the *Sipo*, proclaimed in speech after speech and text after text: the nation could not let its guard down just because the communist and Social-Democratic opposition was now behind bars. It was precisely when the task seemed to be complete that it grew more complicated and more difficult, because the only enemies remaining on the field of battle were the most hardened ones. Heydrich and Himmler maintained this discourse throughout the Shoah, recommending over and over that the tempo of the Final Solution be accelerated as the physical disappearance of European Jewry became a reality. As time went on, they insisted, only the most dangerous remained, only those who had managed to survive. Faced with this "army of professional criminals," the police had but one goal: their "extermination."[115] The resources for this war of eradication were no longer lacking. Daluege first assumed that the police would be carefully screened. Where necessary, its personnel had been turned over in 1933, in order to limit "bureaucratic resistance" as much as possible. He himself had overseen the recruiting of "trustworthy National Socialist civil servants, who would be sweeping things out with an iron broom" by "throwing open the doors of a career in the police force to National Socialist veterans."[116] Overly socialist or liberal colleagues—potential saboteurs—were to be rapidly shown the door. As the author pointed out, it was a "purging of the police," which was "in this way rid of its unreliable elements."[117]

Once recruited, this new and motivated personnel had come up against an obsolete state rule, with its obsolete laws: "In order to apply our National Socialist principles, there was always an article of law missing. This is natural: the new spirit could not build on the old laws of the Weimar system." Against this old and harmful law, Daluege held up the "law of the *fait accompli*, of the National Revolution." January 30, 1933, by the very fact of its occurrence, had established a new political and legal order, which imposed itself de facto. From there, legal texts had followed to support and justify police interventions. In particular, Daluege expressed pride in the Reichstag Fire Decree of February 28, 1933, as well as the November 24, 1933, law against dangerous habitual criminals, which gave unlimited latitude to the police in their interventions. The Criminal Code of 1871 had not permitted "an energetic struggle against criminals." Article 42 of the Law of November 24, 1933, authorized the "unlimited detention for security reasons" of anyone the police deemed to be irremediably dangerous.[118]

The police could thus "act preventively, by averting crimes, which was not possible under the law before."[119] The old police force had been completely tied to the "principle of repression." Now "the principle of prevention and prophylaxis" was dominant: "The reprehensible acts of professional criminals should in a way be prevented in an a priori manner, mechanically."[120] This was possible through *Schutzhaft* and "preventive police detention" (*polizeiliche Vorbeugehaft*).[121]

Yet another absurd state of affairs was being brought to an end, one against which Daluege turned the full force of his irony. He harshly criticized those grotesque situations in which the police had to sit dutifully by and wait until a recidivist burglar committed a new infraction in order to snare him. It was impossible to apprehend notorious cat burglars even when you ran into them with crowbar in hand. Worse, and even more absurdly, the police were required to politely return the instruments of future offenses to their owners, since "no offensive action had yet been reported."[122]

Prevention and Eradication: *Schutzhaft,*
Vorbeugungshaft, and *Sippenhaft*

Among the weapons now at the police's disposal, Daluege was pleased about two procedures in particular: *Schutzhaft* (protective detention) and *Vorbeugungshaft* (preventive detention). During wartime, in addition to these, *Sippenhaft* (familial detention) became increasingly popular.

Schutzhaft had been an exceptional police measure introduced into Prussian law in the autumn of 1848, shortly after the revolutionary unrest of that same year. At the time, it was a legal means of detaining a person for his own safety and security by offering him the protection of the police and of a state penitentiary institution. In 1916, during the First World War, the procedure was made into a law, which specified that *Schutzhaft* was a police act that required judicial oversight. The detainee had to appear before a judge the day after his arrest. These restrictions disappeared in 1933. In the Reichstag Fire Decree of February 28, 1933, *Schutzhaft* was resoundingly upheld by Nazi legal experts and police officers, who removed all judicial oversight from it and left its application to the discretion of the police. The line between the police and the judiciary was blurred to the point of disappearing. This blurring is most evident in a single, significant detail: *Schutzhaft* orders were printed on mauve paper, which, before 1933, had been the color of judicial rulings.

The police had full discretion when it came to *Schutzhaft:* detention was not even subject to administrative oversight. It would make sense that a police procedure not subject to the oversight of the judiciary would fall to the competence of administrative judges, but this ambiguity was banished in Article 7 of the law of February 10, 1936, which specifically excluded *Schutzhaft* from the oversight of administrative courts.

The jurist Hans-Joachim Tesmer became a prosecutor in 1931, and was then appointed head of the Gestapo's *Schutzhaft* bureau. In 1936, he published a paean to "protective detention."[123] In it, he began with an overview of the justifications for this legal institution, whose utilization in Prussia he helped to oversee. In addition to the February 28, 1933, decree, which received reverential treatment in nearly every text of the era that discussed new police practices, Tesmer deftly cited Articles 14 and 15 of the Police Administration Act of June 1, 1931, which provided for "temporary detention by the police." Regarding the order of February 28, 1933, Tesmer, as so many others did, argued that the "communist peril" explicitly mentioned in its preamble more broadly designated any subversive activity that threatened the safety of the state, which offered the law infinite scope in its application. Not only open communists were targeted, but "any elements who, in their behavior, endanger the reconstruction work of the German people in a way that threatens the state and the people." With such solid backing, the police could go about their work of protecting the state and making use of "preventive police detentions," "the most effective arm against enemies of the state."[124]

The measure was "there above all to protect the people and the state against all activities infringing on their safety."[125] The pleasant fiction of an institution created to ensure "the protection of the detainee" had given way to the reality of a "political-police protective measure."[126] In other words, it was at once a political and a police measure, delivering defenseless individuals with no recourse to appeal or arbitration into detention at the entire discretion of the police: "Only those still dreaming of their liberal past will deem these measures too harsh, or even illegal." Such people, he argued, would do better to reflect on the principles that, since 1933, had become the bedrock of the German political community, and to accept that the individual was no longer the law's central concern, nor at the heart of the thinking and practices of the police. Certainly, *Schutzhaft* was a restrictive measure for the individuals it targeted as well as for the people in their lives, but "the advantages resulting for the community . . . far outstrip any inconveniences that may, depending on the situation, affect detainees and their families." It was not surprising, therefore, that *Schutzhaft* had been "welcomed and appreciated by a large portion of our people," most likely the healthiest ones, "as the most effective means of protection" for the community of the people and its state.[127]

The prosecutor Tesmer, a member of the NSDAP and the SS, and now a *Dezernatleiter* (department chief) in the Gestapo, openly acknowledged that *Schutzhaft* was an adjunct to, and even circumvented, judicial sentencing. It was well known that "undertakings hostile to the state cannot be combated through provisions in criminal law alone." The phrasing was sibylline, but suggestive of what had become commonplace in Germany since 1933: the Gestapo often waited outside of courtrooms to arrest defendants who had been discharged or too lightly sentenced by the justice system. The same thing happened at prisons: the Gestapo could, "when necessary, declare safety measures" be taken against a prisoner who had completed his sentence, sending him directly from prison to a concentration camp.[128] That this "safety detention" was double jeopardy was openly accepted and acknowledged by jurists and the police. Anyone who had committed an offense was liable, by predisposition or biological determination, to commit another one. To protect the community of the people and the state, such people should be apprehended and removed from the community.

The logic of *Schutzhaft* was extended through *Sicherungsverwah-*
rung (security confinement), which was instituted by the Gewohnheits-
verbrechergesetz (Law against Dangerous Habitual Criminals) of
November 24, 1933. Article 42 of this law allowed judges, "if public
safety requires it," to aggravate the sentence of a recidivist to separate
him from the *Volksgemeinschaft* for as long as possible. Although it
derogated from common law and from the legal heritage of the Weimar
Republic, this provision had nevertheless been requested by criminal
law reformers for decades, because it was seen as translating scientific teaching into law: anyone who had committed repeated and reprehensible acts was a nonreformable "habitual criminal" to be treated
as a biological threat. In 1941, the law was modified to give judges
recourse to the death penalty in extremely serious cases, and "if the
protection of the community of the people or the need for fair expiation require it."

This "biologization" of the law also produced *Vorbeugungshaft*. A
decree issued on November 13, 1933, gave police officers the right to
arrest as a "career criminal" any person considered to be a potential
recidivist, and therefore likely to strike again, and to send them to a
concentration camp. In March 1937, Himmler launched a broad sweep
of *Berufsverbrecher* (professional criminals). A year later, in spring
1938, he ordered that the German police target "asocials" and *Volks-*
fremde, outsiders or "aliens to the community of the people," that is,
individuals who, because of their vices and their laziness, required a
term in a concentration camp to be brought back in line. This "action
against those unwilling to work" (*Aktion Arbeitsscheu Reich*) followed
a "Basic Decree on the Fight to Prevent Criminality" signed by Himmler
on December 14, 1937. In it, the police chief clarified the provisions of
the November 1933 decree, giving the police carte blanche to arrest "professional or recidivist criminals," and, more generally, any harmful or
useless individuals susceptible to falling into this category. Although it
was used to justify occasional intervention, starting in 1939, the decree
evolved into a more generalized and systematic law, debated over by legal
experts and the police until the end of the war.

Last in this series of new police measures were *Sippenhaf-*
tung (shared responsibility of family or clan) and *Sippenhaft* (family

detention), which were invoked more and more frequently starting in 1943–1944. This signaled the final break with the common law of the past and a full embrace of the biological view of the delinquent and criminal. Himmler had no trouble justifying them, both in terms of the founding principles of so-called Germanic law and in biological terms. *Treue* (loyalty) was so intense for Germanic peoples that, when a man fell, the state—that is, the community of the people—stepped in to help his grieving family. They received help because they had had the honor of counting a hero among their ranks. Himmler also argued that war heroes ought to be compensated with gifts of land, from which their entire families could benefit. Reciprocally, "it is old German practice that the family and the clan be held responsible for each of its members. . . . If one of its members commits treason, and if the clan cannot prove that he has been excluded from their ranks, then the family is considered to share in the responsibility," he explained in a speech delivered six days after the July 20, 1944, attempt to assassinate Hitler.[129] *Sippenhaftung* and *Sippenhaft* were completely logical from a biological standpoint. On August 3, 1944, exactly fourteen days after the attack on the Führer, Himmler described the fates of traitors and their families:

> I shall create absolute familial responsibility. . . . All you have to do is read the Germanic sagas. When . . . familial vengeance was exacted, it was consequential, limitless. . . . They said: this man is a traitor, his blood is bad, it is traitor's blood, it must be eradicated. And this is how vengeance exterminated the entire family, down to the last of its members. The Stauffenberg family will be obliterated down to the last of its members.[130]

On July 25, still reeling from the shock of the attack on the Führer, Himmler declared at Grafenwöhr:

> Read the ancient sagas! When someone perjured himself or committed treason, the clan was captured, on the grounds that their blood was bad. If it had produced a scoundrel, then something was wrong with the blood. And so, it was eradicated.[131]

Goebbels agreed with this idea. An entry in his *Journals* dated October 3, 1944, reads, "I believe that the elimination of this tainted blood from the body of the German people will, in the long term, have only beneficial effects."[132] The blood of the traitors of July 20 was guilty blood. The same was true for other traitors, notably deserters. A successful deserter could be tried and condemned only in absentia. To compensate for this inconvenience, Hitler and the high command imagined a dissuasive measure that would lessen the temptation to cross over: *Sippenhaftung* for deserters' families. In November 1944, the army discontinued court martials for desertion cases and handed them over to the RSHA (Reichssicherheitshauptamt, or Reich Main Security Office). The order, signed by Wilhelm Keitel, specified that

> the family of a deserter who has been found guilty by a military tribunal according to form must answer for the guilty party's crime with its possessions, its freedom, or its life. It is the Reichsführer SS and the chief of German police who determine the scope of this responsibility on a case-by-case basis. To this end, files are to be transmitted to the RSHA without delay.[133]

Little by little, not only deserters were put to death, but also soldiers who had simply lost their way (*Versprengte*). There were more and more of the latter as combat became increasingly violent and the Wehrmacht's combat units fell apart at an accelerating rate.[134] In the shock of an attack, Wehrmacht regiments often scattered, leaving their dazed members to wander behind enemy lines. Considered to be deserters, *Versprengte* and their families were to be treated according to the provisions of the abovementioned decree, signed on November 19, 1944.

In the end, *Sippenhaftung* was expanded to include not only deserters and those considered as deserters, but German prisoners of war as well, or, as the text of the order specified, soldiers of the Wehrmacht captured by the enemy without having proven "to have fought to the very end," that is, until death, which quite logically, did exclude the possibility of capture by the enemy: "The community of worthy and courageous soldiers excludes them from their midst. Their families are responsible for them. Any payment of pensions or benefits is suspended."[135]

Combating Homosexuality

Demands for recognition and commemoration by the community have
led to the extensive revisiting of Nazi attitudes toward homosexuality
in recent years.[136] Nazi repression of homosexuals and the virulence
of its homophobia were undeniable, but they touched only German or
"Germanic" (when it was soldiers in the Waffen-SS) homosexuals. Elsewhere, foreign homosexuals were never targeted, arrested, and de-
ported as homosexuals, but rather as members of the resistance, as
Jews, or for other offenses. Nazis had nothing particularly original to
say about homosexuality. They repeated the anathemas and epithets
of their contemporaries, which were drawn from passed-down norms.
For them, there was no need to revise the words of the infamous paragraph 175 of the 1872 Criminal Code, which defined homosexuality
as "an anti-natural vice" (*Widernatürliche Unzucht*). Nevertheless,
until the criminal law reform of 1935, homosexual acts and intentions
had been misdemeanors (*Vergehen*). After 1935, they were crimes
(*Verbrechen*).

Nazi discourse, with its rhetoric of genesis and its vetting of origin and provenance, did nevertheless develop an original theory of
homosexuality's source. For Josef Meisinger, the director of the "Central Department for the Repression of Homosexuality and Abortion"
of the Reich Ministry of the Interior, homosexuality was "Asiatic
in origin." Like the Jews, the plague, and rats, it, too, came from
the East: "From its original infection site in the Orient, it spread to the
Greeks and the Romans, and then, ultimately, to the Germanics. We
observe in the geography of this propagation that homosexuality is
biologically foreign to the Nordic race." This "plague on the race"
owed much to Christianity, for it could be observed that "monastic
life and homosexuality . . . are phenomena that have been linked for
centuries."[137]

Once again, the shadow of an argument repeated elsewhere may be
observed here. Generally, except in deeply degenerate, diseased individuals, homosexuality was a kind of default sexuality, emerging when
nothing else was possible: hence its presence in single-sex communities or in situations of manifest demographic imbalance between the
two sexes. For this reason, government officials showed little concern

for lesbianism. Since the First World War, the female sex had been so overrepresented in the population that the overwhelming majority of sapphic relationships could be attributed to "women's sexual distress." These women were in fact "anything but abnormal" and their activity could be described as a kind of collective onanism. Women's biological condition willed them to bear children, and so the voice of nature would, if given the chance, quickly make itself heard again: "If these young women have the opportunity to return to the task assigned to them by nature, generally they do not fail to do so."[138] Give them men, and lesbians would return to their better sentiments and sexualities, in keeping with nature's decrees. Theirs was a simple case: Himmler recommended that the militarization of girls be ceased in order to avoid their becoming excessively virile and slipping into homosexuality. In a famous speech at Bad Tölz, the SS chief declared:

> To me it is a catastrophe to see young girls and women marching through the countryside, with their impeccable bags on their backs. It makes me nauseated. It is a catastrophe to see women's organizations, communities, and circles take up activities that destroy all feminine seduction, distinction, and charm. It is a catastrophe that . . . we are transforming women into logical beings, that we are training them for and in everything, that we are masculinizing them so that, over time, the difference between the sexes, the polarity, is blurred. From there, the path to homosexuality is not too far off.[139]

Women were malleable, vulnerable, and close to nature; their sexuality followed its rules so long as they could find men and so long as society and the state did not play at making them into tomboys. For these reasons, lesbianism was not a Nazi preoccupation. This was all the more true because of the war, which had increased the population imbalance between the sexes, making the loss of a few women along the way an acceptable thing. The same was not true of men. Because there were more than enough women, a male homosexual was necessarily someone whose sickness was extreme and whose convictions were staunch. Treatment and rehabilitation were a possibility for the more benign cases, but the rest had to be totally eradicated from the German body. Only from the German body, it should be noted: Slavic,

Jewish, or French homosexuals did not bother the SS at all; to the contrary, since their existence diminished the reproductive capacity of those populations. A "dangerous and infectious plague," the "crime" of homosexuality was "punished by death" in the SS, since "all members of the SS and the German police are on the front lines of the struggle we are waging for the eradication of homosexuality among the German people."[140] This struggle was being waged without anger, without hatred, without any particular feeling at all, Himmler declared. Eugenic purging was to be carried out with the quiet tranquility of a gardener tending his plants:

> For our ancestors . . . these few cases represented the very definition of abnormality. Homosexuals, known as *Urning*, were drowned in the marshes. . . . It was not a punishment, but simply a matter of eliminating an abnormal life. It had to be removed, just as we pull out nettles and throw them in a pile to be burned. There was no vengeance there: the person in question simply had to disappear. That is what our ancestors did. For us, unfortunately, this is no longer possible.[141]

Who could blame a nettle for being a nettle? To weed it out angrily was nonsense: nature and human survival simply required that it be uprooted.

In Nazi discourse, the question of homosexuality was always linked to procreation. The "homosexual problem" was always presented in a coldly statistical light, a calmly arithmetical issue of demographic risk. In his speech on the subject at Bad Tölz, Himmler expressed his worry in percentages: "If I start with the assumption that there are two million homosexuals in Germany, that brings us to 7 to 10 percent of German men. This means that, if we do nothing, our people will die of this epidemic." Homosexuality limited procreation, undermined the German people's biological substance, and endangered its existence and its power as a group. "Some people say to us, what I do is no one's business, it is my affair, my private life. No: anything relating to sexuality is not a private matter, but signifies the life or death of a people; world power or insignificance."[142]

The same was true of abortions. It was no coincidence that Meisinger's services within the Ministry of the Interior dealt with both the "repression of homosexuality and abortion": both of them had the same demographic consequences. They were, at root, an identical crime against the race.

The Struggle against "Asocials"

Starting in 1939, the struggle against "asocials" (*Asoziale*), more and more frequently referred to as "alien to the community" (*Gemein-schaftsfremde*), was inflected by the context of the war. Because of the circumstances and the immediate threat to the existence of the German nation and race, this struggle became a fight to the death.[143] This was the attitude championed by the Reich's new minister of justice, Dr. Otto Thierack, a jurist by training and a prosecutor by profession. In a "brief to judges" (*Richterbrief*), of which more than ten thousand copies were printed, Thierack offered a kind of memorandum on the meaning of the war. The "brutal harshness" required of judges with regard to "profes-sional criminals" was a "debt to our people and the best of our sons, the ones who are putting their life on the line and sacrificing it" for Ger-many.[144] Thierack was echoing Hitler's obsession with social Dar-winism: in his public and private discourse, the Führer deplored the counter-selective role of a war that had shed the best blood of the bravest men, while villains and scoundrels, both behind bars and living as free men, prospered and reproduced back at home. Criminal policy, through the ordered decimation of criminals, should offer the possi-bility of restoring the balance between the good and the bad. Thierack, former president of the Volksgerichtshof, was just as preoccupied as the Führer with the biologically harmful effects of war:

> Every war necessarily provokes a counter-selection. While the most precious blood is sacrificed on the field of battle, the degenerate de-linquent, inferior from a social and biological point of view . . . cannot expect the community to tolerate him in its midst any longer. His exclusion is really a commandment dictated by the preservation of the people's value. In this measure, the exercise of criminal law thus carries out a task of racial hygiene, that of the continuous purifica-tion of the body of the people, so that the bad elements do not end up drowning out the good. In accordance with the mission the Führer has assigned the justice system, which consists of deploying the most

radical means against traitors, saboteurs, dangerous pests, violent
criminals, and asocial professional criminals, the number of death
sentences has constantly risen since the beginning of the war.[145]

Criminal law as it was conceived of after 1933 was a kind of warfare;
the brutality and deadliness required of it were even greater because of
the need to compensate for the biologically disastrous effects of the war
with the outside. Thus, Thierack wrote in his brief to judges, "the war,
which has destroyed so much of our best blood, cannot leave the asocial
criminal untouched." National Socialism and the war had "changed the
nature of our criminal law," the minister reiterated: since 1933, and even
more since 1939, it was no longer intended to "carefully protect citizens'
freedoms," but rather "to protect the community of the people," a
"principle that today stands at the center of our criminal thought."[146]
The minister of justice did not mince words in explaining the judges'
task to them: "Already in peacetime, the professional criminal who repeatedly attacked our community of the people was a parasite on its
body. In wartime, he is dangerous, and a domestic saboteur."[147] Here,
both registers were being mobilized: the martial one—criminals were
traitors who undermined the rear—and the biological one: they were
parasites. The conclusion was unavoidable: "The legislator has drawn
the necessary conclusions from this, and given judges the means to wage
battle against professional criminals until the extermination of this
alien body within our community."[148] All of this was extremely coherent: Thierack cited the law of November 24, 1933, and alluded to the
law of July 14, 1933, explaining that "by undertaking this task, criminal
law is linked organically to the great fundamental laws of our National
Socialist state, those which assure the selection, the purification, and
the health of our people." This "racial-hygienic" purge was "a commandment dictated by the preservation of our people, and, in this way, a
commandment of justice itself."[149]

"Professional criminals" were only the tip of the asocial iceberg,
however. "Elements alien to the community" were generally subtle and
made up a category that was much more difficult to discern. While
"professional criminals" were excessively asocial, the majority of *Gemeinschaftsfremde* were people who had fallen into this state by de-

fault—for lack of work, of commitment, of involvement with the community of the people.

Starting in June 1941 and the beginning of the "great war in the East," there was intense and regular correspondence between the Ministry of Justice and the RSHA in view of drafting a "law regarding the treatment of aliens to the community." In this correspondence, the term *Asozial* was slowly replaced by that of *Gemeinschaftsfremd. Asozial* was a word with foreign roots, which, moreover, referred to "society," and therefore to an understanding of human community that the Nazis violently rejected. *Gemeinschaftsfremd* presented the dual advantage of being authentically German and of designating something that was "alien" to the "community," that is, the *Volksgemeinschaft,* the organic, biological, and natural entity that for the Nazis was the only appropriate definition of the human species. The hardline approach of the RSHA ultimately prevailed in these exchanges, to the great disappointment of Hans Frank, who was scandalized at the ways in which the planned legislation stripped the judiciary of its prerogatives and handed them over to the police.[150] He would explain this in April 1942 to the head of the Reich Chancellery, Heinrich Lammers, in a letter that signaled the beginning of his progressive marginalization.[151] In January of 1945, these exchanges between the RSHA and the Ministry of Justice finally produced a draft law that, because of its timing, was never signed or applied within the Reich, although many of its provisions had been enacted since 1940.

The first article of the draft law offered a broad definition of *Gemeinschaftsfremde:* "An alien to the community is anyone who, through his personality, his lifestyle, flaws in his understanding or in his character, demonstrates his inability to meet the minimum requirements of the community of the people."[152] The measures taken against them were typical of the Nazi arsenal of repressive practices in place since 1933. For the most part they were police measures (Article 2), and, secondarily, judicial ones (Article 3). Article 2 provided for measures, in regular use since 1937, of "police surveillance" and "incarceration in a police camp," a generic and sibylline formulation that included any repressive camp run by the *Schutzhaft.* The precedence of the police over the justice system in the order of the law's articles was a clear indication that "treatment" of "aliens to the community" had largely been removed from the jurisdiction of the courts.

The law targeted "irrecoverable asocials" (*unverbesserlich*), people who, despite the improvement of the economic situation, which had provided work for everyone, and while the community had been mobilized to fight a war for Germany's very survival, had remained criminal or useless. It was only natural to suspect that biological necessity had determined these people would become parasites or criminals: "The fact that someone has not taken up his proper role in the community of the people does not mean he is incapable of doing so. Before the taking of power, there were millions of them. Today, only a few remain."[153] These ferocious diehards could not be convinced to fall into the ranks of the *Volksgemeinschaft*, even with full employment and the improvement of Germany's social situation and general climate—and even in the face of repressive and dissuasive police intervention. While the majority of these people had been recovered thanks to general wellbeing, full employment, and rehabilitation, an incompressible "remainder" persisted. This group, "because of its disposition, is incapable of taking its place within the community."[154]

The draft legislation of January 1945 mentioned the term "tendency or propensity" (*Hang oder Neigung*) six times, and established the notion of *Neigungsverbrecher* (criminals by inclination). With biology in play, past illusions of criminal law (punish to reform) evaporated: it was necessary to lock away, to castrate, or to kill in order to protect the community of the people from the presence and the reproduction of these rotten elements. Any hope of "the individual's integration to his rightful place in the *Volksgemeinschaft*" was unrealistic.[155] Criminal law thus became criminal biology, as indicated in Article 4 of the draft law on "sterilization": "Elements alien to the community whose offspring are feared to be undesirable must be sterilized" according to the procedures and provisions of "the law for the prevention of genetically diseased offspring of July 14, 1933," an "application by analogy" (*sinngemässe Anwendung*) in the draft law.[156]

The logic of the laws on euthanasia and pathological heredity was in this way mapped onto criminal law. In the preamble to the law of 1945, Paul Werner, former prosecutor, SS member, and director of the

"VA" bureau (here "V" is the Roman numeral five) of the RSHA, wrote that the various "Weimar governments failed when faced with elements alien to the community of the people. They did not use the findings of the science of heredity and of criminal biology to lay the groundwork for a healthy . . . criminal policy." Blinded by their "liberal ideas," they "never saw anything but the 'rights' of the individual," whereas, "for National Socialism, the individual is nothing when the community is at stake."[157] Undesirable elements had to be understood in terms of their "specific biological and genetic constitution," and treated accordingly.[158] Warner, basing his argument on empirical studies in criminal biology, remarked that these elements "in their vast majority belong to families known . . . to the police and the law." As the biological and genetic nature of the flaws targeted by the draft legislation had been more than proven, it should now be possible to "sterilize elements alien to the community if their offspring are feared to be undesirable." This diagnosis and "this decision must be ruled on by the hereditary health courts" established by the law of July 14, 1933.[159] The Nazis' rulings claimed to be based on "studies that prove the consistency of an incapacity to live in a community over ten generations."[160] Here they were citing the work of Robert Ritter, in particular his "genetic studies" of "the descendants . . . of vagabonds, crooks, and thieves," published in 1937 with the pithy title *Ein Menschenschlag* (One breed).[161]

In a 1940 speech, Walter Gross, the head of the NSDAP *Rassenpolitischen Amtes*, explained at length that the flaws of asocial individuals could no longer be seen as "damages caused by the [social and familial] environment." To the contrary, alcoholism, laziness, pimping, and delinquency were "exclusively familial and hereditary in nature." It was therefore necessary to break with "the day before yesterday's ideas"— especially since, in wartime, it was unthinkable that useless and harmful individuals would continue to shirk their obligations with regard to their life in the community, particularly those of "work" and of "military service," while "healthy German men are increasingly mobilized by the war and taken from work, family, and reproduction." Nourishing and supporting these asocials had to cease; they were useless mouths, harmful in their uselessness and even in their very existence. The "professionally unemployed, as may be said," had always found well-meaning fools to help them.[162]

One time, it was the Catholic organizations, one time, the Protestant organizations . . . , the province, the mayor, the councilor. It
didn't matter who, there was always someone who paid for them, and
who did it willingly, because it was a duty of humanity, and this is
how, until now, they passed through the net.[163]

Once again, yesterday's—or "the day before yesterday's"—ideas
were the enemies of National Socialist regeneration: "sentimentalism,
as well as obtuse moral conceptions alien to life" had to make way for
science, for this "ongoing progress punctuated by knowledge of the phenomena of the biology of heredity."[164] Gross argued that it was vital to
break with "the crap" of the past:

In every poorhouse in Germany, you find those people of whom you
say, "Well, all right, they cost a lot of money, but we are doing our
best to reform them and put them back on the straight and narrow."
But we, we are saying, "In the name of heaven, why?" . . . And here,
someone answers: "Yes, you're right, the father is deplorable, but
maybe the child inherited valuable dispositions from the mother that
must be saved." My dear friends, this is nonsense.[165]

Two things are necessary: First, to energetically collar asocial individuals. This is the job of the police. Second, to ensure that these
asocial elements do not produce any new ones. . . . This is a necessary biological measure, no longer only a police measure. These elements must be excluded from genetic transmission.[166]

Nipping the Revolution in the Bud

Traumatized by the Great War and by the November Revolution, Nazi
leaders were obsessed by the insurrectional context of 1917–1918. Everything, in their eyes, had to be done to maintain the bond between the
front lines and the rear, and, even more than that, between the people
and the power, since the disconnect between the two had been a key
feature of the revolutionary situation in 1918. An organized pillaging
of Europe was thus undertaken in order to prevent all risk of famine
and discontent. On top of this, repressive, prophylactic executions were
organized of leaders held in concentration camps since 1933 in cases
where unrest or the military situation gave reason to fear an opportunity for insurrection.

As early as 1934, the Nazi leadership began nipping in the bud even the vaguest possibility of attempted revolution: the elimination of the SA hierarchy, whose ambition had been to absorb the Reichswehr, much to the displeasure of its general command, was an indispensable step in the construction of an army capable of waging war on a large scale. On July 3, 1934, a remarkably laconic normative text justified and extended legal immunity to the perpetrators of the murders committed during the Night of the Long Knives and the days that followed it. The "law on measures necessitated by state safety," which Hitler, Frick (minister of the interior) and Gürtner (minister of justice) signed on July 3, 1934, had only one article. Retroactively, it declared that the acts perpetrated "on June 30 and July 1 and 2, 1934," were not illegal: these "measures, necessitated by the peril threatening the state, were fully justified by the law." Murdering SA officers in their sleep and killing Schleicher in his own home in front of his wife became "measures" taken to "suppress highly treasonous and treasonous attacks against our country."[167]

Hitler himself delivered an exegesis of this brief text in a long speech to the Reichstag on July 13, 1934, which was intended as much for the German citizenry as it was for the NSDAP, who might have been surprised or upset by the massacre of so many *alte Kämpfer*, including Ernst Röhm himself. Hitler justified the force of his reaction with three series of arguments. The first was based on the urgency of the situation, for "only a pitiless and bloody intervention might still make it possible to nip the revolt in the bud and to avoid its propagation." To save order, the state, and the nation, "lightning-fast action" was required. Second, Hitler continually pointed to Röhm's "betrayal" of the Nazi movement, Germany, and the Führer all at once, although Hitler had been his superior and his friend: "He betrayed me, and only I could hold him to account." With a few transparent allusions to "the life that the head of the general command and a circle that had come together around him had begun to lead," a life "intolerable in the eyes of our National Socialist understanding" that "violated all of the laws of dignity and an honorable attitude," Hitler also drew attention to the fact that homosexuals such as Röhm, as well as "Ernst, in Berlin, Heines, in Silesia, Heinz, in Saxony, Heinebrecht, in Pomerania," who shared this "disposition" with Röhm, had been violating the moral laws of Nazism, which condemned this unnatural behavior with the utmost firmness. Finally, Hitler had had to swiftly combat treason, which he qualified as mutiny. That SA units had (allegedly) been placed in a state of alert on the evening of June 30, 1934, was, according to Hitler, clear indication of "sedition": "A mutiny! For it is I, and I alone, who am the Supreme leader of the SA," and therefore the only one authorized to give such an order. And "today we are shattering mutiny following the same iron laws of yesteryear": "For all time, mutinous divisions have been recalled to order through decimation."

The harshest possible reaction was all the more necessary given Germany's recent history, which provided evidence of the danger of inaction. Here, again, the memory of 1918 was invoked: "There is only one state that did not apply its military code, and died from it: Germany," the Germany of Wilhelm II, who had not been able to nip sedition in the bud and had allowed subversion to propagate. These words, which came at the end of the speech, echoed those of its opening, in which Hitler recalled the experience of the front and its collapse, which he claimed to share with the members of the Reichstag: "We all suffered from this terrible tragedy, when, as obedient soldiers faithful to our duty, we suddenly faced the revolt of rioters," "true rapists of the nation," which an authority aware of its responsibility ought to have had massacred without any other form of trial. This was exactly what the Führer had done:

> I did not wish to expose our young Reich to the fate of the old one. . . .
> The nation must know that anyone who threatens its existence—
> guaranteed by inner order and security—will be punished! And in
> the future, everyone must know that if he raises his hand against the
> state, he will die.[168]

It went without saying that in such circumstances, there was little recourse to law and the judiciary: emergency constrained, necessity commanded, danger obliged. Declaring that he was "responsible for the fate of the German nation," the Führer proclaimed himself its "supreme judge," of first and last appeal, handing down orders that saved the whole by sacrificing a few rotten parts.

The speech said everything there was to say, and Carl Schmitt's oft-cited article about it adds very little. It merely shows that one of Germany's greatest legal experts was in full agreement with the Führer, who, as the title of the article stated, was "protecting the law." Schmitt's argument was based on his already well-known study, published thirteen years prior, in 1921, of dictatorial power: the "Führer protects the law" by derogating from it, a paradoxical but simple mechanism that had proven effective since ancient Rome. Schmitt, however, went a step further than the Roman *Caveant consules*, affirming that even outside of moments of great danger, "the true Führer is also simultaneously judge. From the quality of Führer results the quality of judge."[169] "Anyone who pretends to separate or oppose the two makes the judge into a counter-Führer or an instrument in the hands of a counter-Führer," a harmful separation of powers that would lead to "the destruction of the law and the state." The Führer—and everything in National Socialist culture proved this—fought ceaselessly for the life of the German people. He therefore always acted in accord with the law, as "all law is derived from the law of the life of the German people."[170] The rest was not law, but "a positivist interlacing of norms," something jurists would do well to realize: "We must not hold ourselves blindly to legal concepts, to arguments, and to jurisprudence that were left to us by an obsolete and diseased era."[171]

Once the Röhms and the Schleichers had been eliminated, once the NSDAP's left-wing internal opposition had been decapitated and potential opposition from the national-conservatives had been warned, a second wave of police prophylaxis targeted all of the potential Karl Liebknechts and Rosa Luxemburgs remaining in Germany. Starting on September 1, 1939—the date the war began—*Schutzhäftlinge* could no longer be freed. Hardened communists and potential leaders could no longer leave their prisons or camps. The goal was to keep these elements under lock and key in order to kill them off if the situation required it: there would never have been a "November Revolution" if its leaders had been prevented from acting by the army and government of Wilhelm II. Hitler repeated this quite often to his tablemates:

> The domination of subhumans in 1918 can be explained by the fact that, on the one hand, four years of war had bled away the nation's best forces at the front, while, at the rear, criminals were being cossetted. The death penalty was, so to speak, no longer executed. The

prison doors had only to be opened for the revolution to find its leaders. I instructed the Reichsführer SS that in cases where unrest might be feared, the concentration camps should be cleaned out and all of that hoi polloi be executed. That way, we will be rid of all the leaders.[172]

This was one of the many meanings of the promise that Hitler made on September 1, 1939: "Never again in German history will there be a November 1918." The prophecy might have meant that there would be no more defeat, or no more capitulation, or then again, no more German revolution. On the twentieth anniversary of the Munich Beer Hall Putsch, Hitler reiterated his promise:

> I do not know if there are any Germans hoping for an Allied victory. . . . Perhaps a few criminals, who believe they will get an easier living out of it. But there can be no doubt that we will settle accounts with all of these people. What happened in Germany in November 1918 will not happen again. In a time when sacrifices are demanded of hundreds of thousands of brave soldiers, we will not back down from the prospect of . . . sentencing a few hundred traitors to death, without any other form of trial.[173]

In a speech at Bad Tölz in February 1942, Himmler expressed his confidence in a people that had been regenerated and purified. Dangerous elements no longer existed, or were kept under lock and key, within shooting range where necessary:

> We can also let go of all fears of agitation within Germany. Our people is no longer what it was in 1914–1919; it is a people which has experienced war as totality. And then, we have Adolf Hitler. In this decisive struggle, our rear is well guarded. The heart of our European citadel is clean: the SD will see to it.[174]

The trauma of 1918, as well as the vast damages wrought on Germany by the Red revolution, fully justified brutality against potential instigators. In application of the Führer's orders, putative revolutionaries were sent before the firing squad in the autumn of 1944, following on the heels of D-Day, the July 20 assassination attempt, and the crumbling of the Army Group Center. And so Ernst Thälmann, who had been held in a concentration camp since the spring of 1933, was transferred to Buchenwald, where he was murdered by the SS on August 18, 1944. On October 11, 1944, at Sachsenhausen, the toll climbed even higher: twenty-seven high-ranking communist leaders were put to death.

CHAPTER SIX

The War Outside:
"Harshness Makes the Future Kind"

German Harshness

WHO WOULD HAVE the effrontery to reproach the German military for the way it fought? If the Germans were "harsh" it was because they had become that way over the course of their history, because of the events they had endured: "We, the National Socialists, have been accused of harshness . . . and our methods have been considered unworthy of the classical era of our cultural history."[1] But the German people, which had been "gullible, magnanimous, on the inside were the most humane of peoples"—until they were attacked, lied to, and tricked. Then they became "morally determined, harsh, and pitiless . . . , defiant of pretty words said to them by outsiders, disdainful of promises, and cold, resolute in the defense of their vital rights, the very ones over which they were being challenged."[2] As might be expected, it had been "over there, at Versailles . . . , that everything began": "It was at this moment that the most tender among us became harsh."[3] This "harshness was born of suffering. Our harshness is the moral attitude of a people that for too long has lived in the realm of ideas," while its neighbors burnished their weapons and filled their granaries. The good old German yokel, easygoing and paternal, had had his eyes opened: "Our harshness is the iron armor of a man under attack. Behind this armor beats a sensitive heart, but we know how to keep it quiet when people think they can profit politically from our kindness."[4]

What moral code, what code of honor, should be followed in this extreme and terrible war? Albrecht Hartl offered his advice and life lessons in various writings for the Wehrmacht and the Waffen-SS. Collected in two volumes, these heavily edifying little sermons used and abused ponderous generalizations to teach combat soldiers the virtues of Nordic man and how not to become paralyzed by their conscience. Everything would go well if the soldier would only remember that "the laws of life, which express themselves in his blood, in nature, and in history, are the guidelines for his actions." The "moral obligations that the laws of his blood impose on him" were "the supreme laws of his action."[5] All of this was obvious, but the spirit—much like, at times, the blood—of Germanic men and women had been muddied and muddled by doctrines preached by "foreign, supra-state powers, which have attempted to destroy, to curb, or to devitalize natural laws."[6] It was by returning to himself and his race, as well as to "consciousness of his unconditional, moral responsibility" to the "laws imposed by his blood, which require him to serve the good of his people, his family, his country," that the soldier would act and fight with peace in his heart.[7] Moreover, he would act efficiently: "He has the sacred duty to enlist and defend his honor against individuals and people who wish him ill. He will do this without meanness or sentimentalism."[8]

His innate and just conscience would tell him that he was always right to act as he did "when he obeys the laws of life." No need for scruples or individual conscience: "Nordic man is never alone." He knew that "what serves his people is right and good."[9] Everything was very simple indeed:

> In all logical consequence, a clear biological concept of race induces criteria of value and the normative order from our racist worldview. Its basic lesson is that we must serve the vital force that is inborn in us, which was given to us by nature (God, Providence), which is superior to us and which will not end with us. Everything else must be subordinate to this: politics, science, ideology.[10]

The conclusion was clear: "The highest and most sacred duty of man is the preservation . . . of his race."[11] Every measure was therefore taken to spare combatants in the Wehrmacht or the SS from excessive or excessively trying questions about the legitimacy of their actions: "Biological thinking has formulated reasonable criteria for evaluating situations. It gives you the strength to make clear decisions and shows you what you can and what you must do," explained an SS instructional pamphlet.[12] From the beginning, adolescents enrolled in *Napolas* (*Nationalpolitische Lehranstalten*, secondary schools established under the Third Reich, also known as NPEA, or *Nationalpolitischen Erziehungsanstalten*) and young recruits heard little else: "A moral man is one who uses all of his strength to serve the purity, the growth, the development of the creative force of our blood, and who protects it."[13]

Ideally, troops, police officers, and members of the SS or the army would not ever have to think for too long. They were continually reminded that they were not there to do so. A soldier obeyed his superior's orders. They, in turn, obeyed their leader, for Germany was a fighting community whose political order had been thought out along military lines. The military *Führerprinzip* (leadership principle) governing the Nazi Party since 1920 was transposed to the entire Reich by an equivalency established in 1933 between the will of the Führer and the law.

In the armed forces, each man swore an oath to Adolf Hitler himself, thereby locking both their consciences and a hierarchical system into place. The practice of this swearing in had begun in 1934, with an oath taken by members of the Wehrmacht. On August 2, 1934, after the Night of the Long Knives, Hitler's pledge to the military's commanders, and the death of Marshal-President Hindenburg, the German Army had to be bound to the Führer's very person, in life and in death. Soldiers had to swear "unconditional obedience" to Hitler "before God," a "sacred oath" that meant "giving one's life" to obey him.

As for the SS, it had been swearing "loyalty and courage," as well as "obedience unto death" to its supreme chief, since the 1920s. The oaths of the Wehrmacht and SS auxiliary forces deployed with the German Army starting in 1941 included all of these elements, with variations linked to the divisions' specific identities: the Muslim Croats of the Thirteenth Mountain Division of the SS Handschar did not forget their "all-powerful God," the Sikhs Indian Volunteer Legion of the Waffen-SS called upon their "Führer Subhas Chadra Bose," while members of the French African phalanx swore allegiance to "Marshal Pétain." Many felt they were bound by these oaths until April 30, 1945, the day Hitler "fell" in his "heroic struggle against Bolshevism." The conspirators of July 20, 1944, were considered to be traitors because they had violated their oaths, and their rehabilitation in national memory was a long and complicated affair in postwar Germany.

The Nazi texts noted that traditional notions and categories of duty, order, and obedience were insufficient in a conflict marked by the extreme commitment of the Bolshevik armies: "The old notions of military duty and obedience are no longer sufficient to ensure this iron-toughness and the strength of soul required in combat with the Russians," read a 1943 edition of *SS-Leitheft*. Superior fanaticism could be the only recourse against and salvation from a fanatical enemy. "The force of Bolshevik aggression can only be shattered by greater harshness and fanaticism from the German Army." As the war dragged on, the "work of ideological education, whether in the army or among the entire German people," took on ever greater significance: "It must incite the entire nation to uncompromising fanaticism and ensure that each person feels he is a soldier and a fighter for Adolf Hitler."[14] Retempering bodies and souls by immersing them in ideological radicalism was the only way to meet the challenges of total war and racial war, the only way to avoid "the destruction of all of Europe's valid biological substance." Only this fanaticism would allow Germany to avoid a moral and military collapse like that of 1917–1918.[15]

In this racial war, which was a natural occurrence just like the grinding of land masses against each other or the clash of salt and fresh water in a river delta, it was necessary to rise to the level of the elements, by force of moral conviction and physical hardiness: "Natural disasters cannot be held back by flimsy netting woven artificially by bourgeois brains, but only by natural forces." Already, in 1933, "the German uprising provoked by Adolf Hitler" had been a "basic natural phenomenon"—an insurrection against death, which was stalking the German people. In such a context it was easy to understand that the war could not be won with "obsolete representations," "allegedly chivalrous virtues," and outdated "moral values." These values "had been weighed in the balance and found lacking," as one source asserted in an explicit, though not cited, reference to the Hebrew Bible.[16] The reference is of course ironic, since biblical values were exactly what had been found lacking. One had no need of a Jewish book to be able to behave and fight correctly: "The ethical behavior of a man is the result of his worldview," and "our ideology is our own moral code."[17]

War in Poland and War in the East

Poland and the East were considered to be recurrent problems for Germany: waves of attacks from the East had assaulted Germanity for millennia. In terms of political biology, Hitler and Himmler believed that, for Germany and Germanity to live, the Polish principle, and, beyond that, the Slavic principle as a national principle, had to die. This obviously did not imply that all Slavic people ought to be killed—they were useful as servile laborers—but rather that they ought to be deprived of everything that made life human: conscience, culture, intelligence. Deprived of a head (or heads) and of a brain (or brains); deprived, too, of all the Jewish leaders who manipulated them, the Polish and Slavic peoples in general would become the submissive and zealous tools to advance German projects in the East.

Hitler employed the same terms to define the Nazi military and police mission in Poland, and then in the Soviet Union, speaking of "eliminating Polish vital forces" and the "destruction of the Russian vital force."[18] In both cases, this meant the murder of the *Intelligenz* by the Einsatzgruppen of the SD.[19] The former was a polysemic term that meant both academic faculty and the intelligentsia as a social group. The "vital forces" that gave life to the Polish and Slavic communities were Poland's intellectual elite and, further to the east, the "political commissars" of the Red Army.

The Third Reich's first war, in Poland, had to be waged with unprecedented swiftness and brutality in order to settle things on the Eastern Front in case Western democracies entered the war, and to dissuade the West from getting involved by generating broad media coverage of the brutality of Nazi warfare. On August 22, 1939, a week before operations began, Hitler called a meeting of key generals of the Wehrmacht high command at Obersalzberg. According to notes taken by General Franz Halder, chief of the Army High Command, Hitler opened the meaning with a cynical dismissal of the question of motives for war: "For propaganda, I will give a reason to attack, it doesn't matter whether it is credible or not. No one asks the winner whether he is telling the truth. When it comes to war, it isn't the law that counts, but the victory."[20]

Hitler went on to explain how the war should be waged and attempted to banish any scruples or pangs of conscience that might arise among his superior officers and generals:

We must close our hearts to all pity. We must proceed brutally. Eighty million people are waiting to receive their right and their due. Their existence must be secured. Might makes right. Proceed with the greatest harshness. Swift decision is necessary.[21]

As we can see, Hitler's relationship to the law was not purely cynical. He conceded that a fallacious pretext was needed to amuse the peanut gallery, and that a bone should be tossed to the world's journalists and chancelleries. But this diplomatic and journalistic playacting was a smokescreen for the Third Reich's fight for the right to exist of eighty million Germans, who needed the East for space to live. Behind the screen, pity was inappropriate. There could be none for individuals as different from Germans as were the Poles, who were members of the inferior Slavic race. This was all the more true because in the twenty years they had dominated Silesia and Pomerania, the Polish people had never had any pity for the Germans.

From the first perspective, the war in Poland had been a resounding success: victory had been rapidly, even thunderously, decisive. The Third Reich's first *blitzkrieg* had impressed (and intimidated) Western military powers both militarily—Poland had been swiftly destroyed—and journalistically, with images of the rapid advance of German tank units and film reels of the bombing and destruction of Warsaw having the hoped-for demoralizing effect. The fate of the Polish capital most likely did weaken the desire to fight and resist among many French, Belgian, and Dutch people.

But beyond achieving these solely military objectives, in the short and the medium term, Nazi Germany carried out its objective of "destroying Poland," which Hitler had set as a goal for both his generals and his occupation policy. Regarding the eradication of the Polish elite, Himmler dismissed all imputations of cruelty or barbarousness, invoking the biological need to proceed radically in order to avoid the resurgence of the Polish problem in every generation:

I know that, for this reason, I have been attacked and am attacked by plenty of people who tell me: acting in this way is not Germanic. I sometimes get the feeling that for some people, being Germanic means playing the nice guy and politely disappearing. That is what would not be Germanic. Pardon me, but what we are doing, I maintain that it is right and I believe that it is right. We were obliged to rob the enemy of its leaders and its thinkers . . . , we could not do otherwise.[22]

Even more than Poland, the entire East was held up as an anomalous space in which none of the laws and practices of war held any sway. Here again, the notes taken by General Franz Halder are a precious source. The chief of the Army High Command had been summoned to a meeting with Hitler on March 30, 1941, where before an audience of two hundred and fifty superior officers and generals, the Führer delivered a rambling, nearly two-and-a-half-hour-long speech on the principles and the ends of the coming war in the East. Hitler enjoined his generals to be aware that a war against the USSR was a "struggle between two worldviews" that were irreconcilable with each other. From a biological standpoint, Germany was facing a population of Slavic subhumans who had been instrumentalized and rendered savage by their Jewish masters, the inventors of Bolshevism: "Communism is an appalling danger that weighs on our future."[23] From this point onward, communist leaders were to be eradicated without hesitation or reservation. This was Hitler's justification for the Kommissarbefehl (Commissar Order), which had not yet been issued, but was at that time being discussed and prepared by the jurists of the Wehrmacht:

> Out of the question to get court martials mixed up in all this. Troop leaders need to know what's going on here. . . . Our soldiers must defend themselves using the same means with which they are attacked. The political commissars and the men of the GPU are criminals. They must be treated as such.[24]

The customary usages of the law of war and of *jus gentium* therefore did not govern or provide norms for relations with the Red Army. Nothing that had been codified in Geneva or The Hague was valid when it came to the soldiers or the general population of the USSR: "We must give up on considering these people as comrades, as soldiers. The Communists have never been comrades, and never will be. This is a war of extermination." Troops therefore needed to be educated and acculturated according to new norms, which had nothing in common with those governing ordinary wars: Germany was facing not merely a strategic enemy, but an ideological and biological enemy that, if it was not destroyed, would never cease to attack Germany and threaten the German people: "If we do not see things in this way, we may well defeat the enemy, but the Communist enemy will stand up to us again in thirty years. We are not waging a war to preserve the enemy." During this speech, the two hundred and fifty members of the Führer's audience, along with the entire Wehrmacht, were plunged into a radically different normative universe. The usual and customary norms were not valid in the East, a wild territory populated by subhumans (the Slavic population) and microbes (the Jews): "The struggle we are about to undertake will be extremely different from the one we waged in the West. In the East, harshness makes the future kind. Officers must make the sacrifice of overcoming their reservations."[25]

Hitler was very aware that the consciences of the officers he was addressing would be unsettled by the idea of a radical war in which the enemy was completely stripped of the legal rights and safeguards that armies, particularly the Prussian army, took pride in honoring. Because these were the generals and commanding officers who would be setting the norms and giving the orders to the troops, it was essential that they accept the need to wage a different kind of war against a different kind of enemy. And so Hitler made a dialectical switch between ignominiousness and nobility, the abject and the sublime: the goal of Germany's extreme harshness in the East was to end a war and a threat that had loomed for millennia. Only the most extreme violence could definitively end Semitic Asia's assault on Germanic Europe: to be "harsh" in the East was therefore to be "kind" to Europe and to future generations. It was the painful and necessary duty of a generation of German soldiers to undertake this heavy task. Some were upset and offended by the brutality and the ferocity of the war as it was waged by the German armies. If older officers, veterans of an empire of cravats and noble names, of Iron Crosses and Christian norms, felt free to balk and to invoke the rules of chivalry, they should be reminded that chivalry could exist only among equals. Chivalrous morality had no meaning among Bolsheviks and Jews, for they were incapable of understanding it, grasping it, or respecting it. Their entire being said and expressed the very opposite, as Himmler pointed out: "The Jew presupposes immorality, treason, and lies as the conditions of his political struggle. Loyal to himself, he even considers it a weakness not to exterminate his enemy."[26] As for the Slavic people recruited into the services of the Bolshevik Jews, they were fanaticized "robots" who devastated and killed mechanically, not "comrades" in humanity.[27]

The East, a Place of Constant Exception

Hitler signed the directive for Operation Barbarossa on December 18, 1940, and plans for the imminent war against the USSR took shape rapidly after that. By March 13, 1941, Field Marshal Wilhelm Keitel, chief of the Supreme Command of the Wehrmacht, informed general officers that their theaters of operation would be divided among the army and special units commanded by Heinrich Himmler, chief of the SS and the German police. The Einsatzgruppen had existed for several years; the first of them had been created around the Austrian Anschluss in March 1938. These mobile and rapid units were to hunt down and arrest potential opponents. Other "intervention groups" had been deployed in the Sudetenland in October 1938, then in Bohemia-Moravia in March 1939, and finally in Poland in September of the same year. Following the orders that had been given to them, the Einsatzgruppen committed their first mass murders in Poland. In the East, the killing was to be organized systematically, and would occur on a larger scale. Keitel warned his troops:

> In the army's zone of operation, Reichsführer SS receives special orders from the Führer. . . . In the context of these tasks, the Reichsführer SS acts entirely independently and is solely responsible.[28]

Military leaders had no right to examine or question the activities of the SS or the German police, who were answerable to Himmler alone. He, in turn, answered only to the Führer. The only stay on this complete freedom of action was entirely operational in nature: "The Reichsführer SS will see to it that military operations are not disrupted in the execution of these tasks."[29] A month and a half later, on April 28, 1941, Von Brauchitsch, chief of the army High Command, detailed the specific nature of the mission and the type of interventions to come:

> The execution of police and security tasks requires . . . the intervention of special commandos of the security police (SD) in zones of

military operations. [The goal is to] seize specified objects . . . as well as particularly important persons (key emigrants, saboteurs, terrorists, etc.).[30]

Here too it was specified that while "commandos of the security police and the SD" are "subordinate to the armies for matters relating to movements, supplies, and housing," their members "carried out their mission under their own full responsibility," in such a way that their logistical subordination to the Wehrmacht did not in any way impede their "disciplinary and judicial subordination to the chief of the security police and the SD," Reinhard Heydrich.[31] In other words, these commandos obeyed RSHA orders only and were not required to respect the rules to which Wehrmacht soldiers were subject. An army officer witnessing a violation of the law of war by a member of one of these commandos, for example, could not have him brought before a court martial: only the SS had that oversight. Here, again, as in the order signed by Keitel, the only rule the army imposed on SS and police commandos was "not to disrupt military operations." Otherwise, the land and its inhabitants were theirs. Really, the directives that regulated the interventions of the SS and police Einsatzgruppen were harbingers of a significant normative shift that would soon affect the Wehrmacht as well. As the weeks passed, the orders issued for the upcoming Operation Barbarossa show that what was once an exception made for the SS and the police was slowly becoming the legal framework of common law. While the first exceptional provisions, in April 1941, concerned only the SS, a series of orders signed in May and June 1941, before the June 22 offensive, absolved troops of any obligation to obey the law of war. German historiographical literature often cites the Kommissarbefehl of June 6, 1941, which no doubt owes its fame to the fact that it explicitly ordered the killing of unarmed men without recourse to evidence or even summary judicial proceedings. Nevertheless, this order targeted Red Army "political commissars"; in other words, a specific and therefore limited group of people. The same cannot be said for a series of orders issued starting on May 13, 1941, signed by Wilhelm Keitel. As head of the Supreme Command of the Armed Forces, the highest military authority after Hitler, Keitel issued a "decree on the exercise of military jurisdiction in the Barbarossa zone" that, read in its entirety, essentially gave German troops in the East carte blanche to engage in any act of violence or repression that contributed in any way to their security. Civilians were exposed with no protection to whatever punishment German soldiers chose to mete out to them. The preamble to this edict specified that war tribunals could only become fully operational once the territories conquered in the East had been entirely pacified. In the meantime, court martials were to "limit themselves to their principal task," which was "first of all to maintain discipline." The pacification of conquered zones would only be possible "if the army pitilessly defends itself against all attack from a hostile civilian population"—and it was by definition hostile, because the enemy in the East was "peculiar."

The first articles of the decree specified that "until further notice, reprehensible acts committed by hostile civilians are no longer within the jurisdiction of military tribunals and court martials." Troops were required to administer justice themselves, on site and without delay. Any hostile act was "to be fought immediately with the most radical expedients until the attacker is completely destroyed." The decree also authorized "measures of collective violence" against any suspicious "locality." Furthermore, "it is expressly forbidden to detain suspects." Civilians in the East had no right to legal protection. Wehrmacht soldiers, by contrast, were fully covered by the second part of the decree: "There is no obligation to pursue acts committed against hostile civilians by members of the Wehrmacht and its cortège." No official action would be taken for war crimes and offenses, unless doing so was "required to maintain troop discipline and safety."[32] In other words, the only exception to this permanent state of legal exception was for the German Army itself: legal action was taken if and only if the act in question represented a danger to the army.

Eleven days later, an order signed by the army's commander in chief, Walther von Brauchitsch, retracted the carte blanche given to the army, modifying Keitel's instructions with the proviso that "it is the task of officers to prevent arbitrary excesses by individual soldiers and to ensure that the troops do not become savage. Soldiers must not come away thinking that it is possible for them to do whatever they please to inhabitants."[33] Individual acts of violence that compromised discipline, and over the long term, troop performance, or that placed troops in danger, were prohibited: stripping local populations of all legal rights did not mean complete power (since the security of the German Army took precedence) and certainly did not mean individual power (because overall troop cohesion and coherence had to be maintained).

From the beginning, the territories and populations of Eastern Europe were placed outside the law. The wild lands of the East were peopled with barbarians and could not be subject to the same rules as Central or Western Europe. Even before military operations began, it was stipulated precisely and carefully in a series of decrees, issued as the invasion was prepared between December 1940 and June 1941, that Soviet civilian populations were outside the law.

The pronouncement of such orders, the thunderous succession of instructions to troops, were prescriptions for a military campaign that, it was hoped, would be sudden and devastating. Historians have remarked that while the invasion of France had unexpectedly turned out to be a *blitzkrieg*, the invasion of the East had just as unexpectedly turned out not to be one. Maximalist orders were necessary to inflict sudden devastation and instant defeat; military and police violence had to be continuously ratcheted up. In spite of expectations, however, the German occupation of Eastern Europe ended up taking longer than expected, due to the *rasputitsa* (spring thaw, or "season of bad roads"), military stalemate, and indecision. As time wore on, the army high command, SS and police leaders, and civilian occupation authorities became stymied. If the USSR had not been beaten with the extreme measures already in place, how to handle new threats that arose as the Blitzkrieg lost its momentum and dragged out into a long slog? Already, the orders issued from December 1940 to June 1941 had made civilian populations into enemies, stripping them of all legal protection. And during this period, these populations did become a threat, either because they participated in guerrilla actions led by the Red Army, or because they provided logistical support (housing, food) for these operations.

More than a year after Operation Barbarossa began, Hitler signed Order 46, to "reinforce the struggle against the scourge of the bands in the East."[34] But how could the Germans "reinforce" the "struggle" against civilian populations and "political commissars" when the struggle had, from the beginning, been extremely forceful? The "scourge" of partisans had "reached a scale that is no longer bearable," the decree proclaimed, demanding "the destruction of these bandits" through "the harshest measures." Faced with an enduring war and unexpected resistance, the Nazi high command had to find its way to new language and new forms of action; in this way, they made superlatives into comparatives, stooping ever lower as they raised their voices ever louder.

Despite its rodomontades, the decree of August 18, 1942, included an unprecedented order for the "fair treatment of the [local] population," indicating a dawning awareness that "a requirement for the destruction of gangs is assuring the population that it will have access to the bare necessities for survival." The order echoed the debates opposing the various German authorities in the East: on one side, the HSSPF (Höhere SS- und Polizeiführer; or supreme chiefs of the SS and the police), who, along with certain Reichskommissare, took a hard line and opposed any form of concession; on the other, the civilian officials working under Rosenberg's Ministry for the Occupied Eastern Territories, at times with support from some officers of the Wehrmacht, who wished to preserve civilian populations for exploitation over the long term. Disagreements between these two camps were numerous and heated.

In practical terms, the decree of August 18, 1942, despite its talk of "reinforcement" and "radicalization," indicated a clear retreat from the extreme position of the 1941 decrees. Compromise with local civilian populations had become necessary; their favor and cooperation were needed. The high command began to see reason: the criminal decrees of 1941 had landed occupying troops and authorities in a disastrous situation. By categorizing these civilian populations as implacable enemies by dint of their very biology and substance, the German occupier had left them a single choice: to die or to resist. Nazi radicalism had been performative. The 1942 decrees, far less extreme than those of 1941, acknowledged this by requiring lucidity, fairness, and differentiation with regard to Eastern populations, rather than lumping them into a single hostile body.

Now, instead of the grand racial sweep of geo-ethnic *Flurbereinigung* (reconfiguration), instead of racist ukases whose hardline positions had led to political misinterpretations denounced by some Nazi authorities, discrimination had become necessary—between good and bad Slavic people, for example.[35] Thus "bandits" were specifically and increasingly harshly targeted, as was made clear in the December 16, 1942, decree regarding "the rigorous struggle against resistance movements in the Balkans and the East."[36] The decree specified that acts of resistance on the Soviet and Balkan fronts, "more than ever, make it a matter of life and death" for Germany and the German people, as if shade and nuance were possible in such a radical, extreme situation. The idea that this war was a matter of life or death, or, as the German expression had it, "of being or nothingness" (Sein oder Nichtsein), had been an incessant drumbeat since the earliest phases of preparation for war in the East in the summer of 1940. Here again, what stands out is the point to which the Nazi leadership found itself with absolutely no room to maneuver. Acts of resistance and guerrilla warfare were the predictable consequence of the Germans' extreme brutality in eastern and southeastern Europe. It was precisely because the German Army and police forces had violated every law of war and humanity that they found themselves faced with the most desperate forms of resistance.

Curiously, even from the Nazis' perspective, and even though decrees issued as early in December 1940 had clearly indicated that the rules of war in the West were not valid in the East, Hitler and Keitel were obliged to repeat this point constantly, most likely as a necessary justification for radicalization. Against any possible misgivings, Hitler affirmed again and again that "this struggle no longer has anything to do with the rules of chivalrous combat or with the provisions of the Geneva Convention"—as if his tactics had ever respected such rules. But while there was nothing new to say when it came to the principles and justifications the Nazis had laid out at the outset, some leeway did remain with regard to the war crimes that German soldiers were invited to commit. The December 16, 1942, decree, for example, was the first to explicitly include women and children as targets, as if the more general term of "civilian population" used in the orders issued before that time, starting in December 1940, was no longer sufficiently clear. "In this struggle, therefore, troops have the right and the duty to resort to any expedient, with no restrictions, including against women and children, so long as they lead to success" in the identification and destruction of enemies in the resistance.

Because the goal was "to avoid the propagation of the plague," it went without saying that "the utmost extreme [sic] brutality" was to be used: Nazi discourse had already exhausted the conventional resources of the German language, so Hitler and Keitel went to every grammatical extreme to intensify their orders, superlativizing even their superlatives.[37]

To stay any misgivings about these orders, and fearing that some people might recoil at such an explicit formulation of practices that, while already being undertaken, had not yet been stated so baldly, Hitler added that "any consideration extended to partisans" of any kind was "a crime against the German people and against the soldier on the front, who must suffer the consequences of attacks carried out by gangs, and could never understand why they would be spared, they or their sidekicks."[38] The dialectical switching made the argument irrefutable: any pangs of conscience were handed back to the person cultivating and formulating them. Here again, it was clearly stated that compassion and pity had only one valid object, which was the German people. Other peoples, non-Germanic ones, were not worthy of this attitude or of this consideration, even less so now that they were fighting pitilessly against Germany and its people. Burning a village and murdering its inhabitants were not crimes; instead they were part of a military police operation that made it possible to stamp out a pocket of partisans and/or served as a dissuasive measure against local populations to bring relief to German troops. Massacring a group of defenseless civilians with no provocation or justification was not a crime. Hesitating to do so, however, was.

And yet, here again, and despite the many decrees issued since December 1940, it was necessary to reaffirm that such acts were good and right, as long as they supported the cause and the safety of the German Army. Misleading appearances notwithstanding, these acts were not reprehensible and must in no case be subject to discipline or punishment. The second point of the December 16 decree specified that "no German must be held responsible for his behavior in the struggle against gangs, either disciplinarily or legally, before a court martial."[39] The indiscriminate repression of civilians was understood and formulated in terms of *Sippenhaftung*, which justified inculpating entire families from a biological standpoint. The blood of the "partisan" and the "terrorist" was contaminated, and therefore guilty. It had to be eradicated, on biological principle. This was the explanation offered in a decree signed by HSSPF Ost Commander Wilhelm Koeppe on June 28, 1944. After the customary preamble lamenting that "security in the General Government has degenerated so much in the past months that it is now necessary to intervene against foreign terrorists and murderers with the most radical expedients and the most extremely severe[40] measures," Koeppe's order stipulated that "not only arrested criminals must be shot, but, beyond that, all men in their family. As for female members of these families, they must, past the age of sixteen years, be held in a concentration camp."[41]

These orders, characterized by their complete biological and rhetorical consequentialism, remonstrated with the German soldier's worst enemy—himself, and his goodness, his friendliness, his naïveté: "In the treatment of bandits and those who voluntarily aid them, the most extreme harshness must be shown. Sentimental considerations are, in this decisive matter, irresponsible."[42] Officers were to ensure that troops were not overcome by compassion: "Each unit officer is responsible for ensuring that bandits and civilians taken prisoner during active combat (including women) are all shot, or, preferably, hanged."[43] The incurable sentimentalism and the inveterate propensity for helpfulness and love made the German soldier easy prey for the enemy's evil. A *Landser* (soldier), like any member of the Germanic people, was vulnerable because he was too good. Orders were formulated along these lines, explicitly warning soldiers against segments of the population that might provoke their tenderness and thus be a danger to them, notably women and children.

A decree signed by General von Roques on January 13, 1942, and addressed to all troops in the Heeresgebiet Süd (Southern Zone) warned them against the Russians' use of adolescent boys, who easily won the trust of men in the Wehrmacht, and then worked covertly as spies:

These adolescents are only able to carry out their intelligence missions because of the misplaced goodness of German soldiers, who allow themselves to be taken in by their moving stories and take them on board their vehicles and feed them in the mess hall. I say again with the utmost severity that this type of enemy has no right

to any benevolence or pity from us and that any teenager who approaches German soldiers is to be immediately sent to the competent authorities of the Geheime Feldpolizei [GFP, or military police]
or the SD.[44]

The justification for these orders was clear. In addition to the extreme danger and the radical and total nature of combat, it was necessary to understand a bit of the history and psychology of a people, and
to function at the same level as the Eastern populations. They were already so accustomed to such violence that it was absurd to try to
respect the usages of the West, which would not be comprehensible to
them. Knowing how to handle a firearm was necessary to communi-
cate with the Russians, just as Russian lords had once cracked the
whip to exact obedience from this servile population. They had never
been accustomed to any kind of consideration. Taking into account
the extremely recent abolition of serfdom—in name alone, since Bolshevism had in fact perpetuated it—it was easy to see that the hides of
the Russian people had been tanned so often that the only option was
to strike again, and harder: "The Russian has for all time been used to
energetic, brutal, and implacable treatment by authority."[45] Accustomed to bowing to blows, the muzhik of the steppe would merely look
away slyly if not confronted with pitiless violence: "Any indulgence or
softness is a weakness and represents a danger," because it encouraged
Russians to stand tall and did not teach them to respect and fear their
new masters.[46]

Hostile Space, Contaminated Space

All of these decrees to troops were crafted against the backdrop of the
same specific imagination, which saw and described the Soviet world
as a contaminated space. These orders were supplemented by *Merkblätter*, a kind of handbook that explained and expanded on a decree,
much as a legal memorandum may explain laws or regulations. Working
with specialists of the war's Eastern Front, I have identified three
Merkblätter, as well as a circular sent to officers on the behavior expected of German soldiers in Russia.[47] These notifications, which the
officers were obliged to read to troops, served as mnemonic devices,

and were to be destroyed after reading. They warned soldiers of the dangers awaiting them and indicated ways to avoid them. Their titles speak volumes: "Take Care," "Warning against Soviet Underhandedness," and "Do You Know the Enemy?"[48] The documents were standardized: while they varied in form and structure, the vocabulary they employed and the themes they discussed were identical.

The first idea they explained was that Soviet territory was intrinsically hostile to the German Army. The Soviet Union was a "conglomerate of Slavic, Caucasian, and Asiatic peoples" where "Jewishness is . . . strongly represented."[49] It was important to be particularly mistrusting of Jews, who constituted the Bolshevik elite, as well as "Asiatic soldiers." The worst, alas, could be expected of these "Asiatics" with their slanted eyes and Mongolian faces. These racial others, so far removed—even more so than Slavic people—from European humans, might do anything. In combat situations, they had "treacherous methods" and were "impenetrable, unpredictable, underhanded, and insensitive."[50] Asiatic subhumans, so common in the USSR, were the perfect incarnation of the eternal nomad of the steppe, who, spurred on by Attila the Hun, Genghis Khan, or Stalin, regularly surged forward to threaten Europe. Imperturbable and cruel, the Asiatic person was a fundamentally twisted and dangerous enemy.

The customs of the Red Army in general were unusual, and therefore surprising to the "chivalrous" European fighting man. German soldiers were to be aware of this, "to adapt to it," to adjust (sich einstellen) by imagining "the most underhanded and most despicable methods."[51] The goal was, as one of the manuals enjoined its readers, to "know the enemy" in all of its startling difference. The Red Army would stoop to every deceit: snipers, guerrilla warfare, parachuting soldiers behind the lines . . . "The immediate destruction of such enemies is well within your rights," advised one of the Merkblätter, particularly since the Rotarmist "acts with no moral compunction" and "is capable of the worst brutality," meaning that showing any "trust and benevolence" was pointless.[52] Generally, "the greatest mistrust is imperative at every moment," even when the fighting seemed to have ended.[53] The Red Army did not respect any of the customs of war: Soviet soldiers might even pretend they were wounded or dead and then jump up suddenly to open fire on German soldiers. Similarly, one had to proceed very carefully with Soviet soldiers who were pretending to give themselves up: "Pretending to be dead or raising their hands above their heads" was a common ruse for them.[54] Putting their "hands up is not enough!": "You are accustomed" to people giving themselves up like this, but the Soviets will trick you if you go by the usages and customs of war. You have to expect to be surprised and tricked all the time, everywhere, by everyone. The same was true for supposedly wounded men lying on the ground: "Approach the dead or wounded with great caution."[55]

What should be retained from these instructions? A man who seemed to be giving himself up was in reality not an enemy laying down his arms, but would fire "at your back to resume the fight."[56] The dead or wounded were actually sprightly individuals pretending to be injured, the better to harm the troops. So should you shoot at a man who was giving himself up, since you could not trust raised hands? Should you open fire on the dead and wounded? The orders did not expressly say so, but this was certainly to be inferred from these terrifying instructions, whose goal was to keep German soldiers on high alert at all times.

This widespread suspicion was not limited to soldiers, the wounded, the dead, and anyone giving himself up. It included civilians as well: "Do not be too confident when entering villages that seem overly calm and safe."[57] Clearly, all of this tended to develop a siege mentality in the German soldier. Never, it went without saying, should you let yourself fall into the barbarous hands of Soviet subhumans, for it would mean intense suffering: "Each German soldier must know that detention in the hands of the Red Army is synonymous with cruel torture and death," as well as "ignoble, sadistic, and brutal treatment."[58] This, according to the texts, was the rule among these monsters. The conclusion was always the same: "So be careful! Be harsh and pitiless."[59] The enemy was unreliable, dishonest, and not particularly tender. Their malignancy and their cruelty required the German Army to exercise the most extreme prudence and justified the most extreme violence. Soviet hostility was intrinsic, and quite literally virulent. The East was potentially deadly territory for the German soldier, poisoned as it was by the activity and the presence of Jews and Bolsheviks. Indeed, among other deadly ruses used by the Red Army were unconventional weapons such as chemical and biological poisons. The *Merkblätter* were clear on this subject: "They poison the food! Do not eat anything you find there, do not drink any well water that has not been sampled and tested. Expect poison everywhere."[60] Analysis by "health officers" and "veterinary officers" was necessary before any decisions could be made about the safety of consuming food or water, the latter of which "must only be drunk boiled."[61]

Moreover, the Soviets had also "poisoned" the very land in Russia, chemically or biologically. Their methods were described and listed in a proclamation specifically devoted to "cunning warfare customs among the Soviets": the enemy, which "would stoop to any crime" and which "unscrupulously uses every possible means," would not hesitate to "poison the land" using chemical shells, "spray vehicles," or individual "copper sulfate spray guns."[62]

The Soviets were expected to employ a chemical or bacteriological scorched-earth policy: instead of destroying things to deprive German soldiers of food and shelter and handicapping them in this way, they would poison everything, with the intent to kill. The text warned that not only "food and fodder abandoned in place will be contaminated" but also "huts and shelters."[63] Going to every length to provoke psychosis, the manual warned against all contact between German skin and Soviet furniture and buildings: "Be careful not to touch doorknobs and pump handles!"[64]

Hostile territory, contaminated earth: the danger of poisoning redoubled the danger of contamination—and in a deliberate fashion. The bacteriological war waged by the Russians was both active and passive all at once, because people in the East were also diseased. Centuries of miserable sanitary conditions and deplorable hygiene, aggravated by Bolshevik mismanagement, had kept Slavic, Asiatic, and Jewish communities in a microbial environment to which they had grown fully immune, through adaptation and habituation. The result was that Eastern peoples were the healthy vectors of thousands of illnesses unknown in the West:

Danger, epidemic! The territory and the population are contaminated by typhus, cholera, and the plague, pathologies that have long disappeared for us thanks to the exemplary hygiene of the German people.

You have been vaccinated against these diseases and should not fear
them, but all the same, avoid all contact with the population.[65]

East to West: Importing Violence to the Western Theaters

The acculturation of German troops and officers to abnormal and
anomalous orders was a massive undertaking: the decrees and instructions discussed above were read and disseminated to the millions of
soldiers who spent time on the Eastern Front between 1941 and 1945.
As the war went on and as fighting in the East became increasingly
difficult, decrees such as these were issued to guide behavior toward
Western armies and populations. This in no way implies that between
1940 and 1943 the behavior of the German Army in the West was as
"correct" as its propaganda claimed. The taking and killing of hostages,
as well as the massacres of French colonial troops perpetrated by the
Waffen-SS and by units of the Wehrmacht, are well known.[66]

Of course from the Nazis' perspective, this behavior was irreproachable. Black soldiers had no business on European soil. Their place was
elsewhere. Indeed, their deployment by the French military to fight in
European theaters of operation was a crime against civilization and
against the race that demanded retribution. In Chasselay, in Lentilly,
and in Clamecy, the "black shame" of 1923 could finally be redressed.
As for the execution of hostages, it was provided for in the law of war: it
was at that time an internationally recognized and normalized procedure, and inspired no particular misgivings in the occupier.

Little by little, however, and in the shadow of an Eastern Front along
which every normative barrier had been broken from the get-go, measures were taken that violated the provisions of the law of war and of
jus gentium (international law or the basic rights extended to foreign
or enemy nations) that would normally have been applicable to the civilized peoples of the West. And so it was that on September 17, 1942,
Admiral Karl Dönitz gave the following order to the submarine fleets
in his command: members of the *Kriegsmarine* were forbidden to help
sailors from enemy ships, by "pulling men out of the sea, by recovering
capsized lifeboats, [or] by giving food and water" to the shipwrecked.
Enemies at sea were to be abandoned to their fate and to die. There was
no solidarity with enemy sailors facing exposure to the elements or

death. Chivalrous camaraderie in the face of a danger (the ocean) that threatened and transcended all combatants had no reason to exist; nor did the basic solidarity that brought crews together in the face of a common enemy: "Lifesaving operations contradict the most elementary demands of this war: the total destruction of enemy ships and their crew." One exception: "Shipwrecked men will be saved on the sole condition that the information they might provide may be useful for our own ships."[67]

Aware that this order went against the sailors' code of honor and shattered the brotherhood of men facing death at sea, Dönitz sketched out a justification in the most imperative and stripped-down form possible: "Be tough. Bear in mind that the enemy does not spare women and children in the bombing of German cities."[68] It was therefore the enemy's behavior that justified and legitimized orders that violated all of the principles of maritime warfare. Dönitz was suggesting that violence should escalate cumulatively, and reflect the enemy's own violence: because the enemy was killing the spouses and children of German soldiers in air raid operations, the *Kriegsmarine* could leave the representatives of this criminal breed to die at sea. Of course, no mention was made of the Nazis' own responsibility for the increasingly extreme nature of the war's violence, particularly against civilians.

Justifying the radicalization of violence as a necessary mirroring of enemy behavior was an import from the war on the Eastern Front and the discourses deployed there to justify it. In a decree issued on September 5, 1941, for land operations in Soviet territory, the AOK 11 indignantly and firmly denounced the underhanded and barbarian practices of the Red Army, which, overwhelmed on all sides by the advance of German troops, promoted partisan resistance behind the lines:

> The German command as well as the troops must adapt as rapidly
> as possible to this unusual form of combat and destroy partisan
> groups . . . with no consideration for any misunderstood humanity.[69]

Over time, it was no longer just enemy soldiers who were excluded from "any misunderstood humanity," but the civilian populations of Western Europe as well. Little by little, they would begin to experience the repressive violence that had been exacted on populations to the East, although never to the same extent. The orders, at least, were explicit. As difficulties increased on the Eastern Front, guarantees that had been extended to the occupied territories in the West began to disappear. The infamous "Night and Fog" decree of December 7, 1941, directed that the "harshest of measures" be taken against "the Communist element and other circles hostile to Germany," which, since "the beginning of the Russian campaign," had "redoubled . . . their attacks on the Reich."[70]

Keitel's implementation letter, signed a few days later, stipulated that acts of opposition were not to be punished with prison sentences or penal servitude, which would be "interpreted as signs of weakness."[71] The only sanction possible was death or disappearance, the point being "to dissuade" through the terror of death or by leaving "the population in ignorance" as to what might have happened to the "guilty parties." Lack of knowledge thus became a weapon of terror, nourishing the darkest of fears. It was "this end that transfer to Germany must serve." The "Night and Fog" decree violated all of the principles of the law of war and *jus gentium*, which stated that any act of hostility toward an occupying force was to be brought to trial before a military or a civil court. Hitler's directive replaced public legal proceedings with a secret police measure that caused the prisoner to vanish without a trace, extending a form of *Schutzhaft* aggravated by silence and secrecy throughout occupied Europe.

The decree remained in force until the end of the war, but was de facto annulled by another directive issued by Hitler in the summer of 1944, as the Reich began to lose its footing. With the Eastern Front collapsing, D-Day, and the Resistance now fighting the German Army openly alongside the Allies, Hitler ordered that any hostile act be punished with immediate execution. As had been the case in the East since the beginning, troops were now to defend themselves in their own courts of the first and final instance, with no formalities, delay, or specific procedure: "Troops and all members of the Wehrmacht, the SS, and the police must execute all terrorists and saboteurs caught in the act of wrongdoing on site and without delay." As for anyone arrested after the fact, "they must be brought to the nearest unit of the security police and the SD." No judicial procedures were provided for; no legal protections afforded. The only exceptions were indeed significant when one recalls the radical orders issued in the East: women, who, as mere "accomplices, must be employed as forced labor. Children must be spared."[72]

On paper, then, a distinction remained between West and East; the West was a territory with standards, protections, safeguards, and scruples still in place. Some will object that, as early as 1940, it was common for the occupying forces to detain and execute hostages in France, Belgium, and Holland. Terrible as it was, this practice nevertheless fell within the law of war and *jus gentium* at that time. While hostages were already being executed in France in 1940, it is important to remember that there was no such practice on the Eastern Front in 1941. Indeed, according to a decree on the "treatment of hostile civilians" issued on August 3, 1941, by the OKH (Oberkommando des Heeres, or Army High Command), "no preventive detention of hostages in view of preventing future wrongdoing is required." In the lines that preceded this one, it was specified that any act of passive or active resistance would be followed by "immediate collective retaliatory measures," by "order of a regiment chief at the least."[73] This was the only qualification given to these radical instructions. Taking hostages on the Eastern Front was seen as a pointless endeavor, a way of mediation and deferring retaliation, which was supposed to be immediate, direct, and brutal (mass executions, the destruction of villages, and so on). As contradictory as it may seem, the repressive practice of detaining and executing hostages actually represented a kind of safeguard for populations in occupied territories to the West.

All the same, in practical terms, civilian populations in the West were progressively stripped of protections to persons and property.[74] On October 28, 1944, in the context of a sustained offensive by the Red Army in the East and the North, Hitler issued an order to the Wehrmacht divisions occupying northern Norway via Alfred Jodl: "The Führer . . . has ordered . . . that, in the interests of its own safety, the entire Norwegian population located to the east of the Lyngen Fjord be evacuated, and all habitations be burned or destroyed." The measure was justified because the Reich was under the obligation to save—in spite of itself—this Germanic population of Nordic blood. Indeed, the decree even specified that its orders were being issued because of

"the feeble inclination of the northern population of Norway to voluntarily evacuate" its land and homes.

Nordic blood would be protected by the Reich, even over territory.
Although certainly of passing inconvenience to the populations whose
houses were being destroyed, the tactic would ultimately lead to victory and contribute to the higher common good. If the Soviets won,
after all, houses would not be the only ones to suffer. There were no
compunctions about this scorched-earth policy: "Sympathy for the civilian population is inappropriate"; more than that, in fact, since clem-
ency for the few in the present moment would be a threat to the future
of the many.

The next day, on October 29, 1944, General Rendulic, the commander of the Twentieth Mountain Army, passed on the Führer's
order with the following message:

> Troops will understand the measures to be taken once it has been
> explained to them that the barbaric methods of the air raid war
> against the German homeland and its cultural patrimony have
> brought far greater misfortune to the German population than the
> measures we must undertake in Norway, their goal being to prevent
> any Russian breakthrough.[75]

From the beginning, orders for Operation Barbarossa provided for
collective retaliation against civilians through mass executions and
the destruction of villages or neighborhoods. No such thing was ordered in the West until late in the war. On February 3, 1944, Field
Marshal Hugo Sperrle, deputy commander in chief on the Western
Front, signed an order detailing directions to be followed in case of hostile action by the Resistance:

> Respond by opening fire immediately! If innocents are harmed in our
> counterattack, this is regrettable, but exclusively the fault of the ter-
> rorists. Cordon off the sector and arrest all civilians within it, without
> consideration for rank or person. Immediately burn all houses from
> which shots were fired. No measure, even ones that may seem too
> harsh, can lead to prosecution.[76]

In fact, "negligent indulgence by leaders must be punished, as it is a
threat to the men's safety."[77] This last clause opened the way to a broad

and generous interpretation of the order's conditions of application, and by the late spring and summer of 1944 it was being applied in the broadest possible sense. In addition to Oradour-sur-Glane, some dozen other villages in France were the sites of mass killings. All of these massacres were the result of the importation of practices already being implemented on the Eastern Front, by units acculturated to extreme violence. These units found themselves on French soil, facing military catastrophe and phenomena similar to those they had encountered in the East. German military capacity was crumbling and "guerrilla" actions were intensifying, in the form of harassment by "terrorists" and "partisans," which the French called "Resistance fighters."

As is well known, the village of Oradour-sur-Glane was destroyed by the Das Reich division of the Waffen-SS. Dortan, at the base of the Jura Mountains, was burned, and its inhabitants massacred, by the Cossack volunteers of an *Ostregiment* of the Wehrmacht. Maillé, in Indre-et-Loire, was destroyed by the recently formed Seventeenth SS-Panzergrenadier Division Götz von Berlichingen, which was led by veterans of the Eastern Front.[78]

Kein Kamerad: The Treatment of Soviet Prisoners of War

The treatment of war prisoners in the East was based on two different but interlocking ways of thinking. First was the logic of racial and ideological war. Its goal was to eliminate the enemy elite, the leadership, and it considered Soviet combatants criminals who should be treated as such. Second was the logic of domination and servitude. Its goal was to enslave Slavic populations and exploit their vital forces to the point of exhaustion. The Kommissarbefehl (Commissar Order), which has been the subject of much study, is perhaps the most famous illustration of this first logic.[79] Probably it is better known and cited more often than the texts discussed earlier because it contained explicit orders to kill, whereas the decrees of May 13 and 19, 1941, merely suspended the competence of military tribunals.

The decree's preamble offered a kind of boilerplate of orders relating to the East, recalling that "in the struggle against Bolshevism, no attitude in keeping with the principles of humanity or of *jus gentium* can be expected of the enemy."[80] This imputation—purely and simply

a projection of Nazi intentions onto the enemy, combined with a probably sincere fear of the Bolsheviks' "Asiatic barbarity"—offered in advance a justification for any and all German atrocities by raising them
to the level of legitimate defense and prevention. To intensify the general atmosphere of anxiety, the preamble did not limit itself to general
statements: it specified that German prisoners of war would suffer
"hateful, cruel, and inhuman treatment."

The Russian and Slavic populace, considered to be amorphous and
passive, was not being held actively responsible for the crimes to come;
they had merely been fanaticized by a Bolshevik elite, which had made
them the instruments of its future conquest of Europe. As usual, Nazi
anthropology was definite in its assertions that the (Judeo-) Bolshevik
heads were the ones that needed to roll. "Political commissars of all
types" were the "true vectors of the resistance" to be feared within
the Red Army and the Soviet system. Because shock operations were
believed to be the key to German success, the Kommissarbefehl should
be read in a tactical light. The goal of the Reich's *blitzkrieg* tactic was
to strike down the Soviet enemy swiftly. To this end, all "resistance"
was to be quelled immediately. The Red Army's fanaticized and fanati-
cizing officers were the central danger, because they were the ones
manipulating the masses. Because these masses had neither character
nor will of their own, the Reich would be able to impose its own tasks
on them once the war was over. The "instigators of Asiatic and barbaric combat methods" presumed to be under the employ of the Red
Army, however, were "political commissaries."[81] These men were "not
recognized as soldiers" and were to "be immediately executed."[82] The
order directed that "the protections extended to prisoners of war by international law and *jus gentium* are not applicable to them." Among
the masses of prisoners taken by German troops, "they must be executed once they have been isolated."[83]

To Hitler and the OKW, which had issued the order, "political commissaries" were necessarily guilty, by dint of their very existence.
Even if no war crimes or insidious acts of resistance could be imputed
to them, they were guilty of bearing "that specific insignia—a red star
with golden hammer and sickle—on their sleeves." Moreover, when the
time came to decide "if they are guilty or not, the personal feeling" of

the German officer regarding the political "mindset and attitude" of the "commissary counts more than any fact that might or might not be proven."[84] The red star designating a political officer was a certain death sentence. In his doctoral thesis, historian Felix Römer examined the transmission and the application of the Commissar Order, explaining how unexpected and shocking it initially was, not only because it violated the traditional laws of war, but also because it went against the code of honor of the German Army itself. In order to preempt doubt and prejudice, the order dismissed the utility of referring to the ways and customs of war out of hand:

> In this struggle, any concern or consideration, any vague attempts to apply international law to these elements, is to be rejected. Such an attitude would represent a danger to our own safety and to the rapid pacification of conquered territories.[85]

Historians have shown that the systematic application of the Commissar Order ultimately backfired for the German Army. Political officers of the Red Army, faced with certain death if captured, were encouraged to keep struggling to the end, down to the very last man, and encouraged those under their orders to do the same. Because of this, as early as September 1941, and at the very highest level, voices were raised within the German Army to suspend the application of this order.[86] It would take nearly a year for these voices to be heeded, in May 1942, when Hitler suspended the Commissar Order "on a provisional basis." It would never again be formally applied.

Nevertheless, the criminalization of the enemy was not limited to the Red Army's "political commissars." A directive from the OKW dated September 8, 1941, firmly recalled that the Soviet adversary was an irreconcilable ideological enemy. Because of their fanaticism, they could be expected to fight violently and unfairly. "Sabotage, fallacious propaganda, arson, murder" were the odious "tactics at their disposition." Because he employed them, "the Bolshevik soldier has lost all right to be treated as an honorable soldier according to the provisions of the Geneva Convention."[87] The Soviets were the ones, in other words, who had intentionally placed themselves outside the community of combatants. Another order stipulated that "the German soldier . . . will maintain the attitude and the distance merited by the Russians' violence and their inhumane savageness in combat."[88]

Hitler had already explained to his generals that the Soviet soldier was not a "comrade." The orders confirm that the suffering and the fate of soldiers on the Eastern Front elicited no sentiment of solidarity, either during or after combat. On September 8, 1941, a directive ordered that "the strictest distance" be maintained between members of the Wehrmacht and Soviet prisoners.[89] This implied that there was to be no human contact with prisoners, who were not to be perceived as men worthy of consideration or holding any rights. A memorandum appended to the order reminded, "any conversation with prisoners of war . . . is strictly forbidden, unless its object is the strictly necessary communication of an order."[90] That is, as had already been stipulated in concentration camp regulations, it was forbidden to speak to prisoners for any reason other than to issue compulsory instructions.

"Any indulgence or kindness is to be absolutely forbidden," the order added. "Treatment must be cold, but correct." This "correctness" did not include any possibility of considering Soviet prisoners as fellow men, as sharing in the collective human experience, or as the subjects of any sort of interaction or empathy. Instead, "prudence and wariness are called for at all times."[91]

German soldiers were not to employ "clubs, whips, or other objects" to make this hierarchy clear to prisoners: "The use of such contact and strike weapons by German soldiers is expressly forbidden," because handling such weapons both implied nearly direct bodily contact with prisoners and demanded a great deal of energy from those employing them. Such weapons were used by maniacal types incapable of containing their anger. German guards were not to lower themselves in this way: "The use of firearms," weapons both noble and distant, "is the rule against Soviet prisoners." Contact arms were ignoble; their use was reserved for "camp police," who were Kapos recruited from among the local population.[92]

German soldiers were therefore neither whip-wielding bullies nor executioners. Another order stipulated that members of the Wehrmacht were not to carry out the death sentences of prisoners of war. They were to be performed by executioners selected "from among the Soviet pris-

oners" themselves. In cases where "none of them manifested his avail-
ability," the prisoner was to be handed over to the "closest State Secret
Police headquarters." In all cases, "execution by a German member of
the Wehrmacht is out of the question."[93] The superior dignity of the
German soldier was on the line: no whips, no ropes. In Hitler's mind,
German soldiers were the overlords, the only ones "authorized to bear
arms."[94]

The fact remained, though, that these circumstances violated the
elementary rules of prisoners of war. Fugitives, for example, could expect certain death: "Fire must be opened without warning" and
"without warning shots."[95] The rule of thumb was "shoot to kill." In
regulations concerning war prisoners, the use of arms was permitted
only in exceptional cases, since prisoners were disarmed and vulnerable; in German prison camps in the East, it was the rule. The decree
of September 8, 1941, even recalled that while the use of firearms
against war prisoners was generally subject to the regulations governing
this practice in peacetime, this could not be the case on the Eastern
Front, because the "peaceful conditions" in question could not exist.
Even when disarmed and imprisoned, Red Army soldiers were still the
enemy. Therefore any "insubordination, active or passive resistance,
must be punished immediately by weapon (bayonet, rifle butt, firearm)."
These instructions were so important that German soldiers who did
not follow them were considered to be guilty of the dangerous "indulgence" discussed above. German guards were to remain aware that
"anyone who does not use his weapon energetically enough is subject
to sanction."[96]

The legal regime imagined for Soviet war prisoners granted them
no rights whatsoever, elevating the exception as the rule. Prisoners
were criminals, or, at best, and quite literally, subhuman: the Slavic
people had no innate value other than their potential employment in
any task the Reich saw fit to assign them. Their use value was nothing
more than a variable in an economic equation that included many
others, notably overall supplies available to the German military and
the Reich. Prisoners of war were plainly at the very bottom of the chain,
negligible remainders in a mathematical operation. At a meeting of
German generals on November 13, 1941, General Halder, chief of the

OKH, instructed General Wagner, who, as quartermaster-general, was responsible for troop supplies, to make note of the following:

> Prisoners of war who do not work must be left to die of hunger. Those who work may be fed from army food supplies on a case-by-case basis. Given the current supply situation, however, this cannot be ordered systematically.[97]

In reality, the severe treatment of Soviet prisoners of war went far beyond these orders and considerations—far enough to exceed all comprehension. Soviet prisoners were exposed to the elements without food or care, abandoned entirely to the harsh climate. Of the five million Soviet soldiers held prisoner by the Germans, 3.3 million of them died in less than a year.[98]

The mass murder of Soviet prisoners of war elicited protests even within the Reich government apparatus. Most remarkable, in that it sums up the arguments of all those dumbfounded by the massacres, is a letter from Alfred Rosenberg himself. On February 28, 1942, the "Reich minister for the Occupied Eastern Territories" sent a long note to OKW chief Marshal Keitel. In it, Rosenberg, who was responsible for the future of the Eastern Territories, reviewed the information he had received from his services about the behavior not only of the Sipo-SD and the Einsatzgruppen, but of the Wehrmacht as well. He reminded the chief of the Armed Forces Supreme Command that "the war in the East is not over yet," and that "desertion by Red Army soldiers" ought to be encouraged through "the treatment of prisoners of war." The minister recalled, furthermore, that the Reich was not planning for chaos and devastation, but rather "to serve its own ends, [which are] occupation and economic development" in the conquered territories. To "this end, the Reich depends on the enduring collaboration of the population" there.[99]

Rosenberg stated in no uncertain terms that "the tragedy, on an unprecedented scale," of the fate of Soviet prisoners endangered both of these goals: the inhuman treatment that was inflicted on them did not make these prisoners into "propagandists for the German and National Socialist cause"—much to the contrary, in fact. Instead of experiencing "in their very bodies, that National Socialism wants to and can bring them a better future" once they had been freed from Bolshevism, prisoners were "abandoned to the harsh climate," to "typhus," and to "death by inanition." "Rain or snow, they are abandoned to the elements. You should be aware that they were not even given the tools that would have allowed them to dig holes and shelters." Prisoners now identified Nazism with the worst kind of misfortune, and were dying by the hundreds of thousands. There was no need to look any further, Rosenberg wrote, for an explanation "of the growing resistance of the Red Army, and, because of it, the death of thousands more German soldiers."

The German High Command, which answered for the blood of its soldiers, was in fact spilling it irresponsibly. Rosenberg was infuriated by the cravenness of the OKW and did not hide it. Blind racism and total ignorance of the USSR had led the generals to approve of or tolerate that "Asiatics be killed, when it is precisely the populations of the Asiatic territories of the Soviet Union (Transcaucasia, Turkistan) who are the firmest opponents of Russian oppression and Bolshevism." These "Asiatic" populations had welcomed the Germans as liberators and were now being executed for racial reasons "based largely on false representations of the peoples of the Soviet Union."[100]

The second major error of the German military had to do not only with the pursuit of war, but also with the use of local populations for the colonization and the territorial development of the East by the Reich: "Of 3.6 million prisoners, only a few hundred thousand are still fully employable" for the work that the Reich needed to assign them. Development of the land and economy of the ex-Soviet territories would require the Slavic peoples' servitude. They therefore had to be nourished and treated correctly, not abandoned to a horrible, lingering death. Rosenberg did not mince words in his indictment of Keitel, the OKW, and the Wehrmacht: "The German economy and the arms industry will suffer the consequences of the errors committed in the treatment of prisoners of war."[101]

PART III

Reigning

CHAPTER SEVEN

The International Order of Westphalia and Versailles: *Finis Germaniae*

WERE GERMANS NO LONGER welcome anywhere? *Flüchtlinge* (Refugees), a popular film directed by Gustav Ucicky and projected throughout the Reich in 1933, certainly supported this idea.[1] It told the story of the German-speaking Mennonites of the Volga, who, after 1917, fled the Soviet inferno for Harbin, China. In Ucicky's film, the Red Army, at war with the impotent Chinese state, chases the German refugees down in order to punish them and send them back to the USSR. As luck would have it, the League of Nations is on the scene, allowing the Germans' voices to be heard. A German representative is seen pleading on their behalf at the headquarters of a "high commission" in the city, demanding international protection for his compatriots. The commission's conclusion is chilling: the Harbin Germans are Soviet citizens; it would therefore be impossible for the League of Nations to come between them and their country! Formal law comes down hard against the substantive, biological, and cultural reality, which is that there is a true difference between these Germans and the Soviet state. The Germans react with violent despair: "To hell with the commission! Here we are, thousands of us, dying like flies!" One of the poor souls awaiting execution by the Cheka or perhaps a fate in the Gulag shouts angrily to the security barricade forbidding him access to the League of Nations headquarters, *"Germans!* Defenseless! Stripped of our rights! They can do anything they want to us, we're outlaws!"

As luck would have it, the commander of the international guards is an elegant, haughty officer who turns out to be German. Arneth, played by Hans Albers, is disgusted by these Germans begging for help—he gave up on Germany long ago. He had fought for his country in the trenches and then been sanctioned for his love of the fatherland—unspoken but

implied here is a stint in the *Freikorps* and involvement in the activities
of the extreme Right. It was better, he had concluded, to sign on as a mercenary far from home than to stand by and witness the mediocrity of the
Weimar Republic. "You're on your own!" Nevertheless, over time,
Arneth-Albers begins to sympathize with the plight of his compatriots,
and decides to help them—after all, they had had no part in the Republic
that had sanctioned him, and they, too, are exiles forgotten by the rest of
the world. Arguing against group members who wish to leave the city
individually and on foot—madness—he imposes a communal solution:
everyone will go by train, in a locomotive parked on a rail siding, just
waiting to be started up. Alas, Soviet bombing has destroyed a portion of
the rail track, which must be replaced. Undaunted, Arneth organizes the
refugees into an iron-clad hierarchy, of which he becomes the Führer. A
true leader, his only goal is the common good; he shoots down a parched
German who tries to drink water meant for the locomotive, because "it
was endangering everyone's life" to allow a single person to benefit. His
words ring out like the bullets in his revolver, in the hallowed tradition
of the Prussian barracks: "Follow me, got it?" In reply, a mechanically
enthusiastic chorus rings out: "*Jawohl!*"

The gripping progress of the Germans is skillfully interwoven
with the apathetic work of the commission, which deliberated over
"legal assessments" in a haze of cigar smoke, sipped coffee served by
liveried servants, and delivered monotonous, self-important speeches.
Just as the Hohe Kommission comes to the definitive conclusion that
the Germans are Soviet citizens and that the international community
can do nothing for them, the train starts up and saves the poor wretches.
Under the iron fist of their Führer, they have become a true *Volksgemeinschaft:* organized, organic, and struggling together toward the
shared goal of the common good and return to the fatherland.

There was no salvation possible under the existing international
order and law, which had evolved from treaties and peace agreements
that were hostile to Germany, a nation hounded over the past centuries by the onslaught of no fewer than three Thirty Years' Wars.

Thirty Years' Wars (1618, 1792, 1914)

The first (and actual) Thirty Years' War had had two causes: Catholic
imperialism and the French will to power, which both hewed to a single

objective, a repeated assault on the North by the South and the West. As discussed above, in the Nazi reading of history the Lutheran Reform had been an attempt, albeit an imperfect and incomplete one, to return to the Nordic essence. If any of Luther's admirers were tempted to see an insurrection of the German spirit in the nailing of the ninety-five theses, the SS was there to remind them that Protestants were actually bad Germans. After all, they had remained Christian and continued to reason with a Bible in hand. Even if they did rely on a German translation by Luther himself, "For thirty years, Germany was a theater of war because . . . the Protestants believed that fighting for dogmas was more important than closing ranks against the foreign enemy."[2]

Nevertheless, the Reform had been a worthy attempt at "revolution" against the "alienation of the Germanic world" by an "ever more Roman Catholic church" and a "universal Habsburg monarchy." The Counter Reform, this "anti-Reform" with no positive project or end other than fighting Lutheranism, had been impelled by "forces alien to the race" (volksfremd), such as Loyola, the founder of the Society of Jesus, who "was not an Aryan, but who was descended from the Basques, a pre-Indo-Germanic group" flanked by a horde of "Spanish Jews who had had themselves baptized and were attempting to cloak their past in extreme Catholic zeal."[3]

In a demonic orgy of witch hunts and inquisitorial violence, Catholic order had once again ruled Bavaria, where a "regime foreign to our people" had been imposed by the Jesuits' battlewagons. In this way, a Roman citadel had emerged in southern Germany. While the pope had not been able to "subjugate the entire German people," he could at least divide them, as France also sought to do. The "pope thus began encouraging German particularism," working "hand in hand with France."[4]

The papacy and the French monarchy had every interest in seeing Europe's great central power explode: racially homogeneous Germany had to be divided religiously and politically. To this end, the war had to last as long as possible. This, according to another article in the SS-Leitheft, had been the diabolical plan of Cardinal-Minister Richelieu, who was at once a man of the pope and of his king, a clever spirit who had sworn to end Germany: "The war must last, and last still more. We must prolong it artificially," he had declared to Louis XIII. His will had been carried out, and he had every reason to rejoice about it: "We have obtained chaos in Germany. Its people is spilling its own blood. It is a triumph for France."[5]

The Peace of Westphalia had been the great victory of Germany's intractable enemies. With "the demilitarization of the German side of the Rhine" and the loss of two "security outposts on our Western front, Switzerland and the Netherlands," "the Reich was now utterly defenseless against the West."[6] In addition to the pope and France, and in concert with them, the "effective winners" of this atrocious war, which had caused the deaths of "half the German population," were the "local princes, individual powers," as well as "the Jewish war profiteers," eternal vultures who had taken advantage of the war to lay the groundwork for the power they now held.[7]

After thirty years of calamity, the 1648 Peace of Westphalia had been a fatal blow to the German organism, which was shattered into "343 independent states, into 40,000 principalities," into an "absurd dust cloud of nations and micro-nations."[8] "Just as Richelieu wanted." Although he had died in 1642, he had left Europe with this legacy; six years later, the Peace of Westphalia was still "his work."[9] The Peace continued the war by other means, such was the force of its destructiveness:

> All of the Cardinal's work had two goals: a powerful and well-organized France and a powerless, dismembered Germany. Richelieu and the Peace of Westphalia: these are the two cornerstones of all policy against Germany. Germany was to remain a field of ruin and a field of battle for the European powers. This is what France wanted until 1940. It is still what England desires today.[10]

Luckily, after three hundred years of distress, the Führer's victories had exorcised and rid Europe of "the spirit of Richelieu."

1648: The Peace of Westphalia and the International Order

For two centuries, Versailles had been the epicenter of the Franco-German conflict. From the other side of the Rhine, Versailles had issued the orders to destroy the Palatinate in 1688. For this reason, Bismarck had chosen to proclaim the new Empire in the Hall of Mirrors on January 18, 1871. In retaliation, Clemenceau, who had lived through the era and remembered it well, had insisted that the Peace of 1919 be signed in the same place. Places were significant: retribution had to be exacted on the site of an offense. Hitler, as we know, was a strong believer in this idea, and for this reason ordered that the Armistice of June 22, 1940, be signed in the Compiègne Wagon, the same railcar in which Marshal Foch had signed the Armistice of November 11, 1918. Oddly enough, the Führer had no interest in Versailles itself, although it was probably the toponym to which he had referred most since the beginning of his political career in 1919. Even so, he never manifested any interest in imitating Bismarck in order to cancel out Clemenceau's gesture. If the Armistice had been signed in the Forest of Compiègne in an echo of November 1918, where to sign the future peace treaty that would someday end the war in the West? In an entry in his *Journals* dated November 17, 1939, following the successful invasion of Poland and as Hitler was giving orders for a lightning assault on Western democracies, Goebbels noted the following answer to this question:

> The Führer is speaking of our war goals. . . . He is envisioning the total liquidation of the Peace of Westphalia, which was signed in Münster, and which he wishes to replace in Münster, too. This would be our ultimate goal. When we have succeeded in this, we can die in peace.[11]

More than Versailles, the Peace of Westphalia was the true source of Germany's ills, according to Nazi authors. It had established an international order that the Peace of 1919 merely confirmed: 1648, as Freisler wrote, was the year "the Versailles of Münster and Osnabrück" was signed.[12] In 1942, Franz-Alfred Six, a university professor and a lieutenant colonel in the SS who was responsible for *Gegnerforschung* (studies of the enemy) within the RSHA, published the texts of the treaties of Münster and Osnabrück, so that everyone would be aware of them.[13] To anyone surprised to see him working on such a scholarly, historic publication in the middle of the war, Six explained that it should not be forgotten that French and Great British policy was an attempt to "reestablish the circumstances that were prevailing in 1648." These circumstances had been characterized by "the powerlessness and the self-mutilation of the Reich."[14] Six added, "at this historic hour, presenting the German people with all of the articles and paragraphs of this peace treaty is a political necessity."[15]

The clauses of this peace had sealed the fate of Germany as a political power. Two historians, Friedrich Kopp and Eduard Schulte, argued this at length in their book published in 1943, contending that in 1648, Germany had "become a defenseless object in the hands of the European powers." From the powerful, coordinated, and cohesive organism it had once been, the Reich had "been demoted to the rank of a mere aggregation of states."[16] The de facto dissolution of the Holy Roman Empire had been achieved through the accession to sovereignty of innumerable German political entities, which had been France's asserted goal. The Peace of Westphalia had "made the division and the powerlessness of Germany into a basic law of European diplomacy" and international order. France had always made sure that this "well-organized German anarchy" was kept in place. "France, under the liberal and terribly humane Republic or under Napoleon, kept pursuing the policy of 1648, without reservation and with the same methods as Richelieu, Mazarin, and Louis XIV." Its regimes had changed, but not its latent state of war against Germany. This war had been pursued under cover of the loftiest and most disinterested of principles: "Even after 1871, France's Third Republic, though allegedly democratic, humane, and idealist, pursued this bellicose policy, the very one that the highly imperialist kings of France had pursued in Westphalia."[17] Under these conditions, it was clear that "the National Socialist movement . . . was at once a protest against Versailles, Münster, and Osnabrück," the "Westphalian diktats," the false " 'peace' of 1648."[18]

From the 1920s on, the francophone jurist Friedrich Grimm was a tireless propagandist for this idea. He believed that France was bound by the "will of Richelieu."[19] For Grimm, the dying wish of the diabolical cardinal had been for "the total destruction of German unity," and as a result, every Frenchman began his morning muttering, while he buttered his toast, *Ceterum censeo Germaniam esse delendam* ("I believe Germany must be destroyed," a variation of a famous saying by Roman statesman Cato the Elder).[20] In order to destroy Germany, it was necessary to sow "disorder" there by fostering various strains of particularism, local secessionist movements, and the mediocre ambitions of petty local potentates looking to play Louis XIV in their provincial fiefs.[21] For Franz Six, the same thing had been going on for three centuries: the "removal of militarily and economically vital territories" and the deployment of "unfailing support for German particularism" had been proven effective by Richelieu and rigorously employed since his time.[22]

In 1942, Carl Bilfinger, a professor of international law at the University of Heidelberg, published a lengthy article on the topic of the Peace of Westphalia and the international legal order it had begun. In what is the most detailed analysis to use this perspective, he argued that the treaties of 1648 marked the birth of international law. A tragic birth, to his way of thinking, because it came at the price of the destruction of internal orders such as that of the Reich. The Holy Roman Empire had been "mutilated" and "dismembered," anatomical and medical metaphors that connoted the biological nature of the organism being killed off.[23] Even more than the principalities' accession to full sovereignty, which Nazi jurists, historians, and ideologues so often lamented, Bilfinger denounced another aspect of the 1648 treaties, that of the "denationalization and the internationalization of sovereign German territories," because the peace treaties had included provisions for foreign intervention if they were not upheld.

Furthermore, and even worse, internal constitutions were required to respect the principles laid out by these peace treaties. Bilfinger denounced the overriding of national law by international law, which to him was a total distortion that opened the door to invasion. He believed that the international order had always conspired to bring about the centrifugal fracture of Germany by encouraging "the freedom of German regions with regard to the Reich," as well as "the liberty of the individual with regard to the state."[24] Liberalism was a well-known French import. And as for separatism, it had been fanned by the constant maneuvers deployed by Paris in Bavaria and the Rhineland territories. The enemy was also organizing the "pillage of German land" through a predatory "occupation," as had happened during the Thirty Years' War, the Napoleonic Wars, and in 1923 in the Ruhr. Everything had been undertaken using the "same methods" for the past "three hundred years." "These methods are violence, interference in German internal affairs, as well as mutilation, theft, and famine," such as had taken place during the Thirty Years' War and the blockade of 1914–1919.[25] Friedrich Grimm and Bilfinger argued along the same lines, that the struggle against 1648 and against Versailles was "a fight for the law," which crafty, shiftless enemies were attacking with violence, lies, and hostility.[26]

Grimm's writing contained something far more interesting than a simple denunciation of the eternal French enemy and its supposedly constant stance since 1648. A lawyer and a legal scholar, Grimm's readings of the Peace of 1648 and that of 1919 were nourished by the Nazi epistemology of the law examined earlier. To Grimm, the international order that France sought and the legal norms that had been imposed on Germany for centuries were destined for failure because they were "formal-legal."[27] Richelieu, according to Grimm, may well have been an abominable enemy for Germany, but he had served his own country as an intelligent and sensible statesman, fully attuned to life's national and international demands. He may well have made use of the law in unprecedented ways, but he had never been its slave: "Richelieu, like all great statesmen, was no friend of the paragraph. His state grew with him. . . . Unwritten law took precedent in his eyes, over any rigid text."[28] Richelieu had served the life of his country, having understood its needs for organic growth. The same could not be said for his distant epigones in the twentieth century, such as Clemenceau or—even more so—Poincaré, who "had a filing cabinet instead of a heart." The "formal jurist Poincaré" and his comrades "knew their files, the lessons they had learned about Richelieu, but they were incapable of envisioning problems as they evolved."[29]

In the end, argued Grimm the Francophile, France was behaving ridiculously and fighting for a dead order because its leaders had not understood their own vital interests: "France is governed by obsolete fogeys. No other country exists in which old men have such a decisive influence over political decisions."[30] These timorous and fragile old people could neither see nor comprehend life. These jurists and these careful, myopic lawyers were ignorant of the realities of the European organism. They did not understand the idiosyncrasies of geopolitics. They had hidden themselves away in a realm that was gray, drab, and lifeless:

> French politics has a formula, a case, for every situation, handled in dusty archives. At the Quai d'Orsay, there is still a "Germany" folder with Richelieu's name on it. They call that the continuity of the state

and its services. Everything in there is neatly and nicely written, and these files and their paragraphs are still exercising their tyranny today. This politics is foreign to all progress, to the pulsing life of blood.[31]

Richelieu, if he were still alive, would refuse to be a prisoner of his own legacy. He would see Europe as it really was. He would choose Germany, a living and vital power, as an ally, instead of exhausting France in a fight against it. Life could not be translated into maxims, nor action into algorithms. Richelieu had been a great statesman, for he had understood his time and his context. It was a fatal error to try, as the French had for the past three centuries, to transform his work into a textbook for geopolitical action, to respect and reiterate the actions of a dead man who, had he been alive, would have acted entirely differently. Richelieu "knew how to constantly adapt to the context." He would not have rigidly followed a path that would lead him over the edge: "It is harmful for ideas to be transformed into rigid maxims for governments alien to life to invoke as 'eternal laws' for their actions."[32]

What was true of Richelieu was true of Bismarck as well. In 1871 the "Iron Chancellor" had opted for federation and a "Lesser German" solution, because at the time it had been the only way to achieve German unity. This did not mean that the "Greater German" ideal or centralization were to be rejected—quite the opposite, in fact. The Führer's role was not to piously reproduce Bismarck's approach. Like his predecessor's job, the Führer's task was to help Germany to live in the context of its time.

The old fossils governing France were writing its death sentence. Grimm pointed the finger at the legal formalism of weak-willed, rigid lawyers muttering mummified dogmas instead of thinking of life: "In Versailles, these incorrigibles believed that they could once again impose the principles of the Peace of Westphalia"—principles that were no less than three hundred years old! French ossification was confining the international order in an obsolete framework. "The undying Richelieu, the undying Peace of Westphalia, this is what has summed up the tragic fate of the German people for centuries, even today."[33]

It went without saying, then, that "Hitler's German mission is to end Richelieu's legacy. . . . Here, perhaps, is the deepest meaning of the great historical events we are witnessing." Indeed, now it had been "three centuries that the fight begun by Richelieu in 1630 against the idea of German unity has endured, through three Thirty Years' Wars."[34] In his book's conclusion, Grimm echoed Hitler's words to Goebbels in November 1939:

> The peace to come will make it possible to put to rest the Peace of Westphalia of 1648. This time, we will not be content with half measures. The Führer's mission is to put an end to the third Thirty Years' War in three centuries' time by striking down Richelieu's idea once and for all. This three-century war, which Richelieu began, will finally come to an end.[35]

Even before a peace treaty could be signed, the armies had spoken, and the balance of power had definitively changed. Whereas

> for centuries, our fate had been sealed, it was recently broken open again, thanks to the Führer, who rebuilt a Great German imperial power, which, through the destruction of France, returned Alsace and Lorraine to the German people, as well as the Netherlands, as well as soon, most likely, Switzerland.[36]

With the occupation of France, "the Peace of Westphalia was liquidated [liquidiert]."[37] As an SS publication asserted, this was why "the religious powers of the past, in addition to the political powers, particularly the 'democracies,' want to provoke a new Thirty Years' War today."[38]

Fabrizierte Konstruktionen: International Legal Absurdity

The fate of Germanity in the Europe established by the Treaty of Versailles was a violation of the most basic laws of nature. First and foremost, the entities created to house German populations were not viable. This was true of Germany, but even more so of Austria, a stunted nation that had been reduced to nothing by the Treaty of Saint-Germain when it broke apart the Austro-Hungarian Empire. While it was true that the multinational empire had been doomed to failure by biology and history, the fate of German speakers within it, who were hemmed into a tiny Alpine state and deprived of *Anschluss* with Germany, was simply criminal: "The Treaty of Saint-Germain deprived the German state of Austria of all the essential and necessary conditions for life." Without any resources or industries to speak of, undermined by a macrocephalic imbalance between Vienna and the truncated *hinterland,* Austria was "a residual state, incapable of leading an autonomous life"—a state that would be "unfit to live if it had to rely on its own strength."[39] The unviable territories created by the treaty were a sin against nature because "their imposed frontiers do not follow those of the peoples."[40] Politics, once again, was violating biology, just as diplomatic maps were violating racial ones. Nowhere had the right of Germanic populations to self-determination actually been respected: not in Germany or Austria, where *Anschluss* had been forbidden; not for the Germans of the Sudetenland, which had been annexed by the newly created state of Czechoslovakia; and not for Germans in Danzig, Memel, Silesia, or Transylvania, to name only a few places. The jurist Kurt Trampler deplored this as the height of madness: "Those who recognize the Czechs' rights . . . ought logically to have recognized the same rights for the German people." It was stupefying to see that the German speakers were the worst off in the former Austro-Hungarian Empire. There was no reason that "the Germans of Austria-Hungary have less right to self-determination than the other peoples of the monarchy."[41] The result had been the massive minority problem in post-Versailles Europe, a biological and a political aberration. The Germans had been "persecuted" everywhere in the states created by Versailles, in which a systematic "war" against the German "school and mother tongue" was being waged, with the explicit goal of "de-Germanification."[42]

The German minorities of Poland or Czechoslovakia had not been lucky enough to be taken care of in this way. Among the irrational states created by the Treaty of Versailles, Czechoslovakia was presented as the nadir. Indeed, it might be more accurate to refer to it as "Czecho-Slovakia," as the Nazi sources did, inserting a hyphen as if to underline its politically artificial, racially mixed, and culturally schizophrenic nature. *Tschecho-Slowakei* was an "anti-natural construction," a "fabricated construction," as Hitler himself put it, falling back on two

Gallicisms (*fabrizierte Konstruktion*) to draw attention to the artificiality and foreignness of "this abnormal artifact," this Wilsonian and French fantasy that had no reason to exist in the heart of Europe.[43]

Fabricating such a fiction had required violence. In the interwar period, Czechoslovakia was presented to the world as a happy island of democracy in a sea of central European dictatorships. Hitler, with implacable sarcasm, was intent on revealing the true nature of this model state:

> This state is a democracy; that is to say, it was founded on the democratic principles of imposing a construction fabricated in Versailles on a vast majority, swiftly and without asking them. This true democracy thus began by oppressing the majority of its inhabitants, violently depriving them of their vital rights.[44]

Hitler was outraged by the lies of the Czechs and of the international community, ridiculing all those "who defend liberty, fraternity, justice, the self-determination of the peoples, etc.," those eternal know-it-alls who

> for fifteen years have acted against the peoples' most natural interests, against all human dignity, who have written diktats imposed with a gun to the head, only to turn around and deplore, in a nice gesture of hypocritical indignation, the unilateral violation of "sacred" laws and even more sacred treaties.[45]

The contradictions of the international order of Versailles had thus been internalized by the Constitution and the functioning of the Czechoslovakian state: "Seven and a half million people are deprived of their right to self-determination, specifically in the name of a certain Mr. Wilson's right to self-determination!" Faced with demands for self-determination and freedom, the Czechs had responded with the most brutal forms of repression: "The misfortune of the Germans of the Sudetenland is unspeakable. They want to exterminate them. They are oppressed in an inhuman and humiliating manner."[46] Hitler hardened and dramatized his message, increasing international tensions, in a speech at the Berlin Sportpalast on September 26, 1938, that left Chamberlain convinced that there were no choices left but resignation or war. In it, Hitler spoke of Benesch's "reign of terror" and of the "war of eradication" being waged by the Czechs in order to "slowly annihilate Germanity" in the Sudetenland.[47] This project had almost succeeded: "a very high death rate" and "extreme childhood misery" had made biological extinction inevitable, as a result of the "programmed economic ruin" imposed by Prague.[48]

What were the Reich's demands? Rights, pure and simple: "nearly twenty years after President Wilson's declaration, it is time for peoples' right to self-determination to be implemented for these three and a half million unfortunates." This, according to Hitler, was the "most natural solution," because it was the most in alignment with the right to life.[49] Today, Hitler promised, on September 26, Germany was determined to fight for its *Lebensrecht*, the "right to life" of its oppressed compatriots. And let it be known, this new Germany was not the Germany of 1918:

> I march at the head of my people like the first of its soldiers. Let the world know that behind me marches an entire people, a people different from the people you knew in 1918! If, before, a wandering scholar succeeded in pouring the poison of democratic slogans into our ears, today, our people is not what it was yesterday![50]

Hitler's speech was delivered against the backdrop of an intensive press campaign orchestrated by Goebbels, who deployed a proven tactic in use since the 1920s: a steady bombardment of propaganda. It is evident in editions of the *Völkischer Beobachter* from that time: from August 1 to October 1, 1938, every one of this major journal's front-page headlines was related to the Sudetenland. Hitler drew frequent parallels between the domestic situation in Germany under the Weimar Republic and international relations in the 1930s. As he did so, the Nazi press was redeploying the schemata, the rhetoric, and the invective used against Weimar, the Social-Democrats, and the KPD before 1933.

The situation in Czechoslovakia was simple: faced with "murderous Czech bandits" and "deadly Hussite thugs," the Sudeten Germans had maintained their "impeccable discipline" and abandoned "the legal right to self-defense," in "the hopes that the state would finally find the means and the methods to put an end to the activities of the irresponsible Marxist and Czech elements."[51] On August 28, 1938, Rudolf Hess offered a tribute to these citizens:

We observe with admiration that you are maintaining iron discipline, despite the worst kinds of harassment, in spite of the terror and the murder . . . , and an unshakable calm, which comes from the clear feeling that you are well within your rights. . . . You have been entrusted with the rights of three and a half million Germans, the rights of millions of members of a great people.[52]

As could only be expected, such heroic abnegation could not be maintained forever, particularly in the face of a "Czecho-Slovak" government that acted in such patent bad faith. Instead of granting "protection and vital rights" to the Sudeten Germans, Prague had struck out at them "with martial law and with new murders."[53] There could be no hesitating: "This criminal state must be destroyed" not only for the sake of the Sudeten Germans, but also to protect Europe.[54] Hitler—a hypochondriac who since the summer of 1938 had been obsessed by his aerophagia (excessive air swallowing), which he was convinced was caused by stomach cancer—saw "Czecho-Slovakia" as a "cancerous ulcer that is destroying the entire European organism."[55] To him, this "work of madness and ignorance" was neither "a nation from the standpoint of ethnology [sic], nor [one] from that of strategy, language, or economics." It was "impossible to keep this artificial construction alive through political or diplomatic maneuvering."[56]

The Czech "mosaic state" had been built on untenable contradictions.[57] Prague had built its state on a "right to self-determination" that it refused to extend to its minorities, stifled as it was by "a centralizing constitution." The world piously celebrated "the philosophers of humanity Masaryk and Benesch," Enlightenment minds anointed by the League of Nations, but "the ideals of humanistic democracy elaborated by the philosopher Masaryk have become murder and terror under the dictatorship of the potentate Benesch, a dictatorship of inferiors, pure and simple."[58]

The Czechs were politically and culturally contradictory because they were biologically diseased. The *Völkischer Beobachter*, faithful to its mission as racial observer, used its racial logic to point out that "Czecho-Slovakia" was undermined by "racial dualism": "In the arteries of the Czech people, the—constructive—Slavo-Nordic element is struggling against the Avar blood that dominates it with its propensity to destroy everything."[59] It was a mixed people, and therefore schizophrenic. This explained the contradictions that ensnared it—and with which it ensnared others. With the biological and medical lens firmly in place to examine the case of the Czechs, Prague could now be likened to Carthage:

> The Prague of Benesch and his consorts has become the Carthage of our times. It is the European outpost of the moral and cultural degeneracy whose point of reference is the Moscow Bolsheviks. Europe, and above all Germany, can have but one duty: the definitive destruction of this hotbed of pestilence. This is the only way that the young twentieth century will succeed, just as Ancient Rome did, in saving civilization from the menace of this half-savage vermin.[60]

The situation in Poland was particularly bad for German speakers. The poor Germans had always been under threat in these Slavic territories, which they had conquered and civilized during the Middle Ages. Bismarck had wanted to intensify colonization, not in order to "eradicate the Poles" but to "avoid the eradication of Germanity."[61] After Versailles, the German territories demanded by the Polish state, such as Silesia, had been the site of "bloody uprisings" and "abominable terror."[62] The League of Nations had ceded to this violence in refusing to grant the Germans of Poland "self-determination in accord with Wilson's program."[63] The Gethsemane of the German minority had come and gone. Their "Via Dolorosa" could now begin, as the government's avowed goal was to "eradicate everything German in the newly Polish state." The author denounced "the total absence of rights afflicting the German racial minority": "The protection of minorities 'guaranteed' by the League of Nations and the Polish Constitution has not prevented the agony of the Germans in Poland."[64] This protection would have been all the more helpful in the Polish context, where "for a thousand years a hatred of the Germans" had reigned, which was now culminating in veritable "extermination measures": "Stripped of rights and dispossessed, they have been condemned to die."[65]

In a 1940 essay, Alexander von Freytag-Loringhoven, a professor of international law at the University of Breslau and a NSDAP deputy to the Reichstag since 1933, also denounced "the Polish reign of terror," this "terror against the German racial group," which had, by

his calculations, racked up a staggering "fifty-eight thousand" innocent German-speaking victims, killed by Polish executioners.[66] It is
interesting to note that, down to the thousand, this number corresponds to the number of Polish civilians killed by the SS Einsatzgruppen
and the German police. By September and October 1939 they had embarked on their efforts to eradicate the country's elite, and, in so doing,
to destroy Poland as a nation.

The learned professor of law, taking care to justify the attack on
Poland by presenting it as an act "of natural law," was hewing scrupulously to official Nazi discourse as presented in a publication of the
German Ministry of Foreign Affairs.[67] The book, *The Atrocities Committed by the Polish People against the Germans in Poland*, was published in French, both because it was the language of diplomacy and
because the French public and French decisionmakers were its target
audience and were also called upon as its witnesses. The thick book,
which came out in 1940, followed a few brief introductory chapters with
nearly three hundred pages of "irrefutable, officially monitored proof" of
Polish atrocities, including some one hundred pages of often unbear-
ably graphic photographs. This book, too, advanced the figure of "fifty-
eight thousand dead and disappeared" Germans.[68] According to the
Auswärtiges Amt, the entire Polish "political system" was "founded
on the old rallying cry of the extermination of the Germans," so much
so that "any manifestation of German national life was interpreted as
being directed against the Polish state."[69] Consequently there was an
imperative for the "eradication of everything that was German," which
had become nothing less than a "national duty." In light of such hatred and such ethnic perversity, the author denounced "moral chaos
leading to murder." Far from meeting its obligation to protect minorities, the Polish government had "itself handed its citizens of German
race over to the bloodthirsty furor of Polish brutes, against any constitution, any law, any moral, any human feeling."[70] Instructions from
Warsaw were carried out at the regional level by "the Voivodes' devastating practices against the German ethnic group."[71]

The book could have been a commentary, or even the script, for a
film by Gustav Ucicky called *Heimkehr* (Return to the fatherland).
Shot in 1940, the same year the book was published, it met with tremendous success when released in German theaters the following

year, in 1941. The film was a detailed portrayal of the trials of the *Aus-landsdeutschtum* at the hands of their Polish tormentors. It opened at the scene of a pogrom, in which the German school in a Polish village is destroyed and its books burned in a sinister auto-da-fé. Marie, the young, pretty, and brave teacher, protests to the mayor, an ominous- and suspicious-looking gentleman with a strong Slavic accent, flanked by huge dogs whose barks punctuate each of his sentences—Polish dogs! Marie protests that "there are laws in Poland, too," and a long con- versation on the idea of citizenship ensues, during which Marie affirms that she is German by essence and Polish by an accident of history. Peaceful and conciliatory, yet determined, she goes everywhere—first on a gracious visit to the mayor, then, moving up the hierarchy, to the Voivode, and then to court—in an attempt to recover her school and her students. In so doing, she ends up in a disagreement with her fiancé, a certain Dr. Fritz Mucius. He contends "that one can only break vio- lence with violence."

The rest of the film proves Mucius right: Marie, Fritz, and their friend Karl Michalek go out to the movies, where, of course, only Fox and MGM films are being screened. Our three German citizens from Poland rise respectfully when the Polish national anthem is played, but they refuse to sing it. They are attacked by a crowd that the camera, in a series of close-ups, depicts as inhuman monsters. Fritz is wounded, and dies after the doctors refuse to care for him. All of the Polish authorities (the mayor, the Voivode, the cinema director, police officers, doctors, judges, and so on) are portrayed as hostile to the Germans, and as plot- ting their extinction. One unfortunate incident follows another. After Fritz's death, Polish characters attack a young German woman, who ends up being killed by a sinister, hairy, broad-headed man, a Slavic beast with a baleful glare and an unbalanced libido. These extremely violent scenes are interspersed with peaceful ones: in a Warsaw sitting room, the Polish government formulates cunningly reassuring lines to feed to the German ambassador, who is worried about the German mi- nority in Poland suffering from a lack of legal standing. A soothing toast, another lynching . . . The Germans' only recourse is to place their faith and hope in Hitler. They meet secretly in a barn to listen to their Führer on the *Reichssender* (radio broadcasts), and are arrested in a Polish police raid. The film's highly suspenseful ending takes place at the bottom of a crypt-like cellar, into which the unfortunates have been thrown. The dark and disturbing space resonates with the singing of children, like angels of the catacombs, led by the ever-consoling Marie. She calms the little ones and moves the adults with a monologue about the far-off German fatherland:

> Not only will the whole village be German, but all around, everything will be German. . . . It'll be so funny when the earth in the meadows, the bit of clay, the stone, the grass, the hay, the hazelnuts, the trees, everything will be German like we are, because it will have grown on the hearts of millions of Germans, all of them returned to the German earth—and become the earth. Because it's not just that we're satisfied to live a German life: we'll die a German death, and even in death, we'll still be Germans, we'll become a bit of Germany.

Just as the Polish assassins begin to flood the cellar and are loading their machine guns for the final massacre, the sounds of fighter planes and tank engines fill the air: "The Germans are here!" Shouts of joy and freedom fill the air; the relief of the prisoners is shared by the teary audience: the Führer's war against Poland's murderous oppression, a criminal state that has deprived its German minority of all legal safeguards and protections, is well and truly a war for life and justice. In the end, the "violent" Fritz, killed by the Poles halfway through the film, is proven right: in the face of these heights of iniquity, Marie's gentleness is for the birds. Defending yourself and securing your right to life requires a fight.

Like the 1941 film, the German official report of 1940 deplored the cultural and economic asphyxiation (by confiscatory fiscal measures, expropriations, and so on) of the German minority, whose "religious services" had been forbidden, and whose "use of the language has become impossible in the street, in stores, in restaurants."[72] This persecution culminated in the autumn of 1939 in a "horrifying storm of bloody killings," perpetrated by a "rabble," by "hordes," by terrifying Slavic "riffraff" whose "penchant for torture and cruelty" was well known.[73] "All of the Germans were killed, regardless of their age, their profession, their social status, their religion, their sex." They had been "brutally mutilated"—and here, the text obliged the reader to wade through the anatomical specifics and a profusion of unbearable details, in the style of a medical inquest.[74] In the course of these massacres, perpetrated by "elements devoid of moral sentiment," "entire families, entire villages have been wiped out."[75] Here, then, if any proof was still needed, was hard evidence of the genocidal will of the Polish people, corroborated by "the number of children from the German minority beaten and shot," and by the fact that "they had gone so far as to murder a woman about to give birth."[76]

The text also underlined that all of this had been premeditated by the "Polish authorities," who had encouraged the massacres with arms and orders. Their rigorous organization had exploited the formidable energy of a mass of subhumans by whipping up their most criminal instincts "through every form of propaganda, the press, the radio, certain priests."[77] Once unleashed, the murderous impulses of the Slavic people had culminated in a saturnalia of violence, moral debasement, and sexual perversion. The text deplored the "attitude . . . in defiance of all laws and all morality" as well as the "shameful" role played by "fanaticized females."[78] There could be no doubt about it: "In the history of twentieth-century political murders, the atrocities committed by the Poles occupy a special place in their enormity and in the scale of their cruelty."[79]

Everything had conspired in this crime: reasons of state, the passion of the vilest of sentiments, premeditation and precipitation, orders from on high, and the chaos of these animal bodies, boors stirred up by hatred. The "depravity of the Polish population's morality, the consequence of immoral and degenerate politics" was not solely responsible for this carnage, however.[80]

> These massacres were organized; they are not the result of a spontaneous explosion of savage hordes. The people were systematically stirred up, a bloody psychosis was nourished and sustained in them, one that fit only too well with the Polish mentality, which is disposed to cruelty, inclined to murder and pillage.[81]

Legal experts were thus justified in denouncing plans for the "total eradication of everything German in this country," and in welcoming the Führer's war as "a fight for the German right to live," for "the law was fully on the side of the Germans."[82] Hitler's proclamation to the soldiers of the Wehrmacht on September 1, 1939, was hardly surprising, in light of all this. He explained that it was up to them to protect the Germans of Poland, who had been "chased from their houses and their farms by a bloody terror." This same Hitler, we recall, had just calmly admitted to his generals that he was seeking "a propaganda reason to launch the war; credible or not, it does not matter."[83] The mission of the "German Army" was to "wage uncompromising battle to defend the honor and the right to life of the German people."[84]

International "Law": A Fact

At a bare minimum, the law should be more than a bald statement of fact—or, at the very least, not be (entirely) derived from the mere state of things. The distinction between de facto and de jure is foundational, if not to the law, then at least to the epistemology of law, and to all reflections on the essence of the phenomenon of law. With his familiar blend of wit and rigor, Jean-Jacques Rousseau devotes several key pages of his *Social Contract* to this distinction. He recalls, not without mischief, that a force (normalized and nomothetic) that resorts to force (to the mere fact of force, that is) is—de facto—lacking in sufficient force to assert its own authority.

In international law, which was formalized as a practice and as a discipline in seventeenth- and eighteenth-century Europe, the distinction between law and the state of things was particularly problematic. More than in any other field, the rule of law, by necessity, appeared to originate in power, and in the balance of power; in other words, from adversarial relationships. The rules of international law generally came from peace treaties, which sanctioned the victory of one set of parties and the defeat of another. In the religious world, a fact (of victory or defeat, for example) could be assigned a transcendent meaning—this was the logic of the ordeal or the trial, for example—relating to divine judgment, from which norms could be legitimately derived. But in the increasingly disenchanted universe of international relations in the modern and the contemporary era, fact and necessity were merely a question of conflict and the balance of power, an immanently and eminently circumstantial matter to which it was difficult to assign a higher meaning, let alone a transcendent one.

Legal experts seemed to know this, and to be resigned to the normative value of the state of fact, sanctioning it in the great peace conferences and peace treaties that characterized the work of modern diplomacy. The watchword of international law as it emerged from the wars and peacetimes of the European seventeenth century, and from the beginnings of the colonial experiment, would appear to have been *Ex factis jus oritur* (law is born of facts), a Latin precept and legal doctrine well known to internationalists. War, quite literally, called the shots, and the law had only to wait until the battle was won to pronounce on the facts. The most celebrated statement of this was the principle of *Uti possidetis*: a belligerent is justified in affirming his ownership of (that is, his rights to) what he possesses (de facto), even if this possession is the result of military conquest (again, de facto).[85] When it came to colonization, European powers asserted the right to take possession of *terrae nullius*, land that, according to them, belonged to no one. Escheat (the fact that they were possessed by no one) reverted this land to the power that chose to occupy it, to possess it (de facto), and thus to own it (de jure).

Nazi legal experts followed the logic that the law sanctions a state of fact, above all in their reasoning that law should transcribe the natural order. To them, however, international law was the exception—because they took exception, so to speak, to the state of fact of the defeat of 1918, which had been sanctioned by the 1919 treaty. Viktor Bruns, a professor at the University of Berlin, and, since 1933, president of the international law section of the "Academy for German Law," approached this issue with the serenity and the lofty remove of an epistemologist of the law. Essentially, he argued that it was time to give up on fantasies and to lucidly examine reality:

> For as long as international law has existed, states have seen treaties as a means of protecting their policies, of exploiting a state of fact, of securing what they have acquired by sanctioning it with the law. Every treaty is the expression of a balance of power and of the overall political situation prevailing at the time of its signature. Every treaty is a kind of freezing of the past.[86]

This was not a problem, so long as no one went around spouting poppycock about the "sacredness of treaties," which were merely the record of a state of facts, and therefore about as sacred as a weather bulletin or a sheet of football scores. From there, Professor Bruns generalized, "All law is dependent on a specific context. It is determined, at its origins and over the duration, by this context." Jurists, in other words, were essentially clerks of court: they noted what fact dictated. The logical, epistemological, and ontological consequence of this was so simple that it could be neatly summed up in a truism: "If the situation underlying the treaty changes, then the treaty regulates a situation that no longer exists."[87] The discrepancy between the text (of the treaty) and the reality (that it claimed to state) was such that the convention had to be revised.

That same year, in 1934, a few months after Germany withdrew from the League of Nations, Carl Schmitt leveled this attack at foreign legal scholars still defending the Treaty of Versailles: "Why should world history freeze itself precisely on June 28, 1919, and why should that be law?" The Paris treaties were nothing but "instruments for the perpetuation of a specific moment, and a perfectly unjust moment, at that."[88]

International law should not be constrained to treating facts in treaties as set in stone. In this strange "un-law," the other result of the principle of *ex factis jus oritur* was that, as one situation succeeded another, the law could be revised. In other words, the provisions of international law were not absolute norms, but rather decrees relating to a specific context, which therefore had to evolve as the context evolved. The high priests of the temple of positivism thus had to temper their *Pacta sunt servanda* with a few extra Latin words: treaties should be respected, but if and only if the doctrine of *clausula rebus sic stantibus* was respected. The two phrases were indissolubly linked, recalled Professor von Rauchhaupt, a major scholar of international law at the University of Heidelberg and the author of a celebrated textbook on the subject.[89] This customary "clause" dictated that norms should be obeyed only so long as they hewed to the state of fact. This passion for the *clausula* principle seems to have been widespread at the time, to judge from the number of German legal scholars writing and publishing about it then. This included at least four doctoral theses submitted between 1934 and 1941, as well as frequently recurring discussions and mentions of it in the contemporary literature on international law.[90]

The doctrine of *clausula rebus sic stantibus*, by stating the possibility of adapting law to fact, ensured that texts did not become dead letters, or, even more important, that death not take hold of the living. What was a norm that did not evolve with the state of things? A sarcophagus, a shirt of Nessus, that petrified the living instead of poisoning it. In the journal of the Academy for German Law, Karl Haushofer, father of German geopolitics and a convert to Nazism, deplored the deathly fixity of jurists who were enemies of Germany: "For the privileged members of the international order, the law is static, fixed in the moment of the letter," whereas "dynamism is a necessity dictated by the laws of nature."[91]

Carl Bilfinger wrote much the same thing in an essay that opposed the "law of the League of Nations" and the "laws of nations." In it, he raised the question of whether "the law of the League of Nations is truly international law."[92] Bilfinger asserted that the answer was no, because it was not "dynamic." With arguments reminiscent of Heraclitus, Bilfinger recalled that in classical international law, "the flow of becoming" and "life in the process of its arrival" are accounted for in the "dynamic element" introduced by *clausula rebus sic stantibus*. By contrast, "the accent placed on safety, the status quo, on the static principle, goes against this understanding of the law . . . based on the principles of dynamics and evolution."[93] A tribute paid to virtue by vice, the Treaty of Versailles, and, consequently, the Covenant of the League of Nations in its Article 19, included the *clausula* doctrine. Bilfinger cited all of Article 19, as if to remind the international community of its duties and to reaffirm Germany's right to see the international legal order evolve.[94]

Pamphlets denounced, essays argued, and textbooks taught. Schmitt's and Bilfinger's opinions were widely shared by their fellow jurists in long and plodding treatises that filled their students' law books. Otto Göppert, for example, a *juris doctor* and high-ranking diplomat, published a text of nearly seven hundred pages on the League of Nations for the edification of German law students. In it, he vituperated against the subordination of the international order to French interests:

"Revision is war," Aristide Briand declared in a speech in 1930. There is no clearer way to express that Article 19 does not exist, so to speak,

in the French view of things. . . . The result is therefore that Article
19 is, in the present circumstances, perfectly inapplicable.[95]

On a more fundamental level, the League of Nations was committing a crime of lèse-legality by refusing to allow treaties to be revised:
the "elasticity" of the law ought to reflect the plasticity of things,
because "the world is not static."[96] The League was violating not only
the spirit of the law, but the letter as well, since "it is clear from Articles
11 and 19 that the territorial order established by the peace treaties
cannot be forever considered sacred or intangible." This was logical,
given that law was based "on the principle of evolution, and not only
that of conservation; on the dynamic element and not only the static element."[97] The international order as created by Versailles had ignored
Article 19 of the League of Nations Covenant and the doctrine of *clausula rebus sic stantibus*, to the point that the League was not a *So-
ciété des nations* (in French in the original text), but rather a "Society
of Nations"; a mere alliance created among certain nations to defend
their individual interests, instead of a universal community to promote the general interest.[98] In this, the author was echoing Carl
Schmitt's harsh rhetoric: Schmitt often pointed out that the League of
Nations (Völkerbund) was not a *Bund* (a federation or a community) but
rather a mere *Bündnis* (coalition), "an old fashioned opportunistic alliance" rather than the innovative community promised and heralded
by Wilsonian messianism.[99] Others, too, pointed out that "there can
only be a league of nations, and not a community of nations," merely
an artificial *Gesellschaft* (society) made up of heterogeneous parts,
rather than a homogeneous, organic, and natural *Gemeinschaft*.[100] In
itself, the existence of this "society" was purely negative. It was an
"enormous hostile alliance" in which "the entire world was in league
against Germany": "The exclusion of Germany from the community
of the peoples . . . is not a rhetorical exaggeration, but must be understood in the most literal and most legally precise sense."[101]

Life (both that of individuals and that of races and states) is characterized by fluidity, lability, evolution. A static legal system that sought
to fix situations in a rigid way thus was a straitjacket that suffocated the
living organisms comprising the international community. Instead of

following the motions of life, the static nature of formal law was obstructive, an infarction for races and nations: "No living law without the possibility of revision," without "life's natural growth," Carl Schmitt insisted.[102] Contemporary international law was thus an intellectual and moral aberration. It was both a biological calamity and an epistemological monstrosity. Schmitt attacked the order of the Treaty of Versailles in the harshest terms. Contemporary international law no longer had any relation to the life of nations and to political reality. Opposing the "order of the law" (a concrete order induced from reality) and "legal fictions" (morbid abstractions created in the diseased minds of a coterie of cosmopolitan jurists), Schmitt regretted that in the law of treaties, "all notions are divorced from concrete situations and stripped of meaning," that they had "lost any real relationship to the concrete order of a peaceful and fair coexistence of peoples respecting one another."[103] Instead of a "concrete order" sanctioned by law, the jurists had plunged the nations into an absurd fantasy. Schmitt's skillfully scathing mockery of the logic of collective security, based on an alliance for peace and an application of the principle of transitivity to antagonisms, was unmatched. Article 42 of the Treaty of Versailles, which demilitarized the Rhine, was, to his mind, "a shocking example of these legal fictions," which he abhorred and denounced, because any violation of this zone represented, according to the Versailles Treaty and the League of Nations Covenant, "a threat to world peace": "If a military marching band performs on a Sunday afternoon in Düsseldorf, a hostile interpretation of Article 42 would turn the event into an attack on Siam and Portugal." The two nations, both members of the League of Nations and thus linked to France through the Covenant, were jointly bound to guarantee its defense. But "if, to the contrary, the French invade the Ruhr with an army of tanks and the latest model of cannon, then, legally, it will not be belligerence, but a pacification measure."[104] Words were violating things as they actually were: "This system of legal relabeling will end up destroying all legality . . . and eradicating the final remains of legal common sense among honest people."[105] This melting of borders, the plasticity of space, was not merely a hypothetical danger. It was also *concretely* absurd: in an article published in 1939, Schmitt recalled that a planned customs union between Germany and Austria had been knocked down with a single vote, from the Cuban Antonio Sánchez de Bustamante, who had voted to oppose it before the International Court of Justice.[106]

Who was to blame? "Positivist" jurists, people who were so upset with reality that they had replaced it with a morbid and deadly phantasmagorical fiction. Yet again, Schmitt pointed a finger at Hans Kelsen and his "Vienna school"—a place name that connoted the Judaized cosmopolitanism of an imperial capital open on all sides, particularly the Eastern European one. This "Vienna school . . . built the international legal community . . . as a system of norms based on the founding principle of *Pacta sunt servanda*."[107] These impenitent logicians had, as they always did, made the law into a pyramid of rules deduced from a founding rule—in this case, absolute respect for the sanctity of treaties, a kind of abstract and decontextualized letter hovering above the situations and contexts from which it had been divorced.

Schmitt took care to distinguish between *rechtlich*, an adjective derived from the German root word *Recht*, and *juristisch*, derived from the Latin *Jura:* anything *rechtlich* was good, because *Recht* was the law as it was induced from concrete situations, whereas *juristisch* had its origins in the tradition and thinking of the Latin *Jus*, an abstract form of law with no relation to reality. This allowed Carl Schmitt to lament without falling into self-contradiction that "a legal order would be troubled by legal fictions."[108] The goal of positivist legal scholars was not to confuse for the sake of misleading, but rather to subject reality, life, and Germany to an order that was hostile to it.

Schmitt observed that rules were being devalued in a kind of normative inflation. He regretted the increasing disproportionality between "the content in law," "the legal substance" of texts, and their number: the less the principles of justice were obeyed, the more texts were promulgated, in a truly morbid movement of normative metastasis.[109] There was a "relationship between the stunting of the substance of the law and the inflation of rules."[110] Paradoxically, the contemporary era, which appeared to be the "formal apogee of the law" had created the most flagrant "material injustice": *Summum jus, summa injuria*.[111] Faced with a well-meaning and honest Germany seeking only to assert its "basic right to life," the cosmopolitan French lackeys in Geneva were weaving dangerous normative snares that they alone understood and mastered.[112]

> French policy and the international law that serves it . . . have, for the past fifteen years and with admirable zeal, spun a conceptual web around the Diktat of Versailles and the Covenant of the League of Nations[, a web made up of] hundreds of definitions, interpretations, constructions, covenants, and draft covenants.[113]

Here, Schmitt was critiquing foreign policy as developed in France by Louis Barthou, who, in 1934, attempted to relaunch the system of pacts and alliances in reverse, before his assassination in Marseille on October 9 of that year. The Eastern Pact imagined by Barthou was intended to revive France's Eastern alliances so that Germany would be surrounded. Its only legacy would be the Franco-Soviet Treaty of Mutual Assistance, which, although it was actually signed (in 1935), would remain a largely incantatory and symbolic agreement. International law, dominated by the French and by logicians of every stripe, valued "pacifism over peace, legality over justice"; that is, a notion that was abstract ("pacifism") and formal ("legality") instead of a reality that was concrete ("peace") and material ("justice"). This was all Germany demanded and everything its enemies "denature through abstract turns of phrase." The Reich's enemies were promoting "a complex system of conceptual determinations and conventional obligations instead of promoting a vital order."[114]

The intellectual work that had given rise to a legal order so utterly hostile to Germany was as biased as the rules it produced. There was no such thing as art for art's sake; even a simple mathematical calculation was never an innocent mental exercise:

> The methods of generalization [at work in the conceptual creations of positivist jurists] are always an expression of expressionist trends, not only from a logical standpoint, but from a political one. Generalization is a means of imposing oneself as the norm. This is why all imperialism is based on polysemic and general concepts and seeks to bind the peoples it dominates in an ambitious system of concepts and norms whose definition, interpretation, and sanctioning it takes charge of itself in decisive moments.[115]

The legal positivism of "logicians of the norm" thus took on the appearance of rational neutrality, of universality. This supposed universality, however, was merely the intellectual and legal translation of French, British, and American strains of political imperialism.

Norms were not mathematically deduced: they were physically induced. In international law as in all other fields of law, Schmitt and his neo-Hegelian sidekicks pressed for a law that would be the faithful transcription of concrete orders that truly existed: family, profession, race, nation, and so on. It was time for the law to look reality in the face and build once again from concrete situations. If the positivists found it pleasing to speak of basic norms, let them be taken at their word and let it be reaffirmed that the foundational norm of all law, the most elementary one, was the "right to life"—in other words, the "vital interests" of the German people. It was necessary to begin with "the most obvious of all basic rights, the right to exist."[116] Epistemologically, international law did not qualify as law. There could be no doubt that it was an epistemology tied to a diseased ontology, that of the Jew, who fled reality to find refuge in abstractions, where he might finally feel at ease: international law was "the typical product of an anti-racial internationalism, excogitated by a Jewish brain."[117] This morbid science supported and tied into a deadly politics. If, in international law, death was seizing the living, it was not only because death, consubstantial with this static understanding of things, was on the prowl, but also because murder was the law's foundation. As it existed, the law was not objectively macabre, but rather actively murderous: its enemies simply wanted to kill Germany through the "law."

In the political arguments and legal pamphlets of the German right wing, an apocryphal saying of Clemenceau's had considerable currency. In 1923, Hitler denounced the "treaty made to kill twenty million Germans and destroy the German nation."[118] This figure was reproduced everywhere. An eleventh-grade history book, for example, explained how "the president of the French Council Clemenceau affirmed with no pity that there were twenty million Germans too many." This number represented the exact difference in population between France and its cumbersome neighbor on the other side of the Rhine. Versailles had continued the war, but by other means. "The war against the German Army had ended, but the one being waged against the German people continued."[119] The "peace" was actually a continuation of the policy implemented by the Allies during the conflict: blockade, famine, mass deaths—with the goal of not only eliminating Germany as a political enemy, but also eradicating the German people as a race.

Everything in the Treaty of Versailles betrayed "the will to exterminate displayed by the enemies" of Germany. The schoolbook cited earlier gave a detailed account of all of the mining and agricultural resources that Germany had been deprived of by the treaty's territorial amputations: "15 percent of our grain and 20 percent of our potatoes" had been taken from the mouths of the Germans, not to mention everything Germany was losing from Alsace and the Moselle Valley, the former duchy of Schleswig, the Memel Territory, Poland, and West Prussia.[120] Once again, this included grain and potatoes, but also livestock, fruit, milk products, beetroots, and so on. After this "peace," Germany was left horrifically mutilated; Germans were now nothing but a "people without a land."[121] Deprived of its soil, its blood would disappear. The German organism was now utterly mangled, like a body deprived of one of its vital members. The conclusion of the textbook lesson was a sentence to be learned by heart: "The goal of the diktat of Versailles was to exterminate the German people."[122]

The law founded in the Treaty of Versailles not only mutilated and amputated the German body; the treaty also violated Germany's integrity through devastating and denaturing invasive procedures. Versailles was "an intrusion into the body of the German people," into "the substance of the German people," not only because "the waterways have been internationalized," but also because the provisions of international law had been inserted into national constitutions.[123] The jurists were particularly outraged at the introjection of international law in their country's law, in Article 178–2 of the Constitution of August 11, 1919, which states: "The provisions of the peace treaty signed on June 28, 1919, in Versailles are not called into question by the present constitution." For Arthur Wegner, "The diktat of Versailles was the Constitution-chaplet of the Weimar interregnum."[124] The internationalist worm, in other words, had tainted the fruit of Germany's constitution. Since the Peace of Westphalia, Germany had been "internationalized," Carl Bilfinger argued.[125] The international safeguards provided for by the Peace of Westphalia and the Treaty of Versailles had made German territories

into porous legal entities without any legal integrity or organic coherence. These bodies had been gashed open and made vulnerable to every
form of aggression and contamination:

> Henceforth Germany was defenseless. It possessed an impotent
> pseudo-government, helpless and characterless, and was abandoned
> to Marxist-democratic, Judeo-liberal trends. It was open to all attacks,
> and its borders were stripped bare.[126]

The Tricks of the Treaty: The Law as Duress

Worse than a necessity, or a state of fact, the Treaty of Versailles had
been an unlawful act, and a violent one, inflicted on Germany in a betrayal of every stated promise, commitment, and principle. In German,
the word *Vertrag* has several meanings. It may designate an international treaty (the "Versailler Vertrag," for example), but it generally
refers to a civil law contract, which is, of course, a mutually binding
agreement based on reciprocal obligations and free, informed, and
mutual consent by both parties. In the absence of any of these criteria,
a contract is null and void.

If the Treaty of Versailles was considered to be a *Vertrag* in all senses
of that word, then, the first critique to be leveled against it was one of
consent: when exactly had the Germans given their consent, and to
what? Clearly, they had not been in a position to consent to anything
when the peace conference began in January 1919: Germany, like the
other defeated powers, had not been invited. Peace talks took place
behind closed doors, among the "Big Four." The only thing plenipotentiary about the German representatives had been their name: the
treaty's contents had been revealed to them at the last minute, with
the obligation to sign before June 28; otherwise the Allies would resume hostilities. For Hitler, this was ample grounds to reject it now.
He denounced the foundational violence of this supposed law in
speech after speech:

> One cannot extort someone's signature from him by holding a pistol
> to his head and threatening to starve millions of people, and then
> proclaim that this document, dressed up with a stolen signature, is
> an official law![127]

The Germans had consented to nothing but the peace conditions laid out by President Wilson in his famous "Fourteen Points" speech to the U.S. Congress in 1918. By Wilson's own argument, "the right of peoples to self-determination" ought to be a guarantee to the German High Command and government that Germany would not suffer from excessive territorial and demographic damages, and that it would be allowed to preserve its national integrity and cohesion.

The German Reich's first communication to the American government at the end of World War I received a response from the State Department signed by Secretary of State Robert Lansing on November 5, 1918. In it, Lansing confirmed that peace would be on the terms Wilson had laid out in his speech that January. Along with all of his colleagues, legal scholar Herbert Wissmann, who had written his doctoral thesis on "Problems in the Revision of the Treaty of Versailles," believed that "Secretary of State Lansing's note . . . constituted a preliminary peace treaty . . . containing all of the legal foundations of the future peace treaty."[128] This exchange between the German and American governments constituted a "pre-treaty valid under international law" because it had led to the formulation of an expression of free and informed consent. "In this way, the principles in President Wilson's 'Fourteen Points' were no longer merely programmatic demands, but became actual norms of international law." An imposing four-page bibliography listed dozens of essays, theses, and legal journal articles that expressed the scholarly consensus that the German-American exchange of notes had been a "completely lawful pre-treaty."[129]

Of course, everything had changed six days later, when the Armistice was signed on November 11, 1918. Although "this German laying down of arms did not in any way signify that the German nation was surrendering itself to the arbitrary will of the victor," the Allies had shown their true face and replaced the law with force.[130] After the Treaty of Versailles was signed on June 28, 1919, "the darkest day in German history," there "could be no question of a freely consented agreement," because Germany had "bowed to illegitimate and illegal coercion."[131]

Wissmann concluded that it was therefore legally accurate to describe the treaty as a *diktat*, a polemical term he believed was the academically suitable one. "The word diktat is a suitable description for what occurred, including from a legal point of view," Arthur Wegner concurred in *Geschichte des Völkerrechts* (History of international law), a reference work in the 1930s.[132] Kurt Trampler, a specialist on the borders of post-Versailles Europe, was unequivocal in his description of the legal status of the exchange of notes between Germany and the United States, and the validity of Lansing's note. "With this note, a legally valid pre-treaty was established that . . . necessarily means that any divergence between the peace treaty and Wilson's points is a violation of convention." The real "treaty" was contained in the note; all the rest was a mere "diktat" that in no case could "abolish the real treaty." The latter "remained law, no matter what. And this law lives as long as the German nation recognizes it as one," unlike the false treaty of June 1919.[133] Germany was bound only by this exchange of notes, this American promise that peace would be based on the principles according to which Germany had ceased to fight, and on these principles alone.

Duress, criminal intent to mislead (German consent had been given based on false claims), and intentional fraud (the Treaty of Versailles had been presented as something it was not): in 1939, Hans Frank was still shocked by this underhanded, dirty trick:

> [To perpetrate] the most ignominious violation in the history of humanity . . . , the legal format of a consensual agreement between two powers equal in rights was chosen to conceal from the naïve reader the most brutal, most arbitrary violation of a great and cultured people.[134]

Semantic creativity flowered in descriptions of the Treaty of Versailles. In addition to the widespread and Latinate *Diktat*, a French word that was Germanized to describe a calamity that had rained down from the West, there was *Schand-* or *Schamfrieden* ("shameful" or "ignominious" peace), *Unfrieden* ("un-peace"), and of course *Kriegsvertrag* (war treaty), since this "diktat, which is only a treaty from a legal formalist standpoint . . . , may be read more as a declaration of war than as an instrument of peace."[135] The Treaty of Versailles had violated the will of the German people by disrespecting its freedom to contract and by circumventing the "pre-treaty" of November 1918, which had claimed to lay down the cardinal principle of a new international order, a people's most sacred right, that of self-determination.

Woodrow Wilson, a former professor of political science at Princeton, a specialist and a follower of Immanuel Kant—the Kant of *Perpetual Peace*—wished to establish the ideals of the Enlightenment as governing principles among nations. His Fourteen Points proposed to create or establish as a regulating ideal a kind of universal society where collective security would be overseen by a permanent parliament of nations practicing public diplomacy and international democracy based in ongoing dialogue, the colloquium of reason, goodwill, and the clear interest of all. A true democrat, Wilson believed that in international law, a people's right to self-determination was the equivalent of the autonomy of the democratic subject at the national level, and therefore was a necessary condition for the existence of the global society he believed would safeguard world peace. Opponents of the Treaty of Versailles argued that while this right had been more or less respected in the creation or re-creation of the Central European states (Poland, Czechoslovakia, Yugoslavia, and so on), it had been denied to the German populations that had been integrated by force into these new states (such as the Germans in Poland, or the Sudeten Germans in Czechoslovakia), as well as to the Austrians, whose annexation by Germany was forbidden by the Treaty of Versailles.

To the Nazis, the Treaty of Versailles had far graver implications than its impact within the specific historical context of 1918–1919. By failing to uphold their commitments, the Allies had not only coerced and tricked Germany; they had misled all of humanity. Their diplomatic and political piracy had made them into enemies of humankind, rendering impossible any society or community of states. Heinrich Rogge, a professor of international law, was one of the thinkers behind this argument, most notably in an article titled "Recht und Moral eines Friedensvertrages" (Law and morals of a peace treaty).[136] He argued that the Treaty of Versailles was not a peace treaty. After all, it did not contain any of the customary features of one. Normally, such a treaty resulted from an initial international negotiation and respected the honor of the defeated parties by allowing them to participate in the peace conference, sparing them humiliation and respecting their sovereignty both during the conference and in the provisions of the treaty itself. Versailles had not met any of these conditions, and was thus the exact antithesis of an acceptable international agreement. According to the author, this had deep anthropological and legal meaning. Law ceded to force during wartime, and negotiations and treaties reinstated it, with "all peace treaties signifying a confirmation by the community of international law." By "depriving the defeated of their rights," the "treaties of Paris shook and even destroyed the foundations of the community of international law."[137]

Was Versailles not merely a continuation of the war by other means? Optimistic, cynical, or resigned observers might be tempted to see it as the "institution of a law of war," a "war treaty whose object is to reestablish peace," that is, an act of violence or force whose goal was to reestablish peace.[138] Rogge, however, believed it was far worse than that: the Treaty of Versailles was missing one last mark of respect, the ultimate symbol of human community, which was respect for the adversary's honor. Before and during the war, the Allies had completely disregarded one of the fundamental doctrines of the law of war: *Etiam hosti fides servanda* (one must be honest even with one's enemy).

For all time, Germany had cultivated honor and respected the rules of honor each time it went to war. As the same author noted several years later, Germany had never succumbed to the temptation of "partisan warfare," as France had in 1870, 1914, and 1940. Indeed, "wherever Germany makes its mark in the art of combat, war is subordinated to the ethics of moderation, discipline, and self-control"—as proven, no doubt, by the Polish invasion, which was over and done with by the time Professor Rogge wrote these lines.[139] Temperate in wartime, Germany was moderate and magnanimous in victory. Returning, relevantly, to Bismarck's policy for Austria in 1866, Rogge recalled that the "Iron Chancellor" had persuaded Wilhelm I not to press his advantage by riding all the way to Vienna once the way had been opened by the Battle of Königgrätz. Rogge defined "Bismarck's peace policy" as "self-disciplined vengeance," a "temperance in victory, an honor paid to the defeated adversary."[140] Bismarck had done everything that the Allies, in their hubris and their desire for vengeance, had not known to do; specifically, to preserve the actual conditions of human coexistence and community.

According to Rogge, a clear "line in the history of law linked Kant and Hitler," and included Bismarck along the way. After all, Kant—who, lest it be forgotten, was German—had been the first to insist, first in *Perpetual Peace* (article 6) and then in *Groundwork of the Metaphysics of Morals* (section 1, 58), on the importance of respecting the honor of one's adversary; in this light, the Treaty of Versailles was "dishonest, in the sense of Kant and of Hitler."[141] National Socialism, which was based on the principle of race, respected the German people as it respected other peoples: "Nazism means a self-limiting of the German people, the people's peaceful turning inward, toward, and within itself. Nazism rejects all imperialism" so familiar to Western powers. As proof of this return to basic principles, Rogge cited Hitler's speech to an assembly of jurists in Leipzig on October 4, 1933, in which he claimed "to reject the dividing line that exists between law and morality." By promoting "the unity of the law and ethics," Hitler was laying the foundations for an enduring, honorable peace.[142] Nothing less.

"By dispossessing the defeated of their rights," the treaties of Paris had broken the bonds among the nations that constituted "the international community."[143] Not only was the Treaty of Versailles not a treaty—and even less a peace treaty—it was something far worse: an act of diplomatic piracy that had destroyed any possibility of a universal society of nations or a peaceful coexistence within an international community, because it had broken the last bonds of trust and respect. Nations had returned to a state of nature: who, now, could criticize Germany, the victim of such a lack of civility and humanity, for engaging in piracy in its desire to right the wrongs that it had suffered?

International Injustice and Natural Justice

Clearly, then, modern and contemporary international law was an artificiality that violated the basic laws of nature and harmed the most natural people of all—the German people. Luckily, Hans Frank proclaimed, "the law of life; that is, the law built from a nation's common biological destiny, is stronger than any purely formal order" and than "any constructivist chicanery."[144] The international order of the future would be as concrete as the international law of the past had been abstract. The leaders of the new Germany had understood this, as Viktor Bruns was happy to report:

> It is neither human will nor human rules that give form to the world, but nature itself, which is the law of man and the limit of his power. . . . The art of princes . . . ought to require that no treaty that violates his own people's right to life should ever be signed.[145]

There was no danger of this with Hitler. Edgar Tatarin-Tarnheyden crucified "normativist logicians" such as Kelsen, who allowed themselves to forget that "ideas are always substantial, and therefore concrete."[146] These warped thinkers assigned too much importance to "concepts" and to "form," when it was clear that a jurist ought to be interested only in the "vital substance" that made up reality. Along with *Lebenssubstanz*, Tatarin employed myriad *Leben*-compounds: the "vital territories" (*Lebensgebiete*) that had been plundered from Germany, the "right to life" (*Lebensrecht*) so vigorously denied it, its "vital interests" (*Lebensinteresse*), which were so consistently ignored.[147] And yet "formal law . . . is valid only as long as it does not contradict the law of life, the very idea of law, justice."[148] The latter three terms were interchangeable, as the only justice was that which gave voice to life, to nature.

In order to remain concrete in international law, it was necessary to take into account the reality of races: had the jurists and politicians still defending the Treaty of Versailles "ever seen a map of the peoples" of Europe?[149] The rules of international law were valid only to the extent that they accorded rights to races and their respective values: "In international law, only that which is in keeping with the right to life of a people endowed with a capacity for hard work and a strong life force can be imposed . . . over the long term." To apply "the letter for the letter" was absurd: the letter of the law was valid only if it expressed reality, if it was a transcription of life.[150] And life commanded that the best resources be attributed to the strongest and the most efficient. Over the formal equality favored by the anemic eggheads over in the Vienna school, from Rostock Tatarin advanced the idea of an "authentic international law" that would not be a "law of states" (*Staatenrecht*) but rather a true "law of the peoples" (*Völkerrecht*).[151] It would be founded on the fundamental principle that we must acknowledge the rightful place of each individual people, and, in particular, the *Lebensraum* it deserves, based on its numbers and on its racial and cultural superiority or inferiority, and its vital force, depending on which it will hold promise or die out.[152]

Using these criteria, there could be no doubt that jurists would award preeminence to Germany, not because it was Germany, but because the international order had to be governed by the trusty principles of Frederick the Great and "the organic idea of *Suum cuique*": "to each his due" would lay the groundwork for an international body that was temperate and well regulated, without excess, defect, or imbalance. Each people was to "take its place in the international legal community according to its vocation" and to the criteria cited above. This organic international community would represent a "transposition of the ideas that the Führer has set as the cornerstone of German politics," a transposition from domestic law to international law of this "organic understanding" that had, in Germany, made possible the emergence of an "authentic community of the people once class and state opposition had been overcome" in 1933.[153]

Only "National Socialist legal thought, racial thought," asserted a "substantive understanding of international law," which was the only valid one, as "it is only in this way that the term 'law of the peoples' (*Völkerrecht*) can be made real."[154] States were the peoples' representatives at the international level, and thus should cease to be "formalist legal entities" and become "people-powers in a unified territorial organization bound to a space that belongs to these peoples."[155] Jurists attentive to reality should also be cognizant of this concrete order of nations, which was the origin of their coexistence and their hierarchy. By the same token, they should pay less attention to states and more attention to peoples, which came first. This was the subject and message of the *habilitation* work of Norbert Gürke, the son-in-law and student of Otto Kollreuter in Munich. In 1935, he published a research thesis titled *Volk und Völkerrecht* (People and international law). Gürke, who would go on to hold professorships in Breslau and in Vienna, opened by noting that while in 1918 the "law of peoples" was an undisputed concept, there was no agreement on the definition of the word "people." For example, democrats, Catholics, and Marxists—in other words, all the breeds culturally dominant in Versailles, Geneva, and Weimar—did not see "the people" as "a vital natural entity."[156] This meant that "the concept of the people was denatured by liberal, democratic, Marxist theories."[157]

Gürke proposed a return to what was obvious and natural, "a racial perspective" that "starts, not with the individual" or with states, but with "the people as vital natural unit."[158] The people, seen as an organic community, a race, or as the text put it, a "vital-racial unit," was "the supreme political value," the "absolute value."[159] The logical conclusion of this assertion was drawn by Gürke's colleague Heinrich Korte, a student of Carl Schmitt and a senior lecturer in public law at the Reichsverwaltungsschule (Reich School of Administration) of Pirna-Sonnenstein (Saxony). In 1942, Korte published a book based on his doctoral thesis titled *Lebensrecht und völkerrechtliche Ordnung* (Law of life and international legal order). The language of the title reflected the work's central thesis, which was that since 1648 and 1919, a de facto opposition had existed between *Lebensrecht* and *Völkerrecht*, because international law had not been based on the natural right of peoples to live.

The author was pleased to report that since 1933, German policy "had as its bedrock the vital interests, the right to life, and the living space" of the German people; it was, in other words, an "understanding based on race and on the laws of life."[160] But practice had preceded theory, and now the time had come to propose an "international law based on the laws of life."[161] Korte warned that "the laws of life" should not be seen as "a substitute for the fundamental law" of positivists; nor should "living space" be seen as "the perpetuation of the spheres of influence" of the past. It was important to realize that these two notions "were of a new, revolutionary-dynamic kind," and that they represented a "renaissance of natural law in the form of a re-grounding of politics in the laws of life."[162] These laws dictated that Germany possess the resources to feed its people: because the Treaty of Versailles had led to "the overpopulation of the living space," and to a "people without a land," Hitler had demanded a "peaceful review . . . against the static policy of the Western powers," against "their rigid foreign policy and their static legitimacy."[163] This "destructive order destined to annihilate German existence" was a sin against any "sane and natural understanding of the law."[164] Because the Führer's requests had been ignored, Germany had resigned from the League of Nations and "demanded the right to autonomous decisions regarding its vital rights," a "vital decision" having to do in particular with its "basic sovereign right to self-defense."[165]

From the perspective of natural reality, French policy was absurd. Instead of taking care of its vast and luxuriant colonial empire, France, armed with the ideas of a bygone era—in this case, the seventeenth century—had stubbornly persisted in seeking to diminish German power on the European continent. Each country might have enjoyed a sane division of living spaces, Germany with its *Lebensraum* in eastern and southeastern Europe, and France with its empire. But no, "Germany had to be taken apart piece by piece, in order to reestablish at Europe's center a situation analogous to the one produced by the Peace of Westphalia." Here, the author nodded to Friedrich Grimm and his theses in a footnote.[166] Germany, which only wanted to "preserve its right to life," acknowledged Great Britain's naval superiority as a necessity for sustaining the British Empire, and took no exception to France devoting itself to its colonies. The Western powers, on the other hand, wanted nothing less than the "destruction" of Germany. And so Germany was forced to fight "in legitimate self-defense" in order to protect its "inalienable rights to life."[167] At a more general level, Germany was fighting for its vital rights in a way that respected the laws of nature. The same could not be said for the British, who had forged a monstrous "artificial construction," an empire spread out over four continents and unified only through waterways opened by its navy. Germany, by comparison, was creating a homogeneous and organically coherent continental space that "obeys the natural laws of territory," the same laws that had long been forgotten by the Western powers with their overseas empires.[168]

Carl Schmitt's concept of *Grossraum*, a homogeneous and distinct area that is clearly delimited from other areas, surfaces in Kort's argument in a way that requires clarification. Reflections on Schmitt's thought could and do fill the pages of many books. He was by far the most brilliant legal thinker in his two fields, constitutional law and international law, and unique among his colleagues for the historical, philosophical, and theological richness of his thought and language. In the context of this book, however, we will limit ourselves to explaining the elements of his thought that were taken up and disseminated by his colleagues and students. His intellectual contributions make it tempting to linger over the author of *The Nomos of the Earth*, published in 1951, and the intriguing works that preceded it in 1920s and 1930s. In this context, however, our focus is Schmitt's impact on Nazi thought, particularly through the idea of *Grossraum*, a geographical and geopolitical concept that was ultimately supplanted by the more right-leaning idea of *Lebensraum*. *Lebensraum*, which began as little more than a slogan, was fashioned into a practical notion by Nazi intellectuals. The concept of space that it was grounded in was ultimately given material form in plans for the conquest and colonization of the East. In public law, Schmitt's idea of the total state underwent a similar fate. With a shift to the Right, it morphed into the Nazi racial state, and even further, into a theoretical dissolution of the very idea of the state, against which Schmitt, in opposition to Höhn, argued in vain.[169] This theoretical shift was accompanied at the practical level by the disintegration of the state into the "agencies," or *Anstalten*, theorized by Höhn, who argued that they were more manageable, rapid, and adaptable. From this ground grew the Nazi polycracy that has been described by historians for decades.

To promote the concept of *Grossraum* and to defend the European policy of the Third Reich, Schmitt took a certain perverse pleasure in holding Americans to their own standards. Fascinated by the Monroe Doctrine, he demonstrated that it prohibited all foreign powers from intervening in the American hemisphere, "a non-interference of extra-American powers in this space, coupled with non-interference of America in non-American space."[170] Originally, therefore, it had been "continentally American and defensive." Wilson had denatured the Monroe Doctrine by "declaring that the Monroe Doctrine should become a global doctrine," proposing in a speech on January 22, 1917, that international relations ought to be regulated by an extension of the principle of nonaggression to the entire world. In making this argument, Wilson had not understood, or perhaps had pretended not to understand, the core of what Monroe had been asserting with regard to the American continent—and for it alone. James Monroe had upheld a "non-interventionist understanding of space," whereas his distant successor, Wilson, sought an "extension of liberal-democratic principles to the entire Earth and all of humanity"—in other words, the very opposite of non-intervention.[171] In 1917, Wilson had used this denatured version of the Monroe Doctrine as a theoretical justification for American interference in European affairs, which had culminated in the United States entering the Great War in 1917, a development that had proven fatal for Germany. Wilson's "transformation of a spatially conceived principle of non-interference into a spatially undifferentiated general system of interference" substituted the original doctrine for the liberal-democratic ideal "of 'free' world trade and a 'free' world market."[172] This was evidence of a regrettable contamination of American policy by the mercenary and imperialist spirit of the British. Schmitt proposed (re)founding an "international law for greater-space regions," governed, as the programmatic title of his 1939 book suggested, by "a prohibition of intervention for powers external to that space."[173]

Carl Schmitt was not alone in his orthodox reading of the Monroe Doctrine: Hitler himself did so in a famous speech on April 28, 1939, delivered as a lengthy response to President Roosevelt in which he afforded himself the luxury of claiming to be more American than the Americans: "we Germans are defending exactly the same doctrine for matters regarding Europe, or, in any case, for the interests and the dominion of the Greater German Reich."[174] Schmitt spoke of a "German Monroe Doctrine," although he cautioned, "we are thus not simply imitating an American model if we make reference to the Monroe Doctrine. We are merely excavating the healthy core of an international legal *Grossraum*."[175]

What better way to Germanize this reasoning than to devote a long article to the concept of *Reich?* Schmitt explained from the outset that the idea was "untranslatable" and that the Latin or Western equivalents of *imperium* and *empire* were not satisfactory. In opposition to these erroneous translations, the Reich was an entity "essentially determined by the people" living in it. It induced and created "a fundamentally non-universalistic legal order built on the foundation of respect for every people."[176] It was the very opposite, therefore, of the "ideals of assimilation and melting pots of the empires of Western democracies."[177]

Strangled by the two imperialist, universalist worldviews of the East and the West, the Reich "defends on both of these fronts the sacredness of a vital order that is non-imperialistic, racial, and which respects peoples" and their national identities. As opposed to the "legal order of the League of Nations," which had denatured "the legal order of the peoples," making it into a "global and universalistic law," the Reich sought to defend an "international law" (*Völkerrecht*) in the original sense of that word; that is, "the law of the peoples" (*Recht der Völker*). Schmitt argued against international law created by states, contending that the "creators and vectors of international law" were "no longer states, but empires"—*Reiche*, that is: entities at the intersection of "*Grossraum*, the people, and the political idea." *Reich* was not an abstract legal concept, a paragraph in a dictionary or an entry in a glossary. It was an *Ordnungsbegriff*, a concept based on a concrete order (that of the people), people who, by enacting this order, also generated the order. This "order of the people, based on the people" could easily be extended to the entire earth: it could be "planetary; that is, based on the earth as a space."[178] This global expansion was no idle fancy, thanks to the victories of Germany's armies:

A powerful German Reich has arisen; from what was only weak and feeble there has emerged a strong center of Europe now ready to realize its great political idea: the respect of every people, understood as a reality of life determined through species and origin, blood and soil. . . . Capable, too, of rejecting the interference of foreign powers hostile to the idea of race and people in its *Grossraum*.[179]

Heinrich Korte, an epigone and exegete of Carl Schmitt, inflected Schmitt's thinking with biology. The young teacher, a member of the faculty of the Reich's School of Administration, was far stricter in his Nazi orthodoxy than the great legal theorist, who had been overtaken on all sides. Korte, who manifestly knew how to read, chose not to mention *Grossraum*, which was too loaded a term. Instead he spoke of *Lebensraum*, arguing that Germany, in its foreign and military policy, "is acting in accord with the natural laws of *Lebensraum*." These established and asserted "the domination of the people with biological and political strength, which mobilizes and governs the forces of smaller states in order to foster fruitful cooperation." Blinded by their own worldview and led astray by their own machinations, Great Britain and the United States were mistaken in their belief that German policy was a project of "global conquest."[180]

Germany was neither imperialist nor positivist. "Contrary to the destructive nature of the falsely universalistic orders of Versailles and Geneva, it is creating an order in keeping with life" and setting up the conditions for a real and lasting peace.[181] Gustav Walz, who, in 1942, appeared eager to include Carl Schmitt in the intellectual conversation once again, proposed that it was time to overcome the sterile opposition between "the ideology of *Grossraum* and the racist concept of space," in order to arrive at a "racial order of *Grossraum*." In other words, the Nazi order, an order of nature and of peace, was based on respect for the principle of race, and sought to end imperialism in a world that it would see divided up into carefully delimited, autonomous, and independent *Grossraum*, with the "prohibition of intervention by foreign powers in these spaces."[182]

Against the "law of the League of Nations" (*Völkerbundsrecht*), which misunderstood *Völkerrecht* as international law, rather than understanding it literally as the "law of the peoples," against the dogmatic and abstract "natural law" of the legal positivist tradition, National Socialism had undertaken a return to "the identity of the law of nature and the law of life."[183] It simply wanted to "carry out the laws of life" according to a legal and territorial order governed by nature alone.[184]

> A people's right to life appears as the manifestation of the laws of life, according to which it is the vitality of a race, of a people, of a nation . . . that decides over its existence: the law of life is thus a natural law, a vital interest that a people affirms and reinforces as their national existence in the struggle for life.[185]

National Socialism had saved international law from the transcendent abstractions of "universalist thought," reestablishing "its roots in the people, its immanence."[186] These words echoed those of Helmut Nicolai, who in 1931 explained with his usual eloquence that an international law, shared among all nations, and therefore among all races, was an illusion, because "a shared feeling for the law is only possible if an identity perception based in racial identity exists." Sarcastically, Nicolai considered that if a minimal international law might succeed in rallying certain geographical areas, "it would leave aside a few peoples, such as the Negroes of southern Africa or the Bushmen." "A community of states and peoples is only possible for Germanic peoples."[187]

According to Friedrich Wilhelm von Rauchhaupt, an influential expert in international law, National Socialism had given "a specific and profound meaning to the concepts of the people and the community of the people." Furthermore, he continued, the "title of 'law of the peoples,' once so unfitting, is perfectly suitable and may be rightfully employed."[188] The professor was pleased to note that his field of specialization, once a source of great suffering for "German students with nationalistic sensibilities," had become a "place of assembly, through which all of the members of the community of the people faithful to the fatherland [now] pass." Once an "object" of international law, Rauchhaupt concluded with pleasure, Germany was now fully its "subject."[189]

[CHAPTER EIGHT]

The Reich and Colonization of the European East

IN ONE OF THE two speeches he gave in Posen in October 1943, Heinrich Himmler reminded his listeners that "every last measure we take must obey the law of the war among the races and the peoples. As I was saying to you, there are no rules for the treatment of foreign peoples"—no rules, that is, other than that of the Germanic race's absolute dominion and the unlimited exploitation of those foreign vital forces needed to serve the goals of the Reich.[1] Serving the life of the race was the guiding principle of the Reich's foreign policy. By 1939, it had left the field of international relations to embark on its project of conquest and colonization.

Lebensrecht: The "Most Basic Right"

By its very nature, the Germanic race was the most fertile (demographically) and the most creative (culturally), but it was also the one that had received the smallest share of land and resources. In a telegram sent on April 14, 1939, shortly after the Wehrmacht's invasion of the Czech areas known as Rest-Tschechei—it had entered Prague on March 15—Roosevelt requested reassurance from Hitler that peace would be kept: could the German chancellor now give his word to the president of the United States that there would be no more claims on or annexations in Europe? Could he commit to keeping his word, given that he had just violated the Munich Agreement, through which the international community had shown goodwill and good faith?

Addressing the Reichstag on April 28, 1939, Hitler offered Roosevelt a scathing response. In what would rapidly became one of his most famous speeches, Hitler, who rarely displayed any humor, offered a jocund and lengthy list of countries the Reich did not wish to invade—a *reductio ad absurdum* intended to demonstrate that the international community's fears were entirely unfounded. Hitler suggested that the implacable logic of German policy gave them even less ground for fear. The Führer then renewed his attack on the Treaty of Versailles, "that ignominious subjugation, the most shameful pillage of all time," obtained with "a pistol to the head" of Germany. Given these conditions, he refused to promise peace to "anyone other than the German people, for whose life and very existence [he was] responsible, and which alone was holding [him] accountable."[2] The entire world order had denied the German people's *Lebensrecht*. It was all very fine for Roosevelt to accuse Hitler of bad manners—the American president had been spoiled by Mother Nature:

> I, Mr. Roosevelt, must make due with a more modest and hemmed-in space. You have a hundred and thirty-five million people and 9.5 million square kilometers. You have a country blessed with incredible riches, all the treasures of the land, fertile enough to nourish more than a billion men.[3]

Examined in relative terms, America's good fortune was even more dazzling. "You are lucky enough to have to feed only fifteen individuals per square kilometer. . . . You can, thanks to the extent of your space and the fertility of your fields, offer each American ten times more than a German. Nature made this possible for you," whereas Germany had to support "a hundred and forty inhabitants per square kilometer."[4] The natural balance of things had been upset by the geopolitical map, an imbalance intensified by the theft of Germany's colonies through yet another falsehood: "To justify this monstrous attack on our rights, they invented a 'lie about colonial responsibilities' comparable to the 'lie about the responsibilities of war,'" pretending that German domination had been more intensive, and even more inhumane, than the British or French had been with their own colonial possessions.[5] This had resulted in the amputation of the race's *Lebensraum* in Europe, and the theft, clear and simple, of its possessions overseas. Man's redistribution of nature's resources ought to be revised as soon as possible. Favored by history, Roosevelt had no right and no authority to level accusations at Germany. In this way, the Nazis argued openly that the international order was not only unjust, but artificially unjust. Nature's justice dictated that Germany not only be well provided for, but even better provided for than the others. After all, and once again, the German race was the most culturally fecund and the most biologically fertile of all races. It gave birth to magnificent children and to the most sublime masterworks of human culture. Nature had elected the Germanic race, only to see it bludgeoned by history, and this was what the Nazis claimed to be repairing. It was only right to correct this error by making sure that the German people, a *Volk ohne Raum* (people without room), were finally endowed with the space they needed to spread out, grow, and prosper. Every German foray into international relations was presented as the reparation of an injustice: "With the total victory of the German Army in Poland, the time has come to repair the injustice inflicted in the German East and on its population in 1919," wrote the historian Theodor Schieder, then a young scholar.[6] An expert on Eastern Prussia, he would author several memoranda on Poland and its reconfiguration for *Gauleiter* Erich Koch of Konigsberg and for the SS.

The widespread use of the adverb particle *wieder*, "once again" or "anew" (*wiedergewonnen, Wiederherstellung, Wiedergutmachung,* and so on) indicated that the Reich's actions were all intended to bring about restitution and reconstruction: "The reconstruction of German domination and the German population emerges as . . . compensation for a glaring political injustice." The restitution of land, however, could not take place in a series of individual steps, but rather had to be a "people-to-people reparation, through which the German people is restored its due." To go waving "old property deeds" on a case-by-case basis or to require "individuals" to reclaim their former "land and possessions" was out of the question.[7] The endeavor had to be collective and entirely holistic, to obey a higher law than that of individual interest and property. Far beyond the individual matter of Poland, the Nazis claimed to be undertaking a mission of global biological justice.

Reestablishing natural justice: the doctrine of *suum cuique* also governed relations among races and between blood and soil. And from this perspective, the international order as it had been imposed on Germany in 1648 and in 1919 was an intolerable historical and biological injustice. The imbalance between (insufficient) land and (abundant and creative) blood had reached its zenith with the Treaty of Versailles, which had deprived the most fertile and creative blood of its very means of subsistence.

Jedem das Seine was not merely an inscription over the entrance to Buchenwald. It was also the watchword of German colonization in the East, as German expansion was seen as a work of natural justice that was merely providing the Germanic-Nordic race with what it needed to survive. The term *Lebensraum* ("vital room" or "room to live") has no direct translation; the paraphrase offered here dulls the force of its original meaning, which is the literal designation of a space that the race required for its very survival:

> The millennial tradition of German colonization in the East, which was reduced to dust in Versailles, is now experiencing a powerful renaissance, which will give our people its right to live for the centuries and millennia to come.[8]

The Germanic race was history's country cousin. Culturally fecund and demographically fertile, good and civilizing, almost blindly peaceful and well-meaning, it had never fought back violently against the poor treatment it had received. When it had fought, it had done so to protect Europe from African or Asian invasion. Acting as a shield had caused the race to lose men and blood, weakening its vital forces and leaving it defenseless in 1648 and 1919, when, in paper treaties, the entire world had turned against it. Little by little, the space left to the Germanic race had shrunk away: at its most expansive during Antiquity, when the Germanic peoples had reigned supreme in the North, the East (the Black Sea), and the South (Greece and Rome), their space had been divided up and carved off during the Christian Middle Ages (the priesthood against the Empire), by the violent incursions of Asian invaders (from Attila the Hun to the Turks, not to mention Genghis Khan), and then again after the destruction wrought by the Thirty Years' War, and then the wars of the French Revolution and Empire. The contemporary era had crowned this catastrophic evolution with the "lesser German solution" of 1871, and the Treaty of Versailles.

The Nazis were not the first to complain that Germany did not have enough space and that the exiguity of its territory was hampering the Germanic race's demographic and economic growth. Far from it: nineteenth-century Pan-Germanism had already called for ethnic unification within a single political entity that would govern all Germans—and promoted the conquest and colonization of territories in Eastern Europe. The Pan-Germanic movement sought the annexation and use of land in Bohemia, Moravia, Poland, and elsewhere, which, it asserted, had been conquered and civilized in the past by various orders of Germanic warrior monks. The *Volk ohne Raum* needed its *Raum* back; to this end, it would follow the path opened by the *Drang nach Osten* of the Middle Ages, this "yearning for the East" that the nineteenth-century Pan-Germanics had made into their historiographical leitmotiv. The Nazis, therefore, were not the first to lament the *Volk ohne Raum,* nor to declare that the conquest of the East was a driving ambition. Not even the concept of *Lebensraum* was original to them; it had been invented by natural scientists as a translation and Germanization of the word "biotope" before being adopted as a geopolitical term, adapted first to the study of human phenomena, then to the political arena. The evolving use of this term is characteristic of a movement, widespread in the nineteenth century, to map nature onto history.

The Nazis were merely repeating and radicalizing pre-1914 ideas. Everything that had occurred since then seemed to prove them right. The First World War, with its two million combat deaths—and, they claimed, its million civilian deaths from famine and Spanish influenza—was clear proof that Germany was facing a biological threat. It was not so much Germany as a state that had been under attack before and after World War I, but rather Germany as a people. The world's hostility was not merely political, but actually biological. The space that Germany was claiming was for its nourishment and its defense, a necessity for the life of its species: to go without it meant certain death, either by starvation or military aggression. For the Nazis, the experience of the First World War had been a warning regarding these vulnerabilities: deprived of natural borders, Germany had been left open to enemy attack, particularly from the East, where the greatest danger lay. Surrounded by enemies, it was the ideal blockade victim. And indeed, a blockade had caused the famine of 1917, which, along with the Bolshevik scourge, had led to the November Revolution in 1918.

The words *Lebensrecht* and *Existenzrecht* were therefore to be taken literally; they were not mere expressions, but the cornerstones of a rhetorical edifice solid enough to succeed in swaying other countries' intellectuals, journalists, observers—and even governments. If men such as Georges Bonnet, the French minister of foreign affairs, argued for a second Munich Agreement in September 1939, following Hitler's invasion of Poland, it was not only because he feared repeating the bloodbath of 1914–1918. Bonnet and men like him also thought it foolish to send soldiers to die for Danzig when the Germans needed it to live. For many in the West, Nazi discourse was not some guttural rumbling, peddled over crackling airwaves. It was a credible argument, and if it did not win the full support of its audience abroad, many heard it with understanding and even a measure of goodwill.

The land to the East was, as we have seen, "a living space in an even deeper sense" than a purely economic one. "For us it has not only economic importance, but also vital importance, as it may mean life or death, depending on whether we dominate it or not."[9] The goal of Nazi policy, buttressed by old geopolitical and biological obsessions, was the "safeguarding" (*Sicherung*) of Germanic life and the growth—if possible, exponential growth—of the biological substance it produced. Hitler had a vision of a 100 million Germanic people over the short term and 250 million over the medium term.[10] And in 1944, Roland Freisler went so far as to imagine "the billion Germans of the next two hundred and fifty years."[11]

Replanting the Race

To produce such a volume of biological substance, blood had to be nourished with soil; the *Volk ohne Raum* needed its *Raum*. The race, in other words, needed to put down new roots through a concrete colonial policy. The Nazi project and discourse echoed the many questions that the social, cultural, and demographic—and therefore anthropological—changes of the nineteenth century had raised in European society. They denounced as artificial the new world brought about by the Industrial Revolution, the rural exodus, and the urbanization and proletarization of Europe. It was a world of solitude, of psychological, biological, and "social" decay—a world where, to the Nazis, "society" had replaced traditional community. *Lebensraum* in the East provided an answer not only to the biological threat to the existence of Germany as a people, but also to the questions, the breakage, and the trauma of an Industrial Revolution that had been more rapid and brutal in Germany than perhaps anywhere else.

The world of the Jew, according to the Nazis, was the immense artificiality of the Industrial Revolution. The Jew hated himself, hated the world, hated reality, and hated the nature in and around him. Fleeing nature and reality to find refuge in rabbinical phantasm and abstraction, the Jew lived only in and through artifice, in this way creating a "civilization" that was in no way "culture." The roots of culture stretched deep into the earth, creating a rootedness that connected human beings to nature. The Jew, by contrast, had created an artificial world of cities, which isolated and uprooted men from the earth: the *Asphaltjude* had produced the *Asphaltmensch*.[12] A man of asphalt lived a life that was reticular, horizontal, and rhizomorphous; he had no true roots and lived disconnected from the earth. His existence was desynchronized, cut off from the tempo of nature and the cosmos, exposed to constant artificial light and the ever-present temptations of the city. Such a man did not rest when the sun went down; sleepwalking through the night, he was entirely divorced from nature; deprived of the invigorating air of the countryside, he was exposed to the poisons of pollution; deprived of space, he lived in slums where physical crowding and unhygienic conditions were the rule. Deprived of nature and cut off from the nature within him, he had become a man without instincts, a fragile city plant condemned to die, uprooted from the cement by the Jews, the Civil Code, industry, liberalism, and Marxism.

The period of Weimar Germany, the apotheosis of "civilization's" dominance over nature, of the city over the countryside, and of modernity over tradition, was the decade in which alienation had reached its height, when Germans had been the most divorced from themselves. "The hallmark of this era was the absolute absence of instinct, the forgetting of the most basic demands of politics and economics."[13] Thankfully, this had all come to an end in 1933. Colonization would make it possible to reconcile economic imperatives (the subsistence of the Reich and its agricultural autonomy) and *Rassenhygiene* (the health and care of a race that had returned to its roots and to itself). After the great uprooting of the nineteenth century, the race could now plunge its roots back into the soil again—a familiar soil that had already been cultivated by Nordic man, whose archaeological remains the SS was searching for (and finding!).

Strengthened by the good air, a healthy life, and contact with the earth, the Nordic race would build an agricultural utopia—not only because its vocation was an agricultural and biological one (producing vital substance in the form of wheat, children, and so forth), but because this ambitious undertaking had been conceived of in agricultural terms. In plans for the East, the term *Flurbereinigung*, which refers to the consolidation of farmland, was used frequently. The goal of Eastern colonization was, quite literally, to reclaim fields, to aggregate them into a coherent whole to improve their biological productivity. The clear "dividing lines" announced by Hitler in a major speech on the East he delivered on October 6, 1939, after the successful invasion of Poland, were being drawn much as one would clear out a field in order to parcel out races and roots, to allot the species the space it required.

Colonization, therefore, was a form of agricultural planning based on an agronomic understanding of people, things, and situations: on planting, uprooting, discarding, replanting, and transplanting. The policies of *Umgestaltung* (reconfiguration), *Umvolkung* (geo-ethnic reconfiguration), and *Umsiedlung* (colonization) rolled out by the Reich and implemented by its engineers, were matters of *Umpflanzung*—of the "transplantation" of people, who were, after all, natural beings like plants, who needed land to grow and prosper.[14] The Nazis focused all their longing on the dark, fertile, fecund soil of the East, colonized so long ago by the Varingians. Produce, nourish, procreate, Goebbels noted in his *Journals*, for

> The Führer sees the East as our future India. This is the colonial territory we must occupy. This is where farms for our farmers and the veterans of the *Wehrmacht* must be created. . . .
>
> The goal of our war is the expansion of our *Lebensraum* in the broadest sense. We have set ourselves a goal that will require several centuries. This goal will require great sacrifice for some time, but it is worthwhile for the generations to come. Only for this can we justify such a bloodletting to ourselves and to history: it will give life to millions of German children. . . .
>
> The East is our space. We must pierce through to it, it is there we must invest everything to develop the *Lebensraum* we will need in

the future. There we shall find everything we need to give life to our people, starting with the marvelous dark earth, whose fertility is unmatched. It is there that we must build, organize, and mobilize everything for the life of our nation.[15]

The reference to India and the British Empire was no accident. In the past, Germanic migrations had left behind nothing but biological isolates, haphazardly planted only to be overwhelmed and swept away. The Reich now wished to create something solid and enduring, to replace the scattered plantings of the past with a powerful and coherent biological concentrate. Germans, in their history, had suffered too much from division and dispersion. The Reich was to be the political expression of an imposing monolith: to Hitler's laments about the Germanic *Zersplitterung* of the past, Himmler replied that the time had come to organize the division and scattering of the peoples of the East.[16] Their fate was servitude, or, for some of them, extinction, which was economically inevitable. The *Ostvölker* were to be reduced to a *Volkssplitter* (fragmented people), and thus to experience the circumstances that had, for so long, kept the Germanic tribes from victory.[17]

The Germanic populations sent to the East, those called to colonize these territories in order to nourish the Empire, would know that they were loved and protected. There could be no question of abandoning them to their fates, far from the fatherland, no question of ignoring the Reich's outer edge. The space to be established in the East was also a strategic area that would constitute an armed march between Europe and Asia. The Reich was the colonists' political and military safeguard; it was also the biological structure they were helping to build. None of this, of course, was in any way meant to disparage the work of the Germanic populations of the past. To the contrary, their migrations were what had made the colonization of the East a sacred mission.

The land of the East had been fertilized by the dead, by the Germanic colonizers of the past who had made territories of these lands and had sanctified the soil with their blood: "Anyone who wishes to settle in the East is tilling sacred ground," because "German soldiers, German men, spilled their blood there and now rest, in sacred peace, in these lands. Now, a land acquired by blood is being used anew to produce new blood, families, children."[18] To cultivate the land was to honor a debt to the dead, and at the same time to guarantee the life to come. Hence the abundance of words such as *Aufgabe* (task), *Pflicht* (duty), *Verpflichtung* (obligation), and *Verantwortung* (responsibility), which made colonization into an imperative. This may be contrasted with the French and British colonial discourse, which generally painted colonial life as an overseas adventure by which colonists would reap commercial benefits while engaging in a vague civilizing mission. For the Reich, to conquer, to colonize, and to cultivate were sacred duties dictated by the biological status of the Nordic race—representing both an obligation to its past (with the plow tilling the soil, and the sword delimiting the Nordic territories to the East and erecting the great protective wall against Asia) and a responsibility to its future.

Putting Poland to Use

In the East, there was much work to be done. Russia had remained in a state of static backwardness for centuries, a situation only exacerbated by Bolshevik terror and incompetence. And as for Poland, it was, quite simply, a disaster. Once highly Germanicized, its lands had unfortunately been assigned to a Slavic non-state after 1919. They were now being scandalously neglected, and *Siedlung* ("installation" or "colonization") would require *Aufbau* (structure). Texts and films of the era all described Poland as it appeared to soldiers encountering it during the September 1939 invasion. Luckily, all that would change now:

> in place of savage anarchy and Polish incompetence (*polnische Wirtschaft*), impeccable order and cleanliness are being established, along with a constantly growing economic and cultural life. The East is no longer as it appeared to us during the Polish campaign—the reflection of a rotten, decomposing state, the image of Polish worthlessness, even if much remains to be done to liquidate the Polish legacy and found a new, healthy, attractive life in each district.[19]

To liquidate the Polish legacy meant that "this earth be treated as virgin soil," as a colonial *terra nullius* that belonged to no one but its colonists, the only people capable of cultivating it.[20] Poland was divided into two main zones: to the north were the territories integrated into the Reich (Wartheland and Danzig-West Prussia); to the south, an occupied territory that was to function as a reservation for the Polish populations expelled from the north and for Jews assigned to the ghettos (*Judenreservat*). The north was placed under a policy of full-fledged Germanization and colonization and dependence on the *Heim ins Reich*, whereas the south had a more uncertain and evolving identity. Although early on it was envisioned as a territory to which expelled Jewish and Polish populations would be sent, little by little it was slated for colonization, although this was somewhat hampered by the presence of the populations initially assigned to it. It continued to be used as a forced residence for them, despite the ongoing protests of its very colonially titled "Governor General" Hans Frank.

At any rate, Poland itself had been destroyed as a state and was slated for destruction as a nation. The Nazis' intent was to maintain the Polish population in a state of such cultural backwardness that they would never have the capacity to gain any self-awareness, any comprehension of their identity or their condition, or any understanding that they would, over the mid- and long-term, be exploited like livestock to serve German economic needs. As discussed earlier, the first stages of this project required the extermination of the Polish elite. Any members of the intelligentsia potentially capable of nourishing the Polish language, culture, or identity had to die. The same went for the political elite, as well as anyone in the upper echelons of the country's military and governmental administrations. Employing a vocabulary that was at once colonialist and feudalistic, Hitler affirmed that the Polish population could have just one *Herr*, a term meaning "master" or "lord": "This principle must be respected absolutely: no 'Polish lords.' Wherever they exist, they must be killed, harsh as this may seem."[21] Hitler was unequivocal that this feudalist-colonialist domination could not be shared:

> Once again, the Führer wishes to underline that the Polish population
> must have just one master, the German. There cannot be two masters
> at the same time. This is why all the representatives of the Polish
> intellectual elite must be killed. This probably sounds harsh, but
> what can you do, this is the law of life.[22]

This was the mission of the SS Einsatzgruppen and the German police, who murdered sixty thousand people in Poland in just over a month.[23] Stripped of their elite, Poles were also deprived of any access to intellectual or cultural development. They were to receive only minimal education, of a kind that would allow them to perform the tasks that the German colonists and masters assigned to them. They were, moreover, to retain contact with a dimwitted clergy, who were to teach them submissiveness and obedience. Hitler, like Himmler, wished to rid Germany and the Germans of the Christian "plague," but he believed that Polish priests, like missionaries in overseas colonies, might turn out to be the foolish servants of German domination:

> It is completely justified for the Polish people to preserve their Catholicism. . . . We will pay the priests, and in return, they will preach what we ask them to. . . . The priests are to maintain the Poles in a state of stupidity and foolishness, because it is in our interest for them to do so. If the Poles were lifted to a higher level of intelligence, they would no longer be the workforce we need.[24]

The mistakes of the Second Reich would not be repeated: no rights for Poles. Bismarck and Wilhelm II had been too weak and too inconsistent in the pursuit of their political aims. They had lacked "that harshness necessary for the defense of the idea of the Reich," a "mistake typical of this era of bourgeois decadence," which had been paid for with the First World War, and then the Uprisings of Greater Poland and Silesia.[25] Thanks to the Führer, "the political indecisiveness and the cowardice characteristic of this era have been . . . overcome."[26] Once again, nature's laws were in force: it was a simple fact that the Polish people were a mere instrument, heads of cattle, energy sources to be employed to serve the needs of the Reich. Unreflecting and unaware, they existed to be controlled and commanded. By nature, noted Bormann, the Poles were a Slavic people, and therefore slaves:

> The Pole is, unlike our German worker, born to carry out ignoble tasks. . . . One cannot, the Führer has pointed out, ask a Slav to be more than what nature made him. While our German worker is, by nature, careful and hardworking, the Pole is naturally lazy and must be driven to labor.[27]

Lurking behind this dull stereotype and the eminently colonialist cliché—in other languages and cultures, *polnische Wirtschaft* is easily interchangeable with any number of ethnic slurs—was Hitler's essentialism and his belief in the fixity of species. For all eternity, Polish (Slavic) biology had been inferior and degenerate. Nature had decreed that the Polish people would serve the interests of those in command, because they were incapable of commanding or organizing themselves. Once again, Nazi policy was merely carrying out nature's will, reestablishing the natural order of things. The Poles had become dangerous because kindly souls had given them culture, and because Germanic blood had provided structure and strength to a formless and characterless race. By remedying this artificial state of things, Nazi Germany, according to Hitler and Himmler, would return the Poles to their natural vocation as a Slavic people. In a memorandum on the "treatment of aliens in the East," Heinrich Himmler stipulated that Germany must strictly see to it that the Poles receive only minimal instruction, which would keep them below the level of intelligence necessary to gain self-awareness, develop personalities, and rebel against their masters.

> For the non-German population in the East, there will be no schooling beyond a four-year elementary education. The goal of this schooling will be to teach them to count to a maximum of five hundred, to write their names, and that God commands them to obey the Germans. . . . As for reading, I do not believe it is indispensable.[28]

Deprived of education and of culture, the Poles were also to be stripped of their rights: the Empire of 1871, which had sought to construct a state that included these populations, had seen them turn against it. They had rebelled, using and abusing their own rights to deprive the Germans of theirs. The Nazis wished to end this state of affairs once and for all. Himmler recalled that

> the Polish problem has occupied us for more than a thousand years. . . . Clarity is necessary, and this is how I understand the mission that the Führer has assigned to me: we must, at least in the provinces that now belong to Germany, solve and eradicate the problem of the Polish minority once and for all.[29]

Eradicate the "problem"—but not the population itself, which was to be kept alive and used for servitude, in a reservation managed by the "General Government." Bormann called it "our labor reserve for wretched tasks."[30] The Poles would be educated just enough to be the production tools of the German economy. Moreover, the Polish people would be deprived of good German blood, the Germanic elements lost to history, the slightly miscegenated people whom the SS would identify, select, and send back to Germany so that the Reich could recover the blood that belonged to it. In this way, the excellence of German blood would no longer civilize, strengthen, and improve the Slavic subrace, whether through bodily mixing or the mere presence of racially superior elements in their midst.

> As cruel and tragic as each individual case may seem, this method remains the gentlest and the best when compared to what the Bolsheviks do when they physically eradicate a people, which we reject as anti-Germanic and impossible.[31]

This was the only way to reestablish the natural order. And so, "this population will be a shepherd-less flock to serve us, and . . . each year, seasonal workers [will] come to Germany to work on specific tasks (roadwork, quarries, construction, and so forth)," all of it "under the severe, consistent, and fair management of the German people."[32] It was consistent because it was based on natural inequalities, and fair, because everyone would be fulfilling their proper role and their biological calling—the masters would command and the slaves would obey.

Colonizing a Familiar Climate

The East was a natural zone of expansion for the Nordic race because it was nearby. There was territorial continuity between it and the Altreich, or pre-1937 Reich. It was rich and fertile, and had already been colonized by Germanic tribes, meaning that the land itself was irredentist. Finally, its climate was a familiar one, despite presenting its own topographical particularities. Once again, it was "Adolf Hitler who had understood as no one else had that our people needs the East as a territory for colonization and a natural zone of expansion."[33] The word "natural" was not employed as an image or a metaphor; it was naming a meaningful state of things: nature itself dictated that the racial space be expanded to the East. Konrad Meyer put it in even more biological terms: "the penetration (Durchdringung) of German life into the land of the East."[34] Territorial continuity and climatic familiarity made possible the "construction of a little fatherland (*Heimat*)" and the "nation's *ver sacrum* in the new German land of the east."[35]

It was, however, necessary to draw the line between good and bad colonization. In *Aufbruch des Nordens* (Resurrection of the North), Prince Friedrich Wilhelm of Lippe was severe in his criticism of past colonization. Thanks to National Socialism, "the German essence is finding itself again," where once it had been troubled by imports from elsewhere and by the race's own movements of colonization and emigration.[36] The Germans, a race of conquering peasant-soldiers, had colonized the Balkans and Italy, producing Greece and Rome.[37] Lippe acknowledged that beneath the Mediterranean sun, the Nordic race had been able to deploy the very best of its genius, but condemned this dissociation of *Blut* (blood) from *Boden* (soil). The Nordic race ought to stay tied to its *Heimat* (homeland)—otherwise it risked losing itself:

> Over there, in the far-off South, the source of Nordic life ran dry, slowly but surely. A country alien to the race and an outside influence changed the souls of succeeding generations, which forgot the Nordic fatherland of their ancestors. And the Nordic law began to waver in the breasts of these descendants.[38]

Lippe, in other words, was not preaching colonization. Better to cultivate the land and see to one's own hearth, to breathe the air of one's fathers, to keep the home fires burning, to stay true to oneself: "These Nordic ancestors, placed in an environment that was unfamiliar to the North, lost their Nordic value system little by little under the influence of an alien axiological order."[39] Lippe gave the example of Rome: the original political organization, as well as the original Roman law—which strictly segregated plebeians from patricians and insisted on the total subordination of child to father, wife to husband, and slave to master—were the true expression of the truth of the race, before this true and healthy inspiration was lost to the influence of climate and racial mixing.[40]

Geographical and climatic alienation had also denatured and degenerated the Germanic peoples lost in the Iberian Peninsula: "We are at home in our Reich, and we will never be at home in our African colony. Africa would degenerate our race, and in two hundred years, the Germanic lord would resemble an African," Himmler affirmed, citing the example of the "Spanish": "They were Goths and Vandals, our ancestors, when all's said and done. For seven hundred years, they lived in an emollient and destructive environment, exposed to alien racial influences, and they squandered the legacy of their blood" because none of them "had respected the sacred law" of race.[41] An instructional manual for SD officers was similarly severe and definitive, unceremoniously dismissing this far-off colonization:

> It is time to give up on fantastical plans for massive overseas colonies. . . . The useless waste of Nordic blood in southern zones where the sun shines brightly is a lesson we have understood clearly. We now know that race depends on space, and that any artificial modification of this ancient and proven relationship with the environment is an attack on the laws of nature in which the order we live in is grounded.[42]

This did not mean that Germany was renouncing its overseas colonies and accepting the Versailles edicts it had rejected. Indeed, an abundance of texts demanded the restitution of the colonies that had been taken from the Reich by Articles 118 and 119 of the Treaty of Versailles. These colonies, however, were to be used for economic ends, not included in population policy. There would of course be civil servants and members of the German military stationed in the colonies to ensure that coffee, cacao, bananas, and rare minerals were sent back to Germany, but no farmer-colonists would be settled there.[43] Their place was in the East, in a climate and land that history and experience had proven did not alter Nordic humanity—unlike the African sun, which softened and degenerated it. This peculiar non-colonialist approach to colonization was distinctly unlike the colonial projects of France or Britain. The Eastern project, by contrast, was openly and extremely colonialist, and the Nazi hierarchy took pleasure in highlighting the radical nature of its relationship to the space and the populations in the East, invoking the model that other European countries used for overseas colonies. Hitler, in his famous speech of September 12, 1938, in the midst of the Sudetenland crisis, paused to remind any *Weltdemokratien* wringing their hands over Nazi ambitions and actions of the way they had treated their own colonial populations.[44] A few months later, in March 1939, the Nazis borrowed the term *Reichspro-*

tektorat from the French to designate its annexation of Bohemia and Moravia.

At the same time, contrasts with the African, Asian, Oceanian, and American colonies were strongly underlined. Above all, these differences were geographical and climatic. They were also historical: there was a Germanic claim on the colonies to the East because of the Germanic tribes that had once occupied, colonized, and civilized them. This made the Nazi enterprise nothing but an attempt to restore a broken link in the chain of history, just as it was reestablishing spatial links among territories that were meant to be interconnected:

> Archaeological discoveries document irrefutably and in the eyes of the entire world the Reich's right to the land in the East. Anyone moving to the East is not a colonizer [in the sense of overseas colonies], but an heir to our fathers, who merely had to move away from their land for a time, for . . . no Reich could protect them from its sword.[45]

The Nazi project in the East was thus neither comparable to nor commensurable with French or British colonial policy. As Hitler put it to Albert Speer, "unlike the English, we will not be content to capitalize; we will populate. We are not a nation of shopkeepers, we are a nation of peasants."[46] Commercial colonization there was therefore out of the question—the goal was to settle there sustainably, definitively, and en masse, by establishing a rooted and enduring population. The point was not to juxtapose a colony and a metropole, but rather to incorporate it, in the most literal and organic sense of that word. To achieve this, it was first necessary to make the most of geography by developing lines of communication between the eastern and western Reich: high-speed train lines were included in the *Generalplan Ost*, and the first east-west highways were already under construction in occupied Poland, so that Berlin and the Altreich could be linked as swiftly as possible to the outposts of the eastern colonies. As Konrad Meyer put it,

> the goal, for centuries and centuries, must remain the same: to link the new German *Lebensraum* in the East with the old Reich territory (Altreich), so that we achieve the condition of our ultimate goal: to form the first true Germanic empire of all Germans, by laying its definitive foundations.[47]

Also, and above all, it was necessary to create an organic, substantial, and biological unity between the Reich and its colonies by the large-scale settling of farmers and soldiers in the East. The chief of the RKF planning office in the East and leader of the *Generalplan Ost* affirmed this vigorously: "Anyone still satisfied with the idea that we can Germanize by superimposing a thin layer of landowners on the Polish population understands nothing of eastern history, nor of the suffering of pureblood Germans in the autumn of 1939." It had become clear that "the goal of a planned colonization strategy is the Germanization of the entire space, down to the smallest details," "down to the furthest corners," or, in case the reader had not fully understood, "down to every last nook and cranny," in order to avert "the danger that one far-off day, a foreign race, subdued and servile today, returns to destroy the reconfiguration of German *Lebensraum* in the East." The chief planner proudly noted that the East was the crucible of the Reich and the home of Nazism: "Our policy for the future in the East is, when you look at it closely, no more or less than the realization of the National Socialist idea."[48]

In the same article, Meyer did acknowledge that German men were lacking, and that it would be necessary to move forward in phases, prioritizing which places were to be Germanized first and which were to be left for later. This paucity of humans was highlighted by Himmler in a speech in February 1940 and by Heydrich in October 1941, and over time became an obsession.[49] It was increasingly clear that colonization in the East was a dynamic and progressive process. It would take time, because it was a part of the long history of the race, a biological mass that remained to be produced. Himmler summed up the process in a succinct phrase that, with a swift grasp, made organic incorporation into the empire follow settlement: "Today, a colony; tomorrow, a settlement; the day after that, the Reich!"[50]

It was first necessary to take possession of the land in the East, as the British and French had done in Africa, then to settle colonists there. Only once a generation or two of settlers had put down roots would the East become an organic part of the Empire. The physical incorporation of the territories in the East required *Germanisierung*, to which Hitler devoted an explicit passage in *Mein Kampf:*

One cannot undertake to Germanize only the land, and not the men. What was generally understood by the word Germanization was only the forced and artificial teaching of the German language. But one cannot imagine a greater error than to believe that a Negro or a Chinaman could become Germanic merely because he has learned German and is able to speak it, and to give his vote to a German political party. Our bourgeois nationalists have never understood that this supposed Germanization was, in reality, de-Germanization. . . . This marked the beginning of a bastardization, and, for us, not Germanization, but a destruction of the Germanic element. . . . Or, put better, like the people, the race does not lie in the language, but in the blood. One can only truly speak of Germanization if we succeed in transmuting the blood of inferiors. But this is impossible.[51]

There was no point, then, in attempting to bring about a cultural conversion of Slavic character—or, as another passage in *Mein Kampf* put it, in attempting to dress a monkey up as a lawyer. Mass production of Nordic blood was the only way. It would be repeating the errors of the past to settle a numerically weak colonial elite in the East. Sooner or later, it would be drowned by the indigenous masses. Instead, it was necessary to terrorize the locals, to reduce them to slavery, and to replace their numbers by encouraging as many colonists as possible to put down roots in the Eastern soil. Jürgen Wiepking-Jürgensmann, who was responsible for land reconfiguration for the RKF, summed up the SS viewpoint in an article on building a German landscape in the East:

We must not implement colonial policy. The new land must be densely populated and must everywhere become the land of the German people, which German men will work and fill with their whole being and their whole essence.[52]

Although it may not seem so at first glance, Wiepking-Jürgensmann's mission was a crucial one: if German populations were to be settled in the East and put down roots there, it was necessary to foster feelings of geographical and sentimental familiarity between these colonists and their new *Heimat*. Consequently the landscapers of the RKF were mandated to create or to recreate the landscapes and vistas of the colonists' homeland, by introducing the plant species and grains of the lands from which they had come: "We must give the young farmers familiar landscapes, the fatherland they left behind, without which, in very little time, they will become embroiled and 'easternized' (verostet)."[53]

In addition to the aesthetic aspects of their mission, SS landscapers were to produce microclimates that fostered the growth of the Germanic race and its agricultural enterprises. The author pointed out that while the creation of actual microclimates was beyond the capacities of land planning, it was possible to create on a very large scale, at the most local level, conditions that were less hostile than the overall conditions of the Eastern climate. In a long passage on valleys, humidity levels, wind speed, and the utility of hedges and glades of trees, Wiepking-Jürgensmann explained how to protect the colonist farmers from the rigors of the continental climate so that they would feel at home and "be able to achieve optimal agricultural production."[54]

This landscaping enterprise was particularly important to the Reichsführer SS, as indicated in a directive dated December 21, 1942.[55] Himmler noted with horror that "the landscapes of the conquered territories in the East have suffered greatly from neglect due to the cultural backwardness of alien races," so much so that they had "become steppe-like, desert-like," and had "been devastated by a hunter-gatherer-style agriculture" of the animal-like wanderers who had inhabited it and pillaged it without creating any value there. He drew a clear distinction between the pre-Neolithic, hunter-gatherer Slavic peoples and the Germanic cultivators, who had established agriculture and culture instead of devastating the territories they occupied with a lack of knowledge and understanding. Like trees, the Germans had put down roots and fertilized. Methodical and peace-loving beings, Germanic people did not mutilate nature. They instead inhabited it with respect, maintaining the same harmonious relationship with it that they maintained among themselves and their peoples. Germans were balanced, peaceful beings who left the inferior races to their incompetence and the racially mixed to their schizophrenia, their agitation, and their hatred of nature:

> The Nordic-German man, on the other hand, feels a vital need to engage in a harmonious relationship with nature. In his homeland,

and in the territories he colonized and transformed over the generations, one can observe a harmonious landscape of farms, gardens, and fields, the faithful image of his peaceful being.

It was important, therefore, that the territories conquered in the East take on the stable and serene appearance of the Nordic race. The land should become the expression and the object of a spirit, a culture, and a blood. Then and only then would these territories be the creation and the home of the Germanic people; then and only then would they be pleased to dwell abidingly there:

> For the *Lebensraum* in the East to become a homeland for our colonists, the landscapes must be transformed through planning that respects nature. This is one of the building blocks for the consolidation of the German race in these regions. It is therefore not enough to implant our race in these regions and to exclude alien races from them. The spaces must also take a form that corresponds to our being, so that Germanic men feel at home there. . . . The face of nature must be the most beautiful and the most worthy expression of the racial community as it is inscribed in the land.

Soil and Blood

This land, made familiar and similar to the *Heimat* by the work of the landscapers, was to be appropriated with the help and work of other engineers of the colonization process as well. It should be recalled that Konrad Meyer, in charge of implementing the *Generalplan Ost*, was an agronomist and a geographer specialized in land distribution and rights. Meyer wrote that in the East, "land and soil are attributed in the form of individual private properties *(besonderen Rechts)*.[56] Colonists are settled through the attribution of a temporary fief, which becomes hereditary, and ultimately private, property."[57]

The choice of the word *Lehen* (fief, estate, tenure), with its medieval overtones, in the *Generalplan Ost* seemed inevitable since the goal was to serve

> a precise end, which is the consolidation of the German race. The creation and implementation of individual property rights in the colonized area therefore seems indispensable and correlates with the proven traditions of German colonization and its history.

The millenarian Reich was thus advancing in the more or less mil-
lennial wake of the Teutonic knights and the Sword Brethren colonists
of yore. The September 1933 law that established the *Erbhof* (special
inherited properties under the Reichserbhofgesetz, or state hereditary
farm law) also claimed to be reestablishing ties with the Middle Ages
of the *Bauern* and the *Meiers*. Land planning and the creation of a "special law" in the East extended the logic of the *Erbhof*. In the East, it was
"the Reich, in the person of the Reichsführer SS, the commissioner for
the consolidation of the German race, who holds the land and the soil,"
the property and the earth. Colonists did not immediately gain ownership of their land:

> The goal of the Reich's division of land into fiefs is the creation of a
> new form of private property. Ownership will be gained by the devo-
> tion of hard work, by the achievement of the vassal and his entire
> family, with the help of the Reich.

The Reich made the land available and lent the money. This "settlement debt" was to be reimbursed "over a generation (thirty-three
years)" so long as the generation performed satisfactorily. Access to
ownership in the East was thus dependent on agricultural performance
and biological value, with the peasant-vassal's vital and racial success
measured by the quality and number of children he produced.

The *Generalplan Ost* did specify that "the Reich reserved the right
to refuse the conversion of a temporary fief into a hereditary fief in cases
where families demonstrate that they are unfit to fulfill their mission in
the East (*Ostaufgabe*)." And even before this conversion occurred, "a
temporary fiefdom may be rapidly revoked in cases of improper farming,
personal unreliability, or repeated negligence affecting requirements for
productivity and profitability" of blood and soil. Freisler was extremely
pleased with the law of 1933; according to the terms of the *Generalplan
Ost*, land ownership was relative, not absolute; it was not a direct relationship but one mediated by the *Volk*. The "possession of a colonial fief
represents a duty to the people and the Reich," not unconditional enjoyment of a piece of property. A colonist's *Ostaufgabe* was to farm and to
reproduce, to produce vital substance, both agricultural and human.
The East was to be "the nursery and the hothouse for Germanic blood."
Natalist expectations ran high: tax provisions for *Lehngut* in the East

were calculated by the *Generalplan Ost* based on families with four children. With fewer children, subsistence was challenging, benefits were not granted, and accession to ownership was not guaranteed; more children meant that families were completely tax-exempt. A similar taxation scale was applied to members of the SS who had fewer than four children and had to pay a fee for each "missing" child. Even this was not enough for Himmler:

> Think of Johann-Sebastian Bach! He was the thirteenth child in his family! After the fifth or the sixth, or even the twelfth child, if Mama Bach had said, "that's enough now," which would have been understandable, the works of Bach would never have been written. The same goes for Wagner: he was the sixth child.[58]

Precious Germanic blood! It alone was able to conceive, command, and organize: by nature, the Slavic peoples (Polish, Russian, Ukrainian, Belorussian, and so on) were incapable of imposing form and organization on themselves. Until Germanic blood had been brought to their bodies through racial mixing, they had remained a formless mass: "These hordes only became peoples through the penetration of our blood into their bodies."[59] This had occurred through racial mixing, which it was absolutely necessary to forbid a priori and to eliminate a posteriori by systematically hunting down and killing all miscegenated individuals in which the alien racial element dominated, but whose mostly foreign blood had received a small, decisive dose of Germanic blood. According to Himmler, "our blood became our greatest enemy when it was incorporated into a foreign nationality."[60] This occurred by the mixing of blood and the production of crossbreeds, or when a person whose Germanic blood had remained more or less pure was integrated into the state and military structures of foreign countries such as Poland:

> If I take the war against Poland, I observe that, each time we encountered slightly firm resistance, it was Germans. Take General Rommel, who defended Warsaw, or Admiral Unruh, who defended Hel. . . . I believe that the General who held out for eighteen days between the Weichsel and the Bug had a German name, as well. Do not forget: what is dangerous in history, on this globe, on this earth, is our own blood.[61]

The normative and practical consequences of this observation were twofold. In terms of prevention, it was necessary to prohibit all mixing of blood. It was also necessary to remove all the Germanic blood that could be extracted from Poland and the Eastern Territories in general, for there was quite a bit there. The ebb and flow of history had washed drifting Germanic elements onto Slavic shores, a phenomenon that had been accentuated by the sparse and scattered nature of past colonization, which had never been planned out or overseen by a central authority. This dispersed Germanic blood was to be recovered by all possible means:

> Traveling through the villages and cities of the east, one is sur-prised—I am, at least—by the palette of faces and people. You will find, for example, a blond haired, blue-eyed man with a narrow face gazing at you with hatred, who is a fanatical Pole and who, when you ask him, "My goodness, aren't you a pureblooded German?" will an-swer you, "No, I am Polish." There, you say to yourself, "No doubt about it, it's our blood, our best blood, it can't be subdued. . . ." That's the first type. The opposite types are individuals of whom one can say, there is a pureblooded Hun, he's remained the typical Hun who was here fifteen hundred years ago. . . . And then you'll find many variations, for example when you see blue eyes shining from a typi-cally Mongolian face, or then again when a man appears to belong to our race, and then you notice he has slanted eyes or cheekbones that are a bit too high, and you say to yourself, "Ah! A little bit of alien race interfered there!"[62]

The SS therefore had a considerable task ahead of it, because crossbreeds were dangerous. Lightly crossbred individuals could be recovered and cleansed of alien influence over the course of a few generations. As for pureblooded Germanic people who had been accul-turated to Polish culture and nationalism, they were to undergo a pro-cess of re-Germanization (*Rückdeutschung*) that would teach them their true biological identity and their racial interests. Implementing this policy fell to the Reichsführer SS in his role as RKF. The task was a moral duty, as Himmler explained in another speech, and of the ut-most importance:

> We have the duty, I believe, to take their children, to remove them from their environment, even in cases where we have to kidnap them

or steal them. It is possible that this may shock our European sensibility [sic], and more than one of you will come and say to me: "How
can you be so cruel, to tear a child away from his mother?" And I can
reply: "How can you be so cruel as to leave such a brilliant future
enemy to the other side, when later on he will kill your son or your
grandchildren?" Either we take this blood and we do something with
it by reintegrating it into our body, or, good sirs, you can say that it
is cruel, but what do you want, nature is cruel, we exterminate this
blood. We cannot be responsible, before our sons and our ancestors,
for leaving that blood there, on the other side, so that someday the
enemy will be able to have competent leaders and commanders. It
would be cowardly on the part of our current generation to refuse to
make the decision and leave it to its descendants.[63]

Colonial predation thus was also a matter of blood: lost and drifting
Germanic blood had to be recovered, to ensure that it did not turn
against the Nordic race.

Herrenmenschentum in Action

Colonizers in the East were producers, creators of biological substance.
The productivist and natalist imperative was to get the most from the
earth, in order to achieve food independence for the Reich and to provide children to the Führer. Ideally, the colonial empire would be entirely autonomous, feeding itself and producing its own children, so
that it cost the Reich nothing, or as little as possible. Konrad Meyer
did not hide the fact that he was investigating "to what extent it was
possible to make colonization in the East independent of all financial
and other support from the Reich, as the costs it must currently bear—
as well as projected costs of all kinds—are extraordinarily high."

The financial optimization of the Empire was a project of economic
modernization. Returning the race to the land did not mean returning
to the pre-industrial age, as the many publications and exhibits on the
new Lebensraum hastened to point out. Here the planners claimed to
be avoiding any rationalist hubris and developed a critique of modernization that they put forth in the name of modernity and efficiency.
Nazi spatial planners sought to create a "colonization structure" that
"made possible a lifestyle specific to the German race," rather than imposing a "rigid plan."[64] Holding their set squares and compasses as

others held their swords, the experts of the RKF and the SS were trying not to create a "system that was inflexible, simplistic, and universally applicable," but rather to sketch out flexible guidelines that "can vary depending on the situation." Eggheads and positivist pride had been so thoroughly denigrated by the Third Reich that it was necessary to tread carefully: "There can be no standardized solutions that are valid in every situation. Rationalization, typology, and norming are certainly necessary today, but they must be limited by life itself."[65]

There was no single plan for villages, therefore, but rather general suggestions to be adapted depending on the place, and an overarching guideline: the space produced had to be a living space and a space to live. *Bios* against *ratio:* colonial space was one of harmony between population and land. It was a space for the race to set down new roots, as well as a place of familiarity between man and field. In Germany, the planners wrote, every kind of space possessed its own structural logic, architecture, and population. Each population merely had to be projected from one to the other, from the "flatland regions," the "hilly regions," and the "mountainous regions" of the Altreich to their corresponding regions in the colonies.

> Northern Germans will be assigned to the flatland territories of the Warthe and the Weichsel, inhabitants of central Germany to the hilly areas of the East, and the southern Germans, from the Alps and the Pre-Alps, will be sent to the mountainous regions.[66]

Nazi colonial planning thus respected the borders and distributions that nature and tradition had put in place, rather than creating new and artificial ones. Southern Germans (Franconians, Bavarians, Swabians, and so on) had thousands of years' experience in mountainous climes. Furthermore, their build and their physical strength—nature and race, then—meant that they were specially adapted to live and farm in altitudes and landscapes that would leave a fisherman from Rostock at a loss. Point taken.

Reestablishing harmony between earth and blood, and building an agricultural utopia, did not exclude aims of efficiency. These aims meant that rural areas were subject to the same health requirements and the same performance criteria as industrial and urban areas. On the farm level, planners were careful to uphold one separation—a legitimate one—between the habitations of men and animals. For health reasons, German farmer-colonists were under no circumstances to sleep with their livestock. Better yet, provisions were made for the construction of an "odor-stopping compartment between the living quarters and the stable." Interior design took health into consideration, as well as seeking to foster the highest possible levels of efficiency: "the economy of gestures," bywords of the Bauhaus and the Athens Charter, were translated here in "the reduction of travel distance," the "straight, short passageways," and the ergonomic furnishings that would be "built-in." The fixtures and fittings were both fixed and fitted; the movables immovable. After all, "residents are not expected to move."[67] Truly, the goal was to settle populations, to have them put down roots in their colonial agricultural fiefs, to ensure that "the antagonism between the city and the country" was overcome.[68] The legacy of an era that had confused progress with the uprooting of populations would be brought to an end. The goal of Nazi spatial planning was to settle people and create harmony among territories, not to foster separation, competition, and displacement. The borderline between city and country was to be slowly effaced, because every space was *Lebensraum*, city and country alike. Rural spaces were to be just as efficient and productive as the industrial and urban expanses of asphalt and smokestacks.

The colonist was thus to be a modern producer and feudal lord all at once. Racial domination, the exercise of *Herrenmenschentum* in an empire built on military force, demanded segregation, as well as the absolute subjugation of the colonized populations. When it came to the use of Slavic labor in Germany, Goering ordered the strictest possible discrimination and subordination. Of course the Slavic "human animals," as Himmler called them, would be treated properly so they could furnish the best of their labor. But humane treatment of these subhumans did not under any circumstances imply empathy or compassion. It had to remain completely clear to all involved, *Ostarbeiter* and German alike, that biological hierarchy was unyielding: "No contact with the German population. Above all, no 'solidarity.' German workers are fundamentally superior to the Russians."[69]

What was true of the German proletarian who had remained in the Reich to work was all the more true for the young officer or civil servant sent to the frontiers of German conquest and colonization. Planning for the attack on the USSR, Herbert Backe, the secretary of state for provisions and agriculture, set out his "Twelve Commandments for the Behavior of Germans in the East and for the Treatment of Russians" on June 1, 1941.[70] To "carry out our mission in the East," Backe wished, above all, to call on dynamic, ambitious youth. Thanks to the conquest and the unprecedented expansion of German space, these young men would now have a playing field that matched their talent and biological excellence. The loosening of borders would allow the race and its talents to come into full flower, at long last: "For centuries, England has given young men positions of responsibility in its Empire to help them to develop their leadership skills. Until now, Germany's small size has never permitted this." To encourage civil servants to make the move, Backe specified that in the East, "only performance counts." It was thus necessary to show "initiative" (*Entschlussfreudigkeit*) and "responsiveness" (after all, "better a bad decision than no decision at all"), as well as "flexibility of method." This primer for what today would be called "management" reminded the young pups out on the steppe that there was no point in getting bogged down in "formalities and red tape."[71] The thing that counted was their "total involvement" and their "desire to perform" in a context where their imagination and inventiveness allowed them to be "all the more flexible in the methods used."

Their relationship to the land and to the Slavic people should not be hampered by norms that had no validity in the East: "You should not approach things with Western criteria." The respect and the guarantees granted to people by the German administration had no place in these strange lands: "The Russians are," by nature, "a mass that always wants to be led." At every moment, the question to ask oneself was "what serves Germany" and Germany alone, a categorical imperative for the German civil servant and government official discussed earlier. If reservations or problems of conscience emerged, one was "not to apply German criteria or customs. Forget everything of Germany, except Germany itself." Things could not be clearer: to serve Germany, one had to forget everything that made up the everyday workings of German civil service—all honor, all morality, all respect for fellow men—in the name of the only valid and worthy goal, the good of Germany. It was "only on this condition that your will shall be moral even in its harshness."

The relative nature of values was a leitmotif that structured Nazi discourse about the East. As Himmler recalled, "we must not . . . act based on German criteria," but rather should treat the Slavic people "as they actually are."[72] The only way to make oneself understood was by speaking louder and striking harder. As was the case with policies of economic exploitation, large-scale measures of collective oppression were justified in the eyes of Keitel and the OKW by the fact that life in the East did not have the same value as life in the West: "Remember that in the countries in question, a human life has no value." Killings could and should be multiplied, therefore, using "exceptional harshness" in order to achieve the desired goal of "dissuasion through terror." The most "appropriate" rate, therefore, was "fifty to a hundred communists" to "compensate the death of one German soldier."[73]

Untermenschentum and Slavery

Hitler commanded that the colonized zones in Poland, as in the rest of the East, were to be "deprived of intelligence of their own. The formation of an autochthonous intelligentsia must be prevented."[74] Conrad Meyer regretted, as we have seen, that Germans had colonized only superficially in the past. They had exercised too light a touch, civilizing everything without expelling the foreign blood. It was necessary to ensure that "one day, once again, a foreign race—today submissive and even servile—does not reduce our efforts to reconfigure German *Lebensraum* in the East to nothing." To do this, it was necessary to "Germanize every nook and cranny," as "we should be convinced that the East will remain German, and for good, only when any foreign blood that might threaten the cohesion of our race has been removed."[75] What was written here, for Warthegau and Danzig-West Prussia, could not be valid for the vast territories won from the Soviet Union.

The tone was not as high by the time the June 1942 version of the *Generalplan Ost* was released. The work to be done in the East was enormous. Labor from the *fremdvölkisch* (those alien, *fremd*, to the German *Volk*) was needed, and Germanization could no longer require the removal of all foreign blood:

> Germanization will be considered complete when, on the one hand, the land and the soil have been placed in German hands; and, on the

other, when the professionals, civil servants, employees, and qualified workers, as well as their families, are all German.[76]

And thus the rank and file of farm workers and the riffraff of the
industrial proletariat, the servile labor, remained, working under the
orders of the German colonizers, who were farmers, engineers, or civil
servants. The Empire needed their hands: "As we cannot do without
the collaboration of the population currently living on Eastern soil, the
racial order that we must create in the East must have as its goal the
pacification of the indigenous peoples." This was to be achieved not
through "evacuations" but rather by "transfers of indigenous peoples
to Sovkhoz and Kolkhoze land," following a fair and "appropriate selection based on their profitability."[77] To make this Germanization possible, the territories in the East were to be put through a "pacification"
(*Befriedung*) process that was both brutal and uncompromising. This
would allow German troops to move freely and undisturbed. The police
became less and less distinguishable from the army, adopting both its
lethal violence and its weapons:

> The Führer indicates to the Reich marshal and field-marshal that he
> has always wanted police regiments to be equipped with armored ve-
> hicles. This is particularly necessary for their deployment to the
> new territories in the East. . . . This massive space must naturally be
> pacified as quickly as possible. The fastest way to do this is to im-
> mediately kill anyone who so much as allows himself to look at us
> the wrong way. [Here Hitler is borrowing from Wilhelm II's famous
> *Hunnenrede* (Hun Speech), in which he asserted, "no Chinese will
> ever again dare to look cross-eyed at a German."][78]

In a calm obtained through brutal repression, the Germans could
peacefully go about their work of domination and production, with the
help of tens of millions of slaves. The treatment these slaves were to
receive was not exactly friendly: "We are not here to pep these people
up . . . so much as to empty them of their substance. We do not want
these peoples: we want their country," Goebbels wrote.[79] As for
Himmler, he explained to his generals that the Germans' duty was

> to fill our camps with slaves—here I would like to state things clearly
> and distinctly—with slaves who will work for us and build our cities,

our villages, and our farms without our paying the least attention to the losses sustained.[80]

In any case, Slavic people were servile by nature, and incapable of governing themselves. Their biological idiosyncrasies had destined them for slavery in the exclusive service of others' projects. As Hitler put it, "the Slav is a born slave seeking his master; all he asks is who the master is, that's it. . . . The Slavic people are unfit for independent life."[81] Using Slavic people to achieve one's own ends was thus what nature demanded—here as everywhere else, it was nature that commanded German policy. And let no one object that slavery had been abolished and that the principles of law prohibited the expropriation of the defeated: "Legal relations? That is man's invention! Nature knows no land registries and no deed registrars! Our heavens know only force."[82] The exploitation of Slavic labor was a logical and moral necessity, induced from particularistic principles that were to be deployed with virility and without hesitation. The plenipotentiary for forced labor, Fritz Sauckel, called for a balanced moral approach to things:

> We shall get rid of the last of that rubbish of vapid humanitarianism we are still dragging with us. . . . It is hard to tear men from their fatherland and their children. But we did not want war! The German child who loses his father at the front . . . is far more strongly affected. Let us hereby renounce all inappropriate emotions.[83]

Himmler, in his usual pedagogical vein, warned against and defused any vague notions of moral conflict. Blame did not lie where one might think. Anyone offended by the principles implemented by the SS had not deeply and rationally examined the question:

> When one of you comes to see me and says to me: "I can't use women and children to dig this anti-tank trench. It's inhuman. It will kill them." I answer: "You are the murderer of your own blood, because if this trench is not dug, German soldiers—that is to say, the sons of German women—will be killed. That's our own blood." This is what I would like to instill in my SS and what, I believe, I have managed to teach them: one of the most sacred laws of the future is that our care, our duty, is our people, our blood. This is what we must dream

and think of, this is what we must work for, and nothing else. All the rest is nothing to us.[84]

With that, Himmler swatted the ball back over the net: anyone with moral compunctions would do well to think first of his brothers in blood, brothers the Judeo-Bolsheviks would not hesitate to exterminate if they came out the winners. After all, the leaders of the regime and the thinkers of colonization reassured themselves, the others behaved no differently. Privately, Hitler often referred to the American Indians and the way they had been treated by the nation of pioneers that had colonized their continent. Just like the Americans,

> we must feel no scruples. We do not claim to be wet nurses, and we have no duties toward these people. . . . We have only one duty: to Germanize by bringing in Germans and to consider the indigenous people as Indians.[85]

[CHAPTER NINE]

The Millennium as Frontier

TRENNUNG, OR "SEPARATION," WAS a harmful Eastern import. The regime's lawyers, ethicists, raciologists, and leaders all wished to restore the fused and interconnected community that had originally existed among the members of the *Volksgemeinschaft,* and between its members and nature. But the imperative to return to this state of origin was valid only for members of the Nordic race, as a solid and coherent organism. An organism necessarily has borders and limits. Inside and outside, therefore, became the objects of careful distinction and extreme segregation. In the words of Theodor Schieder, an adviser to the SS on the colonization of Poland, "the supreme law of this reconfiguration is the securing of our people's land in the East through mass colonization, with all classes of the German population in a healthy social order." To achieve this required "the clear segregation of the German people from the Polish in order to avoid the risk of mixing among peoples and races," as well as "extremely large-scale population displacement."[1]

Solidarity of the *Volksgemeinschaft*

Establishing a sharp, clear boundary with the outside precluded any boundaries or dissensions within. The racial community was harmonious. Dissent, as we have seen, had no place among people who were biologically identical. For this reason, if two SS men fought, Heinrich Himmler, a severe and exacting father to his men, placed them under house arrest together. They were to share quarters "for a period of six weeks" so that they would have "the opportunity to talk things out at length and to reflect together on the idea of camaraderie and the duties of German men at war."[2] *Kameraden* could not squabble, not with the enemy at large—and certainly not in the presence of one.

The credibility and authority of the Aryan *Herrenmensch* (lord) could never be undermined. No dissension, dispute, or disagreement among Germans could be tolerated before the Polish, the Jews, or the Russians, and never should a superior scold a German subordinate in their presence: "If you have reason to be dissatisfied with a German, do not let it show in front of the Russians." "German camaraderie" should prevail at all times, with a united front presented to the racial enemy.[3] Furthermore, and in all circumstances, it was necessary to behave coldly and with no emotion, for to have feelings was to be affected by the animal nature of the Jews. A German was never to disagree in front of a Russian or a Jew; to do so was a violation of German dignity. He could not allow himself to be carried away by anger; nor, on the other hand, could he allow himself to soften. He was to be cold, "distant," and "consistent," to master himself as he mastered others. "You must carry out everything as a soldier, but you must do it correctly, properly, without any personal enjoyment, without personal benefit."[4] Himmler, as every one of his biographers has noted, maintained at all times the tone and the posture of a fatherly teacher, and he repeated this lesson throughout his speeches and sermons.

Finally, racial science, which classified, distinguished, and excluded, could not separate German from German: internal homogeneity was as absolute as external heterogeneity. In a speech to the young students of the *Napolas* boarding schools, Himmler emphasized that blonds ought not to imagine that they were better than brunets, based solely on phenotypic traits:

> We have no right to do anything that would make Nordic blood, the Nordic race, which has always been the main, creating, and dominating race . . . into something that separates us. . . . We cannot tolerate someone believing that he has a particularly desirable phenotype and is therefore more valuable and better than someone else, who, for example, has black hair. If we allow this to happen, the result will be that in very little time the struggle of the social classes we have overcome will be replaced by a struggle of racial classes, by a distinction between superior and inferior that would be a true blow to our people. I do not see Nordic blood as something

that separates us, but as the component in our blood that unites all parts of Germany.[5]

The word *trennend* appears three times in this short speech, warning students of the potential ills of a form of racism that could lead to an internal explosion. Racism united and consolidated internal cohesion; it did not divide the body, as the artificially created class struggle had done. In this, Himmler was echoing Hans Günther, who, in his own work, condemned the hubris of blonds. The community of the people was a community of equals. There was, of course, an internal hierarchy to the Nordic race, but it was merely a functional and military one. Its distinctions were based on (natural) talent, (inborn) vocation, and performance (which was induced from all of these and developed through work).

In 1927, the NSDAP issued a memorandum to its members with a list of Nazi categorical imperatives, and a number of points to remember. Nazi morality was openly particularistic. Nazism was egalitarian and respectful to all Germans, but was not valid for non-Germans or for anyone alien to the Germanic-Nordic race, who fell outside its jurisdiction. Having specified that "the National-Socialist worldview is our supreme law on this earth," the text added that members of the NSDAP, while they did belong to an enlightened elite, were not to scorn their racial brothers in their thinking or their actions. This applied both to those outside the party and to those lower down in the NSDAP hierarchy:

> Treat your subordinates as your comrades in race, not as beasts of burden. Do not see them as objects to be exploited, but as allies and collaborators in the struggle for survival and for the life of our entire people! Never treat them in a way that you yourself, as a German and a National Socialist, would not like to be treated, and never see yourself as their master, but always as their Führer.

Moral law was applicable to anyone who was "German" or "National Socialist." It was not applicable to anyone outside of this natural and moral community, of this confraternity of biological being and the "ought-tos" of moral duty: "always see in the very least of the comrades of your people the bearer of your blood . . . and therefore give greater esteem to the lowest street-sweeper than to the king of a foreign country!"[6]

Close, Segregate, Isolate: The Treatment of *Fremdvölkische*

Compulsory military service and mobilization, followed by the opening of multiple theaters of war and the occupation of an empire that extended from the polar circle to the Mediterranean and from Brest to Brest-Litovsk, had drained the Reich of its men: there were a total of eighteen million German men in uniform between 1939 and 1945, some for all six years. The Reich's economy lacked manpower, and Hermann Goering, who was responsible for the "Four-Year Plan" and the war economy, sought to compensate for this deficit with forced labor.

In Western Europe, countries were subject to the forced enlistment of laborers, notably in France, with its infamous Service du Travail Obligatoire, or STO. This program mobilized a considerable portion of the male population between 1943 and 1945, and was supplemented by voluntary workers and prisoners of war. But the majority of workers brought into the Reich came from the East—from occupied and partially annexed Poland, and from the Reich's *eingegliederte Ostgebiete* (Integrated Eastern Territories). In 1945, there were five million Polish and *Ostarbeiter* (Eastern workers) in the Reich. This influx of labor led to the production of norms, laws, rules, and regulations intended to govern the work of these *Fremdvölkische* and the time they spent on German soil.

Initially it was the Polish workers who were targeted, in a series of ten directives issued on March 8, 1940, known as the Polenerlasse (Polish Decrees). They were signed by the "Reichsführer SS and the German chief of police," who thereby affirmed his authority with regard to questions that also fell to the military (for the arms industry), the judiciary, and the Ministry of Armaments: "The large-scale employment of workers of foreign races in Germany is so unprecedented and exceptional" that it was necessary "to regulate not only their work, but also their lifestyle."[7] A handbook to be read to Polish workers, their overseers, and their employers summed up these regulations. First and foremost, the ten articles of the "duties of civilian workers of Polish race during their time in the Reich" made clear that these workers were immobilized and under house arrest. The first four articles of the *Merk-blatt* took away all freedom of movement, forbidding workers to "leave their place of residence" and to "travel by public transportation."[8]

Polish workers were not only immobilized; they were isolated. Articles 6 and 7 strictly forbade "all social contact with the German population, in particular the frequenting of theaters, cinemas, balls, cafés, restaurants, and churches." "Dancing and the consumption of alcohol" were permitted only in "venues specifically assigned to the Poles." As for the opium of the people, so dear to the Polish heart, it, too, was regulated and segregated: German churches were not open to Polish Catholics; or at any rate worship was "not to be shared with the German population."[9] Article 7 was the first and the only one to threaten capital punishment. It concerned sexual relations, which were, of course, strictly forbidden between Poles and Germans: "Anyone entering into sexual contact with a German woman or a German man, or who approaches one in an immoral way, will be punished by death." This, in fact, was the main concern of the Reichsführer SS, who was responsible not only for the security of German blood, but for its purity as well:

> The presence of nearly one million Polish people in the Reich [represents a] burden and a challenge to the biological policy of the German people. We must oppose it with the inner strength of our people. It is, above all, the duty of the party and its organizations to signal to the people the dangers arising from it and to instruct them as to the necessary distance to be kept from Polish workers.[10]

In order for the Germans to preserve their honor and their race and maintain their distance, they had to be able to identify Polish people. To this end, one of the "Polish Decrees" of March 8, 1940, was a "police ordinance regarding the identification of civilian workers of Polish race employed in the Reich." This ordinance directed that Polish workers were to wear "on the right side of their chest" a badge featuring "a five-centimeter square resting on its point with a 0.5 cm purple border and a yellow background inscribed with a 'P' 2.5 centimeters in height."[11] This systematic identification was the first of its kind in the Reich outside of the concentration camps, which had been identifying prisoners using a system of color-coded triangles since 1938. In September 1941, the policy of identification was extended beyond the camps for Jews, who were required to wear a yellow star, and then for "Eastern workers" in February 1942.

The RSHA, by imposing its will on the other sections of the administration involved, succeeded in making the *Einsatz* of Polish people in the territory of the Reich into an issue of biology and safety above all else—indeed, into an issue of biological safety *tout court*. The "Polish Decrees" also regulated labor. Articles 5, and then Articles 8–10 of the March 1940 *Merkblatt* employed general language and stock phrases; for example, "sabotage" and "breaches of discipline" would be "punished most severely." Specifically—indeed, this was the only punishment to receive specific mention—it would be punished by internment in "work rehabilitation camps."[12] However, and just as logically, "anyone working in a satisfactory manner will receive bread and a salary."[13] In this way, the Polish Decrees of March 1940 enacted a special labor law, which was examined and assembled in a book published in 1942 by two lawyers, Johannes Küppers and Rudolf Bannier, titled *Arbeitsrecht der Polen im Deutschen Reich* (Polish labor law in the German Reich).[14] That same year, the two colleagues published another, much slimmer, volume titled *Einsatzbedingungen der Ostarbeiter, sowie der sowjet-russischen Kriegsgefangenen*. In English this would be, more or less, "Conditions for the Use of Eastern Workers and Russo-Soviet Prisoners of War," but the title's use of word *Einsatz* is difficult to translate.[15] It was not describing the "employment" of this Slavic, and therefore racially mediocre, labor, but rather its *use*. The word *Einsatz* functioned to repackage labor as a kind of servile tool, making the text into a kind of operating manual for animated objects. When it came to "ex-Soviet" prisoners, the term "labor law," which had been kept in use for the Poles, disappeared completely from the lawyers' writing. This change from "labor law" to the mere regulation of *Einsatz* highlights once again the way in which the status of Eastern peoples was eroded into that of *Untermenschentum*, or "subhumans," with every step that Germany made to the East.

Because the *Ostarbeiter*, too, were massively employed in the territory of the Reich, they required regulation, as well, which was formalized in a circular signed by the Reichsführer SS on February 20, 1942. The "General Regulations regarding the Recruitment and Employment of Labor from the East" was a harsher iteration of the rules decreed nearly two years earlier for Polish workers. Himmler explicitly specified that these "production forces can only be transported to the Reich in closed convoys" under the "surveillance of the Order Police" (OrPo), and were to be held in "disinfection camps at the Reich's borders" beforehand.[16] Their "housing" was to ensure their "isolation"; they were to be kept "apart from the German population." And so workers were held in "closed camps," preferably behind "barbed wire fences."[17] Moreover, "production forces from former Soviet Territories" were to be kept "under constant surveillance," and were never to leave their quarters and workplaces. All contact with the German population was of course strictly forbidden. To this end, in addition to being held in prison camps, *Ostarbeiter* were required to wear identifying badges, as the Poles were, in compliance with Article A-VIII of the Decree of February 20, 1942. They were assigned an "upright triangle measuring 70×77 mm, with a blue and white border 10 mm wide, bearing the word OST in white letters on a blue background."[18]

The regulations governing Eastern workers were so restrictive, so terse, and so rudimentary that they were summed up in a *Merkblatt* only five points long, instead of the ten points accorded to Polish worker regulations. These *Merkblatt*, published in three languages (Russian, Ukrainian, and German), forbade all movement except under "surveillance," required obedience to "guards" (police officers or overseers), and punished any sexual relations with Germans with death, and any neglectfulness or sabotage in the workplace with imprisonment in a concentration camp.[19] The last article reminded workers that it was obligatory to wear the "OST" badge on the right side of their chest. The *Ostarbeiter* regulations thus followed the same principles governing the Polish workers, but in a more repressive way, which showed through in their succinctness. Surveillance and confinement were constant, and any breach of the rules was punished by imprisonment in a concentration camp rather than a "work education camp" (*Arbeitserziehungslager*). There was nothing friendly in the *Merkblatt*'s language: whereas the Polish had been promised a "salary and bread," satisfactory *Ostarbeiter* who "behaved with discipline" by "working well" would be "treated with dignity"—that is, with the dignity befitting an unfit being. Remuneration was not mentioned at all, which

explained why Küppers and Bannier could not really accurately include
the term "labor law" in their book's title. The identification of the
Ostarbeiter deserves comment, as well: as was the case for concentration
camp *Schutzhäftlinge*, for Polish Jews, the Polish workers, then Jews in
the Reich and in occupied Europe, these badges symbolized the reduction of individuals to mere categories (*Ost*, Jew, asocial, political, and so
on). As such they were stripped of all rights, made into the objects of
policy implemented by subjects elsewhere, and higher up, in the racial
hierarchy. Ulrich Herbert, who devoted a part of his doctoral thesis to
this topic, did not qualify these "decrees" as "legal regulations *sensu
stricto*": "They were more . . . the codification of an attitude, the expression of a theory of racial overlords couched in legal language."[20]
Their purpose was actually to manage and regulate the Empire's slave
population during their time in the metropole. The highly repressive
laws and punishments provided for in these decrees strengthened the
dividing line drawn between Germans and the colonized populations
and thus deepened the conceptual chasm between them. Outside of
the Altreich, where workers lived under exceptional and coercive conditions, a special criminal code was also established for Polish people
living in (former) Poland.

On December 4, 1941, Goering, then president of the Council of
Ministers for the Defense of the Reich, signed a "Criminal Law Decree
against the Polish People and the Jews in the Integrated Eastern Territories."[21] Roland Freisler praised this remarkably short, clear, and repressive decree as a model regulatory text that was highly adapted to the
new era and circumstances and to the National Socialist philosophy of
law.[22] Certainly, a criminal code consisting of twenty-eight articles in
just three pages is some kind of model of efficiency: if the Nazi legal
system had indeed sentenced the paragraph to hang, then this decree
could be its gallows. It did not even bear the stamp of the Ministry of
Justice, and was signed only by Frick, the minister of the interior, and
Lammers, head of the Reich chancellery.

Every one of the principles of the Nazi "renewal" of law was illustrated in this text. By 1941, it had long been commonly accepted that
legality had been defined by the legacy of rabbinic positivism and the
"tyranny of the paragraph," and that the new law, flexible, mobile, and
living (as well as vital) was to bring this tyranny to an end. This is ex-

actly what the December 4, 1941, decree did: Poles were commanded to "behave in compliance with German law" and to "abstain from anything that threatens the sovereignty and the reputation of the German people."[23] This "German law" was largely unknown to the Polish population, because it had not been translated into Polish. Article II nevertheless added that the "Polish people and the Jews will also be sanctioned . . . when they commit an act punishable . . . according to the basic principles of German criminal law."[24] The legal vulnerability of the targeted populations was intensified in the second part of Article I-1, which could be interpreted as giving full creative freedom to judges, and inviting them to use this "general clause" as they saw fit.

The commission of any crime at all was most often punishable by death, or, "in less serious cases," with stiff prison sentences.[25] In addition, the Criminal Code for the Polish People and the Jews of Poland provided for a large, unspecified, and potentially infinite number of crimes of omission (crimes based on a failure to act or obey). Articles I-4-4 and I-4-5 also specified that anyone even so much as hearing about a plan to infringe on "the sovereignty of the German Reich and the German people's reputation" was liable to receive the death penalty. The principle of legality was also violated in sentencing, as "in cases where the law does not provide for the death penalty, the latter should be applied when the act displays a particularly contemptible state of mind." Legality, like equality, no longer existed. The exceptional criminal law established by this decree held the Poles to their mediocrity and the Jews to their extreme racial otherness. The maximum sentence provided for in this criminal code could be relaxed in a single significant attenuating circumstance: while in general, minimum sentencing was applied for all infractions, an exception could be made "if the act was committed exclusively against their own people."[26]

At no point in the proceedings was the accused in any way the equal of the prosecution. Under no circumstances, therefore, could he have a judge removed from a case.[27] Furthermore, while the testimony of Jews and Polish people was admissible as evidence, "they do not take oath." After all, what good was their promise or their word? Yet, completely asymmetrically, perjury before the court "naturally" was subject to "provisions for perjury and lying under oath."[28] It went without saying that the "Poles and the Jews could not participate in civil lawsuits or file any claims" in court, much less bring suit.[29] Finally, rulings against them were "immediately applicable," although "the prosecutor may appeal sentences" that he considered too tepid.[30]

This decree provided the guidelines for police and judicial treatment of the Polish population in Warthegau, in Dantzig–West Prussia, and under the General Government for the Occupied Polish Territories, as well as for the Polish workers in the Altreich, who were subject— based on personal law rather than on territorial law—to this special Polish code. Indeed, they were the principal, and, in practice, the only population affected by these regulations. Nazi authorities never needed this special criminal code in order to brutalize, displace, ghettoize, and murder the Jewish population of Poland. Quite revealingly, in administrative correspondence and legal documents, the decree is not referred to by its complete name, which was far too long and complicated, but rather by the abbreviated (in both form and meaning) title of *Polenstrafrechtsverordnung* (Polish criminal law decree). One notes as well that while state and party lawyers were careful to include all of these provisions, rudimentary as they were, in ad hoc texts, they were not nearly so careful when it came to the peoples of the Greater East. There was no special criminal code for *Ostvölker:* the police and military decrees of 1940–1941, issued in preparation for Operation Barbarossa, were amply sufficient for coercive and crushing rule.

The East as Border

In 1934, the Munich-based jurist Kurt Trampler, who was a specialist in international law and an expert on the status of Austria and the German minorities in southeastern Europe, published a short book titled *Volk ohne Grenzen* (People without boundaries). The "people without a land" created by the Treaty of Versailles had been deprived not only of its *Lebensraum*, but, as a logical consequence, of the limits of its biotope. Trampler sought to call attention to this, because he felt it was a neglected issue. There was plenty of interest in flat expanses on maps and stretches of space, but much less in the lines drawn across them. And yet what good was an organism incapable of distinguishing its inside from its outside? What good was a body exposed? Trampler's language in approaching this legal question was highly biological:

The search for borders is by nature innate in every living being. Every tree seeks to delimit the ground it occupies with its roots. . . . Every animal seeks to protect its shelter and its hunting ground from its enemies. Borders, as nature teaches us, are not arbitrarily drawn lines, but enclose a vital space that a given living being or living species succeeds in occupying through its active vital workings.[31]

The Treaty of Versailles, with the absurd map it had imposed on Europe, had deprived the German people of the natural borders of its biology. The "borders inflicted by Versailles," these "coercive borders," were not the natural borders of the German people, who had been deprived of *Lebensraum*, of consistency, and of biological cohesion. "The Paris diktats . . . made us into a people without borders, a threatened and unsettled people": "The German people has no more borders to circumscribe it and bind it into a true unit." The Reich now needed to fight for "the racial border," a "race border" traced out by "the plough's furrow."[32] The "ploughshare border" dug by agricultural activity, by the farm work of the race's peasants, was the mark imprinted by blood on the soil.[33] Trampler's prized idea was shared by all his colleagues: *Lebensraum* and the natural border were drawn and traced out by the blood working the soil, which struggled on and with its land to make it into a hospitable place to live. The right to live and to abide on the land was won by the axe, the plow, and the scythe:

The political territory of German Austria . . . became German because the brush hoes and plows of German farmers transformed this virgin land into farmland . . . [through] agricultural acquisition, . . . [through the true] work of colonization.[34]

The diplomats and lawyers in Versailles had been perfectly aware of what they were doing. "The German borders were shattered" because the goal of the powers at Versailles had been "to destroy the natural strength of the German people." Pan-German will had not been strong enough to overcome the Allies and impose the *Anschluss*. If the Austrian and German governments had not been dogged enough, it was because "they lacked the concept of a German life community."[35] The war and its subsequent "peace" had created a "mutilated Reich," deprived of a "well-circumscribed German space. The living area of the German people, which was now defenseless, was stripped of all protections and exposed to any outside attack."[36] It was therefore time to devote everything to ensuring that "the border of the race, the Reich, and our military protection" all coincided.[37] The author was outraged to note that through a diplomacy of squares and compasses, of grand and abstract principles, the diplomats had attempted to impose an unnatural falsehood on the people of Europe and their actual, concrete realities:

> The violent destruction of biological borders is a violation of the basic, inalienable rights of the people. Racial borders should not be moved by force. The vital, creative work of a people must determine its borders. The space a people succeeds in occupying through its vital work, through peaceful labor, constitutes its inalienable racial space.[38]

Not only had the Third Reich been a revolution within Germany, it had sparked an international revolution as well: "the German revolution against the Europe of constraints," against "this anti-natural repression of the biological uniqueness" of the German people.[39] This revolution was to bring about a "new order," because through it, the German people were "setting the first cornerstone of a true peace, which would not need arbitrarily drawn borders."[40] Hitler was keeping faith with the history of the German people in Europe, which was many millennia long:

> Here we return to our people's original mission: to be a people of order, a people unified in reaching towards the future, firmly rooted in its soil, fighting for its eternal rights and for the rights of all other peoples peacefully reaping the benefits of respect.[41]

With the Ostgrenze, "the Eastern frontier," Trampler's wishes would be fulfilled beyond his wildest imaginings. Nature laughed at the artificial creations of men; the realities of the people had nothing to say to borders drawn by diplomats and statesmen—particularly when they had been drawn to endanger life and stifle nature. In another book, Trampler expanded on the case he knew best, that of Austria as it emerged from the Treaties of Versailles and Saint-Germain-en-Laye in 1919–1920. Trampler asserted that the Austrians had followed a strictly Pan-German vision in their actions. The Vielvölkerstaat (multinational state) of the "aging dynasty" of the Habsburgs, which was "more and more biologically and intellectually alienated," was breathing its last and could do nothing "against the vital growth of the peoples" in its empire.[42] These peoples, through a vote by their deputies on October 21, 1918, had officially separated, and the German-speaking representatives had affirmed their will "to maintain the integrity of the German population zone of the ex-Danubian monarchy," by voting to be annexed by Germany on November 12 of the same year.[43] The author noted with satisfaction that these resolutions had been voted for by the Social Democrats, who at that time were in the political majority in Austria. In so doing, "they had in every respect acted . . . as National Socialists."[44] They were far more closely aligned with the National Socialists than those traitorous German Social Democrats, who, meeting in "the alleged Council of the People's Deputies in Berlin," had done nothing to support their racial comrades. Whereas Austrian Chancellor Renner, a Social Democrat, had proclaimed, "We are of one stock and united in our fate," the Germans, led astray by "the liberal worldview," had been incapable of understanding the biological and racial perspective of the deputies who had come together in Vienna.[45] "The liberal-democratic culture had made the Reich's population more and more alienated from the reasoning" of the Austrian deputies. According to this reasoning, "a man with the same language and the same culture, with the same blood and the same destiny, even outside the borders of the Reich, [is] a racial comrade just the same as the citizen of the Reich himself."[46]

The malignant powers at Versailles and the foolish Social Democrats in power in Germany had abandoned the Austrian Germans to a natural (or rather, an unnatural) disaster. Worse still, they knew that they had been allotted nonviable land as their territory. And as for the German speakers not included in the preposterous territory of this stunted Austria, they had been left in the evil clutches of the everlasting enemies of Germanity. Now transformed into majorities in countries created to suit their whims, they persecuted their Germanic populations as dangerous minorities who should be slowly eradicated. The signature extorted from Germany at Versailles had been written with a poison pen: "If ink were stronger than blood, then this signature would have marked the funeral" of Germans in Europe.[47]

In the face of such dire and deadly artificiality, the Third Reich was restoring nature, and, above all, the natural bonds linking the members of a single race: it had brought an end "to the corruption of values, of chaos" by ensuring that, in the domestic and international political order, "the natural bond of each man to his people, understood as the strongest of natural communities, be restored to its former rights." In a foreshadowing of the now famous images of Wehrmacht soldiers toppling frontier posts at the Austrian, Czechoslovakian, and Polish borders, Trampler prophesied that "all of the intellectual evolution of our time indicates that, for the life and the moral vitality of our people, the barrier that marks the political frontier is less and less important." This was because Nazi Germany, in all ideological and political coherence, considered "the people as a natural unit."[48] It considered all German-speaking minorities in their respective states as fully German, and the Reich as their natural homeland. It had already been the ambition of nineteenth-century Pan-Germanism to bring these "Germans" together in a single state whose borders would be natural, historical, and rightful. The Third Reich adopted this ambition. Even before resorting to arms (or the threat of arms) to redraw the European map, it had decided to ignore the political borders established by the peace treaties of 1919–1920 and to impose what, in the Reich's eyes, was the only valid idea of the nation—not the "liberal-democratic" one of political participation in a state, but rather one of simple, natural, and substantive participation in the biological organism of the people or race.

In a speech to the Reichstag on February 20, 1938, Hitler announced that henceforth Germany would ignore political borders and acknowledge only biological entities. He regretted the "painful consequences of the madness that was Versailles, which wrought havoc on the European map," and recalled that "more than ten million Germans," who had "fought shoulder-to-shoulder with the German soldiers of the Reich until 1918," had been "deprived of union with the Reich against their own will." Then he warned, "Political and legal separation away from the Reich can only lead to our people's absolute dispossession of their rights." The Germans who had been scattered into foreign nations by the Treaty of Versailles, which had ignored the promises of "President Wilson's Fourteen Points," remained "our comrade peoples (*Volksgenossen*)."[49] All too often, it would seem, these poor unfortunate *Volksgenossen*, minorities in the countries created by Versailles, were victims of "persecution" from the majorities in power. Germany could not and would not tolerate this. Just as "England defends its interests throughout the world," even where "pureblooded" Englishmen were not present, "today's Germany will defend its interests." This meant, first and foremost, "the protection of our German comrades who are not able to demand that their human, political, and ideological freedoms be respected."[50]

Hitler was affirming in this speech that true citizenship was biological citizenship, and not merely a question of legal or political status. By extending his protection to German minorities in Europe and around the world, he was also employing racial grounds to refute the principle of national sovereignty. His speech was an open declaration that race dictated political action and that international policy could not be directed by anything but biology. Artificially constructed maps and political borders were no longer recognized. Professor Alexander von Freytag Loringhoven, an eminent scholar in international law and president of the Kolonialrecht section of the "Academy for German Law," placed this gesture in the context of the overall failure of the "League of Nations, which was to exercise oversight" with regard to the respect of minorities and their rights, but had not protected them. And since this international order had failed in its duties, the Führer had replaced it. It was therefore only right for Hitler to demand and proclaim "the right of motherlands to protect the segments of their populations living in foreign nations."[51]

And so Nazi policy, drawing what it saw as healthy inspiration from the natural principles of *Lebensraum,* organic cohesion, and biological solidarity, was seeking to end the unbearable problem of the minority issue that had been created by the treaties of 1919–1920. The lawyer Gustav Adolf Walz, in a cogent article published in 1937, straightforwardly demonstrated that the word *Minderheit* ("minority") was the product of a liberal-democratic culture that thought and reasoned only in the quantitative terms of mathematical relations.[52] In a democratic regime, a majority decided and the minority had to bow to its will. The political minority, through either tacit or explicit consent, had to fall in with majority decisions or risk repression if it chose to contest them. Either way, its existence was neither acknowledged nor encouraged: it was supposed to dissolve into obedience to a law dictated by the majority. The same thing was true of the biological minorities, notably the German ones, who were scattered across Europe into new nations and separated from the Reich by the artificial borders of Versailles. National Socialism and its "racist principle" offered a solution to this problem by promoting the creation of coherent and homogeneous racial groupings.[53] Better yet, both domestically and internationally, Nazism refused to persecute, to suppress, or to oblige minorities to undertake "assimilation." Instead, it was resolutely committed to segregationist "dissimilation," whereby biological entities that were alien to one another were kept strictly separate.[54]

The Spatial Border: The *Ostwall*

Throughout history, Europe, like Germany, had suffered from its lack of a strictly defined territory, of visible natural borders. This openness engendered a natural fear of military invasion, as well as demographic fears of submersion by massive immigration, intensified by a biological fear of infiltration through surreptitious insinuation and mixing:

> Observing the different continents in an atlas, one notes Europe's peculiar situation immediately. America, Africa, and Australia are coherent geographical entities separated from the outside. . . . Europe, on the other hand, is, geographically speaking, a mere appendage to the landmass of Greater Asia. . . . What separates it from Asia is not water, but blood.[55]

In addition, "wherever natural borders are missing, man must replace them with the strength of his people and with a political organization," such as the Reich. Deprived of "natural protection on its eastern and western flanks, the most threatened ones," it had nevertheless succeeded in "affirming the presence of its people on a land."[56] One could not help but note that the "Slavic peoples, by comparison, have been less gifted in the creation of nations."[57] The most ancient history and the most current events, since Versailles, attested to this:

> Up until now, these people have not had any success in creating their own states (see the Poland of the Treaty of Versailles, Czechoslovakia, Yugoslavia, and the Soviet Union, which were organized by the Jews and other alien races).[58]

The result of this was the *Ostaufgabe,* this Eastern mission so unique to the German people. It was nothing less than a way to fulfill Germany's political, cultural, and racial duty to protect European and Nordic civilization, a task that Germans had undertaken for millennia.

Despite what one sometimes hears and reads, the Third Reich had no ambitions for world domination. What interested it was the European continent. In the heat of the German Army's succession of rapid-fire victories, one certainly did hear talk of pushing all the way to India, and confrontation with the United States seemed inevitable at some point. But, overall, the idea of sharing spheres of influence as had been laid out in the Anti-Comintern Pact and the Pact of Steel was to be more or less respected—unless, of course, Italy failed to uphold it, in which case Germany would intervene, as it did starting in 1941, to compensate for the Duce's shortcomings. As it happened, Eastern colonization was being planned realistically, in a manner that took the military situation into account. Certainly, the second version of the *Generalplan Ost,* completed in June 1942, did set staggering goals for the geo-ethnic reconfiguration and development of the East. At the same time, however, it defined with relative coherence the three zones of colonization—Ingermanland (Ingria), Ukraine, and Gotenland (the Crimea)—which in the end kept a respectful distance from the Urals and the so-called "Asiatic" zone.

The project for Eastern conquest and colonization was circumscribed and finite, not undefined or indefinite. From the beginning in 1940, and even in the first euphoric weeks of the 1941 campaign, plans for the East and discussion among the Nazi elite mentioned the limits of conquest and colonization. As in the Middle Ages, the Nazis planned *Marken* (marches) for the Eastern frontier of the new Eastern territories. Colonists in this march zone would form a "biological protective wall in the East," made up of SS veterans, who, like retiring Roman legionaries, would be sent to serve the land when they completed their military service.[59] The plow would follow the sword, Himmler proclaimed: "And so in the East, thanks to our SS comrades at the front, a new German peasantry is assembling, a living Eastern wall, whose strength and domestic security are guaranteed by the 'peasant-soldiers' (*Wehrbauern*) of the SS."[60]

A hard life awaited them, but it was vital for Germanic colonists to settle and put down roots in the land of the marches. The most experienced soldiers, declared Himmler, were to be placed at the outposts there:

> In the twenty years that follow the war's end, I have made it a goal—and I hope we will succeed in it—to move the Germanic border 500 km to the East. This means that we will have to resettle farmer families—a racial migration of the best German blood, accompanied by the harnessing of the Russian masses to help in the tasks we must carry out. This means that once the bells have tolled for peace, the most difficult era of our life will begin. We will have twenty years ahead of us to secure the peace. Just as I am demanding today that you be unwavering in your faith and courageous in your struggle, I will ask of you then that you be the faithful servants of our safety and our blood, true peasants and faithful partisans of our empire. . . . After that, the East will be cleansed of all foreign blood and our families will colonize it as its farmer-overlords.[61]

To ensure that these veterans would be good farmers, future peasant-soldiers were to participate in comprehensive agricultural training, after which they would become *SS-Neubauernanwärter* (SS candidate farmers) sponsored by the RuSHA. Lengthy theoretical and technical training was planned for men and veterans who did not come from rural backgrounds, including

> a four-week course in an SS camp in the East, followed by a year as a farm hand in a well-managed farm run by an SS veteran, followed by five years as a land worker on selected properties, alternating with courses in Eastern SS camps.[62]

Thus familiarized with the land and farming, the SS veterans would be settled in the place of their struggle and would constitute "a protective wall of peasant-soldiers . . . against the Asian tidal wave."[63] The marches would be under absolute military and police control by the Reich. In Hitler's own words, as noted by Martin Bormann during a summit meeting of Rosenberg, Keitel, and Goering on July 16, 1941,

> the establishment of an enemy military power west of the Urals is now out of the question, even if we have to wage war for a hundred years. The Führer's successors must know this: the Reich's security can only be assured if there is no foreign army to the west of the Urals.[64]

The possibility of arming indigenous populations was dismissed from the outset, although in practice this position would shift as the military situation deteriorated: "The iron principle must be and must remain: no one but the Germans should be allowed to bear arms."[65]

The Limits of the Nazi Biotope: The Eastern Marches and Buchenwald

Where should these marches occur and what time limit should be set for the Eastern conquest? What criteria were used to set the limits of the Reich's expansion? Certainly, there were practical military considerations: as conditions in the East evolved throughout the war, goals were reconsidered and redefined. But essentially, and yet again, the limits of Nazi expansion were set by nature. Let us recall that the East was a vital living space in what, to the Nazis, was a strictly literal and scientific sense, meaning it was a biotope for the Nordic race. The species' living space was thus defined by the laws of nature. An ideological pamphlet distributed by the NSDAP to civil servants and soldiers in the East indicates that history had been the first to answer the questions posed earlier: archaeological discoveries showed that Germanic outposts had never crossed over a certain line. This line was topographically invisible, since no natural borders, no mountains or rivers, had ever delineated the Germanic realm from Asia. Archaeological research showed, nevertheless, that there were no traces of Germanic presence beyond a certain Eastern line. This was not mere chance.

This historical response was in fact a decree from nature: if the Germanics had not ventured to the east of this line, it was because there actually was a natural border—although an invisible one, because it was climatic. It was the borderline between the maritime climate and the continental climate, and it was marked by the eastern limits of where the beech tree (Buche) grew: "Here again, nature traced a line that is above all a climatic line. . . . In the forest and flower cover, it is most clearly indicated by the eastern limit of the native beech," the Rotbuche (Fagus sylvatica).[66]

The European beech tree, a Germanic plant par excellence, grew in the West. No such species existed in the East: "To the west of this line extends the Middle-European zone, friendly, open, colorful, and easily circumscribable, which enjoys the blessing of a varied maritime climate. Beyond lies the hostile land of the East, with its continental climate."[67] This climatic borderline was to be respected; nature had drawn it for German tree and German man alike, for, as we know, they were more or less one and the same, and could live only in fertile and fertilized soil. Lippe and other authors, including Himmler and Hitler, were unequivocal when it came to the decisive (and restrictive) influence of nature on human undertakings. This was why, according to Himmler, Africa and Spain were not to be colonized. A mild climate could be favorable at times—Hitler believed that Germanic photosynthesis in Greece and Rome proved this—but it became dangerous in excess. It mutated the Germanic organism, rather than benefiting it. Again, the tree indicated the borderline: cross over, and the race would be lost in an *Unland*. "Although this spatial border is not visible, it has only rarely been crossed by Nordic peoples."[68]

Blood followed sap, and man's steps should go no further than the roots of the beech: the colonization of "*Warthegau*, occupied anew, all of the experiments, and all of the plans for demographic policy in other territories, uniquely in the East," had been made "by confirming and applying the laws of nature."[69]

The Physical Edge: Famine, Exploitation, Exhaustion

The future living space of some was to be the mass gravesite of others. A photograph of a Wehrmacht company on the Eastern Front summarizes this philosophy starkly. The group is posed for the camera in front of a blackboard on which is painted the rather unambiguous slogan, "Russia must die, so that we may live."[70]

The Eastern march represented a physical edge as well as a geographical limit: the exploitation of Slavic populations consisted of physical servitude so extreme that for some, it would result in the complete exhaustion of their vital forces. Nazi planners were consistent optimizers. The economists, agronomists, geographers, demographers, and other specialists working for the RKF, the Ostministerium, or in the administration of Goering's "Four-Year Plan" carefully reified, quantified, and calculated the physical and economic productivity of the Reich-occupied Eastern territories. It was clear to them that the Slavic people were not a human population worthy of that name, or of any rights that might be accorded to such humans. They were a servile mass and were to be treated and exploited as such. In this sense, the way the engineers of the Nazi colonial project thought about their empires did not differ too greatly from their British, Belgian, or French counterparts. But the immensity of the spaces, the demographic numbers, and the work carried out seemed to intensify the managerial coldness of their gaze. The norms of planning were dispassionately calculated with optimization as their driving goal: the Slavic people were a biomass to be regulated according to the needs of the German economy, the jobs to be filled in the Reich, and the infrastructures to be built in the vast territories to the East.

Everything was reified and quantified—so many variables for so many equations. The sub- or infra-human variable of the Slavic biomass was an element in an operation of managerial mathematics, projecting means and ends over the medium and long term. It was the only option: the *Grossraum Ost* was vast, and the economic and military tasks ahead were titanic. For maximal clarity and precision, and for the purposes of organized and centralized decision-making, directives did not go into detail, preferring instead to generalize from the outset: the sources all use the word *Slawentum*, which refers to a demographic mass that was to be regulated and whose labor force was to be exploited. According to the logic of managerial profit-building, it was necessary to optimize this labor force by extracting at least a passable level of performance at the lowest possible price; that is, with the smallest possible nutritional input. A meeting of secretaries of state held in preparation for Operation Barbarossa decided that starting on May 2, 1941, more than a month and a half before the operation's launch, "oil seeds," "oil cakes," "fats," and "meats" of all types were to be sent promptly to the Reich once military needs had been met. It went without saying that "fighting can only continue if, in the war's third year"—that is, 1941—"the entire Wehrmacht is fed by Russia."[71]

As a result, "most likely millions of people, the exact number is unknown, will die of hunger."[72] This logical consequence, an accounting line item, was also a conscious and deliberate one, given that the Slavic population, as things stood, was too high in the Eastern colonial territories. As the rigorous stewards of natural, nutritional, and physical resources, Nazi planners established a new "iron law" to govern the development of the Eastern territories. The iron law of salaries, as revealed and condemned by Marx, consisted in maximizing profit while reducing the price of the labor factor to its bare minimum—in other words, the salary paid was to be barely sufficient for the upkeep and reproduction of the labor force. This logic was applied and taken to the extreme by the Nazi colonists, and the scale of the consequences, given the land and the size of the populations to be enslaved and exploited in the application of these accounting formulae, was vast.

Once again, behind the slide rules and the arithmetic planning, nature's law was being borne out: the Slavic populations had no right to the land, which they occupied without possessing it. Only racial excellence and the expression of this excellence through cultivation and colonization conferred property rights, and these they did not have. Their presence was a factual one, not a rightful one. As Hitler put it, "It is completely absurd that the Russian masses, backward as they are, culturally useless, would monopolize this land and these infinite spaces, which belong to the best of the earth."[73] Famine was openly and concertedly planned for. There could be no moral compunctions about it, because nature was just regarding all things and all proportions. Just as a Russian life did not have the same value as a German life (in both absolute and relative terms), a Slavic body and stomach did not have the same needs, or even the same substance, as did its German counterparts. Herbert Backe, always eager to remind his civil servants that German values did not apply in the East, offered them this advice, in all its historical, sociological, and gastric relativism:

> For centuries, Russian man has tolerated poverty, hunger, and small means. His stomach is elastic, so no misplaced pity! Do not try to apply the German standard of living as a criterion, and do not attempt to change the Russian lifestyle.[74]

Heinrich Himmler, an expert in the "treatment of alien racial elements in the East," also justified without qualification the exploitation unto death of Slavic vital energy:

> Everything that brings us closer to victory is right. Everything that keeps these savage people in our service is right, and it is right for a Russian to die instead of a German. It is right, and we can defend it before God and men.[75]

The Reichsführer SS reiterated these basic elements from his moral catechism in one of his Posen speeches, delivered to his commanding officers and generals on October 4, 1943:

> The SS follows an absolute principle: we must be honest, correct, loyal, and good comrades toward men of our own blood—and toward no one else. I could not care less how a Czech or a Russian is doing. . . . I am only interested in whether other people are doing well or dying of hunger to the extent that we need them as slaves of our culture—otherwise, I could not care less. To me, the question of whether or not ten thousand Russian women die of exhaustion while building an anti-tank trench is interesting only in terms of whether the trench is ready for Germany or not.[76]

Getting upset about famine in the East was to be (guiltily) ignorant of the fact that nature was finite, and that race relations were a zero-sum game. If some were to eat and survive, then others must perish. It was also to forget a little too quickly the starvation and suffering of the German population during First World War—in particular during the *Kohlrübenwinter* (turnip winter) of 1916–1917, which had resulted, among other things, in the November Revolution of 1918. The German-Soviet Pact, signed on August 23, 1939, was an attempt to prevent famine and blockade, through the exchange of German manufactured goods for Soviet raw materials, including grain shipments, and Stalin followed through scrupulously on the agreement. The launch of Operation Barbarossa however, unleashed a policy of widespread predation on the USSR.[77]

On November 8, 1941, Reichsmarschall Goering, who was in charge of the "Four-Year Plan" and thus of economic exploitation of the East, called a meeting in his majestic offices at the Air Ministry. During the meeting, which included Alfred Rosenberg, the Reich minister for the Occupied Eastern Territories, as well as the Reich commissars for the *Ostland* and the Ukraine, Goering shared a major concern: "We cannot impose an additional reduction in rations on the German population," in the third year of the war. Thinking back, it was easy to calculate that the third year of the preceding war, 1916, had marked the beginning of the military, nutritional, and political hardships of the preceding Reich. Goering wanted to go to every possible length to prevent the recurrence of this type of situation. The Reichs-marschall declared that "the fate of the major cities, particularly Leningrad, is of no importance at all to me. This war will see the most mass deaths since the Thirty Years' War." What mattered was that "supplies to all of Europe" be assured through the spoliation of the East, without any consideration for the physical and demographic consequences for the Slavic populations.[78]

Here, Goering was merely following the reports and recommendations of his services. In February 1941, he and Hitler had decided to create the WO Ost (Wirtschaftsorganisation Ost, or Economic Organization for the East), an impressive structure comprising twenty thousand civil servants working under the Reichsmarschall's command. On May 23, 1941, the WO Ost's "Agriculture Department" sent Goering a report outlining principles for the agricultural and nutritional exploitation of the Soviet Union. The report's authors opened with the observation that the Bolshevik Revolution of 1917 and the USSR's subsequent isolation in international politics had caused a breach in Europe's agricultural and economic organization. The Soviet Union's retreat from international commerce and its increasing autarchy had upset the continental balance by depriving the European subcontinent of the vast lands and supplies of the Russian hinterlands. The "destruction" of this natural and agricultural "balance" had led to a harmful "disruption" of the Reich's food supplies.[79]

To reestablish the "balance" between the Eastern *Hinterland* and the West, it was necessary to completely reorganize Soviet production, which, according to the WO Ost experts, was divided into "dependent areas" (*Zuschussgebiete*) and "surplus areas" (*Überschussgebiete*) at the macro-geographic level. With the most cavalier approach to geography, the experts designated the northern part of the territories as "dependent areas," and "forested zones" (*Waldzone*), and the southern half as productive "surplus areas" and "zones of black earth." Here again, Eastern policy was sketched out in the most general of terms, with little in the way of specifics or details. The Reich's specialists wielded their squares and compasses with no concern for nuance: the Soviet territories to be conquered and colonized were reduced to a binary juxtaposition of rich and fertile lands to the south and a north too poor to feed itself, and therefore dependent and vaguely parasitical.

The experts were unsparing in their assessment of the northern zone: if it could produce nothing on its own, then let it die. The report submitted to Goering was categorical on this point: "Beyond supplying the German troops stationed in this zone, preserving activity in this territory is of no interest to Germany. The population of the forested zone will thus endure the harshest famine, particularly the cities."[80] Feeding the Soviet population in the northern half of the occupied territories was absurd and a threat to the Reich's own population:

> Attempts to prevent famine and death among these populations by importing surplus from the zones of black earth would only be to the detriment of Europe, and would weaken Germany's capacity to resist, particularly to withstand blockades, during this war. We must be perfectly clear on this point.[81]

In the advice and reports produced by the military and civil servants working in the WO Ost, the trauma of 1916–1917 was explicitly evoked as an imperative to ensure the Reich's *Blockadefestigkeit* (capacity to withstand blockades), and thus to avoid repeating the famine that Germans had experienced during that time. It was to this end, and to this end alone, that a portion of the Soviet population *might* be granted access to food and other staples. In the southern zone, "in the black-earth territories, the main surplus zone for grain and oil crops, our main and primary goal is to maintain and consolidate production." To this end, it was recommended that "the major production structures (kolkhozes and sovkhozes)" be preserved. The workforce employed in these agricultural facilities "can have access to fit living conditions" so long as it kept them motivated and strong enough to work to produce more calories for the Reich.[82]

"Keep Your Distance"

Hitler warned his generals that the Eastern enemy were *kein Kamerad* (not comrades). Nor were the *Untermensch* fully human; from a legal standpoint, their inferior biological status translated to quasi-nonexistence. They were objects, and did not understand, feel, and experience the same things that Germans did. To Himmler, these subhumans were not carved from the same wood, and had to be spoken to in a language they understood:

Let us be careful to abstain from attributing a German soul to these people, or German criteria, or German tact—everything that, by all rights, we should display at home and which we always will. We do not believe that these foreigners think the same things that we do, so let us avoid saying, in a rush of foolish compassion, "We can't actually do that to the Russians or to the Poles." We may be doing something to them, but we are doing good for our families, and that is why we are doing it.[83]

Objectively then, morality was not universal, because it could not be applied equally to all objects: a Russian could not be thought of as a German. Morality was no more universal in a subjective sense, as each race followed the ethic dictated by its blood. Walter Gross argued that the time had come to recognize "racial determinism, and therefore, the racial subjectiveness of the values with which peoples and men can alone judge their actions," which "will protect us from the presumptuousness shown by the false objectivity of liberalism."[84] The boundaries of law and morality were ontological, and drawing them served a biological end that Himmler pointed out constantly—to consolidate one life force by exploiting, weakening, and even ending another:

Whereas for Germans I forbid all mistreatment of mothers and children and [I] battle abortion by all possible means, for Slavs I say: I am not their protector; let them do what they will. My jurisdiction doesn't extend that far! What other peoples do, they are answerable for to themselves. The only interest they hold for me is their utility to Germany; otherwise, I couldn't care less. I defend the law as a German, and for my people.[85]

Hierarchy and the imperative of segregation were reaffirmed: "Keep your distance from the Russians: they are Slavs, not Germans." Any familiarity was forbidden, as was sharing a table or a drink: one did not eat or drink with Russians—just as in the KL (Konzentrationslager, or concentration camps), any proximity between guards and prisoners was forbidden, and subject to strict punishments for SS members: "Any contact, even the most insignificant, with inmates, is formally prohibited and will lead to immediate dismissal from the SS, as well as protective detainment, and even incarceration in a concentration camp." These excerpts from the Lagerordnung (camp regulations) show that any contact at all between prisoners and guards risked blurring, or even abolishing, the border between the two species, so much so that any human interaction "beyond those required by service" led to the immediate dismissal of SS members, who were not only excluded but then subject to the same legal provisions (those of *Schutzhaft*) as the prisoners they had joined in their fall from grace.[86] There could be no conversation with them, either: Russians were "born dialecticians" and had "inherited a philosophical penchant" that led them to want to chatter and argue. It would be pointless, however, to attempt to convince them of anything. Russians, as Herbert Backe, pointed out, were not conversational companions, nor did they have any inclination to understand a shred of National Socialism. Their incomprehension mattered not at all, in the end—all that was required of them was efficiency. "We have no intention of converting the Russians to National Socialism," Backe wrote. "We want to use them as tools."

Faced with these back-talkers and whiners, a German had "to be a man of action who commanded what was necessary, with no argument, without useless chatter or philosophical consideration." He had to be a man, since Russians, in a word, and by nature, were women. "A Russian is impressed only by action, as he himself is soft and feminine." All the more reason, therefore, to avoid being "soft and sentimental," so as not to allow those doleful, plaintive, and weepy Russians to drag you down the slippery slope of feeling and compassion:

> If you cry with a Russian you will make him happy, for then he will be able to disdain you. Because by nature they are women, the Russians want to find a man's fault so that they can disdain him. So do not let yourselves be made unmanly. Maintain a Nordic attitude.[87]

The latter injunction did not mean, however, that one should do Slavic women the honor of showing them one's virility. Quite to the contrary, in fact: men were to remain men—that is, fair and inflexible—in front of the great feminine masses of the Russian population, but never, ever were they allowed themselves to be seduced or compromised sexually. Can this stance be interpreted as a simple extension of the Nuremberg Laws? No, because Slavic people were not poisonous in the same way that Jews could be. Physical contact and sexual mixing with Jews had a pathological impact on an Aryan's physical body.

The same could not be said of Slavic people, although they were often dirty and diseased.

The code of norms applicable to SS and German police officers recalled the absolute prohibition of "any sexual relations with anyone alien to the race"—a prohibition that applied only to foreigners.[88] The Reichsführer SS, who himself had a none-too-discreet double life, exhorted his men to maintain active sex lives, both within and outside the bonds of marriage, in order to produce as much healthy biological substance as possible. Indeed, the various instructions he gave to this end were the subject of debate and indignation outside the SS. Seeking to avoid any mixing of fluids and the contamination of his men and the race, Himmler stated explicitly in the code of law of the SS that "sexual relations with women of foreign races, such as Polish, Czech, or Russian women (including Ukrainians) are strictly forbidden," but not absolutely. Sometimes the soldiery deserved a warrior's rest. Because temptation ran high—it was only human, after all—"relations with these women are authorized, on the other hand, if they take place in official bordellos." In other words, a purely instrumental use of these women of alien race was permitted, because in these military bordellos there was no risk that "conception or any form of attachment [would] occur." It was out of the question for SS or police officers to feel any tenderness for foreign women—or any feelings at all—let alone forget themselves to the point that they might imagine having children with one of them. This type "of attachment to the non-German population" would represent "a sin against our own blood," and disrespect "for our race and the integrity of our blood." "Anyone guilty of this thereby shows that he has not understood the basic principles of National Socialism."[89]

The goal of this strict prohibition was to maintain an unbridgeable distance between the colonizers and the colonized, as well as to avoid the conception of mixed-race children, who, thanks to miscegenation, would be born armed with Germanic qualities:

> It is no small thing, when one of us spends the night someplace in Russia with an Asiatic woman and produces a child. For this original sin will be manifested in the form of a descendant who, armed with the organizational talent of the Germanic and the brutality of the Asiatic, will come and attack Europe. It is our descendants who

will have to expiate with their blood what one of us committed so carelessly.[90]

The most terrifying of the German-Asiatic or Mongol-Germanic bastards, the plague of plagues, had been Genghis Khan, the monster of extermination who had rained devastation on Europe like an apocalyptic demon. According to Himmler, there could be no doubt that "this man was an Indogermanic-Mongolian bastard, who was reported to be tall, with gray eyes and red hair." It was his Germanic genius that had allowed him to "swiftly organize the innumerable masses of inner Asia and to lead them in an attack on Europe."[91]

The problem of "racial bastards" was not limited to the colonies— it was also an issue in the "metropole" of the Altreich. As Dr. Walter Gross, who was responsible for racial policy in the NSDAP, explained to the Hitler Youth in a 1943 brochure, the price of German victory was the presence on its soil of an unprecedented number of foreign elements, which threatened the purity of its blood. Germany was thus facing the "problems caused by foreigners on the very soil of the Reich, and racial policy demands that cannot be met without a clear awareness of our own blood, self-respect, and racial pride."[92] Gross exhorted the Youth not to repeat the errors committed "during the great invasions and the Crusades," when "racial pride and distance from elements present on foreign soil" had not been maintained.[93] Thankfully, times had changed:

> Today, Germany is led by men who are aware of the importance of questions relating to blood, and who are doing everything in their laws and their decrees, through the measures they are taking and the education they are providing, to learn History's lessons and prevent victory in war from leading us to . . . biological defeat.[94]

Gross solemnly called on the moral responsibility of each and every German: the temptation to engage in sexual relations with foreigners was great, and there had never been such opportunity to do so as after the victories of the Third Reich. What "might seem humanly comprehensible" constituted "in reality a betrayal of our own race and the blood of our ancestors."[95] And "loyalty to the blood of our people is, at this hour in our history, the supreme duty and the most serious of tasks."[96]

"Six Thousand Years of Jewish Hatred"

Loyalty to blood required the practice of unprecedented levels of violence—or, rather, returning to and rehabilitating a precedent set generations before:

> We must deploy a radical German racial policy. Just as the Sword
> Brethren did not triumph using kid gloves . . . , by the same token,
> our men posted on the Eastern Front must fight fanatically for our
> worldview and impose our racial interests with absolute violence if
> necessary.[97]

Here, Hitler's words were intended for all the *Ostvölker*, thirty million of whom, according to the *Generalplan Ost*, were to die over the
short and medium term. Slavic peoples, however, unlike the Jews, were
not slated for complete eradication. Yet it should be recalled that in
the eyes of the Nazi leadership and to staunch anti-Semites, the Shoah
was a war. For thousands of years, they believed, Jews had sought to
destroy Nordic humanity. In its mandatory ideological instruction,
the SS taught its men that "six thousand years of racial war" had been
caused by "six thousand years of Jewish hatred."[98] The great prayer of
the Jews, these henchmen of a fanatical God, had always been "Exterminate them, like the seventy thousand Persians" massacred during
the great anti-Nordic pogrom of Purim, which the Jews still celebrated
as holiday.[99] It was the Jews who had started the Great War, caused the
defeat and the November Revolution, and weakened Germany. By the
same token, it was the Jews who had started this Second World War.[100]
Hitler affirmed it in his famous speech on January 30, 1939, seven
months before the Reich invaded Poland:

> If the international Jewish financiers should once again succeed in
> plunging the nations into a world war, the result will not be the Bol-
> shevization of the world and thus the victory of the Jewry, but the
> destruction of the Jewish race in Europe.[101]

"Once again": November 1918, this domestic revolution, which had
led to Germany's defeat, was the work of the Jews. This is yet another
of the multiple meanings that may be ascribed to Hitler's promise that
never again "in German history would there be a November 1918."

There would be no more defeat; and, barring that, no more capitulation; in any case, no more victories for the Jews. Because Germany was still always under attack, and because the Nordic race was, in spite of itself, constantly in a state of war, then any declaration of war (against Poland or against the USSR) was superfluous. The unleashing of the German Army was merely the manifestation of a latent state of conflict, a legitimate defense against the substantive attacks during millennia of hatred from Germany's enemies, notably the Jews. Operation Barbarossa was a defensive and protective move to protect the imperiled Germanic race: "The imperative of our own survival commanded us to stand up for our rights and to act."[102] The goal of Bolshevism, a Jewish doctrine, was to "reduce Europe to a watery stew of humanity" without a racial elite, making it a degenerate putty for the Jews to manipulate as they wished. Europeans would be slaves to their misdeeds, while the "countries of Europe" became "the servile provinces of international Jewry."[103]

It was only natural that "the fight against the Bolsheviks" was to be undertaken "in the same pitiless way that the Bolsheviks themselves wage war"; in other words, radically. "Bolshevik doctrine requires the most brutal extermination of anything that is not Bolshevik." If, therefore, "they strike us violently, we must reply with even greater violence."[104] As everything about the radicalization of contemporary conflicts proved—the First World War being the prime example—the stakes of war are extreme, even total. In 1941, Robert Ley, head of the DAF (*Deutsche Arbeitsfront,* or German Labor Front), warned that in case of defeat, "the German people would be entirely exterminated, you and I, everyone, men, women, and children. The baby in its mother's womb would be killed. The Jew would know no compassion, no pity at all."[105]

These dire apocalyptic warnings became more and more terrifying as time passed and the prospect of defeat became more real. Backed into a corner, down to the last man, it was better to have taken things to extremes oneself, and to be fully informed of the horror of the peril. On January 30, 1944, in the ritual speech he delivered every year on the same date, to commemorate the Nazi accession to power, Hitler declared that if "Germany did not win this war, . . . the eternal Jew, this ferment of destruction, would celebrate its second triumphal *Purim* on the ruins of a devastated Europe."[106]

The truth about the Bolshevik horror and the dark projects fomented in the East was revealed in texts published in the West: wherever its members happened to be, the Jewish people were united in their inexplicable hatred of Nordic man. On July 24, 1941, as genocidal operations in the East were beginning to accelerate, the *Völkischer Beobachter* ran the headline "Massive Jewish Extermination Program; Roosevelt Orders the German People to be Sterilized; Germans to be Exterminated within Two Generations."[107]

The newspaper cited *Germany Must Perish*, a self-published book by an isolated man named Nathan Kaufmann. The historian Geoffrey Herf has devoted several enlightening pages to this text, and notes that while there was no question it was blown out of proportion, Goebbels and Hitler nevertheless did actually take it as evidence of a Jewish truth.[108] Goebbels decided to have it translated and published for distribution to every soldier on active duty: "It will be highly instructive for every German man and woman to see what would become of the German people if, as in November 1918, we showed any signs of weakness."[109] Wolfgang Diewerge, who was put in charge of its publication, condemned the work of "the American Jew Theodore Nathan Kaufmann, of the Manhattan Ghetto."[110] Diewerge bluntly stated the overt goal of the war that Jews had declared on Germany. The Jews intended to succeed where they had failed between 1618 and 1648, and then again between 1914 and 1918—that is, in "the eradication of the German people and its eighty million members," through the "sterilization of all men of an age and capacity to procreate, as well as women and children."[111] This "extermination program" dictated by "the Talmud" was the harsh reality of this new world war, which, let it be repeated, was hiding its real face behind the generous and general motives stated by Roosevelt and Churchill on the Potomac.[112]

> This rehash of Versailles would bear as little resemblance to the Potomac statements as the first Versailles did to Wilson's promises. In a single voice, the international Jewry of New York, Moscow, and London is demanding the total destruction of the German people.[113]

Once again, it was clear that no one would see anything to protest about: "The 'global conscience' would allow this mass crime to be perpetrated against a nation of culture" because "it had already accepted plenty of other things, and, in any case, 'global conscience' is a Jewish invention, not an Aryan one."[114] The author dismissed the potential disbelief of his readers: "This plan is not an invention of the mind, but pure Jewish *Realpolitik*."[115] This present, imminent danger only confirmed and intensified an ancient peril. In 1942, Hitler justified extreme Nazi brutality toward the Jews by making reference to ancient history. Fighting and even killing the Jews was fulfilling a duty to the past:

> Once again, the Führer expresses his opinion: he has decided to unsparingly wipe out all Jews in Europe. There can be no vague inclinations to sentimentality here. The Jews deserve the catastrophe they are currently living. They will, with the destruction of our enemy, experience their own annihilation. We must accelerate this process coldly and without hesitation; in so doing we will render an inestimable service to suffering humanity, which the Jewry has tormented for millennia.[116]

This responsibility to a racial past was also a responsibility to the future: the present generation had to undertake and complete the task. The Nazis were confronting a danger that had lasted for millennia because no one else had ever dared to do so. Their predecessors in this struggle had had neither the racial science nor consciousness of the danger—and indeed, had not had any consciousness at all, as Judeo-Christianity had perverted it. By acting here and now, they were sparing their children and grandchildren the burdensome task of one day having to carry out this unpleasant work:

> The time is ripe, now, to offer a final solution to the Jewish question. Future generations will have lost the energy and the keen instinct it requires. It is thus in our interest to move forward in this matter in a radical and consistent manner. The burden we are now shouldering will be a boon and a godsend to our descendants.[117]

The present generation, which was able to act, had to seize the opportunity of this conflict to wage a radical racial war, a total biological war that would rid the Nordic race once and for all of its enemy. Himmler insisted on this point:

> In a village, when I was obliged to give the order to march against the partisans and Jewish commissars—I say this here, and my words

are intended exclusively for this audience—I systematically gave the order to kill the women and children of these partisans and commissars as well. I would be a coward and a criminal with regard to our descendants if I allowed the hate-filled children of these subhumans who were killed in the fight of humans against subhumans to grow up.[118]

To do one's duty to history and biology, to act with full responsibility to the past and to the future, required that the enemy's future be destroyed. The biological radicalism of the fight against the Jews required that their descendants be killed, and, as one of the genocide's practitioners, Lieutenant-Colonel Jäger, specified, this meant right down to the womb.[119] The treatment of Jewish children appeared to be a problem to those participating in the crime. Himmler himself did not hide this, as Goebbels noted:

With regard to the Jewish question, he offers a frank and unvarnished report. He is convinced that we can resolve the Jewish question throughout Europe by the end of the war. He proposes the harshest and most radical solution: exterminate the Jews and all they possess, down to their children. This certainly is a logical solution, even if it is violent. We must take it upon ourselves to resolve this problem in our time. Future generations most likely will not deal with the problem with the same passion and courage as we have.[120]

It was up to the present to wipe the slate clean of the past and future of the Jews. Himmler was aware of the gravity and the difficulty of this decision, but he was not lacking in arguments when it came to convincing his men to kill what might appear to them to be innocent and defenseless beings:

There is a question you have certainly asked yourselves, to which I would like to respond. This question is the following: "You see, I understand that we would kill grown Jewish men, but women and children?" I must tell you something: one day, these children will grow up. Let us imagine for a moment that we are dishonest enough to say: "No, no, we are too weak for this, but our children can take care of it someday. They should be able to finish the job, too." Well, then the Jewish hatred of these avengers, little today and grown tomorrow, will plague our children and our descendants, so that one day they will have the same problem to resolve; but it will be in a

time when there will be no more Adolf Hitler. We cannot be responsible for that. It would be cowardly, and that is why we have preferred
a clear-cut solution, as harsh as it may be.[121]

It was clear that this responsibility toward the future went hand in
hand with the eradication of future generations of the Jewish race, with
the extinction of its future. The sweet little babies of today would be
tomorrow's inexorable enemies. Appearances were deceiving—*Jud
bleibt immer Jud* (a Jew is always a Jew)—and behind their innocent
mask, their substance was criminal. Adorable and endearing, those
Jewish children? "A little piglet is also totally adorable." That did not
mean that, one fine day, it would not grow up to be a repugnant and
dangerous "old sow."[122]

German "Un-Cruelty"

The imbeciles and the cowards who were upset by the violence of these
procedures and chattered on at every turn about humanity were the real
criminals. An SS brochure for SD and police officers quoted Houston
Stewart Chamberlain's condemnation of those who, "by waving the flag
of 'humanity' condemn the human species to extinction."[123] The Jews
had been the first to be cruel. The Jews were such hateful and egotistical
creatures that they would kill each other, had they not had the good
fortune to have outside enemies, who were just as necessary to their
survival as the oxygen they breathed. This was Hitler's claim in *Mein
Kampf*:

> Jews act in concord only when a common danger threatens them or
> a common prey attracts them. Where these two motives no longer
> exist then the most brutal egotism appears and these people who be-
> fore had lived together in unity will turn into a swarm of rats that
> bitterly fight against each other.
>   If the Jews were the only people in the world they would be wal-
> lowing in filth and mire and would exploit one another and try to ex-
> terminate one another in a bitter struggle.[124]

Jews only worked together to serve their own interests and against
their enemies. Hedonistic materialists, they were incapable of "idealism" or the least shred of community sentiment when they lacked

an enemy. This was the message of an uncompleted film whose rushes have been preserved in the film department of the Bundesarchiv, the German Federal Archives. *Ghetto* was shot in the Warsaw Ghetto in May 1942, two years after *Der Ewige Jude* (The eternal Jew, 1940). The systematic murder of Jews by the General Government began in the spring of 1942, as well. Most likely the film's goal was to preserve a minimal record of life in the ghettos, which, little by little, were to be emptied. Most likely, too, the film was intended for distribution—as *Der Ewige Jude* was—in an attempt to help justify the Reich's anti-Jewish policy.

The film crew captured a population that was exhausted, starved, and sick, rehashing all of the same clichés employed by every contemporary news report and "documentary" whose subject—and target—was the Jews. The ugliness of the images, which were of emaciated, unsettling, sinister-looking faces, was accentuated by the shaving of heads, filmed in closeup. Overcrowded and filthy buildings were explored in minute detail. Indifferent passersby walked past cadavers in the street, people who had died on the sidewalk of starvation. The film, presented as raw footage, was in fact carefully orchestrated by the cameramen, as shown in reports by the ghetto commandant, Heinz Auerswald, as well as in the journals of Adam Czerniaków, the head of the Judenrat (Jewish Council), and in the testimony of Willy Wist during investigations leading up to the Auerswald Trial in the late 1960s.[125]

Among other things, to illustrate the alleged luxuriant wealth of the ghetto, a ball, with a buffet and champagne, was staged at 8:30 a.m.; people were forced to sit and eat lavishly in a restaurant, served with food that the film crew had brought into the ghetto; and a woman was taken to a clean apartment and compelled to primp and preen for hours on end. The film sought to show that in the face of misery and death, the materialistic and hedonistic Jews had no *Volksgemeinschaft*, that they were incapable of generosity and solidarity. As his racial brothers lay dying in the street, the Jew continued to sip his champagne. This sordid inequality in life continued in death: the film crews also staged an opulent funeral, complete with abundant flowers and a luxurious catafalque supporting a gleaming coffin, then panned over images of bodies being loaded into carts and dumped unceremoniously into mass graves. The violence of this staged Jewish existence provoked indignation and disgust.

Before they mentioned "cruelty," kind and compassionate souls would do well to take a good look at the Jews, and to this end the Nazis produced an abundance of literature denouncing their horrors and their evils. To begin with, as legal experts and police officials were constantly pointing out, they were substantively criminal. In the words of Kurt Daluege, the OrPo chief, "the Jew is a criminal" because of his flawed biology.[126] This made preventive action necessary. An article on "Jewish Criminality" by Johann von Leers gave a laundry list of criminal cases involving Jewish people, presented as proof of a criminal ontology.[127] Jewish people were immoral and criminal by nature, child and adult alike, baptized or not. It was essential, therefore, to establish procedures by which they could be identified and recognized. A vast body of rules required the identification of people who were Jewish, as part of a campaign to assign and reduce them to the biological category of Jewishness.

In the realm of culture, and a full five years before Jewish men, women, and children were required to wear a yellow star, Carl Schmitt suggested that in order to bolster effective resistance to the Jewish invasion of German intellectual life, the works of Jewish intellectuals should be shelved in separate "Judaica" sections in libraries. Furthermore, he proposed, the word *Jude* should be added in citations of Jewish authors. This "library cleansing" and the purging of books was no idle proposition. Its goal, in "observing who is Jewish and who is not" was to tie intellectual production to its biological origins. In this way, any idea proposed by a Jewish person (for example, egalitarianism or universalism) could be read and perceived as the symptom of the physical being that had secreted it, rather than as thinking worthy of intellectual interest. "A Jewish author, in our eyes, holds no 'purely scientific' authority." Here, Schmitt was using quotation marks because "pure science" did not exist. His observation was "the point of departure for addressing the issue of citation. A Jewish author is, in our eyes, and supposing that he is cited at all, a Jewish author. To include the word and the label 'Jew' is for us not an extraneous addition, but essential information" because it revealed the nature of the author.[128]

Here, Carl Schmitt was merely promoting "solutions" to the "Jewish question" that had been proposed in European academic circles by others before him. Later, following strict civil status norms, the Reich minister of the interior would decide to include the notation "of Jewish race" in civil records, despite racial theorists' insistence that Jewishness was a "non-race" or a "counter-race" with no homogeneity, an unstable biological condition that was impossible to define. On August 18, 1938, a ministry circular decreed that German children were to be given "only German names."[129] Exceptions would be made for "non-German names" adopted into usage and tradition, names that "popular consciousness no longer considers as foreign." These exceptions were generally religious ones, and therefore generally biblical, and therefore generally Jewish—although the circular did not mention this—such as "Hans, Joachim, Julius, Peter, Elisabeth, Maria, Sofie, Charlotte." "Jewish children" were to receive "Jewish names," a list of which was appended to the circular. Parents of Jewish boys could choose names such as Ahaseurus, Bahya, Nehab, Sabbatai, or Zebulon—all names that had fallen out of use, and were distinctive in ways that made obvious the discriminatory and often defamatory intent.[130] Little girls could be named Bathsheba, Gole, or Hanasse; or, if those did not please, Pessel or Zippora. The other names for boys and girls offered on the list were in the same vein. The circular was retroactive in nature, as well: Jewish children and adults born before its publication with names not appearing on the list were obligated to add a given name as of January 1, 1939: "to wit, for men, the name Izrael and, for women, Sarah."[131] The ordinance also stipulated, and again, retroactively, that all "name changes" would be canceled in cases where applicants had sought to "hide their Jewish origin."[132] This was a very common occurrence due to Jewish nature, which was sly and calculating, eager to dissemble whenever possible, even though "a Jew will always be a Jew and no baptism can change anything about that."[133]

The ontology of the Jews was so difficult to understand or define that other methods for identifying Jews were soon put into practice. On October 5, 1938, an order was issued dictating that every Jewish citizen's passport was to be stamped with a red "J" three centimeters in height.[134] And starting on September 1, 1941, Jews in the Altreich were required to wear a yellow star at all times.

Against Jewish Criminality

The Jew's criminal nature was broadly advertised. The newspaper *Der Stürmer* specialized in depictions of the Jew as rapist, thief, murderer, child-killer, and impenitent participant in the white slave trade. In 1938, Julius Streicher's publishing house put out a book called *The Poisonous Mushroom*, which radicalized these shopworn stereotypes for German children.[135] With the help of graphic illustrations, this edifying tale begins with a walk in the forest, where little Franz's mother is teaching him the gentle art of collecting edible fungi. All at once, the mother cries out in horror, "In the name of heaven, Franz, that isn't a mushroom. . . . And it's twice as dangerous, because it's easy to mistake it for [an edible] one." This lesson allows the mother to develop a subtle analogy with "humanity's poisonous mushrooms," which are just as difficult to identify, and often imperceptible, despite their radical difference.[136] "They are Jews, and they will remain Jews. They are poisonous to our people," as "a single Jew can destroy an entire village, an entire city, even an entire people."[137] This was the message of *The Jew Süss*, released in cinemas a few years later. These "demons in human form" were a "calamity" that, thankfully, schools taught students to identify.[138]

Jews were ugly, smelled bad, were mean, "and they want to be human beings."[139] To this end, they "have themselves baptized," with the complicity of the Church, which was guilty of collaborating with an enemy of the race: a baptized Jew "would not be any more German than a baptized Negro."[140] Little Franz learns that Jews are "manipulative" tradesmen and "liars," both "insolent and intrusive," not letting their customer-prey out of their clutches until they sold off all of their mediocre junk at usurious prices.[141] They were also sexual criminals with a decided taste for raping children, as well as young women, as could be seen in cases of Jewish doctors taking advantage of their patients, and bosses who imposed themselves on their servants. They were shady lawyers, mistreated animals—all in all, "murderers of whole peoples," "race destroyers" who "quite simply wanted all other peoples to die."[142] Adults were fed literature that was even more hair-raising and incomparably more detailed, but with the same general thrust. To know the Jews, one merely had to take a scientific approach and study their own law books. Armed with purported quotes from the Talmud and the *Schulchan Aruch,* the authors of such texts pretended to show the Jews as they were, in their own words. The best example of this approach is *Jüdische Moral* (Jewish morality), a text published by the NSDAP in 1943. Written to show that its title was an oxymoron, its anonymous authors insisted on their objectivity and impartiality: they had worked "without any anti- or pro-Jewish prejudice," *sine ira et studio* (without anger and fondness), without "even an ounce of tendentious preconceptions" using "irreproachable materials" from Jewish sources, not pamphlets or anti-Semitic forgeries.[143] The picture they painted was, of course, terrifying—a Jewish law that was particularistic and criminal to the point of murderousness.

The high morality that rabbis, Semites, and their friends were always boasting about, the sublime laws of Moses, were valid only for Jews: "Moral principles exist only among Jews," "within the Jewish community alone."[144] The Jews claimed that "man . . . can only be Jewish," and that by the same token, Gentiles were not men.[145] They therefore rejected Gentiles as humans: "Non-Jews . . . have lost their original human nature and become animals, so that they do not deserve to be called men."[146] Jews were only "obliged to behave in a truly ethical manner toward other Jews." So-called "Jewish morality" was really "a morality among Jews" and an "anti-morality toward anything that is not Jewish."[147] Indeed, not only were Jews not required to respect non-Jews; they were moreover permitted to give free rein to their "deep hatred of everything that is not Jewish."[148] Let it be clear, the text asserted, their racial ethos was one of hatred, since Yahweh was "the vengeful God."[149] The Jews were all possessed by the very "thirst for vengeance unique to the Old Testament" that they denounced in Hitler.[150]

This scorn and hatred were manifest in specific prescriptions and prohibitions. It was "permitted to kill a Gentile" and "forbidden to save his life."[151] A *Goy* was "totally without rights" according to Jewish morality and law. "The theft and pillage of Gentile property is allowed," as are the trafficking and rape of Gentile women![152] Horrified, the authors gave up on including any more quotations, explaining that they were "Jewish filth that we refuse to pull from the void, even by alluding to it." By the same token, what the Jews said about their own women "cannot be reproduced herein, for reasons of basic decency."[153] This was pure paralipsis, because it was followed by a welter of quotations professing to show that Jews were impulse-driven animals dominated by their desires and their vices. To them, women, including Jewish women, were "slaves, beasts of burden, domestic objects and objects of lucre."[154] A non-Jewish woman was seen as "a toy," or "livestock." All of this was "entirely foreign to our way of thinking," since Nordic men respected women.[155] Reading such horrors, one could only rejoice over the impermeable line that the Nuremberg Laws had drawn between these beasts and women of good Nordic race. People who thought themselves clever were always talking about "the 'honest' Jew who couldn't actually lower himself to all that." But "there is no 'honest' Jew, because even if a Jew happens to be behaving 'honestly,' it is only to take advantage of those gullible old Gentiles, and to use them for his own ends."[156]

Jews themselves were extremely careful to preserve their "unity as a people." "The purity of the Jewish 'race' is protected by very strict matrimonial laws." This left Jews to go about their "unbridled depravity" on the condition that they did not conceive any children with Gentile women, which "the Talmud sanctions as a racial sin."[157] Jews reified, used, and abused. What was true of their (im)moral and debauched lives was also true of their trade and financial practices, parasitic and mediating activities monopolized by a breed that was, it was well known, lazy and reluctant to do any kind of work. Jews were humanity's "parasite," and resembled the parasites ravaging "the biological life of nature."[158] "Everything in [them] is oriented toward the exploitation and the domination of the non-Jewish world."[159] The answers to the rhetorical questions raised by this intriguing volume were obvious: Jewish morality "is not an ethics or a morality according to our understanding." It "repels all good human common sense, and, consistently applied, is called to provoke the ruin of everything that is not Jewish."[160] The Talmud truly was, as little Franz's mother had explained to him, a criminal's Bible, "the secret law book of the Jews," which, in a yeshiva led by a disturbing rabbi, teaches its students to steal, rape, and kill.[161]

The logical outcome of this reification and this scorn for others was universal enslavement and widespread murder by the Jews, who were armed with their hatred of everything that was not Jewish. The Ten Commandments were "the world's most immoral law code." According to their interpretation by the Talmud, the "key to understanding Jewish nature," which Jews were required "to keep secret from Gentiles," "the commandment 'Thou shalt not kill' means not killing any man of Israel. The *Goyim*, the children of Noah, and heretics are not children of Israel."[162]

Fritz Hippler's infamous film *Der Ewige Jude* brought all of these ideas to the screen. The movie condemned "the morality of the Jewish race, totally opposed to the laws of Aryan ethics." Jewish law was made up of filth ("put like a good German would, their houses are dirty"), laziness (Jews, as illustrated on screen, worked reluctantly and poorly), and materialism ("for the Jew, the only true value is money"). Horrifying statistics showed audiences that the Jews, who made up just 1 percent of the world's population, comprised 34 percent of all drug traffickers and 98 percent of the white slave trade! A series of terrifying faces was then shown, "refut[ing] the liberal theory of the equality of everything bearing a human face." The physical features of the Jewish prophets were hardly more appealing: "And it was none other than these Abrahams and Jacobs who were supposed to promote a high-level morality" with their Ten Commandments and their Talmud? And "what does the Talmud teach," except for lying and murder?

The camera then panned slowly over a yeshiva: "This is not a course in religion" that was being taught, because "rabbis are political educators." Judaism "is not a religion, but the conspiracy of a pathologically treacherous and poisonous race against the health of the Aryan race and its moral law." Faced with this plague, the "new Germany" would respect "the eternal law of nature, which commands that the purity of the race be protected." It was hardly surprising, then, at a lecture at Friedrich Wilhelm University in Berlin on December 1, 1941, to hear Goebbels affirm:

> Jewry . . . is now being subjected to the progressive extermination it had planned for us, and which it would have launched without hesitation had it had the power to do so. So now it is perishing in accordance with its own law: an eye for an eye, a tooth for a tooth.[163]

Hitler echoed this in a radio speech delivered at the Reichstag on January 30, 1942: "For the first time, the old Jewish law is now going to be applied: an eye for an eye, a tooth for a tooth."[164] As the *Völkischer Beobachter* reiterated, Jewish cruelty was merely being turned against the Jews themselves:

> Happily, the circumstances of the Jews have evolved in many countries toward their exclusion and elimination: they are thus paying for their crimes against the peoples of this world. . . . This is only just, and it is a terrible blow to the guilty party. . . . The war of vengeance that the Jews launched against Germany has been turned against them. They must now follow the path they themselves traced out.[165]

The Shoah: A War

In *Meine Psyche,* Rudolf Höss, the former commandant of the Auschwitz-Birkenau concentration camp, confessed to his confusion when he first received the order for mass killings, particularly of women and children. Then again, would a "squadron commander in the Air Force" who received orders to bomb a city have been able to disobey these orders by arguing that "his bombs would mostly be killing women and children? No: he would have been court-martialed. . . . I am convinced . . . that the two situations are comparable. I was a soldier, an officer, just like him."[166] In this comparison, Höss sought to acknowledge that his combat activity was as unconventional as the indiscriminate bombing of unarmed populations. In so doing, however, he was invoking the suffering of a German civilian population that was, in the Nazis' eyes, the victim of a war fomented by the Jews, and thereby justifying his work of genocide: once again, an eye for an eye, a tooth for a tooth.

Höss described the traumatizing experience of an air raid alert, the mass of bodies and faces contorted with fear, the anguish of humans huddled in their bomb shelters, terrified of death. He had "observed the faces, the attitudes in air-raid shelters, in cellars." He had seen how these poor unfortunate souls "clung to one another, sought protection from their fellow man when the whole building shook" under the bombs.[167] Höss's evocation of this scene, observed by chance during leaves of absence obtained to visit German cities struck by enemy bombing, creates a striking parallel to another scene, which the *Lagerkommandant* also describes at length in his confessional memoir: "I had to be present for all of the procedures. . . . I had to observe death itself through the peephole of the gas chamber."[168] Eichmann evoked the same traumatic experience: "After the Berlin bombings, I said to myself, 'He was right, the Führer, to have all those dogs killed.' If you had seen the horror! It is our own blood, our own children, it is me [they are killing]!"[169]

Since the Jews had declared war and were responsible for the misfortune of the German people, it was only fair and right for them to die the same horrible death as the German mothers and children killed by the bombs. Were the people committing genocide murderers? Clearly, no: Höss repeated several times that he was neither a prison ward nor a butcher. In the SS, he explained, "we also were soldiers, just the same as the other armies of the Wehrmacht."[170] Let there be no doubt about it: Rudolf Höss was a human being, moved and affected by the procedures at Birkenau. Because he was its leader, because he was in charge of it all, he had to oversee it all, and inspect it all. He had therefore been exposed to the tragedy of murder—but he had had to keep a stiff upper lip. As a concentration camp commandant, he was convinced that the SS's work of reform and repression was necessary: "Before the war, concentration camps were reform centers for enemies of the state," and "all kinds of asocials." They "had therefore fulfilled a precious mission for our people," a "cleansing process" that was as "necessary as any preventive fight against criminality."[171]

> As an old National Socialist, I was deeply convinced of the necessity of concentration camps. True enemies of the state had to be placed in detention, and asocials and professional criminals, against whom it was impossible to fight under the usual laws, had to be imprisoned so that the people could be protected from their harmful behavior.[172]

Just like Theodor Eicke, he felt anger toward SS members who complained about having to work as "executioners": "The destruction of the state's enemies within was just as much a duty as the extermination of the enemy outside, on the front, and no one had the right to qualify this work as dishonorable."[173] The higher necessity was not self-evident. In hindsight, Höss felt he was "poorly qualified for the service."[174] He had been a prisoner himself in the 1920s, under Weimar, giving him excessive empathy for the prisoners. As the head of a center for mass murder (Birkenau), Höss had had to work even harder at self-control:

> I also saw a woman who, as they were closing the doors of the gas chamber, was pushing her children out and shouting as she wept, "Then at least let my children live!" Yes, there were lots of little heartrending scenes like that, which affected everyone who saw them.[175]

Höss was aware of his responsibility: "I could show nothing of what I was feeling, as everyone's eyes were on me."[176] As a result, he obliged himself

> to seem cold and insensitive . . . as I observed procedures that would pierce the heart of anyone with human sensitivities. I could not even turn away when I was overcome by overly powerful human emotions. I had to look coolly on, when the mothers went into the gas chambers with their children, who were crying or laughing,[177]

unaware of what awaited them. Relieved, Höss could now show his feelings and let himself go to comfortable self-pity: public opinion, which would see him as a sadist and a monster, might understand "that he had a heart, and that this heart was not bad."[178] Only a heroic idea of duty and a deep awareness of the necessity of these procedures had allowed him to carry out his task without failing or weakening:

> I always heard . . . this question, in the discussions I overheard: "Is it really necessary, what we're doing here? Is it necessary to destroy hundreds and thousands of women and children?" And I, who had often . . . asked myself that question, deep down, I had to make do with the Führer's orders and take comfort in them. I had to tell them that this destruction of Jewry was necessary to free Germany forever, to free our descendants from their worst enemies forever.[179]

It was thus out of conviction, and fully aware of what he was doing, that he had carried out this difficult task, even if now he contested the suitability of this mass murder:

Today, I do see that the extermination of the Jews was a bad idea, fundamentally bad. This extermination of the Jews made the whole world hate Germany. We did not serve the cause of anti-Semitism with this approach. To the contrary, it advanced the cause of the Jewry.[180]

Höss, as was the case of so many, had not changed: "I remain a National Socialist in the sense that I still believe in this idea of life. It isn't easy to give up . . . an idea, a worldview you believed in for twenty-five years."[181] Indeed.

Biological Danger, Medical Treatment

A foreign substance as necessarily harmful, as virulent, and as irreconcilable could justly be described as a pathological plague: what, in nature, was as aggressive, blind, and constantly hostile as a virus or a bacterium? Hermann Esser, a journalist from Bavaria, one of the founding members of the DAP (Deutsche Arbeiterpartei), the German Workers' Party, the precursor of the NSDAP, vice-president of the Reichstag starting in 1933, and secretary of state for the Ministry of Propaganda, expanded on this idea in a widely read pamphlet, *Die jüdische Weltpest* (The global Jewish plague), published in 1939 by Franz Eher, the NSDAP's publisher. The irreducibility and the intensity of the Jewish threat were "a constant hardship for the world, an unprecedented threat to humanity." Fighting it was a "moral duty."[182] It was also a public health imperative:

> Such a breed, which, through its own rules and laws, places itself outside any community of the people and which shows the most cynical brutality toward non-Jews, has lost all right to be considered with "pity." Against blight and epidemics, it is not the moaning of merciful apostles of pity that is effective, but the use of the most radical expedients of segregation and elimination.[183]

Acting in this way was a matter of "survival instinct, legitimate defense, the defense of the right to life." It was "an ethical duty and a moral right." The author denounced the "compassionate idiots" who "unctuously condemned anti-Semitism as going against Christian brotherly love" as "sentimental dandies," as "false apostles of mercy," as "tightrope walkers of a double morality, all puffed up with their own self-importance."[184]

This was exactly what *Der Ewige Jude* stated and showed on screen: the Jews were a blight from Asia, just like rats and the plague. Several animated sequences showed the spread of rats and the Black Death across the globe, following the schemas and the routes of the Jewish diaspora. The Jews were "foreign bodies in the organism of the people," parasites who got in through "bodily wounds" they had spotted; wounds whose weakness they had sized up in order to invade and destroy from within. The "Polish campaign" of autumn 1939 had revealed the Jews as they really were, destitute, deformed, dirty, dressed in caftans, and wearing side locks. The eyes of the Germans, misled by "assimilated Jews" who dressed up and lived as Europeans, were now open. In the face of such danger, the limits of emotionally driven and disorganized anti-Semitism were clear: striking out blindly at Jews in great orgies of violence and saturnalian pogroms might satisfy impulse, but never reason. Even less would such an approach actually solve the biological problem posed by the Jews' existence. Already in 1920, Hitler had chosen his path—rational anti-Semitism:

> We do not depend on our feelings (sentimental anti-Semitism), but are determined by a cool calculation of the facts. And, on this matter, it must be said that the Jew is, as Mommsen put it, the ferment of decomposition. It matters little whether people are good or bad: he provokes the crumbling of every race he inhabits as a parasite. It would be absurd to reproach a tuberculosis bacillus for its action. . . . But it would be just as unjustified not to fight, in the name of my own life, this tuberculosis, and not to destroy its vector. . . . Fighting the Jew is driving him away.[185]

More than twenty years later, in 1941, Hitler had not changed his mind; much to the contrary, in fact: "We will rid ourselves entirely of the destructive Jews. . . . In these matters I am proceeding coolly. I feel that I am only carrying out history's will."[186] Treatment, applied "coolly," was medical in nature, because it was a response to a biological problem. Really, as an SS publication put it, the goal was "to extract the Jewry from the body of our people," an "act of self-defense against a present danger."[187] This understanding required giving up on the idea of the good Jew, the neighbor, the friend, or the children's piano teacher. It was possible that some Jews might be less bad than others, "but when you lie down in a hotel bed infested with bedbugs, you don't ask one specific bedbug, 'Tell me, are you a good or a bad bedbug?' You crush it."[188] Carrying out history's will, to employ Hitler's words, meant applying nature's decrees, and behaving consistently in the face of a biological danger.

Doctors were not being cruel or bad when they amputated a limb infected with gangrene—this, we recall, was the job of the police. By the same token, gardeners pulling up nettles and burning them were not guilty of any crime—this, we recall, was the image Himmler chose to describe the fight against homosexuals. By the same logic, the Reich could not be accused of barbarousness or sadism if it rigorously "treated" (behandeln) a nuisance or a biological threat:

> We are the first to have resolved the issue of blood with concrete actions. . . . The same thing goes for anti-Semitism as for de-lousing. Destroying lice is not an ideological question. It is a matter of cleanliness. Anti-Semitism, in the same way, has not been a worldview, but an issue of hygiene—indeed, one that will soon be resolved. We will soon be rid of our lice. We still have twenty thousand nits among us. Then it will be over and done with, in all of Germany.[189]

Buttressing such considerations was a famous passage by Paul de Lagarde, a major reference for anti-Semites since the end of the nineteenth century, which was cited piously and often in these sources:

> One would have to have a heart of stone not to feel compassion for the poor German and—it amounts to the same thing—not to hate and despise the Jews and those who—out of humanity!—speak to the Jews and are too cowardly to crush this vermin.
>
> You don't negotiate with trichina or bacilli. You don't cultivate trichina or bacilli. You exterminate them, as quickly and carefully as possible.[190]

What had been a virulent and hate-filled—but still largely metaphorical—discourse in the nineteenth century became literal truth in Nazi Germany.

Little remains of the Jews themselves. . . . True, they are being subjected to a barbarous procedure, but one they fully deserve. The Führer's prophecy, with which he threatened them if they launched
another world war, is beginning to come true in a truly terrible way.
We cannot allow ourselves to be overcome by sentimentality in these
matters. The Jews, if we do not defend ourselves, will end up exterminating us. It is a fight to the death between the Aryan race and
the Jewish bacillus. No other government, no other regime, would
have the strength to resolve this question for all time. Yet again, the
Führer is leading the charge and is the unwavering prophet of a radical solution that is imposed by the way things are and is thus inevitable. Thank God, and thanks to the state of war, we have a range of
possibilities open to us which we would not have recourse to in
peacetime. We must employ them. . . . The Jewry has no reason to
laugh: its European representatives must pay dearly for the fact that
its other representatives, in England and in America, are organizing
and propagating war against Germany—but we must consider this a
justifiable price to pay.[191]

These notes were written by Joseph Goebbels in March 1942, as Operation Reinhard was beginning. The decision to murder all of the
Jews in Europe had most likely been made in December 1941, when
the Reich was alarmed for two reasons.[192]

The first was military and geopolitical. The initial counterattacks
by the Red Army, and the early arrival of winter, had bogged down the
advance of the German Army. At the same time, the attack on Pearl
Harbor had precipitated the entry of the United States into the global
conflict. Germany, which declared war on the United States on
December 11 of that year, found itself where it had been in 1917–1918,
embroiled in a high-pressure war on two fronts, both of them threatening to endure, and even to end in defeat. The Jews—who, according
to Hitler, were responsible for all of it—were once again in the winning position they had held in 1918. Now as then, storm clouds were
gathering: a war of attrition, a revolution at home—and a Jewish
victory.

The second reason had to do with public health. Nazi policy had always made it a rule to expel the Jews from Germanic *Lebensraum*. The
Third Reich's anti-Semitic policy aimed to push hundreds of thousands

of people to emigrate. Mass deportation plans had been developed to accompany the Reich's expansion, such as the Madagascar Plan, and then the plan to deport and abandon the Jews in "the East," near the polar circle. The Royal Navy's control of the sea made the former plan impossible, while ongoing Soviet resistance made the latter one unrealistic. The RSHA thus found itself in charge of a Jewish population of about eleven million, according to its estimates, living in an area under German dominion. This had led to a public health problem: cramming millions of people into ghettos and subjecting them to famine and exhaustion had caused the outbreak of contagious illnesses such as typhus, which threatened to infect German soldiers and civilians in Poland as well. The human and health problems engendered by Nazi policy made Europe's Jews into a medical and public health concern, as a film made for German residents of Poland explained:

> An old site of typhus infection may be found in . . . Poland, everywhere one encounters the Jewish population. Unimaginable filth and the constant exchange of lice-infected clothing are responsible for the uncontrollable propagation of the epidemic. . . . In this way they are endangering German soldiers in contact with this flea-infested population. . . . A mere glance at the regrettable state of their housing should warn soldiers of the invisible danger threatening them in the Jewish quarters, right in the midst of the dirtiest possible surroundings.[193]

Operation Reinhard, through which the General Government implemented the decision to murder all of the Jews in Europe, was a biomedical process, as Robert Ley explained in a speech in May 1942:

> Jews are humanity's greatest danger. If we do not succeed in exterminating them, we will lose the war. Sending them somewhere [else] is not enough. It would be like trying to imprison a louse in a cage somewhere. It would find a way out, and, cropping up from underneath, would begin to make us itch again. You must annihilate them, exterminate them, for what they have done to humanity.[194]

Who would be foolish enough to accuse nature of cruelty? Nature was above good and evil: it simply *was*. Moreover, as we have seen, the Germans considered themselves "correct" in their approach to the

Jewish question. In the writing and speeches of Himmler and Goebbels, the adjectives *anständig* (decent) and *human* are used frequently to describe Nazi actions and decisions. Himmler in particular often asserted that the measures taken by the Nazis were not only right and just, but also fair in their scope and proportion. No useless suffering or upsetting excesses could be observed anywhere, he claimed: this was merely what a response to the Jewish question required in terms of rigor and consistency. "This process has been carried with consequence, but without cruelty. We are not tormenting anyone. We know that we are fighting for our existence and for the preservation of our Nordic blood."[195]

Natural necessity underpinned an apodictic ethics that could not be debated and required no thought in its application, since it was inscribed in the stars in the sky and in the cells of the Germanic body. An empty and ersatz counterfeit of Kant's categorical imperative—a kind of mathematical algorithm employed to incite and justify unconditional obedience—was continually deployed under the Third Reich. In the words of an SS handbook written for SD and police officers,

> the foundational value of Germany's future, the highest moral law of the State, the people, and each and every one of us, may be summed up in this sentence: "Always act as if the law of your will were a fundamental law of Nordic racial legislation," [which requires you to do everything so that the race can live].[196]

Thus, the transgression of moral limits implied by the Final Solution was only transgressive according to humanist, Judeo-Christian legislation, whose origins and meaning in the eyes of the Nazis have been thoroughly explored in this book. "Nordic racial legislation" might indeed have seemed transgressive and immoral. But it was actually the purest of all law, no more and no less than the practical and ethical translation of the laws of nature. Far from a crime, the Nazis saw the Final Solution as the highest possible expression of natural morality. As harsh or paradoxical as this morality might seem to contemporary generations, it had to be imposed if the Nordic race wished to live:

The earth would not be what it is without Nordic blood, Nordic culture, and Nordic minds. If we wish to preserve our Nordic race, we must eliminate the others. . . . You, the leaders of tomorrow, are responsible for carrying out this task. You must lay the moral and spiritual foundations among your men that will prevent them from becoming soft and weak again, and that will prohibit them from accepting Jews or any other subrace into the Reich.[197]

Conclusion

"Our program replaces the liberal idea of the individual and the Marxist concept of humanity with the people, a people defined by its blood and rooted in its soil. This may be a simple and concise sentence, but its consequences are colossal," Hitler wrote in *Mein Kampf,* which was composed in prison in 1924–1925 and then published in 1927.[1] Germany was the first to suffer these consequences, as it was stripped of political pluralism, labor unions, the rule of law, and safeguards to citizens. Next came the rest of Europe, which was subjected to violent practices, unprecedented in human history, aimed at enslaving and annihilating certain peoples. Clearly, it cannot be argued that all this calamity and misfortune emerged from this "simple" sentence. It was, however, a warning. Its author was telling us that what the Nazis said, proposed, and wrote ought to be taken seriously. It is all the more noteworthy for the number of times it was repeated and reprinted. (Here it is taken from an ideological instruction pamphlet published by the SS.) In a single gesture, it rejects the legacy of Christianity, the Enlightenment, and the French Revolution (the "individual"), as well as "Bolshevism," an avatar of the individual and a proponent of a universalistic understanding of "humanity," its history, and its destiny. Against the "individual" and "humanity" it staked the *Volk,* its *Blut* (blood), and its *Boden* (soil). These two lines were taught to candidates for the Waffen-SS and the police, who learned them by heart. They outlined a few of the central tenets of the Nazi "worldview," a cross-section of which I have offered herein, through a study of the norms it established and the normative thought it upheld.

In a previous book, I explored the strength of the Nazi narrative. Nazism was a worldview; that is, it was first of all a vision of history, a singular narrative that constantly, everywhere, in each instant and in every possible form, recounted the race's past in its every gesture, trial, glory, and misfortune. The narrative was not primarily poetic in nature—the tellers of the Nazi tale were not in it for the narrative pleasure of commemorating the Ice Ages, the Germanic people of the forests, and the epic of Henry the Lion. Their story, their history, as it was incessantly told, was a normative one: the narrative gave rise to a norm, which told people how to act, and why. What could be done in the face of thousands of years of Nordic suffering, in the urgency of the present moment? Procreate and fight in order to—at long last—reign.

The sources that I read, listened to, and watched in my research for this book led me far back in time, to the origins of the race, when Germanity was at one with nature; when all mediation and all separation were unknown; when the Germanic race was authentic, healthy in body and mind, and unmixed. The strict rules governing the procreation of German children all sought to return the race to the happy time of its birth; Germans were to procreate extensively, of course, but they were to keep their Germanic blood pure. Such a thing could be possible only if the German people were able to unshackle themselves from the norms imposed by Judeo-Christian acculturation, its false God, its imperative of monogamy, its blessing of the mixing of all blood on the pretext that all men could meld together as equals in the love of their creator. Returning the Germanic race to the primal purity of its birth thus implied a "reevaluation of values," a radical cultural critique that made it possible to shake off norms that were hostile to life—norms that prophets with evil intentions, hate-filled revolutionaries, and unthinking humanists had imposed on Germany. The German people had to reevaluate their values, return to nature, and in this way bring about a normative revolution: it was by returning to its own childhood that the race would produce healthy offspring.

Foreign norms undermined this struggle. In spite of itself, the Nordic race had been ripped from the interconnected quietude of its origins by hateful Jews, who, for six thousand years, had been waging a merciless war against it. There was, of course, nothing shocking about this, when we recall that "all life is struggle." The Germanic race had been forced into history, that implacable dialectic of the races—but Christianity, the Enlightenment, and humanist morality had, at the same time, deprived it of adequate weaponry. For history was a war among races, a merciless biological struggle from which, as Goebbels said in 1943, one could only emerge as a "survivor" or be "exterminated." In that perilous hour, against a threat that had been intensified by the Great War, the Germanic race needed to be able to fight without hindrance or handicaps: its combat practices had to follow the laws of nature, the same laws that governed history and dictated that the strong triumph over the weak. It was necessary for the race to act with a decisive violence that would paralyze its enemies and make it possible for the Germans to fight the clock, which was running down against them. Every passing moment was an opportunity for the enemy to grow, for more mixing and more degeneration. Stunning and unprecedented violence was required, not only during invasions, but also when securing conquered territories.

These were the conditions necessary for Germany to put an end to History. Germany had been a victim for centuries, as the last incarnation of a Germanic-Nordic power whose bastions (Rome and Greece, for example) had fallen one by one. It was this long litany of painful misfortunes that the Nazi program sought to stop. Herein was the purely eschatological dimension of Nazism. For the Nazis, there was an after to the moment of genesis, of origins, of birth. There was an after to history, with its racial dialectics, its struggle and contamination. They believed the time had come to emancipate time itself, to open up the vast spaces of the East and the millennium for themselves through conquest and colonization. The millennium was not a flight of fancy, or a mere political slogan: it was an openly stated, carefully thought out, and very serious political program. This reign of the race, a re-rooted race restored to its authenticity, to the earth, and to the purity of its own blood, was also described and standardized down to the very last detail, and assigned an extensive and highly specific moral code.

Everything in these three phases of the Nazi epic obeyed, with the most inexorable logic, norms induced or deduced from the handful of postulates for which the Nazis sought confirmation in History: the whole was more important than the part and the individual was nothing compared to the *Volk* that gave him his meaning and his existence; universal humanity was an illusion, and the only thing that counted as a tangible normative reality was the Germanic *Volksgemeinschaft*, which was united in its blood and its shared values.

The Germanic race had finally been rescued from struggles of conscience, from scruples, and from doubts raised by the introduction of foreign values. Authenticity allowed for automatism: instinct dictated action, and nature, as was only right, wrote and enacted all law. In the modern and contemporary maelstrom of values and schools, in this "war of the gods" that characterized modernity, the Germanic people had been set on a sure path, because "the laws of life, which are manifest in his blood, in nature, and in History, are the guidelines for his action."[2] This sure path was the path of the law of blood: the one their blood dictated to them; the one their blood protected and perpetuated; and the one that commanded that they spill alien blood, which was mediocre and inferior, lacking in any value—an infectious fluid to be driven away and even destroyed.

This study was based on the conviction that it is necessary to take seriously the texts, the images, and the words of the Nazis. This is not easy to do. While reading them, it may be difficult to believe that these authors could seriously have believed or subscribed to the things that they wrote, that their texts could ever have been read without unease, mockery, or indignation. And yet, there can be little doubt that these authors were convinced of what they were saying: the case of the doctors described in the Introduction—who, in 1964, were still repeating what they had been saying since before 1930, and had put into practice over the twelve years that the Third Reich endured—is not an isolated one. Far from it.

The hypothesis that this discourse was generally well received should not be so surprising: many of the threads woven into the arguments studied here were drawn from widely held beliefs and ideas that were neither specifically Nazi nor even strictly German, but rather European and Western. These shared ideas were simply—which is, of course, saying a lot—radicalized and drawn together in the 1920s, and then put into practice starting in 1933 with a swiftness and a violence that claimed to be a response to Germany's alleged distress.

While it may not be wholly intelligent, innovative, or interesting, Nazi discourse does at least seem to respond to or correspond with the acts committed in Germany and in Europe between 1933 and 1945. Rarely in history have word and action been so closely associated as in the Third Reich. Rarely has the distinction between "discourse" and "practice" seemed so tenuous. It is of course to be doubted that every one of the members of the Einsatzgruppen had read the works of Edgar Tatarin-Tarnheyden, Georg Mehlis, or Heinrich Korte; that they fully mastered the concept of "bionomics"; or that they were familiar with the particulars of the landscape plans of the RKF (Reich Commission for the Consolidation of German Nationhood). Nevertheless, the texts I investigated were all based on postulates and assumptions; they followed specific paths of reasoning and formulated concepts that either explicitly or indirectly, by imitation or quotation, were present everywhere, including newsreels, films, ideological teaching materials, tracts, posters, and meeting agendas. Many studies have shown that these ideas found their mark and that they helped to inform the perceptions of civilians, police officers, and troops, giving meaning to their experiences and even their traumas—for example, when the Soviet NKVD emptied its prisons of any potential collaborators before the Wehrmacht's arrival in June and July 1941 and German soldiers witnessed the decaying bodies that they had left behind to rot in the hot sun.[3] Nazi discourse on the "horrors" and "crimes" of "Judeo-Bolshevism" explained this type of event, and many others: the 1918 defeat, the 1923 hyperinflation, the 1929 stock market crash, not to mention the end of the Roman Empire, evangelization, and the Thirty Years' War.

That the Nazi program was made up of words, images, and ideas that, more often than not, were not invented by the Nazis, or even the Germans, made it especially easy for contemporaries to adopt all or part of it. Western anti-Semitism, colonialist racism, social Darwinism, eugenics, imperialism, fear and hatred of Judeo-Bolshevism, fear and scorn of Ostjuden . . . all of these were elements in a European and Western language whose effects could be seen and felt elsewhere (consider the Dreyfus affair in France; the colonial empire; and social engineering policies in Switzerland, Scandinavia, and the United States, among other examples). One form of this language, however, was intensified, consolidated, and radicalized in Germany in the 1920s, then put into practice by the Third Reich in the 1930s and 1940s with unprecedented violence and intensity.

The sources examined for this study provided the conditions that made possible the implementation of the most radical and violent methods ever imagined in the West for the stated purpose of ensuring a people's safety and security. You didn't have to be a dyed-in-the-wool Nazi or be able to recite these texts by heart in order to apply all or part of what they prescribed. Often, they were merely restating ideas that were considered commonplace during that time—and not just in Germany. Concepts such as the war against criminals, preventive detention, or colonization were all promoted and practiced outside Germany as well. The Nazis argued that their projects and actions were not fundamentally different from what others were doing, or, at the very most, that the differences had to do with scale, or with the frank and uninhibited way they declared their principles and aims. The only distinction they fully claimed as such—and it was only the better to boast about it—was the Final Solution: no one had ever diligently mass-murdered an entire people, because no one, until then, had had the stamina for such an undertaking, nor seen the necessity of attempting it.

Many of the works cited in this study were distributed directly to the public as popular films, newspapers, course materials, and so on. Others were theoretical texts written by specialists in fields such as law, ethics, philosophy, biology, politics, and epistemology that were not intended for, or accessible to, laypeople. In an effort to stay close to reality and social practices, it is tempting for the historian to leave such texts to "the nibbling criticism of mice." And yet this welter of texts usually required thought and work from their authors; this is visible in their sheer mass, as well as, at times, in their distribution. These texts were written by people who manifestly had a great deal to say, and who were participating fully in the reality of their time, on two levels: first, they were expressing both fears and plans; and second, they were working for the future, to spark a revolution in thinking and mores that alone could ensure Germany's survival in the coming centuries.

These reflexive texts reveal more about Nazism than their abandonment by historians would lead one to believe. Certainly, as Marcel Gauchet writes, "historians do not like to take on theoretical texts": they are proud of not being taken in by ideas, of descending from the attic to explore the street and the cellar.[4] In this manner they are taking part in the intellectual and social mission of elucidating a past reality, preferably one that is humble, and even base. At first glance, a lawyer's blustering about mediation and immediateness seem to be of little interest for understanding Nazism. Such abstract reflections, produced by the dominant, the educated, the knowledgeable, fall to the philosopher, to whom we ascribe all sorts of abstruse perversions, or to the historian of ideas, that hybrid creature, neither historian nor philosopher, an easy object for our mockery. Historians have better things to do. And yet, as Gauchet points out, with such texts "we come as close as we can to history as its actors thought about it—I do not say lived it; obviously, that is a level one does not reach."[5] These texts are a privileged source for the historian, because "history has a reflexive level at which it illuminates itself again entirely."[6] At the end of this journey, and after a decade spent reading them, it seems to me that the sources I consulted shed new light on Nazism and its practices by familiarizing us with the fears, the postulates, and the projects that comprised it.

Nevertheless, two considerations must be borne in mind when approaching them, having to do, again, with the relationship between discourse and practice, and with temporality. Let us begin with a temporal consideration, one oriented toward the future: these sources, while revelatory of a time and a place, formulate plans for a normative revolution that was only partially accomplished. The Nazis, in their constant struggle against time, were aware of this handicap. Both in public and in private, Hitler placed his hopes in Germany's youth. Adults, the present generation, were old men crippled with values and beliefs that were hostile to life, filled with harmful ideas. One could hardly expect these generations to change. One had to wait for new shoots to grow, generations that had known only National Socialism and its teachings. These generations would be made up of men who were not new, but rather regenerated, bathed once again in the ethos of their blood, familiar in their earliest memories with the values of their race.

In the meantime, it was necessary to make do with tens of millions of Germans who had been denatured by priests and pastors, idealists and Jews, alienated by a long march of dissolving and destructive "isms" (liberalism, humanism, universalism, and so on). Commenting on the sometimes negative reactions elicited by the introduction of the yellow star in Germany in 1941, Joseph Goebbels regretted that the German people were "not yet ripe" and remained "handicapped by their sentimentalism."[7] Only an elite with both intelligence and character could understand that what the Third Reich was doing was just, beautiful, good, and kind. This elite was the group of SS generals and commanding officers to whom Himmler spoke openly at Poznań, in October 1943, of the Final Solution and its moral and practical implications. Himmler assured his men that they were not rotten murderers, as the morality they had inherited from their fathers might claim. Rather, they were soldiers who were eradicating a deadly evil so that Germany could live; they were a heroic generation accomplishing something that no other generation before them had had the courage and the strength to do; and they were sacrificing themselves so that future generations would no longer be threatened by a mortal danger.

The second temporal consideration is one oriented toward the past: by reading the sources drawn together here and granting them historical importance, I in no way mean to postulate that they were programmatic to the point of being carved in stone, nor to profess any sort of naïve intentionalism. An interest in what was written does not mean that "all was written." Far from it: a historian working with these texts is making a contribution to the overall work of the historical community, which is attempting to reconstitute developments over time by recalling the dialectic that exists between discourse and practice, condition and context.

It is easy to say and to write. Ideas have the privilege of unlimited and free radicalism. That such ideas became imperative, and even performative, is a matter of context, of specific times and places, that the historian must recreate. No doubt the most striking example (in terms of the radicalism of the ideas it advanced and of the crimes committed) is biomedical anti-Semitism. Since the nineteenth century, the claim had been advanced in writing that Jews were "bacilli"—and Nazi ideological instruction texts rarely missed an opportunity to quote Lagarde's words on this. Hitler espoused this radical anti-Semitism in *Mein Kampf*, which he had absorbed from the far right-wing circles he had frequented since his youth in Austria. "Bacillus," "parasite," "microbe": the Jew was a biological threat. Research on the Shoah, however, has shown that Nazi anti-Jewish policy adopted the goal of eradication quite late. At first, the word *Vernichten* (to eradicate or annihilate) was used to indicate that the Jews were to be eradicated from German and then European soil through forced emigration.

The ideas advanced by biomedical anti-Semitism only set out the conditions through which such acts could become possible and thinkable, and then desirable, in the specific context of the autumn of 1941. The brutality of the ghettoization of Jews in Poland and then elsewhere in the territories under the General Government's control gave rise to a public health situation so catastrophic that, as Paul Weindling showed, murder came to be justified as a public health measure and deployed as a "medical procedure." If, moreover, we agree on the fact that the decision to exterminate all the Jews in Europe was most likely made in December 1941, then we know that it was made at the moment when, because of the conflict in the East and the entry of the United States into the war, the Nazi leadership found itself in a situation that resembled that of 1917–1918, faced with the possibility of a new "November 1918"—meaning (Jewish) revolution, capitulation, and defeat. Which brings us back to the conclusion that the study of Nazi ideas and their mental universe is particularly helpful for understanding what humans inflicted on other humans.[8]

In studying these normative sources, texts, and images, which say what one must do (to oneself, to others, to the world), I hope to have made a contribution to thinking about the phenomenon of Nazism, to understanding it, in other words, by exploring the thinking of Nazis themselves, what structured and constituted it, and which may be seen and read in these sources.

These texts and images teach us that Germany always acted, in full legitimacy, in a situation of *Not*—three little letters with tremendous importance, a word with many meanings that reappears throughout the sources. First and foremost, the word *Not* articulated the distress of a wounded, traumatized Germany on the way to biological extinction. At the same time, it emphasized the urgency of swift reaction, to stop the distress. And, finally, it affirmed necessity, the total absence of choice: it was impossible not to act, and it was impossible to act in any other way—which in this context meant fighting for the survival of the race. The imperative to procreate, to fight, and to reign was none other than nature's. If inherited norms were evil and harmful, if they were slowly killing off the race, it was because they violated the alleged laws of nature: everything that is diseased must die; all mixing is harmful; all wombs are made to produce the most children possible.

These natural laws were the only legislation that the Third Reich recognized as valid, the only laws that legislators and judges were required
to transcribe. A return to the source was a return to birth; that is, to
nature. What was true of the renewal of the law was valid for all fields
of normativity and action: Russians must be struck down because, by
nature, they were animals who understood nothing else. They should
not be given too much food because, by nature, their stomachs could
retract and adapt. As for the Reich's eastern border, it was set by the
range of the beech, a Germanic tree species.

Nature the legislator was at work in all places, which simplified
everything. No more questioning, no more argument, no more debate
in public or in one's innermost heart: the obligation of ancient morality
and ancient law (If I ought, then I can; I ought, therefore I can) was
replaced by incontrovertible necessity (I cannot not). Universalism
based on universality was no more, because in nature, there was no
such thing: what rule, as one lawyer asked, is shared by both Eskimos
and the Negroes of southern Africa? It was absurd to believe in universal laws. Imperatives were decreed by blood, and prescriptions were
particularistic. The need for scruples and conscience was finally gone.
Conscience was a tortured and diseased authority invented by mixed
and morbid beings, and it hindered action, paralyzing and ultimately
killing the actor.

Consistency, or consequentiality, was promoted over conscience:
one had to be konsequent. Already referring to the Final Solution in the
past tense, Himmler affirmed in November 1942 that "this process was
carried out with consistency, but without cruelty. We are not causing
anyone to suffer, but we know that we are fighting for our existence and
so that our Nordic blood will triumph."[9] This "uncompromising" consequentialism, as a preferred and recurring phrase put it, was present all
the way to the end—to the other's end, but also to one's own.

On March 19, 1945, Hitler signed an order for the destruction of the
infrastructures of the Reich. It was a military tactic, a scorched-earth
policy deployed before the advancing Soviet Army. In the short term,
as Albert Speer, the minister of armaments and war production observed, there was nothing to say, but what about the long term? What
about after the war? What about the survival of the German people?
Wouldn't they need the bridges, the silos, the granaries, and the dams

that would be destroyed under the *Führerbefehl*, the "order of the Führer"? To these objections, Hitler replied that there was no long term, no after the war:

> If we must lose the war, the German people will be lost, too. It is not necessary to take care of the basic elements our people would need to survive. . . . The [German] people has turned out to be the weakest, and the future belongs to the strongest people, the Eastern people, and to it alone. In any case, the mediocre ones will be the only ones left after the war, because all the good ones are dead.[10]

Nature had spoken. Biological logic commanded it: the life of the German people stopped there.

Notes

Introduction

1. "Eingeschläfert," 1960, p. 33. Translations from German into French (as well as from all other non-French languages) are by the author and unless otherwise noted have been translated from French into English by the translator.
2. Klee 2003, p. 33, "Bayer."
3. Ibid.
4. "Aus Menschlichkeit töten?," 1964, p. 42.
5. Ibid., p. 43.
6. Cf. Stangneth 2011.
7. Browning [1992] 2007, p. 260.
8. Heer (ed.) 1995.
9. Bartov 1986; Gerlach 1999; Pohl 1997; Dieckmann 2011.
10. Matthäus et al. 2003.
11. See Römer 2012; Neitzel and Welzer 2011.
12. Wildt 2002.
13. Ingrao [2013] 2015.
14. Herbert [1996] 2010. The term "intellectual in action" was invented by Christian Ingrao.
15. Koonz 2003.
16. Gross and Konitzer (eds.), 2009; Gross, 2010.
17. Reichel [1991] 1993.
18. Haffner [2000] 2004, p. 83.
19. Frick [1933] 1998, p. 9.
20. Chapoutot 2012.
21. "6.000 Jahre Rassenkampf," 1942.

1. Origins

1. Wiwjorra 2006.
2. Gross, Walter, 1942, p. 1.
3. Eckhard 1931.
4. Ibid., p. 3.
5. Ibid., p. 7.
6. Ibid., p. 8.
7. *Der Ewige Jude*, 1940.
8. "Verwirrung im Blut," IV, 1939.
9. Eckhard 1931, p. 19.
10. Stengel von Rutkowski 1941, p. 8.
11. Ibid., p. 16.

12. Graupner 1941, pp. 284, 286–287, 291, 301.
13. Himmler 1942 (a).
14. "Der Sinn unseres Lebens," 1939, p. 28.
15. Ibid.
16. Ibid., pp. 30, 29.
17. Rossner 1941, p. 67.
18. Ibid., p. 66.
19. Stengel von Rutkowski 1943, p. 29.
20. Ibid., p. 30.
21. Astel 1937, p. 11.
22. Quoted in Fest 1993, pp. 169–170. Felix Kersten, like Hermann Rauschning, is sometimes an unreliable source, whom historians such as Joachim Fest use only when the reported words and acts can be corroborated elsewhere or at least seem highly probable.
23. Cf. Kater 1974.
24. Stöpel 1939.
25. Ibid., p. 7.
26. Ibid., p. 11.
27. Ibid., pp. 84–86.
28. Graupner 1941, pp. 294, 297.
29. Ibid., p. 298.
30. Hitler [1943] 1993, p. 144.
31. Cf. Chapoutot 2012.
32. Cf. Jütte 2002.
33. "Deutsche Frauenschönheit," 1942, p. 6.
34. "Ist das Nacktkultur?," 1935.
35. Ibid.
36. *Translator's note:* Johann Joachim Winckelmann (1717–1768) is considered one of the founders of both art history and scientific archaeology. His work, which among other things was the first to distinguish among Greek, Greco-Roman, and Roman art, was highly influential in the neoclassical movement of the late eighteenth and early nineteenth centuries.
37. "Verwirrung im Blut," II, 1939.
38. Schwarz 1940.
39. Sonder 1942, p. 45.
40. Clemens 1941.
41. Funk 1940.
42. Frank 1936 (a), p. 10.
43. Freisler 1941, p. 3.
44. Valentiner 1937, foreword.
45. Gütt, Rüdin, and Ruttke 1934, p. 56.
46. Frick 1936, p. 5.
47. Lehmann 1937, p. 337.
48. Ibid., p. 340.
49. Gütt 1935, p. 23.
50. Ruttke 1939, p. 14.
51. Himmler [1936] 1970, pp. 246–247.

52. Ibid., p. 247.
53. Weitzel 1940.
54. Himmler [1936] 1970, p. 247.
55. Ibid., p. 246.
56. Himmler 1937 (b).
57. Mehlis 1941, p. 35.
58. Ibid., p. 45.
59. Ibid., p. 53.
60. *Die Paragraphensklaverei und ihr Ende*, ca. 1937, p. 17.
61. Merk 1935, pp. 11–12.
62. Ibid., pp. 62, 70.
63. Ibid., pp. 73–74.
64. Nicolai 1932, p. 3. The adjective *lebensgesetzlich* has been in common use since then.
65. Ibid., p. 9.
66. Ibid., p. 10.
67. Ibid., p. 17.
68. Ibid., p. 3.
69. Ibid., p. 11. It goes without saying that by "Slavs," only the original Slavic peoples were meant. To the Nazis, contemporary "Slavs" were the pathetic, disastrous result of racial mixing between Asians and Turko-Mongolians.
70. Ibid.
71. Ibid., p. 13.
72. Ibid., pp. 51, 55
73. "Natur," 1938.
74. Dietze 1936 (a), p. 818.
75. Frank 1935, p. 492.
76. Wagner [1934] 1943, p. 33.
77. Wagner [1936] 1943, p. 176 (my italics).
78. Frank 1934 (a).
79. Mehlis 1941, p. 116.
80. Freisler 1938, p. 56.
81. Ibid., p. 55.
82. Ibid., p. 8.
83. Höhn 1935, pp. 79, 83.
84. Brunner 1939, p. 128.
85. Ibid., pp. 134, 153, 151, 158.
86. Forsthoff 1941, pp. 13, 16.
87. Ibid.
88. Brunner 1939, pp. 509, 510.
89. Stengel von Rutkowski 1935, pp. 163–164.
90. Ibid., p. 166.
91. Ibid., p. 167.
92. Ibid., p. 165.
93. Ibid., p. 168.
94. Astel 1937, p. 8.
95. Ibid., p. 12.

96. Ibid., p. 14.
97. Günther 1934, foreword.
98. Ibid., pp. 12–13.
99. Ibid., p. 13.
100. Rossner 1942, p. 46.
101. Ibid., pp. 20–21.
102. Ibid., p. 25.
103. Ibid., p. 32.
104. Ibid., p. 33.
105. Ibid., p. 13; Günther 1935.
106. Ibid., p. 36.
107. Hauer 1935, p. 398.
108. Günther 1935, p. 36.
109. Stengel von Rutkowski 1937, p. 8.
110. Lippe 1933, p. 7.
111. Ibid., p. 18.
112. Nicolai 1932, p. 9.
113. Ibid., pp. 20–21.
114. Holzner 1940, p. 25.
115. Nicolai 1932, p. 27.
116. Ibid.
117. Ibid.
118. Ibid., p. 7.
119. Ibid.
120. Ibid., pp. 13, 31.
121. Freisler 1938, p. 55; Frank 1933, p. 39.
122. Astel 1935, p. 7.
123. *Schulungs . . .* , n.d., p. 105.
124. Cf. Jouanjan 2010, pp. 211–233.
125. Stier 1934, p. 21.
126. Holzner 1940, pp. 26–27.
127. Ibid., p. 22.
128. Leers 1941.
129. Merk 1935, p. 76.
130. Nicolai 1932, p. 14.
131. Ibid., p. 19.
132. Ibid., p. 18.
133. Frenssen 1942, p. 28.
134. Hans Johst, cited in Rossner 1942, p. 99.
135. Ibid., pp. 77, 78.
136. *Lehrplan für die weltanschauliche Erziehung in der SS und Polizei*, n.d., p. 12.
137. Leers 1939, p. 13.
138. Leers 1941, p. 14.
139. Schmitt, 1934 (b), p. 11.
140. Ibid., p. 29. *Translator's note:* The author is referring to the concept of *stufenbau* proposed by German legal scholar Hans Kelsen in his *Pure Theory*

of Law (*Reine Rechtslehre*, first published in 1934 and then revised extensively and republished in 1960). The 1960 edition was translated into English by Max Knight. See Hans Kelsen, *Pure Theory of Law* (1967; Berkeley: University of California Press, 1978), which was translated from Hans Kelsen, *Reine Rechtslehre*, rev. and exp. ed. (Vienna: Verlag Franz Deuticke, 1960). See also Alf Ross and Henrik Palmer Olsen, "The 25th Anniversary of the *Pure Theory of Law*" *Oxford Journal of Legal Studies* 31, no. 2 (2011): 267–268.

141. Schmitt, 1934 (b), p. 44.
142. Ibid., p. 14. (This translation is from Bendersky, p. 49.)
143. Ibid., p. 7. (The translations of this and the previous quotation are from Bendersky, p. 43.)
144. Ibid., p. 13.
145. Goethe is the Shakespeare of the German language, and as such, is a more reliable lender of credibility than any other author; his name brings a special shine to any and all quotations. The verse used to bolster the argument cited here was not in fact written by Goethe, but by the philosopher Friedrich Heinrich Jacobi.
146. Viergutz 1944, p. 57.
147. Ibid., p. 58.
148. Buch 1936, p. 7.
149. Ibid., p. 6.
150. Viergutz 1944, p. 58.
151. Frenssen 1942, p. 28.
152. Himmler 1936, fol. 2.
153. Bechert 1935, p. 72.
154. Ibid., pp. 71, 72.
155. Ibid., p. 84.
156. Hedemann 1941, p. 2.
157. Freisler 1940 (c), p. 9.
158. Ibid., p. 13.
159. Ibid., p. 22.
160. Ibid., p. 21.
161. Ibid., p. 33.
162. Künssberg 1936, p. 1.
163. Ibid., p. 3.
164. Ibid., p. 7.
165. Nicolai 1932, p. 47.
166. Ruttke 1934, p. 100 and n. 1.
167. Gross, Walter, 1933.
168. "Was wir wollen," 1935, p. 1.
169. Freisler 1941, pp. 12, 1.

2. Alienation

1. "Verwirrung im Blut, IV," 1939.
2. Ibid.

3. Confucius, according to Richard Walther Darré, was of Nordic race. Cf. Darré 1940 (b).

4. "Verwirrung im Blut, IV," 1939.

5. Ibid.

6. "Mitteilungsblätter für die weltanschauliche Schulung der Ordnungspo-lizei," 1943.

7. Cf. Hachmeister 1998.

8. Holzner 1939, pp. 44, 49.

9. Ibid.

10. The exact wording is *"sit amabilis viro suo, ut Rachel; sapiens, ut Rebecca; longaeva et fidelis, ut Sara."* The propitiatory words of the wedding ceremony enumerate the biblical virtues that she must incarnate and cultivate for her husband.

11. Holzner 1939, pp. 46–47.

12. Ibid., pp. 49–50.

13. Ibid., p. 50.

14. Ibid., pp. 56, 61, 63, 62.

15. "Adam, Eva und Methusalem," 1942, p. 20.

16. Ibid., pp. 20–21.

17. Ibid., p. 21.

18. Ibid.

19. Stengel von Rutkowski 1937, p. 27.

20. Lippe 1933, p. 34.

21. Günther 1934, p. 6.

22. Kynast 1927.

23. Lippe 1933, p. 36.

24. Ibid., p. 37.

25. *Translator's note:* "International" here means one of four associations founded between 1864 and 1936 to promote socialist or communist action.

26. "Warum wird über das Judentum geschult?," 1936, p. 10.

27. Ibid.

28. Alexander VI was a member of the house of Borgia, which was rumored to have Jewish roots. The Borgias also had notorious noses, specifically nose bumps, which are seen as Jewish.

29. *Schulungs . . . ,* n.d., pp. 92–93.

30. Eco 1995.

31. Frank 1936 (a), p. 12.

32. Schroer 1936.

33. Schmitt 1934 (b), p. 9. (This translation is from Bendersky, p. 45.)

34. *Lichtbildvortrag,* n.d., p. 7.

35. *SS-Handblätter für den weltanschaulichen Unterricht,* "Thema 2," n.d., p. 4.

36. "600 Bastarde klagen an," 1935.

37. Schmitt (ed.) 1936 (b), p. 28.

38. It is this "liberal-Marxist worldview that placed the individual at the center of his thinking and his legal action" (Frank [ed.] 1935, p. xvi).

39. The law of April 7, 1933, classed *Zulassung*, the authorization to practice law, as a civil servant role in the broad sense of that term. An exception was made for veterans. The last *Zulassungen* were definitively revoked in 1938.

40. Haffner 2000, pp. 145ff.

41. Johnson [1999] 2001. See also Haffner [1914–1933] 2004, p. 125.

42. Heinrich Himmler, cited in Best et al. 1936, pp. 11, 12.

43. Ibid., pp. 15–16.

44. Ibid.

45. Hitler 1934.

46. Freisler 1940 (c), p. 29.

47. *Schulungs . . .* , n.d., p. 73.

48. Buch 1936, p. 5.

49. Buch 1938, pp. 42, 43.

50. Hüttig 1937, p. 33.

51. *Schulungs . . .* , n.d., p. 81.

52. Rosenberg 1940, p. 1.

53. Ibid., p. 4.

54. Ibid.

55. Ibid.

56. Rosenberg [1934] 1936, p. 228.

57. Eilemann 1935, pp. 1, 2.

58. Schilling 1937, p. 26.

59. Ibid., p. 86.

60. Ibid., pp. 164, 168.

61. Ibid., p. 210.

62. Ibid., p. 169.

63. Ibid., pp. 210, 211.

64. On the thinking of Fritz Lenz, see the next section of this chapter.

65. Walz 1938, p. 11.

66. Ibid.

67. Ibid., p. 12.

68. Ibid., p. 13.

69. Ibid., p. 30.

70. Ibid., p. 49.

71. Freisler 1941, pp. 5–6. On the contrast between contemporary labor law and medieval corporatist law, see pp. 6–11.

72. Ibid., p. 11.

73. Jess 1936 (a), p. 6.

74. Jess 1936 (b), p. 41.

75. Banniza von Bazan 1943, p. 5.

76. *Lichtbildvortrag*, n.d., p. 11.

77. Jess 1935, pp. 59–60.

78. Jess 1936 (b), p. 40.

79. Merk 1935, p. 108.

80. Lange 1933, p. iii.

81. Ibid., p. 3.

82. Ibid., p. 5.
83. Ibid., pp. 7, 17.
84. Ibid., p. 7.
85. Ibid., p. 37.
86. Walz 1938, p. 14.
87. Ibid.
88. Ibid., p. 15.
89. "Woran sterben Völker?," 1939, p. 15.
90. *Der Schulungsbrief,* 1937, p. 88.
91. "Woran sterben Völker?," 1939, p. 15.
92. Ibid., p. 16.
93. Lenz 1933, pp. 12–13.
94. Ibid., pp. 8–9.
95. Ibid., pp. 14, 15.
96. Berger 1936, p. 17, 22, 24.
97. Ibid., pp. 6, 10.
98. Ibid., p. 6.
99. Ibid., p. 13.
100. *Um das Menschenrecht,* 1934.
101. *Lichtbildvortrag,* n.d., p. 28.
102. Krieck 1939, p. 31.
103. Dietrich 1935, pp. 6, 14.
104. Ibid., p. 16.
105. Ibid., p. 23.
106. Ibid., p. 33.
107. Ibid.
108. Ibid., p. 17.
109. Ibid.
110. Mehlis 1941, p. 32.
111. Ibid.
112. Rosenberg 1934, p. 47.
113. Mehlis 1941, p. 32. *Translator's note:* I have chosen to translate the French word "Germanité" (*Germanentum* or *Deutschtum* in German) as "Germanity" rather than "Germanness." While the latter is in slightly wider use, it is, according to the *Oxford English Dictonary,* a twentieth-century invention, and therefore does not carry the connotations of the less common word "Germanity," which has been in use since the early to mid-nineteenth century.
114. Frank 1938 (a), pp. 1–2.
115. Cf. Jouanjan 2005.
116. Frank 1936 (b), p. 1.
117. Ibid., p. 1.
118. Ibid., p. 2.
119. Ibid.
120. *Die Paragraphensklaverei und ihr Ende,* ca. 1937, p. 8.
121. Frank 1936 (b), p. 2.
122. Cf. Chapoutot [2008] 2012.

123. Frank 1934 (a).
124. Freisler 1941, pp. 8–9.
125. Frank 1936 (b), p. 2.
126. Merk 1935, pp. 34–35.
127. Ibid., p. 35.
128. Frank 1936 (b), p. 2.
129. Ibid. This Latin aphorism, which means "Live first, then philosophize," is more commonly worded *"primum vivere, diende philosophari"* and has been attributed to Hobbes, Aristotle, and Seneca. Its actual source is unidentified.
130. Frank 1934 (b), p. 3.
131. Goebbels [1924–1945] 2005–2009 (May 5, 1936).
132. Literally "time of combat": the period of struggle against the Weimar Republic, from 1919 to 1923.
133. Hitler [1932–1945] 1962, p. 1628, Speech to the Borsig-Werken Company, Berlin, Dec. 10, 1940.
134. Frank 1935, p. 490.
135. Ibid.
136. Ibid., p. 489.
137. Ibid., p. 490.
138. *Lichtbildvortrag*, n.d., p. 20.
139. Ibid.
140. Graul 1937, pp. 17, 21.
141. Ibid., p. 38.
142. Rossner 1942, p. 50.
143. Darré 1940 (a), p. 54.
144. Himmler [1933–1945] 1974, p. 103.
145. Matthäus 1996. See also Lorenz et al. 1999.
146. Werner 1934.
147. Ibid., p. 16.
148. Ibid., p. 24.
149. Ibid., p. 16.
150. Ibid., p. 29.
151. Ibid., p. 14.
152. Ibid., pp. 29–30.
153. Vesper 1931.
154. Klee 2007, p. 630.
155. Berger 1936, p. 24.
156. Rosenberg 1935, p. 2; Rosenberg 1930, p. 74.
157. Erbt 1934. Dr. Erbt was also the author of a biography of Jesus Christ that argued for his "Nordicness" (Erbt 1926; see also Erbt 1930).
158. Kummer 1935.
159. Ibid., p. 315.
160. Ibid.
161. Ibid., p. 311.
162. Ibid.
163. Ibid., p. 312.

164. Ibid.
165. Ibid., pp. 315, 317.
166. Ibid., pp. 315, 320.
167. *Schulungs . . .* , n.d., p. 90.
168. "Woran sterben Völker?," 1939, p. 21.
169. "Verwirrung im Blut," II, "Artfremde Moral," 1939, p. 13.
170. Ibid.
171. *Schulungs . . .* , n.d., p. 84.
172. Cf. Hockerts 1971, and, for the Cologne region, Johnson [1999] 2001.
173. "Ordensgemeinschaft," 1943, p. 3.
174. Ibid., p. 4.
175. Ibid., p. 3.
176. Himmler [1937] 1970 (a).
177. *Translator's note:* "Michel" is a classic figure of German naiveté—a kindly, foolish bumpkin.
178. Gütt 1934, pp. 53 and 54.
179. Ibid., p. 53.
180. Ibid., p. 56.
181. Ibid., p. 57.
182. "Woran sterben Völker?," 1939, p. 19.
183. Ibid., pp. 20, 19.
184. Berger 1936, p. 17.
185. On so-called "mixed" marriages, cf. Frick [1933] 2010.
186. Himmler [1933–1945] 1974, p. 102.
187. Ibid. "Bolshevism of yesteryear" is a reference to Christianity.
188. Ibid., p. 98.
189. Ibid., p. 99.
190. *Die SS- und Polizeigerichtsbarkeit*, n.d., p. 46.
191. Ibid., p. 47.
192. From *Leben* ("life") and *Born* ("fountain").

3. Restoration

1. Hitler 1937, p. 7.
2. Ruttke 1937, p. 5.
3. Hitler 1937, p. 7.
4. Ruttke 1937, p. 6.
5. Ibid., p. 204.
6. Nicolai 1932, p. 47.
7. Ibid., p. 7.
8. Ibid., p. 10.
9. Ibid., p. 32.
10. Hitler 1926, p. 433. The translations of this and the following quotation are from *Mein Kampf,* trans. James Murphy (London: Hurst and Blackett, 1939).
11. Ibid., p. 434.

12. Frick 1934, p. 13.
13. Ibid.
14. Frank 1936 (a), p. 3.
15. Steinhoff 1939. In German, "Der Heilige Bürokratius" (Saint Bureaucrat) sounds similar to "der Heilige Bonifazius" (Saint Boniface), a leading figure in the Anglo-Saxon mission to evangelize the Germanic peoples of the Frankish empire. The implication was that the Latinate plagues of Catholic religion and the bureaucratic state went hand in hand.
16. Gercke 1935, p. 14.
17. Lenz 1933, p. 16.
18. Volkmar 1935 (b), p. 692.
19. Rosenberg 1932; Ruttke 1934, p. 94.
20. Volkmar 1935 (a), p. 473.
21. Rosenberg 1932. *Translator's note:* The murder of Konrad Pietzuch in the village of Potempa, in Upper Silesia, which took place on August 10, 1932, came to be known as the Potempa Murder or the Potempa Affair, and was probably the most highly publicized of the many acts of Nazi political violence committed before 1933. Pietzuch, an unemployed Polish laborer with Communist sympathies, was brutally beaten and killed in his home by members of the SA, nine of whom were brought to trial, six of whom were found guilty, and five of whom were given the death penalty. Hitler publicly denounced the sentences as a miscarriage of justice and expressed his sympathies with the convicted murderers. The affair immediately became a cause célèbre for National Socialists, and just two weeks after the trial ended, the death sentences were commuted to life imprisonment by the Prussian *Staatsministerium*. See Richard Bessel, "The Potempa Murder," *Central European History* 10, no. 3 (1977): 241–254 and Chapoutot 2010.
22. Volkmar 1935 (a), p. 475.
23. Karl Friedrich Euler, cited in Grundmann (ed.) 1942, p. 272.
24. Cf. Puschner (ed.) 2012.
25. Grundmann 1939, p. 3.
26. Ibid., p. 5.
27. Ibid., pp. 9, 21.
28. Leitpoldt 1941.
29. Grundmann 1940, p. 237.
30. Hitler [1941–1944] 1980, Private conversation, Oct. 21, 1941.
31. Ibid., Private conversation, Nov. 30, 1944.
32. Meyer, Hermann, 1925 (a), p. 41.
33. Meyer, Hermann, 1925 (b), p. 164.
34. Ibid.
35. Himmler [1937] 1970 (b).
36. Grundmann 1939, p. 10.
37. Ibid., pp. 14–15.
38. Ibid., p. 15. The Institute's colloquia would be held in Wittenberg in 1940 and in Eisenach in 1941.
39. Ibid., pp. 16, 18.
40. Ibid., foreword, p. 1.

41. Gross, Raphael [2000] 2005, pp. 108–109.
42. Schmitt (ed.) 1936 (a), pp. 14, 35.
43. *Die Botschaft Gottes,* 1940; *Deutsche mit Gott,* 1941; *Grosser Gott, wir loben Dich,* 1941.
44. *Schulungs . . . ,* n.d., p. 96.
45. Ibid., p. 102.
46. Hedemann 1941, p. 1.
47. Ibid., p. 4.
48. Ibid., p. 27.
49. Ibid., p. 46.
50. Ibid. pp. 21, 53.
51. Stier 1934, p. 34.
52. Ibid., p. 35.
53. *Translator's note:* What to call Schmitt's *Generalklaussel* in English is a thorny question for translators; it has been translated as "vague legal clause," "general clause," "blanket clause," and "general interpretive principle." This question is so thorny because what Schmitt was describing was itself somewhat vague: essentially, that certain norms, such as good faith or public order, offer a kind of release valve or universal exception for judges in situations where following the letter of the law would lead to injustice. Because the Nazi jurists cited herein seized upon this idea as applicable or expandable to the "substantive values" discussed above, for the sake of clarity I have chosen to use Schmitt's original German.
54. Frank (ed.) 1935, p. 14.
55. Ibid., p. 15.
56. Ibid., p. 16.
57. Ibid.
58. Frank 1938 (a), p. 18.
59. Leers 1936 (a).
60. Frank 1933, p. 37.
61. Frank 1937, p. 24.
62. Heuber, ca. 1937, p. 7.
63. Ibid., p. 11.
64. For more on this 1933 summer camp experience, see the detailed account of the young *Referendar* Sebastian Haffner (Haffner 2000, pp. 253ff).
65. "Deulig-Tonwoche," 1933. The image of the scaffold appears at timecodes 2.15–2.25.
66. "Der preussische Justizminister Kerrl besucht das Referendarlager in Jüterbog," 1933. The image of the scaffold was made famous by the flyleaf of a book by Bernd Rüthers (Rüthers 1988). For more on the Jüterbog camp experience, see Schmerbach 2008.
67. Frank 1938 (a), p. 9.
68. Frank 1933, p. 37.
69. According to the legal scholar de Boor, "English legal method" offered a path for "the reform of German law" to follow (Boor 1934).
70. Larenz 1934, p. 40.
71. Larenz 1938, pp. 18, 8.

72. Ibid., p. 15.
73. Ibid., p. 16.
74. Ibid., p. 18.
75. Freisler 1938, pp. 28, 43.
76. Ibid., pp. 28–29.
77. Ibid., p. 78.
78. Significantly, the law referred to *Abmeierung,* an Old High German word completely forgotten by all but a handful of historians of medieval law, which designated a lord's right to take land from the vassal responsible for cultivating it. (*Meier* comes from the Latin *major,* which very loosely designates the holder of any kind of responsibility.) Freisler used this same word (*abmeiern, abgemeiert*) in the text cited earlier.
79. "Beschluss des Grossdeutschen Reichstags" [1942] 1962.
80. Freisler 1941, p. 10.
81. Ibid., p. 6.
82. For "faithful administrator," see "Zweierlei Recht" 1935, p. 7.
83. Freisler 1941, p. 25.
84. Ibid., p. 26.
85. Ibid., p. 25.
86. Darré 1936.
87. Ibid., p. 6.
88. Ibid., p. 12.
89. Ibid., p. 13.
90. Darré [1929] 1940.
91. Darré 1936, p. 14.
92. Ibid., p. 15.
93. Lange 1933, pp. 23, 19.
94. Ibid., p. 20.
95. Ibid., p. 25.
96. Ibid., p. 26.
97. *Der Herrscher* 1937.
98. Freisler 1935, p. 19.
99. Ibid., p. 9.
100. Ibid., p. 23.
101. Ruttke [1934] 1937, p. 58.
102. Schmitt 1934 (b), p. 59.
103. Freisler 1941, pp. 12, 23.
104. Luetgebrune 1934, p. 19.
105. Barth 1940, p. 12.
106. Ibid., p. 30.
107. Ibid., pp. 31, 33.
108. Larenz 1938, p. 23.
109. Ibid., p. 19.
110. Ibid., p. 28.
111. Schmitt 1934 (b).
112. Larenz 1938, p. 33.
113. Ibid., pp. 14, 18.

114. Thierack 1942, p. 2.

115. Hitler [1932–1945] 1962, p. 233, Speech delivered at the Nuremberg Rally, Sept. 12, 1938.

116. Cited in ibid., p. 1905.

117. Fehr 1940, p. 53.

118. Larenz 1934, p. 24.

119. Freisler 1938, p. 41.

120. Ibid.

121. Freisler 1941, p. 12.

122. Boor (de) 1934, pp. 2, 51, 52 59, 1.

123. Reier 1935, p. 20.

124. Ibid., pp. 24–25.

125. Frank 1934 (b), p. 4.

126. Schoetensack 1937, p. 8.

127. "Gesetz zur änderung des Strafrechts und des Strafverfahrens," 1934, pp. 341–348. Article III-1-2 decreed that the people's court be composed of five members, of whom only two "must have the qualification of judge." The professional judges, in the minority, were commonly known as *Berufsrichter*, and the lay judges as *Volksrichter*. *Volksrichter* were not randomly selected citizens, but rather judges nominated by the Ministry of Justice, then named by Hitler. Of the ninety-five *Volksrichter* who sat on the bench of the Volksgerichtshof in 1943, thirty were officers in the Wehrmacht, four were police officers, and forty-eight were officers in the SA, the SS, the NSKK, and the Hitler Youth.

128. Schoetensack 1937, p. 9.

129. Heinrich Himmler, cited in Best et al. 1936, p. 15.

130. Ruttke 1939, p. 21.

131. Ibid., p. 13.

132. "Gesetz zur Verhütung erbkranken Nachwuchses," 1933.

133. Art. 6-1.

134. "Begründung zum Gesetz zur Verhütung erbkranken Nachwuchses" [1933] 1998, p. 2.

135. Arts. 7-1, 7-2.

136. Arts. 9, 10.

137. Art. 12-1.

138. Falk Ruttke, cited in Fickert 1938, p. 15.

139. Ibid., p. 16, n. 4.

140. Gross, Walter [1940] 1988, p. 243.

141. Ibid.

142. Ibid., p. 242.

143. Rüdin (ed.) 1937, p. 134.

144. Ibid., pp. 135, 134.

145. The article is referring to doctors and nurses, the *Betreuer* whose fate—"a life lived for nothing" (*umsonst*)—was lamented at length in articles and documentary films.

146. "Ein menschliches Gesetz," 1935, p. 2.

147. Frick 1933 (a), p. 139.

148. Ibid.
149. "Begründung zum Gesetz zur Verhütung erbkranken Nachwuchses" [1933] 1998, p. 1.
150. Hitler 1926, p. 279.
151. *SS-Handblätter für den weltanschaulichen Unterricht,* "Thema 3," n.d., p. 6.
152. Gross, Walter, 1937, p. 23.
153. Binding and Hoche 1920; Mayer 1927.
154. Klee 1988, and Klee 1989.
155. Goebbels [1938], 1971, vol. 1, pp. 309–332.
156. Gross, Walter, 1937, p. 23.
157. "Grenzen des Mitleids," 1933, p. 18.
158. Ibid., p. 19.
159. "Die humanste Tat der Menschheit," 1936.
160. "Gesetz zum Schutz der Erbgesundheit des deutschen Volkes (Ehegesundheitsgesetz)," 1935; Arts. I-1-d, I-1-c.
161. Ruttke 1939, pp. 22–23.
162. Gütt, Rüdin, and Ruttke 1934, p. 16.
163. Wagner [1934] 1943, p. 34.
164. Ibid., p. 35.
165. Wagner [1935] 1943, pp. 103 and 108.
166. Wagner [1936] 1943, p. 143.
167. "Gnadentod," 1937, p. 4.
168. "Rasse, Glaube, Bekenntnis," 1935, p. 4.
169. Frank 1938 (b), p. 9.
170. Frank 1933, p. 38.
171. Tatarin-Tarnheyden 1934, p. 5.
172. Ibid., pp. 7, 10.
173. Ibid., p. 8.
174. Ibid., pp. 11, 12. Tatarin castigated Kelsen for daring to claim that he was drawing on Kant: "As if a stranger on German soil could understand anything of the deep mysteries of the German soul as they are manifested and expressed in Kant" (p. 11). In other words, Kant was not the formal, abstract logician he was believed to be, as presented by the impudent Jew Kelsen.
175. Ibid., pp. 11, 15.
176. Ibid., p. 16.
177. Ibid., p. 17.
178. Ibid., p. 14.
179. Himmler [1933–1945] 1974, p. 92.
180. Darré 1940 (a), p. 17.
181. Ibid., pp. 18, 20.
182. Ibid., p. 43.
183. Ibid., p. 42.
184. Ibid., pp. 55, 56.
185. Himmler 1942 (a).

4. "All Life Is Struggle"

1. Ruttke 1939, p. 6.
2. Gercke 1935, p. 11.
3. Hitler [1941–1944] 1980, p. 148, Private conversation, Dec. 1, 1941.
4. Hitler [1941–1942] 1976, Private conversation, evening of Apr. 15, 1942.
5. "Cats are a foreign, unpredictable race. They have no place among us. They come from the east. . . . They do not know how to integrate themselves into any community. . . . They are asocial. Germans love dogs," Wilhelm Vesper, a Nazi writer, declared to his son Bernward, who was the future companion of Gudrun Ensslin, one of the founders in the 1970s of the Red Army Faction, a German anarchist guerrilla group. He wrote of the road from Nazism to the Red Army Faction in his superb memoir *Die Reise* (Vesper, 1977, p. 356).
6. Hitler [1941–1944] 1980, p. 148, Private conversation, Dec. 1, 1941.
7. "Du oder Ich!," 1939, p. 11.
8. Ibid.
9. Eichenauer 1934, p. 23.
10. Haacke 1942, p. 7.
11. Ibid., p. 6.
12. Ibid., p. 7.
13. "Ordensgemeinschaft," 1943, p. 4.
14. Himmler 1937 (b).
15. *Alles Leben ist Kampf,* 1937.
16. Eichenauer 1934, p. 127.
17. Ibid., p. 128.
18. Dietze 1936 (b).
19. Dietze 1936 (a), p. 818.
20. Ibid.
21. Ibid., pp. 818–819.
22. Ibid., p. 819.
23. Ibid., p. 820.
24. Ibid., pp. 819–820.
25. Frank 1938 (b), p. 9.
26. Hitler [1942] 1966, p. 307.
27. Hitler [1941–1942] 1976, p. 491, Speech to Wehrmacht officer cadets, Berlin Sportpalast, May 30, 1942.
28. Hitler 1926, p. 314.
29. Stier 1934, p. 15.
30. Hitler [1932–1945] 1962, p. 205, Speech, Berlin Sportpalast, Feb. 10, 1933.
31. Rosenberg 1930, p. 597.
32. Ibid., p. 598.
33. Ibid., p. 597.
34. Staemmler [1933] 1939, p. 11.
35. Buch 1938, p. 44.
36. Ibid.
37. *SS-Handblätter für den weltanschaulichen Unterricht,* "Thema 1," n.d., p. 6.

38. Ibid., p. 3.
39. Ibid., "Thema 2," n.d., p. 2.
40. See Part 3 of this volume.
41. Zschucke 1944, p. 170.
42. Ibid.
43. Rauchhaupt 1936 (a), p. 406.
44. Schmitt [1937] 1940, p. 239.
45. Zschucke 1944, p. 172.
46. See Chapter 3.
47. Eugen Stähle, December 4, 1940, quoted in Klee 1983, p. 16.
48. Indeed, the film poster showed a paragraph sign (§) superimposed on the stern and serious face of Paul Hartmann, who played Thomas Heyt in the movie.
49. *Twelve Angry Men* was directed by Sidney Lumet in 1957.
50. Gütt 1934, p. 53.
51. Wagner [1938] 1943, p. 273.
52. Mehlis 1941, p. 44.
53. Ruttke 1935 (a), p. 23.
54. Ibid., p. 24.
55. Wagner [1936] 1943, p. 177.
56. Ibid., p. 174.
57. Ibid., p. 178.
58. Wagner [1934] 1943, p. 32.
59. Gütt 1935, p. 18.
60. Reiter 1933, p. 28.
61. Kroll, Werner, 1941, p. 126.
62. Frenssen 1942, p. 56.
63. Wagner 1943, pp. 188, 230.
64. Ibid., p. 188.
65. Ibid., p. 183.
66. Ibid., p. 235.
67. Wagner [1933] 1943, p. 14.
68. Ibid., p. 277.
69. Ibid., pp. 234–235.
70. Ibid., p. 285.
71. Reiter 1933, p. 4.
72. Ibid.
73. Ibid., p. 5.
74. "Gott?," *Sigrune*, July 10, 1938, p. 1.
75. Rosenberg 1936.
76. Hitler 1940, p. 56, Speech to the Borsig-Werken Co., Dec. 10.
77. Ibid., p. 57.
78. Ibid.
79. "Zehn Gebote gegen die Ruhr," 1941.
80. "Gebote zur Gesundheitsführung," 1939; this was a separate sheet included with the brochures of *Hitlerjugend* and written by the *Reichsarzt für die Hitlerjugend*.
81. "Zehn Gebote für die Gattenwahl," n.p., n.d.

82. Goebbels [1926] 2002; "Grundsätze für die Sicherheitspolizei," 1943, p. 49; Bauer 1942.

83. The speech's style, notably in its use of the rhetorical flourish of anaphora, was intentionally archaic-sounding, as may be observed in the frequent placement of the verb before the noun: *Wir wollen wahren die ewigen Fundamente unseres Lebens* ("We want to preserve the eternal foundations of our life").

84. Cf. "Sieh dich vor!" [1941] 1995, as well as *"Polen-Erlass"* ("Decree regarding the Polish"). See Chapter 7.

85. *Translator's note:* André Chénier (1762–1794) was a French poet and revolutionary who supported the establishment of a constitutional monarchy and wrote poems, articles, and pamphlets critical of the violent tactics of the sans-culottes and the Jacobins. He denounced their leaders—including Maximilien Robespierre—by name, and composed an *Ode to Charlotte Corday* after the assassination of Jean-Paul Marat. He was arrested shortly thereafter, and guillotined just days before Robespierre himself.

86. Gütt, Rüdin, and Ruttke 1934, p. 10.

87. Frick 1933 (b).

88. Hitler 1926, vol. 2, chap. 15, "Notwehr als Recht."

89. Tirala 1933, p. 114.

90. Frick 1933 (a), p. 138.

91. Ibid., p. 139.

92. Helmut (ed.) 1934, pp. 6, 42.

93. Danzer 1943, pp. 5, 6, and 9.

94. Danzer 1937; Bernsee 1938.

95. Burgdörfer 1936, p. 8.

96. "6.000 Jahre Rassenkampf," 1942.

97. Hitler [1922] 1935, p. 25.

98. Hitler [1932–1945] 1962.

99. Himmler 1942 (a), fols. 180–199, 198.

100. Himmler [1933–1945] 1974, p. 160.

101. Ibid., p. 128.

102. Ibid., p. 125.

103. Frank 1938 (a), p. 39.

104. Eilemann 1935, p. 4.

105. Stier 1934, p. 8.

106. Frank 1938 (a), p. 38.

107. Ibid., p. 10.

108. Nicolai 1932, p. 32.

109. Schmitt [1936] 1940, p. 214.

110. Ibid., p. 227.

111. Ibid., p. 228.

112. Adolf Hitler, cited by Goebbels [1924–1945] 2005–2009 (December 18, 1941). Cf. also Hitler [1928] 1992, "Aussenpolitische Standortsbestimmungen . . . ," p. 94.

113. Himmler 1942 (a).

114. Goebbels [1924–1945] 2005–2009 (December 14, 1941).

115. "Mitteilungsblätter für die weltanschauliche Schulung der Ordnungspolizei," 1944, p. 7.
116. Ibid.
117. Rauschning 1940, p. 50.
118. Ibid.
119. Goebbels [1924–1945] 2005–2009 (May 24, 1942).
120. Hitler [1926] 1998.
121. Hitler [1941–1944] 1980, Private conversation, Oct. 14, 1941.
122. Ibid.
123. Viergutz 1944, p. 60.
124. Ibid., p. 62.
125. Ibid., p. 61.
126. Rauschning 1940, p. 50.
127. Viergutz 1944, p. 65.
128. Himmler [1940] 1974, p. 125.
129. Cf. Pois [1986] 1993.
130. Himmler 1942 (a).
131. Viergutz 1944, p. 64.
132. Rauschning 1940, p. 57.
133. Ibid., p. 56.
134. Gütt 1936, p. 10.
135. Ibid., p. 8.
136. Ibid., p. 18.
137. Gütt, Rüdin, and Ruttke 1934, p. 5.
138. Ibid., p. 6.
139. "Woran sterben Völker?," 1939, p. 16.
140. Ibid., p. 19.
141. Goebbels [1924–1945] 2005–2009 (August 3, 1940), (October 28, 1941).
142. Ibid. (August 2, 1942).
143. Himmler 1943 (a).
144. Goebbels [1924–1945] 2005–2009 (June 4, 1938).
145. Gerlach [1997] 1999; Goebbels [1924–1945] 2005–2009 (December 13, 1941).
146. Prag and Jacobmeyer 1975, pp. 457–458.
147. Ingrid Greiser, quoted in Kaden (ed.), 1993, p. 176. She is also quoted by Friedländer 1998, p. 183.
148. Goebbels [1924–1945] 2005–2009 (March 27, 1942).
149. Hitler [1932–1945] 1962, p. 1238, "Beseitigung der lebendigen Kräfte Polens," Aug. 22, 1939, Halder notes.

5. The War Within

1. "Zweck und Gliederung des Konzentrationslagers," 1941, p. 5.
2. Ibid., p. 6.
3. Ibid., p. 40.
4. Ibid., p. 41.
5. Ibid., pp. 40, 47, 48, 49, and passim. On "without warning," see p. 41.

6. Ibid., pp. 46–50, "Strafordnung."

7. Ibid., p. 46, "Inspektion der Konzentrationslager."

8. Ibid., pp. 46–47.

9. See the translator's note in Chapter 3 for more on the "general clause."

10. Ibid., p. 48, "Strafordnung," item 20.

11. "Disziplinar- und Strafordnung für das Gefangenenlager" [1934], 1983, p. 205.

12. "Besondere Lagerordnung für das Gefangenen-Barackenlager" [1934], 1983, p. 197.

13. Knigge and Stein (eds.) 2009.

14. To my knowledge there are no archival sources offering any explanation for the decision to have this slogan cast and hung over the camp's entrance.

15. Jess 1935, pp. 54–55.

16. Tatarin-Tarnheyden 1936, p. 16.

17. Freisler 1935.

18. Ibid., title page.

19. Ibid., p. 32.

20. Ibid.

21. Freisler 1938, pp. 18, 24.

22. Frank 1935, p. 492.

23. "Gesetz über Verhängung und Vollzug der Todesstrafe," 1933, p. 151.

24. Frank (ed.), 1935, "Einleitung" (introduction), p. xiv.

25. Hitler 1937.

26. Buch 1938, p. 44.

27. Ruttke [1934] 1937, p. 57.

28. Mezger 1935.

29. Ibid., pp. 390–391.

30. Ibid., p. 392.

31. Stier 1934, p. 20.

32. Oetker 1935, pp. 1317–1318.

33. Buch 1938, p. 45.

34. Stengel von Rutkowski 1940, p. 221.

35. Ibid.

36. Schulungs . . . , n.d., p. 111.

37. Freisler 1940 (a), p. 3.

38. Freisler 1939 (a), p. 1851.

39. Freisler 1939 (b).

40. Schulungs . . . , n.d., pp. 111, 113.

41. Frank 1935, p. 491.

42. Ibid., p. 492.

43. Freisler 1940 (c), p. 14.

44. Frank 1935, p. 492.

45. Ruttke [1934] 1937, p. 46.

46. Heydrich 1936, p. 121.

47. Stier 1934, p. 2.

48. Ibid., p. 17.

49. Oetker 1935, p. 1318.

50. Die Paragraphensklaverei und ihr Ende, n.d., p. 16.

51. Cf. Hitler [1932–1945] 1962, pp. 1856–1857.

52. Ibid., p. 1860.

53. Hitler [1942] 1993, p. 176, Speech to the Reichstag.

54. Ibid.

55. Heinrich Himmler, quoted in Best et al. 1936, p. 12.

56. Cf. also Haacke 1942, p. 6.

57. Heinrich Himmler, quoted in Best et al. 1936, p. 13.

58. Ibid., p. 14.

59. *Schulungs . . .* , n.d., p. 119.

60. Ibid.

61. Heinrich Himmler, quoted in Best et al. 1936, p. 14.

62. Ibid., pp. 11–12, 15.

63. Höhn 1936, p. 23.

64. Ibid., p. 24.

65. Ibid.

66. Ibid., p. 25.

67. Ibid., p. 24.

68. Ibid., p. 26.

69. Ibid.

70. PvG (*Polizeiverwaltungsgesetz*), § 14.

71. Ibid., p. 21.

72. Ibid., p. 28.

73. Ibid., p. 30.

74. Ibid. pp. 33–34.

75. Ibid., p. 34. The definition of the police as an "Einsatzkorps im Dienste der volksgemeinschaft" also appears on p. 33.

76. Cf. Johnson [1999] 2001, pp. 53–112.

77. Cf. Herbert [1996] 2010.

78. Best 1936, p. 125.

79. Ibid., p. 126.

80. Ibid.

81. Ibid.

82. Ibid.

83. Best 1940, p. 7.

84. Ibid., p. 8.

85. Ibid., p. 9.

86. Ibid.

87. Ibid., pp. 10–11.

88. Ibid., p. 12.

89. Ibid., pp. 12–13.

90. Ibid., p. 14.

91. Ibid., p. 15.

92. Best 1939, p. 48.

93. Best 1940, p. 18.

94. Law of December 20, 1934, Article I-2-2.

95. Best 1940, p. 20.

96. Ibid., p. 15.

97. Ibid., p. 20.
98. Cf. Baumann 2006, p. 132.
99. Ritter 1942, p. 116.
100. Baumann 2006, p. 134.
101. Höhn 1938, p. 8.
102. Best 1936.
103. *Die SS-und Polizeigerichtsbarkeit,* n.d., p. 46.
104. Stier 1934, p. 24.
105. "Richterbrief Thierack," circular cited in Ayass 1998, p. 322.
106. "Begründung zum Gesetz zur Verhütung des erbkranken Nachwuchses" [1933], 1998, p. 20.
107. Daluege 1936, p. 63.
108. Ibid., p. 12.
109. Ibid., pp. 9–11.
110. Ibid., p. 12.
111. Ibid., p. 13.
112. Ibid., p. 14.
113. Ibid., p. 68.
114. Ibid., p. 69.
115. Ibid., p. 17.
116. Ibid., pp. 18, 19, 25.
117. Ibid., p. 25.
118. Ibid., pp. 18, 20, 22.
119. Ibid., p. 24.
120. Ibid., p. 33.
121. Ibid.
122. Ibid., p. 23.
123. Tesmer 1936.
124. Ibid., p. 136.
125. Ibid., p. 137.
126. Ibid., p. 136.
127. Ibid., p. 137.
128. Ibid.
129. Himmler [1944] 1974, p. 221.
130. Himmler [1944] 1953.
131. Himmler [1944] 1970.
132. Goebbels [1924–1945] 2005–2009 (August 3, 1944).
133. Keitel [1944] 1993.
134. Keitel [1945] 1993.
135. "Führerbefehl über Sippenhaftung . . ." [1945] 1993.
136. Cf. Schlagdenhauffen 2011.
137. Meisinger [1937] 1993, pp. 148, 150.
138. Ibid., p. 153.
139. Himmler 1937 (a).
140. Cf. "Widernatürliche Unzucht ist todeswürdig," 1935; *Die SS . . .* , n.d., p. 47.
141. Himmler [1933–1945] 1974, p. 97.
142. Himmler 1937 (a).

143. The evolving and complex fate of the Gypsies bears witness to this. Excluded by the Nuremburg Laws from sexual relationships and marriage with "Aryans," they were considered racial "others," but not as dangerous as the Jews. Starting in 1939, their fate was increasingly determined by concepts inherited from the Kaiserreich and the Weimar Republic, and in fact present throughout Europe: settlement, social control, and repression of the asocial behaviors and potential dangers of non-integrated nomadic populations. Cf. Zimmermann 1996, and Lewy 2000.

144. Thierack [1943] 1975, p. 58.

145. Thierack [n.d.] 2009, p. 266 n. 16.

146. Thierack [1943] 1975, p. 58.

147. Ibid.

148. Ibid., p. 57.

149. Ibid., p. 58.

150. The matter was given to Paul Werner, a professional prosecutor and the chief of Bureau 5A (responsible for handling "legal questions regarding the criminal police") in the RSHA. On Paul Werner, see Wildt 2002, p. 320.

151. Frank [1942] 1998, p. 302. Upset that "the police be given such vast prerogatives to the detriment of the ordinary courts," the thinker behind the "National Socialist rule of law" was horrified at "this short-circuiting of judicial intervention." It ignored "point 19 of the party platform," which called for "a German communitarian law," which in turn implied "a regular independent judge who would rule according to the National Socialist worldview. This judge is not a barrier to the security of the Reich and the German people; he is one of its essential pillars" (ibid.).

152. "Gesetz über die Behandlung Gemeinschaftsfremder" [1945] 2009, p. 343.

153. "Wer sind die Asozialen?" [1942] 1998, p. 310.

154. Ibid., p. 311.

155. The expression *Einordnung in die Volksgemeinschaft* appeared five times in the draft law.

156. "Gesetz über die Behandlung Gemeinshaftsfremder" [1945] 2009, Article Iv, § 1 and 2, p. 344.

157. Werner [1944] 1998, p. 369.

158. Ibid., p. 370.

159. Ibid., p. 372.

160. "Die Bekämpfung der Gemeinschaftsunfähigen" [1941] 1998, p. 309.

161. Ritter 1937.

162. Gross, Walter [1940] 1998, p. 243.

163. Ibid.

164. "Wer sind die Asozialen?" [1942] 1998, p. 310.

165. Ibid., p. 243.

166. Ibid., p. 244.

167. "Gesetz über Massnahmen der Staatsnotwehr," 1934, p. 529.

168. Hitler [1932–1945] 1962.

169. Schmitt [1934] 1940, p. 200.

170. Ibid.

171. Ibid., p. 201.

172. Hitler [1941–1944] 1980, p. 59, Private conversation, night of Oct. 14–15, 1941.
173. Hitler [1932–1945] 1962, p. 2055, Speech, Nov. 8, 1943.
174. Himmler 1942 (b), fols. 180–199, 198.

6. The War Outside

1. "Unsere Härte," 1943, p. 1.
2. Ibid.
3. Ibid., p. 2.
4. Ibid., pp. 1, 3.
5. Holzner, 1940, p. 12.
6. Ibid., p. 20.
7. Ibid., p. 24.
8. Ibid., p. 28.
9. Holzner, 1941, p. 10.
10. Stengel von Rutkowski 1943, pp. 27–28.
11. Ibid., p. 164.
12. *SS-Handblätter für den weltanschaulichen Unterricht*, "Thema 2," n.d., p. 6.
13. "Die Nationalpolitischen Erziehungsanstalten," 1937.
14. "Unser revolutionärer Wille," 1943, p. 1.
15. Ibid., p. 2.
16. "Ordensgemeinschaft," 1943, p. 2. The phrase is from Daniel 5:27: "You have been weighed in the balance and found lacking."
17. Ibid., p. 3.
18. Hitler [1932–1945] 1962, "Beseitigung der lebendigen Kräfte Polens," and "Vernichtung der Lebenskraft Russlands."
19. See Chapter 8.
20. Hitler [1932–1945] 1962, Remarks made on Aug. 22, 1939.
21. Cited in Halder [1939–1942] 1962–1964, vol. 1, p. 82.
22. Himmler [1940] 1974.
23. Hitler [1941] 1963, vol. 2, pp. 335ff.
24. Ibid.
25. Ibid.
26. Himmler [1933–1945] 1974, p. 57.
27. Goebbels 1943.
28. "Richtlinien auf Sondergebieten . . ." [1941], 1984, p. 301.
29. Ibid.
30. "Regelung des Einsatzes der Sicherheitspolizei . . ." [1941], 1984, p. 305.
31. Ibid., p. 306.
32. "Erlass über die Ausübung der Kriegsgerichtsbarkeit . . . ," 1941.
33. "Behandlung feindlicher Zivilpersonen und Straftaten . . . ," 1941.
34. "Richtlinien für die verstärkte Bekämpfung . . . ," 1942.
35. The Ostministerium, for example, criticized the treatment of "Asiatic" peoples in prison camps. Classified as Mongolian, they were considered to

be the most barbaric and the most hostile of populations, whereas in fact they were one of the groups most receptive to the presence of the Germans: marginalized by the Soviet Empire and persecuted by Stalin, they saw the Wehrmacht as a liberating force. Their mass murder through famine and neglect thus came to be considered a colossal political miscalculation.

36. Hitler [1942] 1993, pp. 126–127, Decree, Dec. 16, 1942.

37. The expression in German is *allerbrutalste Mittel:* the word *allerbrutal* is already a superlative, but the authors of the order nevertheless added the suffix -*st(e-s/r)* to it, which is the linguistic marker used to indicate the superlative. The translation here is therefore as ungainly as the German original: "the most radically or extremely brutal" or "the most most brutal."

38. Ibid., p. 127.

39. Ibid.

40. Again, the adjective used here (*scharf*) is a double superlative, following the same logic explained in note 37.

41. Koeppe [1944] 1993.

42. "Kampfanweisung für die Bandenbekämpfung im Osten" [1942] 1989.

43. Ibid.

44. Roques [1942] 1984, p. 50.

45. "Behandlung feindlicher Zivilpersonen und russischer . . ." [1941] 1984, p. 350.

46. Ibid.

47. Cf. Römer 2008, pp. 85–88; "Richtlinien für das Verhalten der Truppe in Russland" [1941] 1984, p. 312.

48. "Sieh dich vor!" [1941] 1995, p. 65; "Warnung vor heimtückischer Sowjetkriegsführung" [1941], 1984, p. 316; "Kennt Ihr den Feind?" [1941] 1984, p. 318.

49. "Richtlinien für das Verhalten der Truppe in Russland" [1941] 1984, point 3.

50. Ibid., point 2.

51. "Kennt Ihr den Feind?" [1941] 1984.

52. "Sieh dich vor!" [1941] 1995, p. 65, point 5; "Warnung vor heimtückischer Sowjetkriegsführung" [1941] 1984, point 2-1, preamble.

53. "Sieh dich vor!" [1941] 1995, preamble.

54. Ibid., p. 65, point 5.

55. "Kennt Ihr den Feind?" [1941] 1984.

56. Ibid.

57. "Sieh dich vor!" [1941] 1995, point 7.

58. Ibid., point 10; "Warnung vor heimtückischer Sowjetkriegsführung" [1941] 1984, point 2-2-h.

59. "Kennt Ihr den Feind?" [1941] 1984.

60. Ibid.

61. "Warnung vor heimtückischer Sowjetkriegsführung" [1941] 1984, point 1-b, point 1-a-2, "Schutz dagegen."

62. Ibid., preamble and points 1-a-2-1, 1-a-2-2.

63. Ibid., point 1-a-2-6.

64. Ibid.

65. "Kennt Ihr den Feind?" [1941] 1984.

66. Scheck 2007.

67. Dönitz [1942] 1993.

68. Ibid.

69. Kaden et al. (eds.), 1993, vol. 1, p. 144.

70. "Führerbefehl zur Verfolgung von Straftaten . . ." [1941] 1993.

71. "Erste verordnung GFM Wilhelm Keitel zur Durchführung des Nacht- und Nebelerlasses" [1941] 1993.

72. "Führerbefehl zur Bekämpfung . . ." [1944] 1993.

73. "Behandlung feindlicher Zivilpersonen und russischer . . ." [1941] 1984, p. 350.

74. Cf. Lieb 2007, pp. 243, 263. Cf. also Lambauer 2010.

75. Rendulic [1944] 1993.

76. Lieb 2007, pp. 263ff.

77. Ibid.

78. Ibid.

79. In addition to the article and the published thesis of Felix Römer (Römer 2008), see Broszat et al. 1965; Krausnick 1977; Hürter 2006; Förster 1983.

80. "Richtlinien für die Behandlung politischer Kommissare" [1941] 1993, vol. 1, p. 137.

81. Ibid.

82. Ibid., p. 138.

83. Ibid.

84. Ibid.

85. Ibid., p. 137.

86. "Anfrage OKH zwecks Aufhebung des Befehls vom 6. Juni 1941," September 23, 1941, cited in Alfred Streim, *Sowjetische Gefangene in Hitlers Vernichtungskrieg. Berichte und Dokumente, 1941–1945* (Heidelberg: Müller, 1981), pp. 96ff. This note, addressed from the OKH to the OKW and to the Führer, argued that "a weakening of the will to fight could be achieved on the Russian side if the commissars, who are clearly the principal source of the uncompromising resistance we are encountering, could see the way opening to a ceasefire or to being taken prisoner. For the moment, all a commissar can expect is certain death. This is the reason he fights to the death, and that he forces Red Army soldiers to resist to the very last, often in the most brutal ways." Hitler and Keitel dismissed the request three days later. It would take until May 6, 1942, for Hitler to heed these arguments and to alter his position and soften his orders: "In order to encourage Soviet troops' inclination to desert and capitulate when surrounded by our men, the Führer orders . . . that, initially and experimentally, political commissars and officers be left alive" (p. 96).

87. "Anordnungen für die Behandlung . . ." [1941] 1984, p. 351.

88. "Behandlung feindlicher Zivilpersonen und russischer . . ." [1941] 1984, p. 350.

89. Ibid., p. 351.

90. "Merkblatt für die Bewachung . . ." [1941] 1984, p. 354.

91. "Behandlung feindlicher Zivilpersonen und russischer . . ." [1941] 1984, p. 352.

92. Ibid.
93. "Vollstreckung von Todesstrafen . . ." [1941] 1984, p. 363.
94. Bormann [1941] 1984, p. 23.
95. Ibid., p. 351.
96. Ibid.
97. "Merkpunkte aus der Chefbesprechung . . . ," 1984, p. 362.
98. Streit 1978.
99. Ibid.
100. "Brief Reichsminister Rosenberg . . ." [1942] 1984, p. 399.
101. Ibid., p. 400.

7. The International Order of Westphalia and Versailles

1. An excellent adventure film, this UFA production came across as ideologically neutral enough that a French version, titled *Au bout du monde* and
   sometimes referred to as *Les Fugitifs* (The ends of the earth; or The fugitives), was shot and distributed in 1933, starring the multilingual German
   actress Käthe von Nagy, with Henri Chomette in the role played by Hans
   Albers in the German original. Still today, *Flüchtlinge* is seen as a harm-
   less example of filmmaking in that era, and is not considered to be a
   Vorbehaltsfilme.
2. *Schulungs . . .* , n.d., p. 40.
3. "Deutschlands Weg durch den Dreissigjährigen Krieg," 1938, p. 59.
4. Ibid., pp. 60, 61, 63, 64.
5. "Der Kardinal kocht eine Teufelssuppe . . . ," 1942, p. 5.
6. "Deutschlands Weg durch den Dreissigjährigen Krieg," 1938, p. 67.
7. Ibid., pp. 67, 68.
8. "Der Kardinal kocht eine Teufelssuppe . . . ," 1942, p. 6.
9. Ibid., p. 7.
10. Ibid.
11. Goebbels [1924–1945] 2005–2009 (November 17, 1939).
12. Freisler 1940 (b), p. 65.
13. Cf. Hachmeister 1998. 3.
14. Six (ed.) 1942, p. 5.
15. Ibid., p. 11.
16. Kopp and Schulte 1943, pp. viii, 101.
17. Ibid., pp. 108, 115, 121, 122.
18. Ibid., pp. ix–x, 107, 110.
19. Grimm 1940.
20. Grimm (ed.) 1940, p. 14.
21. Grimm 1940, p. 17.
22. Six (ed.) 1942, p. 7; cf. also Baustaedt, 1936, p. 13.
23. Bilfinger 1942, p. 6.
24. Ibid., p. 29.
25. Ibid., p. 30.
26. Grimm 1939.

27. Grimm 1940, p. 43.
28. Ibid., p. 25.
29. Ibid., pp. 91, 93.
30. Ibid., p. 119.
31. Ibid.
32. Ibid., pp. 120, 119.
33. Ibid., pp. 125, 118.
34. Ibid. pp. 96, 132.
35. Ibid., p. 132.
36. Ibid.
37. Ibid.
38. *Schulungs . . .*, n.d., p. 41.
39. Trampler 1935, pp. 33, 34.
40. Ibid., p. 31.
41. Ibid., pp. 9, 5.
42. Ibid., pp. 41, 39, 41.
43. *Völkischer Beobachter*, September 20, 1938, p. 2; Hitler [1932–1945] 1962, pp. 900–901, Speech to the Reichstag, Feb. 20, 1938.
44. Ibid.
45. Ibid., pp. 898, 899.
46. Ibid., p. 901.
47. Ibid., p. 927.
48. Ibid., pp. 928, 901.
49. Ibid., p. 929.
50. Ibid., p. 932. The *wandernder Scholar* in question was President Wilson, the former professor of political science and traveling statesmen who took Europe by surprise when he set up his headquarters in France, in Versailles, no less, for many months. The expression "wandering professor" is a clear reference to that of the "wandering Jew."
51. *Völkischer Beobachter*, September 18, 1938, p. 1, September 20, 1938, p. 1, August 27, 1938, p. 1.
52. Ibid., August 29, 1938, pp. 1–2.
53. Ibid., September 14, 1938, p. 1.
54. Ibid., September 18, 1938, p. 1.
55. Hitler 1938, p. 1.
56. Ibid., p. 2.
57. Ibid.
58. "Der Tscheschiche Weltbetrug," 1938.
59. Ibid. The Avars, or Avares, were a nomadic Mongolian-Turkish people, who, like the Huns, arrived in Europe around the middle of the sixth century and disappeared over the course of the ninth century.
60. "Prag-Karthago," 1938.
61. Lüdtke 1941, p. 154.
62. Ibid., p. 161.
63. Ibid., p. 169.
64. Ibid., 179.
65. Ibid., pp. 185, 180.

66. Freytag-Loringhoven 1940, pp. 21, 113, 112.
67. Ibid., p. 21.
68. Schadewaldt, 1940, p. 7.
69. Ibid., p. 14.
70. Ibid., p. 15.
71. Ibid., p. 16.
72. Ibid.
73. Ibid., pp. 18–20.
74. Ibid., p. 19.
75. Ibid., pp. 25, 23.
76. Ibid., p. 27.
77. Ibid., pp. 25, 17.
78. Ibid., p. 26.
79. Ibid., p. 27.
80. Ibid., p. 28.
81. Ibid., p. 31.
82. Lüdtke 1941, p. 196; Freytag-Loringhoven 1940, p. 21.
83. Hitler [1932–1945] 1962, pp. 1307, 1237, Speech to the Reichstag, Sept. 1, 1939.
84. Ibid., p. 1307.
85. *Uti possidetis, uti possideatis* (As you possess, thus may you possess).
86. Bruns 1934, p. 10.
87. Ibid., p. 21.
88. Schmitt 1934 (a), pp. 19, 20.
89. On the maxim *Pacta sunt servanda* and the principle of the *clausula*, see Rauchhaupt 1936 (b), p. 23.
90. See, among others, Schesmer 1934, Schmitz-Ost 1941, Seemann 1939, Schuchmann 1936.
91. Haushofer 1938, p. 418.
92. Bilfinger 1938, p. 10.
93. Ibid., p. 31.
94. "The Assembly may from time to time advise the reconsideration by Members of the League of treaties which have become inapplicable and the consideration of international conditions whose continuance might endanger the peace of the world" (The Covenant of the League of Nations, June 18, 1919). Bilfinger cites the text in German; the text here is cited in the original English as made available online by The Avalon Project of Yale Law School.
95. Göppert 1938, p. 439.
96. Ibid., p. 443.
97. Ibid., p. 429.
98. Ibid., pp. 431, 1–2.
99. Schmitt 1934 (a), p. 28.
100. Mehlis 1941, p. 39.
101. Wegner 1936, p. 315.
102. Schmitt 1934 (a), p. 20.
103. Ibid., p. 23.

104. Ibid., p. 21.
105. Ibid., p. 22.
106. Schmitt [1939] 1940 (b), p. 295.
107. Schmitt 1934 (b), p. 11.
108. Ibid., p. 22.
109. Ibid., p. 12.
110. Ibid., p. 14.
111. Ibid., p. 15.
112. Schmitt 1935 [2005], p. 436. A few years later, when France was no longer a threat, the British took their place as the whipping boys of German legal literature. For example, Gustav Adolf Walz, a professor at the University of Breslau, published a book in 1942 titled *Völkerrechtsordnung und Nationalsozialismus* (The international legal order and National Socialism) in which he condemned "the international peace imposed by the League of Nations" as a *pax Britannica*, rather than as the *pax gallica* he would no doubt have described before 1940 (Walz 1942, p. 42).
113. Schmitt 1935 [2005], p. 436.
114. Ibid.
115. Ibid., pp. 438-439.
116. Schmitt 1934 (b), pp. 7, 11, 8.
117. Walz 1942, p. 39.
118. Hitler [1923] 1939, p. 1543.
119. Füssler 1940, p. 344.
120. Ibid., pp. 347, 352.
121. Ibid., p. 351.
122. Ibid., p. 354.
123. Wegner 1936, pp. 318, 316, 321.
124. Ibid., p. 323.
125. Bilfinger 1942, p. 6.
126. Frank 1939, p. 1538.
127. Hitler [1932-1945] 1962, p. 1313, Speech to the Reichstag, Sept. 1, 1939.
128. Wissmann 1936, p. 4.
129. Ibid., p. 7.
130. Ibid., p. 4.
131. Ibid., pp. x, 17.
132. Wegner 1936, p. 344.
133. Trampler 1935, p. 7.
134. Frank 1939, p. 1538.
135. Rauchhaupt 1936 (b), p. 122.
136. Rogge 1936-1937.
137. Ibid., p. 740.
138. Ibid., p. 742.
139. Rogge 1940, p. 279.
140. Rogge 1935, p. 20.
141. Ibid., p. 17.
142. Ibid., pp. 113, 114, 115.
143. Rogge, 1936-1937, p. 742.

144. Frank 1939, p. 1539.
145. Bruns 1934, p. 24.
146. Tatarin-Tarnheyden 1936, p. 7.
147. Ibid., pp. 9, 12.
148. Ibid., p. 13.
149. Ibid., p. 9.
150. Ibid., p. 14.
151. Ibid., pp. 16, 15.
152. Ibid., p. 16.
153. Ibid.
154. Ibid., p. 18.
155. Ibid., p. 17.
156. Gürke 1935, p. 2.
157. Ibid., p. 3.
158. Ibid., preface, p. iii.
159. Ibid., p. 15.
160. Korte 1942, p. 2.
161. Ibid., p. 3.
162. Ibid., p. 40.
163. Ibid., pp. 48, 54.
164. Ibid., p. 49.
165. Ibid., pp. 50, 51, 31.
166. Ibid., p. 59, n. 70.
167. Ibid. pp. 67, 69.
168. Ibid., p. 74.
169. Notably Schmitt [1939] 1940 (a), p. 309.
170. Ibid., p. 295. English translation from Stephen Legg, ed., *Spatiality, Sovereignty, and Carl Schmitt: Geographies of the Nomos* (London: Routledge, 2011), p. 46.
171. Schmitt [1939] 1940 (b), p. 296 (Legg 2011, p. 47).
172. Ibid., p. 297 (Legg 2011, p. 48).
173. Schmitt 1939 (Legg 2011, p. 116).
174. Hitler [1932–1945] 1962, Speech to the Reichstag, April 28, 1939, pp. 1148–1179. Heinrich August Winkler notes that the chancellor's cabinet had read Schmitt's April 1, 1939, presentation in Kiel and that this had inspired the drafting of Hitler's speech (Winkler, 2000, vol. 2, p. 67).
175. Schmitt [1939] 1940 (a), p. 302 (Legg 2011, p. 52).
176. Ibid., p. 303.
177. Ibid., p. 304. English translation from Claudio Minca and Rory Rowan, *On Schmitt and Space* (London: Routledge, 2015), p. 179.
178. Ibid. Translation from Minca and Rowan.
179. Ibid. Translator's translation.
180. Korte 1942, p. 76.
181. Ibid., p. 79.
182. Walz 1942, p. 130.
183. Ibid., pp. 89, 119.
184. Ibid., p. 120.

185. Korte 1942, pp. 118, 119.
186. Ibid., pp. 88, 89.
187. Nicolai 1932, p. 44.
188. Rauchhaupt 1936 (b), pp. 18, 19.
189. Ibid., p. 7.

8. The Reich and Colonization of the European East

1. Himmler 1943 (c).
2. Hitler [1932–1945] 1962, p. 1172, Speech to the Reichstag, Jan 30, 1939.
3. Ibid., p. 1177.
4. Ibid., p. 1178.
5. *Schulungs . . .* , n.d., p. 53.
6. Schieder 1992.
7. Ibid.
8. *Schulungs . . .* , n.d., p. 64.
9. *Kurzthemen zu . . .* , 1942, p. 3.
10. Hitler [1941–1942] 1976, p. 284, Speech, May 12, 1942. Cf. also Hitler 1926, pp. 349–351.
11. Freisler [1944] 1993.
12. Schmitz-Berning 1998, "Asphalt," pp. 71–72.
13. *Schulungs . . .* , n.d., p. 54.
14. Cf. notably Schmidt 2003, p. 177.
15. Goebbels [1924–1945], 2005–2009 (December 13, 1941; October 1, 1942; and October 2, 1942).
16. Cf. *Mein Kampf* and the numerous speeches in which Hitler described the suffering of a German nation that had been scattered for centuries.
17. Himmler [1940] 1987.
18. "Der Runenspeer von Kowel," p. 6; "Erde, die mit Blut gewonnen ist . . ."
19. Ibid.
20. "Im Osten wächst neues Volk auf neuem Land," p. 4.
21. Bormann [1940] 1984, p. 19.
22. Ibid.
23. Cf. Böhler 2009.
24. Bormann [1940] 1984, p. 19.
25. Gross, Walter, 1943, p. 25.
26. Ibid., p. 26.
27. Bormann [1940] 1984, p. 19.
28. Himmler [1940] 1987.
29. By "mission," Himmler meant being named head of the RKF (Reichskommissariat für die Festigung deutschen Volkstums), the "Reich Commissariat for the Consolidation of German Nationhood."
30. Bormann [1940] 1984, p. 18.
31. Himmler [1940] 1987.
32. Ibid.
33. *Schulungs . . .* , n.d., p. 53.

34. Meyer, Konrad, 1942.

35. Meyer, Konrad, 1941, p. 7.

36. Lippe 1933, p. 4.

37. Ibid., p. 6.

38. Ibid.

39. Ibid., p. 7.

40. Ibid., pp. 16–17.

41. Himmler 1942 (b).

42. *Schulungs . . .* , n.d., p. 61.

43. For a detailed list of colonial products considered indispensable to the German economy, see, for example, ibid., p. 56.

44. Hitler [1932–1945] 1962, p. 899.

45. "Der Runenspeer von Kowel," p. 7.

46. Speer 1975, p. 87.

47. Meyer, Konrad, 1941, p. 7.

48. Ibid.

49. The numerical inferiority of the Indo-Germanic race, an eminently valuable historical corollary, was one of Himmler's obsessions. He called constantly on the German nation to increase its birthrate, and returned again and again, with great anxiety, to German losses and the bloodletting on the Eastern Front, as the war wore on (see notably Himmler 1941, fol. 4, and 1943 [a], fols. 73, 164).

50. "Heute Kolonie, morgen Siedlungsgebiet, übermorgen Reich!," in Himmler 1942 (b), fol. 186.

51. Hitler 1926, p. 428.

52. Wiepking-Jürgensmann 1940, p. 132.

53. Ibid.

54. Ibid.

55. Quotes from this directive reproduced here are taken from Mäding 1943, pp. 51–62 ("Allgemeine Anordnung Nr. 20/vI/42 über die Gestaltung der Landschaft in den eingegliederten Ostgebieten," December 21, 1942).

56. The translation "land and soil" for *Grund und Boden* is an attempt to express as clearly as possible the German expression's distinction between land (in the sense of what is dealt with under the law—land, property, or real estate, in other words) and the earth itself (that is, the physical reality of the land as it is worked by people—the soil, in other words).

57. Meyer, Konrad, 1942, for this and the following citations.

58. Himmler 1942 (b).

59. Himmler [1940] 1974, p. 125.

60. Ibid., p. 127.

61. Ibid.

62. Ibid., p. 125.

63. Himmler, 1943 (b), fol. 289.

64. Ibid., fol. 48.

65. Ibid., fol. 51 bis.

66. Ibid., fol. 51.

67. Ibid.

68. *Planung und Aufbau im Osten*, 1942, fol. 47.
69. "Ausführungen des Reichsmarschalls in der Sitzung" [1941] 1984, p. 383.
70. "12 Gebote für das verhalten der Deutschen im Osten und die Behandlung der Russen." Backe would replace Richard Walther Darré as minister of agriculture in 1942.
71. Cf. Wildt 2011.
72. Himmler 1943 (b), fol. 288.
73. Keitel [1941] 1993.
74. Hitler [1941] 1963, vol. 2, pp. 335ff.
75. Meyer, Konrad, 1941, p. 7.
76. Meyer, Konrad, 1942.
77. Ibid.
78. Ibid.
79. Goebbels [1924–1945] 2005–2009 (August 22, 1938).
80. Himmler [1933–1945] 1974, p. 159.
81. Hitler [1941–1944] 1980, pp. 62, 63, Private conversation, Sept. 17, 1941.
82. Ibid., p. 91, Private conversation, Oct. 17, 1941.
83. Sauckel [1943] 1984, p. 167.
84. Himmler 1943 (a), fols. 90–91.
85. Hitler [1941–1944] 1980, pp. 90, 91, Private conversation, Oct. 17, 1941.

9. The Millennium as Frontier

1. Schieder [1939] 1992.
2. "Befehl des Reichsführers SS über Kameradschaft," 1942, p. 19.
3. Backe [1941] 1984, point 4, p. 380.
4. Himmler 1935.
5. Himmler 1938.
6. Hitler [1927] 1943.
7. Himmler, Mar. 1940, p. 9.
8. "Pflichten der Zivilarbeiter . . . ," 1940, arts. 1, 3.
9. Ibid., art. 6.
10. Himmler Mar. 1940, p. 9.
11. "Polizeiverordnung . . . ," 1940.
12. "Pflichten der Zivilarbeiter . . . ," 1940, art. 5.
13. Ibid., art. 9.
14. Küppers and Bannier 1942 (a).
15. Küppers and Bannier 1942 (b).
16. "Allgemeine Bestimmungen über Anwerbung . . . ," 1942, A-II-1 and 2.
17. Ibid., A-IV-1.
18. Ibid., A-VIII.
19. "Merkblatt für Arbeitskräfte . . . ," n.d., arts. 1–4.
20. Herbert 1985, pp. 76–77.
21. "Verordnung über die Strafrechtspflege gegen Polen und Juden in den eingegliederten Ostgebieten" (Göring 1941).

22. Freisler 1942, pp. 25ff.
23. Göring 1941, art. I-1.
24. Ibid., art. I-2.
25. Ibid., art. I-3.
26. Ibid., art. III-3.
27. Ibid., art. VII.
28. Ibid., art. IX.
29. Ibid., art. XI.
30. Ibid., art. VI-1.
31. Trampler 1934, p. 3.
32. Ibid., p. 4.
33. Ibid., p. 5.
34. Trampler 1935, p. 22.
35. Ibid., pp. 24, 25, 28.
36. Ibid., p. 31.
37. Ibid., p. 44.
38. Ibid., p. 54.
39. Ibid.
40. Ibid., p. 55.
41. Ibid.
42. Ibid., pp. 10, 3.
43. Ibid., pp. 9, 13.
44. Ibid., p. 8.
45. Ibid., p. 13.
46. Ibid., p. 14.
47. Ibid., p. 37.
48. Ibid., p. 43.
49. Hitler [1932–1945] 1962, p. 801, Speech, Mar. 23, 1933.
50. Ibid., p. 802.
51. Freytag-Loringhoven 1940, p. 20.
52. Walz 1936–1937.
53. Ibid., p. 599.
54. Ibid., p. 600.
55. *Kurzthemen zu . . .* , 1942, p. 4.
56. Ibid.
57. Ibid., p. 5.
58. Ibid.
59. *Schulungs . . .* , n.d., p. 63.
60. Himmler n.d., p. 68.
61. Himmler 1942 (b).
62. Himmler n.d., p. 16.
63. Heydrich [1941] 1994.
64. Bormann 1941 [1984], p. 23.
65. Ibid.
66. *Kurzthemen zu . . .* , 1942, p. 5.
67. Ibid.

68. Ibid.
69. Stengel von Rutkowski 1943, p. 7.
70. Cited in Müller 1991, p. 10.
71. Überschär and Wette 1984, p. 377.
72. Ibid.
73. Hitler [1941–1944] 1980, p. 66.
74. Backe [1941] 1984, p. 382.
75. Himmler 1943 (b), fol. 284.
76. Himmler 1943 (a), fols. 90, 91.
77. Cf. Gerlach 1999; Aly and Heim 1993.
78. Überschär and Wette 1984, pp. 385–386.
79. "Allgemeine wirtschaftspolitische . . ." [1941] 1984, p. 377.
80. Ibid., p. 378.
81. Ibid.
82. Ibid.
83. Himmler 1943 (b).
84. Gross, Walter [1935] 1936, p. 29.
85. Himmler 1943 (c).
86. "Zweck und Gliederung des Konzentrationslager," 1941, p. 6.
87. Backe [1941] 1984, p. 381.
88. *Die SS . . .* , n.d., p. 46.
89. Ibid., p. 49.
90. Himmler, 1942 (b), fol. 189.
91. Ibid., fol. 188.
92. Gross, Walter, 1943, p. 28.
93. Ibid., p. 29.
94. Ibid., p. 30.
95. Ibid.
96. Ibid., p. 31.
97. Hitler [1941–1942] 1976, p. 285, Speech, May 12, 1942.
98. *Lichtbildvortrag*, n.d., p. 38.
99. Ibid., p. 39.
100. Cf. Herf [2006] 2011.
101. Hitler [1932–1945] 1962, p. 1058, Speech to the Reichstag, Feb. 20, 1938.
102. *Kampf dem Bolschewismus*, n.d., p. 15.
103. Ibid., p. 1.
104. Ibid., p. 15.
105. Ley 1941.
106. Hitler [1932–1945] 1962, pp. 2083–2084, Speech, Jan. 30, 1944, (cited in full in Chapter 4).
107. *Völkischer Beobachter*, July 24, 1941, p. 1.
108. Cf. Herf [2006] 2011, pp. 107–108.
109. Goebbels [1924–1945] 2005–2009, p. 108, July 3, 1941.
110. Diewerge 1941, p. 1.
111. Ibid., p. 2.
112. Ibid., p. 3.

113. Ibid., p. 5.
114. Ibid., p. 6.
115. Ibid., p. 8.
116. Goebbels [1924–1945] 2005–2009 (Feb. 15, 1942).
117. Ibid. (March 7, 1942).
118. Himmler [Dec. 1943] 1974, p. 201.
119. See the text of the Jäger Report in Wette 2011.
120. Goebbels [1924–1945] 2005–2009 (Oct. 9, 1943).
121. Himmler [1944] 1978, pp. 207–208.
122. Battenberg 1931, p. 44.
123. Chamberlain [1903] n.d., p. 75.
124. Hitler 1926, p. 331. The English translation here and in the following citations was accessed at http://www.greatwar.nl/books/meinkampf/meinkampf.pdf.
125. Cf. Hersonski 2010.
126. Daluege 1935.
127. Leers 1936 (b).
128. Schmitt (ed.) 1936, pp. 29–30.
129. "Richtlinien über die Führung von Vornamen . . . ," 1938.
130. It is worth noting that the name "Joseph" was not included in any of the lists in the circular—not in that of forbidden Jewish names, and not in that of Jewish names that were to be tolerated because of their common usage. Its presence among the given names of the Nazi inner circle (Adolf, Heinrich, Hermann, etc.) in the person of Joseph Goebbels, so named by his Rhineland Catholic family, made the exception obvious enough.
131. "Richtlinien über die Führung von Vornamen . . . ," 1938, point A-5, p. 1346.
132. Ibid., point C-15, p. 1348.
133. "Jud bleibt immer Jud," 1938.
134. "Verordnung über Reisepässe von Juden," 1938.
135. Hiemer 1938.
136. Ibid., p. 4.
137. Ibid., p. 6.
138. Ibid., p. 7.
139. Ibid., pp. 11, 12.
140. Ibid., p. 22.
141. Ibid., pp. 27, 26.
142. Ibid., p. 31.
143. *Jüdische Moral*, 1943, pp. 6, 9.
144. Ibid., p. 2.
145. Ibid., p. 3.
146. Ibid., pp. 4, 5.
147. Ibid., p. 5.
148. Ibid., p. 6.
149. Ibid., p. 7.
150. Hitler [1932–1945] 1962, p. 1058, Speech to the Reichstag, Jan. 30, 1939.
151. *Jüdische Moral*, 1943, pp. 10, 11.

152. Ibid., p. 14.
153. Ibid., pp. 17, 18.
154. Ibid., p. 17.
155. Ibid., pp. 21, 19, 18.
156. Ibid., pp. 21, 22.
157. Ibid., p. 20.
158. Ibid., pp. 22, 23.
159. Ibid., p. 22.
160. Ibid., p. 6.
161. Hiemer 1938, chap. "Was ist der Talmud?," p. 15.
162. Esser 1939.
163. Goebbels [1941] 2011 (b), pp. 119, 120.
164. Ibid., p. 136.
165. "Die jüdischen Kriegshetzer besiegeln Judas Schicksal," 1941.
166. Höss 1958, p. 138.
167. Ibid.
168. Ibid., p. 128.
169. Eichmann [1957] 1960.
170. Höss 1958, p. 138.
171. Ibid., p. 148.
172. Ibid., p. 67.
173. Ibid., p. 72.
174. Ibid., pp. 66–67.
175. Ibid., p. 125.
176. Ibid., p. 128.
177. Ibid.
178. Ibid., p. 150.
179. Ibid., p. 127.
180. Ibid., p. 148.
181. Ibid., p. 147.
182. Esser 1939, p. 5.
183. Ibid.
184. Ibid.
185. Hitler [1905–1924] 1980, p. 156.
186. Hitler [1941–1944] 1980, pp. 90, 91, Private conversation, Oct. 17, 1941.
187. Lichtbildvortrag, n.d., p. 39.
188. Battenberg 1931, p. 39.
189. Himmler [April 1943] 1974.
190. Cited in Esser 1939.
191. Goebbels [1924–1945] 2005–2009 (March 27, 1942).
192. Gerlach [1997] 1999.
193. Kampf dem Fleckfieber!, 1942.
194. Ley 1942.
195. Himmler 1942 (b), fol. 185.
196. Schulungs . . . , n.d., p. 76.
197. Himmler 1942 (a).

Conclusion

1. Cited in *SS-Handblätter für den weltanschaulichen Unterricht*, "Thema 3," n.d., p. 1.
2. Holzner 1940, p. 12.
3. Cf. Bartov 1999, and Ingrao 2006.
4. Gauchet [2003], 2008, p. 241.
5. Ibid., p. 242.
6. Ibid.
7. Speer 1975, p. 401.
8. Revault d'Allonnes 1995.
9. Himmler 1942 (a), fol. 185.
10. Cited in Speer 1969, p. 446.

Bibliography

Abbreviations

BABL   Bundesarchiv Berlin-Lichterfelde

BA-FA   Bundesarchiv-Filmabteilung

BA-MA   Bundesarchiv-Militärarchiv

UFA   Universum-Film Aktiengesellschaft

Primary Sources

"12 Gebote für das Verhalten der Deutschen im Osten und die Behandlung der Russen," BABL, RW, 31 292, fols. 1–2.

"600 Bastarde klagen an," *Das Schwarze Korps*, May 8, 1935, p. 11.

"6.000 Jahre Rassenkampf," in *Dieser Krieg ist ein weltanschaulicher Krieg*, Schulungsgrundlagen für die Reichsthemen der NSDAP für das Jahr 1941/42; Der Beauftragte des Führers für die überwachung der gesamten geistigen und weltanschaulichen Schulung und Erziehung der NSDAP, Berlin, 1942, pp. 39–54, BABL, RD NSD, 16 29.

"Adam, Eva und Methusalem. Zur Entjudung der deutschen Vorstellungswelt," *SS-Leitheft*, no. 8 b, 1942, pp. 20–21.

Alles Leben ist Kampf, Rassenpolitisches Amt der NSDAP, 1937, BA-FA, 2812, 25 min.

"Allgemeine Anordnung Nr. 20/VI/42 über die Gestaltung der Landschaft in den eingegliederten Ostgebieten," Dec. 21, 1942, cited in Mäding, 1943, pp. 51–62.

"Allgemeine Bestimmungen über Anwerbung und Einsatz von Arbeitskräften aus dem Osten," Feb. 20, 1942, Erlass-Sammlung des Chefs der Sicherheitspolizei und des SD, pp. 24–35.

"Allgemeine wirtschaftspolitische Richtlinien für die WO Ost," Gruppe Landwirtschaft, May 23, 1941, cited in Überschär and Wette, 1984.

"Anordnungen für die Behandlung sowjetischer Kriegsgefangener," Oberkommando der *Wehrmacht*, Sept. 8, 1941, cited in Überschär and Wette, 1984, pp. 351–354.

Astel, Karl, *Rassendämmerung und ihre Meisterung durch Geist und Tat als Schicksalsfrage der weissen Völker*, Munich, Eher, 1935.

———, *Die Aufgabe. Rede zur Eröffnung des Winter-Semesters 1936–1937 anlässlich der neu nach Jena einberufenen Dozenten Bernhard Kummer und Johann von Leers*, Jena, Fischer, 1937.

"Ausführungen des Reichsmarschalls in der Sitzung am 7.11.1941 im RLM, Oberkommando der *Wehrmacht*," Nov. 11, 1941, cited in Überschär and Wette, 1984, pp. 380–382.

"Aus Menschlichkeit töten?—Spiegel-Gespräch mit Professor Dr Werner Catel über Kinder-Euthanasie," *Der Spiegel*, no. 8, 1964.

Backe, Herbert, "Zwölf Gebote für das Verhalten der Deutschen im Osten und die Behandlung der Russen," June 1, 1941, cited in Überschär and Wette, 1984, pp. 380–382.

Banniza von Bazan, Heinrich, "Liberté, égalité, fraternité. Rassenbiologische Folgen der französischen Revolution," *Neues Volk*, 1943, pp. 4–5.

Barth, Robert, "Das 'gesunde Volksempfinden' im Strafrecht." Dissertation zur Erlangung des Doktorgrades der Rechts- und Staatswissenschaftlichen Fakultät der Hansischen Universität in Hamburg, Hamburg, Selbstverlag, 1940.

Battenberg, Ludwig, *Fieberkurve oder Zeitenwende? Nachdenkliches über den Nationalsozialismus*, Munich, Lehmann, 1931.

Bauer, Vinzenz, *Zehn Gebote für den Streitrichter*, Berlin, Deutscher Rechtsverlag, 1942.

Baustaedt, Bertold, *Richelieu und Deutschland*, Berlin, Ebering, 1936.

Bechert, Rudolf, "Deutsche Rechtsentwicklung und Rechtserneuerung," in Frank (ed.), 1935, pp. 71–84.

"Befehl des Reichsführers SS über Kameradschaft," *SS-Leitheft*, no. 10 a, [18 Mar.] 1942, p. 19.

"Begründung zum Gesetz zur Verhütung des erbkranken Nachwuchses," *Deutscher Reichsanzeiger*, no. 172, July 26, 1933, cited in Ayass, 1998.

"Behandlung feindlicher Zivilpersonen und russischer Kriegsgefangenen," Oberkommando des Heeres, Aug. 3, 1941, cited in Überschär and Wette, 1984.

"Behandlung feindlicher Zivilpersonen und Straftaten Wehrmachtsangehöriger gegen feindliche Zivilpersonen," May 24, 1941, BA-MA, RH 22/155.

Berger, Friedrich, *Volk und Rasse als Grundlage und Ziel deutscher Erziehung*, Stuttgart, Gutbrod, 1936.

Bernsee, Hans, "Kampf dem Säuglingstod," *Politische Biologie*, no. 5, 1938.

"Beschluss des Grossdeutschen Reichstags," Apr. 26, 1942, cited in Hitler [1932–1945], 1962.

"Besondere Lagerordnung für das Gefangenen-Barackenlager," KL Esterwegen, Aug. 1, 1934, cited in Kosthorst, 1983, vol. I, pp. 197–205.

Best, Werner, "Die Geheime Staatspolizei," *Deutsches Recht*, 1936, nos. 7–8, pp. 125–128.

———, "Die Schutzstaffel der NSDAP und die deutsche Polizei," *Deutsches Recht*, 1939, pp. 44–48.

———, *Die deutsche Polizei*, Darmstadt, Wittich, 1940.

———, Hans Frank, Heinrich Himmler, and Reinhard Höhn, *Grundfragen der deutschen Polizei. Bericht über die konstituierende Sitzung des Ausschusses für Polizeirecht der Akademie für deutsches Recht am 11. Oktober 1936*, Hamburg, Hanseatische Verlagsanstalt, 1936.

Bilfinger, Carl, *Völkerbundsrecht gegen Völkerrecht*, Munich, Duncker & Humblot, 1938.

———, "Völkerrecht und Staatsrecht in der deutschen Verfassungsgeschichte," in Ernst-Rudolf Huber (ed.), *Idee und Ordnung des Reiches, I. Gemeinschaftsarbeit deutscher Staatsrechtslehrer*, Hamburg, Hanseatische Verlagsanstalt, 1942, pp. 1–47.

Binding, Karl, and Alfred Hoche, *Die Freigabe der Vernichtung lebensunwerten Lebens*, Leipzig, 1920.

Boog, Horst, et al., *Das Deutsche Reich und der Zweite Weltkrieg*, vol. IV, *Der Angriff auf die Sowjetunion*, Stuttgart, Deutsche Verlags-Anstalt, 1983.

Boor (de), Hans-Otto, *Die Methode des englischen Rechts und die deutsche Rechtsreform*, Berlin, Vahlen, 1934.

Bormann, Martin, "Aktenvermerk, Besprechung beim Führer," Oct. 2, 1940, cited in Überschär and Wette, 1984, pp. 18–19.

———, "Aktenvermerk, Treffen im Führerhauptquartier," July 16, 1941, cited in Überschär and Wette, 1984, pp. 22–23.

"Brief Reichsminister Rosenberg an den Chef OKW, Generalfeldmarschall Keitel," 28 Feb., 1942, cited in Überschär and Wette, 1984, pp. 399–400.

Brunner, Otto, *Land und Herrschaft. Grundfragen der territorialen Verfassungsgeschichte Südostdeutschlands im Mittelalter*, Brno, Rohrer, 1939.

Bruns, Viktor, *Völkerrecht und Politik*, Berlin, Junker & Dünnhaupt, 1934.

Buch, Walther, "Recht ist, was dem Volke dient," *Neues Volk*, 1936, no. 11, pp. 5–7.

———, "Quellen deutschen Rechts," *Rasse und Recht*, 1938, pp. 41–45.

Burgdörfer, Friedrich, "Völker am Abgrund," *Politische Biologie*, no. 1, 1936.

Chamberlain, Houston Stewart, *Die Grundlagen des neunzehnten Jahrhunderts*, 1903, cited in *Schulungs . . .* , n.d.

Clemens, Hans, "Nacktheit," *Deutsche Leibeszucht*, July 1941, p. 133.

Daluege, Kurt, "Der Jude: kriminell," *Neues Volk*, 1935, no. 7, pp. 22–27.

———, *Nationalsozialistischer Kampf gegen das Verbrechertum*, Munich, Zentralverlag der NSDAP, 1936.

Danzer, Paul, "Geburtenkrieg," *Politische Biologie*, no. 3, 1937.

———, *Geburtenkrieg*, 4th ed., Munich, Lehmann, 1943.

Darré, Richard Walther, *Das Bauerntum als Lebensquell der nordischen Rasse* [1929], 8th reprint, Munich, Lehmann, 1940.

———, *Blut und Boden. Ein Grundgedanke des Nationalsozialismus*, Berlin, Reichsdruckerei, 1936.

———, (a) *Neuordnung unseres Denkens*, Goslar, Verlag Blut und Boden, 1940.

———, (b) *Vom Lebensgesetz zweier Staatsgedanken (Konfuzius und Lykurgos)*, Goslar, Verlag Blut und Boden, 1940.

Das Schwarze Korps, Zeitung der Schutzstaffeln der NSDAP—Organ der Reichsführung SS, Munich, Franz Eher Verlag, 1935–1945.

Deisz, Robert, *Das Recht der Rasse. Kommentar zur Rassengesetzgebung*, Munich, Zentralverlag der NSDAP, 1938.

Der Biologe. Monatsschrift des Reichsbundes für Biologie und des Sachgebiets Biologie des NSLB, Munich, Lehmann, 1931–1944.

Der Ewige Jude (Fritz Hippler), 1940, Reichspropagandaleitung der NSDAP, BA-FA, BSP, 16921, 65 min.

Der Herrscher (veit Harlan), UFA, 1937, BA-FA, 10274, 99 min.

"Der Kardinal kocht eine Teufelssuppe. Eine Geschichte von des Reiches tiefster Erniedrigung," *SS-Leitheft*, no. 8 b, 1942, pp. 4–7.

"Der preussische Justizminister Kerrl besucht das Referendarlager in Jüterbog," Aug. 1933, BABL, Bestand Bild 102 AktuelleilderCentrale, Georg Pahl, Bild 102–14899.

"Der Runenspeer von Kowel. Der Siedler im Osten ist kein 'Kolonist,'" *SS-Leitheft* 6, no. 2b, [1941], pp. 6–10.

Der Schulungsbrief. Deutsches Monatsblatt der NSDAP und DAF, 1937, vol. III.

"Der Sinn unseres Lebens," *SS-Leitheft*, no. 4, 1939, pp. 27–30.

"Der Tscheschiche Weltbetrug," *Völkischer Beobachter*, Sept. 22, 1938, p. 5.

"Deulig-Tonwoche," no. 083, Aug. 8, 1933, BA-FA.

"Deutsche Frauenschönheit," *Neues Volk*, 1942, no. 1, pp. 4–6.

Deutsche Justiz. Rechtspflege und Rechtspolitik; amtliches Blatt der deutschen Rechtspflege, Berlin, von Decker, 1933–1945.

Deutsche Leibeszucht. Blätter für naturnahe und arteigene Lebensgestaltung, Berlin, Wernitz, 1937–1943.

Deutsche mit Gott. Ein deutsches Glaubensbuch, Weimar, Verlag Deutsche Christen, 1941.

"Deutschlands Weg durch den Dreissigjährigen Krieg," *SS-Leitheft*, no. 1, 1938, pp. 59–69.

"Die Bekämpfung der Gemeinschaftsunfähigen," *Informationsdienst*, no. 126, 1941, Rassenpolitisches Amt der NSDAP, reproduced in Ayass, 1998, pp. 307–309.

Die Botschaft Gottes, Institut zur Erforschung des Jüdischen Einflusses auf das Deutsche Kirchliche Leben, Weimar, Verlag Deutsche Christen, 1940.

"Die humanste Tat der Menschheit," *Neues Volk*, 1936, no. 7, p. 5.

"Die jüdischen Kriegshetzer besiegeln Judas Schicksal," *Völkischer Beobachter*, Süddeutsche Ausgabe, Oct. 28, 1941, p. 2.

"Die Nationalpolitischen Erziehungsanstalten," *SS-Leitheft*, no. 2, 1937, p. 35.

Die Paragraphensklaverei und ihr Ende, Berlin, Nationalsozialistischer Rechtswahrerbund, n.p., n.d., ca. 1937.

Die SS- und Polizeigerichtsbarkeit. Ein Leitfaden, Hauptamt SS-Gericht, n.p., n.d., BABL, RD NSD, 41 41.

Dietrich, Otto, *Die philosophischen Grundlagen des Nationalsozialismus. Ein Ruf zu den Waffen deutschen Geistes*, Breslau (Wrocław), Hirt, 1935.

Dietze, Hans-Helmut, (a) "Naturrecht aus Blut und Boden," *Zeitschrift der Akademie für Deutsches Recht*, 1936, pp. 818–821.

———, (b) *Naturrecht in der Gegenwart*, Bonn, Röhrscheid, 1936.

Diewerge, Wolfgang, *Das Kriegziel der Weltplutokratie*, Berlin, Zentral-verlag der NSDAP, 1941.

"Disziplinar- und Strafordnung für das Gefangenenlager," KL Esterwegen, Aug. 1, 1934, cited in Kosthorst, 1983, vol. I, pp. 205–211.

Dönitz, Karl, "Funkspruchbefehl an alle U-Boot-Kommandanten" [Order regarding the saving of enemy crews], Sept. 17, 1942, cited in Kaden et al. (ed.), 1993, vol. III, p. 109.

"Du oder Ich! Gedanken über die Härte im Kampf und den Willen zum Sieg," *SS-Leitheft*, no. 10 b, 1939, pp. 11–12.

Eckhard, Albert, *Kampf der NSDAP gegen Tierquälerei, Tierfolter und Schächten*, Hanover, Giesel, 1931.

Eichenauer, Richard, *Die Rasse als Lebensgesetz in Geschichte und Gesittung. Ein Wegweiser für die deutsche Jugend*, Leipzig, Teubner, 1934.

Eichmann, Adolf, interviewed by Willem Sassen [Sept. 1957], *Life Magazine*, vol. XLIX, nos. 22 (Nov. 28, 1960) and 23 (Dec. 5, 1960).

Eilemann, Johannes, *Weltanschauung, Erziehung und Dichtung. Einige Kapitel einer arteigenen Ethik*, Frankfurt, Moritz Diesterweg, 1935.

"Eingeschläfert," *Der Spiegel*, no. 34, 1960, pp. 31–33.

"Ein menschliches Gesetz," *Das Schwarze Korps*, July 18, 1935, booklet 13.

"Einsatz Jugendlicher zu Erkundungszwecken durch die Russen," Jan. 13, 1942, in Überschär and Wette, 1984.

Erbt, Wilhelm, *Jesus, der Heiland aus nordischem Blute und Mute*, Stuttgart, Roth, 1926.

——, *Der Anfänger unseres Glaubens*, Leipzig, Pfeiffer, 1930.

——, *Weltgeschichte auf rassischer Grundlage*, Leipzig, Armanen-verlag, 1934.

"Erde, die mit Blut gewonnen ist . . . Aus der Rede des Reichsführers SS in Breslau," *SS-Leitheft* 6, no. 2b, [1941], p. 1.

"Erlass über die Ausübung der Kriegsgerichtsbarkeit im Gebiet Barbarossa und über besondere Massnahmen der Truppe," May 13, 1941, Bundesarchiv-Militärarchiv, RW 4/v. 577.

"Erste Verordnung GFM Wilhelm Keitel zur Durchführung des Nacht- und Nebelerlasses," Dec. 12, 1941, cited in Kaden et al. (ed.), 1993, vol. I, p. 163.

Esser, Hermann, *Die jüdische Weltpest. Judendämmerung auf dem Erdball*, Munich, Zentralverlag der NSDAP, 1939.

Fehr, Hans, "Die Plastik des Rechts," in Freisler and Hedemann, 1940, pp. 51–62.

Fickert, Hans, *Rassenhygienische Verbrechensbekämpfung*, Leipzig, Wiegandt, 1938.

Flüchtlinge (Gustav Ucicky), 1933, UFA, BA-FA, 10180, 81 min.

Förster, Jürgen, "Das Unternehmen 'Barbarossa' als Eroberungs- und Vernichtungskrieg," in Boog et al., 1983, pp. 413–447.

Forsthoff, Ernst, *Grenzen des Rechts. Vortrag gehalten auf der KantFeier der Albertus-Universität am 12. Februar 1941*, Königsberg, Gräzer und Unzer, 1941.

Frank, Hans, *Rede gehalten auf der ersten Kundgebung der Berufsgruppe Verwaltungsbeamte im BNSDJ am 14. September 1933 in Berlin*, Berlin, Verlag von Reimar Hobbing, 1933, pp. 31–45.

——, (a) "Nationalsozialismus im Recht," *Zeitschrift der Akademie für deutsches Recht*, 1934, p. 8.

————, (b) *Neues Deutsches Recht. Rede vor dem diplomatischen Korps und der ausländischen Presse am 30. Januar 1934 bei einem Empfangsabend des aussenpolitischen Amtes der NSDAP*, Munich, Zentralverlag der NSDAP, 1934.

————, "Die nationalsozialistische Revolution im Recht," *Zeitschrift der Akademie für deutsches Recht*, 1935, pp. 489–492.

————, (a) "Ansprache des Reichsrechtsführers," in Schmitt (ed.), 1936.

————, (b) "Die Zeit des Rechts," *Deutsches Recht*, 1936, pp. 1–3.

————, *Deutsches Verwaltungsrecht*, Munich, Eher, 1937.

————, (a) *Rechtsgrundlegung des nationalsozialistischen Führerstaates*, Munich, Eher, 1938.

————, (b) "Vorwort," in Deisz, 1938.

————, "Danzigs Kampf. Ein Kampf um das Recht. Rede des Reichsleiters Reichsministers Dr Hans Frank anlässlich der Osttagung Deutscher Rechtswahrer in Zoppot vom 21.–25. August 1939," *Deutsches Recht*, 1939, pp. 1537–1540.

————, "Schreiben des Reichsministers ohne Geschäftsbereich und Präsidenten der Akademie für Deutsches Recht Dr Hans Frank an den Reichsminister ohne Geschäftsbereich und Chef der Reichskanzlei Dr Heinrich Lammers, 7. April 1942," cited in Ayass, 1998, p. 302.

————, (ed.), *Nationalsozialistisches Handbuch für Recht und Gesetzgebung*, Munich, Zentralverlag der NSDAP, 1935.

Freisler, Roland, *Schutz des Volkes oder des Rechtsbrechers? Fesselung des Verbrechers oder des Richters? Einiges über das zweckmässige Mass der Bindung des Richters an gesetzliche Strafbestände*, Berlin, von Decker, 1935.

————, *Nationalsozialistisches Recht und Rechtsdenken*, Berlin, Spaeth & Linde, 1938.

————, (a) "Gedanken zum Kriegsstrafrecht und zur Gewaltverbrecherverordnung," *Deutsche Justiz*, 1939, pp. 1849–1856.

————, (b) "Vortrag zur Volksschädlingsverordnung," Tagung des Reichsjustizministeriums am Oct. 24, 1939, BABL, R, 22 4158.

————, (a) *Das Recht im Reich: Rede. I, Gehalten vor den Verwaltungs Akademien der Nordmark*, Kiel, Verwaltungs-Akademie der Nordmark, 1940.

————, (b) "Gedanken zu Gehalt und Gestalt in der Rechtsarbeit," in Freisler and Hedemann, 1940, pp. 63–86.

————, (c) *Wiedergeburt strafrechtlichen Denkens*, Berlin, von Decker, 1940.

————, *Grundlegende Denkformen des Rechts im Wandel unserer Rechtserneuerung*, Berlin, von Decker, 1941.

————, "Die Polenstrafrechtsverordnung," *Deutsche Justiz*, 1942, pp. 25ff.

————, "Gegen Klamroth und andere," *Volksgerichtshof*, Aug. 15, 1944, cited in Kaden et al. (ed.), 1993, vol. III, p. 233.

————, and Justus Hedemann, *Kampf für ein deutsches Volksrecht. Richard Deinhardt zum 75. Geburtstage*, Berlin, von Decker, 1940.

Frenssen, Gustav, *Lebenskunde*, Berlin, Grote, 1942.

Freytag-Loringhoven, Alexander von, *Kriegsausbruch und Kriegsschuld 1939*, Essen, Essener Verlagsanstalt, 1940.

Frick, Wilhelm, (a) "Ansprache des Herrn Reichsministers des Innern Dr Frick," *Volk und Rasse*, 1933, pp. 137–142.

———, (b) "Richtlinien für die Geschichtslehrbücher," *Zentralblatt für die gesamte Unterrichtsverwaltung in Preussen*, Prusse Ministerium für Wissenschaft, Kunst und Volksbildung, Berlin, Weidmann, no. 15, Aug. 5, 1933, pp. 197–199.

———, Speech, Berlin, Apr. 25, 1933, cited in Mayer, 2010, p. 100.

———, Speech, Berlin June 28, 1933, cited in Ayass, 1998, pp. 6–13.

———, "Reichsreform und Rechtserneuerung," *Zeitschrift der Akademie für deutsches Recht*, 1934, pp. 12–13.

———, "Das nordische Gedankengut in der Gesetzgebung des Dritten Reiches," in Wilhelm Frick and Arthur Gütt, *Nordisches Gedankengut im Dritten Reich*, Munich, Lehmann, 1936, pp. 5–8.

"Führerbefehl über Sippenhaftung von Familienangehörigen kriegsgefangener Soldaten," Mar. 5, 1945, cited in Kaden et al. (ed.), 1993, vol. III, p. 270.

"Führerbefehl zur Bekämpfung von Terroristen und Saboteuren in den besetzten Gebieten," July 30, 1944, cited in Kaden et al. (ed.), 1993, vol. I, p. 253.

"Führerbefehl zur Verfolgung von Straftaten gegen das Reich oder die Besatzungsmacht in den besetzten Gebieten," Dec. 7, 1941, cited in Kaden et al. (ed.), 1993, vol. I, p. 162.

Funk, Fritz, "Heimkehr zum eigenen Wesen," *Deutsche Leibeszucht*, Mar. 1940, p. 423.

Füssler, Wilhelm, *Geschichte des deutschen Volkes für die deutsche Jugend*, Giessen, Roth, 1940.

"Gebote zur Gesundheitsführung—Du hast die Pflicht, gesund zu sein!" *Die Jungenschaft. Blätter für Heimabendgestaltung im deutschen Jungvolk*, May 1939, vol. XV.

Gercke, Achim, "Rasse und Recht," in Frank (ed.), 1935, pp. 11–16.

Germanien. Monatschrift für Vorgeschichte zur Erkenntnis deutscher Wesens, Deutsches Ahnenerbe eV, Verlag Ahnenerbe-Stiftung, 1929–1944.

"Gesetz über die Behandlung Gemeinschaftsfremder," Jan. 1945, facsimile reproduced in Schädler, 2009, pp. 343–345.

"Gesetz über Massnahmen der Staatsnotwehr," July 3, 1934, single article, *Reichsgesetzblatt*, vol. I.

"Gesetz über Verhängung und Vollzug der Todesstrafe," Mar. 29, 1933, *Reichsgesetzblatt*, vol. I.

"Gesetz zum Schutz der Erbgesundheit des deutschen Volkes (Ehegesundheitsgesetz)," Oct. 18, 1935, *Reichsgesetzblatt*, vol. I.

"Gesetz zur änderung des Strafrechts und des Strafverfahrens," Apr. 24, 1934, art. III, *Reichsgesetzblatt*, vol. I.

"Gesetz zur Verhütung erbkranken Nachwuchses," July 14, 1933, art. I, *Reichsgesetzblatt*, vol. I.

Ghetto, 1942, BA-FA, 112445.

"Gnadentod. Ein Leserbrief," *Das Schwarze Korps*, Mar. 18, 1937.

Goebbels, Joseph, *Die Tagebücher von Joseph Goebbels, 1924–1945*, 29 vols., Institut für Zeitgeschichte Munich, Saur, 1987–2008; in French, *Journal*, excerpted in 5 volumes, Tallandier, 2005–2009.

———, "Zehn Gebote für jeden SA-Mann," *Nationalsozialistische Briefe*, Sept. 15, 1926, cited in Reichardt, 2002, p. 673.

——, Speech, Reichenberg, Nov. 19, 1938, cited in Heiber (ed.), 1971.

——, (a) July 3, 1941, cited in Herf [2006] 2011.

——, (b) Lecture, Berlin, Friedrich-Wilhelm University, Dec. 1, 1941, cited in Herf [2006] 2011.

——, Speech, Berlin, Feb. 18, 1943, *Völkischer Beobachter*, Feb. 19, 1943, pp. 1–2.

——, et al., *Ich kämpfe! Sonderdruck zum 10. Jahrestag der Machtergreifung, 30. Januar 1943*, Munich, Zentralverlag der NSDAP, 1943.

Göppert, Otto, *Der Völkerbund. Organisation und Tätigkeit des Völkerbundes*, Stuttgart, Kohlhammer, 1938.

Göring, Hermann, "Verordnung über die Strafrechtspflege gegen Polen und Juden in den eingegliederten Ostgebieten," Dec. 4, 1941, *Reichsgesetzblatt*, 1941, vol. I, pp. 1759–1761.

Graul, Werner, *Golgotha des Norden. Bilder und Gedanken zur Geschichte des politischen Christentums*, Erfurt, Thiel & Böhm, 1937.

Graupner, Heinz, "Die Einheit alles Lebendigen," in L. Stengel von Rutkowski (ed.), *Das naturgesetzliche Weltbild der Gegenwart*, 1941, pp. 271–301.

"Grenzen des Mitleids," *Neues Volk*, 1933, no. 7, pp. 18–19.

Grimm, Friedrich, *Das deutsche Nein. Schluss mit den Reparationen! Ein letzter Appell*, Hamburg, Hanseatische Verlagsanstalt, 1932.

——, "Der Rechtskampf des nationalsozialistischen Deutschlands gegen Versailles," *Deutsches Recht*, 1939, pp. 1540–1544.

——, *Das Testament Richelieus*, Berlin, Zentralverlag der NSDAP, 1940; in French, *Le Testament de Richelieu*, Flammarion, 1941.

——, (ed.), *Frankreichs Kriegsziel—"Les Conséquences politiques de la paix," de Jacques Bainville*, Hamburg, Hanseatische Verlagsanstalt, 1940.

Gross, Walter, "Revolution des Geistes," *Neues Volk*, no. 10, 1933, pp. 5–6.

——, *Heilig ist das Blut*, Berlin, Rassenpolitisches Amt der NSDAP, 1935.

——, "Der Rassengedanke in der weltanschaulichen Auseinandersetzung unserer Tage—Antrittsvorlesung, 26. November 1935 in der Aula der Universität Berlin," in Gross, Walter, *Rasse, Weltanschauung, Wissenschaft. Zwei Universitätsreden*, Berlin, Junker & Dünnhaupt, 1936, pp. 17–32.

——, "Geistige Grundlagen der nationalsozialistischen Rassenpolitik," *Neues Volk*, 1937, no. 1, pp. 22–23.

——, "Vortrag auf einer Kundgebung des Gaus Oberdonau des Rassenpolitischen Amtes der NSDAP, Linz," Mar. 14, 1940, cited in Ayass, 1998, pp. 242–244.

——, "Nationalsozialistische Lebensführung," *Neues Volk*, 1942, no. 1, pp. 1–2.

——, *Deine Ehre ist die Treue zum Blute deines Volkes*, Schriftenreihe für die Wochenendschulungen der Hitlerjugend, Heft 3, Reichsjugendführung, Berlin, 1943, BABL, RD NSD, 43 155-3.

Grosser Gott, wir loben Dich, Weimar, Der neue Dom, 1941.

Grundmann, Walter, *Die Entjudung des religiösen Lebens als Aufgabe deutscher Theologie und Kirche*, Weimar, Verlag Deutsche Christen, 1939.

——, *Christentum und Judentum. Studien zur Erforschung ihres gegenseitigen Verhältnisses. Sitzungsberichte der ersten Arbeitstagung des*

Institutes zur Erforschung des jüdischen Einflusses auf das deutsche kirchliche Leben vom 1. bis zum 3. März 1940 in Wittenberg, Leipzig, Wigand, 1940.

———, (ed.), *Germanentum, Christentum und Judentum. Studien zur Erforschung ihres gegenseitigen Verhältnisses*. vol. 2: *Sitzungsberichte der zweiten Arbeitstagung des Institutes zur Erforschung des jüdischen Einflusses auf das deutsche kirchliche Leben vom 3. bis zum 5. März 1941 in Eisenach*, Leipzig, Wigand, 1942.

"Grundsätze für die Sicherheitspolizei," *Die Deutsche Polizei. Taschenkalender für die Sicherheitspolizei*, Reichsführer-SS und Chef der Deutschen Polizei-Kameradschaftsbund Deutscher Polizeibeamten, Berlin, Verlag Deutsche Kultur-Wacht Oscar Berger, 1943, p. 49.

Günther, Hans Friedrich Karl, *Frömmigkeit nordischer Artung*, Leipzig, Teubner, 1934.

———, "Die Auflösung der germanischen Rassenpflege durch das mittelalterliche Christentum," *Germanien*, 1935, no. 2, pp. 33–42.

Gürke, Norbert, *Volk und Völkerrecht*, Tübingen, Mohr, 1935.

Gütt, Arthur, "Schlusswort," in Helmut (ed.), 1934, pp. 52–59.

———, *Dienst an der Rasse als Aufgabe der Staatspolitik*, Berlin, Junker & Dünnhaupt, 1935.

———, *Verhütung krankhafter Erbanlagen. Eine Übersicht über das Erbkrankheitsgesetz mit Texten*, Langensalza, Beyer und Söhne, 1936.

———, Ernst Rüdin, and Falk Ruttke, *Gesetz zur Verhütung erbkranken Nachwuchses vom 14. Juli 1933 nebst Ausführungsverordnungen*, Munich, Lehmann, 1934.

Haacke, Ulrich, "Pflicht, die Tugend der Preussen," *SS-Leitheft*, no. 3, 1942, pp. 6–10.

Haffner, Sebastian, *Geschichte eines Deutschen. Die Erinnerungen, 1914–1933*, Stuttgart, DTV, 2000; in French, *Histoire d'un Allemand. Souvenirs, 1914–1923*, translated by B. Hébert, Arles, Actes Sud, 2004.

Halder, Franz, *Kriegstagebuch. Tägliche Aufzeichnungen des Chefs des Generalstabes des Heeres 1939–1942*, 3 vols., Stuttgart, Kohlhammer, 1962–1964.

Hauer, Wilhelm, "Die biologische Wurzel des religiösen Artbildes," *Der Biologe*, 1935, no. 12, pp. 397–404.

Haushofer, Karl, "Recht und Dynamik im Fortleben der Völker," *Zeitschrift der Akademie für deutsches Recht*, 1938, pp. 418–420.

Hedemann, Justus Wilhelm, *Das Volksgesetzbuch der Deutschen. Ein Bericht*, Munich, Beck, 1941.

Heimkehr (Gustav Ucicky), 1941, Tobis and UFA, BA-FA, 10264, 88 min.

Helmut, Otto (ed.), *Volk in Gefahr. Der Geburtenrückgang und seine Folgen für Deutschlands Zukunft*, Munich, Lehmann, 1934.

Heuber, Wilhelm, *Die Paragraphensklaverei und ihr Ende*, Berlin, Nationalsozialistischer Rechtswahrerbund, n.p., n.d., ca. 1937.

Heydrich, Reinhard, "Die Bekämpfung der Staatsfeinde," *Deutsches Recht*, 1936, nos. 7–8, pp. 121–123.

———, Speech, Prague, Oct. 2, 1941, cited in Madajczyk, 1994, p. 21.

Hiemer, Ernst, *Der Giftpilz*, Nuremberg, Der Stürmer Verlag, 1938.

Himmler, Heinrich, Speech, Breslau (Wrocław), Jan. 19, 1935, BABL, NS, 19 1092, p. 5.

———, "Die Pflichten des SS-Mannes und des SS-Führers—Grundsätze über die Heiligkeit des Eigentums," Nov. 9, 1936, BABL, NS, 19 1791.

———, Speech, Dachau, Nov. 8, 1936, cited in Ackermann, 1970.

———, (a) Speech, Bad Tölz, Feb. 18, 1937, BABL, NS, 19 4004.

———, (b) "Plan der Reichsführung SS zur Erschliessung des germanischen Erbes," 1937, BABL, NS, 19 320, fol. 1.

———, (a) Speech delivered at the wedding of Luitpold Schallermeier, Mar. 4, 1937, cited in Ackermann, 1970.

———, (b) "Weltanschauliche Schulung," June 28, 1937, cited in Ackermann, 1970, p. 257.

———, Speech, Plön, Nov. 20, 1938, published in *Das Schwarze Korps*, Nov. 20, 1938, p. 3.

———, Speech, Feb. 29, 1940, cited in Himmler, *Geheimreden*, 1974, pp. 116–130.

———, "Erläuterungen," Mar. 8, 1940, in *Documenta Occupationis teutonicae*, vol. X, pp. 8–11.

———, "Einige Gedanken über die Behandlung der Fremdvölkischen im Osten," May 15, 1940, in Kühnl, 1987, pp. 328ff.

———, "Aussprache des Reichsführers SS und Chef der Deutschen Polizei Heinrich Himmler anlässlich der Besprechung der Kommandeure der Gendarmerie am 17. Januar 1941," BABL, NS, 19 4008, fol. 4.

———, (a) "Der Reichsführer SS vor den Oberabschnittsführern und Hauptamtchefs im Haus der Flieger in Berlin am 9. Juni 1942," BABL, NS, 19 4009, fol. 65.

———, (b) Lecture, delivered at the SS Junkerschule of Bad Tölz, Nov. 23, 1942, BABL, NS, 19 4009.

———, Speech to SS leaders, Kharkov, April 24, 1943, cited in Himmler, *Geheimreden*, 1974, pp. 200–201.

———, (a) Speech, Posen, Oct. 4, 1943, BABL, NS, 19 4010.

———, (b) "Sicherheitsfragen—vortrag, gehalten auf der Befehlshabertagung in Bad Schachen am 14. Oktober 1943," BABL, NS, 19 4008.

———, (c) Speech, Posen, Oct. 24, 1943, BABL, NS, 19 4011.

———, Speech to commanding officers of the Kriegsmarine, Weimar, Dec. 16, 1943, cited in Himmler, *Geheimreden*, 1974.

———, Speech to a group of generals, Sonthofen, June 21, 1944, cited in Himmler, *Discours*, 1978.

———, Speech to the officers of a grenadier division, Bitsch, July 26, 1944, cited in Himmler, *Geheimreden*, 1974.

———, Speech, Grafenwöhr, July 25, 1944, cited in Ackermann, 1970, p. 151.

———, Speech to a group of Gauleiters, Aug. 3, 1944, published in *Vierteljahreshefte für Zeitgeschichte*, no. 1, 1953, pp. 357–394.

———, *Geheimreden 1933 bis 1945 und andere Ansprachen*, ed. Bradley F. Smith and Agnes F. Peterson, Frankfurt, Propyläen Verlag, 1974; in French, *Discours secrets*, translated by M.-M. Husson, Gallimard, "Témoins," 1978.

———, *Dich ruft die SS*, Hauptamt SS, Berlin, Hillger, n.d., BABL, NSD, 41 127.

Hitler, Adolf, *Hitler. Sämtliche Aufzeichnungen, 1905–1924*, ed. E. Jäckel and A. Kuhn, Stuttgart, Deutsche Verlagsanstalt, 1980.

———, Letter to Konstantin Hierl, July 3, 1920, reproduced in ibid.

———, Speech, Apr. 12, 1922, reproduced in Ristow, 1935.

———, Speech, Apr. 17, 1923, cited in Grimm, 1939.

———, *Hitler. Reden, Schriften, Anordnungen. Februar 1925 bis Januar 1933,* 12 vols., Munich, Saur, 1992–2003.

———, "Aussenpolitische Standortsbestimmungen nach der Reichstagswahl Juni–Juli 1928," in ibid., vol. II, A.

———, Speech, Munich, Mar. 12, 1926, cited in Kroll, 1998.

———, *Mein Kampf,* Munich, Zentralverlag der NSDAP, 2 vols., 1926; in English, *Mein Kampf,* translated by James Murphy (London, Hurst and Blackett, 1939).

———, "Der Führer fordert," Jan. 9, 1927, cited in Goebbels et al., 1943.

———, *Hitlers zweites Buch. Ein Dokument aus dem Jahr 1928,* ed. G. L. Weinberg, Stuttgart, Deutsche Verlagsanstalt, 1961.

———, *Hitler. Reden und Proklamationen, 1932–1945,* ed. M. Domarus, Wurtzbourg, Verlagsdruckerei Schmidt, 1962.

———, Speech, Berlin Sportpalast, Feb. 10, 1933, reproduced in ibid.

———, Speech, Mar. 23, 1933, reproduced in ibid.

———, Speech to the Reichstag, Feb. 20, 1938, cited in ibid.

———, Speech delivered at the Nuremberg Rally, Sept. 12, 1938, ibid.

———, Speech to the Reichstag, Jan. 30, 1939, cited in ibid.

———, Speech to the Reichstag, Apr. 28, 1939, ibid.

———, "Beseitigung der lebendigen Kräfte Polens," Aug. 22, 1939, Halder notes, ibid.

———, Remarks made on Aug. 22, 1939, ibid., p. 1238.

———, Speech to the Reichstag, Sept. 1, 1939, cited in ibid.

———, "Vernichtung der Lebenskraft Russlands," July 31, 1940, Halder notes, cited in ibid., p. 1238.

———, Speech to the Borsig-Werken Company, Berlin, Dec. 10, 1940, reproduced in ibid.

———, Speech, Nov. 8, 1943, cited in ibid.

———, Speech, Jan. 30, 1944, ibid.

———, "Schlussansprache des Führers vor dem Parteikongress," *Völkischer Beobachter,* Sept. 11, 1934.

———, Speech to the Reichstag, Jan. 30, 1937, in *Stenographische Berichte über die Verhandlungen des Deutschen Reichstag,* 1937, vol. 459, pp. 2–17.

———, Interview with the *Daily Mail,* cited in the *Völkischer Beobachter,* Sept. 20, 1938.

———, Speech, Mar. 30, 1941, cited in Halder, 1963, vol. II, pp. 335ff.

———, *Hitlers Tischgespräche im Führerhauptquartier: 1941–1942,* ed. H. Picker, 1951; reprint Stuttgart, Seewald, 1976.

———, Private conversation, evening of Apr. 15, 1942, cited in ibid.

———, Speech, May 12, 1942, reproduced in ibid.

———, Speech to *Wehrmacht* officer cadets, Berlin Sportpalast, May 30, 1942, reproduced in ibid.

———, *Adolf Hitler. Monologe im Führerhauptquartier, 1941–1944. Die Aufzeichnungen Heinrich Heims,* ed. W. Jochmann, Hamburg, Knaus, 1980.

——, Private conversation, Sept. 17, 1941, cited in ibid.

——, Private conversation, Oct. 14, 1941, ibid.

——, Private conversation, night of Oct. 14–15, 1941, ibid.

——, Private conversation, Oct. 17, 1941, ibid.

——, Private conversation, Oct. 21, 1941, ibid.

——, Private conversation, Dec. 1, 1941, ibid.

——, Private conversation, Nov. 30, 1944, ibid.

——, Speech, Berlin, February 15, 1942, reproduced in Kotze and Krausnick, 1966.

——, Speech to the Reichstag, Apr. 26, 1942, reproduced in Kaden et al. (ed.), vol. I, 1993.

——, Decree, Dec. 16, 1942, cited in Kaden et al. (ed), vol. III, 1993.

——, Interview with Admiral Horthy, Apr. 18, 1943, in Kaden et al. (ed), vol. III, 1993.

Höhn, Reinhard, *Rechtsgemeinschaft und Volksgemeinschaft*, Hamburg, Hanseatische Verlagsanstalt, 1935.

——, "Altes und neues Polizeirecht," in Best et al., 1936, pp. 21–34.

——, "Volk, Staat und Recht," in Höhn, Reinhard, Theodor Maunz, and Ernst Swoboda, *Grundfragen der Rechtsauffassung*, Munich, Duncker & Humblot, 1938, pp. 1–29.

Holzner, Anton, *Das Gesetz Gottes*, Berlin, Nordland, 1939.

——, *Ewige Front*, Berlin, Nordland, 1940.

——, *Zwinge das Leben* (*Ewige Front*, II), Berlin, Nordland, 1941.

Höss, Rudolf, *Kommandant in Auschwitz. Autobiographische Auszeichnungen von Rudolf Höss*, Stuttgart, Deutsche Verlagsanstalt, 1958.

Hüttig, Werner, "Rasse und Raum," *Neues Volk*, 1937, no. 9, pp. 33–35.

Ich klage an (Wolfgang Liebeneiner), 1941, Tobis, BA-FA, 10298, 120 min.

"Im Osten wächst neues Volk auf neuem Land. Umsiedlung und Ansiedlung im Zusammenklang," *SS-Leitheft* 6, no. 2b, [1941], pp. 2–6.

"Ist das Nacktkultur?" *Das Schwarze Korps*, Apr. 24, 1935, p. 12.

"Jason und Medea. Die Tragödie der rassischen Mischehe," *SS-Leitheft*, no. 6 a, 1941, pp. 18–20.

Jess, Friedrich, *Rassenkunde und Rassenpflege*, Dortmund, Grüwell, 1935.

——, (a) "Gleichheits- und Verschiedenheitslehre im Lichte der Erblichkeitsgesetze," *Neues Volk*, 1936, no. 2, pp. 6–7.

——, (b) "Gleichheits- und Freiheitswahn," *Neues Volk*, 1936, no. 4, pp. 40–41.

"Jud bleibt immer Jud," *Das Schwarze Korps*, May 26, 1938, p. 10.

Jüdische Moral, Schriftenreihe zur weltanschaulichen Schulungsarbeit der NSDAP, Amt Parteiamtliche Lehrmittel, no. 20, 1943, BABL, RD NSD, 16 31–20.

Kaden, Helma et al. (ed.), *Dokumente des Verbrechens*, 3 vols.: vol. I, *Schlüsseldokumente*; vol. II, *1933-May 1941*; vol. III, *Juni 1941–1945*, Berlin, Dietz, 1993.

"Kampfanweisung für die Bandenbekämpfung im Osten" [Instructions for the fight against gangs in the East], Nov. 11, 1942, cited in Klee and Dressen, 1989.

Kampf dem Bolschewismus. 28 Fragen und Antworten über den Bolschewismus, Reichsführer SS—SS-Hauptamt, n.p., n.d., BABL, RD NSD, 41 96.

Kampf dem Fleckfieber! 1942, Heeres-Filmstelle, Forschungsgruppe der Militärärztlichen Akademie, BA-FA, 14552 1–4, 32 min.

Keitel, Wilhelm, "Befehl vom GFM Wilhelm Keitel zur Unterdrückung der Zivilbevölkerung in den okkupierten Ländern," Sept. 16, 1941, cited in Kaden et al. (ed.), 1993, vol. I, p. 146.

———, "Befehl von GFM Wilhelm Keitel über die Sippenhaftung gegen Familienangehörige von überläufern aus der Truppe," Nov. 19, 1944, cited in Kaden et al. (ed.), 1993, vol. I, p. 256.

———, "Befehl vom GFM Wilhelm Keitel zur standrechtlichen Erschiessung versprengter deutscher Soldaten," Mar. 1945, cited in Kaden et al. (ed.), 1993, vol. I, p. 259.

"Kennt Ihr den Feind?" 1941, cited in Überschär and Wette, 1984.

Klee, Ernst, and Willi Dressen, *"Gott mit uns." Der deutsche Vernichtungskrieg im Osten, 1939–1945,* Frankfurt, Fischer, 1989.

Koeppe, Wilhelm, decree, June 28, 1944, cited in Kaden et al. (ed.), 1993, vol. I, p. 250, and vol. III, p. 216.

Kopp, Friedrich, and Eduard Schulte, *Der westfälische Frieden. Vorgeschichte, Verhandlungen, Folgen,* Munich, Hoheneichen, 1943.

Korte, Heinrich, *Lebensrecht und völkerrechtliche Ordnung,* Berlin, Duncker & Humblot, 1942.

Krieck, "Philosophie," in Wilhelm Pinder and Alfred Stange, *Deutsche Wissenschaft. Arbeit und Aufgabe,* Leipzig, Hirzel, 1939, pp. 29–31.

Kroll, Werner, "Jüdische Wunderdoktoren entlarvt! Das jüdische Ferment der Zersetzung in den Heilberufen," in Walbaum (ed.), 1941.

Kummer, Bernhard, *Midgards Untergang. Germanischer Kult und Glaube in den letzten heidnischen Jahrhunderten,* Leipzig, Klein, 1935.

Künssberg, Eberhard Freiherr von, *Rechtliche Volkskunde,* Halle, Max Niemeyer Verlag, 1936.

Küppers, Hans, and Rudolf Bannier (a), *Arbeitsrecht der Polen im Deutschen Reich,* Berlin, Otto Elsner Verlagsgesellschaft, 1942.

———(b), *Einsatzbedingungen der Ostarbeiter, sowie der sowjetrussischen Kriegsgefangenen,* Berlin, Reichsarbeitsblatt—Sonderveröffentlichung, 1942.

Kurzthemen zu. Der Schicksalskampf im Osten, Schulungsunterlage, no. 15, Der Reichsorganisationsleiter der NSDAP, Hauptschulungsamt, 1942, BABL, RD NSD, 9 33–15.

Kynast, Karl, *Apollon und Dionysos. Nordisches und Unnordisches innerhalb der Religion der Griechen. Eine rassenkundliche Untersuchung,* Munich, Lehmann, 1927.

Lange, Heinrich, *Liberalismus, Nationalsozialismus und bürgerliches Recht,* Tübingen, Mohr, 1933.

Larenz, Karl, *Rechtserneuerung und Rechtsphilosophie,* Tübingen, Mohr, 1934.

———, *Über Gegenstand und Methode des völkischen Rechtsdenkens,* Berlin, Junker & Dünnhaupt, 1938.

Leers, Johann von, (a) *Blut und Rasse in der Gesetzgebung. Ein Gang durch die Völkergeschichte*, Munich, Lehmann, 1936.

———, (b) "Die Kriminalität des Judentums," in Schmitt (ed.), 1936, pp. 5–60.

———, *Deutsche Rechtsgeschichte und deutsches Rechtsdenken*, Berlin, Deutscher Rechtsverlag, 1939.

———, "Haben die verschiedenen Rassen ein verschiedenes Rechtsempfinden?" *Volk und Rasse*, 1941, pp. 12–14.

Lehmann, Ernst, "Biologie und Weltanschauung," *Der Biologe*, 1937, no. 11, pp. 337–341.

Lehrplan für die weltanschauliche Erziehung in der SS und Polizei, SS-Hauptamt, n.p., n.d., BABL, RD NSD, 41 61.

Leitpoldt, Johannes, *Jesu Verhältnis zu Griechen und Juden*, Leipzig, Wigand, 1941.

Lenz, Fritz, *Die Rasse als Wertprinzip. Zur Erneuerung der Ethik*, Munich, Lehmann, 1933.

Ley, Robert, Speech, Sept. 3, 1941, cited in Herf [2006] 2011, p. 145.

———, Speech, Amsterdam, May 10, 1942, cited in Herf [2006] 2011, p. 145.

Lichtbildvortrag. Judentum, Freimaurei, Bolschewismus, vol. 3: *Der Bolschewismus: ein Werkzeug des Judentums*, Berlin, Rasse- und Siedlungshauptamt der SS, n.d., BABL, RD NSD, 41 88, 1–3.

Lippe, Friedrich Wilhelm Prinz zur, *Aufbruch des Nordens*, Leipzig, Klein, 1933.

Lüdtke, Franz, *Ein Jahrtausend Krieg zwischen Deutschland und Polen*, Stuttgart, Lutz, 1941.

Luetgebrune, Walter, "Volksgeist und neues Recht," *Zeitschrift der Akademie für deutsches Recht*, 1934.

Mäding, Erhard, *Regeln für die Gestaltung der Landschaft. Einführung in die Allgemeine Anordnung Nr. 20/VI/42 des Reichsführers SS, Reichskommissars für die Festigung deutschen Volkstums, über die Gestaltung der Landschaft in den eingegliederten Ostgebieten*, Berlin, Deutsche Landbuchhandlung, 1943.

Mayer, Joseph, *Gesetzliche Unfruchtbarmachung Geisteskranker*, Frieburg, Herder, 1927.

Mehlis, Georg, *Führer und Volksgemeinschaft*, Berlin, Junker & Dünnhaupt, 1941.

Meisinger, Josef, "Bekämpfung der Abtreibung und Homosexualität als politische Aufgabe," Berlin, Apr. 6, 1937, cited in Grau (ed.), 1993, pp. 147–153.

Merk, Walther, *Vom Werden und Wesen des deutschen Rechts*, Langensalza, Beyer & Söhne, 1935.

"Merkblatt für Arbeitskräfte aus den besetzten altsowjetrussischen Gebieten," n.p., n.d.

"Merkblatt für die Bewachung sowjetischer Kriegsgefangener," Oberkommander der Wehrmacht, Sept. 8, 1941, cited in Überschär and Wette, 1984.

"Merkpunkte aus der Chefbesprechung in Orscha am 13.11.1941," cited in Überschär and Wette, 1984.

Meyer, Hermann, (a) *Der deutsche Mensch. Völkische Weltanschauung und Deutsche Volksgemeinschaft*, vol. I: *Völkische Weltanschauung*, Munich, Lehmann, 1925.

————, (b) Ibid., vol. II: *Deutsche Volksgemeinschaft*, Munich, Lehmann, 1925.

Meyer, Konrad, "Siedlungs- und Aufbauarbeit im deutschen Osten," *Die Bewegung*, 1941, no. 8.

————, "Generalplan Ost. Rechtliche, wirtschaftliche und räumliche Grundlagen des Ostaufbaues," June 1942, BABL, R, 49 157a, fols. 1–84.

Mezger, Edmund, "Die Biologie im neuen deutschen Strafrecht," *Der Biologe*, 1935, no. 12, pp. 388–393.

"Mitteilungsblätter für die weltanschauliche Schulung der Ordnungspolizei," Herausgegeben vom Befehlshaber der Ordnungspolizei in Münster (Westfalen), Gruppe B, Feb. 20, 1943, vol. 27–28, p. 7.

————, ibid., May 1, 1944, vol. 42.

"Natur," *Der neue Brockhaus*, Leipzig, F. A. Brockhaus Verlag, 1938, vol. III, p. 346.

Neues Volk. Blätter des rassenpolitischen Amtes der NSDAP, Berlin, Verlag Neues Volk, 1933–1944.

Nicolai, Helmut, *Die rassengesetzliche Rechtslehre. Grundzüge einer nationalsozialistischen Rechtsphilosophie*, Munich, Eher, 1932.

Oetker, Friedrich, "Grundprobleme der nationalsozialistischen Strafrechtsreform," in Frank (ed.), 1935, pp. 1317–1361.

"Ordensgemeinschaft," *SS-Leitheft*, no. 2, 1943, pp. 1–5.

"Pflichten der Zivilarbeiter und arbeiterinnen polnischen Volkstums während ihres Aufenthalts im Reich," Reichsführer SS, Mar. 8, 1940.

Planung und Aufbau im Osten. Erläuterungen und Skizzen zum ländlichen Aufbau in den neuen Ostgebieten, Der Reichskommissar für die Festigung deutschen Volkstums, Stabshauptamt, Berlin, Deutsche Landbuchhandlung, 1942, BABL, R, 49 157, fols. 47–73.

Politische Biologie. Schriften für naturgesetzliche Politik und Wissenschaft, Munich, Lehmann, 1936–1940.

"Polizeiverordnung über die Kenntlichmachung der im Reich eingesetzten Zivilarbeiter und -arbeiterinnen polnischen Volkstums," *Reichsgesetzblatt*, 1940, vol. I, p. 555.

"Prag-Karthago," *Völkischer Beobachter*, Sept. 23, 1938, p. 7.

"Rasse, Glaube, Bekenntnis," *Das Schwarze Korps*, July 17, 1935.

Rasse und Recht. Monatsschrift herausgegeben von Dr Erich Ristow, Stuttgart, Kohlhammer, 1937–1938.

Rauchhaupt, Friedrich Wilhelm von, (a) "Leitgedanken des deutschen Wehrrechts," *Deutsches Recht*, 1936, pp. 401–406.

————, (b) *Völkerrecht*, Munich et Leipzig, Voglrieder, 1936.

Rauschning, Hermann, *Gespräche mit Hitler*, Zurich, Europa-Verlag, 1940.

Recht der Rasse. Monatsschrift herausgegeben von Dr Falk Ruttke und Dr Erich Ristow, Stuttgart, Kohlhammer, 1935.

"Regelung des Einsatzes der Sicherheitspolizei und des SD im Verbande des Heeres," Apr. 28, 1941, cited in Überschär and Wette, 1984.

Reier, Herbert, *Volk, Richter und Führung im germanischen Staat. Vortrag, gehalten in der rechtswissenschaftlichen Arbeitsgemeinschaft im NS-Juristenbund, Abteilung Jungjuristen*, Berlin, Klein, 1935.

Reiter, Hans, "Nationalsozialistische Revolution in Medizin und Gesundheitspolitik," *Neues Volk*, 1933, no. 10, pp. 3–5 and 28.

Rendulic, Lothar, Oct. 29, 1944, order to the 20th Mountain Army, cited in Kaden et al. (ed.), 1993, vol. III, p. 239.

"Richtlinien auf Sondergebieten zur Weisung Nr. 21 (Fall Barbarossa) vom 13.3.1941, Oberkommando der Wehrmacht, Feldmarschall Keitel" [1941], cited in Überschär and Wette, 1984.

"Richtlinien für das Verhalten der Truppe in Russland," May 19, 1941, cited in Überschär and Wette, 1984.

"Richtlinien für die Behandlung politischer Kommissare," known as the "Kommissarbefehl," Oberkommando der Wehrmacht, June 6, 1941, cited in Kaden et al. (ed.), 1993.

"Richtlinien für die verstärkte Bekämpfung des Bandenunwesens im Osten," Oberkommando des Heeres, Nov. 11, 1942, cited in Überschär and Wette, 1984.

"Richtlinien über die Führung von Vornamen, Reichsministerium des Innern, Runderlass," *Ministerialblatt des Reichs- und Preussischen Ministeriums des Innern*, Aug. 18, 1938, pp. 1345–1348.

Ristow, Erich, "Der Führer über Staat und Recht," *Recht der Rasse*, 1935, pp. 23–29.

Ritter, Robert, *Ein Menschenschlag. Erbärztliche und erbgeschichtliche Untersuchungen über die—durch 10 Geschlechterfolgen erforschten—Nachkommen von Vagabunden, Jaunern und Räubern*, Leipzig, Thieme, 1937.

———, "Das Kriminalbiologische Institut der Sicherheitspolizei," *Kriminalistik*, 1942.

Rogge, Heinrich, *Hitlers Friedenspolitik und das Völkerrecht*, Berlin, Schlieffen Verlag, 1935.

———, "Recht und Moral eines Friedensvertrages," *Völkerbund und Völkerrecht*, 1936–1937, pp. 736–742.

———, "Der deutsche Kriegsbegriff," *Zeitschrift der Akademie für deutsches Recht*, 1940, pp. 277–279.

Roques, Karl von (General), "Einsatz Jugendlicher zu Erkundungszwecken durch die Russen," Jan. 13, 1942, cited in Überschär and Wette, 1984.

Rosenberg, Alfred, *Der Mythus des 20. Jahrhunderts*, Munich, Hoheneichen, 1930.

———, "Mark gleich Mark, Mensch gleich Mensch," *Völkischer Beobachter*, Aug. 26, 1932, pp. 1–2.

———, "Deutsches Recht," Lecture, Berlin Sportpalast, Dec. 18, 1934, by invitation of the Nationalsozialistische Kulturgemeinde and the Bund Nationalsozialistischer Juristen, reprinted in *Gestaltung der Idee (Blut und Ehre II)— Reden und Aufsätze der Jahre 1933–1935*, Munich, Franz Eher Verlag, 1936, pp. 222–234.

———, "Eine neue deutsche Rechtsphilosophie," *Zeitschrift der Akademie für deutsches Recht*, 1934, pp. 47–48.

———, Speech to the "Bremer Tagung des Reichsbundes für Vorgeschichte," Sept. 28, 1935, reprinted in the *Völkischer Beobachter*, Jan. 30, 1935.

———, Lecture to a conference of prehistorians, Lübeck, Oct. 1936, reprinted in the *Völkischer Beobachter*, Oct. 19, 1936.

———, "Eine Abrechnung mit den Ideen von 1789—Rede, gehalten in der französischen Abgeordnetenkammer am 28. November 1940," *Völkischer Beobachter*, Nov. 29, 1940, pp. 1 and 4.

Rossner, Ferdinand, "Rasse als Lebensgesetz," in Walter Kopp, *Rassenpolitik im Kriege. Eine Gemeinschaftsarbeit aus Forschung und Praxis*, Hanover, Schaper, 1941, pp. 65–82.

———, *Rasse und Religion*, Hanover, Schaper, 1942.

Rüdin, Ernst (ed.), *Rassenhygiene im völkischen Staat. Tatsachen und Richtlinien*, Munich, Lehmann, 1934.

———, "Aufgaben und Ziele der deutschen Gesellschaft für Rassenhygiene," *Volk und Rasse*, 1937, pp. 132–138.

Ruttke, Falk, "Rassenhygiene und Recht," in Rüdin (ed.), 1934, pp. 91–103; reprint in Ruttke, 1937.

———, "Volkspflege," *Recht der Rasse*, 1935, pp. 14–21.

———, *Rasse, Recht und Volk. Beiträge zur rassengesetzlichen Rechtslehre*, Munich, Lehmann, 1937.

———, *Die Verteidigung der Rasse durch das Recht*, Berlin, Junker & Dünnhaupt, 1939.

Sauckel, Fritz, speech, Jan. 6, 1943, cited in Überschär and Wette, 1984, pp. 380–382.

Schadewaldt, Hans, *Les Atrocités commises par les Polonais contre les Allemands de Pologne. Document rédigé et publié sur l'ordre du ministère des Affaires étrangères du Reich, avec pièces authentiques à l'appui*, Berlin, Volk & Reich Verlag, 1940.

Schesmer, Ekkehard, *Die Lehre von der "clausula rebus sic stantibus" und das heutige Völkerrecht*, Düsseldorf, Nolte, 1934.

Schieder, Theodor, "Aufzeichnung über Siedlungs- und Volkstumsfragen in den wiedergewonnenen Ostprovinzen—erster Entwurf, 7.10.1939," cited in Ebbinghaus and Roth, 1992, pp. 84–91.

Schilling, Kurt, *Geschichte der Staats- und Rechtsphilosophie. Im Überblick von den Griechen bis zur Gegenwart*, Berlin, Junker & Dünnhaupt, 1937.

Schmitt, Carl, *Frieden oder Pazifismus? Arbeiten zum Völkerrecht und zur internationalen Politik, 1924–1978*, Berlin, Duncker & Humblot, 2005.

———, (a) *Nationalsozialismus und Völkerrecht*, Berlin, Junker & Dünnhaupt, 1934.

———, (b) *Über die drei Arten des rechtswissenschaftlichen Denkens*, Hamburg, Hanseatische Verlagsanstalt, 1934; in English, *On the Three Types of Juristic Thought*, translated by Joseph W. Bendersky, Westport, Prager Publishers, 2004, pp. 43–49.

———, "Der Führer schützt das Recht" [1934], in *Positionen und Begriffe*, 1940, pp. 199–203.

———, "Paktsysteme als Kriegsrüstung. Eine völkerrechtliche Betrachtung" [1935], in *Frieden oder Pazifismus?* [1924–1978], 2005, pp. 436–439.

———, "Vergleichender überblick über die neueste Entwicklung des Problems der gesetzgeberischen Ermächtigungen: 'Legislative Delegationen'" [1936], in *Positionen und Begriffe*, 1940, pp. 214–234.

————, "Totaler Feind, totaler Krieg, totaler Staat" [1937], in *Positionen und Begriffe*, 1940, pp. 235–239.

————, (a) "Der Reichsbegriff im Völkerrecht" [1939], in *Positionen und Begriffe*, 1940, pp. 303–312; English translations cited in Legg, Stephen (ed.), *Spatiality, Sovereignty, and Carl Schmitt: Geographies of the Nomos*, London, Routledge, 2011, pp. 46–48, 52, and 116; and in Minca, Claudio, and Rory Rowan, *On Schmitt and Space*, London, Routledge, 2015, p. 179.

————, (b) "Grossraum gegen Universalismus. Der völkerrechtliche Kampf um die Monroe-Doktrin" [1939], in *Positionen und Begriffe*,1940, pp. 295–302.

————, *Völkerrechtliche Grossraumordnung mit Interventionsverbot für raumfremde Mächte. Ein Beitrag zum Reichsbegriff im Völkerrecht*, Berlin, Deutscher Rechtsverlag, 1939.

————, *Positionen und Begriffe. Im Kampf mit Weimar-Genf-Versailles, 1923–1939*, Hamburg, Hanseatische Verlagsantalt, 1940.

————, (ed.), *Das Judentum in der Rechtswissenschaft. Ansprachen, Vorträge und Ergebnisse der Tagung der Reichsgruppe Hochschullehrer des NSRB am 3. und 4. Oktober 1936*, Berlin, Deutscher Rechtsverlag, 1936.

————, (a) "Eröffnung der wissenschaftlichen Vorträge durch den Reichsgruppenwalter Staatsrat Prof. Dr Carl Schmitt," in Schmitt (ed.), *Das Judentum in der Rechtswissenschaft*, 1936.

————, (b) "Schlusswort des Reichsgruppenwalters Staatsrat Prof. Dr Carl Schmitt," in Schmitt (ed.), *Das Judentum in der Rechtswissenschaft*, 1936, pp. 28–35.

Schmitz-Ost, Udo, "Das Institut der *clausula rebus sic stantibus* als Ausdruck zwischenstaatlicher Dynamik in politischen Verträgen," doctoral thesis, University of Heidelberg, 1941.

Schoetensack, August, *Grundfragen des neuen Strafverfahrensrecht. Denkschrift des Ausschusses für Strafprozessrecht der Strafrechtsabteilung der Akademie für deutsches Recht*, Stuttgart, Kohlhammer, 1937.

Schroer, Hermann, "Das Verhältnis des Juden zum Gesetz," in Schmitt (ed.), 1936, pp. 18–25.

Schuchmann, Walther, *Die Lehre von der "clausula rebus sic stantibus" und ihr Verhältnis zu Art. XIX des Völkerbundpaktes*, Düsseldorf, Nolte, 1936.

Schulungs-Leitheft für SS-Führeranwärter der Sicherheitspolizei und des SD, Berlin, Document Center Library Collection, n.p., n.d., probably 1941, A3345-B, microfilm, reel 127, images 269–332, BABL, RD, 19 11.

Schwarz, Josef, "Lichtsehnsucht und Sonnesglück," *Deutsche Leibeszucht. Blätter für naturnahe und arteigene Lebensgestaltung*, Berlin, Leibeszucht, July 1940, p. 477.

Seemann, Friedrich, "Die *clausula rebus sic stantibus* als völkerrechtliche Revisionsnorm," doctoral thesis Göttingen, 1939.

"Sieh dich vor!" [1941], cited in Heer (ed.), 1995, p. 65.

Sigrune. Blätter für nordische Art, Erfurt, Verlag Sigrune, 1933–1944.

Six, Franz-Alfred (ed.), *Der westfälische Friede von 1648. Deutsche Textausgabe der Friedensverträge von Münster und Osnabrück*, Berlin, Junker & Dünnhaupt, 1942.

Sonder, Ulrich, "Der natürliche Mensch," *Deutsche Leibeszucht. Blätter für naturnahe und arteigene Lebensgestaltung*, Apr. 1942, p. 45.

Speer, Albert, *Erinnerungen*, Berlin, Propyläen, 1969.

———, *Spandauer Tagebücher*, Berlin, Propyläen, 1975.

SS-Handblätter für den weltanschaulichen Unterricht, "Thema 1—Allein die nationalsozialistische Weltanschauung sichert uns ein artgemässes Leben," n.p., n.d.

———, "Thema 2—Gesetze des Lebens. Grundlage unserer Weltanschauung," n.p., n.d.

———, "Thema 3—Wir kämpfen für die Ewigkeit unseres Volkes," n.p., n.d.

Staemmler, Martin, *Rassenpflege im völkischen Staat. Ein Mahnruf an alle, die sich mitverantwortlich fühlen für die Zukunft unseres Volkes* [1933], Munich, Lehmann, 1939.

Steinhoff, Hans, *Robert Koch, Bekämpfer des Todes*, 1939, Tobis, BA-FA, 187456, 113 min.

Stengel von Rutkowski, Lothar, "Der Weg zur lebensgesetzlichen Schule," *Volk und Rasse*, 1935, pp. 163–169.

———, *Das Reich dieser Welt. Lieder und Verse eines Heiden*, Erfurt, Wölund, 1937.

———, "Kritische Bemerkungen zu dem Buch von Werner Sombart: 'vom Menschen,'" *Der Biologe*, 1939, no. 5, pp. 187–189.

———, "Die Frage der Willensfreiheit vom Standpunkt der Kulturbiologie," *Der Biologe*, 1940, nos. 7–8, pp. 213–221.

———, "Weltbild und Weltanschauung," in Stengel von Rutkowski (ed.), *Das naturgesetzliche Weltbild*, 1941, pp. 7–21.

———, *Was ist ein Volk? Der biologische Volksbegriff. Eine kulturbiologische Untersuchung seiner Definition und seiner Bedeutung für Wissenschaft, Weltanschauung und Politik*, Erfurt, Stenger, 1943.

———, (ed.), *Das naturgesetzliche Weltbild der Gegenwart*, Berlin, Nordland, 1941.

Stier, Günther, *Das Recht als Kampfordnung der Rasse*, Berlin, Heymann, 1934.

Stöpel, Joachim, *Über den altindischen Tierschutz*, Leipzig, Edelmann, 1939.

Streim, Alfred, *Sowjetische Gefangene in Hitlers Vernichtungskrieg. Berichte und Dokumente, 1941–1945*, Heidelberg, Müller, 1981.

Tatarin-Tarnheyden, Edgar, *Werdendes Staatsrecht. Gedanken zu einem organischen und deutschen Verfassungsneubau*, Berlin, Heymann, 1934.

———, *Völkerrecht und organische Staatsauffassung*, Berlin, Verlag für Staatswissenschaften und Geschichte, 1936.

Tesmer, Hans-Joachim, "Die Schutzhaft und ihre rechtlichen Grundlagen," *Deutsches Recht*, 1936, nos. 7–8, pp. 135–142.

Thierack, Otto, "Dr Thierack an die deutschen Richter," *Völkischer Beobachter*, Sept. 1, 1942.

———, "Richterbrief," *Mitteilung der Reichsministers der Justiz*, no. 4, Jan. 1, 1943, reproduced in Boberach (ed.), 1975, pp. 51–58.

———, "Die Strafrechtspflege im fünften Kriegsjahr," n.p., n.d, BABL, R, 3001–4692, fols. 1–3, fol. 2, cited in Schädler, 2009, p. 266, n. 16.

Tirala, Lothar Gottlieb, "Die biologische Erneuerung des deutschen Volkes," *Volk und Rasse*, 1933, pp. 114–115.

Trampler, Kurt, *Volk ohne Grenzen. Mitteleuropa im Zeichen der Deutschenverfolgung*, Berlin, Verlag Grenze und Ausland, 1934.

———, *Deutschösterreich, 1918/19. Ein Kampf um Selbstbestimmung*, Berlin, Heymanns, 1935.

Um das Menschenrecht (Hans Zöberlein), 1934, Arya-Film GmbH, BA-FA, BSP, 1936, 82 min.

"Unsere Härte," *SS-Leitheft*, no. 1, 1943, pp. 1–3.

"Unser revolutionärer Wille," *SS-Leitheft*, 1943, pp. 1–2.

Valentiner, Theodor, "Die seelischen Ursachen des Geburtenrückganges," *Politische Biologie*, no. 2, 1937.

"Verordnung über Reisepässe von Juden," Oct. 5, 1938, *Reichsgesetzblatt*, vol. I, 1938, p. 1342.

"Verwirrung im Blut," II. "Artfremde Moral," *Das Schwarze Korps*, June 13, 1939, booklet 24, p. 13.

———, IV. "Diesseits und Jenseits," *Das Schwarze Korps*, June 29, 1939, booklet 26, p. 11.

Vesper, Wilhelm, *Das harte Geschlecht*, Hamburg, Hanseatische Verlagsanstalt, 1931.

Viergutz, Rudolf, *Über Grundfragen der Religion zugleich Voraussetzungen werdender deutscher Volksreligion*, Leipzig, Klein, 1944.

Völkerbund und Völkerrecht, ed. C. von Freytag-Loringhoven, Berlin, Heymanns, 1934–1938.

Volk und Rasse. Illustrierte Monatsschrift für deutsches Volkstum, Rassenkunde, Rassenpflege, Munich, Lehmann, 1933–1945.

Volkmar, Erich, (a) "Das dynamische Element bei der Neubildung des deutschen Rechts," *Zeitschrift der Akademie für deutsches Recht*, 1935, pp. 472–480.

———, (b) "Dynamik im Recht? Hat die Unterscheidung von statischer und dynamischer Rechtsauffassung im nationalsozialistischen Staat noch eine Bedeutung?" *Zeitschrift der Akademie für deutsches Recht*, 1935, pp. 691–692.

"Vollstreckung von Todesstrafen an sowjetischen Kriegsgefangenen," Oberkommander der Wehrmacht, Dec. 29, 1941, cited in Überschär and Wette, 1984.

Wagner, Gerhard, "Arzt und Volk im Dritten Reich," 1933, reproduced in *Reden und Aufrufe*, 1943, pp. 12–17.

———, "Das Gesundheitswesen im Dritten Reich," May 27, 1934, reproduced in *Reden und Aufrufe*, 1943, pp. 31–47.

———, Speech to the Nuremberg Reichsparteitag, Sept. 1935, reproduced in *Reden und Aufrufe*, 1943, pp. 100–120.

———, Speech to the Nuremberg Reichsparteitag, Sept. 1936, reproduced in *Reden und Aufrufe*, 1943.

———, "Gesundes Leben—Frohes Schaffen," speech, Berlin, Sept. 24, 1938, reproduced in *Reden und Aufrufe*, 1943, pp. 269–285.

———, *Reden und Aufrufe. Gerhard Wagner, 1888–1939*, ed. Leonardo Conti, Berlin, Reichsgesundheitsverlag, 1943.

Walbaum, Jost (ed.), *Kampf den Seuchen! Deutscher Ärzte-Einsatz im Osten. Die Aufbauarbeit im Gesundheitswesen des Generalgouvernements*, Krakau (Kraków), "Deutscher Osten" Verlag, 1941.

Walz, Gustav Adolf, "Minderheitenrecht oder Volksgruppenrecht?" *Völkerbund und Völkerrecht*, 1936–1937, pp. 594–600.

——, *Artgleichheit gegen Gleichartigkeit. Die beiden Grundprobleme des Rechts*, Hamburg, Hanseatische Verlagsanstalt, 1938.

——, *Völkerrechtsordnung und Nationalsozialismus*, Munich, Eher, 1942.

"Warnung vor heimtückischer Sowjetkriegsführung," 1941, cited in Überschär and Wette, 1984.

"Warum wird über das Judentum geschult?" *SS-Leitheft*, no. 3, 1936, pp. 7–11.

"Was wir wollen," *Recht der Rasse*, 1935, pp. 1–2.

Wegner, Arthur, *Geschichte des Völkerrechts*, Stuttgart, Kohlhammer, 1936.

Weitzel, Fritz, *Die Gestaltung der Feste im Jahres- und Lebenslauf in der SS-Familie*, Wuppertal, Völkischer Verlag, 1940.

Werner, Manfred, *Natur und Sünde. Eine Studie zu der angeblichen* anima naturaliter christiana *an Hand der grönländischen Missionsgeschichte*, Leipzig, Klein, 1934.

Werner, Paul, "Begründung" (draft), Mar. 17, 1944, cited in Ayass, 1998.

"Wer sind die Asozialen?" Parteikanzlei der NSDAP, Munich, June 25, 1942, reproduced in Ayass, 1998, pp. 310–311.

"Widernatürliche Unzucht ist todeswürdig," *Das Schwarze Korps*, May 22, 1935, p. 13.

Wiepking-Jürgensmann, Heinrich, "Deutsche Landschaft als deutsche Ostaufgabe," *Neues Bauerntum*, 1940, pp. 132–135.

Wissmann, Herbert, *Revisionsprobleme des Diktats von Versailles*, Berlin, Verlag für Staatswissenschaften und Geschichte, 1936.

"Woran sterben Völker? Auslese und Gegenauslese," *SS-Leitheft*, no. 3, 1939, pp. 15–21.

"Zehn Gebote für die Gattenwahl," n.p., n.d, Rassenpolitisches Amt der NSDAP, Reichsausschuss für Volksgesundheitsdienst, Reichsministerium des Innern.

"Zehn Gebote gegen die Ruhr," cited in Walbaum (ed.), 1941, pp. 31–32.

Zeitschrift der Akademie für deutsches Recht, Munich, Beck, 1936–1945.

Zeitschrift für die gesamte Staatswissenschaft, Tübingen, Mohr, 1933–1945.

Zeitschrift für Wehrrecht, Berlin, Schweitzer, 1936–1944.

Zschucke, Otto, "Das Wehrrecht, sein Wesen, sein Inhalt und seine Gliederung," *Zeitschrift der Akademie für deutsches Recht*, 1944, pp. 170–172.

"Zweck und Gliederung des Konzentrationslagers," *Dienstvorschrift für Konzentrationslager (Lagerordnung)*, Berlin, Reichsicherheitshauptamt, 1941.

"Zweierlei Recht," *Das Schwarze Korps*, Apr. 17, 1935.

Secondary Sources

Ackermann, Josef, *Heinrich Himmler als Ideologe*, Göttingen, Musterschmidt, 1970.

Aly, Götz, and Susanne Heim, *Vordenker der Vernichtung. Auschwitz und die deutschen Pläne für eine neue europäische Ordnung*, Frankfurt, Fischer, 1993.

Ayass, Wolfgang, *"Gemeinschaftsfremde." Quellen zur Verfolgung von Asozialen, 1933–1945,* Coblenz, Bundesarchiv, 1998.

Bartov, Omer, *The Eastern Front 1914–45: German Troops and the Barbarisation of Warfare,* New York, St. Martin's Press, 1986.

——, *L'Armée d'Hitler. La Wehrmacht, les nazis et la guerre,* translated by J.-P. Ricard, Hachette, 1999. [First published in English as *Hitler's Army. Soldiers, Nazis, and the War in the Third Reich,* New York, Oxford University Press, 1991.]

Baumann, Imanuel, *Dem Verbrecher auf der Spur. Eine Geschichte der Kriminologie und Kriminalpolitik in Deutschland, 1880 bis 1980,* Göttingen, Wallstein, 2006.

Bessel, Richard, "The Potempa Murder," *Central European History,* vol. 10, no. 3, 1977, pp. 241–254.

Bialas, Wolfgang, *Moralische Ordnungen des Nationalsozialismus,* Göttingen, Vandenhoeck & Ruprecht, 2014.

Boberach, Heinz (ed.), *Richterbriefe. Dokumente zur Beeinflussung der deutschen Rechtssprechung, 1942–1944,* Boppard, Boldt, 1975.

Böhler, Jochen, *Der Überfall. Deutschlands Krieg gegen Polen,* Frankfurt, Eichborn, 2009.

Broszat, Martin et al., *Anatomie des SS-Staates, II. Konzentrationslager, Kommissarbefehl, Judenverfolgung,* Olten, Walter-Verlag, 1965.

Browning, Christopher R., *Ordinary Men: Reserve Police Battalion 101 and the Final Solution in Poland,* New York, HarperCollins, 1992; in French, *Des hommes ordinaires. Le 101e bataillon de réserve de la police allemande et la Solution finale en Pologne,* translated by É. Barnavi, Les Belles Lettres, 1994; reprint Tallandier, "Texto," 2007.

Chapoutot, Johann, *Le Meurtre de Weimar,* Presses universitaires de France, 2010.

——, *Le National-Socialisme et l'Antiquité,* Presses universitaires de France, 2008; reprint 2012. [English translation: *Greeks, Romans, Germans: How the Nazis Usurped Europe's Classical Past,* translated by Richard R. Nybakken, Berkeley, University of California Press, 2016.]

——, "Les nazis et la "nature": protection ou prédation?" *Vingtième Siècle. Revue d'histoire,* vol. 1, no. 113, 2012, pp. 29–40.

Delmas-Marty, Mireille, and Henry Laurens, *Terrorismes. Histoire et droit,* Paris, CNRS Éditions, 2010.

Dieckmann, Christoph, *Deutsche Besatzungspolitik in Litauen,* Göttingen, Wallstein, 2011.

Ebbinghaus, Angelika, and Karl-Heinz Roth, "Vorläufer des Generalplans Ost. Eine Dokumentation über Theodor Schieders Polendenkschrift vom 7.10.1939," *Zeitschrift für Sozialgeschichte des 20. und 21. Jahrhunderts,* 1992, vol. VII, no. 1.

Eco, Umberto. "Ur-Fascism," *New York Review of Books* 22 (11), June 22, 1995.

Fest, Joachim, *Das Gesicht des Dritten Reiches,* Munich, Piper, 1993.

Friedländer, Saul, *Das Dritte Reich und die Juden,* Munich, Beck, 1998; in French, *Les Années d'extermination. L'Allemagne nazie et les Juifs, 1939–1945,* Paris, Éditions du Seuil, 2008.

Gallus, Alexander, and Axel Schildt, *Rückblickend in die Zukunft*, Göttingen, Wallstein, 2011.

Gauchet, Marcel, *La Condition historique*, Paris, Stock, 2003; reprint, Gallimard, "Folio," 2008, p. 241.

Gerlach, Christian, *Sur la conférence de Wannsee. De la décision d'exterminer les Juifs d'Europe* [1997], translated by J. Schmidt, Paris, Liana Lévi, 1999.

———, *Kalkulierte Morde. Die deutsche Wirtschafts- und Vernichtungspolitik in Weissrussland 1941 bis 1944*, Hamburg, Hamburger Edition, 1999.

Grau, Günther (ed.), *Homosexualität in der NS-Zeit. Dokumente einer Diskriminierung und Verfolgung*, Frankfurt, Fischer, 1993.

Gross, Raphael, *Carl Schmitt et les Juifs* [2000], translated by D. Trierweiler, Presses universitaires de France, 2005. [Published in English as *Carl Schmitt and the Jews*, translated by Joel Golb, Madison, University of Wisconsin Press, 2007.]

———, *Anständig geblieben. Nationalsozialistische Moral*, Frankfurt, Fischer, 2010.

———, and Werner Konitzer (eds.), *Moralität des Bösen. Ethik und nationalsozialistische Verbrechen*, Frankfurt, Campus Verlag-Fritz Bauer Institut, 2009.

Hachmeister, Lutz, *Der Gegnerforscher. Die Karriere des SS-Führers Franz Alfred Six*, Munich, Beck, 1998.

Heer, Hannes (ed.), *Vernichtungskrieg. Verbrechen der Wehrmacht 1941 bis 1944—Ausstellungskatalog*, exhibition catalog, Hamburg, Stiftung Institut für Sozialforschung, 1995.

Heiber, Helmut (ed.), *Goebbels Reden*, 2 vols., Düsseldorf, Droste, 1971.

Herbert, Ulrich, *Fremdarbeiter. Politik und Praxis des "AusländerEinsatzes" in der Kriegswirtschaft des Dritten Reiches*, Berlin, Dietz, 1985.

———, *Best: biographische Studien über Radikalismus, Weltanschauung und Vernunft*, 1996; in French, *Werner Best. Un nazi de l'ombre (1903–1989)*, translated by D. Viollet, Tallandier, 2010.

Herf, Jeffrey, *The Jewish Enemy. Nazi Propaganda during World War II and the Holocaust*, Cambridge, MA, Harvard University Press, 2006; in French, *L'Ennemi juif. La propagande nazie, 1939–1945*, translated by P.-E. Dauzat, Paris, Calmann-Lévy, 2011.

Hersonski, Yael, "A Film Unfinished," 2010, documentary, Germany, MDR-SWR, 90 min.

Hockerts, Hans-Günther, *Die Sittlichkeitsprozesse gegen katholische Ordensangehörige und Priester, 1936–1937. Eine Studie zur nationalsozialistischen Herrschaftstechnik und zum Kirchenkampf*, Mainz, Matthias-Grünewald, 1971.

Hürter, Johannes, *Hitlers Heerführer. Die deutschen Oberbefehlshaber im Krieg gegen die Sowjetunion 1941–1942*, Munich, Oldenburg, 2006.

Ingrao, Christian, *Les Chasseurs noirs. La brigade Dirlewanger*, Paris, Perrin, 2006.

———, *Croire et Détruire*, Fayard, 2010; in English, *Believe and Destroy: Intellectuals in the SS War Machine*, translated by Andrew Brown, Cambridge, MA, Polity Press, 2013, reprint 2015.

Johnson, Eric, *Nazi Terror. The Gestapo, Jews and Ordinary Germans*, New York, Basic Books, 1999; in French, *La Terreur nazie. La Gestapo, les Juifs et les Allemands ordinaires*, translated by C. Beslon and P.-A. Dauzat, Paris, Albin Michel, 2001.

Jouanjan, Olivier, *Une histoire de la pensée juridique en Allemagne (1800–1918). Idéalisme et conceptualisme chez les juristes allemands du XIXe siècle*, Presses universitaires de France, 2005.

———, "*Gefolgschaft* et *Studentenrecht:* deux gloses en marge du *Discours de rectorat*," *Les Études philosophiques*, no. 93, 2010.

Jütte, Daniel, "Die Entstehung und Auswirkungen des nationalsozialistischen Reichstierschutzgesetzes von 1933," *Berichte des Institutes für Didaktik der Biologie der Westfälischen Wilhelms-Universität Münster*, suppl. 2, 2002, pp. 167–184.

Kater, Michael H., *Das Ahnenerbe der SS 1935–1945. Ein Beitrag zur Kulturpolitik des Dritten Reiches*, Stuttgart, Deutsche Verlagsanstalt, 1974.

Kershaw, Ian, in French, *L'Opinion allemande sous le nazisme. Bavière, 1933–1945*, translated by P.-E. Dauzat, Paris, CNRS Éditions, 1995; reprint, 2002. [First published in English as *Popular Opinion and Political Dissent in the Third Reich, Bavaria 1933–1945*, New York, Oxford University Press, 1983.]

Klee, Ernst, *Die Euthanasie im NS-Staat. Die "Vernichtung lebensunwerten Lebens*," Frankfurt, Fischer, 1983.

———, "Die Kirchen und die 'Vernichtung lebensunwerten Lebens,'" ARD, 1988.

———, "*Die SA Jesu Christi*." *Die Kirchen im Banne Hitlers*, Frankfurt, Fischer, 1989.

———, *Das Personenlexikon zum Dritten Reich. Wer war was vor und nach 1945?* Frankfurt, Fischer, 2003.

———, *Das Kulturlexikon zum Dritten Reich. Wer war was vor und nach 1945*, Frankfurt, Fischer, 2007.

Knigge, Volkhard, and Harry Stein (eds.), *Franz Ehrlich. Ein Bauhäusler in Widerstand und Konzentrationslager*, Weimar, Stiftung Gedenkstätten Buchenwald und Mittelbau-Dora, 2009.

Koonz, Claudia, *The Nazi Conscience*, Cambridge, MA, Harvard University Press, 2003.

Kosthorst, Erich, *Konzentrations- und Strafgefangenenlager im Dritten Reich: Beispiel Emsland*, 3 vols., Düsseldorf, Droste, 1983.

Kotze, Hildegard von, and Helmut Krausnick, *Es spricht der Führer. Sieben exemplarische Hitler-Reden*, Gütersloh, Mohn, 1966.

Krausnick, Helmut, "Kommissarbefehl und 'Gerichtsbarkeit Barbarossa' in neuer Sicht," *Vierteljahreshefte für Zeitgeschichte*, no. 25, 1977, pp. 682–738.

Kroll, Frank-Lothar, *Utopie als Ideologie. Geschichtsdenken und politisches Handeln im Dritten Reich*, Paderborn, Schöning, 1998.

Kühnl, Reinhard, *Der deutsche Faschismus in Quellen und Dokumenten*, 6th ed., Cologne, Pahl-Rugenstein, 1975–1987, 1987.

Lambauer, Barbara, "Le terrorisme selon l'Allemagne nazie et sa répression," in Delmas-Marty and Laurens, 2010, pp. 89–164.

Lewy, Guenther, *The Nazi Persecution of the Gypsies*, Oxford University Press, 2000.

Lieb, Peter, *Konventionneller Krieg oder NS-Weltanschauungskrieg? Kriegführung und Partisanenbekämpfung in Frankreich, 1943–44*, Munich, Oldenbourg, 2007.

Lorenz, Sönke, Dieter Bauer, Wolfgang Behringer, and Jürgen Michael Schmidt, *Himmlers Hexenkartothek. Das Interesse des Nationalsozialismus an der Hexenverfolgung*, Institut für geschichtliche Landeskunde und historische Hilfswissenschaften der Universität Tübingen, Bielefeld, Verlag für Regionalgeschichte, 1999.

Madajczyk, Czesław, *Vom Generalplan Ost zum Generalsiedlungsplan*, Munich, Saur, 1994.

Matthäus, Jürgen, " 'Weltanschauliche Forschung und Auswertung'—Aus den Akten des Amtes VII im Reichssicherheitshauptamt," *Jahrbuch für Antisemitismusforschung*, no. 5, 1996, pp. 287–330.

———, Konrad Kwiet, Jürgen Förster, and Richard Breitman, *Ausbildungsziel Judenmord? Weltanschauliche Schulung von SS, Polizei und Waffen-SS im Rahmen der Endlösung*, Frankfurt, Fischer, 2003.

Mayer, Michael, *Staaten als Täter. Ministerialbürokratie und "Judenpolitik" in NS-Deutschland und Vichy-Frankreich: ein Vergleich*, Munich, Oldenbourg, 2010.

Müller, Rolf-Dieter, *Hitlers Ostkrieg und die deutsche Siedlungspolitik. Die Zusammenarbeit von Wehrmacht, Wirtschaft und SS*, Frankfurt, Fischer, 1991.

Neitzel, Sönke, and Harald Welzer, *Soldaten. Protokolle vom Kämpfen, Töten und Sterben*, Frankfurt, Fischer, 2011.

Pohl, Dieter, *Nationalsozialistische Judenverfolgung in Ostgalizien 1941–1944. Organisation und Durchführung eines staatlichen Massenverbrechens*, Munich, Oldenbourg, 1997.

Pois, Robert A., *National-Socialism and the Religion of Nature*, New York, St. Martin's Press, 1986; in French, *La Religion de la nature et le national-socialisme*, translated by J. Merchant and B. Frumer, Éditions du Cerf, 1993.

Prag, Werner, and Wolfgang Jacobmeyer, *Das Diensttagebuch des deutschen Generalgouverneurs in Polen 1939–1945*, Stuttgart, Verlagsanstalt, 1975.

Puschner, Uwe (ed.), *Die völkisch-religiöse Bewegung im Nationalsozialismus: eine Beziehungs- und Konfliktgeschichte*, Göttingen, Vandenhoeck & Ruprecht, 2012.

Reichardt, Sven, *Faschistische Kampfbünde. Gewalt und Gemeinschaft im italienischen Squadrismus und in der deutschen SA*, Cologne, Böhlau, 2002.

Reichel, Peter, *Der schöne Schein des Dritten Reiches*, Carl Hanser Verlag, 1991; in French, *La Fascination du nazisme*, translated by O. Mannoni, Paris, Odile Jacob, 1993.

Revault d'Allonnes, Myriam, *Ce que l'homme fait à l'homme. Essai sur le mal politique*, Paris, Flammarion, 1995.

Römer, Felix, *Der Kommissarbefehl. Wehrmacht und NS-Verbrechen an der Ostfront 1941–1942*, Paderborn, Schöningh, 2008.

————, *Kameraden. Die Wehrmacht von innen*, Munich, Piper, 2012.

Rüthers, Bernd, *Entartetes Recht. Rechtslehren und Kronjuristen im Dritten Reich*, Munich, Beck, 1988.

Schädler, Sarah, *"Justizkrise" und "Justizreform" im Nationalsozialismus. Das Reichsjustizministerium unter Reichsjustizminister Thierack (1942–1945)*, Tübingen, Mohr, 2009.

Scheck, Raffael, *Une saison noire. Les massacres des tirailleurs sénégalais, mai-juin 1940*, translated by Éric Thiébaud, Tallandier, 2007. [First published in English as *Hitler's African Victims: The German Army Massacres of Black French Soldiers in 1940*, Cambridge, Cambridge University Press, 2006.]

Schlagdenhauffen, Régis, *Triangle rose. La Persécution des homosexuels nazis et sa mémoire*, Autrement, 2011.

Schmerbach, Folker, *Das "Gemeinschaftslager Hans Kerrl" für Referendare in Jüterbog, 1933–1939*, Tübingen, Mohr Siebeck, 2008.

Schmidt, Ute, *Die Deutschen aus Bessarabien. Eine Minderheit aus Südosteuropa (1814 bis heute)*, Cologne, Böhlau, 2003.

Schmitz-Berning, Cornelia, *Vokabular des National-Sozialismus*, Berlin, De Gruyter, 1998.

Stangneth, Bettina, *Eichmann vor Jerusalem. Das unbehelligte Leben eines Massenmörders*, Hamburg, Arche, 2011.

Streit, Christian, *Keine Kameraden. Die Wehrmacht und die Sowjetischen Kriegsgefangenen, 1941–1945*, Stuttgart, Deutsche Verlagsanstalt, 1978.

Überschär, Gerd, and Wolfram Wette. *"Unternehmen Barbarossa." Der deutsche Überfall auf die Sowjetunion 1941*, Paderborn, Schöningh, 1984.

Wette, Wolfram, *Karl Jäger. Mörder der litauischen Juden*, Frankfurt, Fischer, 2011.

Wildt, Michael, *Generation des Unbedingten. Das Führungskorps des Reichssicherheitshauptamtes*, Hamburg, Hamburger Edition, 2002.

————, "Der Fall Reinhard Höhn. Vom RSHA zur Harzburger Akademie," in Gallus and Schildt, 2011, pp. 254–274.

Winkler, Heinrich August, *Der lange Weg nach Westen*, 2 vols., Munich, Beck, 2000.

Wiwjorra, Ingo, *Der Germanenmythos. Konstruktion einer Weltanschauung in der Altertumsforschung des 19. Jahrhunderts*, Darmstadt, Wissenschaftliche Buchgesellschaft, 2006.

Zimmermann, Michael, *Rassenutopie und Genozid. Die nationalsozialistische "Lösung der Zigeunerfrage,"* Hamburg, Christians, 1996.

Glossary

Akademie für Deutsches Recht: Academy for German Law.

Altreich: "Old Reich," or "old empire." Nazi term used to designate Germany as its borders existed in 1937.

Amstgericht: local court.

Arbeitserziehungslager: work education camp.

Artgleichheit: racial identity.

BA-FA (Bundesarchiv-Filmabteilung): German Federal Archives–Department Film Archives.

Ballastexistenzen: useless or "ballast" existences.

BA-MA (Bundesarchiv-Militärarchiv): German Federal Archives–Department Military Archives.

BGB (Bürgerliches Gesetzbuch): German Civil Code.

Bildungsbürgertum: the cultivated bourgeoisie.

BNSDJ (Bund Nationalsozialistischer Deutscher Juristen): National Socialist Association of Legal Professionals.

DAF (Deutsche Arbeitsfront): German Labor Front.

DAP (Deutsche Arbeiterpartei): German Workers' Party, the precursor of the NSDAP.

Deutsche Christen: German Christians, a movement within the Protestant church that supported Nazism.

Drang nach Osten: thrust toward the East or yearning for the East.

EGG (Erbgesundheitsgerichte): hereditary disease courts.

Einsatzgruppen: "task forces" or "deployment squads"; paramilitary death squads.

Entjudung: de-Judaization.

Fremdvölkisch: alien (*fremd*) to the body of the German people (*Volk*).

Gauleiter: high-level official of the NSDAP in charge of a *Gau*, a party political district.

Gegenrasse: counter-race.

Gegnerforschung: within the SD, a service for the identification and eradication of ideological enemies.

Gemeinschaft: community.

Gemeinschaftsfremde: elements alien to the community.

Gesellschaft: society.

Gestapo (Geheime Staatspolizei): the state secret police, founded in April 1933.

GFM (Generalfeldmarschall): field marshal.

GFP (Geheime Feldpolizei): the Wehrmacht military police.

Gleichartigkeit: equality.

Grossraum: the idea of a homogenous and clearly delimited space, defined by Carl Schmitt.

Heimtücke: treachery.

Herrenmensch: "overlord" or "master race."

Hitlerjugend: Hitler Youth.

HSSPF (Höhere SS- und Polizeiführer): the supreme chief of the SS and the police forces in a given region.

IKL (Inspektion der Konzentrationslager): Concentration Camps Inspectorate.

Judenfrei **or** *Judenrein:* free or "cleansed" of Jews.

Judenrat: Jewish Council.

Kammergericht: court of appeals.

Kampfzeit: combat narrative.

KL (Konzentrationslager): concentration camp.

Kohlrübenwinter: Turnip Winter.

Kommissarbefehl: Commissar Order (June 1941).

Kriminalbiologische Gesellschaft: Institute for the Study of Criminal Biology.

Kriminalbiologisches Institut der Sipo: Institute for Criminal Biology of the Security Police.

Lagerordnung: camp regulations.

Landgericht: court or tribunal.

Lebensborn: literally, "fountain of life."

Lebensraum: literally, "living space."

Lebensrecht: "the law of life" or "the right to life."

Leistung: performance, production.

Männerbund: "virile community."

Merkblatt: memorandum or handbook.

Napolas (Nationalpolitisches Lehranstalt): NSDAP secondary education institution.

NSDAP (Nationalsozialistische Deutsche Arbeiterpartei): National Socialist German Workers Party.

NSKK (Nationalsozialistisches Kraftfahrkorps): National Socialist Motor Corps.

NSLB (Nationalsozialistischer Lehrerbund): National Socialist Teachers League.

Obersturmbannführer: lieutenant-colonel in the SS.

OKH (Oberkommando des Heeres): Supreme High Command of the German Army.

OKW (Oberkommando der Wehrmacht): High Command of the Armed Forces.

OrPo (Ordnungspolizei): Order Police, the regular police force of the Third Reich.

Ostarbeiter: Eastern workers.

Ostgrenze: Eastern border or frontier.

Polizeiliche Vorbeugehaft: preventive police detention.

Rassenkunde: racial anthropology.

Rassenpolitisches Amt der NSDAP: NSDAP Office of Racial Policy.

Rassenschande: "racial shame," violations of the Nuremberg Laws.

Rassenseelenkunde: "science of the racial soul."

Recht der Völker: law of the peoples.

Rechtserneuerung: renewal of the law.

Referendar: intern or junior staff member.

Reichsärzteführer: "Reich Doctors' Leader."

Reichsarzt für die Hitlerjugend: Chief physician of the Hitler Youth.

Reichsführer SS: special title and rank given to the leader of the SS, Heinrich Himmler.

Reichsgericht: The Supreme Criminal and Civil Court of the Reich, located in Leipzig.

Reichsgesundheitsamt: Reich Central Health Office.

Reichskirche: Church of the Reich.

Reichsmarschall: Marshal of the Reich, a special title given to Hermann Goering.

Reichsnährstand: government body established to regulate food production.

Reichswehr: the name of the German army until 1935.

RKF (Reichskommissariat [-kommisar] für die Festigung deutschen Volkstums): Reich Commission (and Commissioner) for the Consolidation of German Nationhood (Heinrich Himmler).

RLM (Reichsluftfahrtministerium): Ministry of the Air.

RSHA (Reichssicherheitshauptamt): Reich Main Security Office.

RuSHA (Rasseund Siedlungshauptant der SS): SS central office "for race and colonization."

SA (Sturmabteilung): "Storm Detachment," the original paramilitary wing of the Nazi Party.

Schutzhaft: protective detention.

SD (Sicherheitsdienst): SS Intelligence Service.

Sicherungsverwahrung: safety detention.

Sipo (Sicherheitspolizei): security police.

Sippenhaft: family detention.

Sittengesetz: moral law.

Sommerlager: summer camp.

Sonderauftrag: special mission.

Sondergerichte: special court.

Sonderweg: "special path."

SS (Schutzstaffel): "protection squadron."

Sturmbannführer: major (SS ranking).

Sturmführer: lieutenant (SS ranking).

UFA (Universal Film-Aktiengesellschaft): film production company created by the German state in 1917.

Unrasse: "un-race" or "non-race."

Untermensch: "subhuman."

Vernichten: annihilate.

VGH (Volksgerichtshof): people's tribunal.

Völkerrecht: international law.

Volk ohne Raum: people without a land.

Volksgemeinschaft: community of the people.

Volksgerichtshof: people's court.

Vorbehaltsfilme: Nazi films subject to authorization before showing.

Vorbeugungshaft: preventive detention.

Waffen-SS: the military wing of the SS.

Wehrrecht: "military justice"; area of the law dealing with defense.

Weltanschauung: worldview.

Wertordnung: value system.

WO Ost (Wirtschaftsorganisation Ost): Eastern Economic Organization.

Zulassung: permission to practice (law).

Index

Abmeierung (lord's right to take land from a vassal), 129–130, 429n78

Abortion: as crime, 111; homosexuality and, 230–231

Abstinence, 106

Agencies. *See Anstalten*

Aktion T4 program, 2

Alexander VI, 70, 422n28

Alien to body of German people. See *Fremdvölkisch*

Alien to community. See *Gemeinschaftsfremde*

Alles Leben ist Kampf (film), 155–156, 159

American Indians, 352

Animals: Himmler on, 29; Hitler on, 24; hunting and, 30–31; India and the protection of, 29–30; Jews' supposed cruelty toward, 23–25, 29–30; National-sozialistische Deutsche Arbeiterpartei and, 23–24; Nazis and, 31–32; Germanic origins and, 23–32; Reichstierschutzgesetz and, 30; "Trouble in the Blood: This World and the Next" on, 25

Anstalten (agencies): restructuring of state into, 316

Anti-Comintern Pact, 369

Anti-nature, 29, 64–65, 106–109, 147

Anti-Semitism. *See* Jews

Arbeit macht frei (work sets you free), 195

Arbeitsrecht der Polen im Deutschen Reich (Küppers & Bannier), 358

Archaic, pre-Christian rites, 37–38

"Artfremde Moral" *(Schwarze Korps, Das)*, 107

Aryans: and Gypsies, 439n143; and Jesus, 118–120; and Jews, 68, 75, 146–147, 193, 379, 394, 401; as masters, 354; in Nazi hierarchy, 31; Nine Commandments of, 104; as victims, 191–192. *See also* Germanic race

Asians: invasion by, 324, 370; in Nazi hierarchy, 31

"Asiatic" peoples, 259. *See also* Slavs

Asocials: Frank and, 233, 439n151; Walter Gross on, 235–236; Gypsies as, 439n143; "irrecoverable," 234; professional criminals as, 231–232; sterilization and, 234–235; struggle against, 231–236;

Thierack and, 231–232; war and, 231–232 Paul Werner and, 234–235. *See also Gemeinschaftsfremde*

Association of National Socialist Jurists (NSRB), 95

Astel, Karl: natural selection and, 54; nature versus non-nature and, 28–29; scientific values and, 48

Atrocities Committed by the Polish against the Germans in Poland, The (German Ministry of Foreign Affairs), 292

Aufbruch des Nordens (Lippe), 335

Austria, 286–287, 364–366

Avars (Mongolian-Turkish people), 444n59

Backe, Herbert: Eastern European colonization and, 348; hunger and, 374; Slavs and, 379

Bacteriological analogies, 31, 172, 261, 398

Badges for identification, 357–358, 359–360, 390

Bannier, Rudolf, 358

Barbarossa zone, 251–252

Barth, Robert, 134–135

Barthou, Louis, 303

Bartov, Omer, 10

"Basic Decree on the Fight to Prevent Criminality," 225

Bayer, Wilhelm, 1, 2, 3

Beech tree, 371–372

Believe and Destroy (Ingrao), 10

Believers in God. See *Gottgläubige*

Berger, Friedrich: morality and, 104; race and, 88–89

Best, Werner: *Die Deutsche Polizei* by, 212–213; Gestapo and, 211–216; as intellectual in action, 10, 16–17; *Kriminalbiologie* and, 217–218

Bilfinger, Carl, 283–284, 299, 305

Biologe, Der, 50

Biology: bionomics and, 150; borders and, 362–363; in criminal law, 199–200; duty to history and, 385–386; Kriminalbiologische Gesellschaft and, 216–217; "Political Biology," 35–36, 178; political borders and, 366–367

Biomedical anti-Semitism, 412–413

Bionomics, 150

Bionomy, 112

Bismarck, Otto von, 280, 281, 285, 310

Blacks ("Negroes"): in Nazi ideology, 31, 68, 74, 77–78, 320, 391; as soldiers, 262

Blockadefestigkeit (capacity to withstand blockades), 377

Blood: climate and, 341–345; Darré and, 151–152; gold and, 78–79; law of, 408; mixing of, 52–53, 343–345; over ink, 112; "Trouble in the Blood: This World and the Next," 25

Blut und Rasse in der Gesetzgebung (von Leers), 124

Bomb shelters, 395–396

Boniface, Saint, 427n15

Bonnet, Georges, 326

Bordellos, 380

Borders: biology and, 362–363; climatic line and, 371–372; East and, 362–368; Eastern marches and, 371–372; Eastern wall and, 369–370; Europe and, 368; political, 366–367; racial, 363–364; spatial, 368–371; *Volk ohne Grenzen* and, 362–364; Walz and, 367–368

Borgias, 70, 422n28

British Empire, 315

Browning, Christopher, 7

Brunner, Otto, 45–46

Bruns, Viktor: international law and, 297–298; natural law and, 312

Buch, Walther, 59–60, 165; credo of judges and, 199; equality and, 77

Buchenwald: Eastern marches and, 371–372; *Jedem das Seine* and, 195

Buddhism, 29

Burgdörfer, Friedrich, 178–179

Capacity to withstand blockades. See *Blockadefestigkeit*

Caracalla, 94–95

Carl Peters (film), 115

Carolingian alienation, 138

Catel, Werner, 2–3

Catholic Church: as instrument of Jews, 70; monasticism and, 106–108; rituals of 93

Catholicism: monasticism, and anti-nature, 106–108; political, 66, 70

Cats, 157, 432n5

Chamberlain, Houston Stewart, 387

Chéniers, André, 176, 434n85

Christianity: as anti-nature, 64–65; as communism of antiquity, 110–111; confrontation with, 158–159;

de-Judaizing, 117–121; division of faiths by, 109–110; eradicating, 183–188; Germanic religious sentiment contrasted with, 25–29; Himmler and, 110, 158–159, 183–184; Hitler and, 183–184, 185–186; as invented by Jews, 100; materialism of, 26; "Midgards Untergang" and, 104–105; monasticism and, 106–108; *Der Mythus des 20. Jahrhunderts* and, 164; Nazi values contrasted with, 71; positive, 119; religion of death and, 173–174; SS compared with, 107–108; universalism and, 86; Manfred Werner and, 102–103; witch hunts and, 100–102. See also Catholic Church

Chrysippus, 58

Citizenship, as biological, 366–367

Civil law contract. See *Vertrag*

Clauss, Ludwig Ferdinand, 51

Clausula rebus sic stantibus (things thus standing), 299–300

Clemenceau, Georges, 280–281, 304

Climate: and colonization, 334–341; Eastern zone as fertile, 334–335; Germanic race and, 54; Iberian Peninsula and, 335–336; landscaping and, 340–341; Konrad Meyer and, 334; Nordic, 157–158; shaping, 340; soil and blood related to, 341–345

Collective individualism, 87–88

Colonization: for economic reasons, 336; Iberian Peninsula and, 335–336; overseas, 337; Rome and, 335. See also Eastern European colonization

Commissar Order. See *Kommissarbefehl*

Communism: Christianity, ancient, and, 86, 110–111; industrialization of Germany and, 14; universalism and, 86–87

Community of achievement. See *Leistungsgemeinschaft*

Community of people. See *Volksgemeinschaft*

Community of struggle. See *Kampfgemeinschaft*

Concentration camp: *Arbeit macht frei* and, 195; guard duties and powers, 194–195; Höss and, 396; *Jedem das Seine* and, 195–197; precepts of, 194; protection and rehabilitation, 194–197; segregation and, 378–379

Confucius, 64, 422n3

Consent, 306–307

Consequentialism versus conscience, 414

Criminal Biology Society. *See* Kriminalbiologische Gesellschaft

Criminal law: armored divisions of, 201–206; biology in, 199–200; community protection via, 198–199; elimination and, 199; Freisler and, 197–198, 203, 360; individualist liberalism and, 197; no crime without punishment and, 198; Oetker and, 200; as polemical, 203; probability and, 218–219; Stengel von Rutkowski and, 201; as war, 197–201

"Criminal Law Decree against the Polish and the Jews in the Integrated Eastern Territories," 360–362

Criminals: as asocials, 231–232; "Basic Decree on the Fight to Prevent Criminality," 225; Daluege and, 219–220, 389; "Jewish Criminality," 389; Jews as, 389, 391–395; *Sicherungsverwahrung* and, 225; Soviet prisoners of war as, 269–270

Cult of nature, 187–188

Czechoslovakia: as *fabrizierte Konstruktion*, 287–288; Hess and, 289–290; Hitler on, 288–289, 290; racial dualism in, 290–291; self-determination and, 288–289; Versailles and, 287–291

Czerniaków, Adam, 388

Daluege, Kurt: civil servant recruitment by, 221; foreign immigrants and, 220; Jew as criminal and, 389; *Kriminalbiologie* and, 219–222; *Nationalsozialistischer Kampf gegen das Verbrechertum* by, 219; old versus new law and, 221–222; professional criminals and, 219–220

Danzer, Paul, 178

Darré, Richard, 18; blood and, 151–152; property and, 131; witch hunts and, 101

Darwin, Charles, 155

"Death to paragraph." *See* Paragraph

De Boor, Hans-Otto, 137

Decalogue. *See* Ten Commandments

De-Judaizing Christianity: Deutsche Christen and, 117, 121; Grundmann and, 117–118, 120; Jesus as Aryan and, 118–120; Herbert Meyer and, 119; Schmitt and, 121; *Volkstestament* and, 121

De Lagarde, Paul, 400

Demographic mass to be exploited. See *Slawentum*

Dependent areas, 376

Desertion, 227

Deutsche Christen (German-Christian movement): establishment of, 117; *Volkstestament* and, 121

Deutsche Mensch, Der (Meyer, Herbert), 119

Deutsche Polizei, Die (Best), 212–213

Dienst (service), 54

Dietrich, Otto, 90–91

Dietze, Hans-Helmut, 159–161

Diewerge, Wolfgang, 384

Dix, Otto, 11

Dönitz, Karl, 262–263

Doppelmoral (moral double-speak), 107

Downfall (film), 5–6

Dr. Mabuse the Gambler (Lang), 11

East: as border, 362–368, 371–372; climatic border and, 371–372; compromise in, 254–255; Einsatzgruppen deployed in, 250; "General Regulations regarding the Recruitment and Employment of Labor from the East," 358–359; Germanization of, 338–339; German military acculturation related to, 250–258; Goering exploiting, 375–376; Order 46 and, 253–254; as place of constant exception, 250–258; troops stymied in, 253; "Twelve Commandments for the Behavior of Germans in the East and for the Treatment of Russians," 348; war in, 246–250; women and children targeted in, 255

Eastern European colonization: archaeology and, 337; Backe and, 348; blood mixing and, 343–345; climate and, 334–341; communication lines and, 337; economic autonomy and, 345; efficiency aims and, 346–347; as finite, circumscribed project, 369; Germanization and, 338–339; good versus bad, 335; health considerations and, 347; *Herrenmenschentum* in action and, 345–349; Hitler on, 337; *Jedem das Seine* and, 324; land ownership and, 342–343; landscaping and, 339–341; *Lebensraum* and, 324; *Lebensrecht* and, 321–326; Lippe on, 335; livestock and, 347; management primer for, 348; Pan-Germanic movement and, 324–325; physical edge and, 372–377; planning, flexible, and, 345–346; Poland and, 330–334; police and, 350; as progressive process, 338; replanting race, 326–330;

Eastern European colonization *(continued)*
restitution and reconstruction via, 323;
Schieder on, 353; settlement debt and,
342; soil and blood related to, 341–345;
taxation and, 343; Wiepking-
Jürgensmann on, 339–340
Eastern marches, 371–372
Eckhard, Albert, 24, 25
Education of young Germans: acculturation
and, 68; cultural contamination and, 65;
The Law of God and, 65–67, 422n10
Eichenauer, Richard, 159
Eichmann, Adolf: bomb shelters and, 396;
mass murder and, 3; not guilty plea of, 4
Eicke, Theodor, 194
Ein Menschenschlag (Ritter), 235
Einsatz (use of subhuman labor), 358
*Einsatzbedingungen der Ostarbeiter,
sowie der sowjetrussischen Kriegsge-
fangenen* (Küppers & Bannier), 358
Einsatzgruppen (task forces), 250
Emil and the Detectives (Kästner), 12
Enabling Act, 215
Equality: environment and, 77–78; French
Revolution and, 77–78; *Racial Equality
against Equality in Principle*, 80–81
Erbgesundheitsgerichte (hereditary health
courts), 2, 140
Erbt, Wilhelm, 104, 425n157
Eroticism, 106
Esser, Hermann, 398–399
Etiam hosti fides servanda (one must be
honest even with one's enemy), 310
Eugenic murder: Hitler establishing,
167–168; homosexuality and, 230; *Ich
klage an* and, 168–169; as mercy, 170;
performance capacity and, 171; Stähle
and, 168; Wagner and, 170–171.
See also Final solution
Eugenics. *See* Sterilization
Europe, 368. *See also* Eastern European
colonization
Ewige Jude, Der (Hippler): animals and,
24; *Ghetto* and, 388; Jewish morality
and, 394; Jews as plague and, 399
Ewige Wald, Der (film), 100
Ex factis jus oritur (law is born of facts), 297

Fabrizierte Konstruktion (fabricated
construction): Czechoslovakia and,
287–288; Versailles and, 288
Fallrecht (law on case-by-case basis), 137
Familial detention. See *Sippenhaft*
Fehr, Hans, 136

Fidelity: heart and, 56–57; honor as, 54–55
Final solution: common concepts related
to, 409–410; as expression of natural
morality, 403–404; German un-cruelty
and, 387–390; Himmler and, 191,
386–387, 403–404, 412; Höss on,
397–398; *Meine Psyche* and, 395–398;
Operation Reinhard and, 401–402; as
right and just, 403
"Final Solution" (Himmler), 191
Flüchtlinge (Ucicky), 277–278, 443n1
Folklore, law as, 60–63
Forested zones, 376–377
Formalism, 76, 115, 183, 197; Jews and,
74–75; judicial freedom lacking, 198;
Kantian, 176; legal, 285
Forsthoff, Ernst, 46
Fourteen Points, 309
France: Barthou and, 303; black soldiers
and, 262; Friedrich Grimm on,
284–285; Peace of Westphalia and, 282;
Service du Travail Obligatoire and, 356
Frank, Hans, 53; asocials and, 233,
439n151; community protection via
criminal law and, 198–199; death to
paragraph and, 126; idealistic law and,
98–99; "Jewry in the German Legal
Sciences" by, 72; judge as soldier and,
202–203; on law as serving people, 113;
on law of life, 311; liberal-Marxist and,
74, 422n38; no crime without punishment and, 198; pity and, 192; Poland
and, 331; procreation and, 148–149; race
and, 92, 124–125; Roman law and,
93–94, 97–99; on Romano-Byzantine
bastardization, 97; on soul of people
and law, 124–125; state and, 114;
Versailles, Treaty of, and, 308
Franssen, Gustav, 172
Freisler, Roland, 53, 61; criminal law and,
197–198, 203, 360; "Criminal Law
Decree against the Polish and the Jews
in the Integrated Eastern Territories"
and, 360; death to paragraph and,
125–126; *Fallrecht* and, 137; free law
and, 137; on French Revolution, 76;
German population and, 326; judge
and, 133–134, 202; judge as soldier of
home front and, 202; on meaning of
criminal law, 203; Middle Ages and,
81–82; property and, 129–130;
separation and, 44–45
Fremdvölkisch (alien to body of German
people): Polish Decrees and, 356–358;

Service du Travail Obligatoire and, 356; treatment of, 356–362

French Revolution, 58; blood and gold related to, 78–79; de-Nordification from, 82–83; Dietrich and, 90–91; equality and, 77–78; Freisler on, 76; Grundmann and, 117–118; Hitler on, 76; Jess and, 82; Jewish Revolution and, 76–81; Lange and, 83–85; mathematics and, 79–80; Middle Ages and, 81–82; Nazi Revolution and, 78–79; Rosenberg and, 78; Rousseau and, 82; Schilling and, 79. *See also* National Socialist Revolution

Frenssen, Gustav, 55–56, 60

Frick, Wilhelm: nineteenth-century history and, 13–14; "Nordic Thought in the Legislation of the Third Reich" and, 36; *Notzustand* and, 177–178; state and, 114

"Frömmigkeit nordischer Artung" (Günther), 48–49

Führerprinzip (leadership principle), 244

Führer und Volksgemeinschaft (Mehlis), 39

Gegnerforschung, 101

Gemeinschaftsfremde (alien to community), 231; draft law explaining, 233; police versus judiciary related to, 233–234, 439n151

Generalklauseln (general clauses), 123, 134, 428n53

Generalplan Ost, 369

"General Regulations regarding the Recruitment and Employment of Labor from the East" (Reichsführer SS), 358–359

Genet, Jean, 12

Genghis Khan, 381

"Gentilism," 88

Gentilist morality, 16

Gercke, Achim, 115

German-Christian movement. *See* Deutsche Christen

German exceptionalism, 4–5

Germanic democracy: loyalty and, 182–183; Schmitt and, 183

Germanic immediacy: Germanic people as moral and, 39–40; origins and, 39–44

Germanic race: bodily rhythms and, 56–57; climate and, 54; community and, 54–55; fidelity and, 54–55; foreign norms and, 406–407; law as folklore for, 60–63; law of blood and, 408; legal system as lifeblood of, 42; natural selection and, 54; as only moral race, 53–57; origins of, 406; values interconnected for, 55–56; as victim, 407; word and action related to, 408–409; world order and, 57–58

Germanic religious sentiment, 25–29

Germanité, 424n113

German Ministry of Foreign Affairs, 292

Germany Must Perish (Kaufmann), 384–385

Gestapo: Best and, 211–216; as above law, 211–212; mission of, 211

Ghetto (film), 388–389

Goebbels, Joseph: on German sentimentalism, 411; *Germany Must Perish* and, 384; holistic view and, 145; Jewish bacillus and, 401; Jews and, 394; killing Jews as duty and, 385; sentimentalism and, 191–193; *Sippenhaft* and, 226–227; on slaves, 350; Ten Commandments and, 175

Goering, Hermann: "Criminal Law Decree against the Polish and the Jews in the Integrated Eastern Territories" signed by, 360; exploitation of East and, 375–376; forested zones and, 377; hunting and, 30–31; police and, 209–210; Slavs and, 375–376; Wirtschaftsorganisation Ost and, 376

Goethe, Johann Wolfgang von, 420n140

Gold clause, 116

"Golgotha of the North" (Graul), 100

Good and evil as artificial values, 59

Göppert, Otto, 299–300

Gottgläubige (believers in God), 39

Graul, Werner, 100

Graupner, Heinz, 26–27

Greenland, 102–103

Greiser, Ingrid, 192

Grimm, Friedrich: on France, 284–285; Peace of Westphalia and, 282, 284–286

Grimm, Jacob, 61

Gross, Raphael, 11

Gross, Walter, 62; on asocials, 235–236; bastards and, 381; morality and, 378; Slavs and, 378; sterilization and, 141, 145

Grossraum (homogenous and clearly delimited space), 315; *Lebensraum* and, 318–319; Monroe Doctrine and, 316–317; Nazi thought and, 316; order of people and, 318; *Reich* and, 318; Walz and, 319

Grundmann, Walther, 117–118, 120

Guardian of the law. See *Rechtswahrer*

Günther, Hans, 48–50, 69
Gürke, Norbert: habilitation work of, 313;
  vital-racial unit and, 314; *Volk und
  Völkerrecht* by, 313–314
Gütt, Arthur, 37; on medical ethics, 172;
  Notzustand and, 177; science and,
  189–190; *Volk in Gefahr* and, 108–109
Gypsies, 439n143

Haffner, Sebastian, 75
Halder, General, 271–272
Handbooks. See *Merkblätter*
Harlan, Veit, 132
Harshness: Bolshevik aggression and, 245;
  Führerprinzip and, 244; German,
  192–193, 242–245, 332, 348–349; Hartl
  and, 242–243; judicial, 231; "makes the
  future kind," 249; of nature, 156;
  Versailles creating, 242
Harte Geschlecht, Das (Vesper), 103
Hartl, Albrecht: Germanic persons and,
  52; harshness and, 242–243; religion
  and, 66. *See also* Holzner, Anton
Hauer, Wilhelm, 50
Haushofer, Karl, 299
Hedemann, Justus Wilhelm, 60–61,
  121–122
Heimkehr (Ucicky), 292–294
Heimtücke (insidious treason), 202
Helmut, Otto: *Notzustand* and, 178; *Volk
  in Gefahr* by, 108–109
Heraclitus, 162
Herbert, Ulrich, 10
Heredity, science of and scientists, 1–2, 28,
  36–37, 115, 143, 174, 190, 235–236
Hereditary health courts. See
  Erbgesundheitsgerichte
Herrenmenschentum (master-race
  domination): in action, 345–349;
  segregation and, 347
Herrscher, Der (Harlan), 132–133
Hess, Rudolf, 289–290
Heydrich, Reinhard, 221, 251
Hierarchy of living things, 31
Himmler, Heinrich, 6; on animal cruelty,
  29; archaic rites and, 37–38; "Basic
  Decree on the Fight to Prevent
  Criminality" and, 225; blood mixing
  and, 343–345; Christianity and, 110,
  158–159, 183–184; consequentiality and,
  414; on duty to history and biology,
  385–386; Eastern wall and, 369–370; on
  elderly, 38; on elite eradication in
  Poland, 247–248; final solution and, 191,

386–387, 403–404, 412; on Genghis
  Khan, 381; German numerical
  inferiority and, 449n49; *Gottgläubige*
  and, 39; on holism of life, 27; homosexuality and, 110–111, 230; on Jesus,
  119–120; on Jews as lice, 400; Judeo-
  Bolshevik menace and, 180; justice of
  peace and, 139; landscaping and, 340; on
  law, 75–76; lesbianism and, 229;
  mixed-race children and, 380–381; on
  moral compunctions, 351–352; on
  Nordic superiority, 187; normative
  archaeology and, 37–38; *Ostarbeiter* and,
  359; on phenotypic traits, 354–355;
  Poland and, 333; on police, 206–207;
  procreation and, 151, 152; Revolution
  and, 240; on rules for treatment of
  foreign peoples, 321; on segregation,
  347; sentimentalism and, 191; *Sippenhaft* and, 226; on slaves, 350–351; Slavic
  exploitation and, 374–375, 378;
  solidarity and, 353–354; on SS, 108; on
  taxation for having fewer children, 343;
  unwritten law and, 60; women and,
  100–102
Hippler, Fritz, 24
Hippocratic Oath, 171
Hitler, Adolf: American Indians and, 352;
  animal cruelty and, 24; on apes, 156;
  biological citizenship and, 366–367; on
  blood over ink, 112; on cat and mouse,
  157; Christianity and, 183–184, 185–186;
  Clemenceau and, 304; Compiègne
  Wagon and, 281; consent and, 306–307;
  on Czechoslovakia, 288–289, 290;
  dictatorship and, 138; *Downfall* and,
  5–6; on Eastern European colonization,
  337; on environment and struggle, 156;
  eugenic murder established by, 167–168;
  eye for an eye and, 395; *Fabrizierte
  Konstruktion* and, 287–288; on French
  Revolution, 76; on function of state,
  114; on Germanization of East,
  338–339; on Germans as lost, 415;
  Germany Must Perish and, 384; on
  giving no compassion, 256–257;
  heredity laws and, 2; honor and, 311; on
  imperial dynasties, 181; Jesus as Aryan
  and, 118–120; on Jews, character of, 387,
  395; on Jews as bacteria, 31; Judaism
  blamed for war by, 382; judge and, 136,
  204–205; judicial branch taken over by,
  205–206; jurists and, 97–98; killing
  Jews as duty and, 385; Kommissarbefehl

and, 442n86; on laws of life, 163; *Lebensrecht* and, 321–322; "Legitimate Defense as Law" and, 177; *Mein Kampf* and, 114, 162–163, 177, 181, 387, 405; Monroe Doctrine and, 317; Münster and, 281; on natural law, 161–162, 163; on natural selection, 161–162; *Notzustand* and, 179; Order 46 and, 253–254; order for Reich destruction signed by, 414–415; Peace of Westphalia and, 281, 286; pity and, 192, 193; Poland and, 295–296; political borders ignored by, 366–367; Potempa Murder and, 427n21; rational anti-Semitism and, 399; religion and, 186–187; Revolution and, 76, 112–113, 237–240; Röhm and, 237–238; Roosevelt and, 321–322; service to Germany and, 89; on Slavic eradication, 248–250; social Darwinism and, 231; on struggle, 162; Ten Commandments and, 174–175; Versailles and, 281; war in Poland and, 246–247; Western theater executions and, 264–265; Wirtschaftsorganisation Ost and, 376

Höhn, Reinhart, 45, 53; *Anstalten* and, 316; *Kriminalbiologie* and, 217; police and, 207–211; state and, 115

Holzner, Anton, 65–66

Homosexuality: abortion and, 230–231; as anti-natural vice, 228; as Asian in origin, 228; combating, 228–231; as default sexuality, 228–229; eugenic murder and, 230; within versus without the German state, 229–230; Himmler and, 110–111, 230; lesbianism and, 229; procreation and, 230; Röhm and, 237–238

Honor, 54–55, 310–311

Höss, Rudolf, 6; as cold and insensitive, 397; concentration camps and, 396; on final solution, 397–398; *Meine Psyche* by, 395–398

"Humane Law, A" *(Schwarze Korps, Das)*, 142

Humanity, 3, 87, 91, 141; Aryan, 104; crime against, 1; Indo-Germanic, 48; Jewish criminality, 391, 393, 398, 400, 402; jurists as plague of, 97; *jus gentium* principles of, 267; *Mein Kampf* on, 405; misunderstood, 263; new era of, 79, 80; Nordic, 143, 336

Hunger, 373–375

Hunting, 30–31

Hyperinflation, 116

Iberian Peninsula, 335–336

Iceland, 103

Ich klage an (Liebeneiner), 168–169

India, protection of animals in, 29–30

Ingrao, Christian, 10

Insidious treason. See *Heimtücke*

Instinct, 73, 137; axiological, 60; communal, 165; for good, 51–53; Jewish, 295, 327; Nordic, 43, 51–53; normative archaeology and, 36–37; replacing, 175; survival, 147, 398; *Volksgemeinschaft* and racial, 123; Walz proposal and, 85

Institute for the Exploration and the Elimination of the Jewish Influence in German Religious Life, 117, 120

International law: as abstract, 311–312; absurdity of, 286–296; authentic, 312–313; Bilfinger and, 299; Bruns and, 297–298; *Clausula rebus sic stantibus* and, 299–300; customary clause and, 298–299; Czechoslovakia and, 287–291; de facto and de jure, 296; elasticity of, 300; evolving context and, 298; *Ex factis jus oritur* and, 297; *Fabrizierte Konstruktion* and, 287–288; fact and, 296–306; German natural resources and, 305; Göppert and, 299–300; Haushofer and, 299; Kommissarbefehl and, 269; law of the peoples and, 313; *Lebensrecht und völkerrechtliche Ordnung* and, 314–315; Nicolai and, 319–320; Poland and, 291–296; race and, 312; reality and, 304; Schmitt and, 298, 300, 301–304; static, 300–301; Treaty of Saint-Germain and, 286–287; *Volk und Völkerrecht* and, 313–314

"It's Him or Me" *(SS-Leitheft)*, 157

Jäger, Karl, 6

Jedem das Seine (to each his due): Buchenwald and, 195–197; Eastern European colonization and, 324

Jess, Friedrich: French Revolution and, 82; *Rassenkunde und Rassenpflege* and, 197

Jesus, as Aryan, 118–120

Jesu Verhältnis zu Griechen und Juden (Leipoldt), 118

"Jewish Criminality" (Von Leers), 389

Jewish Revolution, 76–81

"Jewry in the German Legal Sciences" (Frank), 72

Jews: as anti-nature, 64–65; artificial laws of, 73; badges and, 390; as biological danger, 398–404; Catholic Church and, 70; cats and, 157, 432n5; as chaotic, 74; Christianity as invented by, 100; against criminality of, 391–395; as criminals, 24, 218–220, 389, 391–395; De Lagarde on, 400; emigration, forced, and, 412; *Der Ewige Jude* and, 24, 388, 394, 399; formalism and, 74–75; Germanic religious sentiment contrasted with, 25–29; *Germany Must Perish* and, 384–385; *Ghetto* and, 388–389; Goebbels and, 394, 401; hierarchy of living things and, 31; Hitler on character of, 387, 395; *Jüdische Moral* and, 392–393; killing Jews as duty, 385; Ley and, 383; library cleansing and, 389; as lice, 400; materialism of, 26; miscegenation and, 73–74; mixed blood and, 52–53; morality and, 392–394; *Der Mythus des 20. Jahrhunderts* and, 164; names and, 390, 453n130; non-race and, 73; Operation Reinhard and, 401–402; as parasites, 393; people of law and, 72–76; as poisonous, 391; public health and, 401–402; Roman law and, 99; self interest of, 387–388; sexual contact and, 379–380; six thousand years of hatred of, 382–387; supposed cruelty toward animals, 23–25, 29–30; Ten Commandments and, 394; World War II and, 382
Jew Süss, The, 391
Jodl, Alfred, 265
Johst, Hans, 56
Joseph, as given name, 453n130
Judge: asocials and, 231–232; Barth and, 134–135; British legal system and, 137; Carolingian alienation and, 138; credo of, 199; as doctor, 200; *Fallrecht* and, 137; Freisler and, 133–134, 202; Hitler and, 136, 204–205; Larenz and, 135; lay, 138–139, 430n127; role of, 133–139; as soldier of home front, 202–203; Thierack and, 136, 231–232
Jüdische Moral (Nationalsozialistische Deutsche Arbeiterpartei), 392–393
Jüdische Weltpest, Die (Esser), 398–399

Kampfgemeinschaft (community of struggle): biological urgency and, 180–181; loyalty and, 182–183; military and, 181–182; Nature and, 182

Kant, Immanuel, 46, 158, 311, 403, 431n174
Kästner, Erich, 12
Kaufmann, Nathan, 384–385
Keitel, Wilhelm, 250; Barbarossa zone and, 251–252; deserters and, 227; Kommissarbefehl and, 442n86
Kelsen, Hans: *Pure Theory of Law* by, 420n140; Schmitt and, 302; Tatarin-Tarnheyden and, 149–150, 312, 431n174
Kerrl, Hans, 125–126
Koch, Karl-Otto, 196
Koch, Robert, 115
Kohlrübenwinter (turnip winter), 375
Kolberg (film), 115
Kommissarbefehl (Commissar Order): backfiring of, 269, 442n86; international law and, 269; political commissaries and, 268–269; preamble of, 267–268; Römer and, 269; as shocking, 269; Soviet prisoners of war and, 267–269
Koonz, Claudia, 11
Kopp, Friedrich, 282
Korte, Heinrich: laws of life and, 314; *Lebensraum* and, 318–319; *Lebensrecht und völkerrechtliche Ordnung* by, 314–315; Treaty of Versailles and, 314–315
Krieck, Ernst, 89
Kriminalbiologie (science of crime fighting): classification and, 217; Daluege and, 219–222; Höhn and, 217; political divergence and, 217–218; rise of, 216–217; Ritter and, 217; sterilization and, 219; Thierack and, 217
Kriminalbiologische Gesellschaft (Criminal Biology Society), 216–217
Kroll, Werner, 172
Kummer, Bernhard, 104–105
Küppers, Johannes, 358
Kynast, Karl, 69

Labor/Laborers: forced, 356–360; needed in Eastern colonies, 349–352; Poles and Slavs as, 246, 333–334, 347, 351, 357–362; women and children as, 351–352
Land ownership, 342–343; property law and, 131
Landscaping, Eastern European colonization and, 339–341
Land und Herrschaft (Brunner), 45–46
Lang, Fritz, 11, 12
Lange, Heinrich: liberalism and, 83–85; property and, 131–132

Lansing, Robert, 307
Larenz, Karl: judge and, 135; renaissance of German law and, 127–129
Law: alienation of, 92–99; armored divisions of, 201–206; of blood, 408; British, 137; death to paragraph and, 125–126; as duress, 306–311; as folklore, 60–63; free, 137; Gestapo as above, 211–212; heredity, 2; Himmler on, 75–76; idealistic, 98–99; judge, role of, 133–139; jurists and, 97–98; legal proverbs and, 62; of life, 311; moral, 355–356; Nazism perspective on, 113–114; norms and, 122; old versus new, 221–222; people over person in, 112; of the peoples, 313; "People's Code of Law," 60–61; as polemical, 203; Pure Theory of Law, 420n140; Das Recht als Kampfordnung der Rasse and, 204; renaissance of German, 126–133, 429n78; as serving people, 113; of sterilization, 139–140; substantive values and, 122–123; unwritten, 60; Walz and, 80–81; war and, 166. See also Criminal law; International law; Legal system; Natural law; Roman law
Law against Dangerous Habitual Criminals. See Sicherungsverwahrung
Law for the Restoration of the Professional Civil Service, 83
"Law is born of facts." See Ex factis jus oritur
Law of God, The (Holzner), 65–67, 422n10
Law of life. See Lebensrecht
Law on case-by-case basis. See Fallrecht
Law on inherited farms. See Reichserbhofgesetz
Lay judge, 138–139, 430n127
Leadership principle. See Führerprinzip
League of Nations, 300, 445n94
Leben-compounds used, 312
Lebensborn, 111
Lebensgesetzlich (belonging to the laws of life / vital-legal), 40, 419n64
Lebensraum (living space): dwindling of, 324; Eastern European colonization and, 324; evolving use of term, 325; Grossraum and, 318–319; Pan-Germanic movement and, 324–325; World War I and, 325
Lebensrecht (law of life or right to life), 112; Eastern European colonization and, 321–326; Hitler and, 321–322; as literal, 325–326

Lebensrecht und völkerrechtliche Ordnung (Korte), 314–315
Legal system: British, 137; Germanic, 41–42; as lifeblood of Germanic race, 42; nature as higher authority in, 42–43; origins, 42; revolution in, 43–44
"Legitimate Defense as Law" (Hitler), 177
Lehmann, Ernst, 35–37, 178
Leipoldt, Johannes, 118
Leistungsgemeinschaft (community of achievement), 167–171
Lenz, Fritz, 16; collective individualism and, 87–88; gentilism and, 88; humanity and, 87
Lesbianism, 229
Levin, Rudolf, 101–102
Ley, Robert, 383
Liberalism: individualist, 197; Lange and, 83–85; Mein Kampf and, 405
Liberal-Marxist, 74, 422n38
Library cleansing, 389
Liebeneiner, Wolfgang, 168–169
Lippe, Prince Friedrich Wilhelm of, 335
Live first, then philosophize. See Primum vivere, secundum philosophari
Living space. See Lebensraum
Lord's right to take land from vassal. See Abmeierung
Loyola, 279
Lutheran reform, 69

M (Lang), 12
Maritime warfare, 262–263
Marriage, 107, 108, 439n143; mixed, 70, 86, 110, 146; Nuremberg Laws on, 146; Reichsführer SS on, 380
Marx, Karl, 196
Master-race domination. See Herrenmenschentum
Mathematics, 79–80
Mayer, Joseph, 144
Medical ethics: Franssen on, 172; German people and, 173; Gütt on, 172; Kroll on, 172; prevention and, 172–173; Reiter on, 172; religion of death and, 173–174; Wagner on, 171; whole versus part in, 171–172
Mehlis, Georg, 171; Führer und Volksgemeinschaft by, 39; relativism and, 92; universalism and, 91
Meine Psyche (Höss), 395–398
Mein Kampf (Hitler): on imperial dynasties, 181; on Jews as egotistical, 387; "Legitimate Defense as Law" in, 177;

Mein Kampf (Hitler) *(continued)*
    liberalism and Enlightenment rejected
    in, 405; rebellion against laws of nature
    and, 162–163; state denunciation in, 114
Meisinger, Josef, 228
Merk, Walther: right and, 40; on Roman
    law, 96
Merkblätter (handbook for decrees):
    civilians and, 260; disease and, 261–262;
    explained, 258–259; know the enemy
    injunction in, 259–260; poison and, 261;
    Soviet territory as hostile and, 259;
    unconventional weapons and, 260–261
Metaphysics, 28–29
Meyer, Herbert, 119
Meyer, Konrad: climate and, 334; on
    colonization as progressive, 338;
    Eastern communication lines and, 337;
    land and soil and, 341, 449n56
Mezger, Edmund, 199
Michels, 108, 426n177
Middle Ages, 81–82
"Midgards Untergang" (Kummer), 104–105
Militärgeschichtliches Forschungsamt
    (MGFA), 10
Minderheit (minority), 367–368
Mixed marriages: baptism and, 70;
    forbidden, 110, 146; racial abomination
    of, 86
Monasticism, 106–108
Monetary nominalism, 116
Mongolian, 440n35
Mongolian-Turkish people. *See* Avars
Monroe Doctrine, 316–317
Moral double-speak. *See Doppelmoral*
Morality: Berger and, 104; final solution
    and, 403–404; Gentilist, 16; Jews and,
    392–394; nudity and, 33–34; Slavs and,
    378. *See also* Nordic morality
Morality trials. *See Sittlichkeitsprozesse*
Münster, 281
Mythus des 20. Jahrhunderts, Der
    (Rosenberg), 164

Names, regulations on, 390, 453n130
National Socialist German Workers'
    Party. *See* Nationalsozialistische
    Deutsche Arbeiterpartei
National Socialist law and legal thought.
    See Nationalsozialistisches Recht und
    Rechtsdenken
National Socialist Revolution: as peaceful,
    149; Tatarin and, 149–150; values
    reevaluation and, 149–152

Nationalsozialistische Deutsche
    Arbeiterpartei (NSDAP), 3; animal
    cruelty and, 23–24; *Jüdische Moral* of,
    392–393; mental illness within, 4;
    Testament of Dr. Mabuse and, 12
Nationalsozialistischer Kampf gegen das
    Verbrechertum (Daluege), 219
Nationalsozialistisches Recht und
    Rechtsdenken (National Socialist law
    and legal thought), 128
"Natur" *(Neue Brockhaus)*, 42–43
Natural law: Bruns on, 312; Buch on, 165;
    Dietze and, 159–161; Hitler on, 161–162,
    163; man and, 161–167; *Mein Kampf*
    and, 114, 162–163; *Der Mythus des 20.*
    Jahrhunderts and, 164; *Rassenpflege im*
    völkischen Staat and, 164–165; Stengel
    von Rutkowski and, 26, 28; struggle
    and, 162, 165–166; war and, 165–166
Natural selection: Germanic race and, 54;
    Gütt and, 108–109; Hitler on, 161–162;
    pity and, 190; SS and, 109, 190
Nature: anti-, 64–65, 106–108; cult of,
    187–188; Dietze and, 159–161;
    Kampfgemeinschaft and, 182; man as,
    155–161; as manifestation of divine, 26;
    monasticism and, 106–108; non-nature
    versus, 28–29; nudity and, 32–35;
    physis and, 29; separation from, 59–60;
    state and, 113–116; as struggle, 155–161;
    thwarting, 108–111; Viergutz on, 58–59
Natur und Sünde (Werner, Manfred),
    102–103
Nazi Conscience, The (Koonz), 11
Nazi Party. *See* Nationalsozialistische
    Deutsche Arbeiterpartei
Nazism: animals and, 31–32; anti-
    intellectualism of, 72; author's
    approach to studying, 15–17; Christian
    values contrasted with, 71; eschato-
    logical dimension of, 407; French
    Revolution and, 78–79; *Grossraum* and,
    316; hierarchy of living things of, 31;
    imperatives of, 19–20; mental universe
    of, 1–20; narrative of, 405–406;
    perspective on Law, 113–114; as
    rereading of history, 17; Ten Com-
    mandments of, 175–176; theoretical
    texts and, 410–411; Thirty Years' War
    and, 279–280; word and action related
    to, 408–409. *See also specific topics*
Neue Brockhaus, 42–43
New Testament of the People. *See*
    Volkstestament

Nicolai, Helmut, 40, 42, 319–320
Night and Fog decree, 264
Night of the Long Knives, 237
Nine Commandments, Aryan, 104
"No crime without law." See *Nullum crimen sine lege*
Nordic morality, 43, 109; biological purity and, 51–52; instinct for good and, 51–53; mixed blood and, 52–53
Nordic piety: "Frömmigkeit nordischer Artung" and, 48–49; origins and, 48–51; *Das Reich dieser Welt: Lieder und Verse eines Heiden* and, 51
Nordic race. See Germanic race
Nordic Romans, 94
"Nordic Thought in the Legislation of the Third Reich" (Frick), 36
Normative archaeology: toward, 35–39; *Gottgläubige* and, 39; Himmler and, 37–38; origins and, 35–39; "Political Biology" and, 35–36; race, primal instinct of, and, 36–37
Norway, 265–266
Not (distress, urgency, and necessity), 176, 413
Notzustand (state of emergency), 176; Burgdörfer and, 178–179; as demographic, 177–179; Frick and, 177–178; Helmut and, 178; Hitler and, 179; Judeo-Bolshevik menace creating, 179–180; Tirala and, 177
Nudity: as form of asceticism, 34; Greek concept of beauty and, 33–34; morality and, 33–34; nature and, 32–35; origins and, 32–35; Suren and, 32–33
Nullum crimen sine lege (no crime without law), 198
Nuremberg Trials, 3

Oetker, Friedrich, 200, 204
Ohlendorf, Otto, 3, 4
One must be honest even with one's enemy. See *Etiam hosti fides servanda*
Operation Barbarossa, 250, 373, 383
Operation Reinhard, 401–402
Oradour-sur-Glane, 267
Order 46, 253–254
Order police. See Ordnungspolizei
Ordinary Men (Browning), 7
Ordnungspolizei (order police), 219
Origins: animals and, 23–32; Germanic immediacy and, 39–44; of Germanic race, 406; Germanic race as only moral race, 53–57; law as folklore, 60–63;

legal system, 42; Nordic piety and, 48–51; normative archaeology and, 35–39; norms, people, and life, 58–60; nudity and, 32–35; of state, 113; unity, separation, mediation, and, 44–48; world order and, 57–58
Ostarbeiter (Eastern workers): badges worn by, 359–360; "General Regulations regarding the Recruitment and Employment of Labor from the East" and, 358–359; Himmler and, 359; regulation of, 359–360

Pact of Steel, 369
Paganism, 104–106, 183–184, 188
Pan-Germanic movement, 324–325
Paragraph: condemnation of, 52, 67, 75–76, 97–99, 133, 139, 150, 198, 284–285, 360; "Death to," 125–126, 433n48; use in written law, 41–42, 207
Peace of Westphalia: Bilfinger and, 283–284; as blow to Germany, 280; France and, 282; German fate sealed by, 282; Friedrich Grimm and, 282, 284–286; Hitler and, 281, 286; international order and, 280–286; Six and, 281, 282–283
"People's Code of Law" (Hedemann), 60–61
People's courts. See Volksgerichtshof
People's Law Code, 121–122
Performance capacity, 171
Peter Schädl (fictional character), 66–67
Phenotypic traits, 354–355
Philosophischen Grundlagen des Nationalsozialismus (Dietrich), 90–91
Physis versus metaphysics, 28–29
Pietzuch, Konrad, 427n21
Pity: for Aryans, 191–192; correct use of, 188–193; Frank and, 192; Goebbels and, 191–193; Hitler and, 192, 193; Jewish question and, 191; natural selection and, 190; sentimentalism and, 190–192
Poincaré, 284
Poison, 261
Poisonous Mushroom, The (children's book), 391
Poland: atrocities in, 292; "Criminal Law Decree against the Polish and the Jews in the Integrated Eastern Territories" and, 360–362; as decomposing, 330; Eastern European colonization and, 330–334; Einsatzgruppen deployed in, 250; elimination of vital force of, 246;

Poland (continued)
    elite eradication in, 247–248, 331; first
    blitzkrieg of, 246–247; Frank and, 331;
    German law and, 360–362; Ghetto and,
    388–389; Heimkehr and, 292–294;
    Himmler and, 247–248, 333; Hitler and,
    246–247, 295–296; massacres of
    German minority in, 294–295;
    population as production tools,
    333–334; population held down in,
    331–334; public health and, 402;
    Schieder and, 323; segregation and, 353;
    slavery and, 332; use of, 330–334;
    Versailles and, 291–296; war in,
    246–248; zones of, 330–331. See also
    Polish Decrees
Police: absolutism and, 210; Best and,
    211–216; community and, 207; Die
    Deutsche Polizei, 212–213; Eastern
    European colonization and, 350;
    Enabling Act and, 215; function of,
    206–216; Gemeinschaftsfremde and,
    233–234, 439n151; Gestapo and, 211–212;
    Goering and, 209–210; Himmler on,
    206–207; Höhn and, 207–211; old versus
    new law and, 221–222; Ordnungspo-
    lizei, 219; paragraphs of law and,
    207–208; prevention and, 222; public
    order and, 209; purging of, 221;
    Schutzhaft and, 222–225; sexual contact
    and, 380; Sippenhaft and, 225–227;
    Untermenschentum and, 350; Vorbeu-
    gungshaft and, 225
Polish Decrees: Einsatz and, 358;
    Fremdvölkisch and, 356–358; house
    arrest and, 356–357; identification
    using badges and, 357–358; isolation
    and, 357; labor regulated in, 358;
    segregation and, 356–358
"Political Biology" (Lehmann), 35–36, 178
Positive Christianity, 119
Potempa Murder, 116, 427n21
Prague, 291
Prevention of disease, 172–173
Preventive detention. See
    Vorbeugungshaft
Primum vivere, secundum philosophari
    (live first, then philosophize), 97
Probability, criminality and, 218–219
"Problems in the Revision of the Treaty of
    Versailles" (Wissmann), 307
Procreation, 19–20; females, German, and,
    146; Frank and, 148–149; Himmler and,
    151, 152; homosexuals and, 230;

Nuremberg Laws on, 146; of pure and
    strong, 146–149; Das Schwarze Korps
    and, 148; Wagner and, 147, 148
"Protection of Animals in Ancient India,
    The," 30
Protective detention. See Schutzhaft
Proverbs, legal, 62
Prussian Army, 158, 167
Public health, 401–402, 413
Pure Theory of Law (Kelsen), 420n140

Race: annihilating, 108–111; Berger and,
    88–89; Blut und Rasse in der Gesetzge-
    bung and, 124; dependent on space,
    336; finding way within, 121–125; as
    foundational, 121; Frank and, 92,
    124–125; international law and, 312;
    Jews as non-race, 73; mixed-race
    children, 380–381; norms and, 122;
    People's Law Code and, 121–122;
    primal instinct of, 36–37; Rassenkunde
    und Rassenpflege, 197; replanting,
    326–330; substantive values and,
    122–123; value system and, 51; Walz
    and, 85; worldview determined by, 50.
    See also Germanic race;
    Herrenmenschentum
"Racial bastards," 52, 73, 380–381
Racial duty, 27–28
Racial Equality against Equality in
    Principle (Walz), 80–81
Rasse als Lebensgesetz, Die, (Eichenauer),
    159
Rassengesetzliche Rechtslehre, Die, 40
Rassenkunde und Rassenpflege (Jess), 197
Rassenkunde und Rassenpflege (science
    and care of the race), 197
Rassenpflege im völkischen Staat
    (Staemmler), 164–165
Rassenseelenkunde (science of racial
    soul), 51
Recht als Kampfordnung der Rasse, Das
    (Stierl), 204
Rechtliche Volkskunde (von Künssberg),
    61–62
Rechtswahrer (guardian of the law), 94
"Recht und Moral eines Friedensver-
    trages" (Rogge), 309–310
Reich, concept of, 317–318
Reich Animal Protection Act. See
    Reichstierschutzgesetz
Reich dieser Welt: Lieder und Verse
    eines Heiden, Das (Stengel von
    Rutkowski), 51

Reich Main Security Office. *See* Reichssicherheitshauptamt

Reichserbhofgesetz (law on inherited farms), 129

Reichssicherheitshauptamt (RSHA), 3, 10

Reichstag Fire Decree, 221, 223

Reichstierschutzgesetz (Reich Animal Protection Act), 30

Reier, Harbert, 138

Reiter, Hans: Jewish doctors and, 174; on medical ethics, 172

Religion: cult of nature as, 187–188; of death, 173–174; Hartl and, 66; Hitler and, 186–187; Viergutz and, 186. *See also* Paganism; *specific religions*

Renaissance of German law: *Abmeierung* and, 129–130, 429n78; community and, 127–128; criteria for creating, 126; freedom and, 127; *Der Herrscher* and, 132–133; Larenz and, 127–129; legal position and, 129; person and, 127–128; property and, 129–132

Rendulic, General, 266

Renner, Austrian Chancellor, 365

Revolution: Himmler and, 240; Hitler acting against, 237–240; Jewish, 76–81; in legal system, 43–44; Night of the Long Knives and, 237; nipping bud of, 236–241; Schmitt and, 238–239; Sturmabteilung and, 237–238; Tatarin-Tarnheyden and, 149. *See also* French Revolution; National Socialist Revolution

Richelieu, Cardinal-Minister, 279, 280, 282, 284–285

Right to life. See *Lebensrecht*

Ritter, Robert: *Ein Menschenschlag* by, 235; *Kriminalbiologie* and, 217

Robert Koch, Bekämpfer des Todes (film), 115

Rogge, Heinrich, 309–311

Röhm, Ernst, 237–238

Roman law: alienation of, 96; Association of National Socialist Jurists on, 95; Caracalla and, 94–95; Frank and, 93–94, 97–99; "Golgotha of the North" and, 100; Jews and, 99; law of life and, 97; legal personality concept and, 95–96; Lippe and, 335; Merk on, 96; Nordic Romans and, 94; reception of, 92–99; Romano-Byzantine bastardization of, 97; state and, 116

Römer, Felix, 269

Roosevelt, Franklin, 321–322

Rosenberg, Alfred, 375; French Revolution and, 78; on monetary nominalism, 116; *Der Mythus des 20. Jahrhunderts* by, 164; Nine Commandments and, 104; Soviet prisoners of war and, 272–273; universalism and, 91–92

Rothenburgsort Pediatric Hospital, 1–2

Rousseau, Jean-Jacques, 82

Rüdin, Ernst: *Notzustand* and, 177; sterilization and, 141–142

Russians, 258, 348

Ruttke, Falk, 62; gold clause and, 116; on life, 155; *Notzustand* and, 177; performance capacity and, 171; sterilization and, 140–141

Sachsenspiegel, 41

Sauckel, Fritz, 351

Saul-Paul, 119

Schieder, Theodor: Poland and, 323; on segregation, 353

Schilling, Kurt, 79

Schizophrenia, 52, 73–74, 287, 291, 340

Schmitt, Carl, 73; de-Judaizing Christianity and, 121; *generalklauseln* and, 123, 134, 428n53; Germanic democracy and, 183; Höhn and, 115; international law and, 298, 300, 301–304; on Jewish law, 74; Kelsen and, 302; League of Nations and, 300; library cleansing and, 389; Monroe Doctrine and, 316–317; *Reich* and, 317–318; Revolution and, 238–239; "Totaler Feind, totaler Krieg, totaler Staat" by, 167; *Über die drei Arten des rechtswissenschaftlichen Denkens* and, 135; Versailles and, 301; world order and, 57–58

Schulte, Eduard, 282

Schutzhaft (protective detention): community and, 224; history of, 222–223; police and, 222–225; police discretion and, 223; Reichstag Fire Decree and, 223; *Sicherungsverwahrung* and, 225; Tesmer and, 223–224

Schwarze Korps, Das, 25; "A Humane Law" and, 142; procreation and, 148; sin and, 107

Science: Gütt and, 189–190; sterilization and, 140. See also *Kriminalbiologie*

Science and care of the race. See *Rassenkunde und Rassenpflege*

Science of crime fighting. See *Kriminalbiologie*

Science of racial soul. See
Rassenseelenkunde
Security Service. See Sicherheitsdienst
Segregation: badges and, 357–358, 359–360;
concentration camps and, 378–379;
Fremdvölkisch and, 356–362; Herrenmenschentum and, 347; keeping
distance and, 377–381; moral law and,
355–356; phenotypic traits and, 354–355;
Poland and, 353; Polish Decrees and,
356–358; Schieder on, 353; sexual
contact and, 357; Volk ohne Grenzen
and, 362–364; Volksgemeinschaft and,
353–356
Sentimentality and sentimentalism, 158,
173, 190–193, 236, 243, 257, 385, 398,
401, 411
Separation: first, 44; Freisler and, 44–45;
higher education and, 48; Land und
Herrschaft and, 45–46; from nature,
59–60; Stengel von Rutkowski and,
47–48
Service. See Dienst
Service du Travail Obligatoire (STO), 356
Settlement debt, 342
Sexual contact, 357, 379–380
Shipwrecked men, 262–263
Sicherheitsdienst (SD), 10
Sicherungsverwahrung (Law against
Dangerous Habitual Criminals), 225
Sin, 102–103, 105–106, 107
Sippenhaft (familial detention): desertion
and, 227; German prisoners of war and,
227; Goebbels and, 226–227; Himmler
and, 226; police and, 225–227;
Versprengte and, 227
Sittlichkeitsprozesse (morality trials), 107
Six, Franz-Alfred, 281, 282–283
Slavery: Goebbels on, 350; Himmler on,
350–351; Poland and, 332; Slavs and,
351; Untermenschentum and, 349–352
Slavs, 42; Backe and, 379; as biomass,
372–373; elimination of vital force of,
246; as feminine, 379; forested zones
and, 376–377; Goering and, 375–376;
Walter Gross and, 378; Himmler and,
374–375, 378; Hitler on eradicating,
248–250; hunger and, 373–375; keeping
distance from, 377–381; morality and,
378; Nazis' definition of, 419n69;
sexual contact with, 379–380; slaves
and, 351; state creation and, 368; war
against, 246–250; Wirtschaftsorganisation Ost and, 376

Slawentum (demographic mass to be
exploited), 373
Soldiers who lost their way. See
Versprengte
Solidarity: Himmler and, 353–354; moral
law and, 355–356; phenotypic traits
and, 354–355; of Volksgemeinschaft,
353–356
Sonderauftrag Hexen, 101
Sondergerichte (special courts), 201;
Heimtücke and, 202; war metaphor
and, 202
Sonderweg (special path), 5
Soviet prisoners of war: "Asiatics" and,
273; criminalization of, 269–270;
distance maintained with, 270;
execution parameters for, 270–271;
Halder and, 271–272; Kommissarbefehl
and, 267–269; no rights for, 271–272;
political commissaries and, 268–269;
protests of treatment of, 272–273;
Rosenberg and, 272–273; shoot to kill,
271; treatment of, 267–273; weapons
used against, 270
Soviet Union: "know the enemy"
injunction and, 259–260; Merkblätter
on, 259; poison and, 261; unconventional weapons and, 260–261
Special courts. See Sondergerichte
Special path. See Sonderweg
Sperrle, Hugo, 266
SS (Schutzstaffel): on biological thinking,
165; conception out of wedlock and,
111; gender and, 107–108; "General
Regulations regarding the Recruitment
and Employment of Labor from the
East" and, 358–359; Himmler on, 108;
"It's Him or Me" and, 157; natural
selection and, 109, 190; oath swearing
in, 244; pity and, 190; sexual contact
and, 380; Ten Commandments and, 175
SS-Leitheft, 157
Staemmler, Martin, 164–165
Stähle, Eugen: eugenic murder and, 168;
Ten Commandments and, 174
Stangl, Franz, 6
State: films critiquing, 115; Frank and,
114; Frick and, 114; function of, 114;
Gercke and, 115; German versus
Roman, 115–116; gold clause and, 116;
Höhn and, 115; nature and, 113–116;
origins of, 113; Roman Law and, 116;
Slavs and, 368; as subordinate to life,
114; Volkmar and, 115–116

State of emergency. See *Notzustand*

Stengel von Rutkowski, Lothar: criminal law and, 201; on Lutheran reform, 69; natural law and, 26, 28; *Das Reich dieser Welt: Lieder und Verse eines Heiden* and, 51; separation and, 47–48

Sterilization: asocials and, 234–235; birth right and, 139–146; compassion and, 140–141; *Erbgesundheitsgerichte* and, 140; goal of, 145–146; Walter Gross and, 141, 145; holistic view and, 144–145; as humane, 143–144; "A Humane Law" and, 142; *Kriminalbiologie* and, 219; law of, 139–140; Mayer and, 144; Rüdin and, 141–142; Ruttke and, 140–141; science and, 140; Western societies and, 144

Stierl, Günther, 200, 204

Stoics, 58, 81

Streicher, Julius, 391

Struggle: *Alles Leben ist Kampf* and, 155–156, 159; confrontation with Christianity, 158–159; Dietze and, 159–161; environment and, 156; of gods, 12–13; Hitler on, 162; "It's Him or Me" and, 157; for life, 165–166; Nordic climate and, 157–158; against oneself, 158; war and, 157. See also *Mein Kampf*

Stufenbau, 420n140

Sturmabteilung (SA), 8, 237–238

Sudetenland, 214; Germans in, 287–289; killings in, 250

Suren, Hans, 32–33

Surplus areas, 376

Task forces. See Einsatzgruppen

Tatarin-Tarnheyden, Edgar, 197; authentic international law and, 312–313; bionomics and, 150; Kelsen and, 149–150, 312, 431n174; law of the peoples and, 313; *Leben*-compounds used by, 312; peaceful revolution and, 149; reality versus concepts and, 312

Taxation, 343

Ten Commandments, 104; Goebbels and, 175; Hitler and, 174–175; Jews and, 394; of Nazism, 175–176; repudiation and use of, 174–176; Stähle and, 174

Tesmer, Hans-Joachim, 223–224

Testament of Dr. Mabuse, The (Lang), 12

Thälmann, Ernst, 240–241

Thief's Journal, The (Genet), 12

Thierack, Otto: asocials and, 231–232; judge and, 136, 231–232; *Kriminalbiologie* and, 217

Things thus standing. See *Clausula rebus sic stantibus*

Thirty Years' War: causes of, 278–279; Nazi perspective on, 279–280; Peace of Westphalia and, 280

Tirala, Lothar, 177

"To each his due." See *Jedem das Seine*

"Totaler Feind, totaler Krieg, totaler Staat" (Schmitt), 167

Trampler, Kurt, 287, 308; Austria and, 364–366; *Volk ohne Grenzen* by, 362–364

Treachery Act, 214

Treaty of Saint-Germain, 286–287

"Trouble in the Blood: This World and the Next" (*Schwarze Korps, Das*), 25

Turnip winter. See *Kohlrübenwinter*

"Twelve Commandments for the Behavior of Germans in the East and for the Treatment of Russians" (Backe), 348

Über die drei Arten des rechtswissenschaftlichen Denkens (Schmitt), 135

Ucicky, Gustav, 277–278, 292–294

Um das Menschenrecht (film), 89

Unconventional weapons, 260–261

Unity of living things, 26–27

Universalism: Christianity and, 86; collective individualism and, 87–88; communism and, 86–87; contradictions of, 86–92; Dietrich reframing, 90–91; humanity and, 87; Krieck and, 89; Mehlis and, 91; Rosenberg and, 91–92

Untermenschentum (person considered racially or socially inferior): pacification of, 350; police and, 350; slavery and, 349–352

Unwritten law, 60

Use of subhuman labor. See *Einsatz*

Value conservation clause, 116

Van der Lubbe, Marinus, 198

Verbrechen der Wehrmacht (exhibit), 9

Versailles, 280–281

Versailles, Treaty of, 242; biology borders and, 363; consent and, 306–307; Czechoslovakia and, 287–291; as dictate, 307–308; *Fabrizierte Konstruktion* and, 288; Fourteen Points and, 309; Frank and, 308; German constitution and, 305–306; German natural resources and,

Versailles *(continued)*
305; Hitler and, 281; honor and,
310–311; Korte and, 314–315; law as
duress and, 306–311; as misleading and
fraudulent, 308; Poland and, 291–296;
"Problems in the Revision of the
Treaty of Versailles," 307; Rogge and,
309–311; Schmitt and, 301; semantic
creativity related to, 308–309; tricks of,
306–311; *Vertrag* as, 306
Versprengte (soldiers who lost their way),
227
Vertrag (civil law contract), 306
Vesper, Wilhelm: on cats, 432n5; *Das
Harte Geschlecht* by, 103
Viergutz, Rudolf: on nature, 58–59;
religion and, 186
Virginity, 106
Vital-racial unit, 314
*Völkerrechtsordnung und Nationalsozial-
ismus* (Walz), 446n112
Volk in Gefahr (Helmut), 108–109
Volkmar, Erich, 115–116
Volk ohne Grenzen (Trampler), 362–364
Volksgemeinschaft (community of people),
123; camaraderie among, 354; moral
law and, 355–356; solidarity of, 353–356
Volksgerichtshof (people's courts):
establishment of, 201–202; war
metaphor and, 202
Volkstestament (New Testament of the
People), 121
Volk und Völkerrecht (Gürke), 313–314
Von Brauchitsch, Walther, 250–251,
252–253
Von Freytag-Loringhoven, Alexander,
291–292
Von Harbou, Thea, 132
Von Künssberg, Eberhard, 61–62
Von Leers, Johann, 55; *Blut und Rasse in der
Gesetzgebung* and, 124; "Jewish
Criminality" by, 389; world order and, 57
Von Rauchhaupt, Friedrich Wilhelm, 298,
320
Vorbeugungshaft (preventive detention),
225

Wagner, Gerhard, 43; eugenic murder and,
170–171; on medical ethics, 171;
prevention and, 173; procreation and,
147, 148; religion of death and, 173–174;
on role of doctor, 171
Walz, Gustav Adolf: *Grossraum* and, 319;
Minderheit and, 367–368; *Racial

Equality against Equality in Principle*
by, 80–81; racial identity and, 85;
*Völkerrechtsordnung und Nationalso-
zialismus* by, 446n112
War: asocials and, 231–232; bacteriological,
261; criminal law as, 197–201; in East,
246–250; German prisoners of, 227;
Judaism blamed for, 382; law integrated
into, 166; maritime, 262–263; metaphor,
202; natural law and, 165–166;
noncustomary approach to, 248–252; in
Poland, 246–248; against Slavs,
246–250; struggle and, 157; Thirty
Years' War, 278–280; "Totaler Feind,
totaler Krieg, totaler Staat" and, 167;
World War I, 325; World War II, 382;
Zeitschrift für Wehrrecht and, 166–167.
See also Soviet prisoners of war
Weber, Max, 12
Wegner, Arthur, 305, 307–308
Wehrmacht company, 372
Weindling, Paul, 413
Werner, Manfred, 102–103
Werner, Paul, 234–235
Western theaters: black soldiers and, 262;
civilians targeted in, 263–264, 266–267;
Hitler decrees executions in, 264–265;
Night and Fog decree and, 264;
Norway, 265–266; protections stripped
away in, 265; shipwrecked men and,
262–263; violence imported to, 262–267
Wiepking-Jürgensmann, Jürgen, 339–340
Wildt, Michael, 10
Wilhelm I, 310
Wilson, Woodrow, 289, 307, 444n50;
Fourteen Points of, 309; as interven-
tionist, 317; Monroe Doctrine and,
316–317
Winckelmann, Johann Joachim, 418n36
Wirtschaftsorganisation Ost (WO Ost), 376
Wissmann, Herbert, 307
Witch hunts, 100–102
Women: conception out of wedlock and,
111; procreation and, 146; targeted in
East, 255; witch hunts and, 100–102
"Work sets you free." *See Arbeit macht
frei*
World order, 57–58
World War I, 325
World War II, 382

Zeitschrift für Wehrrecht, 166–167
Zones of black earth, 376–377
Zulassung, 423n39